AF412505

Springer Series
SYMBOLIC COMPUTATION – *Artificial Intelligence*

N.J. Nilsson: Principles of Artificial Intelligence. XV, 476 pages, 139 figs., 1982

J.H. Siekmann, G. Wrightson (Eds.): Automation of Reasoning 1. Classical Papers on Computational Logic 1957–1966. XXII, 525 pages, 1983

J.H. Siekmann, G. Wrightson (Eds.): Automation of Reasoning 2. Classical Papers on Computational Logic 1967–1970. XXII, 638 pages, 1983

L. Bolc (Ed.): The Design of Interpreters, Compilers, and Editors for Augmented Transition Networks. XI, 214 pages, 72 figs., 1983

M.M. Botvinnik: Computers in Chess. Solving Inexact Search Problems. With contributions by A.I. Reznitsky, B.M. Stilman, M.A. Tsfasman, A.D. Yudin. Translated from the Russian by A.A. Brown. XIV, 158 pages, 48 figs., 1984

L. Bolc (Ed.): Natural Language Communication with Pictorial Information Systems. VII, 327 pages, 67 figs., 1984

R.S. Michalski, J.G. Carbonell, T.M. Mitchell (Eds.): Machine Learning. An Artificial Intelligence Approach. XI, 572 pages, 1984

A. Bundy (Ed.): Catalogue of Artificial Intelligence Tools. Second, revised edition. IV, 168 pages, 1986

C. Blume, W. Jakob: Programming Languages for Industrial Robots. XIII, 376 pages, 145 figs., 1986

J.W. Lloyd: Foundations of Logic Programming. Second, extended edition. XII, 212 pages, 1987

L. Bolc (Ed.): Computational Models of Learning. IX, 208 pages, 34 figs., 1987

L. Bolc (Ed.): Natural Language Parsing Systems. XVIII, 367 pages, 151 figs., 1987

N. Cercone, G. McCalla (Eds.): The Knowledge Frontier. Essays in the Representation of Knowledge. XXXV, 512 pages, 93 figs., 1987

G. Rayna: REDUCE. Software for Algebraic Computation. IX, 329 pages, 1987

L. Bolc, M.J. Coombs (Eds.): Expert System Applications. IX, 471 pages, 84 figs., 1988

C.-H. Tzeng: A Theory of Heuristic Information in Game-Tree Search. X, 107 pages, 22 figs., 1988.

L. Bolc   M. J. Coombs   (Eds.)

Expert System Applications

With Contributions by
C. Bock W. J. Clancey J. Cuena P. E. Johnson
J. B. Moen H. Prade R. Sauers T. Shibahara T. Tanaka
W. B. Thompson J. K. Tsotsos J. Wang

With 84 Figures and 12 Tables

Springer-Verlag
Berlin Heidelberg New York
London Paris Tokyo

Volume Editors

Leonard Bolc
Institute of Computer Science, Polish Academy of Sciences,
PKiN, pok. 1050, Warsaw, Poland

Michael J. Coombs
Computing Research Laboratory, New Mexico State University,
P.O. Box 30001, Las Cruces, NM 88003, USA

ISBN 3-540-18722-7 Springer-Verlag Berlin Heidelberg New York
ISBN 0-387-18722-7 Springer-Verlag New York Berlin Heidelberg

Library of Congress Cataloging-in-Publication Data.
Expert system applications/L. Bolc, M.J. Coombs, eds.; with contributions by
C. Bock ... [et al.].–(Symbolic computation. Artificial intelligence) Includes Index.
1. Expert systems (Computer science) I. Bolc, Leonard, 1934- . II. Coombs, M.J.
III. Bock, C. (Conrad) IV. Series. QA76.76.E95E955 1988 006.3'3–dc 19 87-35565

Printing: Druckhaus Beltz, Hemsbach; Bookbinding: Schäffer, Grünstadt

2145/3140-543210

Preface

While expert systems technology originated in the United States, its development has become an international concern. Since the start of the DENDRAL project at Stanford University over 15 years ago, with its objective of problem-solving via the automation of actual human expert knowledge, significant expert systems projects have been completed in countries ranging from Japan to France, Spain to China. This book presents a sample of five such projects, along with four substantial reports of mature studies from North American researchers.

Two important issues of expert system design permeate the papers in this volume. The first concerns the incorporation of substantial numeric knowledge into a system. This has become a significant focus of work as researchers have sought to apply expert systems technology to complex, real-world domains already subject to statistical or algebraic description (and handled well at some level in numeric terms). A second prominent issue is that of representing control knowledge in a manner which is both explicit, and thus available for inspection, and compatible with the semantics of the problem domain.

William J. Clancey and Conrad Bock (Stanford University, USA), in their paper "Representing Control Knowledge as Abstract Tasks and Metarules", present an expert systems architecture with enhanced transparency. This is achieved by explicitly representing control knowledge in separation from the domain knowledge upon which it operates. Control knowledge is specified in terms of metarules that index facts, and are used to decide which information to gather about a case, and which conclusions to draw. This approach to control is illustrated via the NEOMYCIN program, contrasts being drawn between the inaccessible control knowledge implicit in the original MYCIN domain rules, and between the use of metarules in TEIRESIAS (a knowledge acquisition and explanation facility for MYCIN) which do not achieve a complete separation of knowledge types.

Clancey and Bock also present a generic expert system shell, HERACLES, which they have abstracted from NEOMYCIN and are applying to the study of reasoning strategies. Metarules in HERACLES are expressed in the form of predicate calculus, organized into rule sets and may be compiled into arbitary data structures (from Lisp code) for efficient execution. Examples are given of the generality and explanatory power afforded by this representation.

Ron Sauers (NBI Inc., USA), in his paper "Controlling Expert Systems", also discusses control issues for rule-based expert systems: the problem of designing a control scheme that ensures effective ordering of rule application, yet at the same time allows for easy extension of the rule-base to encompass new problem domains. Sauers first examines the control schemes typically found in rule-based expert systems, including conflict resolution strategies, the use of metarules, goal-directed behaviour, and blackboard architectures. These are then evaluated in terms of their intended use, and the way they are used in practice for implementing real systems. Finally, the author derives a set of desirable characteristics for rule-based control schemes. These are then employed in the design of a new control architecture, the Context-Driven Control Scheme, which is illustrated by application to a number of difficult control problems.

Henri Prade (University of Toulouse, France) discusses the quantitative treatment of uncertain inference in "A Quantitative Approach to Approximate Reasoning in Rule-based Expert Systems". This paper offers a synthetic and comparative overview of different quantitative approaches to managing uncertainty in rule-based systems. Part one considers three existing theoretical models: probability theory; Shafer's belief functions; fuzzy set and probability theory. These are discussed at length, along with the more empirical method used by MYCIN. A careful distinction is made between uncertainty (which pertains to the impossibility of deciding whether a statement is definitely true or definitely false) and vagueness or imprecision (which refers to the presence of vague predicates or vague quantifiers in a statement). Part two focusses on different patterns of deductive reasoning in the presence of uncertainty or vagueness. The goal of a possibility theory-based approach is emphasised as a means of integrating uncertainty and vagueness within a common framework. Finally, problems of combining uncertain and vague information (obtained from different sources) are discussed in detail.

Takushi Tanaka (The National Language Research Institute, Japan) discusses the design of electronic circuits via the goal-oriented composition of basic components in his paper "Structural Analysis of Electronic Circuits in a Deductive System". The understanding of circuits is seen as a process of finding the hierarchical functional blocks, and from these rediscovering the designer's original intentions. In this respect, circuit design shares common characteristics with natural language: they both carry information of the speaker/designer's intentions mapped onto their structures. In addition, a circuit schematic not only represents a physical object, but also functions as a written language for electronic engineers.

Tanaka's paper presents a new method for analysing circuit structures by means of logic programming. A circuit is viewed as a sentence and its elements as words. Analysis of a circuit is thus analogous to parsing a language, with structures defined by deductive rules which are analogous to a definite clause grammar. By the application of these rules, an object circuit is understood by decomposition into a parse tree of functional units.

José Cuena (Madrid Polytechnic University, Spain), in "Building Expert Systems Based on Simulation Models: An Essay in Methodology", considers the problem of incorporating knowledge previously generated by a simulation model into an expert system. This is of interest because of the significant investment in numerical simulation made by engineers over the past twenty years, and subsequent concern to augment them with expert systems, rather than to replace them. It is also a difficult task, because knowledge-based technology constitutes a qualitative change with respect to traditional computer science. Instead of programs being understood as a set of algorithmic functions operating on different data structures, artificial intelligence systems are frequently viewed as sets of specifications to be interpreted by an inference engine. Cuena offers a methodology for coupling these two conceptions in a single application.

Jue Wang (Academia Sinica, China) presents "An Approach to Designing an Expert System Through Knowledge Organization". The system, KORG, first automatically transforms information supplied by a domain expert into a sematic network representation. Connections within the semantic network then serve as data for an automatic programmer, which structures the knowledge into an expert system. A medical consulting program serves as an example for the approach.

Paul E. Johnson, James B. Moen and William B. Thompson (University of Minnesota, USA) consider "Garden Path Errors in Diagnostic Reasoning". Experts often use only a small portion of relevant diagnostic knowledge when solving a problem. They initially propose a solution known to be associated with dominant signs and symptoms, and thereafter preferentially use knowledge related to this first hypothesis. Although this strategy is frequently effective, there is the risk of applying the wrong knowledge when given misleading symptoms. In this case, experts will commit errors, since the knowledge applied will not deal with conflicting information which would tend to disconfirm the initial solution. The paper discusses such "garden path" errors as they affect both human diagnosticians and expert systems, and presents mechanisms for their avoidance incorporated in two generations of a diagnostic program.

John K. Tsotsos and Tetsutaro Shibahara (University of Toronto, Canada) describe two studies – ALVEN and CAA – of "Knowledge Organization and Its Role in Temporal and Causal Signal Understanding". Both projects deal with temporally rich data interpretation tasks, although their focus is on different aspects of interpretation. The ALVEN program processes sequences of time-varying X-ray images (in order to assess performance of the left ventricle of a human heart), while CAA considers an entire signal as if time were an additional spatial dimension (in order to detect and classify abnormalities in heart rhythm from causal relationships between the electrophysiology of the heart and a related electrocardiogram signal).

Warsaw, Poland and Las Cruces, New Mexico   *L. Bolc*
January 1988   *M. J. Coombs*

Table of Contents

Representing Control Knowledge as Abstract Tasks and Metarules

William J. Clancey and Conrad Bock

Stanford Knowledge Systems Laboratory
701 Welch Road, Building C
Palo Alto, CA 94304, USA

ABSTRACT

A poorly designed knowledge base can be as cryptic as an arbitrary program and just as difficult to maintain. Representing inference procedures abstractly, separately from domain facts and relations, makes the design more transparent and explainable. The combination of abstract procedures and a relational language for organizing domain knowledge provides a generic framework for constructing knowledge bases for related problems in other domains and also provides a useful starting point for studying the nature of strategies. In HERACLES inference procedures are represented as abstract metarules, expressed in a form of the predicate calculus, organized and controlled as rule sets. A compiler converts the rules into Lisp code and allows domain relations to be encoded as arbitrary data structures for efficiency. Examples are given of the explanation and teaching capabilities afforded by this representation. Different perspectives for understanding HERACLES' inference procedure and how it defines a relational knowledge base are discussed in some detail.

1 INTRODUCTION

An important feature of knowledge-based programs, distinguishing them from traditional programs, is that they contain well-structured statements of *what is true about the world* that are separate from *what to do to solve problems*. At least in principle, this separation makes it possible to write programs that interpret knowledge bases from multiple perspectives, providing the foundation for explanation, learning, and teaching capabilities (Davis, 1976, Szolovits, et al., 1978, de Kleer, 1979, Swartout, 1981, Moore, 1982, Clancey, 1983a, Genesereth, 1983). The basic considerations in realizing this design are:

1. *Abstraction:* To enable multiple use, inference procedures should be stated separately, not instantiated and composed with the domain facts they manipulate;

2. *Interpretability:* Both factual and procedural knowledge should be stated in a language that multiple programs can interpret (including a natural language translator), incorporating levels of abstraction that facilitate manipulation (an issue of *perspicuity*);

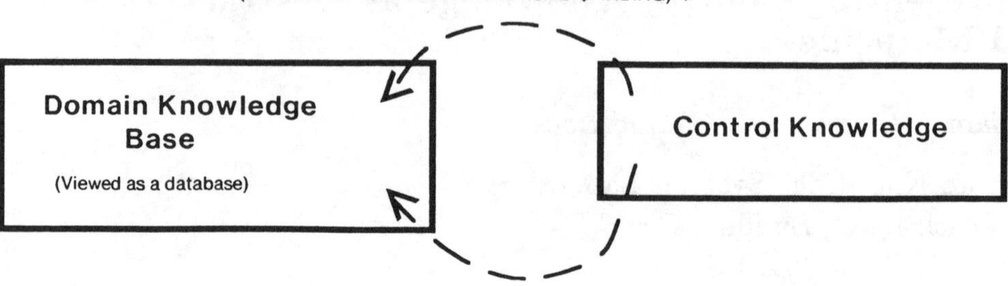

Figure 1-1: Separation of domain and control knowledge in NEOMYCIN

3. *Rationale:* Underlying constraints that justify the design of procedures and models of the world supporting domain facts may be useful for explanation as well as problem solving.

In the GUIDON program (Clancey, 1979, Clancey, 1982a) we explored the advantages and limitations of MYCIN's simple, rule-based architecture as a knowledge representation for a teaching program. To resolve some of the difficulties, we devised a new architecture for a program called NEOMYCIN. In NEOMYCIN (Clancey and Letsinger, 1984, Clancey, 1984a, Clancey, 1984b), the medical (domain) knowledge and diagnostic procedure of MYCIN are expanded (to provide more material for teaching) and represented separately and explicitly. Figure 1-1 shows this idea in a simple way. We also refer to the diagnostic procedure as *strategic* or *control knowledge*. The procedure indexes the domain knowledge, deciding what information to gather about a problem and what assertions to make. The representation of this procedure in a manner that facilitates explanation, student modeling, and ease of maintenance is the main subject of this paper. The complexity of the diagnostic procedure, its abstract nature, and the requirements of the teaching application for interpretability and explicit rationale distinguish this research from previous work.

The development of a good procedural language can be viewed from several perspectives, reflecting the evolutionary process of finding a good representation, using it, and generalizing:

1. *Specify diagnostic procedure.* We studied MYCIN's rules and identified two recurrent, implicit strategies: a hypothesis refinement strategy (Section 2.1) and a question-asking strategy (Section 2.2). We significantly augmented the procedure to incorporate a more complete model of human diagnostic reasoning that is useful for teaching (Section 3).

2. *Represent diagnostic procedure.* To meet our design criteria, we chose to represent the control knowledge as sets of rules, organized into subprocedures called *tasks.* To make explicit how domain knowledge is used by the control rules, we chose a predicate calculus language coupled with procedural attachment (Section 4). This

combination makes explicit the relations among concepts, allows variables for generality, and allows arbitrary representations of domain knowledge for efficiency.

3. *Re-represent metarules.* Observing that the interpreter for the control knowledge was still implicit in Lisp code, we re-implemented it as a simple rule-based system (Section 6). The experiment failed: Expressing knowledge in rules and predicate calculus does not mean that the notation is readable by people or easily interpreted for multiple purposes. A notation is not inherently *declarative*; instead, this is a relation between *a notation* and *an interpreter that decodes the notation for some purpose* (Rumelhart and Norman, 1983). The nature of the knowledge to be decoded, and thus the *expressibility* of a given notation, may change with the purpose.

4. *Make the representation practical.* To make the control knowledge interpretation process more efficient, a compiler was written to compile control rules into Lisp code, replacing relational expressions by direct access to domain data structures (Section 5).

5. *Exploit the representation.* Given a "rough draft" notation that brings about appropriate problem solving performance, we developed explanation and student modeling programs to demonstrate the adequacy of the notation for meeting our design goals. We discovered that some additional knowledge, not required for problem solving, is useful for interpreting the control knowledge for other purposes (Section 7).

6. *Generalize* NEOMYCIN. In studying NEOMYCIN, we determined that the control knowledge is a general procedure for *heuristic classification* (Clancey, 1985). In comparing NEOMYCIN to other programs, we determined that it does diagnosis by selecting a *system identification* from a taxonomy pre-enumerated in the knowledge base. Thus, the program's architecture embodies a general problem solving method for constructing or interpreting arbitrary systems by selecting from pre-enumerated solutions.

Extracting the domain knowledge from NEOMYCIN, as was done in creating EMYCIN from MYCIN, we named the framework HERACLES, "Heuristic Classification Shell," consisting of the classification procedure and interpreter, the relational language for stating domain knowledge and procedural attachments, compiler, and explanation program. We used the HERACLES framework to construct another, non-medical knowledge system in the domain of cast iron defects diagnosis (Section 7.2). We demonstrate the generality of the task language by using it to state the explanation program (Section 7.5).

7. *Study the metarules.* We studied the collected body of control knowledge and discovered patterns revealing how the meaning of a procedure is tied up in the relational classification of domain knowledge (Section 8). We found that the predicate calculus notation is extremely valuable for revealing these patterns. We

examined the difficulties of achieving the ideal separation between domain and control knowledge to characterize situations in which it is impractical or impossible.

The body of this paper unfolds the development of NEOMYCIN, HERACLES, explanation, modeling, and application programs, as indicated above. The central theme is that *an important design principle for building knowledge-based systems is to represent all control knowledge abstractly, separate from the domain knowledge it operates upon.* In essence, we are applying the familiar principle of separating programs from data, but in the context of knowledge-based programming. We argue that the advantages for construction and maintenance of such programs are so pronounced that benefits will accrue from using this approach, even if there is no interest in using the knowledge base for explanation or teaching. The many scientific, engineering, and practical benefits are summarized in Section 10. This work is extensively compared to other research in Section 9.

2 WHAT IS ABSTRACT CONTROL KNOWLEDGE?

We begin with a simple introduction to the idea of abstract control knowledge and examples of alternative representations. "Control knowledge" specifies when and how a program is to carry out its operations, such as pursuing a goal, focusing, acquiring data, and making inferences. A basic distinction can be made between the facts and relations of a knowledge base and the program operations that act upon it. For example, facts and relations in a medical knowledge base might include (expressed in a predicate calculus formulation):

```
(SUBTYPE INFECTION MENINGITIS)
   -- "meningitis is a kind of infection"

(CAUSES INFECTION FEVER)
   -- "infection causes fever"

(CAUSES INFECTION SHAKING-CHILLS)
   -- "infection causes shaking chills"

(DISORDER MENINGITIS)
   -- "meningitis is a disorder"

(FINDING FEVER)
   -- "fever is a finding"
```

Such a knowledge base might be used to provide consultative advice to a user, in a way typical of expert systems (Duda and Shortliffe, 1983). Consider, for example, a consultation system for diagnosing some faulty device. One typical program operation is to select a finding that causes a disorder and ask the user to indicate whether the device being diagnosed exhibits that symptom. Specifically, a medical diagnostic system might ask tne user whether the patient is suffering from shaking chills, in order to determine whether he has an infection. The first description of the program's operation is *abstract*, referring only to domain-independent relations like "finding" and "causes"; the second description is *concrete*, referring to domain-dependent terms like "shaking-chills" and "infection". ("Domain-independent" doesn't mean that it applies to every domain, just that the term is not specific to any one domain.)

The operation described here can be characterized abstractly as "attempting to confirm a diagnostic hypothesis" or concretely as "attempting to determine whether the patient has an infection." Either description indicates the *strategy* that motivates the question the program is asking of the user. So in this example we see how a strategy, or control knowledge, can be stated either abstractly or concretely. The following two examples illustrate how both forms of control knowledge might be represented in a knowledge base.

2.1 An implicit refinement strategy

In MYCIN (Shortliffe, 1976), most knowledge is represented as domain-specific rules. For example, the rule "If the patient has an infection and his CSF cell count is less than 10, then it is unlikely that he has meningitis," might be represented as:

```
PREMISE:
    ($AND (SAME CNTXT INFECTION)
          (ILESSP (VAL1 CNTXT CSFCELLCOUNT) 10))
ACTION:
    (CONCLUDE CNTXT INFECTION-TYPE MENINGITIS TALLY -700)
```

The order of clauses is important here, for the program should not consider the "CSF cell count" if the patient does not have an infection. Such clause ordering in all rules ensures that the program proceeds by top-down refinement from infection to meningitis to subtypes of meningitis. The disease hierarchy cannot be stated explicitly in the MYCIN rule language; it is implicit in the design of the rules. (See (Clancey, 1983a) for further analysis of the limitations of MYCIN's representation.)

CENTAUR (Aikins, 1980), derived from MYCIN, is a system in which disease hierarchies are explicit. In its representation language, MYCIN's meningitis knowledge might be encoded as follows (using a Lisp property list notation):

```
INFECTION
    MORE-SPECIFIC     ((disease MENINGITIS)
                       (disease BACTEREMIA)...)
    IF-CONFIRMED      (DETERMINE disease of INFECTION)

MENINGITIS
    MORE-SPECIFIC     ((subtype BACTERIAL)
                       (subtype VIRAL)...)
    IF-CONFIRMED      (DETERMINE subtype of MENINGITIS)
```

In CENTAUR, hierarchical relations among disorders are explicit (meningitis is a specific kind of infection), and the strategies for using the knowledge are domain-specific (after confirming that the patient has an infection, determine what more specific disease he has). This design enables CENTAUR to articulate its operations better than MYCIN, whose hierarchical relations and strategy are procedurally embedded in rules.

However, observe that each node of CENTAUR's hierarchy essentially repeats a single strategy-- try to confirm the presence of a child disorder--and the overall strategy of top-down refinement is not explicit. Aikins has *labeled* CENTAUR's strategies, but has not stated them abstractly. By representing strategies abstractly, it is possible to have a more explicit and non-redundant design. This is what is done in NEOMYCIN.

In NEOMYCIN domain relations and strategy are represented *separately* and strategy is represented abstractly. A typical rule that accomplishes, in part, the abstract task of attempting to confirm a diagnostic hypothesis and its subtypes is shown below.

```
<Domain Knowledge>

INFECTION
    CAUSAL-SUBTYPES     (MENINGITIS BACTEREMIA ...)

MENINGITIS
    CAUSAL-SUBTYPES     (BACTERIAL VIRAL ...)

<Abstract Control Knowledge>

TASK: EXPLORE-AND-REFINE
ARGUMENT: CURRENT-HYPOTHESIS

METARULE001
IF the hypothesis being focused upon
        has a child
        that has not been pursued,
THEN pursue that child.

(IF (AND (CURRENT-ARGUMENT $CURFOCUS)
         (CHILDOF $CURFOCUS $CHILD)
         (THNOT (PURSUED $CHILD)))
    (NEXTACTION (PURSUE-HYPOTHESIS $CHILD)))
```

NEOMYCIN uses a deliberation/action loop for deducing what it should do next. *Metarules*, like the one shown above, recommend what task should be done next, what domain rule applied, or what domain finding requested from the user (details are given in Section 4.1). The important thing to notice is that this metarule will be applied for refining any disorder, obviating the need to "compile" redundantly into the domain hierarchy of disorders how it should be searched. When a new domain relation is declared (e.g., a new kind of infection is added to the hierarchy) the abstract control knowledge will use it appropriately. That is, *we separate out what the domain knowledge is from how it should be used.*

Metarules were first introduced for use in expert systems by Davis (Davis, 1976), but he conceived of them as being domain-specific. In that form, principles are encoded redundantly, just like CENTAUR's control knowledge. For example, the principle of pursuing common causes before unusual causes appears as specific metarules for ordering the domain rules of each disorder (see (Clancey, 1983a) for detailed discussion).

The benefits of stating metarules abstractly are illustrated further by a second example.

2.2 An implicit question-asking strategy

Another reason for ordering clauses in a system like MYCIN is to prevent unnecessary requests for data. A finding might be deduced or ruled out from other facts available to the program. For example, the rule "If the patient has undergone surgery and neurosurgery, then consider diplococcus as a cause of the meningitis" might be represented as follows.

```
PREMISE: ($AND (SAME CNTXT SURGERY)
               (SAME CNTXT NEUROSURGERY))
ACTION: (CONCLUDE CNTXT COVERFOR DIPLOCOCCUS TALLY 400)
```

We say that the surgery clause "screens" for the relevance of asking about neurosurgery. Observe that neither the relation between these two findings (that neurosurgery is a *type of* surgery) nor the strategy of considering a general finding in order to rule out one of its subtypes is explicit. An alternative way used in MYCIN for encoding this knowledge is to have a separate "screening" rule that at least makes clear that these two findings are related: "If the patient has not undergone surgery, then he has not undergone neurosurgery."

```
PREMISE: ($AND (NOTSAME CNTXT SURGERY))
ACTION: (CONCLUDE CNTXT NEUROSURGERY YES TALLY -1000)
```

Such a rule obviates the need for a "surgery" clause in every rule that mentions neurosurgery, so this design is more elegant and less prone to error. However, the question-ordering strategy and the abstract relation between the findings are still not explicit. Consequently, the program's explanation system cannot help a system maintainer understand the underlying design.

In NEOMYCIN, the above rule is represented abstractly by a metarule for the task of finding out new data. This metarule (shown below) is really an *abstract generalization* of all screening rules. Factoring out the statement of relations among findings from how those relations are to be used produces an elegant and economical representation. Besides enabling more-detailed explanation, such a design makes the system easier to construct and more robust.

Consider the multiple ways in which a single relation between findings can be used. If we are told that the patient has neurosurgery, we can use the subsumption link (or its inverse) to conclude that the patient has undergone surgery. Or if we know that the patient has not undergone any kind of surgery we know about, we can use the "closed world assumption" and conclude that the patient has not undergone surgery. These inferences are controlled by abstract metarules in NEOMYCIN.

<*Domain Knowledge*>

```
(SUBSUMES SURGERY NEUROSURGERY)
(SUBSUMES SURGERY CARDIACSURGERY)
```

<*Abstract Control Knowledge*>

```
TASK: FINDOUT
ARGUMENT: DESIRED-FINDING

METARULE002
IF the desired finding
      is a subtype of a class of findings and
      the class of findings is not present in this case,
THEN conclude that the desired finding is not present.

(IF (AND (CURRENT-ARGUMENT $SUBTYPE)
         (SUBSUMES $CLASS $SUBTYPE)
         (THNOT (SAMEP CNTXT $CLASS)))
    (NEXTACTION
         (CONCLUDE CNTXT $SUBTYPE 'YES TALLY -1000)))
```

The knowledge base is easier to construct because the expert needn't specify every situation in which a given fact or relation should be used. New facts and relations can be added in a simple way; the abstract metarules explicitly state how the relations will be used. The same generality makes the knowledge base more robust. The system is capable of making use of facts and relations for different purposes, perhaps in combinations that would be difficult to anticipate or enumerate.

3 DESIGN CRITERIA FOR NEOMYCIN

In designing an architecture for an intelligent system, we generally start with a set of behaviors that we wish the system to exhibit. For teaching, there are three dominating behavioral criteria:

1. *Solve problems.* The system should be able to solve the problems that it will teach students how to solve. This is the primary advantage of using the knowledge-based approach.[1]

2. *Explain own behavior.* The system must be able to state what it is doing: What domain knowledge it uses to solve the problem, its goals, and the methods it tries. The system might also need to state the rationale for domain facts and procedures, that is, to say why they are correct with respect to some set of constraints or assumptions (Clancey, 1983a).

3. *Model student behavior.* The system must be able to recognize when its procedures and knowledge are used by another problem solver. Specifically:

    a. *The program should be able to solve problems in multiple ways.* For example, a diagnostic program should be able to cope with an arbitrary ordering of student requests for data, and evaluate arbitrary partial solutions at any time (Brown, et al., 1982a).

    b. *The program should solve problems in a manner that students can understand and emulate.* This is obviously necessary if the program is to convey a useful problem solving approach and to recognize it or its absence in other problem solvers.[2] Consequently, the problem solving procedure should be at least an ideal model of what people do, and may need to incorporate alternative and non-optimal methods.[3]

Both explanation and student modeling are made possible by representing the problem solving procedure in a general way, separate from the domain knowledge, in a notation that can be translated to natural language. The ability to apply domain knowledge in an arbitrary order enables the modeling program to follow what the student is doing, as well as to make prescribe good behaviors in teaching interactions.

---

[1] In contrast, traditional CAI programs, except in mathematics and fact recall problems such as geography, are not designed to solve problems independently. They present material, evaluate, and branch according to possible situations pre-enumerated by the program "author" (Clancey, 1982b).

[2] Of course, the knowledge-based tutor is not the only way to use computers for teaching, and the cost/benefit of this approach is not known. See (Papert, 1980, Clancey, 1982b, Brown, 1983) for discussion.

[3] (Johnson, 1983) describes alternative models of reasoning as the basis of designing a knowledge system: mathematical optimization, simulation, and ad hoc rationalization.

With emphasis on problem solving performance and only superficial explanation requirements, most early knowledge systems do not state control knowledge separately and explicitly in the manner of NEOMYCIN. Figure 3-1 summarizes the simple rule and frame-based approaches to knowledge representation. Rule-based systems have a simple (opaque) interpreter, and can easily index what facts and rules were used to make Sssertions. While the literature (e.g., (Davis, et al., 1977)) makes a major issue of the separation of the knowledge base from the "inference engine," the control knowledge is in fact implicit in the rules. Frame-based systems represent domain facts in a well-structured way, but typically control knowledge is represented in arbitrary Lisp code that cannot be explained automatically. In NEOMYCIN, meeting the behavioral goals of explanation and modeling requires a combination of approaches:

- Following the design principle of the rule-based approach, *all knowledge is stated in a simple syntax* that programs can interpret for multiple purposes. In particular, the conditional-action form of control knowledge (or any procedure) makes rules a suitable representation.

- Following the design principle of the frame-based approach, *domain knowledge is stated separately from control knowledge,* so that domain concepts and relations are explicit. In particular, the concept-relation form of domain knowledge makes frame-like structures a suitable representation. Moreover, rules are themselves organized hierarchically with additional knowledge about how they are to be applied.

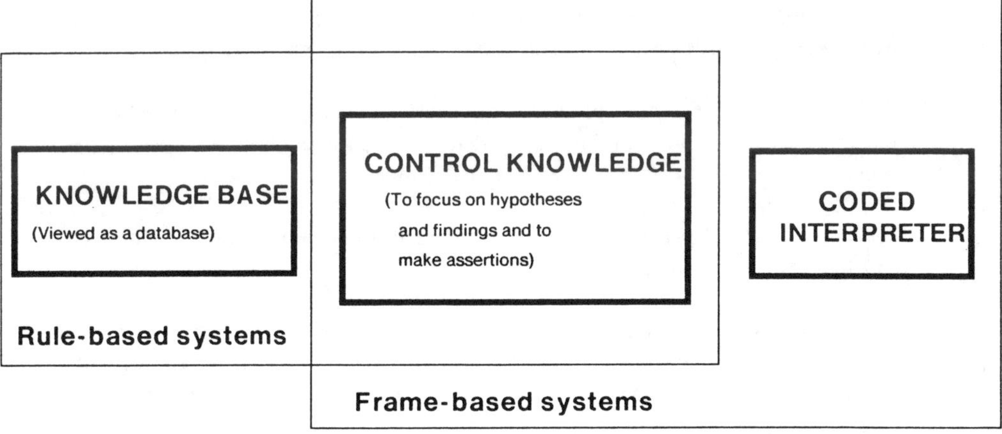

Figure 3-1: Alternative representations of control knowledge

Here we summarize in more detail how this architecture and the design criteria are realized in NEOMYCIN:

- The diagnostic procedure mentions no specifically medical concepts or relations.

- Clauses of domain rules are arbitrarily ordered. Most rules (136/169) have only one clause; the remaining are definitions or patterns that trigger diagnoses.

- There is no uncontrolled backchaining at the domain level. When new problem information is required to evaluate a domain rule, the program does not arbitrarily apply domain rules, but selects among them. This is also called *deliberate subgoaling* (Laird, 1983).

- The diagnostic procedure is decomposed into subprocedures that facilitate explanation. Our rudimentary theory characterizes diagnosis as a process of shifting focus to manipulate a set of possible solutions (the "differential"), including means to generate this set, categorize and refine it, and test it for completeness (Clancey, 1984b).

- There is a fixed set of procedural (opaque) primitives:

  - ask for problem data,

  - assert a domain fact (in metarules that are generalized domain rules),

  - attempt to apply a domain heuristic rule, and

  - invoke a subprocedure.

- Domain knowledge reflects expert experience, consisting of *procedurally-defined associations*, collectively called *domain schema knowledge*:

  - *trigger rules* describe patterns of findings that immediately suggest a hypothesis, perhaps causing an intermediate question to be asked

  - *follow-up questions* are process characterizations that are immediately requested, e.g., upon finding out that the patient has a fever, the program/expert asks for the patient's actual temperature.

  - *heuristic finding/hypothesis rules* make direct connections between findings and hypotheses, omitting causal details.

  - *general questions* are broad characterizations of the patient's history that are intended to cover everything that the patient might have experienced that could cause a disease, e.g., travel, hospitalizations, medications, immunosuppression.

- The diagnostic procedure of NEOMYCIN is based on protocol analysis and previously formalized studies of medical problem solving (Clancey, 1984a, Clancey, 1984b). The procedure reflects a variety of cognitive, social, mathematical, and case experience constraints, none of which are explicit in the program.

- Our methodology assumes that there will be an accumulation of procedural knowledge over time that will be applicable in other domains.

To summarize, NEOMYCIN expands upon MYCIN's knowledge, representing domain and control knowledge separately: The domain knowledge is experiential (schemas) and the control knowledge is a general heuristic classification inference procedure.

4 ARCHITECTURE OF HERACLES

To make control knowledge explicit, many changes and additions were made to MYCIN. Because none of these are specific to NEOMYCIN, but are characteristics of the general framework, called HERACLES, we will hereafter refer to HERACLES and use specific examples from the NEOMYCIN knowledge base. The architecture (refer to Figure 4-3) consists of:

- control knowledge:

  o metarules,

  o tasks,

  o task interpreter.

- domain knowledge:

  o terms and relations

  o procedural attachment (implementation specification)

  o implementation data structures.

Briefly, a task is a procedure, namely a controlled sequence of conditional actions. Each conditional action is called a *metarule*. Metarule premises are stated in the relational language, which is indexed to domain knowledge data structures via procedural attachments. Associated with each task is additional knowledge specifying how its metarules are to be applied. The relational language we have chosen is called MRS (Genesereth, 1983, MRSDICT, 1982). Its relevant features are: a prefix predicate, calculus notation, use of pattern variables with backtracking, use of backchaining in application of rules to determine the truth of propositions, and procedural attachment to allow arbitrary means for assertion or truth evaluation, thus enabling multiple representation of knowledge. (See Appendix II for further details.)

4.1 Metarules

Figure 4-1 shows a typical metarule, for the task "test hypothesis." Such rules were originally called *metarules* to distinguish them from the domain rules, and because most of them directly or indirectly have the effect of selecting domain rules to be applied. Given the set of primitive actions, the term "inference procedure rule" is more accurate.

Metarule premises consist of a conjunction of propositions. There are three kinds of relations: domain, problem solving history, and computational functions. In addition, a relation may be a composite inferred from rules, which we call a *metarule premise relation* (see Figure 4-2). The indicated metarule will collect the set of unapplied domain rules that

---

```
Premise: (MAKESET (ENABLING.QUESTIONS CURFOCUS $RULE) RULELST)

Action:  (TASK APPLYRULES RULELST)

Task:    TEST-HYPOTHESIS
```

Figure 4-1:   Typical NEOMYCIN metarule

```
Premise:  (AND (ENABLINGQ $HYP $FOCUSQ)
               (NOT (TRACEDP ROOTNODE $FOCUSQ))
               (EVIDENCEFOR? $FOCUSQ $HYP $RULE $CF)
               (UNAPPLIED? $RULE))

Action:   (ENABLING.QUESTIONS $HYP $RULE)
```

Figure 4-2:   Typical rule for concluding about a metarule premise relation

mention an unrequested finding that is a necessary cause to the hypothesis under consideration (e.g., receiving antibiotics is a necessary cause of partially treated meningitis).

4.1.1 Groundwork: Domain knowledge, problem-solving history, and Lisp functions

In creating HERACLES from EMYCIN, the original "rule," "context," and "parameter" structures were given new properties, but remain as the primitives of the knowledge representation. For example, parameters are now called *findings* and *hypotheses*, depending on whether they are supplied to the program or inferred. They are hierarchically related. Rules are annotated to indicate which are definitions and the direction of causality if appropriate. Inverse pointers are automatically added throughout to allow flexible and efficient indexing during problem solving. (See Appendix I for a complete listing of domain terms and relations. Further discussion appears in (Clancey, 1984a) and (Clancey, 1984b).)

The problem solving history consists of the bookkeeping of EMYCIN (record of rule application and parameter determination), plus additional information about task and metarule application.

Simple Lisp functions, such as arithmetic functions, are not translated into tasks and metarules. In addition, complex functions in the modified domain (EMYCIN) interpreter, such as the rule-previewing mechanism, are still represented in Lisp. Metarules also invoke a few complicated interface routines, for example to allow the user to enter a table of data.[4]

The domain data structures, problem-solving history, and Lisp functions are collectively called the *Heracles groundwork*. Procedural attachment is used to interface relations appearing in metarules with the HERACLES groundwork.

---

[4]The original EMYCIN function FINDOUT *was* made into a task to enable the explanation and modeling programs to account for how HERACLES infers findings when it doesn't ask the user. In addition, portions of the rule interpreter and all forward reasoning (e.g., application of domain antecedent rules) are re-represented as metarules.

4.1.2 Procedural attachment--Motivation and advantages

A key improvement of HERACLES over early versions of NEOMYCIN is the use of a relational language with procedural attachment in the metarules. Formerly, arbitrary Lisp functions were invoked by metarule premises, inhibiting explanation and student modeling because this code could not be interpreted easily by programs (excluding, of course, the implementation-level Lisp interpreter and compiler).

The advantages of using MRS for representing the premises of metarules are:

- Tasks and metarules themselves make procedural steps and iteration explicit; the MRS encoding makes metarule premises explicit.

- Prefix Predicate Calculus (PPC) provides a simple syntactic structure of relations, terms, and logic combinations that facilitates writing programs to interpret it.

- Backtracking with variables allows matching constraints to be stated separately from the operations of search and database lookup, so complex interactions are restated as simple conjuncts.

- Using rules to infer metarule premise relations allows intermediate levels of abstraction to be cogently represented as rules.

- The messy implementation details of the domain and problem solving history data structures are hidden, yet these underlying structures make efficient use of storage and are indexed for efficient access.

- The PPC syntax facilitates stating metaknowledge. Patterns among relations can be stated explicitly, making it possible to write interpretation procedures that treat relations abstractly. For example, the metarule compiler need only reason about the half-dozen categories of domain data structures, rather than deal with the relations directly. This idea is central to the possibility and advantage of using abstract procedures (see Section 8).

At run time an MRS program deduces what method (inference procedure) to use to evaluate the truth of a statement, and then applies the indicated function. The original program we implemented in MRS, called MRS/NEOMYCIN, was much too slow to be practical (see Section 6). In the current version of HERACLES the metarules are compiled, replacing all of the relations and procedural attachments with direct lookup in the domain knowledge base and problem-solving history (Section 5). To do this, the compiler needs information about how each relation is actually represented in the Lisp data structures and functions of the HERACLES groundwork. Table 4-1 gives the possible forms of implementation, with examples.

There is a miscellaneous category of relations for which the compiler produces relation-specific code. Examples are: a relation for satisfying another relation as many times as possible (MAKESET); the quadruple relation among a finding, hypothesis, domain rule, and certainty factor (EVIDENCEFOR); and relations that can be easily optimized by the compiler (e.g., MEMBER and NULL).

14

Table 4-1:   Implementation of HERACLES groundwork

implementation	example	interpretation
FLAG	NEW-DIFFERENTIAL	T or NIL Lisp var
VARIABLE	STRONGCOMP.WGHT	Lisp variable
LIST	DIFFERENTIAL	Lisp list
PROPMARK	ASKFIRST	T or NIL property
PROPLIST	CHILDREN	list-valued property
PROPVAL	PROMPT	arbitrary property
METARULE-PREMISE-RELATION	TAXREFINE?	determined by a rule
FUNCTION	SAMEP	Lisp function

In summary, we use a relational specification for perspicuity, Lisp data structures and functions for convenience and efficiency, and compile the metarules to avoid the expense of run-time pattern matching and indirect lookup. The resulting metarules are easier to read, maintain, and explain automatically than the original Lisp code.

4.2 Tasks

A HERACLES *task* consists of an ordered sequence of metarules and additional knowledge about how they should be applied by the *task interpreter*. The program begins a consultation by executing the top-level task, CONSULT. The tasks then direct the application of metarules; when metarules succeed, primitive actions are taken and other tasks invoked. See Figure 4-3.

Currently there are 75 metarules in HERACLES, organized into 29 tasks. The invocation structure, integrating hypothesis- and data-directed reasoning, is shown in Figures 4-4 and 4-5.

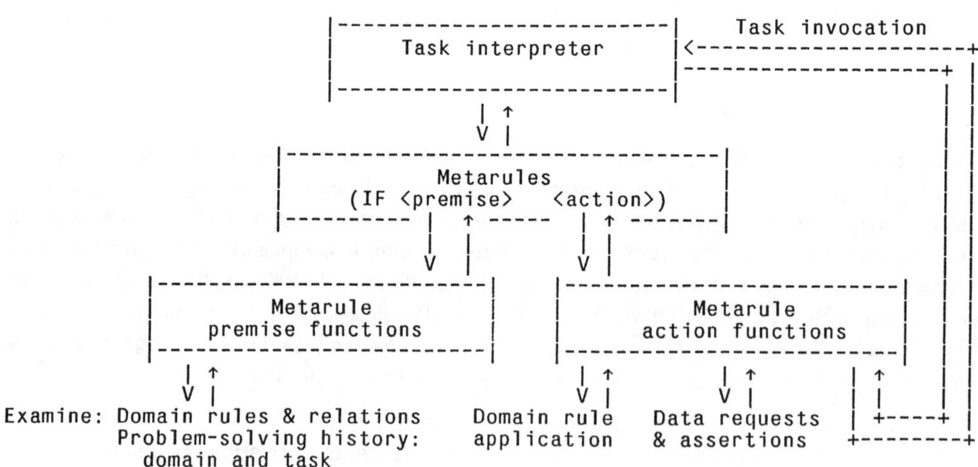

Figure 4-3:   Flow of control in HERACLES

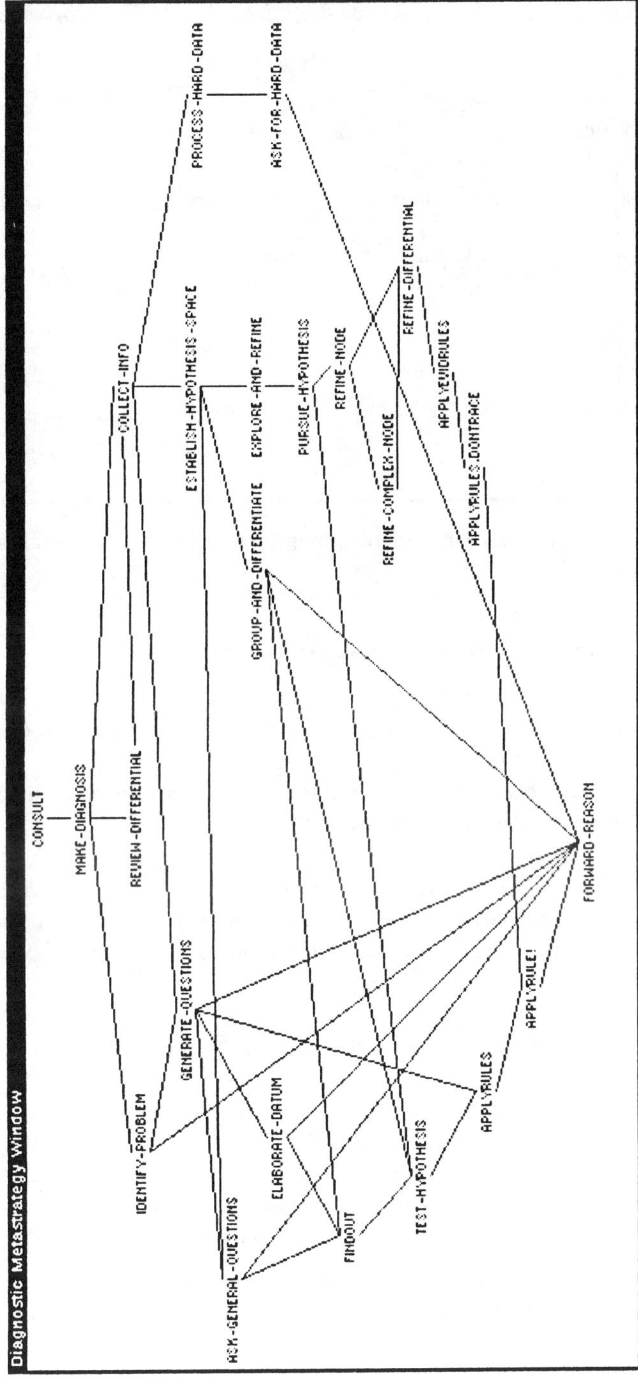

Figure 4-4: Heracles classification tasks [shown as a lattice]

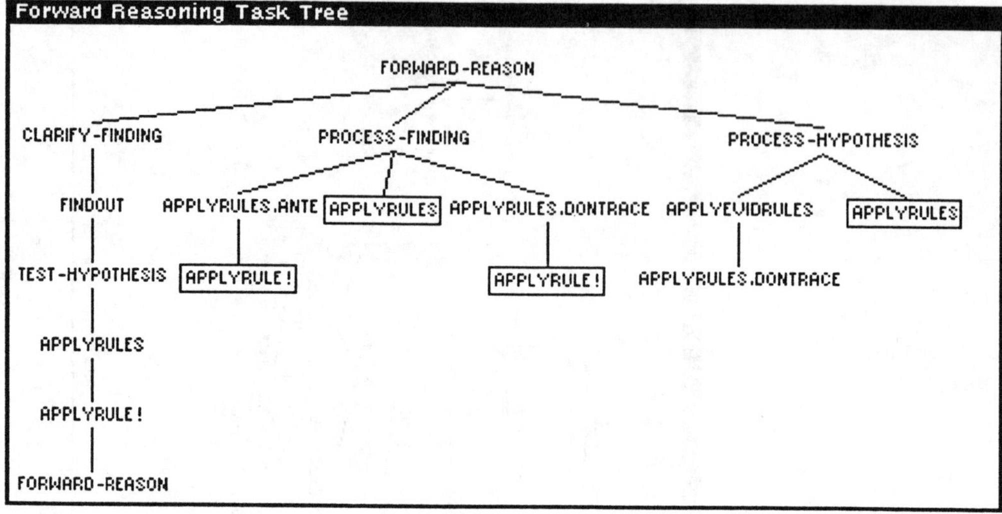

Figure 4-5:   Heracles forward reasoning tasks [shown as a hierarchy]

4.3 The task interpreter

The information used by the task interpreter is:

- The *task focus*, which is the argument of the task (e.g., the focus of the task TEST-HYPOTHESIS is the hypothesis to be tested). Only one focus is allowed.

- The main body of ordered metarules, which are to be applied to complete the task. (Called the *do-during* metarules.)

- The *end condition*, which may abort the task *or any subtask* when it becomes true. Aborting can occur only while the do-during metarules are being applied. The end condition is tested after each metarule of a task succeeds. A task may also be marked to prevent abortion.

- Ordered metarules to be applied before the do-during rules.

- Ordered metarules to be applied after the do-during rules.

- The *task type*, which specifies how the do-during metarules are to be applied. There are two dimensions to the task type: *simple* or *iterative*, and *try-all* or not-try-all. The combinations give four ways of applying the do-during rules:

  - *Simple, try-all*. The rules are applied once each, in order. Each time a metarule succeeds, the end condition is tested.

  - *Simple, not-try-all*. The rules are applied in sequence until one succeeds or the end condition succeeds.

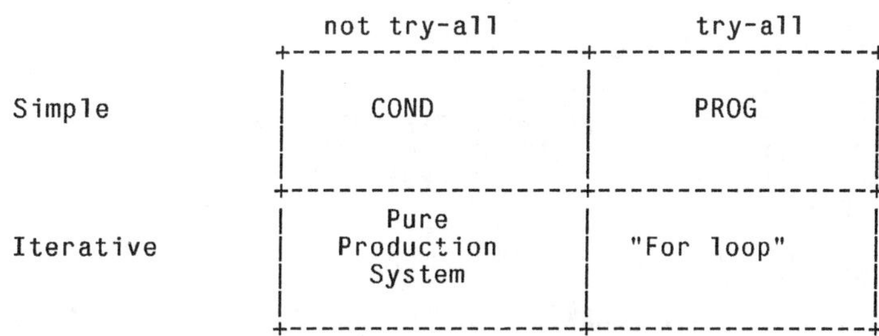

Figure 4-6: Common equivalents for four ways of controlling metarules

o *Iterative, try-all*. All the rules are applied in sequence. If there are one or more successes, the process is started over. The process stops when all the rules in the sequence fail or the end condition succeeds.

o *Iterative, not-try-all*. Same as for iterative try-all, except that the process is restarted after a single metarule succeeds.

The four combinations of control are shown in Figure 4-6 with their common equivalents.

The experiment of representing the task interpreter in *metacontrol* rules is described in Section 6.

Only a few tasks have end conditions. Studying them reveals the following interpretations:

1. *The end condition is the negation of a pre-requisite for doing the task.* For example, the pre-requisite of examining subcategories of hypotheses (EXPLORE-AND-REFINE) is that all more general categories have already been considered. The end condition of EXPLORE-AND-REFINE is (NOT (WIDER-DIFFERENTIAL)), indicating that there is no new hypothesis that lies outside of previously considered categories.

2. *The end condition is the goal the task seeks to accomplish.* For example, the goal of probing for additional information (GENERATE-QUESTIONS) is to suggest new hypotheses. The end condition of GENERATE-QUESTIONS is (DIFFERENTIAL $HYP), indicating that the program has at least one hypothesis under consideration.

Figure 4-7 gives the metarules and control information for the task GENERATE-QUESTIONS (with auxiliary rules to conclude about metarule premise relations). Figure 4-8 shows a partial history of task invocation for a typical NEOMYCIN consultation (After gathering laboratory data (PROCESS-HARD-DATA, PHD), new hypotheses are shown being explored. PURSUE-HYPOTHESIS (PUH) Is invoked three times, leading to application of four domain rules and an attempt to find out five findings.)

<u>GENERATE-QUESTIONS</u>

```
TASK-TYPE:        ITERATIVE
ENDCONDITION:     ADEQUATE-DIFFERENTIAL
LOCALVARS:        ($FOCUSPARM RULELST)
ACHIEVED-BY:      (RULE003 RULE359 RULE386 RULE425)
ABBREV:           GQ
```

<u>RULE003</u>

```
Premise:  (NOT (TASK-COMPLETED ASK-GENERAL-QUESTIONS))
Action:   (TASK ASK-GENERAL-QUESTIONS)
```
Comment: *Ask general questions if not done already.*

<u>RULE359</u>

```
Premise:  (PARTPROC.NOTELABORATED? $FOCUSPARM)
Action:   (TASK ELABORATE-DATUM $FOCUSPARM)
```
Comment: *Ask for elaborations on partially processed data.*

<u>RULE386</u>

```
Premise:  (MAKESET (PARTPROC.SUGGESTRULES? $RULE)
                        RULELST')
Action:   (TASK APPLYRULES RULELST)
```
Comment: *Apply rules using known data as if they were trigger rules.*

<u>RULE425</u>

```
Premise:  (NOT MORE-DATA-COLLECTED)
Action:   (DO-ALL (COLLECT.MORE.DATA)
                    (TASK FORWARD-REASON))
```
Comment: *Simply ask the user for more information.*

<u>Auxiliary metarule premise rules</u>

```
Premise:  (AND (PARTPROC.DATA $DATUM)
               (YNPARM $DATUM)
               (SAMEP ROOTNODE $DATUM $CF)
               (NOT (ELABORATED $DATUM))
               (OR (PROCESSQ $DATUM $ANY)
                   (SUBSUMES $DATUM $ANY)))
Action:   (PARTPROC.NOTELABORATED? $DATUM)

Premise:  (AND (PARTPROC.DATA $PARM)
               (SUGGESTS $PARM $SUGHYP)
               (EVIDENCEFOR? $PARM $SUGHYP $RULE $CF))
Action:   (PARTPROC.SUGGESTRULES? $RULE)
```

Figure 4-7:   Metarules and control information for task GENERATE-QUESTIONS

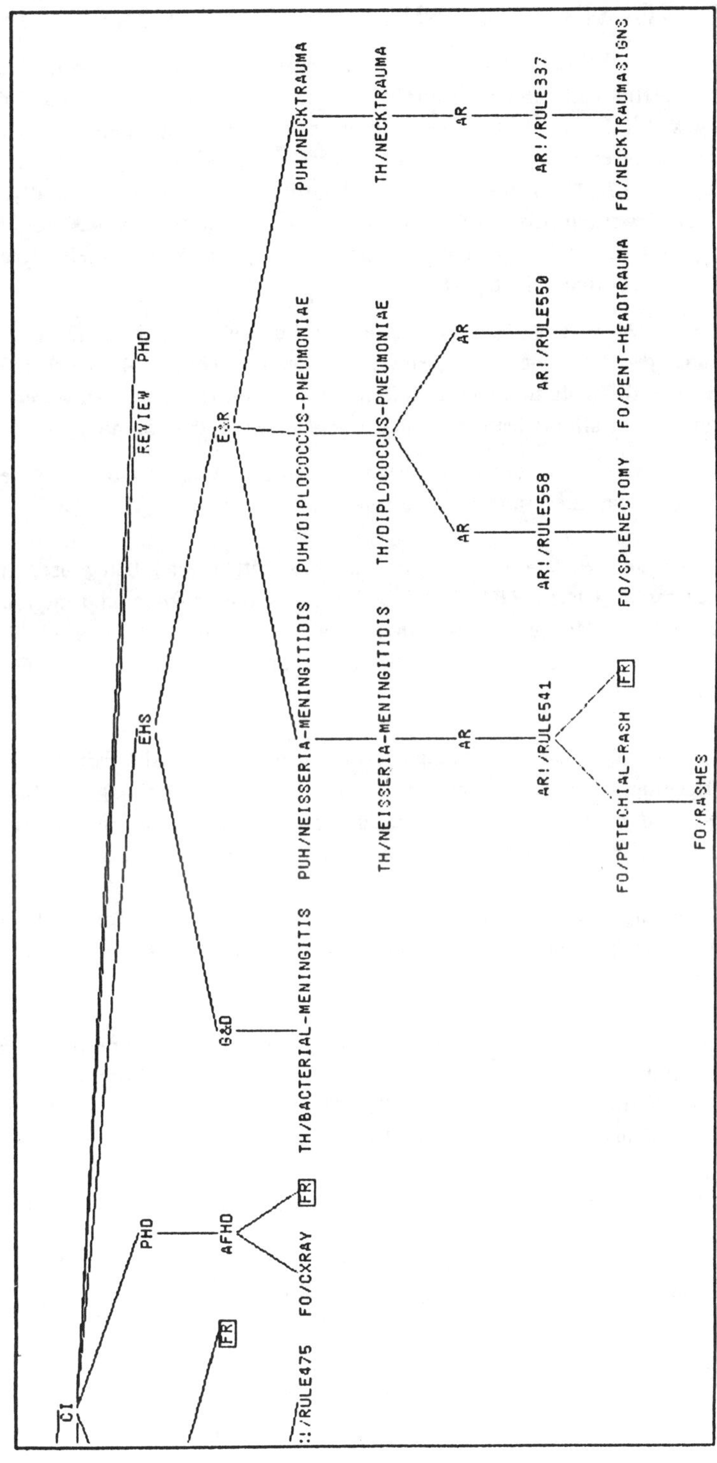

Figure 4-8:   Excerpt of task invocation for a typical NEOMYCIN consultation
--tasks are abbreviated; task foci appear as medical terms

5 THE METARULE COMPILER: MRS -> INTERLISP

Originally in MRS/NEOMYCIN, the MRS interpreter was used for pattern matching, including resolution, backtracking, and procedural attachment. In addition, the task interpreter itself was encoded in MRS rules, controlled by a simple deliberation-action loop (described in Section 6). Even after we reverted to a Lisp task interpreter for efficiency, with the metarules accessed directly as Lisp structures, the program was still too slow to use. Finally, after studying the rules and hand-written Lisp code equivalents, we found that it was possible to compile the metarule premises, including metarule-premise relations and their rules and procedural attachments into ordinary Lisp code.

In the compiled version, each metarule premise generally becomes a Lisp function; each relation concluded by a metarule premise relation rule (Figure 4-2) becomes a Lisp function. In general, it is difficult to write a compiler for MRS-style rules. However, several features of our rules and a few simplifications made it easy to write the compiler:

- Only one rule concludes about each metarule premise relation. Where necessary, rules were combined into a single rule with a disjunction.

- Relations are either predicates or functions, rather than being used in both ways. For example, (CHILDREN $HYP $CHILD) is only used as a functional generator, never as a predicate to test whether a given candidate is a child of a given hypothesis. This was not a deliberate design choice--all of the 166 relations in HERACLES satisfy this property.

- Functional relations are all single-valued (except EVIDENCEFOR). Consequently, backtracking (to find matches for variables in conjunctions) can be expressed as nested *find* or *therexists* loops; failure of the inner loop and return to the next outer loop for a new variable match is equivalent to backtracking.

- Rule conjuncts are ordered manually so that a variable is found (by a functional relation) before it is tested (by a predicate relation). This is a natural way to write the rules.

- Inverse relations are chosen so that Lisp atom with the property corresponding to the relation is the first variable in the relation. For example, the functional relation CHILDREN, as in (CHILDREN $HYP $CHILD), is used when $HYP is known. Again, this occurred naturally rather than being a deliberate design choice.

- As a trivial simplification, redundant clauses are not factored out of disjuncts, in the form
    ```
    (AND <common clauses> (OR d1 d2, ... dn)).
    ```
  Consequently, a few rules are slightly awkward.

5.1 An example

To compile the metarule shown in Figure 4-1, the compiler checks to see what kind of relation ENABLING-QUESTIONS is. Here is what it discovers:

```
(ENABLING.QUESTIONS
 [LAMBDA ($HYP)
   (PROG ($RULE)
     (RETURN (for $FOCUSQ
               in (GETP $HYP (QUOTE ENABLINGQ))
               join (AND (NOT (TRACEDP ROOTNODE $FOCUSQ))
                         (for RULECFLST
                           in (EVIDENCEFOR $FOCUSQ $HYP)
                           as $RULE is (CAR RULECFLST)
                           collect $RULE
                           when (UNAPPLIED? $RULE])))
```

Figure 5-1:   Compiler-generated code for metarule premise rule (Figure 4-2)


```
ENABLING.QUESTIONS

IMPLEMENTATION: METARULE-PREMISE-RELATION
MULTIPLEMATCH:  T
USED-BY:        (RULE566)
UPDATED-BY:     (RULE9325)
```

In writing a function to replace rule9325 (Figure 4-2), the compiler observes that this is a functional relation (not a PREDICATE), so it must return $RULE.   Moreover, it is MULTPLEMATCH, so all matches for $RULE are returned.   The code appears in Figure 5-1. The main difficulty is keeping track of what variables are bound and knowing when to do an iteration versus simply checking if a match exists.   For example, if $RULE were an argument to this function, the code would have been very different.

In general, the compiler's code is a little easier to understand than the manually-written original because it doesn't use constructs like *thereis* and *never*, which require some mental gymnastics to logically invert and combine.

5.2 More details

The compiler recursively pieces together code for each relation.   A second pass ensures that a value is returned from inner loops and Lisp variables are properly bound.   Important subprocedures:

- Produce code for the EVIDENCEFOR relation, (EVIDENCEFOR $FINDING $HYPOTHESIS $RULE $CF)--$HYPOTHESIS and $RULE or $RULE alone might be unknown at the time of matching.

- Gather and compile clauses that test a particular variable (the iterative variable for a compiled loop).

- Modify "find" iterations (on the compiler's second pass) to return the correct value, changing *suchthat* to *collect* or *join*, etc.

Besides the IMPLEMENTATION property described in Section 4.1.2, relations may have PREDICATE and MULTIPLEMATCH properties.   PREDICATE only applies to relations that have an implementation of METARULE-PREMISE-RELATION or FUNCTION (ordinary

LISP function). MULTIPLEMATCH only applies to a metarule-premise-relation. It means that the MRS rule should be "matched as many times as possible." In essence, the compiler changes *find ⟨var⟩ in ⟨list⟩ suchthat...* to *for ⟨var⟩ in ⟨list⟩ collect ⟨var⟩ when....*

Different code is produced depending on whether the result variable, the last variable in the proposition, is bound when a clause is compiled. For example, the code for the clause (TRIGGERPARMS $RULE $PARM) might be:

- (find $PARM in (GETP $RULE 'TRIGGERPARMS) suchthat ...) if $PARM is not bound yet,

- (FMEMB $PARM (GETP $RULE 'TRIGGERPARMS)), if $PARM is bound, or

- (GETPROP $RULE 'TRIGGERPARMS) if $PARM is not bound and it is not tested later in the rule.

All relations compile in a similar way--finding a variable, testing it, setting it, or simply checking to see if a value exists.

Looking for tests to place in the "suchthat" part of an iteration is tricky. The compiler obviously must include later clauses that mention the iteration variable. But it must also include earlier clauses that set a variable mentioned in these later tests, plus later tests of such variables.

The relation MAKESET is used in many metarules. It expects its inner relation to be of type MULTIPLEMATCH, returning a list. Many rules also use a variation of SETQ that only sets the result variable if it is non-NIL. This is convenient because usually in a metarule premise this variable is the focus of the task. We do not want to lose the old focus until we get a new one.[5]

In conclusion, we have found that the PPC notation as a specification language for metarules is convenient, intuitively natural, and allows efficient compilation. The development of the explanation program (Section 7) and the subsequent study of patterns in the domain relations (Section 8) reveal that the notation also has unexpected advantages for helping us to understand the nature of procedures.

6 MRS/NEOMYCIN: A METACONTROL EXPERIMENT

In a program called MRS/NEOMYCIN we attempted to use MRS in a direct way to represent the task interpreter in rules.[6] Our intention was that the new representation would lead to better explanation capability, as well as enhance the debugging capability for knowledge acquisition.

---

[5] In MRS/NEOMYCIN a stack was maintained by the deliberation-action loop, obviating the need for Lisp variables and allowing the focus to be retrieved and reset in a cleaner way (Section 6).

[6] The design and implementation of MRS/NEOMYCIN is primarily the work of Conrad Bock, in partial fulfillment of the Master's degree in Artificial Intelligence at Stanford University. Details about the implementation appear in Appendices II through V.

This experiment failed because the linear sequence of rules into which we translated the interpreter disguises the iterative control so that it is difficult to read, maintain, and explain automatically. In this section we briefly summarize the implementation and reflect on what we learned about making procedures explicit.

6.1 MRS/NEOMYCIN implementation

To specify procedural rule application in rules, MRS was augmented with a form of backward chaining (called "RULEFOR") that dynamically calculates rules to be used in deduction. Specifically, *metacontrol rules* calculate what metarules to use at any time. At the top is a deliberation-action loop. In principle, deliberation only involves domain knowledge and problem-solving state lookup; assertions about the problem are only made by metarule and domain rule actions. Specifically, we forbid hidden side-effects, such as saving computations in rule premises for use by rule actions. Adhering to this discipline simplifies the explanation program and other uses of the control knowledge. Modifications were made to MRS to cope with recomputation inefficiencies that resulted (allowing caching and a history of rule application).

Some of the elements of MRS/NEOMYCIN have survived in HERACLES and have already been described: the relational specification of domain knowledge and problem solving history; metarule premise relations; and procedural attachment (which survived as IMPLEMENTATION categories, rather than the original procedures for asserting, unasserting, and evaluating the truth of statements). The additional constructs in MRS/NEOMYCIN that we used for representing metacontrol in predicate calculus are:

- *Metacontrol rules* (MC "metacontrol" and DR "do-during rulefor" rules), corresponding to the primitive conditional actions of the task interpreter--apply metarules for a task, detect the end condition, and do bookkeeping.

- *Stack of tasks and focus arguments* so that the task interpreter can be invoked recursively (tasks can invoke other tasks).

- *History* of metarules and metacontrol rules applied or failed in a task (for bringing about sequential and iterative computation).

- *Metametacontrol rules* (the NR "nextaction rulefor" rules) that refer to the metacontrol rules by name and invoke them in the proper sequence (do-before, do-during, do-after, then bookkeeping), allowing a normal backchaining interpreter to be used at the highest level.

- *Deliberation-Action loop*, a small Lisp program that invokes MRS to deduce what metarule action to do next.

As can be seen, this is a fairly complex framework for reasoning about control, greatly elaborating upon Davis's original idea of using metarules for refining search (Davis, 1980). In particular, domain-independent metarules invoke base-level rules, MC and DR rules order and choose metarules, and NR rules control the ordering process. This framework, a re-representation of the NEOMYCIN task interpreter, is especially of interest because it provides a control language within MRS in terms of a *tasking mechanism.* We believed that this architecture and its primitives would significantly increase the usefulness of MRS for representing control knowledge.

6.2 Problems with perspicuity and efficiency

In constructing MRS/NEOMYCIN, we invented a way to shoe-horn a complex procedure, the task interpreter, into the deductive mechanisms of MRS, using MRS's metalevel control mechanism (deducing how some thing should be deduced) to control application of metarules and access to domain and problem solving history structures. However, our design was impractical: It was an order of magnitude two slow for available (1982) computers, and most serious of all, the resulting program is conceptually more difficult to understand. What went wrong?

The chief deficiency of MRS/NEOMYCIN is the complexity of the rules representing the task interpreter. It is difficult for people to understand nested iteration that is expressed as levels of rules controlling other rules. Certainly, a program would be in no better position to understand the task interpreter from this kind of specification.

The representation used in MRS/NEOMYCIN was developed to allow machine interpretation, specifically, to allow the augmented MRS reasoning mechanisms to deduce what metarules should be applied at what time. Similar to the goals of AMORD (de Kleer, 1979), we wanted a representation that would make control knowledge explicit in the form of assertions about the control state. While this was achieved, we must not confuse MRS/NEOMYCIN's ability *to carry out the procedure* with understanding it. Predicate calculus is often proposed as a means of making knowledge explicit, but just *stating the steps of the procedure in rules* doesn't make the *meaning of the process* explicit. For example, referring to Figure 6-1, consider the difficulty of understanding that NR rule 4 and DR rule 3 bring about simple try-all application of metarules.[7] The abstract properties of the program's *output* are not immediately obvious from the primitive terms and their combination in rules. AMORD's rules suffer from the same problem: levels of abstraction are missing that would make it clear what the rules and control primitives are doing. This level of specification is analogous to an assembly level program.

We observe three different levels for understanding a procedure:

- *Understanding what the procedure is:* an ability to execute (or simulate) the procedure, that is, to compute the result of applying the steps of the procedure over time;

- *Understanding what the procedure accomplishes:* an ability to describe patterns in the result *abstractly* in terms of the procedure's overall design or goal, and

---

[7] To infer a NEXTACTION, NR 4 causes Metacontrol rule 4 to be applied once for simple, try-all tasks. To infer a DODURING action, concluded by a metarule, DR 3 then selects metarules that haven't been applied. The combined effect is that each metarule is applied once.

NEXTACTION RULEFOR rule 4   **(NR-4)**

```
[IF (AND (CURRENT-TASK $CURTASK)
         (TASKTYPE $CURTASK SIMPLE)
         (TASK-TRY-ALL $CURTASK)
         (THNOT (APPLIED-IN-TASK $CURTASK MC-4)
    (RULEFOR (NEXTACTION $ACTION) MC-4]
```

MetaControl rule 4   **(MR-4)**

```
(IF (AND (DODURING $ACTION)
         (DONT-STOP-TASK $CURTASK))
    (NEXTACTION $ACTION))
```

DODURING RULEFOR rule 3   **(DR-3)**

```
(IF (AND (CURRENT-TASK $CURTASK)
         (TASKTYPE $CURTASK SIMPLE)
         (TASKRULE $CURTASK $MRULE)
         (THNOT (APPLIED-IN-TASK $CURTASK $MRULE)))
    (RULEFOR (DODURING $ACTION) $MRULE))
```

Figure 6-1:   Control rules specifying "simple, try-all" metarule application

- *Understanding why the procedure is valid:* an ability to relate the design of the procedure to its purpose and constraints that affect its operation, that is, understanding the rationale for the design.

The same distinctions apply to the metarule level, and are perhaps more easily understood there. For example, consider the actions of HERACLE's metarules for focusing on hypotheses. First it pursues siblings of the current focus, then it pursues immediate descendents. This is transparent from the ordering of the metarules and the relations mentioned in the premises. Thus, the language adequately expresses the *execution knowledge* of the desired procedure. Now, if you simulate this two step procedure in your mind, you will see a pattern that we call "breadth-first search." MRS/NEOMYCIN can certainly "read" these steps, but it doesn't assign the concept "breadth-first search" to this pattern. Knowing the abstract definition of "breadth-first search," you are able to verify that the program has this design by identifying and classifying patterns in what the program does. The definition of "breadth-first search" and its relation to these two metarules, the *design knowledge* of the procedure, is not expressible in MRS/NEOMYCIN. Finally, mathematical properties of hierarchies and the goal of making a correct classification efficiently, constrain the program, suggesting this design choice. This *rationale knowledge* is also not expressible in MRS/NEOMYCIN. Thus, knowing why the program does what it does requires two kinds of inference: abstraction to characterize patterns and a proof arguing that this design satisfies certain constraints.

The original LISP code of the task interpreter, with abstract concepts such as "repeat-until," "first," and "finally," is more readable to a programmer than the metacontrol rules. All we have gained is a simple interpreter that disciplines design of the system, the deliberation-action loop. Our other goal, writing a program with the flexibility that enables reasoning about control (allowing for dynamic changes in metacontrol), could hardly be said to have been accomplished. How could MRS/NEOMYCIN automatically integrate incremental additions to its control knowledge without an understanding of the procedure's design and rationale? This same criticism can be made about the statement of control regimes given by de Kleer in AMORD and by Genesereth in MRS (Genesereth, 1983). MRS/NEOMYCIN and these other programs are in no better position to explain what they are doing than programs written in Lisp. These programs can make fine-grained statements about what they are doing, but they have no conception of the abstract design that lies behind their actions nor the motivation for this design.

A solution to the problem of readability (for understanding design) is use a higher-level language and a compiler, as in traditional programming languages. The task language is itself a step in the right direction, but tasks merely *name* subprocedures. Reasoning about them and changing them requires additional knowledge about what the tasks mean and how the metarules accomplish them. We take up this issue further in Section 8. Moreover, even if we wrote the task interpreter in the task language itself, and wrote a compiler that converted this language directly into MRS control rules, we would need yet another compiler to make the MRS implementation fast enough to be practical.[8]

In summary, we achieved a "declarative" representation of the task interpreter, *with respect to the* MRS *interpreter*--all control knowledge is represented uniformly as a set of rules, facts in a propositional database, and procedural attachments. But the representation leaves out levels of abstraction that people find to be useful for understanding the design of a procedure, namely listing conditional actions in sequence, when appropriate, and indicating the control for iteration over sequences ("for loops"). These are the two main characteristics of the HERACLES task language, or rule sets in general, accounting for the value of this construct.

7 USE OF ABSTRACT PROCEDURES

7.1 Procedural Explanations

Our first explanation program for HERACLES (Hasling, et al., 1984) demonstrated how the MYCIN HOW/WHY line of reasoning capability could be adapted to describing the inference procedure. With translation of metarules premises to PPC, we are now able to generate much more detailed, selective descriptions of reasoning. Figure 7-1 demonstrates this capability.

```
Has Mary taken medications recently?
** WHY

We are attempting to determine whether Mary has received
antimicrobial medication.

Antimicrobial medication is a necessary factor in causing
partially-treated-bacterial meningitis, a hypothesis we are
attempting to confirm.
```

Figure 7-1:   Excerpt of HERACLES explanation

---

[8]The slowness of MRS/NEOMYCIN is chiefly due to the indirection inherent in retrieving procedural attachments and unnecessary recomputation. For example, each time that a metarule succeeds in providing an action to the deliberation-action loop, the list of metarules is re-deduced, leaving out the ones that have been applied already. The program achieves sequential application in this painful way because it is missing the metaknowledge that the list of applicable rules will never change.

As opposed to simply reading back tasks and metarules in response to successive WHY questions, the new program reasons about which tasks and which metarule clauses to mention. The explanation heuristics include omitting: tasks with rules as arguments, computational relations, relations believed to be known to the user, and relations that might be inferred from known relations. The first time a term in a relation is mentioned (usually a finding or hypothesis), it is described in terms of the active task for which it is a focus, if any. Using a second pass, introduction of pronouns and more complex sentence structure is possible. This explanation should be contrasted with the MYCIN-style response, which involves merely printing the domain rule the program is currently applying, with no strategic or focusing structure. Given the abstract inference procedure, it is straightforward to describe reasoning in terms of previous explanations, for example, "We are still trying to determine..." or "Following the same principle as in question 5, we are...." Development of the explanation system to exploit the new representation in this manner has just begun.

7.2 CASTER: A knowledge system built from HERACLES

As a test bed for developing HERACLES and testing its generality, a small knowledge system has been built that diagnoses the cause of defects in cast iron (using molds made from sand) (Thompson and Clancey, 1986). With the diagnostic procedure already in place, we needed only to define the domain knowledge, using the relational language. We defined a hierarchy of disorders in terms of stages in the process of metal casting (analogous to NEOMYCIN's etiological hierarchy of diseases) and a causal network relating findings to etiologies. It is evident now that we do not understand very well the principles for constructing such a causal network in a consistent and complete way. The HERACLES framework is helping us to focus on these and other domain relations that need to be articulated in more detail.

7.3 Strategic modeling

We have developed a prototype student modeling program called IMAGE; it interprets HERACLES' metarules to explain a sequence of data requests using a mixture of top-down predictive simulation and bottom-up recognition (London and Clancey, 1982). The capabilities of the program are not clear because the space of possible models and heuristic modeling operators have not been precisely defined. Yet, the program does demonstrate the value of stating the diagnostic procedure in a language that can be interpreted by multiple programs. Originally, we believed that making the procedure explicit would be important for teaching it to students. However, now it is becoming clear that the main value of the architecture is for modeling missing domain knowledge or detecting misconception. By observing over time, the program will be able to detect that the student knows a procedure *in general*, so when the student's behavior diverges from the program's, it can infer how his factual knowledge is different. Thus, we make a distinction between knowing a procedure and having factual knowledge that allows applying it to a specific problem situation.

It is also becoming clear that the modeling program needs additional knowledge about the metarules. For example, it is useful to know what metarules it might make sense to delete or reorder. In some cases, leaving something out indicates a different preference for ordering choices; in other cases it indicates a different procedure entirely. This additional information would also help a tutoring program know which deviations from HERACLES' behavior are worth bringing to the student's attention.

28

7.4 Guidon2 programs

A family of teaching programs, collectively called GUIDON2, are under development that use NEOMYCIN as teaching material, analogous to the way GUIDON was built on MYCIN. The first of these programs is called GUIDON-WATCH; making use of sophisticated graphics for watching NEOMYCIN solve a problem (Richer and Clancey, 1985). For example, the program highlights nodes in the disease networks to show how the search strategy "looks up" to categories before it "looks down" to subtypes and causes. Other programs on the drafting board would allow a student to issue task/focus commands and watch what NEOMYCIN does, explain NEOMYCIN's behavior, and debug a faulty knowledge base. This work has all been directly inspired by Brown's proposals for similar tutoring environments for algebra (Brown, 1983).

7.5 Using the task language for other procedures

Recognizing that the task/metarule language could be developed into a good high-level language for procedures in general, whose structure could be exploited for explanation, modeling, etc., we are writing our new explanation program in terms of tasks and metarules. The explanation program is *constructive*, because it pieces together what to say rather than selecting it whole from built in responses. Consequently, some kind of database is needed for posting partial explanations, as well as operators to examine and modify the evolving response. An example explanation rule, for the task that decides what relations in a HERACLES metarule to mention, is given in Figure 7-2.

Our experience indicates that some modifications to the task language may be useful, such as allowing multiple arguments to a task and designating some tasks to be generators that take a list and pass elements on to a subtask in order (several tasks in HERACLES, for example, APPLYRULES, are of this form). Ultimately, we believe that it will be useful for the design of the explanation procedure to be explicit enough to allow it to reflect upon itself to produce alternative explanations when the student does not understand the first response.

```
Premise:  (AND (RELTYPE? $REL 'COMPUTATIONAL)
               (NOT (USER-KNOWN $REL))
               (NOT (EXPLAINED-IN-SUBDIALOG $REL))
               (PREFERENCE THIS-USER 'COMPUTATIONAL-DETAILS))

Action:   (MENTION $REL TASK-INSTANCE)
```

Figure 7-2: An explanation heuristic rule

8 STUDYING ABSTRACT PROCEDURES AND RELATIONS

To review, in HERACLES there are approximately 75 metarules that constitute a procedure for doing diagnosis. The metarules reference:

- Domain knowledge: types of findings and hypotheses, and relations among them;

- Control knowledge about metarules and tasks:

  o (static) the argument of a task, whether metarules are to be applied iteratively, when to return to the head of the list, and the condition under which a task should be aborted,

  o (dynamic) whether a task completed successfully, whether a metarule succeeded or failed, etc.

- Domain problem-solving history: "active" hypotheses, whether a hypothesis was pursued, cumulative belief for a hypothesis, hypotheses that "explain" a finding, rules using a finding that are "in focus", a strong competitor to a given hypothesis, etc.

- Computational predicates and functions: comparison, numerical, and primitive inference routines.

These concepts form the vocabulary for a model of diagnosis, the terms in which expert behavior is interpreted and strategies are expressed (see Appendix I for a complete listing). This vocabulary of *structural relations* and the *body of abstract control knowledge* can itself be studied, as well as applied in other problem domains. It is the beginning of a "descriptive base" (cf. (Miller, 1983), page 182) from which generalizations can be made about the nature of a useful knowledge organization for problem solving.

In the sections that follow we consider a number of issues about the nature of relations and abstract procedures, emphasizing how relations or classifications define procedures and how these relations are derived.

8.1 The nature of an abstract inference procedure

The idea of an abstract procedure is directly related to the idea of separating programs from data, which itself derives from idea of general mathematical laws and formulae. An abstract procedure is one in which problem-specific values are replaced by terms characterizing the type of each value, which become the formal parameters of the procedure. The particular values, for example a list of patient-specific symptoms, becomes a data base upon which the abstract procedure operates. Thus, the MYCIN system is an abstract procedure relative to a case library that it can diagnose. The familiar idea is that a general procedure references *relations*, not individuals directly, which is how the data base must be indexed.

The diagnostic procedure of HERACLES is abstract in the sense that metarules mention only non-medical terms, such as *finding* and *hypothesis*, and relations. These terms are variables, instantiated by domain-specific concepts. The metarules are also abstract in the sense that premises are simple logical patterns; backtracking to satisfy variables and indexing the domain representation is left to the interpreter. Specifically, *traditional programming constructs of iteration, variable assignment, and data structure manipulation have been obviated by the use of prefix predicate calculus as a procedural specification language.* We have replaced what to do at the Lisp computational level by what is true at the "knowledge level" of the procedure we are describing. Finally, the metarules are abstract characterizations of the procedural knowledge that is stated in a domain-specific, implicit way in MYCIN's rules. In this case, the ordering of specific values, such as the order in which to gather data to confirm a hypothesis, has been abstracted to metarules based on *preference relations* such as *trigger finding* and *necessary precursor.*

What is the nature of HERACLES' abstract procedure? What does it do? Studying it, we find a surprisingly simple pattern. There are only three types of task foci: hypotheses, findings, and domain rules. The purpose of each task is to *select* a new focus (for example, moving from a hypothesis to desirable findings). Metarules do this by *relating a current focus to other findings, hypotheses, and rules in the knowledge base.* Thus, domain-specific orderings ("Does the patient have an infection? Is the infection meningitis?") are replaced by:

- a task, something the program is trying to do with respect to its known findings or believed hypotheses;

- a focus (one or more findings, hypotheses, or rules);

- relations among findings, hypotheses, and rules that enable them to be selected preferentially.

An unexpected effect of stating the diagnostic procedure in this way is that there is no more backward chaining at the domain level. That is, the only reason MYCIN does backward chaining during its diagnostic (history and physical) phase is to accomplish top-down refinement and to apply screening rules. This is an important result. By studying the hundreds of rules in the MYCIN system, factoring out domain relations from control knowledge, we have greatly deepened our understanding of the knowledge encoded in the rules. The previously implicit relations between clauses and between a premise and action that made backchaining necessary are now explicit and used directly for selecting the next primitive action (question to ask, assertion to be made, domain rule to apply).

8.2 The advantages of PPC notation for studying procedures

Below we will consider what the relations of HERACLES reveal about the nature of procedures. But first it is worth pausing to consider the advantages of the prefix predicate calculus notation. None of patterns we have discovered were as evident in the original Lisp version of NEOMYCIN's metarules. When the rules were re-expressed in MRS we stopped thinking so much about programming and started to think about the knowledge we were encoding, viz,

- Most of the "flags" in the program were replaced by unary relations. For example, the Lisp free variable PROBLEM-IDENTIFIED became the statement, (TASK-COMPLETED IDENTIFY-PROBLEM). We discovered that for every flag there was some implicit concept that was being characterized by an implicit relation. Here, we recognized that PROBLEM-IDENTIFIED could be restated as the proposition, "The task IDENTIFY-PROBLEM has completed." Implicitly, the task IDENTIFY-PROBLEM was being ,characterized by the the relation TASK-COMPLETED. Thus, a new relation was added to the program. This kind of analysis provides a better understanding of the domain and procedural knowledge. It also greatly facilitates program design. For example, context shifting, as required

for student modeling, can be handled in a more general way using the predicate
calculus notation instead of free variables. Put another way, PPC notation helps us
to separate *task-specific control knowledge* from the *implementation of the task
interpreter*.

- We found that all domain Lisp properties were relations among findings,
hypotheses, and domain rules. The entire domain knowledge base can be viewed as
a hierarchical, relational database. Rather than "parameters" and "rules" we began
to think in terms of findings, hypotheses, and rules and classifications of these.
Similarly, we found that the focus of each task was typed.

- We discovered that all of the predicates in EMYCIN's rule language could be
expressed as relations about propositions. For example, (SAME CNTXT PARM
VALU), "parm of context is value," could be restated in PPC as (with a partially
instantiated example):

```
(AND (BELIEF (<parm> $CNTXT $VALU) $CF)
     ( > $CF 200)).

(AND (BELIEF (SITE CULTURE-1 BLOOD) $CF)
     ( > $CF 200)).
```

This reveals that EMYCIN's "parameters" are domain-specific relations characterizing
various objects (the contexts), and the rule premise functions (e.g., SAME) are
relations between a domain proposition and a certainty factor. (See (Clancey, 1985)
for further logical analysis of MYCIN's parameters.)

8.3 The relation between classifications and procedures

The PPC notation helps us see patterns: relations among "rule premise functions," among data
structures (the IMPLEMENTATION relation used by the compiler), among tasks. The relations
in PPC are the patterns that we observe. We observe that different tasks (e.g., explanation,
diagnosis, compilation) require that knowledge be used in different ways, as evidenced by the
different *second order relations* required by the different procedures we have written:

- The EMYCIN interpreter needs to know only a handful of simple relations. The
most important are:

```
(PROMPT $PARM $STRING)
(ASKFIRST $PARM)
(MULTIVALUED $PARM)
(LEGAL-VALUE $PARM $VALU)

(MENTIONS $RULE $PARM $CNTXT)
(CONCLUDES $RULE $PARM $CNTXT)
(ANTECEDENT $RULE)

(ASKED ($PARM $CNTXT $VALU))
(APPLIED $RULE $CNTXT)
(BELIEF ($PARM $CNTXT $VALU) $CF)
```

- The EMYCIN explanation program needs to know how parameters and rules interact
during problem solving, e.g., (RULE-FAILED $RULE $CLAUSE).

- HERACLES' classification procedure requires hierarchical and triggering and relations, e.g., (SUBSUMES $FINDING1 $FINDING2).

- The task interpreter needs to know how metarules should be applied, e.g., (TASK-TYPE $TASK $TYPE).

- The rule compiler needs to know the IMPLEMENTATION, whether a relation is a predicate or a function, and whether matching should be exhaustive.

- HERACLES' explanation program uses knowledge about how relations can be inferred from one another and belief about what the listener knows (Section 7).

Relations discriminate, they make distinctions that are essential for satisfying procedural objectives, and making distinctions is what control knowledge is all about. It has been known for some time that *classification* is at the core of problem solving (Bruner, et al., 1956). We are constantly faced with choices, and they are arbitrated by classification distinctions that we make about data, operators, beliefs, states, etc.

Relations are a means for indexing domain-specific knowledge: They *select* hypotheses to focus upon, findings to request, and domain inferences that might be made. As such, relations constitute the organization, the access paths, by which strategies bring domain-specific knowledge into play. For example, the metarules given above mention the CHILDOF and SUBSUMES relations. METARULE001 (in Section 2.1) looks for *the children of* the current hypothesis in order to pursue them; METARULE002 looks for *a more general finding* in order to ask for it first.

These relations constitute the language by which the primitive domain concepts (particular findings and disorder hypotheses) are related in a network. *Adding a new strategy often requires adding a new kind of relation to the network.* For example, suppose we desire to pursue common causes of a disorder before serious, but unusual, causes. We must partition the causes of any disorder according to this distinction, adding new relations to our language-- COMMON-CAUSES and SERIOUS-CAUSES.

Similarly, *the applicability of a strategy depends on the presence of given relations in the domain.* For example, a strategy might give preference to low-cost findings, but in a particular problem domain all findings might be equally easy to attain. Or a given set of strategies might deal with how to search a deep hierarchy of disorders, but in a given domain the hierarchy might be shallow, making the strategies inapplicable. By stating strategies abstractly, we are forced to explicate relations. On this basis we can compare domains with respect to the applicability of strategies, referring to structural properties of the search space.

Lenat has found a similar relationship between heuristics (strategies) and slots (structural relations) in his program for discovering new heuristics (Lenat, 1982). In particular, the ability to reason about heuristics in EURISKO depends on breaking down complex conditions and actions into many smaller slots that the program can inspect and modify selectively. The same observation holds for domain concepts whose representation is refined by the synthesis of new slots (e.g., adding a PRIME-FACTORS slot to every number). The program even reasons *about relations* by creating a new slot that collects relations among entries of an important slot.

More generally, it is interesting to view the domain knowledge base of relations as a *map* for accomplishing some task. The map makes certain distinctions that are useful for the task at hand. For example, if we wanted to understand the conditions for the spread of a blight, we might use maps that reveal soil and climate conditions. In this sense, NEOMYCIN's relational knowledge base is a map, a view of the world, that has practical value for diagnosis.

8.4 The meaning of relations

The need to make new distinctions is tantamount to requiring new kinds of knowledge for each procedure. In representing a procedure, using new relations, we are making new statements about what is true in order to specify what to do (what operators to apply to what focus). That is, we are organizing knowledge so that it is accessible, reviewable, and selectable by procedures. Thus, an existing knowledge base must be continuously structured in richer ways for explanation, student modeling, knowledge acquisition.

But what comes first--the distinctions or the procedure? The procedure itself exists in order to "treat instances" the "right way," where the instances are the arguments to subprocedures. Thus, we classify instances and say instances of a certain class are to be treated a certain way. In so doing, we define classes in terms of their *functional significance*.

For example, we found in NEOMYCIN that certain findings, such as "headache" were triggering new hypotheses, when there was much stronger evidence for hypotheses that accounted for these findings already. In addition, we noticed that the findings in question were so non-specific, that it wasn't even clear that they needed to be explained. Thus, we made a distinction between findings: non-specific (perhaps a sign of nothing treatably abnormal) and "red-flag" (a finding that is so abnormal, it must be explained). With this new relation partitioning the findings, we wrote a metarule, "If a non-specific finding is not already explained by hypotheses suggested by redflag findings, then trigger new hypotheses, if any." Notice that "explained by" is another relation among findings and hypotheses, defined in terms of evidence and subsumption.

The new relations (red-flag, explained-by) are defined in terms of primitive relations (finding, suggests), but what they *mean* is bound up as well in how they are used procedurally, that is their association with diagnostic operators such as making an assertion and asking a question. Hence, the relations are not *natural distinctions* as we might categorize cats and dogs separately; they are functionally defined. The categories exist because they are procedurally useful.

Other relations have a similar procedural interpretation, for example, follow-up question, triggers, general question. The definition of these relations is captured by how they are used:

- this operation, a subtask, is (or is not) applicable to operands (the argument of the task, its focus) of type X (e.g., follow-up question, non-specific finding);

- give preference to operands of type X for this operation (e.g., triggering finding is pursued first in confirming a hypothesis).

This suggests that knowledge to derive the metarules includes being able to derive what operations might be applicable to specific task operands. That is, we must know what operations we want to do (e.g., apply a domain rule to change our belief in a hypothesis) and a

34

type characterization of applicable operands. Thus, put the most general way, the situation or premise parts of metarules are searching for operands to which to apply inference operators.

Is there some conceptual definition that could be used to generate these operand distinctions, given other more-primitive, domain relations? Indeed, when we start studying the domain relations (for explanation purposes) we discover that there are implicit implication relations among them (Figure 8-1). For example, a follow-up relation implies that the characterizing finding discriminates the first finding in terms of the *process* that is occurring. At a more general level yet, we find that the follow-up finding *presupposes* the first finding. This suggests that we could define perhaps statistical correlations related to specificity or ability to discriminate hypotheses that could generate these "procedural" relations.

It is apparent that these relations, and even the more primitive relations in HERACLES, such as CAUSES and SUBSUMES, are just a step removed from EMYCIN's domain-specific clause orderings. They specify fairly closely *what to do* or in control terms, *what to infer*. We would

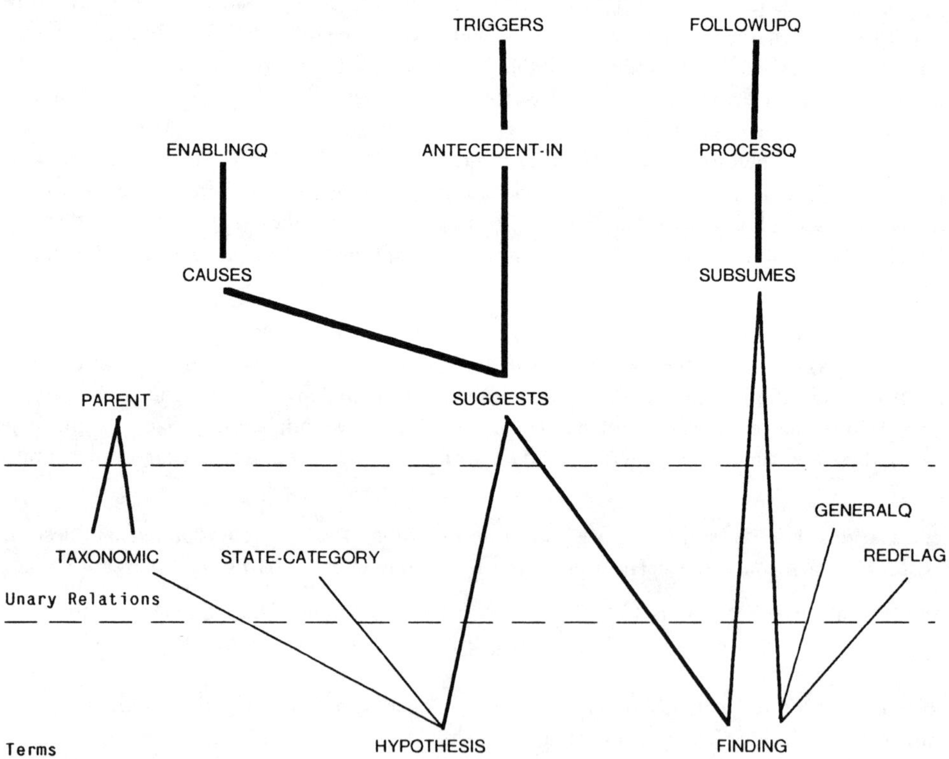

Figure 8-1: Implication relations among HERACLES domain relations
     [higher relations are defined in terms of lower relations]

like to move closer to *what is true about the world* that makes these relations valid. The knowledge we have stated is in the form of *schemas* indicating typical associations that are valuable for problem solving. In a principled way, we would like to state mathematically (statistically) what characteristics of a case population and what structural (hierarchical) constraints make one finding a better general question than another or should cause a group of findings to trigger a disease. To the extent that these are the relations in which experiential knowledge is stated, we are seeking a model of learning that relates cognitive, social, mathematical and world constraints to produce the distinctions we have recorded in NEOMYCIN's knowledge base (e.g., triggers, follow-up questions, general questions, and red-flag findings). Given such a model, we might also be able to automatically configure a knowledge base given primitive relations from which the procedural relations can be derived.

It is also possible to proceed in the other direction, to view MYCIN as a model of "compiled knowledge" and NEOMYCIN as a specification of the primitive relations that get instantiated and composed from practice (Anderson, et al., 1981, Laird, et al., 1984). While NEOMYCIN's knowledge is computationally equivalent to MYCIN--in terms of focus choice and conclusions-- it suggests perhaps a misleading model of learning. It is unlikely that people start only with general principles and instantiate and compose them with experience. The medical knowledge of NEOMYCIN most likely accumulated incrementally, by case experience, not uniformly compiled from explicitly learned generalizations and structural models of the world. Thus, problem solving behavior may appear systematic and principled, but the problem solver may be totally unaware that he is following patterns.

The mechanism of learning may proceed in a way that is analogous to early language learning. We learn how to speak, without being aware of the grammatical rules we are following. Indeed, it is interesting to compare the domain relations to linguistic categories (noun, direct object, demonstrative pronoun, etc.) and the metarules to rules of grammar. Metarules, like rules of grammar, have an abstract, hierarchical nature. Just as the rules of grammar can be used to parse a linguistic utterance, the metarules can be used to parse a sequence of classification actions, as in student modeling, providing a "deep structure" interpretation of behavior (Clancey, 1984b). Is our awareness of the deep structure of language any different from our awareness of the deep structure of diagnosis by classification? Are the learning, representation, and processing mechanisms the same? Answers to these questions are beyond our reach today.

8.5 The difficulties of making a procedure's rationale explicit

It might be objected that for some domains there are no patterns for using knowledge--no abstract procedures--all facts and relations are inseparable from how they will be used. For example, the procedure for confirming any given disorder (more generally, interpreting signals or configuring some device) might be completely situation-specific, so there are no general principles to apply. This would appear to be an unusual kind of domain. We are more familiar with problems in which simple principles can be applied over and over again in many situations.

Teaching and learning are made incredibly difficult if there is no carry-over of procedures from one problem to another. Domains with a strong perceptual component, such as signal interpretation, might be like this. Perceptual skills rely on pattern matching, rather than selective, controlled analysis of data; they are might be poor candidates for representing procedures abstractly.

We also know that in many domains, for efficiency at runtime, procedures have been compiled for solving routine problems. These procedures are written down in the familiar "procedures manuals" for organization management, equipment operation, configuration design, troubleshooting, etc. It is important to recognize that these procedures are based upon domain facts, constraints imposed by causal, temporal, and spatial interactions, problem-solving goals, abstract principles of design, diagnosis, etc. Except where a procedure is arbitrary, there must be some underlying rationale for the selection and ordering of its steps. Knowing this rationale is certainly important for reliably modifying the procedure; such procedures are often just prepared plans that an expert (or a user following a program's advice) may need to adapt to unusual circumstances. At one level, the rationale can be made explicit in terms of an abstract plan with its attendant domain structural relations; a redundant, compiled form can be used for efficient routine problem solving.

In theory, if the rationale for a procedure or prepared plan can be made explicit, a program can reconstruct the procedure from first principles. This approach has two basic difficulties. First, the procedure might have been learned incrementally from case experience. It simply handles problems well; there is no compiled-out theory that can be articulated. This problem arises particularly for skills in which behavior has been shaped over time, or for any problem in which the trace of "lessons" has been poorly recorded. The second difficulty is that constructing a procedure from first principles can involve a great deal of search. Stefik's (Stefik, 1980) multi-leveled planning regime for constructing MOLGEN experiments testifies to the complexity of the task and the limited capabilities of current programs. In contrast, Friedland's (Friedland, 1979) approach of constructing experiment plans from skeletal, abstract plans trades flexibility for efficiency and resemblance to human solutions. While skeletal plans may sometimes use domain-specific terms, as precompiled abstract procedures they are analogous to HERACLES's tasks.

Importantly, as mentioned in Section 6.2, the *rationale for the abstract plan* itself is not explicit in any of these programs. For example, HERACLES's metarules for a given task might be ordered by preference (alternative methods to accomplish the same operation) or as steps in a procedure. Since the constraints that suggest the given ordering are not explicit, part of the design of the program is still not explicit. For example, the abstract steps of top-down refinement are now stated, but the sense in which they constitute this procedure is not represented. (Why should pursuing siblings of a hypothesis be done before pursuing children?) As another example, the task of "establishing the hypothesis space" by expanding the set of possibilities beyond common, expected causes and then narrowing down in a refinement phase has mathematical, set-theoretic underpinnings that are not explicit in the program. Similarly, Stefik's abstract planning procedure of "least-commitment" is implicit in numeric priorities assigned to plan design operators (Clancey, 1983a). Automatically constructing procedures at this high level of abstraction, as opposed to implicitly building them into a program, has been explored very little.

We have considered how relations might be defined in terms of more primitive relations, but is there any hope of formalizing what operators to apply and their applicable operands?

Essentially, we would like to represent what a task means, what goal it seeks to accomplish, how the subtasks do this, and why the subtasks and metarules are ordered in a particular way. For example, TEST-HYPOTHESIS is an example of a task in which the metarules capture an ordered set of operand preferences. The goal of the task is to gather evidence that changes belief. This can be accomplished by applying a APPLYRULE operator to a domain rule that makes an assertion about the hypothesis. We could apply any domain rule, but we have some constraints to satisfy, such as seeking the strongest belief first (to focus on the correct diagnosis as quickly as possible). We transform our constraints into preferences that classify possible domain rules. Specifically, we make distinctions about domain rules in terms of findings they mention, the strength of belief in the conclusion, or the justification of the rule. Then we write metarules to select domain rules on the basis of these distinctions. Representing goals and operators as concepts that can be related by the program (for example, so the program can be said in some sense to understand what it means to "gather evidence that changes belief") and relating constraints so they can be reformulated as classifications of domain concepts, are major research problems. ((Clancey, 1984b) lists all of HERACLES' metarules with prosaic descriptions of the constraints they satisfy.)

It is not difficult to find portions of HERACLES' diagnostic procedure whose design is obscure. In most cases, we are still groping for some idea of *what to do*, what the procedure is, and have insufficient experience for deriving a better representation that would express the design of the procedure more clearly. For example, the end conditions previously described encode the procedure implicitly. The rebinding of the list of new findings to bring about depth-first, focused forward-reasoning is also obscure. Probably most disturbing of all, the premises of FINDOUT metarules invoke this task recursively and indirectly through the domain interpreter (should we view them as abstract domain rules, rather than metarules?). At the very least, we now have a good criterion for identifying an implicit procedure: Any encoding that affects the *choice* of operators, operands, or possible inferences that is not accomplished by an explicit classification relation that makes a distinction among them. For example, the relation among metarules is not explicit, so this part of the procedure is implicit (known only to the designer).

For the moment, we are driven by practical needs in writing teaching programs and worry about deficiencies only as they become important to that goal. Indeed, we have found that a good heuristic for representing procedures abstractly is to work with good teachers, for they are most likely to have extracted principles at a level of detail worth teaching to students.

9 RELATED WORK

The study of problem solving procedures has played a central role in AI and Cognitive Science. The design of HERACLES has been influenced by a great deal of this previous research.

9.1 Cognitive studies

The idea of formalizing a diagnostic procedure as a separate body of knowledge was inspired by studies of goals and strategies (Greeno, 1976, Schoenfeld, 1981), "deep structure" analyses of problem solving sequences (Brown et al., 1977), psychological studies of medical problem solving (Feltovich, et al., 1984, Rubin, 1975, Elstein et al., 1978), and problem space descriptions of behavior (Newell and Simon, 1972). These researchers share the view that *sequences of problem solving steps* could be explained in terms of underlying reasoning principles or strategies. This prompted us to redescribe MYCIN's knowledge in terms of orderly sequences of problem-solving tasks, applied to a medical knowledge base of possible operators, as reported in (Clancey, 1983a, Clancey, 1984a, Clancey, 1984b).

9.2 Explicit control knowledge

If one views the cognitive studies as establishing a conceptual base for describing problem solving, research in AI can be characterized as providing a *technological* base for constructing programs. In particular, the work of Davis concerning *metaknowledge*, specifically *metarules*, provided a formalism and way of thinking about program design that strongly affected the design of NEOMYCIN. In turn, the explicit control formalism of PLANNER (Hewitt, 1972) influenced Davis's work. In some sense, this work has all been influenced in a general way by the structured programming philosophy of abstract data types and hierarchical design (Dahl, et al., 1972). Later descriptions of hierarchical planning (Sacerdoti, 1974) inspired the hierarchical task decomposition of the diagnostic procedure of NEOMYCIN.

The idea of a problem solving architecture with explicit bodies of control and domain knowledge has several sources. For example, representing control knowledge abstractly moves us closer to our ideal of specifying to a program *what* problem to solve versus *how* to solve the problem (Feigenbaum, 1977). Dating back at least to McCarthy's Advice Taker (McCarthy, 1960), many researchers have taken the ideal form of a program to be one that could accept new pieces of information incrementally. For a system with this architecture, improving a program is a well-structured process of stating knowledge relations or, separately, HOW the knowledge will be used. This is to be contrasted with doing both simultaneously in an intermingled, redundant way, as in MYCIN's rules.

An analogy can be made with GUIDON (Clancey, 1979) (Clancey, 1982a), whose body of abstract teaching rules makes the program usable with multiple domains. Traditional CAI programs are specific to particular problems (not just problem domains) and have both subject matter expertise and teaching strategies embedded within them. The separation of these in GUIDON, and now the abstract representation of strategies in NEOMYCIN, is part of the logical progression of expert systems research that began with separation of the interpreter from the knowledge base in MYCIN. The trend throughout has been to state domain-specific knowledge more declaratively and to generalize the procedures that control its application.

Probably the earliest, large-scale realization of the ideal separation between knowledge and search control is in HEARSAY, with its well-defined sources of knowledge, multi-leveled abstract description of solutions on a blackboard, and control knowledge for focusing on data and solution elements (Erman, et al., 1980). Several general problem solving architectures have been developed to improve upon this structure, notably including HEARSAY-III (Erman, et al., 1981) and BB1 (Hayes-Roth, 1984). The emphasis in HERACLES has not so much to build a general architecture, but to proceed in a bottom-up way to specify the knowledge and distinctions important for explanation and student modeling. Then, with a developed vocabulary of knowledge relations and a diagnostic procedure, we have proceeded empirically to characterize the meaning of this general control knowledge and how it might be generalized. We find that the complex control requirements of diagnosis require a rich relational vocabulary for relating domain rules, a conclusion that is paralleled in recent extensions to HEARSAY that achieve finer-grained control by making explicit the relations among knowledge sources (Corkill, et al., 1982).

9.3 Logic specification of procedures

A considerable amount of research is specifically concerned with using logic formalisms to represent inference procedures. None of this work was known to us during the development of NEOMYCIN, but the connections are obvious and worth considering.

Perhaps from the most general point of view, this research could be characterized as an attempt to extend logic to make deduction more efficient. For example, under one conception, a data base of facts requires a *smart interpreter* that has knowledge about different deductive methods and different kinds of problems to control its search. AMORD was one of the earliest attempts to represent different inference procedures in logic (de Kleer, 1979). The idea of *partial programs*, continuing in the Advice Taker tradition, is a continuation of this effort to find a suitable language for incrementally improving a program's behavior (Genesereth, 1984).

Similar problems with efficient deduction arise in database systems that combine relational networks with logic programming (e.g., see (Nicolas, 1977)). To conserve space, it is not practical to explicitly store every relation among entities in a database. For example, a database about a population of a country might record just the parents of each person (e.g., (MOTHEROF $CHILD $MOTHER) and (FATHEROF $CHILD $FATHER)). A separate body of *general derivation axioms* is used to retrieve other relations (the *intensional database*). For example, siblings can be computed by the rule:

```
(IF (AND (PERSON $PERSON)
         (MOTHEROF $PERSON $MOTHER)
         (PERSON $PERSON2)
         (MOTHEROF $PERSON2 $MOTHER))
    (SIBLING $PERSON $PERSON2))
```

Such a rule is quite similar to the abstract metarules that NEOMYCIN uses for deducing the presence or absence of findings. NEOMYCIN differs from database systems in that its rules are grouped and controlled to accomplish abstract tasks. Only a few of NEOMYCIN's metarules make inferences about database relations; most invoke other tasks, such as "ask a general question" and "group and differentiate hypotheses." Moreover, the knowledge base contains judgmental rules of evidence for the disorder hypotheses. These differences aside, the analogy is stimulating. It suggests that treating a knowledge base as an object to be inspected, reasoned about, and manipulated by *abstract procedures*--as a database is checked for integrity, queried, and extended by general axioms--is a powerful design principle for building knowledge systems.

9.4 Hybrid systems

HERACLES is a prime example of a *hybrid* system, combining Lisp, predicate calculus, procedural, and rule representations of knowledge. Simple rule and frame systems, in contrast with traditional programs, are valued for their syntactic simplicity, facilitating the writing of interpretation programs for problem solving, explanation, knowledge acquisition, etc. Yet, in the past decade it has become obvious that different representations are advantageous for efficiency and perspicuity. Other researchers have found similar pragmatic advantages to the kind of hybrid design we find in HERACLES. For example, in SOPHIE-III multiple representations are nicely integrated by a common database that allows dependency-directed inference (Brown, 1977, de Kleer, 1984). Rich (Rich, 1982) reports a system that combines predicate calculus with other representations. Furthermore, an initial motivation for MRS was to facilitate multiple representation systems, an early meaning for the acronym. It is now common to find knowledge engineering tools with hybrid architectures, such as the combination of rule and object-oriented programming in LOOPS (Bobrow and Stefik, 1983) and STROBE (Smith, 1984).

Recently, the idea of developing a *knowledge-specification language* that is integrated with implementation data structures by a compiler, as in HERACLES' metarules, has become popular. GLISP programs are "compiled relative to a knowledge base of object descriptions, a form of abstract datatypes" (Novak, 1982). In the context of automatic programming research, the AP5 language (Cohen and Goldman, 1985) integrates a relational view of Lisp data with predicate calculus, in a manner very similar to HERACLES. STROBE uses an object-oriented language in its control rules, resulting in a syntax somewhere between Lisp and predicate calculus. Preference for these different languages, based on ease of readability, may depend more on familiarity than abstract properties of the formalisms.

Comparing the object-oriented and relational approaches, the ability of an object to respond to a message is analogous to having a relation defined for an instance of a term. Sending a message to an object is analogous to inferring the truth of a proposition when one or more of the terms are bound. The object-oriented view is useful for implementation (e.g., note how our compiler relies on a relation being implemented as a property of the first term), but we believe that a relational view provides a more elegant and revealing perspective for making statements about the knowledge in a system. Metaknowledge takes the form of relations about relations, but statements about messages are neither objects nor messages.

9.5 Rule sets

Rule sets have become popular for hierarchically controlling rules. The control primitives of HERACLES are very similar to those developed contemporaneously in LOOPS. However, this formalism is used in HERACLES for controlling rules that invoke domain rules in a much more complex way, not for organizing the domain rules themselves, as in LOOPS. LOOPS has an agenda mechanism for controlling tasks, which might be advantageous for modeling a process like diagnosis. However, LOOPS lacks the pattern-matching language that we have found to be essential for the indexing and selection operations of an abstract inference procedure. Georgeff (Georgeff, 1982) proposes a framework for procedural control of production systems that bears some resemblance to HERACLES rule sets, but again, he organizes domain rules directly. The task and rule set idea of HERACLES has been applied in STROBE, but here with some abstract metarules for controlling search (Young, et al., 1985).

9.6 Explanation

Aside from its obvious origin in the original explanation research of Shortliffe and Davis, HERACLES research has developed in parallel with the work of Swartout, with complementary conclusions and methodology. An interesting distinction is that Swartout has focused on explaining numerical procedures (how a drug's dosage is computed), while we have focused on the more general procedures of classification reasoning. Consequently, we have easily stated our procedures abstractly, while it is less obvious that a procedure that is more like a recipe for doing something has a meaningful or useful generalization. The level of abstraction aside, both XPLAIN and HERACLES achieve explanations through the separate and explicit representation of domain facts and the procedure for their inclusion and ordering in problem solving. Furthermore, Swartout demonstrated that an automatic programming approach, as difficult as it first seemed, was a natural, direct way to ensure that the program had knowledge of its own design (Swartout, 1981). That is, providing complete explanations means understanding the design well enough to derive the procedures yourself.

As discussed in Section 8.5, the search process of diagnosis, particularly for focus of attention, is so complex that we do not know exactly what the program should do, let alone justify what it currently does in any principled way. However, we believe that the methodology of constructing the program from a specification would be good approach for studying and making more explicit the constraints that lie behind the tasks and metarules.

9.7 The meaning of procedures

This research has clarified for us that there is a useful distinction at a "knowledge level" between facts (what we declare to be true) and procedures (sequential descriptions of what we do). Pursuing our ideal of making explicit the rationale that lies behind every piece of knowledge in our programs, we considered in Section 8 the meaning of HERACLES' inference procedure. This kind of analysis, particularly the search for unspecified constraints, has been strongly influenced by the work of van Lehn and Brown (VanLehn and Brown, 1980), specifically in their very detailed analysis of mathematical procedures. In this restricted domain they have derived alternative procedures from constraints that define operators and the representations being manipulated. This level of precision remains an ideal that directs continuing HERACLES research. Brown's preliminary study of the *semantics of procedures* (Brown, et al., 1982b) reveals a combination of orthogonal constraints very similar to what we have discovered in analyzing HERACLES metarules.

10 SUMMARY OF ADVANTAGES

The advantages of representing control knowledge abstractly can be summarized according to engineering, scientific, and practical benefits:

- **Engineering.**
  - The explicit design is easier to debug and modify. Hierarchical relations among findings and hypotheses and search strategies are no longer procedurally embedded in rules.

- Knowledge is represented more generally, so we get more performance from less system-building effort. We do not need to specify every situation in which a given fact should be used.

- The body of abstract control knowledge can be applied to other problems, constituting the basis of a generic system, for example, a tool for building consultation programs that do diagnosis.

- **Science.** Factoring out control knowledge from domain knowledge provides a basis for studying the nature of strategies. Patterns become clear, revealing, for example, the underlying structural bases for backward chaining. Comparisons between domains can be made according to whether a given relation exists or a strategy can be applied.

- **Practice.**

  - A considerable savings in storage is achieved if abstract strategies are available for solving problems. Domain-specific procedures for dealing with all possible situations needn't be compiled in advance.

  - Explanations can be more detailed, down to the level of abstract relations and strategies, so the program can be evaluated more thoroughly and used more responsibly.

  - Because strategies are stated abstractly, the program can recognize the application of a particular strategy in different situations. This provides a basis for explanation by analogy, as well as recognizing plans during knowledge acquisition or student modelling.

There is certainly an initial cost to stating procedures abstractly, whose benefit is unlikely to be realized if no explanation facility is desired, only the original designers maintain or modify the knowledge base, or there is no desire to build a generic system. But even this argument is dubitable: a knowledge base with embedded strategies can appear cryptic to even the original designers after it has been left aside for a few months. The quality of a knowledge base depends not only on how well it solves problems, but also how on easily its design allows it to be maintained. Easy maintenance--the capability to reliably modify a knowledge base without extensive reprogramming--is important for several reasons:

- Knowledge-based programs are built incrementally, based on many trials, so modification is continually required, including updates based on improved expertise (it was very difficult to add knowledge about new infections to MYCIN because of the implicit search procedure in existing rules).

- A knowledge base is a repository that other researchers and users may wish to build upon years later;

- A client receiving a knowledge base constructed for him may wish to correct and extend it without the assistance of the original designers.

- Also, anyone intending to build more than one system will benefit from expressing knowledge as generally as possible so that lessons about structure and strategy can speed up the building of new systems.

A knowledge base is like a traditional program in that maintaining it requires having a good understanding of the underlying design. Problems encountered in understanding traditional programs--poorly-structured code, implicit side-effects, and inadequate documentation--carry over to knowledge base maintenance. The architecture advocated here--statement of inference procedures abstractly, in a well-structured language--avoids procedural embedding, forcing the knowledge engineer to state domain knowledge in a well-structured way, so it can be flexibly indexed by his procedures.

11 CONCLUSIONS

This research began with the conjecture that the procedure for diagnosis could be separated from the medical knowledge base, and that this would offer advantages for explanation, student modeling, and knowledge engineering. NEOMYCIN, its generalization to HERACLES, and the associated prototype programs (Section 7) demonstrate that the separation and explicit representation of procedural knowledge has merit and is possible. The architecture is convenient, and all indications are that it provides a good basis for further investigation in the nature of procedural knowledge and its use for different purposes.

It is worth noting that our methodology, driven by failures of our programs to meet behavioral objectives, has been very valuable. We select a level of explicitness desirable in our knowledge bases through by using them in'diverse programs (e.g., explanation, modeling). Then we note the limitations for interpreting this knowledge representation, particularly what distinctions need to be made explicit so the procedural knowledge (for diagnosis, compiling, explaining, modeling) can make intelligent choices among alternatives. This continues our approach begun in MYCIN of developing a language, building specific programs for difficult problems, studying the knowledge we have collected, and then repeating the cycle. Our conjectures about problem solving architecture gain credence through experimentation: a given task/metarule is applied in multiple contexts in a given problem, interpreted for different behaviors (e.g., explanation and modeling), and carried over to other domains in new HERACLES systems. In this way, we exploit the idea of abstract control knowledge and gain confidence in the generality of our results. Rather than just building one "expert system" after another, we are developing theories about kinds of knowledge and methods for solving problems.

Critiquing HERACLES today, what does it need to be a more general, useful system for modeling human classification problem solving? We would incorporate, at least: KL-ONE style definitions of concepts and general subsumption algorithm (Schmolze and Lipkis, 1983); hierarchies as lattices allowing multiple parents; conceptual graph definitions of relations (Sowa, 1984); an agenda mechanism for tasks; and dependency reasoning for belief maintenance (de Kleer, 1984). Each of these components is getting so complex, it is unlikely that the community of AI researchers can afford much longer to redundantly re-implement them in every architecture. At some point, we may need to develop interface languages that allow us to share modules, permitting individual decisions about the level of implementation, domain structures, and control, with compilation used to piece together hybrid systems like HERACLES. If this is to be so, the kind of separation and explicit representation of different kinds of knowledge, organized around a relational language, as we advocate, may become an essential principle for building knowledge systems.

I Metarule relational language

The relations used in HERACLES' metarules and rules for metarule premise relations are listed here. They are categorized as domain, dynamic belief, dynamic search or focus bookkeeping, and computational. Inverses (e.g., causes and caused-by) are omitted here, but included in the knowledge base. The important primitive terms are $PARM, $RULE, $CF, and $CNTXT. All other terms and relations are defined in these terms. Indentation indicates hierarchical definition of new terms. For example, a nonspecific finding is a kind of finding. These relations are generally implemented as Lisp structures; the dynamic belief relations are all implemented as Lisp functions.

<u>Domain Relations Pertaining to Findings and Hypotheses</u>

```
(FINDING $PARM)
        (SOFT-DATA $FINDING)
        (HARD-DATA $FINDING)
        (NONSPECIFIC $FINDING)
        (REDFLAG $FINDING)
(HYPOTHESIS $PARM)
        (STATE-CATEGORY $HYP)
        (TAXONOMIC $HYP)
                (PARENTOF $TAXPARM $PARENT)
                (COMPLEX $TAXPARM)


(CAUSES $HYP1 $HYP2)
(SUBSUMES $FINDING1 $FINDING2)
(PROCESSQ $FINDING1 $FINDING2)
(CLARIFYQ $FINDING1 $FINDING2)
(SOURCE $FINDING1 $FINDING2)
(SCREENS $FINDING1 $FINDING2)
(PROCESS-FEATURES $HYP $SLOT $VAL $FINDING)


(ALWAYS-SPECIFY $FINDING)
(ASKFIRST $FINDING)
(PROMPT $FINDING $VAL)


(BOOLEAN $PARM)
(MULTIVALUED $PARM)
(TABLE $BLOCKPARM $FINDING)


(ENABLINGQ $HYP $FINDING)
(SUGGESTS $PARM $HYP)
(TRIGGERS $PARM $HYP)
```

<u>Domain Relations Pertaining to Rules</u>

```
(ANTECEDENT-IN $FINDING $RULE)
(APPLICABLE? $RULE $CNTXT $FLG)
(EVIDENCEFOR? $PARM $HYP $RULE $CF)
(COMMONCASERULES $HYP $RULE)
(UNUSUALCASERULES $HYP $RULE)


(PREMISE $RULE $VAL)
(ACTION $RULE $VAL)
```

```
(ANTECEDENT $RULE)
(TRIGGER $RULE)
(SCREEN $RULE)
```

<u>Dynamic Belief Relations</u>

```
(BELIEF $HYP $CF)
(CUMCF-VALUE $HYP $CF)
(MAX-CONSIDERED-HYP-CUMCF $CF)

(PREVIEW $CNTXT $RULE)

(DEFINITE $CNTXT $PARM)
(DEFIS $CNTXT $PARM $VALUE)
(DEFNOT $CNTXT $PARM $VALUE)
(NOTKNOWN $CNTXT $PARM)
(SAME $CNTXT $PARM $VALUE $CF)
(SAMEP $CNTXT $PARM)
```

<u>Dynamic Search or Focus Relations</u>

```
(CONSIDERED $HYP)
(DESCENDENTS-EXPLORED $TAXPARM)
(EXPLORED $TAXPARM)
(PARENTS-EXPLORED $TAXPARM)
(PURSUED $HYP)
(REFINED $HYP)
(REFINED-COMPLEX $HYP)

(APPLIEDTOP $RULE $CNTXT)
(DONTASKP $CNTXT $PARM)
(TRACEDP $CNTXT $PARM)
 (CLARIFIED $FINDING)
 (ELABORATED $FINDING)
 (SPECIFICS-REQUESTED $FINDING)
 (SUBSUMPTION-CONCLUDED $FINDING)
 (USERSUPPLIED $FINDING)

(TASK-COMPLETED $TASK)
```

<u>Dynamic Relations with Changing Values</u>

```
(CURFOCUS $HYP)
(DIFFERENTIAL $HYP)
(NEW.DIFFERENTIAL)
(WIDER.DIFFERENTIAL)
(DIFFERENTIAL.COMPACT)
```

(NEXT-HARD-DATAQ $FINDING)
(NEW.DATA $FINDING)
(PARTPROC.DATA $FINDING)

<u>Computational Relations</u>

(ABS $ARG $RESULT)
(CFCOMBINE $CF1 $CF2 $RESULT)
(EQ $ARG1 $ARG2)
(GREATERP $ARG1 $ARG2)
(LESSP $ARG1 $ARG2)
(MINUS $ARG1 $ARG2 $RESULT)
(MINUSP $ARG)
(NULL $ARG)
(TIMES $ARG1 $ARG2 $RESULT)

(FIRST-ONE $LIST $RESULT)
(LENGTH $LIST $RESULT)
(MAKESET $PROP $COLLECTVAR $RESULTVAR)
(MEMBER $MEM $SET])
(SINGLETON? $LIST)

(PREDICATE $REL)
(IMPLEMENTATION $REL $VAL)
(MULTIPLEMATCH $REL)
(UNIFY $PATTERN $FACT)

<u>Metarule Premise Relations (Composites)</u>

(ACTIVE.HYP? $HYP)
(ALWAYS-SPECIFY? $FINDING)
(ANTECEDENT.RULES? $PARM $RULE)
(ANY.ANCESTOR? $HYP1 $HYP2)
(BESTCOMPETITOR $CURRENTHYP $BETTERHYP $BHCF)
(BESTHYP $HYP)
(CHILDOF $HYP $CHILD)
(CLARIFY.QUESTIONS $FINDING $PROCPARM)
(DIFF.EXPLAINED $FINDING)
(DIFF.NOTPARENTS-EXPLORED?)
(DIFF.NOTPURSUED?)
(ELIGIBLECHILD)
(ENABLING.QUESTIONS $HYP $RULE)
(EXPLAINEDBY $FINDING $HYP)
(EXPLORE.CHILD? $HYP $H)
(EXPLORE.HYP? $HYP)
(EXPLORE.SIBLING? $OLDFOCUS $HYP)

```
(NEXTGENERALQ? $FOCUSQ)
(PARTPROC.NOTELABORATED? $FINDING)
(PARTPROC.SUGGESTRULES? $PARM $RULE)
(POP-FINDING)
(POP-HYPOTHESIS)
(POP-REDFLAG-FINDING $FOCUSFINDING)
(PROCESS-QUESTIONS? $PARM $PROCTYPEPARM)
(REFINABLE? $HYP)
(REFINABLENODE? $OLDFOCUS $FOCUSCHILD)
(REMAINING.QUESTIONS $HYP $RULE)
(SINGLE.TOPCAUSE $FOCUS)
(SOURCEOF $PARM $SOURCE)
(STRONG-COMPETITOR? $CURRENTHYP $BESTCOMP)
(SUBSUMPTION.SUBTRACED $CNTXT $PARM)
(SUBSUMPTION.SUPERFO $CNTXT $PARM)
(SUBSUMPTION.SUPERTRACED $CNTXT $PARM)
(SUBSUMPTION.SUPERUNK $CNTXT $PARM)
(SUGGESTRULES? $PARM $RULE)
(SUPERS.NOTRACED $PARM $SUPERPARM)
(TAXANCESTOR $HYP1 $HYP2)
(TAXREFINE? $HYP)
(TOP.UNCONFIRMED? $ANCESTOR)
(TOPUNCON $ANCESTOR $HYP)
(TRIGGERQ $HYP $RULE)
(TRIGGERS? $FINDING $RULE)
(UNAPPLIED? $RULE)
(UNCLARIFIED-FINDING $NEW.DATA $FINDING)
(UNEXPLOREDIFF.COMPACT? $HYP)
(UPDATE.DIFF.RULES? $FINDING $RULE)
(WAITINGEVIDRULES? $HYP $RULE)
(WEAK.EVIDENCE.ONLY? $HYP)
```

II Description of MRS

The description of MRS is sufficent to understand MRS/NEOMYCIN, but is not intended to be a tutorial. More detail is given in (MRSDICT, 1982). The aspects of MRS of concern to us are the *database, inference procedures,* and *procedural attachment.*

II.1 The Database

The *database* is the only data structure in MRS. It is a collection of predicate calculus statements, such as

        (COLOROF FIDO BROWN)

to indicate that Fido is brown, or

        (AND (DOG FIDO) (COLOROF FIDO BROWN))

to indicate that Fido is a brown dog. The first element of a statement is called the *relation*, COLOROF, for instance, because it specifies the relationship among the objects that follow it in the statement. It is similar to the links in semantic nets. Frequently, a statement is referred to by its relation, for instance, a "COLOROF statement." To *assert* or *unassert* a statement means to add or remove it from the database, respectively.

Universal quantification is allowed and is represented with variables beginning with dollar signs. For example,

        (IF (DOG $X) (BARKS $X)) ,

or, in long form,

        (ALL X (IF (DOG X) (BARKS X))) ,

which means: "For all objects X in the universe, it is true that 'If X is a dog, then X barks.' " This is an example of a *rule*. A rule may be referred to by the relation of its conclusion. For example, the above rule is a "BARKS rule."

II.2 Inference Procedures

An *inference procedure* is a piece of Lisp code that indicates whether a given statement is deducible from the database statements. The inference procedure of interest here, called *TRUEP*, performs its inference using *backward chaining*. A sketch of it is given in this section; more detail appears in the next section.

Suppose we have in the database the statements

        (IF (DOG $X) (BARKS $X))
        (IF (SPANIEL $X) (DOG $X))
        (SPANIEL FIDO) .

Backward chaining allows deduction of the statement (BARKS FIDO), as follows. The universal variables of the first rule are instantiated to give

        (IF (DOG FIDO) (BARKS FIDO)) .

Then, the premise of the instantiated rule is backchained.[9] This leads to the instantiation of the second rule, which gives

        (IF (SPANIEL FIDO) (DOG FIDO)) .

---

[9]To use backward chaining to deduce a statement is to *backchain* that statement. For instance, in the example (BARKS FIDO) is being backchained. It is called the *goal*. Rules can also be the object of the verb "backchain", as in "the rule is backchained to deduce (BARKS FIDO)." This means that the rule concludes the statement being backchained, so its premise, in turn, is backchained to try to satisfy the rule. Other terminology includes *backchaining*, which is short for backward chaining, and *backchainer*, which is an inference procedure than performs backward chaining.

Since (SPANIEL FIDO) is in the database, (BARKS FIDO) can be deduced from the database.

Here's an example using an AND relation in the premise. Suppose we have in the database the three statements:

```
(IF (AND (DOG $X)
             (NOT (MUZZLED $X)))
       (BARKS $X))
(DOG FIDO)
(NOT (MUZZLED FIDO)).
```

The rule would be instantiated to give

```
(IF (AND (DOG FIDO)
             (NOT (MUZZLED FIDO)))
       (BARKS FIDO)).
```

Since both clauses of the premise AND are on the database, we can deduce (BARKS FIDO). This example of backward chaining only had one "link" in the chain, whereas the previous example had two links.

II.3 Detail of MRS inference

A more detailed explanation of backchaining in MRS is presented here.

For backchaining to run, another inference procedure is necessary, namely *database lookup*. This is used to deduce statements that are already on the database. For instance, if (COLOROF FIDO BROWN) is on the database, then executing

```
(LOOKUP '(COLOROF FIDO BROWN))
```

will return true. Database lookup also provides *variable matching* if the statement contains an existential variable, such as in

```
(LOOKUP '(COLOROF FIDO ?COLOR))
```

or, in long form,

```
(LOOKUP '(EXIST COLOR (COLOROF FIDO COLOR))).
```

Executing this deduces the statement: "there exists a color that is the color of Fido." Rather than just returning true to indicate that it can be deduced (which is correct though not helpful), TRUEP returns a *binding list* giving the constant that is in the same position as ?COLOR, namely BROWN:

```
((?COLOR . BROWN))
```

As shown, a binding list is a Lisp association list.

Every inference procedure has a form that returns all the bindings that can be deduced from the database. For instance, if Fido were multi-colored, which is asserted on the database with multiple COLOROF statements for Fido, then

```
(LOOKUPS '(COLOROF FIDO ?COLOR))
```

would return a list of binding lists:

```
(((?COLOR . BROWN)) ((?COLOR . WHITE))).
```

The naming convention is to pluralize the original inference procedure name, for example, the generic deduction function TRUEP becomes TRUEPS.

The backchainer actually does a database lookup before backchaining rules. Suppose the database contains

```
(IF (DOG $X) (BARKS $X))
(IF (SPANIEL $X) (DOG $X))
(SPANIEL FIDO).
```

and the backchainer is executed on the statement (BARKS FIDO). First, it tries to lookup (BARKS FIDO) and gets nothing. Then it does a lookup for rules that it can use:

        (LOOKUP '(IF ?PREMISE (BARKS FIDO))).

This matches the first rule giving the binding list

        ((?PREMISE DOG FIDO)).

Note that the the first rule has been fully instantiated, so the premise of the rule has become (DOG FIDO).[10] Now the backchainer is called on the statement (DOG FIDO). The process repeats and leads to backchainer being called on (SPANIEL FIDO). Here, the database lookup succeeds and the backchaining stops.

If the backchainer had originally been executed on the statement (BARKS ?X), to find an object that barks, the lookup for the rule would have been

        (IF ?PREMISE (BARKS ?X))

and the binding list returned would have been:

        ((?PREMISE DOG $X)(?X . $X)).

Unfortunately, we do not want to deduce (DOG $X), but (DOG ?XX) where ?XX is some newly generated existential variable. This is called the *variable flip*. In general, during backchaining the premise of looked up rules have their existentials changed to universals, and vice versa, to take care of this problem.

II.4 Procedural attachment

A central feature of MRS is that the name of the Lisp function used to assert, unassert, or evaluate the truth of a given statement (briefly, to "truep" a statement) can be deduced at run time. The name of the Lisp function may be deduced from any of the information present in the MRS database. When the function deduced is always the same for a given statement, this feature reduces to what is commonly known as *procedural attachment.*

Though the name of the attached procedure may be deduced in any manner from the database, the most common way is to look on the database for a statement of the form

        (TO <assert/unassert/truep> <statement> <function name>) .

In the case of TRUEP, the attached procedure is an inference procedure. For example, suppose that during backchaining, one of the rules needed to test that M is an element of list L is:

        (IF (MEMBEROF L M) <conclusion>) .

A special function MEMBEROF-TRUEP is specified as the procedural attachment by the statement:[11]

        (TO TRUEP (MEMBEROF $LIST $MEMBER) MEMBEROF-TRUEP) .

So during the backchaining of the above rule, the MEMBEROF-TRUEP function is called to deduce the statement (MEMBEROF L M). MEMBEROF-TRUEP searches the list L for the member M.

------

[10]Unparenthesized because the binding list uses dotted pairs.

[11]Recall that the dollar signs indicate universal quantification, so this statement says, "to TRUEP *any* three-element statement that begins with MEMBEROF, use MEMBEROF-TRUEP."

The procedural attachments used in MRS/NEOMYCIN are described in Appendix XXX. In HERACLES these are replaced by the IMPLEMENTATION relation (Section XXX) used by the compiler.

III Details of MRS/NEOMYCIN

This appendix describes in some detail the architecture and operation of MRS/NEOMYCIN. Note that metarules have a somewhat different form than examples taken from HERACLES, shown elsewhere in this paper.

In summary, a simple deliberation/action loop manages the system at the highest level. There are three metalevels of reasoning. Metarules recommend action in terms of domain rules to apply, questions to ask the user, or abstract tasks requiring application of more metarules. Metacontrol rules, corresponding to the interpreter for metarules, deduce what action to take next. The highest level of rules orders and selects the metacontrol rules, referring to them by name.

Sequential and iterative application of rules is accomplished by ordering rules in the database, keeping records of which rules have been applied or failed, and by using a form of backward chaining that dynamically calculates the rules to be used in deduction.

III.1 From NEOMYCIN and MRS to MRS/NEOMYCIN

MRS/NEOMYCIN was created from NEOMYCIN by changing the representation of the metacontrol portion. Specifically (refer to Figure 4-3):

- To conform to the MRS rule format, the NEOMYCIN metarules, which evaluate their actions upon application, become, in MRS/NEOMYCIN, simply *recommendations for action*:
  ```
  (IF <premise statement> (DODURING <action>))
  ```
  This rule states that if the premise statement is true, then the statement (DODURING <action>) is true. The actions in MRS/NEOMYCIN are domain-rule application, data request, and task invocation.

- The code that controls the application of metarules, that is, the task interpreter, is translated into MRS rules. These rules are called the *metarule control rules*, or simply *metacontrol rules*. Here it was necessary to augment MRS, as explained later.

- Most of the functions that are used as predicates in the premises of the metarules are translated into MRS rules. They are called the *metarule premise rules*. These rules are applied during the backchaining of the metarules.

Deliberation/Action Loop

With most of the NEOMYCIN control now expressed in rules, an interpreter is needed to execute them. This brings us to the heart of MRS/NEOMYCIN and the first MRS augmentation: the *deliberation/action loop* (DA loop, (Doyle, 1980) (Genesereth, 1983)). As its name

```
(LAMBDA (ACTION)
  (if (TASK? ACTION) then (PUSH-TASK-STACK ACTION)
                          (DALOOP)
                          (POP-TASK-STACK)
                     else
                          (EVAL ACTION)))
```

Figure III-1:   Definition of DOACTION.

```
(LAMBDA NIL
  (loop.until.null
    (DOACTION (TRUEP '(NEXTACTION $ACTION)))))
```

Figure III-2:   Definition of DALOOP.

implies, it deliberates about the next action to take and then takes it. If the action is primitive (a domain-rule application or data request), it is passed to the NEOMYCIN groundwork to be executed. If the action is abstract (a task), the DA loop must deliberate further to determine the next primitive action.[12]   The function that performs actions is called DOACTION, defined in Figure III-1. It is the action part of the deliberation/action loop.

As will be described below, the abstract actions (the tasks) require keeping a stack of tasks, as with traditional procedures. A task is performed with a call to the deliberation/action loop, because more deliberation is necessary to reduce an abstract action to primitive actions. The primitive actions are done with Lisp function calls to the NEOMYCIN groundwork (two functions, in particular, APPLYRULES and FINDOUT).

The definition of the deliberation/action loop appears in Figure III-2. DALOOP deduces the next action to take and then passes it in a recursive call to DOACTION. The loop continues until it is unable to deduce what action to take and then quits. Since DALOOP is called from DOACTION, this means the task is finished and that the task stack is popped.

Deducing the NEXTACTION

In general, the deduction of the appropriate next action can be done by any inference procedure available in MRS. In MRS/NEOMYCIN, backward chaining is used. While the metarules are the rules that specify the next action in their conclusions, they are not backchained directly by the DA loop. The catch is that deciding which metarules are correct to backchain at any given time requires more deduction. This is because only the metarules associated with the current task are to be applied, and they are to be applied by a nontrivial

---

[12]The DA loop has its roots in the principle that deliberation on the course of action and the actual acting should occur separately. Deliberation is defined here as those computations that do not change the database; actions are defined as those that do. This definition is relative to the levels of domain, strategy, and database actions. For example, deliberating with diagnostic metarules requires that the result be written somewhere (an MRS action); similarly, a strategic diagnostic action leads to substantial domain-level deliberation.

procedure, the task interpreter described in Section XXX. The deduction of which metarules to backchain is done using the *metarule control rules* (MC rules). (See Figure III-3. Ellipsis ("...") indicates that only parts of the rule premises are shown.)

However, there is a problem. The task interpreter, like each diagnostic task, is a procedure that itself must be controlled by rules: The rules corresponding to it, the metacontrol rules, cannot be simply backchained. The highest level rules actually conclude not what metarules to apply but which rules constituting the task interpreter (MC rules) to apply.

The form of backward chaining that deduces at run time which rules should be backchained will be called *RULEFOR* backward chaining.[13] It is one of the MRS augmentations and is distinguished from normal backward chaining wherein *all* rules concluding about the goal are backchained. RULEFOR backchaining decides what rules to use by deducing *RULEFOR statements*, namely,

(RULEFOR <statement> <rule>) ,

where <statement> is the statement being backchained, in this case (NEXTACTION <action>), and <rule> is the rule to be used.

In Figure III-3 observe that there are two layers of RULEFOR deduction: first, to determine which task interpreter (MC) rules to apply, and second, to determine which metarules to apply. When metarules are applied, their premises are backchained. Statements in metarule premises are concluded by *metarule premise rules*. These are the rules that replace the Lisp functions originally in NEOMYCIN's metarule premises. The backchaining stops when these premise rules access the data structures and functions in the NEOMYCIN groundwork.

To summarize, we have linearized the steps of an iterative procedure by referencing by name in rules that invoke them conditionally. MC rules correspond to steps of the task interpreter. Some steps must only be done once at the beginning, some are applied iteratively, others are applied once at the end. MC rules conclude what the NEXTACTION should be, for example, a DODURING action. The rules that conclude what MC rule to invoke are the NEXTACTION RULEFOR (NR) rules. Each NR rule refers to a single MC rule by name. The NR rules are an ordered set of rules that can be backchained normally.

The sample trace of MRS/NEOMYCIN in the following section gives examples of all kinds of rules (NR, MC, DR, metarule, metarule premise rule, domain rule) and shows their interaction. Details about these rules are given in Appendix IV.

III.2 Sample Trace of MRS/NEOMYCIN

Presented here is a trace from a MRS/NEOMYCIN run. Comments are in italics. The example uses a task called PROCESS-DATUM which does forward reasoning with new data. The statements describing it are given in Figure III.1 (only 2 of 7 metarules are shown). The task is simple/try-all, so all of its DODURING metarules will be tried once. The task is invoked

---

[13]The name comes from "The RULE FOR <statement> is <rule>," meaning that <rule> is to be used in the backchain deduction of <statement>.

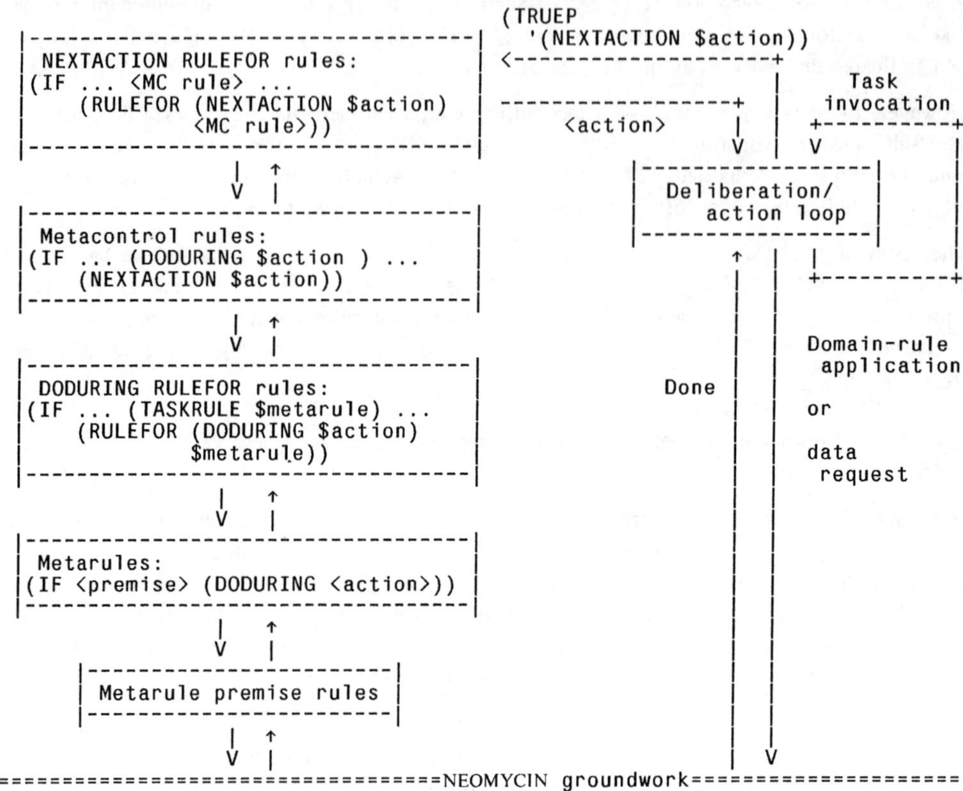

Figure III-3: MRS/NEOMYCIN control flow (showing deduction of DODURING metarules). [$x = variable; <x> = instantiation of $x]

```
(TASKTYPE PROCESS-DATUM SIMPLE)
(TASKGOAL PROCESS-DATUM PARTIALLY-PROCESSED)
(END-CONDITION PROCESS-DATUM DONT-ABORT)
(TASK-TRY-ALL PROCESS-DATUM)

(TASKRULE PROCESS-DATUM
          (IF (AND (CURRENT-ARGUMENT $FOCUS-DATUM)
                   (MAKESET (CLARIFY-QUESTION $FOCUS-DATUM $CLARIFY-Q)
                            $CLARIFY-Q CLARIFY-Q-SET))
              (DODURING (FINDOUT CNTXT (MEMBERSOF 'CLARIFY-Q-SET)))))


(TASKRULE PROCESS-DATUM
          (IF (AND (CURRENT-ARGUMENT $FOCUS-DATUM)
                   (MAKESET (RULES-IN-FOCUS? $FOCUS-DATUM $RULE)
                            $RULE RULE-SET))
              (DODURING (APPLYRULES (MEMBERSOF 'RULE-SET]
```

Figure III-4: Some of the statements describing the task PROCESS-DATUM.

by some metarule which causes the DALOOP to execute:

```
(DOACTION '(PROCESS-DATUM NEUROSIGN-CHRONICITY))
```

Starting abstract action PROCESS-DATUM on NEUROSIGN-CHRONICITY

The task PROCESS-DATUM is pushed onto the task stack. This is done with the relation CURRENT-TASK by asserting the statement

(CURRENT-TASK PROCESS-DATUM) .

Similarly, NEUROSIGN-CHRONICITY is put on the CURRENT-ARGUMENT stack.

Starting DA loop

The DA loop executes

(TRUEP '(NEXTACTION $ACTION))

to find out what action should be passed to DOACTION. This invokes the RULEFOR backchainer which is attached to the NEXTACTION statements. The backchainer executes

(TRUEPS '(RULEFOR (NEXTACTION $ACTION) $RULE))

to find out what MC rules to use in deducing the NEXTACTION statement. (The plural form, TRUEPS, indicates that all of the rules that can be deduced from the database are returned.) The attached procedure for Normal backchaining is used to deduce the RULEFOR statements, which leads to backchaining the NEXTACTION RULEFOR (NR) rules. (Only NR rules 3 and 4 are shown below.)

For brevity, we will skip ahead to the third iteration of the DALOOP, after the MC rules intializing the task have completed and it is time to try the DOBEFORE rules.

This time around, all of the MC rules are candidates for concluding NEXTACTION, except for MC rules 1 and 2, which have already been applied (which is why NR rules 1 and 2 fail). Therefore, the deduction of the NEXTACTION statement begins with MC rule 3 (MC-3) ...

```
Applying NR rule 1 ...
... failed
Applying NR rule 2 ...
... failed
Applying NR rule 3 ...

    [IF (AND (CURRENT-TASK $TASK)
             (THNOT (FAILED-IN-TASK $TASK MC-3]
         (RULEFOR (NEXTACTION $ACTION) MC-3]

... succeeded
Applying NR rule 4 ...

    [IF (AND (CURRENT-TASK $CURTASK)
             (OR [AND (OR (AND (TASKTYPE $CURTASK ITERATIVE)
                               (THNOT (TASK-TRY-ALL $CURTASK)))
                          (AND (TASKTYPE $CURTASK SIMPLE)
                               (TASK-TRY-ALL $CURTASK)))
                      (THNOT (FAILED-IN-TASK $CURTASK MC-4]
                 [AND (TASKTYPE $CURTASK SIMPLE)
                      (TASK-TRY-ALL $CURTASK)
                      (THNOT (APPLIED-IN-TASK $CURTASK MC-4]
         (RULEFOR (NEXTACTION $ACTION) MC-4]

... succeeded
Applying NR rule 5 ...
... succeeded
Applying NR rule 6 ...
... succeeded
```

```
Applying MC rule 3 ...

   (IF (DOBEFORE $ACTION)
       (NEXTACTION $ACTION))
```

The DOBEFORE, DODURING, DOAFTER statements have a RULEFOR backchainer attached. So rather than backchaining the DOBEFORE rules directly, we first backchain (RULEFOR (DOBEFORE $ACTION) $RULE) to determine which rules concluding (DOBEFORE $ACTION) should be tried. The rules concluding (RULEFOR (DOBEFORE $ACTION) $RULE) are the DOBEFORE RULEFOR (DR) rules. In this case, there is only one rule, DR rule 1.

```
Applying DR rule 1 ...

(IF (AND (CURRENT-TASK $CURTASK)
         (DOBEFORE-TASKRULE $CURTASK $MRULE)
         (THNOT (APPLIED-IN-TASK $CURTASK $MRULE)))
    (RULEFOR (DOBEFORE $ACTION) $MRULE))

... failed
```

DR rule 1 fails because the current task, PROCESS-DATUM, has no DOBEFORE rules associated with it (see description of PROCESS-DATUM at beginning of this section). That is, clause 2 of DR 1 cannot be deduced to be true.

```
... failed (MC rule 3)
```

MC rule 3 fails because its premise (DOBEFORE $ACTION) cannot be deduced. The deduction of the NEXTACTION statement continues with MC rule 4 ...

```
Applying MC rule 4 ...

   (IF (AND (DODURING $ACTION)
            (DONT-STOP-TASK PROCESS-DATUM))
       (NEXTACTION $ACTION))
```

RULEFOR backchaining is used to determine which metarules concluding DODURING should be tried...

```
Applying DR rule 2 ...

   (IF (AND (CURRENT-TASK $CURTASK)
            (TASKTYPE $CURTASK ITERATIVE)
            (TASKRULE $CURTASK $MRULE))
       (RULEFOR (DODURING $ACTION)
               $MRULE))

... failed
```

DR rule 2 fails because PROCESS-DATUM is not an iterative task.

```
Applying DR rule3 ...

   (IF (AND (CURRENT-TASK $CURTASK)
            (TASKTYPE $CURTASK SIMPLE)
            (TASKRULE $CURTASK $MRULE)
            (THNOT (APPLIED-IN-TASK $CURTASK $MRULE)))
       (RULEFOR (DODURING $ACTION)
               $MRULE))

... succeeded
```

DR rule 3 succeeds because PROCESS-DATUM is a simple task and has task rules that have not been applied. Since the RULEFOR backchainer uses TRUEPS on the RULEFOR statements, and all the DODURING metarules of PROCESS-DATUM have not been applied, all the metarules are returned as rules to use in deducing (DODURING $ACTION) for MC rule 4.

```
Applying  PROCESS-DATUM metarule 1 ...

   (IF (AND (CURRENT-ARGUMENT $FOCUS-DATUM)
            (MAKESET (CLARIFY-QUESTION $FOCUS-DATUM $CLARIFY-Q)
                $CLARIFY-Q CLARIFY-Q-SET))
       (DODURING (FINDOUT CNTXT (MEMBERSOF 'CLARIFY-Q-SET))))

... failed
```

This metarule uses the MRS *augmentation MAKESET (see section   III.4). Here the statement*

$$(CLARIFY\text{-}QUESTION\ NEUROSIGN\text{-}CHRONICITY\ \$CLARIFY\text{-}Q)$$

is TRUEPS'd, giving all the follow-up questions to ask about the datum NEUROSIGN-CHRONICITY.

CLARIFY-QUESTION is concluded by the metarule premise rule

$$(IF\ (AND\ (PROCESSQ\ \$DATUM\ \$QPARM)$$
$$(THNOT\ (TRACEDP\ CNTXT\ '\$QPARM)))$$
$$(CLARIFY\text{-}QUESTION\ \$DATUM\ \$QPARM)).$$

Here procedural attachment is used. Recall that the domain knowledge of NEOMYCIN *has not been translated to predicate calculus. The questions ($QPARM) that describe the process of a disorder (duration, severity, etc.) are stored as the PROCESSQ property of the disorder. Similarly, TRACEDP is a function that examines a property list to see if a question has been asked before.*

If there are any questions, they are collected and put in the set called CLARIFY-Q-SET. Then FINDOUT asks the questions specified in the set. However, there are no questions in this case, so PROCESS-DATUM metarule 1 fails.

```
Applying PROCESS-DATUM metarule 2

   (IF (AND (CURRENT-ARGUMENT $FOCUS-DATUM)
            (MAKESET (RULES-IN-FOCUS? $FOCUS-DATUM $RULE)
                $RULE RULE-SET))
       (DODURING (APPLYRULES (MEMBERSOF 'RULE-SET))))

... succeeded

... succeeded (MC rule 4)
```

MC rule 4 succeeded partially because metarule 4 was able to deduce (DODURING $ACTION). Not shown is that the second clause of MC rule 4 needed to be deduced, namely

$$(DONT\text{-}STOP\text{-}TASK\ PROCESS\text{-}DATUM).$$

This is the clause that decides whether the task should be aborted or not. It is deduced by the following rule:

$$(IF\ (OR\ (END\text{-}CONDITION\ \$CURTASK\ DONT\text{-}ABORT)$$
$$(ALLE\ (IF\ (AND\ (ONSTACK\ \$TASK\ CURRENT\text{-}TASK)$$
$$(END\text{-}CONDITION\ \$TASK\ \$EC))$$
$$(THNOT\ \$EC))))$$
$$(DONT\text{-}STOP\text{-}TASK\ \$CURTASK))$$

The rule states that the end condition of all the tasks on the task stack must be undeducible, or the current task must have an end condition of DONT-ABORT. The latter is the case with PROCESS-DATUM.

Now that an MC rule has succeeded, DA loop passes the action to DOACTION. The action consists of applying the domain rules that MAKESET put in the set RULE-SET, namely RULE407 and RULE403. These are rules that use the new datum NEUROSIGN-CHRONICITY to make conclusions about hypotheses that are currently "in focus."

```
Starting primitive action (APPLYRULES (MEMBERSOF 'RULE-SET))

Applying RULE407/PATIENT-2; RULE407 succeeded.
Conclude: MENINGITIS of PATIENT-2 is BACTERIAL-MENINGITIS (-.15)
Conclude: MENINGITIS of PATIENT-2 is VIRUS (-.09)
Conclude: CHRONIC-MENINGITIS of PATIENT-2 is YES (.24)

Applying RULE403/PATIENT-2; RULE403 succeeded.
Conclude: MENINGITIS of PATIENT-2 is BACTERIAL-MENINGITIS (.2)
Conclude: MENINGITIS of PATIENT-2 is VIRUS (.604)

Finished primitive action (APPLYRULES (MEMBERSOF 'RULE-SET))
```

After doing a single DODURING action, control returns to the DA loop, and the NEXTACTION statement is deduced again. NR rule 4 will again conclude that MC rule 4 should be tried--this is a try-all task so more than one metarule is allowed to succeed. MC rule 4 fails because it is unable to deduce (DODURING $ACTION)--there are no unapplied metarules. (Specifically, MC rule 4 fails because DR rule 3 fails to find any metarules that can be tried to conclude DODURING.)

The remaining NR rules will be tried, causing the DOAFTER metarules to be applied and goal of the task to be set. (Note that NR rule 4 will fail on subsequent iterations because MC rule 4 has failed.) When the task completes, DOACTION will pop the task and argument stack and erase the APPLIED-IN-TASK and FAILED-IN-TASK statements pertaining to PROCESS-DATUM.

III.3 Summary of Techniques for Procedural Application of Rules

The purpose of the metarule control rules is to mimic the task interpreter, the piece of the Lisp code which applies the metarules in NEOMYCIN. The task interpreter is nicely expressed in a procedural language like Lisp; it contains iterative application of rules, sequential application of rules, setting of variables to save results of computation, and if-then-else statements. These are difficult to express with rules. General examples below review how these constructs are handled in MRS/NEOMYCIN.

Non-try-all Application of Rules

The simplest form of rule application used in the NEOMYCIN task interpreter is that of a "pure production system" in which the first applicable rule[14] in the database is used every time backward chaining is done on the same statement. For instance, suppose the database contains the rules

```
(IF P1 G)
(IF P2 G)
(IF P3 G) .
```

---

[14]"Applicable rules" has different meanings for normal and RULEFOR backward chaining. For normal backchaining it means all the rules in the database that conclude about the statement being deduced. In RULEFOR backchaining it means the rules deduced at runtime as being applicable. If the same rule is deduced as being applicable at each call to the RULEFOR backchainer, then the same looping effect is achieved as with normal backchaining.

At each call to the backchainer, these rules are tried in order,[15] starting at the beginning, until one succeeds. This technique implements iterative non-try-all application of rules. If controlled to occur only once, it will implement simple non-try-all tasks. Avoiding unnecessary computation when all of the rules are failing is discussed below.

Try-all (Sequential) Application of Rules

To apply rules sequentially, RULEFOR backward chaining is used. The technique is to mark that rules that have been applied already so that the RULEFOR backchainer will apply the next one in order.

For example, suppose that G is the goal. Let the database contain the rule
```
(IF (AND (RULE-IN-SEQUENCE $RULE)
         (NOT (APPLIED $RULE)))
    (RULEFOR G $RULE)) .
```
This rule states "for all objects $RULE, if $RULE is a rule in the sequence and has not been applied, then $RULE can be used to deduce G." Each time the RULEFOR backchainer is called, the first unapplied rule is backchained. Note that this requires the RULE-IN-SEQUENCE relation to find the rules in the order required. The APPLIED statements must be asserted into the database by the RULEFOR backchainer, since it is the only mechanism that knows when a rule is applied.

Note that sequential execution is different from iterative execution. The two are usually thought of together as the common DO loop (corresponding to iterative try-all tasks). In MRS/NEOMYCIN, iteration is brought about by a combination of the "loop.until.null" in DALOOP and the control rules that apply metarules until DODURING cannot be deduced.

Applying Rules Until They Fail

To avoid unnecessary recomputation, it is useful to avoid trying rules that cannot succeed after they have failed once. Again, RULEFOR backward chaining is used. Suppose that G is the goal and that POSSIBLE-RULE specifies the rules that might be used to deduce G. Let the database contain the rule
```
(IF (AND (POSSIBLE-RULE $RULE)
         (NOT (FAILED $RULE)))
    (RULEFOR G $RULE)) .
```
When G is being deduced, this rule will make the RULEFOR backchainer omit rules that have failed. As with the APPLIED statements used in sequential application, the FAILED statements must be recorded by the RULEFOR backchainer.

Applying Rules Once

Applying rules only once is straightforward. Using the previous example:
```
(IF (AND (POSSIBLE-RULE $RULE)
         (NOT (APPLIED $RULE)))
    (RULEFOR B $RULE)) .
```
Applying rules in sequence is a special case of this.

---

[15]See ordered database access entry in Appendix III.4 for how statements are ordered by the system designer.

Caching Results

One way to avoid recomputation is to save the results of deduction. For example, consider the rule

```
(IF (AND A B) C) .
```

If the truth of A is important and does not change often, the result of trying to deduce A should be saved for efficiency. The solution in MRS/NEOMYCIN is to modify MRS's principle deductive function, TRUEP, to assert the result of the deducing statements the user wants cached. Then rules applied later can use the result.

For example, suppose that A has been indicated by the user as a statement to be cached. Then the application of the above rule would record the statement (CACHE A ⟨result⟩) in the database. Another rule could refer to this later, for instance,

```
(IF (AND D (CACHE A T))
     E) .
```

For this rule to succeed, the previously deduced value of A must be T.

If-then-else Statements

MRS rules by their definition do not have "else" clauses, which are a method of avoiding recomputation. Caching technique is used to overcome the problem. First, the premise part of the IF is indicated for caching by the user, then the result can be referred to in another rule. For example,

```
(IF-THEN-ELSE A B C)
```

becomes

```
(IF A B)
(IF (NOT (CACHE A T)) C) ,
```

where the rules must be ordered, with no intervening rules that might change the result of deducing A.

III.4 MRS Augmentations

The MRS augmentations that were made in the course of building MRS/NEOMYCIN are summarized here:

- *The deliberation/action loop.* This is the "interpreter" of MRS/NEOMYCIN.

- *RULEFOR backward chaining.* This form of backchaining is used by the DALOOP to select dynamically the metacontrol and metarules to be used in deducing the next appropriate action.

- *Caching.* Caching is used to avoid unnecessary recomputation, such as for if-then-else statements. wherein all the statements deduced during the course of backchaining are asserted onto the database. To avoid confusion, the form of caching described in this paper should be called *selective caching*. It is so called because the user selects the statements that should have their deduction results cached.[16]

---

[16]In MRS/NEOMYCIN, this is done by putting the relation name on a global list. For more generality, the caching should be indicated by a statement on the database or rules that allow deduction of that statement.

To make this more useful, a relation is needed that pulls the binding values out of the binding lists that are the results of deduction (see section II.3 for explanation of bindings). So the CACHE statement is used like this:

```
(AND (CACHE <statement> $RESULT)
     (VARVALUE <variable name> $RESULT $VARVALUE)
     ...)
```

where the ellipsis contains references to $VARVALUE. }

- *APPLIED and FAILED marking mechanisms.* These are used to bring about sequential and iterative rule application within a task. When the task is done, all the APPLIED and FAILED statements are erased. This is done so that the statements cannot confuse the operations of later calls to the task. Note that these statements would need to be included on the stack to allow tasks to be invoked recursively.

- *Ordered database access.* This is used to order the metarules. Since the MRS database in principle has no order imposed on the statements, the order must be specified in another set of statements. For instance, asserting the following statements would order statements F1, F2, and F3:

```
(ACCESSBEFORE (F1 A B) (F2 A B))
(ACCESSBEFORE (F2 A B) (F3 A B))
```

The inconvenience the ordering statements cause the programmer can be eliminated with a programmer interface function. The statements above are asserted as follows:

```
(ASSERT '(ORD* (F1 A B) (F2 A B) (F3 A B))) .
```

The function attached to ORD* statements asserts the statements shown along with their ordering relations. Also, a special procedural attachment is needed for TRUEP that sorts the original statements according to the ordering rules.

This method is too slow to use. A less elegant method is used in MRS/NEOMYCIN which employs the LIFO property of the MRS database. The ordered relations are put into the database in reverse order, so that TRUEP will find them in the order specified by the ORD* statement.

- *Extensional ALL (ALLE).* This construct allows statements like "All cows I know about are not purple." This is different from "All cows are not purple." The second requires some proof showing that cows, by their nature, cannot be purple. The first merely requires a database check.

Our cow example would give:

```
(ALLE (IF (COW $X) (NOT (PURPLE $X)))) .
```

In general, it allows statements of the form:

```
(ALLE (IF <premise> <conclusion>)) .
```

If the ALLE statement is true, it means that for all objects satisfying <premise>, <conclusion> is true. In MRS/NEOMYCIN, ALLE is used to check that none of the tasks on the task stack has its end condition satisfied.

- *Lambda statements.* NEOMYCIN's task structure requires a stack of tasks, analogous to traditional procedure-call stacks. That is, when a new task is invoked, the old task name and arguments are saved so that control can be returned to it when the new task is finished. Traditionally, this is called "lambda binding." In MRS/NEOMYCIN, this is implemented by procedural attachment (to CURRENT-TASK, CURRENT-ARGUMENT, and ONSTACK statements).

- *Set collection (MAKESET).* Frequently it is necessary to collect all the objects in the database that fulfill a given requirement. The solution used bends the rule about separation of deliberation and action. A relation MAKESET is defined with the format

```
(MAKESET <statement> <collectvar> <setname>) ,
```

where <collectvar> is a global variable. A procedure is attached so that when a MAKESET statement is TRUEP'd, <statement> is TRUEPS'd and the bindings for <collectvar> are collected. The bindings are asserted as members of the set named <setname>. They can be retrieved with the function MEMBERSOF. The mechanism is used in the following metarule for applying domain rules that trigger hypotheses suggested by a recent datum given to the program:

```
(IF (MAKESET (TRIGGERS? $FOCUSDATUM $TRIGRULE)
             $TRIGRULE TRIGRULESET)
    (DODURING (APPLYRULES CNTXT (MEMBERSOF 'TRIGRULESET)))) .
```

IV The metacontrol rules

It is the purpose of the metacontrol rules to infer what action the task interpreter would do next. Elaborating a bit on the procedure listed in section 4.3, we list five kinds of actions that take place when each task is executed:

1. *Initialization actions.* There are two of these:

   a. Initializing the cached value of (DONT-STOP-TASK <current task>), the statement corresponding to the end condition.

   b. Initializing the end condition of the current task, if it is indicated by atom (as opposed to arbitrary LISP code).

2. *DOBEFORE actions.* These correspond to the actions concluded by the DOBEFORE metarules of the current task. The DOBEFORE metarules have the form

```
(IF <premise> (DOBEFORE <action>))
```

3. *DODURING actions.* These correspond to the actions concluded by the DODURING rules of the current task. The DODURING metarules have the form

```
(IF <premise> (DODURING <action>))
```

4. *Goal setting action.* This records that the current task was completed if it was not aborted.

5. *DOAFTER actions.* These correspond to the actions concluded by the DOAFTER rules of the current task. The DOAFTER metarules have the form

```
(IF <premise> (DOAFTER <action>))
```

These actions are reflected in six rules that actually conclude NEXTACTION statements:

1. For the DONT-STOP-TASK initialization (the $CURTASK is bound to the current
   task before this rule is applied):

```
(IF (TRUTH)
    (NEXTACTION (ASSERT '(CACHE (DONT-STOP-TASK $CURTASK) T]
```

2. For the end condition initialization:

```
(IF (AND (END-CONDITION $CURTASK $EC)
         (ATOM $EC))
    (NEXTACTION (UNASSERT (QUOTE $EC))))
```

3. For the DOBEFORE actions:

```
(IF (DOBEFORE $ACTION)
    (NEXTACTION $ACTION))
```

4. For the DODURING actions:

```
(IF (AND (DODURING $ACTION)'
         (DONT-STOP-TASK $CURTASK))
    (NEXTACTION $ACTION))
```

5. For setting the goal of the current task:[17]

```
(IF (AND (CACHE (DONT-STOP-TASK $CURTASK) T)
         (TASKGOAL $CURTASK $CURGOAL)
         (CURRENT-ARGUMENT $CURARG))
    (NEXTACTION (ASSERT (QUOTE ($CURGOAL $CURARG]
```

6. For the DOAFTER actions:

```
(IF (DOAFTER $ACTION)
    (NEXTACTION $ACTION))
```

These six rules are called the *metarule control rules* (MC rules) because when they are
backchained by the DA loop to deduce the NEXTACTION statement, the appropriate metarules
are backchained. This occurs because the metarules conclude the DOBEFORE, DODURING,
and DOAFTER statements which are the premises of MC rules 3, 4, and 6.

The important thing to notice is that the MC rules cannot be backchained in the normal
way--they must be controlled. In particular, MC rules 1 and 2 should only be applied once, at
the beginning of the task. Similarly, MC rule 5 should only be applied once. MC rules 3 and
6, which bring about the DOBEFORE and DOAFTER actions need to be applied exhaustively,
so each metarule that recommends a DOBEFORE or DOAFTER action is tried once, in

---

[17]Caching is needed here because the decision of whether to mark the goal is based on the result of deducing
DONT-STOP-TASK, the relation that tells if the current task should be aborted. Normally, the DONT-STOP-TASK
statement could just be re-deduced (though this would be inefficient). However, the DONT-STOP-TASK statement
might be false in MC rule 4, causing the task to abort, but later found to be true as a result of doing the DOAFTER
rules of the current task or by the subtasks specified by the last DODURING rule of the current task. Therefore, the
result of the original deduction is cached when DONT-STOP-TASK is asserted into the database and used in MC rule
5.

sequence. Finally, MC rule 4 will be applied a different number of times, depending on whether this is a simple/iterative or try-all/not-try-all task. So how can we bring about this invocation of the MC rules?

The solution used in MRS/NEOMYCIN is to *embed the MC rules in rules that can be backchained normally and which conclude when the MC rules should be applied*. As the MC rules conclude what NEXTACTION to take, this set of normally backchained rules concludes what MC rule to use for deducing NEXTACTION. That is, these control rules conclude
```
(RULEFOR (NEXTACTION  $ACTION) <MC rule>)
```
. So we say that RULEFOR backchaining is used to deduce (NEXTACTION $ACTION). On each execution of
```
(TRUEP '(NEXTACTION $ACTION))
```
by the DA loop, the RULEFOR backchainer is invoked and it executes
```
(TRUEPS '(RULEFOR (NEXTACTION $ACTION) $MC-RULE))
```
to deduce what MC rule to backchain.[18] The attached procedure for RULEFOR statements is a normal backchainer. The rules that are backchained in deducing these RULEFOR statements are called the *NEXTACTION RULEFOR rules*. They constitute our solution for linearizing the 6 MC rules into a normally backchained set of rules; they are described in the next section.

RULEFOR backchaining is also used on the DOBEFORE, DODURING, and DOAFTER statements because more deliberation is required to choose the appropriate metarule. For example, when MC rule 3 is backchained, its premise is backchained. The metarules that are used to deduce the premise are the DOBEFORE metarules of the task currently being executed as opposed to all the DOBEFORE metarules, and each of these should only be applied once, in order. By backchaining
```
(RULEFOR (DOBEFORE $ACTION) $METARULE)
```
we deduce which metarule that concludes DOBEFORE should be invoked next. This is explained in more detail in section IV.2.

It can now be seen that are two layers of RULEFOR backchaining in the metacontrol of MRS/NEOMYCIN. See figure IV-1. The first layer consists of the six MC rules and the NEXTACTION RULEFOR rules that control when they are applied. The second layer consists of the metarules and the RULEFOR rules that control when they are applied. The interface between the layers occurs when the MC rules are backchained, thereby invoking the metarules.

IV.1 NEXTACTION RULEFOR rules

The NEXTACTION RULEFOR rules (NR rules) are listed in order below, with annotations. After the first three rules are presented, an explanation is given showing how they create the procedural behavior of the task interpreter.

---

[18]The plural form, TRUEPS, indicates that *all* of the rules that can be deduced from the database are returned.

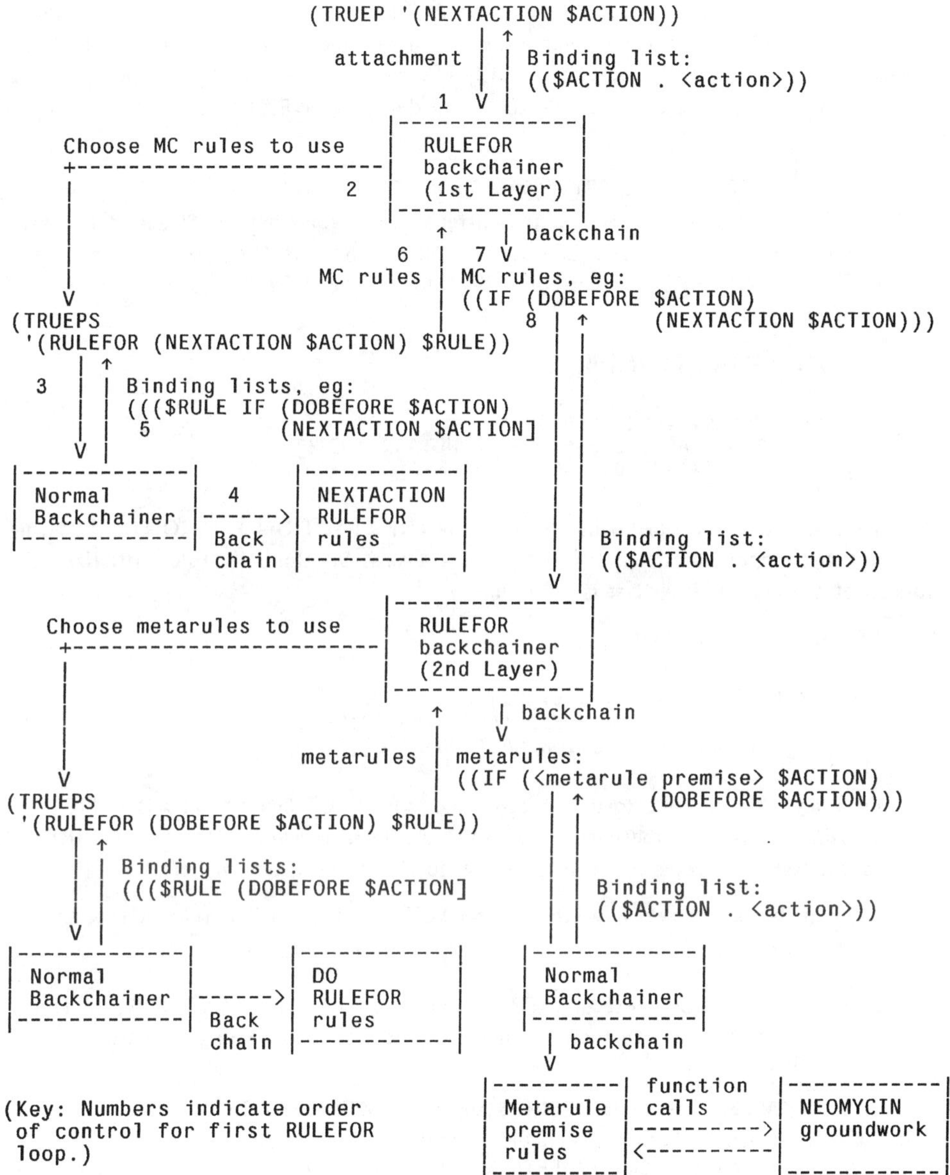

Figure IV-1: Deduction of NEXTACTION statement.

NEXTACTION RULEFOR rule 1

```
[IF [AND (CURRENT-TASK $CURTASK)
         (THNOT (APPLIED-IN-TASK $CURTASK MC-1]
    (RULEFOR (NEXTACTION $ACTION) MC-1]
```

The first thing to note is that the rule in the RULEFOR statement is the same as the rule in the APPLIED-IN-TASK statement, namely metacontrol rule 1. In this way, the MC rules are embedded in all of the NEXTACTION RULEFOR rules, a reference by "name", as opposed to content.[19] NR rule 1 says that the rule to use in deducing (NEXTACTION $ACTION) is MC rule 1:

```
(IF (TRUTH)
    (NEXTACTION (ASSERT '(CACHE (DONT-STOP-TASK $CURTASK) T))))
```

if it has not[20] been applied already in the current task. Note that the $CURTASK variable is bound to the current task by the first clause of NR 1. So this NR rule initializes the cached value of (DONT-STOP-TASK <current task>) to T. The DONT-STOP-TASK statement is explained after NR rule 4.

NEXTACTION RULEFOR rule 2

```
[IF [AND (CURRENT-TASK $CURTASK)
         (THNOT (APPLIED-IN-TASK $CURTASK MC-2]
    (RULEFOR (NEXTACTION $ACTION) MC-2]
```

NR rule 2 says that the rule to use in deducing (NEXTACTION $ACTION) is MC rule 2 if it has not been applied already in the current task. So this NR rule initializes the end condition of the current task if it is an atom.

NEXTACTION RULEFOR rule 3

```
[IF (AND (CURRENT-TASK $TASK)
         (THNOT (FAILED-IN-TASK $TASK MC-3]
    (RULEFOR (NEXTACTION $ACTION) MC-3]
```

NR rule 3 says that the rule to use in deducing (NEXTACTION $ACTION) is MC rule 3 if it has not *failed* before in the current task. This rule takes care of the DOBEFORE actions of the current task by succeeding until there are no DOBEFORE actions left.

Now we can begin to see how the NEXTACTION RULEFOR rules create procedural behavior:

1. The first time DALOOP executes TRUEP on (NEXTACTION $ACTION) to find the next action, NR rule 1 concludes that MC rule 1 is the rule to backchain:
```
(IF (TRUTH)
    (NEXTACTION
        (ASSERT '(CACHE (DONT-STOP-TASK $CURTASK) T))))
```
MC rule 1 is then backchained, concluding that the next action is
```
(ASSERT '(CACHE (DONT-STOP-TASK $CURTASK) T))
```

-----

[19]A label is used here for brevity; the rule itself actually appears in MRS/NEOMYCIN.

[20]The relation is actually *THNOT*. The statement (THNOT <statement>) means that <statement> can not be deduced from the database. This is easily confused with (NOT <statement>) which means that it can be deduced from the database that <statement> is not true.

2. The second time around DALOOP, NR rule 1 fails because MC rule 1 has been applied already. NR rule succeeds, so the action returned is the one specified by MC rule 2, assuming the end condition is an atom.

3. The third time around DA loop NR rules 1 and 2 fail, and NR rule 3 succeeds, assuming the current task has any DOBEFORE actions.

4. Each time around the DA loop, NR rule 3 succeeds until the DOBEFORE actions for the current task run out, whereupon MC rule 3 will fail. Then, on the next DA loop, NR rule 3 will fail, because MC rule 3 has failed once already.

This brings us to the fourth and most complicated rule.

NEXTACTION RULEFOR rule 4

```
[IF (AND (CURRENT-TASK $CURTASK)
         (OR [AND (OR (AND (TASKTYPE $CURTASK ITERATIVE)
                           (THNOT (TASK-TRY-ALL $CURTASK)))
                      (AND (TASKTYPE $CURTASK SIMPLE)
                           (TASK-TRY-ALL $CURTASK)))
                  (THNOT (FAILED-IN-TASK $CURTASK MC-4]
             [AND (TASKTYPE $CURTASK SIMPLE)
                  (TASK-TRY-ALL $CURTASK)
                  (THNOT (APPLIED-IN-TASK $CURTASK MC-4]
     (RULEFOR (NEXTACTION $ACTION) MC-4]
```

We see here that procedural control represented in rules can be difficult to read. NR rule 4 takes care of the DODURING rules of the current task. Note that MC rule 4:
```
(IF (AND (DODURING $ACTION)
         (DONT-STOP-TASK $CURTASK))
    (NEXTACTION $ACTION))
```
appears three times. This is the rule specified by the RULEFOR relation, and NR rule 4 is trying to deduce whether this rule is appropriate now, similar to the previous NR rules. However, the other NR rules just had one consideration, but NR rule 4 has two. That's why **MC rule 4 appears twice in the premise of NR rule 4. The two considerations correspond to the the two clauses of the outermost OR clause in the premise of NR rule 4:**[21]

1. If the current task is iterative and not try-all or a simple try-all task and if MC rule 4 has not already failed during the current task, then it is appropriate to backchain MC rule 4 to deduce the NEXTACTION statement. By stopping only after MC rule 4 fails, multiple DODURING metarules of the current task can be applied. The difference between iterative not try-all (return to the head of the list on each loop) and simple try-all (proceed to the next unapplied metarule on each loop) is controlled by the DODURING RULEFOR rules.

------

[21]Iterative try-all tasks are not handled by the metacontrol rules. This was an oversight that was not detected for some time, for this type of task did not occur in this earlier version of NEOMYCIN. Allowing for this kind of task would require a predicate "APPLIED-IN-LOOP", analogous to APPLIED-IN-TASK.

```
(IF (OR (END-CONDITION $CURTASK DONT-ABORT)
        (ALLE (IF (AND (ONSTACK $TASK CURRENT-TASK)
                       (END-CONDITION $TASK $EC))
                  (THNOT $EC))))
    (DONT-STOP-TASK $CURTASK))
```

Figure IV-2:   Rule concluding DONT-STOP-TASK statement

2. If the current task is simple and not try-all, and if MC rule 4 has not already been
applied in the current task, then MC rule 4 is appropriate to backchain in deducing
the NEXTACTION statement.   By stopping after one application, at most one
DODURING rule of the current task is backchained to find the next action.[22]

As for the content of MC rule 4, it says that the DODURING action should be done next if
(DONT-STOP-TASK <current task>) is true.   The truth of (DODURING $ACTION) means
that a metarule has succeeded; $ACTION is at this point bound to the action specified by the
metarule.   If NR 4 succeeds, the DA loop will extract $ACTION from the instantiated
(NEXTACTION $ACTION) and invoke the function DOACTION.

The DONT-STOP-TASK statement tells whether the task is to be aborted or not.   The rule
used to deduce the DONT-STOP-TASK statement is shown in figure IV-2.   (Note: the binding
for $CURTASK is deduced in the first clause of NR 4.)   This rule will succeed if the end
condition of the current task is DONT-ABORT, or if the end conditions of all the tasks on
the current task stack cannot be deduced to be true.[23]   The results of deducing DONT-STOP-
TASK statements are cached and used in MC rule 5.

NEXTACTION RULEFOR rules 5 and 6

These NR rules are directly analogous to NR rules 1 and 2.   The APPLIED-IN-TASK filter
is used to ensure that MC rules 5 and 6 are applied only once.

IV.2 Second layer RULEFOR rules

When MC rules 3,4 and 6 are backchained, their premise statements are deduced:
```
(DOBEFORE $ACTION)
(DODURING $ACTION)
(DOAFTER $ACTION)
```
These statements are concluded by the metarules.   Since the metarules are applied procedurally,
as specified in section 4.3, a RULEFOR backchainer is attached to the above statements.   The
rules that conclude the RULEFOR statements for the above statements are called the *DO
RULEFOR rules* (DR rules) (as in "DO before") and are given below with annotations.

---

[22]Technically, the DONT-STOP-TASK clause is not needed for this case. It will only be deduced once and could
not be false on the first evaluation. (No action has occurred yet, so no end condition could become true.)

[23]See section III.4 for explanation of ALLE and ONSTACK relations.

DO RULEFOR rule 1

```
(IF (AND (CURRENT-TASK $CURTASK)
         (DOBEFORE-TASKRULE $CURTASK $MRULE)
         (THNOT (APPLIED-IN-TASK $CURTASK $MRULE)))
    (RULEFOR (DOBEFORE $ACTION) $MRULE))
```

DR rule 1 states that if a DOBEFORE metarule (given by relation DOBEFORE-TASKRULE) has not been applied already in this task, then it should be the metarule used to deduce the DOBEFORE action. At each application of the MC rule 3 of layer one, DR rule 1 is applied, thereby choosing the DOBEFORE rules sequentially.

DO RULEFOR rules 2 and 3

```
(IF (AND (CURRENT-TASK $CURTASK)
         (TASKTYPE $CURTASK ITERATIVE)
         (TASKRULE $CURTASK $MRULE))
    (RULEFOR (DODURING $ACTION) $MRULE))

(IF (AND (CURRENT-TASK $CURTASK)
         (TASKTYPE $CURTASK SIMPLE)
         (TASKRULE $CURTASK $MRULE)
         (THNOT (APPLIED-IN-TASK $CURTASK $MRULE)))
    (RULEFOR (DODURING $ACTION) $MRULE))
```

These two rules take care of the DODURING metarules for iterative and simple tasks respectively. When the RULEFOR backchainer deduces
```
(RULEFOR (DODURING $ACTION) $RULE)
```

DR rule 2 returns all the DODURING metarules in the task, whereas DR rule 3 returns the ones not yet applied. Combined with the NR rule 4 from the first layer, the effect is that iterative tasks have their DODURING metarules applied in order until one succeeds, whereas simple tasks have the next unapplied DODURING metarule applied.

Each application of MR 4 finds the next metarule that successfully concludes DODURING. DR rule 2 ensures that for simple try-all tasks this is the next rule in sequence (via the APPLIED-IN-TASK filter). For iterative not-try-all tasks, this is simply the first rule at the head of the list, as asserted into the database. That is, we are relying on the fact that the MRS matcher returns the entire list of metarules in stashed order when deducing DODURING. In summary, APPLIED-IN-TASK is used to bring about *sequential* execution of rules, while FAILED-IN-TASK (as used in NR rules 3, 4, and 6) brings about *exhaustive* application of rules.[24] DO RULEFOR rule 4 for DOAFTER metarules is directly analogous to DO RULEFOR rule 1.

---

[24]Note that the THNOT APPLIED-IN-TASK statement of DR rule 3 is extraneous for simple not-try-all tasks, since NR 4, and hence DR 3, will only be tried once in this case.

IV.3 Ordered data base access

To bring about the right ordering of NR rules (and hence MC rules) and metarules, an ordered data base access is used (see section III.4). In particular, the metarules are asserted with the ORD* relation and the ordered lookup function is attached to:

```
(DOBEFORE-TASKRULE $TASK $MRULE)
(TASKRULE $TASK $MRULE)
(DOAFTER-TASKRULE $TASK $MRULE)
```

The metarules have the form:

```
(IF <metarule premise> (DOBEFORE <action>))
(IF <metarule premise> (DODURING <action>))
(IF <metarule premise> (DOAFTER <action>))
```

V Interface to NEOMYCIN groundwork

As mentioned previously, not all of NEOMYCIN was translated into the augmented MRS. To interface to the NEOMYCIN functions and data structures, a set of procedural attachments were written. They provided complete flexibility in the re-representation of NEOMYCIN.

This appendix has two sections, one for the attachments that accessed NEOMYCIN data structures and one for the attachments that accessed the NEOMYCIN functions.

V.1 Procedural attachments that access data structures

These attachments divide into two classes: the TRUEP(s) functions used to query the database; and the (un)ASSERT functions, used to change the database. They further divide according to the type of data structure they access. See table V-1[25]

- The FLG functions are used to access variables that are used as flags; The TRUEP(s) versions return the truth binding(s) or NIL depending on whether the flag is set or not. No matching is allowed.
  ```
  (TRUEP '(WIDERDIFFLG)) = T)
  ```

Table V-1:   Table of procedural attachments that access data structures

TRUEP{s}	{un}ASSERT	Arguments	# of times used
FLG-TRUEP{s}	FLG-{un}ASSERT	[<flag name>]	2
PROPMARK-TRUEP{s}	PROPMARK-{un}ASSERT	[<mark name> <atom name>]	14
LISTMEM-TRUEP{s}	LISTMEM-{un}ASSERT	[<list name> <member name>]	3
PROPVAL-TRUEP{s}		[<property> <atom> <value>]	15
VAR-TRUEP{s}	VAR-ASSERT	[<variable name> <var value>]	3

---

[25]Note that this classification is not exactly the same as HERACLES' IMPLEMENTATION categories, because the compiler required PROPVAL to be broken into atomic and list values.

- The MARK functions are used to access properties of atoms that have values of T or NIL only. The TRUEP(s) versions return the truth binding(s) or NIL depending on whether the mark is set or not. No matching.
  ```
  (TRUEP '(PURSUED MENINGITIS)) = T)
  ```

- The LISTMEM functions are used to access lists. The TRUEP(s) versions allow matching on the second argument, returning binding(s) giving the element(s) of the list.
  ```
  (TRUEP{s} '(DIFFERENTIAL $HYP))
             = (T ($HYP . MENINGITIS)) or
             = ((T ($HYP . MENINGITIS))
               (T ($HYP . VIRUS)))
  ```

- The PROP functions are used to access properties of atoms that have arbitrary values; The TRUEP(s) version allow matching on the second argument. They return binding(s) that give the property value, if the value is an atom; or the elements of the property value, if the value is a list. ANTECEDENT-IN, used on domain data parameters, is an example of a property that has a list as a value:
  ```
  (TRUEP{s} '(ANTECEDENT-IN HEADACHE $RULE))
             = (T ($RULE . RULE424)) or
             = ((T ($RULE . RULE424))
               (T ($RULE . RULE208)))
  ```

- The VAL functions are used to access variables that have arbitrary values, for example, CURFOCUS. The TRUEP(s) versions allow matching on the second argument, returning bindings that give the value of the variable. For example,
  ```
  (TRUEP{s} '(CURFOCUS $FOCUS)) = (T ($FOCUS . HEADACHE)) or
                                = ((T ($FOCUS . HEADACHE)))
  ```

V.2 Procedural attachments that access functions

Hereafter, the functions being accessed will be referred to as the "target functions." For example, GREATERP is a target function.

Since the target functions rarely return bindings, which is the whole reason for TRUEPing a statement, some procedural attachments need to be in between the TRUEP and the target function to take care of this. These attachments are for TRUEP(S) only; it makes no sense to (un)ASSERT a target function as we did with data structures. The target functions are just used for their results.

It is assumed that the relation of the statement being TRUEPed is the name of the target function, for example,
```
(TRUEP '(GREATERP 1 2))
```

would access GREATERP. It is also assumed that the arguments to the target function appear in the statement in the correct order to be passed to the target function.

These attachments have two dimensions: *result* and *application*. In table V-2, the result dimension is on the horizontal axis, the application dimension on the vertical.

Table V-2:   Table of procedural attachments that access functions

	PRED	FUN	FUNLIST
EVAL	PRED-TRUEP(S)		
NL	NLPRED-TRUEP(S)	NLFUN-TRUEP(S)	NLFUNLIST-TRUEP(S)
ASIS	ASISPRED-TRUEP(S)	ASISFUN-TRUEP(S)	ASISFUNLIST-TRUEP(S)
Args	(<fn> <args>...)	(<fn><args>...<result>)	(<fn><args>...<result>)

The result dimension (PRED, FUN, and FUNLIST) describes how the target function's result is reflected in the bindings returned:

- In the PRED functions, T is returned if the target function returns non-NIL; NIL otherwise. GREATERP would use a 'PRED attachment.
  ```
  (NLPRED-TRUEP '(GREATERP 2 1)) = T
  ```

- In the FUN functions, the result of the target function is matched against the last element of the statement. CFCOMBINE would use a FUN attachment.
  ```
  (NLFUN-TRUEP '(CFCOMBINE 500 800 $CFCOM))
      = (T ($CFCOM . 900))
  (NLFUN-TRUEP '(RULEGET 'RULE424 'PREMISE $PREM))
      = (T ($PREM AND (SAME CNTXT STIFF-NECK)
                      (SAME CNTXT HEADACHE)))
  ```

- In the FUNLIST functions, the result of the target is assumed to be a list. The elements of the result are matched against the last element of the statement.
  ```
  (NLFUNLIST-TRUEP
     '(PICK.TOKENS 'PARM ($AND (SAME CNTXT STIFF-NECK)
                               (SAME CNTXT HEADACHE))
                   $PREMISEPARM))
     = (T ($PREMISEPARM . HEADACHE))
        or
     = ((T ($PREMISEPARM . STIFF-NECK))
        (T ($PREMISEPARM . HEADACHE)))
  ```

The application dimension (EVAL, NL, and ASIS) describes how the target function is to be evaluated:

- EVAL functions apply the target function to its arguments with evaluation of the arguments. This was not used.

- NL functions apply the target function to its arguments without evaluating the arguments.
  ```
  (NLPRED-TRUEP '(YNPARM MENINGITIS)) = NIL
  ```

- ASIS functions evaluate the statement as is. This is for using target functions without knowing anything about how the arguments should be evaluated. The programmer can just use them as they are used in the code being translated. For example,
  ```
  (IF (AND (APPLICABLE? (QUOTE $RULE) ROOTNODE (QUOTE TRUTH))
           (THNOT (APPLIEDTOP (QUOTE $RULE) ROOTNODE)))
  (UNAPPLIED? $RULE))
  ```
  where APPLICABLE? and APPLIEDTOP have ASISPRED-TRUEP(S) attached.

There's one oddball: NL-TRUEP(S). It is like the other NL functions in that it doesn't evaluate the arguments to the target function. It is unlike them in that the CAR of the argument should be a function that returns a binding list. It is used as the truep attachment for UNIFY, the MRS matching function.

Acknowledgments and Historical Notes

NEOMYCIN was designed and implemented in November 1980, following 10 months of studying MYCIN with Reed Letsinger and the late Timothy Beckett, MD. Letsinger spent a year extending the original metarules and knowledge base as part of his MSAI practicum. The program was first presented in Pittsburgh at the ONR Annual Contractors' Meeting for research in instructional systems in January 1981, and then at IJCAI in August (Clancey and Letsinger, 1984). Sections 2 and 11 of this chapter originally appeared in (Clancey, 1983b).

Conrad Bock designed and implemented the procedural attachment mechanism and translated the original functions into MRS rules in the summer of 1982. Large portions of the appendices describing the MRS/NEOMYCIN implementation appear in (Clancey and Bock, 1982). We thank Avron Barr, Greg Cooper, Lee Erman, and Diane Kanerva for commenting on an earlier version of this material.

David Wilkins (a student visiting Stanford from Michigan) brought Conrad's system up-to-date in the summer of 1983, and converted the metarules to replace the impractically slow deliberation/action loop, metacontrol rules, and stack mechanism by a modified task interpreter written in Lisp which invoked MRS only for evaluating metarule premises. This was also too slow, so we reverted to the original Lisp metarules.

In the fall of 1984, we were finally ready to use the MRS representation for explanation. Diane Warner Hasling helped convert Bock's and Wilkin's MRS expressions into Lisp property list format, and wrote code to analyze the relations. This led to a set of rules that was clean enough to compile; Clancey wrote the compiler.

As acknowledged in the individual sections, Diane Hasling, Bob London, Mark Richer, and Tim Thompson have made major contributions to the explanation and modeling routines and Heracles over the past 5 years. We thank Bruce Buchanan for serving as general scientific advisor and political councilor to the project.

All of the programs described here currently run in InterLisp-D on Xerox 1000 Series machines, connected to a VAX-UNIX file server. Computational resources have been provided by the SUMEX-AIM facility (NIH grant RR00785), managed by Tom Rindfleisch.

This research has been supported in part by ONR and ARI Contract N00014-79C-0302. As of March 1985, the research is supported in part by the Josiah Macy, Jr. Foundation, award B852005.

References

Aikins J. S. *Representation of control knowledge in expert systems*, in *Proceedings of the First AAAI*, pages 121-123, 1980.

Anderson, J. R., Greeno, J. G., Kline, P. J., and Neves, D. M. Acquisition of problem-solving skill. In J. R. Anderson (editor), *Cognitive Skills and their Acquisition*, pages 191-230. Lawrence Erlbaum Associates, Hillsdale, NJ, 1981.

Bobrow, D. G. and Stefik, M. The LOOPS Manual. (Xerox PARC).

Brown, J. S. *Remarks on building expert systems (Reports of panel on applications of artificial intelligence)*, in *Proceedings of the Fifth International Joint Conference on Artificial Intelligence*, pages 994-1005, 1977.

Brown, J. S. *Process versus product--a perspective on tools for communal and informal electronic learning*, in *Education in the Electronic Age, proceedings of a conference sponsored by the Educational Broadcasting Corporation, WNET/Thirteen*, July, 1983.

Brown, J. S., Collins, A., and Harris, G. Artificial intelligence and learning strategies. In O'Neill (editor), *Learning Strategies*, . Academic Press, New York, 1977.

Brown, J. S., Burton, R. R., and de Kleer, J. Pedagogical, natural language, and knowledge engineering techniques in SOPHIE I, II, and III. In D. Sleeman and J. S. Brown (editors), *Intelligent Tutoring Systems*, pages 227-282. Academic Press, London, 1982.

Brown, J. S., Moran, T. P., and Williams, M. D. The semantics of procedures: A cognitive basis for training procedural skills for complex system maintenance. (Xerox Corporation, CIS working paper, November 1982).

Bruner, J. S., Goodnow, J. J., and Austin, G. A. *A Study of Thinking*. New York: John Wiley & Sons, Inc. 1956.

Clancey, W. J. Tutoring rules for guiding a case method dialogue. *The International Journal of Man-Machine Studies*, 1979, *11*, 25-49. (Republished in Sleeman and Brown (editors), *Intelligent Tutoring Systems*, Academic Press, 1982).

Clancey, W. J. GUIDON. In Barr and Feigenbaum (editors), *The Handbook of Artificial Intelligence*, chapter Applications-oriented AI research: Educationpages 267-278. William Kaufmann, Inc., Los Altos, 1982.

Clancey, W. J. Applications-oriented AI research: Education. In Barr and Feigenbaum (editors), *The Handbook of Artificial Intelligence*, pages 223-294. William Kaufmann, Inc., Los Altos, 1982.

Clancey, W. J. The epistemology of a rule-based expert system: A framework for explanation. *Artificial Intelligence*, 1983, *20(3)*, 215-251.

Clancey, W. J. *The advantages of abstract control knowledge in expert system design*, in *Proceedings of the National Conference on Artificial Intelligence*, pages 74-78, Washington, D.C., August, 1983.

Clancey, W.J. Methodology for Building an Intelligent Tutoring System. In Kintsch, Miller, and Polson (editors), *Method and Tactics in Cognitive Science*, pages 51-83. Lawrence Erlbaum Associates, Hillsdale, NJ, 1984.

Clancey, W. J. *Acquiring, representing, and evaluating a competence model of diagnosis.* HPP Memo 84-2, Stanford University, February 1984. (To appear in M. Chi, R. Glaser, and M. Farr (Eds.), *The Nature of Expertise*, in preparation.).

Clancey, W. J. Heuristic Classification. *Artificial Intelligence*, December 1985, *27*, 289-350.

Clancey, W.J. and Bock, C. *MRS/NEOMYCIN: Representing metacontrol in predicate calculus.* HPP Memo 82-31, Stanford University, November 1982.

Clancey, W. J. and Letsinger, R. NEOMYCIN: Reconfiguring a rule-based expert system for application to teaching. In .Clancey, W. J. and Shortliffe, E. H. (editors), *Readings in Medical Artificial Intelligence: The First Decade*, pages 361-381. Addison-Wesley, Reading, 1984.

Cohen, D. and Goldman, N. Efficient compilation of virtual database specifications. (U.S.C. Information Sciences Institute).

Corkill, D. D., Lesser, V. R., and Hudlicka, E. *Unifying data-directed and goal-directed control: An example and experiments*, in *Proceedings of the National Conference on Artificial Intelligence*, pages 143-147, August, 1982.

Dahl, O. J., Dijkstra, E. W., and Hoare, C. A. R. *Structured Programming.* New York: Academic Press 1972.

Davis R. *Applications of meta-level knowledge to the construction, maintenance, and use of large knowledge bases.* HPP Memo 76-7 and AI Memo 283, Stanford University, July 1976.

Davis, R. Meta-rules: reasoning about control. *Artificial Intelligence*, 1980, *15*, 179-222.

Davis, R., Buchanan, B., and Shortliffe, E. H. Production rules as a representation for a knowledge-base consultation program. *Journal of Artificial Intelligence*, 1977, *8(1)*, 15-45.

de Kleer, J. Qualitative and quantitative reasoning in classical mechanics. In P. H. Winston and R. H. Brown (editors), *Artificial Intelligence: An MIT Perspective*, pages 9-30. The MIT Press, Cambridge, 1979.

de Kleer, J. *Choices without backtracking*, in *Proceedings of the National Conference on Artificial Intelligence*, pages 79-85, Austin, August, 1984.

Doyle. J. *A Model for Deliberation, Action and Introspection.* Technical Report 581, M.I.T. Artificial Intelligence Laboratory, 1980.

Duda, R. O. and Shortliffe, E. H. Expert systems research. *Science*, 1983, *220*, 261-268.

Elstein, A. S., Shulman, L. S., and Sprafka, S. A. *Medical problem solving: An analysis of clinical reasoning.* Cambridge: Harvard University Press 1978.

Erman, L. D., Hayes-Roth, F., Lesser, V. R., and Reddy, D. R. The Hearsay-II speech understanding system: Integrating knowledge to resolve uncertainty. *Computing Surveys*, 1980, *12(2)*, 213-253.

Erman, L. D., London, P. E., and Fickas, S. F. *The design and example use of Hearsay-III*, in *Proceedings of the Seventh International Joint Conference on Artificial Intelligence*, pages 409-415, August, 1981.

Feigenbaum, E. A. *The art of artificial intelligence: I. Themes and case studies of knowledge engineering*, in *Proceedings of the 5th International Joint Conference on Artificial Intelligence*, pages 1014-1029, Cambridge, August, 1977.

Feltovich, P. J., Johnson, P. E., Moller, J. H., and Swanson, D. B. The role and development of medical knowledge in diagnostic expertise. In W. J. Clancey and E. H. Shortliffe (editors), *Readings in Medical Artificial Intelligence: The First Decade*, pages 275-319. Addison-Wesley Publishing Company, Reading, 1984.

Friedland, P. E. *Knowledge-based experiment design in molecular genetics*. Technical Report STAN-CS-79-771, Stanford University, October 1979.

Genesereth, M. R. *An overview of meta-level architecture*, in *Proceedings of The National Conference on Artificial Intelligence*, pages 119-124, August, 1983.

Genesereth, M. R. *Partial programs*. HPP Memo 84-1, Stanford University, November 1984.

Georgeff, M. P. Procedural Control in Production Systems. *Artificial Intelligence*, 1982, *(18)*, 175-201.

Greeno, J. G. Cognitive objectives of instruction: Theory of knowledge for solving problems and answering questions. In Klahr₁ (editor), *Cognition and Instruction*, . Erlbaum Associates, Hillsdale, NJ, 1976.

Hasling, D. W., Clancey, W. J., Rennels, G. R. Strategic explanations in consultation. *The International Journal of Man-Machine Studies*, 1984, *20(1)*, 3-19. Republished in Development in Expert Systems, ed. M. J. Coombs, Academic Press, London.

Hayes-Roth, B. *BBI: An architecture for blackboard systems that control, explain, and learn about their own behavior*. HPP Memo 84-16, Stanford University, December 1984.

Hewitt, C. E. *Description and theoretical analysis (using schemata) of PLANNER: a language for proving theorems and manipulating models in a robot*. Technical Report 258, MIT AI Laboratory, 1972.

Johnson, P. E. What kind of expert should a system be? *The Journal of Medicine and Philosophy*, 1983, *8*, 77-97.

Laird, J. E. *Universal Subgoaling*. PhD thesis, Computer Science Department, Carnegie-Mellon University, 1983.

Laird, J. E., Rosenbloom, P. S., and Newell, A. *Towards chunking as a general learning mechanism*, in *Proceedings of the National Conference on Artificial Intelligence*, pages 188-192, Austin, August, 1984.

Lenat, D. B. The nature of heuristics. *Artificial Intelligence*, 1982, *19(2)*, 189-249.

London, B. and Clancey, W. J. *Plan recognition strategies in student modeling: prediction and description*, in *Proceedings of the 2nd American Association for Artificial Intelligence*, pages 335-338, 1982.

McCarthy, J. *Programs with common sense*, in *Proceedings of the Teddington Conference on the Mechanization of Thought Processes*, pages 403-410, 1960. (Reprinted in Semantic Information Processing, M. Minsky (Ed), MIT Press, Cambridge, 1968).

Miller, J. *States of Mind*. New York: Pantheon Books 1983.

Moore, R. C. *The role of logic in knowledge representation and commonsense reasoning*, in *Proceedings of the National Conference on Artificial Intelligence*, pages 428-433, Pittsburgh, August, 1982.

Genesereth, M. R., Greiner, R., and Smith, D. E. *MRS Dictionary*. MEMO HPP-82-24, Stanford University, 1982.

Newell, A. and Simon, H. A. *Human Problem Solving*. Englewood Cliffs: Prentice-Hall 1972.

Nicolas, J. M. and Gallaire, H. Data base: Theory vs. interpretation. In H. Gallaire and J. Minker (editors), *Logic and data bases*, pages 33-54. Plenum Press, New York, 1977.

Novak, G. S., Jr. *Data abstraction in GLISP*. HPP Memo 82-34, Stanford University, 1982.

Papert, S. *Mindstorms: Children, Computers, and Powerful Ideas*. New York: Basic Books, Inc. 1980.

Rich, C. *Knowledge Representation Languages and Predicate Calculus*, in *Proceedings of the National Conference on Artificial Intelligence*, pages 193-196, AAAI, 1982.

Richer, M.H. and Clancey, W.J. GUIDON-WATCH: A graphic interface for viewing a knowledge-based system. *IEEE Computer Graphics and Applications*, November 1985, *5(11)*, 51-64.

Rubin, A. D. *Hypothesis formation and evaluation in medical diagnosis*. Technical Report AI-TR-316, Artificial Intelligence Laboratory, Massachusetts Institute of Technology, January 1975.

Rumelhart, D. E. and Norman, D. A. *Representation in memory*. Technical Report CHIP-116, Center for Human Information Processing, University of California, June 1983.

Sacerdoti, E. D. Planning in a hierarchy of abstraction spaces. *Artificial Intelligence*, 1974, *5(2)*, 115-135.

Schmolze, J. G. and Lipkis, T. A. *Classification in the KL-ONE knowledge representation system*, in *Proceedings of the Eighth International Joint Conference on Artificial Intelligence*, pages 330-332, August, 1983.

Schoenfeld, A. H. *Episodes and executive decisions in mathematical problem solving*. Technical Report, Hamilton College, Mathematics Department, 1981. Presented at the 1981 AERA Annual Meeting, April 1981.

Shortliffe, E. H. *Computer-based medical consultations: MYCIN*. New York: Elsevier 1976.

Smith, R. G. Programming with rules in Strobe. (Schlumberger-Doll Research).

Sowa, J. F. *Conceptual Structures*. Reading, MA: Addison-Wesley 1984.

Stefik, M. *Planning with constraints*. STAN-CS-80-784 and HPP Memo 80-2, Stanford University, January 1980.

Swartout W. R. *Explaining and justifying in expert consulting programs*, in *Proceedings of the 7th International Joint Conference on Artificial Intelligence*, pages 815-823, Vancouver, August, 1981.

Szolovits, P., Hawkinson, L., and Martin, W. A. An overview of OWL, a language for knowledge representation. In G. Rahmstort and M. Ferguson (editor), *Proceedings of the Workshop on Natural Language Interaction with Databases*, pages 140-156. International Institute for Applied Systems Analysis, Schloss Laxenburg, Austria, 1978. (also appeared as MIT Techreport, TM-86, June 1977).

Thompson, T. and Clancey, W. J. A qualitative modeling shell for process diagnosis. *IEEE Software*, March 1986, *3(2)*, 6-15.

VanLehn, K. and Brown, J. S. Planning nets: a representation for formalizing analogies and semantic models of procedural skills. In R. E. Snow, Frederico, P. A., and Montague, W. E. (editor), *Aptitude learning and instruction: Cognitive process and analyses*, pages 95-138. Lawrence Erlbaum Associates, Hillsdale, NJ, 1980.

Young, R. L., Smith, R. G., and Pirie, G. Organizing a knowledge-based system for independence. (Schlumberger-Doll Research).

Controlling Expert Systems

Ron Sauers

NBI Inc.
Boulder, CO 80301, USA

ABSTRACT

Control is the term we use to refer to the process of deciding which rules in the
rule base of an Expert System should be considered for application in some given
problem solving context. Expert system programmers specify sets of heuristics
for each problem to be solved, and a rule interpreter must determine how they
should be used to find a satisfactory solution. Human experts are good at making
control decisions; rule interpreters are not.

The ability to perform heuristic reasoning is an important feature of rule-based
expert systems. However, this is often in direct conflict with the ability to extend
the rule base. Thus, the most fundamental problem which we face in developing
a control mechanism for an expert system is this: how do we impose a control
scheme on a set of rules, without sacrificing the integrity of the rule base? We
want the rule base to be extendible; yet, at the same time, we need to ensure that
the rules are applied in the correct sequence in real problem solving situations.

In this paper, we will examine some of the control mechanisms used in real rule-
based expert systems. We will identify a set of requirements for a control scheme
which facilitates the representation of modular rule based programs, and allows
for the rapid development of expert systems which are both correct and extendible. Finally, a new control scheme which meets these requirements will be proposed and discussed.

1 INTRODUCTION

This paper is concerned with the problem of control in Rule-Based Expert Systems. **Control** is the term we use to refer to the process of deciding which rules in the rule base should be considered for application in some given problem solving context.

Imposing control on the rules in an Expert System is an important problem. Furthermore, imposing control correctly is extremely difficult. In this section, we will attempt to define the major problems associated with controlling an expert system. We begin by briefly investigating some of the advantages of using a rule-based formalism for Expert System programming.

A **rule-based system** is usually thought of as having several distinct components. The **rule base** consists of a set of **rules**, expressed roughly in the form

```
IF    condition1, condition2, ...
THEN  action1, action2, ...
```

The IF portion, or **left-hand side**, of a rule describes a problem solving situation, in the form of a set of conditions which must be true of the environment in order for this rule to be applicable. These conditions are often referred to as the **antecedents** of the rule.

The THEN portion, or **right-hand side**, of a rule describes a set of changes to be made in the environment, in the form of a set of actions to be performed when this rule is applied. These actions are often referred to as the **consequents** of the rule.

Each rule in the rule base is used to represent a modular chunk of expert problem solving knowledge. Rules are often problem solving **heuristics**. A heuristic is interpreted as a "rule of thumb"; that is, application of the rule is likely to (but may not always) lead to a solution of the problem described by the rule antecedents.

A rule may represent heuristic knowledge by virtue of the fact that its utility in any given problem solving situation is unknown. Thus, even though the knowledge contained in a particular rule may be true in a given context, the application of that rule in that context may not necessarily get us closer to a solution to the problem at hand.

A rule-based system also includes a **working memory**, which is a list of declarative data items representing facts which are true in the problem solving environment. The antecedents of each rule test for the existence or absence of particular patterns of data in working memory. The consequents add new data items, or modify existing ones.

Finally, a rule-based system includes an **interpreter**. The interpreter is responsible for matching the contents of working memory against the rules in the rule base, and determining which rules are applicable in the current problem solving context. Based on this determination, the interpreter is responsible for updating working memory to reflect the changes specified by the selected rules. The interpreter continues processing in this fashion, until either the problem has been solved, or it is determined that the problem cannot be solved using the current set of problem solving heuristics.

Two basic reasoning schemes are commonly used in expert systems. In **forward chaining** reasoning systems, the interpreter begins with a set of initial facts, which get matched against the rule antecedents. Rules are executed in a forward fashion, moving from antecedents to consequents. The consequents of one rule cause changes in the environment, which are then matched to the antecedents of the next rule, and so on.

A set of IF-THEN rules executed in a strictly forward chaining fashion is often referred to as a **production system**. (In some circles, the term *production system* refers strictly to forward-chaining rule-based systems; in others, the terms *production system* and *rule-based system* are used interchangeably.) Here, the individual rules are called **productions**, and are often thought of as stimulus/response pairs.

In **backward chaining** reasoning systems, the interpreter begins with a set of facts which, in essence, represent the solution to a problem. These facts are matched against the consequents of the rules. The system reasons backwards across each rule, determining which set of facts must have been true in order for the solution to have been derived by the consequents. The antecedents of one rule provide new subproblems, which are matched against the consequents of the next rule, and so on.

Backward chaining systems often provide a backtracking mechanism. Before an important decision is made, the state of the problem solving environment is saved. When the system makes an incorrect decision, it can return to the previous problem solving environment and try solving the problem using a different method. Backward chaining systems are often computationally expensive, since unconstrained backtracking can result in extensive amounts of search.

Now, one of the major advantages of rule-based programming is, in theory, the ability to solve problems in a heuristic fashion. Since it has been found that the reasoning process of human experts is often driven by heuristics, a rule-based formalism is most often the representation of choice for expert reasoning systems. The programmer specifies a set of rules for each problem to be solved, and the system manages to determine how they should be used to find a satisfactory solution.

Determining how the heuristics should be used is the **control** problem. At any given time, some subset of the rules in the rule base will be applicable. The interpreter must decide which is the best to use in each particular situation. Human experts are good at making these sorts of decisions; rule-based interpreters are not.

The information used by an expert system interpreter to decide on a particular rule will be referred to as **control information**. Control information may be obtained from any number of sources. Some is **domain dependent** information: it is intimately related to the particular rules in the rule base, and is therefore specific to a particular application. Other control information is **domain independent**: it is useful across a wide variety of applications.

Domain dependent control information must be provided by the programmer, usually at the time the rule base is developed. Domain independent information can be derived automatically by the expert system interpreter (or, in some systems, the rule compiler), through examination of the individual rules.

If possible, the ability to rely on domain independent control information would be convenient from the point of view of the programmer, since it transfers some of the burden of control to the interpreter. For this reason, many rule-based programming languages attempt to provide domain independent control mechanisms.

However, control decisions are complex, and domain independent information is often inadequate to guarantee that the choice of rules to be applied is always correct. Thus, in many cases, the programmer finds it necessary to provide additional control information, embedded in the rules themselves. For example, the consequent of one rule might create a piece of control information which serves to enable only the next rule in some sequence. The new control information is inserted into working memory and, for all practical purposes, it is indistinguishable from other domain-level data items.

Another advantage of the use of rule-based programming is the **extensibility** of the resulting system. Each rule is highly modular in design; thus, in order to extend the system, we merely need to add heuristics which describe how problem solving may be performed in the new domain.

Extending the rule base to a larger application domain is a normal facet of expert system development. Theoretically, new rules are easily integrated into the existing system, since the interpreter is able to use control information to decide when each of the new heuristics should be applied in place of a previously existing one.

In reality, however, it is usually the case that the existing control information is no longer adequate to enable the system to correctly integrate the new rules. Thus, new control information must also be added to the system.

Adding control information often requires modifying some subset of the existing rule base. The number of changes required may be extensive, since the rule base in expert system applications is large. Furthermore, since control information may be embedded in the rules themselves, it is often difficult to determine which ones must be changed.

Most importantly, modularity of the individual rules is decreased as the rule base is extended. The more control information is added to the system in this fashion, the more closely coupled the individual rules become. Control is imposed on the system at the expense of modularity.

Therefore, the most fundamental problem which we face when developing a control mechanism for a rule-based system is this: how do we impose a control scheme on a set of rules, without sacrificing the integrity of the rule base? We want our rules to be modular, and we want the rule base to be extendible. Yet, at the same time, we need to make sure that the rules are applied in the correct sequence in real problem solving situations.

In this paper, we will specifically address this problem. We will examine some of the most important control mechanisms used in real rule-based expert systems, and will attempt to analyze them from two different perspectives. First, we will be concerned with the principles which led to the development of the various control schemes, and with how they were to behave in theory.

Second, and perhaps more importantly, we will be concerned with the point of view of the programmer of an expert system; that is, how the particular control schemes behave in practice, and how they affect the development of a rule-based program. Our main goal is to identify those characteristics of the various control schemes which allow the programmer to specify control constraints most naturally. In addition, we must determine how to represent control constraints in such a way that the rule base is easily extendible.

Our discussion of control mechanisms begins in section two, which introduces conflict resolution as a control scheme. From this discussion, we will discover several important requirements which must be met by a control scheme if it is to meet the needs of expert system designers. These will be discussed in section three.

In section four, we will discuss some typical alternative control mechanisms. In section five, we will attempt to summarize our discussions of the various control methodologies, with the goal of identifying a set of design considerations for an integrated control scheme.

In section six, a new architecture for the development of expert systems will be proposed. The proposed system has a unique, thoroughly integrated control scheme which facilitates the representation of modular rule-based programs, and allows for the rapid development of Expert Systems which are both correct and extendible. Finally, in section seven, we will analyze our proposed control scheme with respect to the design considerations developed in our previous discussions.

2 CONFLICT RESOLUTION

Conflict Resolution is one method by which a rule-based interpreter may select one of a set of applicable rules to be applied in some problem solving situation. Pure conflict resolution is a relatively simple control methodology. It is important for historical reasons, since it was the control methodology used in most of the earliest, forward chaining production system languages. It is also widely used in state-of-the-art expert system development systems, although it is often integrated into a more sophisticated control scheme.

The most widely known systems which rely on conflict resolution as a control strategy are the **OPS** systems, developed at Carnegie-Mellon University [Forgy and McDermott, 1977]. The first OPS system was developed in the mid-1970's, and has led to several generations of systems to the present date. OPS5 [Forgy, 1981] was the production system language used to develop R1 [McDermott, 1982], the VAX configuration expert system which moved expert system technology into the commercial applications marketplace. The OPS series was one of the earliest to investigate the production system architecture as a domain independent formalism. It also provided a framework for the most important research to date concerning the efficiency of rule-based system implementations [Forgy, 1979].

The remainder of this section will present an overview of the process of conflict resolution as it is known today. In the next section, the role of conflict resolution in a more complete rule-based control scheme will be discussed, and we will attempt to derive some general principles concerning its applicability and limitations.

2.1 The Recognize/Act Cycle

The execution of most forward chaining, rule-based programs occurs in the form of a linear sequence of **recognize/act** cycles, roughly as follows:

[1] Determine the set of rule **instantiations** which are applicable in the current context.

This is the **recognize** phase of the cycle. Conceptually (although not necessarily on an implementation level), this corresponds to **matching** the antecedent of each rule against the data elements in working memory.

For now, we will consider an **instantiation** of a rule to be a mapping between the antecedent clauses of that rule and data items in working memory. Thus, if a single rule can match more than one set of data items, it can have multiple instantiations. The set of applicable instantiations of all rules together at any given time is known as the **conflict set**. (The concept of an instantiation will be further discussed in section 2.4.)

[2] Select a single instantiation from the conflict set for application on this cycle.

This is the process of **conflict resolution**. Thus, conflict resolution, as it concerns us here, involves comparing instantiations to determine which is the most applicable in a given problem solving context. Conflict resolution usually results in the selection of a single member of the conflict set, known as the **current instantiation**. If no instantiation is applicable, execution halts.

[3]   Apply the current instantiation in the current context.

This is the **act** phase of the cycle. Applying an instantiation is often referred to as **firing** a rule. This results in changes to the problem solving environment. For example, new data items may be inserted into working memory, or old data items may be removed. These changes, in turn, enable new rule instantiations, or disable old ones. The recognize/act process continues in the new problem solving context.

In this simple control scheme, the burden of making control decisions falls on the process of conflict resolution. The decision to prefer one instantiation over another is extremely important in the context of problem solving. An incorrect decision may eliminate the possibility of finding an adequate solution path, or may even result in an incorrect solution being selected as adequate.

Furthermore, the conflict resolution decision is a difficult one to make. This is especially true in systems which attempt domain independence, since conflict resolution must make all decisions based only on surface-level, syntactic characteristics of the problem solving environment. Traditionally, such conflict resolution strategies rely on information from one or more of the following sources:

[1]   **Production Memory.** Relationships between productions or sets of productions can be derived or imposed, and these relationships can be used to prefer one rule over another.

[2]   **Working Memory.** Conflict resolution strategies can test for relationships between data elements, or for relationships between sets of data elements and rule instantiations.

[3]   **State Memory**. State memory is a memory which is internal to the production system interpreter. It is basically a history of past execution. In theory, state memory is a sequence of snapshots of the problem solving environment at the start of each recognize/act cycle. However, in practice, it may be as simple as a record of the sequence of names of rules which have been applied.

In summary, it is important to realize that the burden traditionally placed on conflict resolution as a control methodology is an enormous one. Furthermore, the decisions made by conflict resolution strategies are potentially high-risk decisions, made by bringing fairly low-level, domain independent information to bare on the problem solving process.

2.2 Conflict Resolution Strategies

Conflict resolution **strategies** are rules which are used to perform conflict resolution. (Here, the term *rules* is used loosely, since conflict resolution strategies themselves are rarely implemented in a rule-based formalism.) Each conflict resolution strategy C can be expressed as a function which takes as input a list of rule instantiations $I_1 \dots I_n$ (the current conflict set), and returns some subset of those instantiations. Thus,

$$C(I_1 \dots I_n) = J_1 \dots J_m,$$
where m is not greater than n,
and each J is one of $I_1 \dots I_n$.

A single conflict resolution strategy usually tests rule instantiations along a single dimension. Several strategies may be combined in order to obtain a more sophisticated overall procedure. The strategies C_1, C_2, ... C_k are ordered, and are applied to the conflict set in such a way that the $J_1 \dots J_m$ output from strategy C_i becomes the input $I_1 \dots I_n$ to the next strategy C_{i+1}. Thus, if the first strategy does not identify a unique instantiation from the conflict set, the second strategy is applied, and so on.

All conflict resolution strategies can be placed into one of two classes. **Elimination strategies** are used to prevent an instantiation from being applied, independent of which other instantiations appear in the conflict set. An elimination strategy E can be expressed in terms of a boolean function e', which operates on a single instantiation I as follows:

$$e'(I)$$
= *true* if I should be eliminated
from the conflict set, and
= *false* otherwise.

The function e' will be referred to as the **root** function of elimination strategy E.

Selection strategies are used to prefer one instantiation in the conflict set over another. A selection strategy S can be expressed in terms of a root function s', which operates on two instantiations I_1 and I_2 as follows:

$$s'(I_1, I_2)$$
= I_1 if I_1 should be preferred over I_2,
= I_2 if I_2 should be preferred over I_1, and
= *neither* otherwise.

Each selection strategy can be thought of as dividing the conflict set into an ordered set of partitions $P_1, P_2, \ldots P_n$, where all instantiations in a single partition are equivalent according to some criterion, known as the **selection criterion** of the strategy. Furthermore, each instantiation in partition P_i is preferred over every instantiation in partition P_{i+1}.

On some level, an elimination strategy can be thought of as a selection strategy which always divides the conflict set into two partitions: the set of those instantiations which should be eliminated, and the set of those which should not. However, there is one important difference between selection strategies and elimination strategies which make this view incorrect. A selection strategy can remove an instantiation from the conflict set only in the presence of some other instantiation which is preferred according to the selection criterion. Thus, the application of an elimination strategy to a non-empty conflict set can result in an empty conflict set; the application of a selection strategy cannot.

Elimination strategies are somewhat drastic in their effect on the application of an instantiation. In practice, it is often the case that if an instantiation is eliminated from the conflict set on one cycle, it is also prohibited from firing on all subsequent cycles. This is because of the fact that elimination strategies usually test some fundamental property of the state memory of the production interpreter. Selection strategies are far more common than elimination strategies in real systems.

It is often interesting to measure the **selectivity** of a selection strategy. Selectivity is a measure of how often a strategy prefers one instantiation over another. If a strategy is strongly selective, then its selection criterion can usually distinguish between two instantiations. If a strategy is weakly selective, then two instantiations are usually judged equivalent with respect to the selection criterion. A strongly selective strategy can be expected to place a fairly strict ordering on the conflict set; a weakly selective strategy usually places most of the conflict set in the same partition.

The next few sections discuss some of the most commonly found types of conflict resolution strategies. We will look specifically at the use of these strategies in real systems, attempting to identify their advantages and limitations.

2.3 Prioritization Strategies

Prioritization strategies are the simplest of conflict resolution strategies. They are selection strategies whose selection criteria depend on some pre-determined measure of the relative importance of the various rules in production memory. This importance measure is explicitly defined by the programmer at the time the rules are developed.

The simplest scheme for rule prioritization assigns each rule a rank according to when it was defined. For example, the first production defined has priority over all others, then the second production is preferred, and so on. This strategy was used in some of the earliest production systems. It is also common in domain specific systems with a small number of rules with a very limited application.

One advantage of this strategy is its ease of implementation. From the programmer's point of view, it is also easy to learn, and allows for the rapid development of small systems in well-structured problem domains.

The most obvious disadvantage is the amount of burden it places on the applications programmer to precisely specify rule ordering. As the size of the rule base increases, this strategy becomes increasingly impractical. Furthermore, the ability to effectively use this strategy depends on intimate knowledge of the relationship between each rule and the problem solving process. Thus, strict prioritization makes the rule base difficult to modify or extend over time. Finally, this strategy is poor from a software engineering standpoint, since it makes large programming efforts involving many programmers virtually impossible.

A more general, and less selective, scheme for rule prioritization considers two rules equivalent unless a preference relation between them has been explicitly defined. For example, the programmer may specify that *rule-1* should be preferred over *rule-2*. This method of prioritization imposes a partially connected, directed graph structure on the rule base, where rules may be thought of as nodes in the graph, and arcs represent preference relations among the rules.

This scheme has many of the same disadvantages as the strict prioritization scheme. However, the amount of control information which must be specified by the programmer is not as great. In real applications, rules tend to form relatively small clusters, where each cluster contains rules which are generally applicable in the same problem solving context. Rules which are applicable in mutually exclusive contexts do not require explicit preference relations.

On the other hand, this scheme may also result in a system where increasing numbers of ad hoc control constraints are added over time. Constraints are added by the programmer in response to bugs encountered during testing. In this case, the resulting system is at least as unmanageable as one developed under the strict prioritization scheme.

One final scheme for rule prioritization which we will consider here is the assignment of one priority value from a pre-determined set to each rule. This basically corresponds to the explicit definition of the partitions desired as a result of the application of the selection criterion of the strategy. This scheme can be shown to be effective in some situations, especially with a small number of targeted partitions.

For example, we might define two partitions, one labelled **rules** and one labelled **meta-rules**. Then, by convention, we might prefer rules assigned to the meta-rules partition.

The degree to which this scheme is effective depends on the degree to which **semantics** are associated with each partition. That is, the assignment of a rule to a particular partition must have some well-defined meaning to the programmer.

In addition, the semantics associated with each partition might be defined by the rule formalism itself. In this case, the partitions also have meaning to the rule interpreter. For example, **rules** might manipulate object-level data, and **meta-rules** might manipulate object-level rules. (Meta-rules of this sort are actually used in real systems; see section 4.1.)

2.4 Refraction Strategies

The most common use of elimination strategies in conflict resolution is for the implementation of **refraction strategies**. Refraction strategies are conflict resolution strategies which test for equality among instantiations. They are meant to restrict the application of an instantiation in the event that it is similar to another which has already been fired.

Refraction strategies differ along two dimensions. First, they differ according to the criterion used to determine whether or not two instantiations are the same. This we will refer to as the **equivalence criterion** of a refraction strategy.

Second, they differ according to how long equivalent instantiations are prevented from being applied. This we will refer to as the **duration** of the strategy.

For example, one common refraction strategy is that which prevents the same rule from firing on consecutive cycles. Two instantiations are equivalent with respect to this strategy if and only if they are instantiations of the same production. The duration of this strategy is one cycle. This definition of refraction attempts to ensure that, when possible, diverse knowledge sources are brought to bear on each task.

If we extend the duration of this strategy to the length of the problem solving session, we obtain a strategy which prevents the same rule from firing twice. Thus, each production behaves as a **one-shot** rule. This is equivalent in function to removing each rule from production memory after it has been applied.

Another common refraction strategy is that which prevents the same *instantiation* of a rule from being applied twice (although two different instantiations of the same rule may be applied). In this case, the duration of the strategy is the entire problem solving session. Equivalence is defined according to the definition of an instantiation presented above (see section 2.1). That is, two instantiations are equivalent if and only if they are instantiations of the same rule, and each condition in the antecedent of the rule matched the same data item from working memory in both instances.

This is the most strict definition of equivalence among instantiations. It also is potentially expensive to enforce. Ironically, however, this is the most natural definition of equivalence in systems which are most concerned with efficiency. Such systems use once-and-for-all pattern matching algorithms, such as the **RETE** algorithm [Forgy, 1983], to determine the conflict set. Under such schemes, every instantiation is created exactly once, at the time it is initially entered into the conflict set. Equivalent instantiations (according to the strict definition) can never be produced. Thus, the system needs only to ensure that the same *physical* instantiation never be applied twice.

From a programmer's standpoint, the strict definition of equivalence among instantiations is convenient. It avoids having each rule explicitly disable the instantiation of itself which is currently being fired:

```
Rule27:
   IF    (a  =x  =y)
         not(already-fired rule-27)
   THEN (already-fired rule-27)
         . . .
```

However, the definition is too strict in many situations. For example, asserting the same fact twice in working memory will result in the creation of two distinct data items with the same information content. Under the strict definition of equivalence, this will result in the formation of two distinct instantiations which, by any less strict definition, would be equivalent.

As another example, consider the following rule fragment:

```
   IF   (decision =x)
        (justification ?)
   THEN     . . .
```

Here, as in most of the examples to be presented, conditions and actions are represented as **patterns**. Each pattern is intended to correspond to a single data item in working memory, either to be matched (for conditions) or created (for actions). Patterns may contain constant elements (e.g. *decision* and *justification*), or variables (e.g. *=x*). Variables acquire **bindings** when they are matched; if the same variable is mentioned twice in a given rule, it must bind to the same value both times. The special symbol *?* matches anything, but never acquires a binding; it is used in "don't care" situations.

The rule fragment shown above tests for the existence of some named decision (the first condition), for which there exists a valid justification (the second condition). This might be used in a system where a wide variety of possibly conflicting decisions are made by various rules, which must therefore provide a justification for each decision. The important point here is that we don't care what the justification for the decision is, as long as a justification exists. This type of phenomenon occurs frequently in real systems.

In this example, a decision with more than one justification would cause the creation of multiple instantiations which are distinct under the strict definition of equivalence. The problem here is that two data items do not need to be strictly equivalent in order for them to be equivalent with respect to their usage by the rule in question.

In response to problems of this nature, some systems have adopted a less strict definition of equivalence. Under this relaxed definition, two instantiations are equivalent if and only if they are instantiations of the same rule, and the set of **variable bindings** formed are the same in each instance; that is, each variable in the first instantiation is bound to a value which is equal to the binding of that variable in the second instantiation.

This definition of equivalence is most meaningful in a system which allows productions to selectively test features of data items, ignoring features which are not important with respect to the logic of the rule. For example, in the rule formalism of the production fragment given above, the use of the *?* symbol indicates a feature which is not important. In the OPS5 formalism, features are described using attribute/value pairs, and unimportant features are simply not mentioned in the rule definition.

The definition of refraction which is most appropriate in any given system depends on the semantics of the rule formalism. In many cases, it also depends on the application domain. In some instances, the most appropriate definition changes from rule to rule, and the rule formalism must provide some means for overriding the default strategy. In any case, most production systems which use conflict resolution as a control methodology include some definition of refraction in their control strategy.

2.5 Recency Strategies

Recency strategies are selection strategies which prefer instantiations based on the relative age of matched data items. In theory, a recency strategy could prefer relatively old data items, or relatively new data items. In practice, however, only the latter type of recency strategy is found. New data items are important mainly for the following reasons:

[1]   Recent data items are more likely to be correct than old ones.

This heuristic is often used to decide which of two contradictory data items is correct at any given time. Recent data items are considered more likely to be correct because they are more likely to reflect the current problem state. In the absence of a sophisticated truth maintenance system, this is a reasonable heuristic to follow.

However, we must be careful to restrict the use of this heuristic. For example, if two data items are not inconsistent, there is no justification for believing that one is more likely to be correct than the other based only on recency measures.

[2]   Focusing on recent data items enforces the data-driven nature of the rule base.

Rule-based systems must perform in dynamic environments. During the course of solving one problem, a new problem of greater priority may arise. The system must be able to change the focus of its resource in response to new demands imposed by the environment.

A system which exhibits this behavior is said to display **sensitivity** [McDermott and Forgy, 1978]. New demands imposed by the environment are measured not by the contents of the data base, but by *changes* in the data base. Thus, we can increase the sensitivity of a rule-based system by focusing on recent data items.

The behavior of a recency strategy depends in part on the definition of the age of a data item. Two definitions are the most common. Under the first definition, the age of every data item is unique. The relative age of a data item is set at the time the data item is inserted into working memory. Thus, if the consequent of some rule causes the creation of several new data items, the relative age of the data items depends on the ordering of the clauses in the rule definition. OPS5 uses this method for determining the age of a data item.

The second definition is less strict. Under this definition, the age of a data item depends on the *cycle* during which it was created. Thus, if the consequent of some rule causes the creation of several new data items, they will all have the same relative age. Each will be more recent than any data items created on the previous cycle.

The definition of a recency strategy must also specify which data items in an instantiation are to be considered for the purposes of conflict resolution. For example, one common definition of recency considers all data items matched in an instantiation. Under this definition, the system partitions the conflict set according to the recency of the most recent data item in each instantiation. If this does not result in the selection of a unique instantiation, then the most recent instantiations are partitioned according to the second most recent data item, and so on. If the data items of one instantiation are exhausted before those of another, the latter instantiation is preferred. (Note that, under this definition, recency is very closely linked with specificity; see section 2.6.)

Another common, less strict version of recency considers only the most recent data item from each instantiation. A related version considers only the least recent data item. Both of these strategies are far less selective than the strategy presented above.

One problem with virtually every definition of recency is that not all changes in the environment are able to affect control. In particular, recency strategies catch only recently *created* data items. In many cases, recently *removed* data items are equally important. Thus, if a recency strategy is to display sensitivity to changes in the environment, all modifications to working memory should be taken into account.

An interesting variation on the standard versions of recency is that which considers only the *first* data item in each instantiation. For example, OPS5 has an alternate conflict resolution procedure, designed to facilitate **means/ends analysis,** which includes such a recency strategy. In practice, most large OPS5 programs make use of the means/ends analysis conflict resolution strategy.

The following is an example of a typical rule written to take advantage of this type of strategy:

```
IF     (goal =x)
       (decompose =x (=y followed-by =z))
THEN (goal =z)
       (goal =y)
```

Here, the first term in the antecedent of every rule (that is, the one used to determine recency) is, by convention, the specification of a **goal,** towards which the rule can be applied. The antecedent of this particular rule recognizes that the goal (the first condition) can be decomposed into an ordered sequence of two subgoals (the second condition).

The consequent of the rule sets two subgoals by inserting two new "goal" data items into working memory. Assuming the unique-age definition of the age of a data item, the last term in the rule consequent results in the most recent data item. Thus, all rules which match against goal $=y$ will be considered on the next cycle. Later, rules which match against goal $=z$ will be considered.

It is important to note the use of control information in this example. Implicit in this rule, and hidden to the system, is the fact that 'goal' data items are characteristically different from other domain-level data items. The goals are being used as **control tokens**. Also implicit is the fact that goals $=y$ and $=z$ are subgoals of $=x$, and that $=y$ and $=z$ are ordered and must be pursued sequentially. The correctness of this rule depends heavily on the use of a particular conflict resolution strategy. In fact, OPS5 programs which rely on the means/ends analysis procedure will not behave correctly if the default conflict resolution strategies are used.

Recall the original intent of recency strategies: to increase the level of sensitivity which a rule displays towards its environment. Here, instead of increasing sensitivity to the environment, rule sequence is intentionally manipulated by the programmer at the expense of sensitivity.

The use of implicit control information demonstrated in this example is characteristic of programming in rule based systems which use recency as a conflict resolution strategy. Rules are **coupled** through direct communication via control tokens placed in working memory. This is accompanied by a loss of modularity, and an increase in the level of effort required to maintain and extend the rule base.

Of course, the control token approach is advocated by some as a valid rule based programming methodology. In the production system literature, control tokens are often referred to as **signals,** used intentionally for communication between rules. It can be shown [McDermott and Forgy, 1978] that signals can be used in conjunction with particular sets of conflict resolution strategies, in effect providing some common traditional programming constructs. For example, such a scheme could be used to produce external production sequencing (as shown in the example above), or it could be used to produce iteration.

However, it could also be argued that this use of control information indicates that the missing control constructs should have been provided explicitly as part of the original rule formalism. Furthermore, examination of a typical production-oriented expert system will find implicit control information manipulated in a more ad-hoc fashion. In general, the more a system relies on the use of implicit control information, the more difficulties the applications programmer will encounter in developing and maintaining his system.

2.6 Specificity Strategies

Specificity strategies are selection strategies which prefer rules that test more specific features of the environment over rules which test more general features. Specificity strategies differ according to the metric used to measure the level of specificity of a rule with respect to another rule.

Specificity strategies are meant to recognize **special case** relationships between rules. To see why this is necessary, assume that the following rule appears in the rule base:

```
IF   (condition1 ...)
     (condition2 ...)
THEN (action1 ...)
```

Frequently, a rule based system may be in operation for some time, after which the domain of application is extended to include a new class of problems. Now, the system developers may find that the old rule base behaves incorrectly in some situations (in particular, whenever *condition3* is true). Thus, we may find the need for the following rule:

```
IF   (condition1 ...)
     (condition2 ...)
     (condition3 ...)
THEN (action2 ...)
```

The original rule base contained a rule (the first one) that will instantiate in every situation that the new rule will instantiate in. The new rule is a more specific case of the old one, and thus should be preferred whenever there is a conflict. In the absence of a specificity strategy, we are forced to change the original rule to

```
IF   (condition1 ...)
     (condition2 ...)
     (not (condition3 ...))
THEN (action1 ...)
```

in order to explicitly avoid the conflict. The changes of this sort which need to be made when extending the rule base may be extensive. Furthermore, unless we have intimate knowledge of the original rule base, we may not be aware of all conflicts requiring attention. Similarly, the new problem domain may require the addition of the rule

```
IF   (condition1 ...)
THEN (action3 ...),
```

which we would like to apply only in situations where we don't know what else to do. Without relying on specificity, we would have to determine the set of rules $rule_1 \ldots rule_N$ which apply to the same problem solving context, and express the new rule in the following fashion:

```
IF    (condition1 ...)
      and (rule1 is not applicable ...)
      and (rule2 is not applicable ...)
            . . .
      and (ruleN is not applicable ...)
THEN (action3 ...)
```

At this point, we have created a very fragile rule base which contains closely coupled rules. Any attempts at further modification may prove disastrous.

The most important reason for the use of specificity strategies, then, is to increase the modularity and extensibility of the rule base. Modularity and extensibility are important; thus, it would seem that the use of a specificity strategy is to our advantage.

We can quickly see, however, that relying on specificity for program correctness is often self-defeating. For example, we have defined several rules above among which there are special case relationships. Now, suppose that we discover a programming error, requiring a change in the first of these rules. Unless the same change is also made in the remaining rules, the special case relationships have been destroyed, and the rules will no longer operate correctly.

In a more traditional programming language, modularity is achieved through the use of subroutines. If two procedures share functionality, we can write a subroutine which can be called by both. If a subroutine changes, its effects are automatically felt by all procedures which call it.

The effectiveness of a specificity strategy may be increased if a subroutine-like facility is provided. Thus, we could have written our rules in the following form:

```
Rule1:                              Rule2:
   IF    (subroutine1 ...)             IF    (subroutine1 ...)
   THEN ...                                  (condition3 ...)
                                       THEN ...
```

Specificity strategies may compare the specificity of rules, or the specificity of instantiations. The simplest method for determining the specificity of a rule is by assigning each rule an absolute specificity value, independent of the other rules in the rule base. For example, the specificity of a rule might be equal to the number of conditions in the antecedent of the rule. Or, the specificity may be some weighted sum of the number of positive conditions, the number of negated conditions, the number of constants which appear in the conditions, etc.

This is a very crude measure of specificity. First, a rule might be preferred over a totally unrelated one, based on the fact that it has more conditions. Rules are preferred based on much weaker justification than the existence of a special case relationship. Thus, this definition is much more selective than a strict measure of specificity would be.

In addition, this measure of specificity relies on the assumption that the number of symbols required to express the rule is in some way correlated with the amount of knowledge embedded in the rule, thereby making bigger rules the preferred ones.

There are several obvious problems with this assumption. First, it is rarely the case that the semantics of a rule can be inferred from its syntactic representation, especially when relying solely on domain independent syntactic features. The meaning of a matched data item, and its importance with respect to the problem solving process, cannot be derived from its shape.

Second, the number of symbols required to express the logic of a given rule depends highly on the expressive power of the rule formalism. In a given formalism, a complex concept may be simple to express, whereas a simple one may have a complex representation. Furthermore, the rule formalism may be utilized differently by individual programmers. Experienced programmers may find a concept easy to express, whereas inexperienced programmers produce a much more contrived representation.

Based on these considerations, we find that it is necessary to use a more precise definition of the specificity of a rule. The definition must more closely capture special case relationships. In particular, we need to explicitly compare individual pairs of rules, measuring their relative specificity.

One such definition, presented in [McDermott and Forgy, 1978], is as follows: a rule *rule$_1$* is more specific than another rule *rule$_2$* if

[1]   The two rules are not equal,

[2]   *Rule$_1$* has at least as many antecedent clauses as *rule$_2$*, and

[3]   For each antecedent clause in *rule$_2$*, with constant elements $C_1 \ldots C_n$, there exists a corresponding antecedent in *rule$_1$*, with constant elements $C'_1 \ldots C'_m$, such that $C_1 \ldots C_n$ is a subset of $C'_1 \ldots C'_m$.

A number of systems, including OPS4 [Forgy, 1979] and OPS5 [Forgy, 1980], use a specificity definition similar to this one, which much more closely captures special case relationships between rules than did the previous definitions.

However, this definition has problems of its own. In some cases, programmers rely on specificity strategies in an awkward fashion, making the real meaning of the rules unclear. For example, in extreme cases, frustrated programmers have been known to produce this sort of rule:

```
IF    ( a  =x  =y )
      ( a  =x  =y )
      ( b  =y  =z )
          .  .  .
```

Notice that the first two conditions are identical. This is, presumably, a somewhat desperate attempt to inform the system that this rule should be preferred over one with a fewer number of antecedent clauses. It certainly does not do justice to the original intent of the strategy.

In addition, there are subtle special case relations between rules that this definition of specificity will fail to recognize. For example, the rule

```
IF    ( a  =x  =x )
          .  .  .
```

is a special case of the rule

```
IF    ( a  =x  =y )
          .  .  .
```

since the former rule matches only in those instances for which $=x$ and $=y$ are the same in the latter rule.

Examples of this sort may not arise frequently. In addition, precisely recognizing special case relations between rules is an expensive (and often difficult) task. For example, consider the following two rules:

```
Rule1:                        Rule2:

IF    ( a  =x  =y )           IF    ( a  =x  =y )
      ( a  =y  =x )                 ( a  =y  =x )
      ( b  =x  =y )                 ( b  =y  =x )
      ( c  =x  =y )                     .  .  .
          .  .  .
```

In this example, *Rule1* is a special case of *Rule2*. (Substitute $=x$ for $=y$ and $=y$ for $=x$ in *Rule2*, and switch the order of the first two clauses.) The level of difficulty encountered in deriving precise special case relationships increases as the rule formalism becomes more complex.

All definitions of specificity presented so far measure the specificity of rules. One advantage of measuring special case relationships on the rule level is that all such relationships can be determined once-and-for-all. This might be done during the rule compilation phase which occurs in many systems.

Some definitions of specificity, however, measure the specificity of *instantiations* of rules. The most common of these definitions considers an instantiation I_1 more specific than another instantiation I_2 if and only if the antecedent clauses of I_1 match a proper superset of the data items matched by instantiation I_2. Other related definitions are possible, including those which also take into account negated antecedent clauses (which do not match when the rule is instantiated).

Note that this last type of definition really combines information about rules (the existence of negated conditions) with information about instantiations. Let us once again look at pure rule-level specificity by examining another example. Following are two rules:

```
Rule1:                         Rule2:
   IF    (is-a =x =y)             IF    (is-a =x =y)
         (color-of =x =c)         THEN    . . .
   THEN    . . .
```

In this example, *Rule1* is clearly a special case of *Rule2*. Now, suppose working memory contains the following data items:

```
1.  (is-a Clyde elephant)
2.  (is-a Harry penguin)
3.  (color-of Clyde grey)
         . . .
```

Now, using these data items, three instantiations of the above rules are possible:

```
Rule1-inst1:
    IF      1.  (is-a Clyde elephant)
            3.  (color-of Clyde grey)
    THEN          . . .

Rule2-inst1:
    IF      1.  (is-a Clyde elephant)
    THEN          . . .

Rule2-inst2:
    IF      2.  (is-a Harry penguin)
    THEN          . . .
```

Based on rule specificity, *Rule1-inst1* will be preferred over *Rule2-inst1*. This is desirable, since *Rule1-inst1* is a special case (and is more specific) than *Rule2-inst1*. However, rule specificity also prefers *Rule1-inst1* over *Rule2-inst2*. This is not desirable, since, although *Rule1* is a special case of *Rule2*, *Rule1-inst1* is *not* a special case of *Rule2-inst2*. In this example, pure rule-level specificity is clearly inadequate.

This motivates another definition of specificity, which we will refer to as **subsumption**. Subsumption is the most sophisticated attempt at recognizing special case relationships that we will examine. An instantiation I_1 (of rule R_1) will be said to subsume another instantiation I_2 (of rule R_2) if and only if

[1] R_1 is a special case of R_2.

If so, there exists a function S which maps each antecedent clause C_i of R_2 to a unique antecedent clause C'_j of R_1 in such a way that each C'_j is at least as specific as the corresponding C_i.

Note that this function may not be unique. For the purpose of this discussion, assume that it *is* unique. The definition of subsumption presented here is easily extendible to the case where S is a set of functions.

Now, let V be the variable transformation function with respect to S. That is, let V be the complete set of variable transformations required such that, for each antecedent clause C_i in R_2, the instantiation of C_i is equivalent to the instantiation of the corresponding clause $S(C_i)$ in R_1. (This depends on the definition of equivalence used; see section 2.4.)

[2] I_1 is a special case of I_2.

Here, the special case relationship between the instantiations is also well defined. Let B_1 and B_2 be the sets of variable bindings formed for instantiations I_1 and I_2 respectively. Then, I_1 is a special case of I_2 if and only if the binding of every variable v_i in B_2 is equal to the binding of the corresponding variable $V(v_i)$ in B_1 (that is, the corresponding variable as defined by the variable transformation function V).

For example, suppose that we have the following two rules:

```
    Rule1:                        Rule2:
      IF      (a  =x  =y)           IF      (a  =y  =z)
              (b  =y  =z)                   (b  =z  ?)
              (c  =y  =z)         THEN         . . .
    THEN         . . .
```

Here, *Rule1* is a special case of *Rule2*. An instantiation I_1 of *Rule1* is a special case of an instantiation I_2 of *Rule2* if and only if the binding of $=y$ in I_2 is equal to the binding of $=x$ in I_1, and the binding of $=z$ in I_2 is equal to the binding of $=y$ in I_1.

Subsumption, according to this definition, is expensive to determine. Most of the work (that is, the determination of the functions S and V defined above) can be done at rule compile time. However, the actual comparison of variable bindings in the individual instantiations must be done at rule execution time.

Now, what does all of this buy us? Subsumption allows us to recognize all special case relationships between rule instantiations, provided the relationships can be recognized using only **syntactic** information. However, users of rule based systems will quickly find that this is often inadequate. For example, consider the following two rules:

```
Rule1:                          Rule2:
   IF    (is-a =x bird)            IF    (is-a =x penguin)
   THEN (flying =x)               THEN (waddling =x)
```

Suppose we also know that

```
   1. (is-a Harry bird)
   2. (is-a Harry penguin)
```

The problem here is that *Rule2* is a more specific version of *Rule1*, but only because *penguin* is more specific than *bird*. This is a **semantic** distinction, and cannot be recognized based only on syntactic features of the two rules. Thus, our rule base may not be able to correctly determine whether Harry flies or waddles.

We could, of course, make the following change in *Rule1*:

```
   Rule1:
      IF    (is-a =x bird)
            (not (is-a =x penguin))
            (not (is-a =x ostrich))
            . . .
```

The fact that this change is required shows us that the rule base is not easily extendible: each time we extend the problem solving domain to include a new non-flying bird, we must change *Rule1*.

In addition, it can be shown that this sort of change does not always work. For example, suppose that Harry is a penguin, but we don't know it yet. Then, *Rule1* might be applied anyway. Thus, this rule is not correct unless we can guarantee that *Rule57* (for example), which is responsible for inferring that Harry is a penguin, is applied first.

The problem here is that it is difficult to distinguish between a fact which is false, and a fact which we have not yet determined is true. This is known as the **negation vs. absence** problem, and is one of the more esoteric problems which must be faced by users of forward chaining production systems.

Alternatively, we could make the following change in *Rule2*:

```
Rule2:
   IF    (is-a =x bird)
         (is-a =x penguin)
         . . .
```

This change is awkward, and is a good example of letting the conflict resolution strategy dictate how we are to write our rules. In addition, it does not solve the extensibility problem.

In summary, we have seen that recognizing special case relationships between rules is an important problem which must be addressed if we want to increase the extensibility of the rule base. However, using specificity measures is inadequate. The control problem we have encountered here is really beyond the scope of conflict resolution, and must be handled elsewhere in the system.

2.7 Secondary Strategies

All conflict resolution strategies discussed up to this point have one important feature in common: they affect the **correctness** of a rule based program, with respect to the control scheme. That is, if an elimination strategy dictates that a given rule or instantiation should be eliminated on a given cycle, then it is not correct for the system to apply that rule or instantiation at that point in the problem solving process. Similarly, if a selection strategy prefers one instantiation over a second one, then it is not correct for the latter to be applied.

Conflict resolution strategies which affect the correctness of a program in this way will be referred to as **primary** strategies. In some sense, primary strategies actually define the control scheme of a given system, especially in cases where control is dictated completely by conflict resolution. Application programmers may (and, in practice, always do) rely on the primary conflict resolution scheme for correctness of the rule base. Thus, it is very important that the choice of primary strategies used in a particular system be made carefully.

After every available primary conflict resolution strategy is applied to the conflict set, it would be *correct* for the system to apply *any* of the instantiations which remain. It is rare, however, for the system to apply *all* instantiations which remain. In fact, in most forward chaining systems, only one instantiation may be applied on any given cycle. This restriction is made for several reasons, the most important of which are:

[1] We want to maximize the sensitivity of the system.

The greater the percentage of time spent in the **act** phase of the recognize/act cycle, the less sensitive, in theory, the system becomes to the demands of its problem solving environment. In order to maximize sensitivity, we must minimize the amount of time spent between **recognition** cycles, and therefore limit the amount of time spent executing rule consequents.

[2]   Efficiency dictates that only one instantiation be applied on each cycle.

This is a much more practical constraint. Due to the heuristic nature of rule-based programming, it is often the case that two logically correct rules might assert conflicting data items. In order to fire both correctly, the system must maintain two different world views: multiple models of the problem solving environment, each of which may then lead to a valid solution. On the next cycle, the system must independently consider both world views. This practice soon leads to an exponential increase in the amount of work to be performed by the system. Thus, without a high degree of parallelism on the hardware level, applying all correct instantiations is cost prohibitive.

The need arises, then, for the use of **secondary** conflict resolution strategies: strategies which choose among correct alternative instantiations. Secondary conflict resolution strategies do not affect program correctness in any way. In fact, the behavior of secondary strategies is often unpredictable. Programs which rely on secondary strategies for correctness are themselves incorrect.

The most common secondary conflict resolution strategy is **randomness**. This is a selection strategy which prefers arbitrary instantiations. No conflict resolution strategy is more selective than randomness. In effect, it imposes a strict ordering among the remaining instantiations in the conflict set, so that a single instantiation is preferred over all others. For this reason, no further conflict resolution need be performed. Randomness is always the last strategy in a sequence of conflict resolution procedures, and is used only to ensure that a single instantiation is identified.

An important question arises: is random behavior in a rule based system desirable? In order to address this, let us first examine the role of randomness in a typical conflict resolution procedure. The OPS5 conflict resolution procedure [Forgy, 1981] is fairly standard. It uses the following ordered sequence of strategies:

[1]   Refraction (of instantiations which are physically the same, for the duration of the problem solving session).

[2]   Recency (of all data items in each instantiation, where each data item has a unique age).

[3]   Specificity (defined at the rule level).

[4]   Randomness (as presented above).

These strategies are applied to the conflict set in order, until one strategy results in the selection of a unique instantiation. Of these strategies, refraction or recency is usually decisive; that is, one of these is usually the last in the sequence to be executed. Because of the fact that OPS5 uses such a strict definition of recency, it is highly selective, and in most cases is sufficient to produce a unique selection. The definition of specificity used is also highly selective. In the relatively few cases that recency is not decisive, specificity usually suffices.

Thus, randomness is *rarely* the decisive strategy. When randomness is required, the system is usually in one of the following situations:

[1] The order in which the remaining instantiations are applied is completely irrelevant.

In this case, one instantiation is selected at random and applied on this cycle. Another instantiation from this set is applied on the next cycle, and so on, until all of the "random" instantiations have been applied. Then, other instantiations, such as those which are less specific, are enabled.

[2] All of the remaining instantiations provide an adequate solution.

In this case, the selection of an arbitrary instantiation corresponds to the choice of one solution path. Since OPS does not provide a backtracking scheme, only one solution path will be searched. Although all paths are *correct* (secondary strategies do not affect correctness), one path may have been better than another. Random behavior guarantees that the probability of stumbling upon the best solution is no less than that of finding any of the others.

[3] The existing primary conflict resolution strategies were not sufficient to guarantee correctness.

In this case, the previous strategies did not remove an incorrect instantiation from the conflict set, and, therefore, the rule base contains an error. The programmer will most likely modify the program so that this situation does not arise. In practice, many "bug fixes" of this sort are awkward. For example, explicitly testing for the error situation (and negating it) is common.

In light of this discussion, we can say that randomness in a rule-based system is theoretically desirable, although in practice it is rarely used. Furthermore, it is sometimes inconvenient from the point of view of the applications programmer, who would rather have relied on the primary strategies to ensure correctness.

The desirability (and practicality) of a randomness strategy is significantly increased when the system provides a **backtracking** scheme. In fact, this is true for *all* secondary strategies. A backtracking scheme records the state of the problem solving environment at key decision points. This allows the system to recover from the application of a rule which did not lead to a satisfactory solution. In this situation, we might say that the original rule **failed**. One difficult problem associated with backtracking schemes is the identification of a method for measuring the **success** of a rule. In order to measure success, the system must have description of the solution state to be achieved.

In backward chaining systems, the solution state is, in effect, given at the start of the problem. At each intermediate stage, the system defines subproblems to be solved. Thus, backtracking is relatively straightforward. In fact, in backward chaining systems, conflict resolution in general plays a much smaller role, if any, in the problem solving process.

In forward chaining systems, a backtracking effect can be achieved by maintaining an explicit description of the solution paths which have been traversed in working memory. Recognizing solution states is performed by the rule base itself, in a strictly domain dependent fashion.

Alternatively, a system might provide the means for explicitly representing solution states as part of the rule formalism. Systems which maintain explicit representations of solution states provide more sophisticated control mechanisms than do those which rely on pure conflict resolution. We will see examples of such systems in section 4.

Randomness is by far the most common secondary conflict resolution strategy. However, alternatives are possible. For example, one class of alternative secondary strategies are those which are provided mainly for purposes of efficiency (see, for example, [Sauers and Walsh, 1983]).

Expert systems in long-term, real-time applications are becoming increasingly common. In such systems, useful performance data becomes available over time. If this data is incorporated into the state memory of the system, then it is available for testing by conflict resolution strategies. Thus, it is feasible to construct secondary strategies which prefer instantiations based on the amount of some critical system resource which would be required to apply that instantiation. The decision is based on past experience with the system, as reflected in dynamic, self-maintained performance measures.

We must be careful, though, to make sure that such strategies are applied only in situations where the expected benefit is sufficient. The cost of applying this sort of secondary strategy depends on the cost of actually executing the strategy, and also on the cost of monitoring and maintaining the performance data required by the strategy. Making a judgment about the expected cost of a rule in one situation may require comparing that situation to previous ones along fairly subtle dimensions.

Methods for estimating the expected benefit of dynamic control information have been developed (see for example, [Barnett, 1984]). Further research along these lines will directly benefit rule based technology in the future.

3 SOME PRELIMINARY RESULTS

Several important intermediate observations may be made as a result of our discussion of conflict resolution. Some concern the applicability and limitations of the conflict resolution approach to control. Others concern the identification of desirable attributes of a rule-based control scheme. In this section, we will summarize our discussion of the conflict resolution process, and attempt to identify its place in an overall rule-based control scheme. The observations presented here should be kept in mind during our presentation, in section four, of alternative approaches to the problem of controlling expert systems.

3.1 Correctness and Logical Consistency

During our discussion of primary and secondary conflict resolution strategies (see section 2.7), the notion of **correctness** with respect to the control scheme was introduced. Basically, the programmer may rely on the control scheme to ensure the correctness of a rule-based program.

According to common practice, a **conflict** exists between two rule instantiations whenever those two instantiations are applicable on the same cycle. If, according to the conflict resolution scheme, it is incorrect for two rules to be applied on the same cycle, then a potential conflict has been avoided.

We have seen that the existence of a conflict on any particular cycle does not necessarily mean that there exists a *logical* conflict between competing rules. In fact, it is often the case that rules in question are logically consistent, and the conflict is imposed artificially, by virtue of the fact that the rule based interpreter allows only one rule to be fired on any given cycle.

In addition, it is often the case that a rule does not explicitly specify, in its antecedent clauses, precisely the conditions required to guarantee that the rule is logically correct. This is a direct result of relying on the control scheme for correctness. Any given rule needs to include only that subset of logical conditions which guarantees that the rule will be applied correctly in the current system; that is, the rule is applied correctly with respect to the other rules in the rule base, for some targeted set of problems to be solved.

Thus, correctness, as defined by the conflict resolution scheme, is not necessarily correlated with the problem of recognizing inconsistencies in the rule base.

Now, recognizing logical inconsistencies in the rule base is beyond the current state of the art. If we fire two rules on one cycle, they might cause an inconsistency which cannot be detected until much later in the problem solving process. Furthermore, the process of recognizing *semantic* inconsistencies in any given application domain would itself require the use of an expert system.

Thus, it is not reasonable to expect conflict resolution to recognize (or resolve) logical conflicts. In fact, we have no choice but to place the burden for resolving logical conflicts on the applications programmer. The most that we can ask of conflict resolution in this regard is to ease the programmer's burden.

To this end, we might select a primary conflict resolution scheme which allows the programmer to more naturally express logical consistency in terms of the control scheme. For example, recency strategies have this property if we restrict the application of recency to those cases where we must choose between instantiations which match against conflicting data items. Specificity strategies have this property if they are good at recognizing special case relationships between rules.

Note that conflict resolution strategies of this type are more likely to be weakly selective than strongly selective. This is because their selection criteria are not generally applicable to most pairs of instantiations.

However, independent of which strategies are provided to the programmer, using conflict resolution to prevent the simultaneous application of logically conflicting rules is not reliable. This is ironic, since the layman would guess this to be the precise task for which conflict resolution was targeted.

Notice that, with the sole exception of refraction, all conflict resolution strategies we have investigated are standardly used, in practice, to achieve effects other than those for which they were originally intended. This would seem to indicate that programming practice was developed in response to conflict resolution, rather than conflict resolution being developed as an aid to the programmer.

3.2 Semantic Knowledge

Many of the problems with standard conflict resolution strategies were a result of the fact that the information available to the system for resolving conflicts was insufficient. Current strategies rely on domain independent information, derived purely from rule **syntax**. In most cases, syntactic information is insufficient for either recognizing or resolving conflicts. Thus, we need a means for incorporating **semantic** information, particular to the specific domain of application, into the conflict resolution process.

One area where such semantic information can be useful is in describing the declarative knowledge in working memory. Programmers impose meaning on the symbols used to represent knowledge. For the most part, this meaning is hidden from the system; it is implicit, and exists by virtue of the fact that the knowledge is manipulated by the rule base in a particular way. If the system and programmer, by convention, impose the same semantics on selected symbols, then rules can rely on those semantics for correctness. For example, many systems use an **is-a** construct to represent information about type hierarchies. Rules can then use this information in such a way as to provide a simple inheritance mechanism.

We can make semantic information about working memory available to the system in several ways. First, we can integrate a more sophisticated formalism for representing declarative knowledge with the formalism for expressing rules. Such systems have already been developed (see, for example, [Allen and Wright, 1983]). If the interpreter knows about the constructs in the knowledge representation formalism, then it can use the semantic information inherent in the constructs to make control decisions.

Alternatively, we can develop a completely domain-dependent knowledge representation scheme, specific to the particular application. Many systems have been developed successfully in a completely domain specific fashion (see, for example, [Davis 1976]). This approach has become increasingly popular, at least in part because of the absence of a domain-independent approach which works consistently.

Another area where semantic information can be useful is in describing the relationship between a rule and the problem solving process. For example, we have seen how a rule based system can be used to implement a form of means/ends analysis (see section 2.5). In this scheme, some rules serve to **decompose** a problem into subproblems, and others provide **solutions** to subproblems. We have also seen cases where one rule represents a preferred solution to a problem, and another provides an alternate solution path which should be taken only as a last resort.

This type of information can be used directly by conflict resolution strategies. For example, we might want to prefer rules which provide solutions to problems over rules which decompose them into subproblems. Or, we might want to prefer most rules over those which represent last resort solutions.

3.3 Explicit Representation of Control Knowledge

We have seen that it is important to distinguish between object-level information, and control information. Furthermore, the distinction should be made **explicitly**. Implicitly represented control information is not readily accessible by the system, and is therefore of little use with respect to conflict resolution. For example, knowing that **solution** rules should be preferred over **decompose** rules is not useful unless the system can identify those data items which represent problem solving goals.

Also, explicit representation of control knowledge is important for a system which must reason about its own behavior. For example, a system may want to reason about the goals it was pursuing at any given time. In addition, if all domain-dependent control knowledge is represented explicitly, then it is less important to include domain-dependent mechanisms in the system interpreter. Thus, it may still be possible to reason about application-specific control in a task independent fashion.

It has been shown that explicitly representing control knowledge can significantly reduce the amount of search required in solving a given problem (see, for example, [de Kleer, Doyle, Steele, and Sussman, 1983]). Control information can be used to restrict the applicability of rules, avoiding the combinatorial explosions which are typical of search-intensive tasks.

The explicit representation of control knowledge is also important from the point of view of the programmer who must develop and maintain the system. The resulting representation is conceptually cleaner and more modular, and therefore allows the system to be modified more easily.

Finally, it has been shown that explicitly representing control knowledge is important with respect to automated explanation of the behavior of a rule-based system

[Clancey, 1983]. Automated explanation is an important topic which has received much attention in the research community. Unfortunately, it is beyond the scope of this paper.

3.4 Higher-Level Control Constructs

We have seen that, in the traditional approach, conflict resolution is assigned the burden of much more than the resolution of conflicting rules. For example, we rely on conflict resolution strategies to increase the degree to which the rule base is extendible. More importantly, conflict resolution is used to provide what would be, in most other contexts, higher-level control mechanisms. For example, we rely on conflict resolution to provide a means for iterating over a set of data items, and for forcing the execution of a set of rules in sequence.

These sorts of control mechanisms are much more easily provided by explicit control constructs, which can easily be included as part of the rule formalism. Furthermore, this method would be more in line with the belief that control information should be represented explicitly.

Thus, it appears that conflict resolution should play a much more restricted role in an overall control scheme than it has been traditionally assigned. In many situations, conflict resolution strategies are inadequate simply because they are being used to solve a problem which requires much more contextual control information than can be provided. Such problems are beyond the scope of conflict resolution, and are best solved through the use of additional control mechanisms.

4 ALTERNATE CONTROL SCHEMES

Our analysis of the conflict resolution process has identified the need for alternative mechanisms for enforcing control in a rule-based system. This section provides an overview of some of the alternative control schemes which have been developed and used in real systems. The selection presented here is by no means complete. However, this selection is typical, in that most control mechanisms commonly found in rule-based Expert Systems have much in common with one or more of those described here.

4.1 Meta-Rules

Most of the rules which have been discussed up to this point are considered **object-level** rules. That is, they test against data objects in the application domain, and manipulate those objects during problem solving. We can also speak of **meta-level** rules. A meta-level rule is one which tests and manipulates other rules. Object-level rules provide knowledge about the task domain, whereas meta-level rules provide knowledge about how to use this knowledge.

The use of meta-rules was introduced in the TEIRESIAS system [Davis, 1976]. TEIRESIAS uses meta-level knowledge about the application domain to guide the acquisition of new object-level rules, through interaction with the user. Meta-rules were used to decide which object-level rules should be invoked in situations where more than one could have applied.

Note that this is precisely the task assigned to conflict resolution (see section 2). Thus, the use of meta-rules in a control scheme is, on some level, a rule-based approach to conflict resolution. Traditionally, meta-rules can be used to decide whether or not the application of a single rule will be useful (similar in spirit to elimination conflict resolution strategies), or to decide which of two competing rules is more likely to be useful (similar to selection strategies).

However, note that meta-rules traditionally test for the **utility** of object-level rules, as opposed to the **correctness** of the application of a particular rule. Thus, the traditional use of meta-level rules is much like the use of a **secondary** conflict resolution strategy (see section 2.7).

It is interesting to note that rules in TEIRESIAS were executed in a **backward chaining** fashion. In such systems, conflict resolution (or the functional equivalent) is usually not required, since exhaustive search of the solution space is permitted for each problem to be solved.

Exhaustive search was performed in TEIRESIAS, also. The use of meta-rules was intended to limit the application of rules to situations where they were likely to benefit the solution of the current problem. Thus, meta-rules were in part designed to allow the use of rule-based technology in applications where exhaustive search is not practical. In such applications, control is as much of a problem for backward chaining systems as it is for forward chaining systems, which we have focused on throughout most of our discussion.

Representing control knowledge in the form of meta-rules has several other advantages. First, control knowledge is explicit, in a form which allows it to be readily manipulated by the interpreter. Furthermore, a uniform representation is used for both object-level knowledge and control knowledge. Thus, control knowledge can be manipulated in the same manner as object-level knowledge; no additional mechanisms need to be developed.

Since the parallel between the use of meta-level rules and the conflict resolution process is so well-defined, an obvious question arises: can similar techniques be used to develop a conflict resolution scheme which is itself rule-based? For example, the following rule might be used to describe an elimination strategy:

> IF I_1 is an applicable instantiation,
>   and I_1 has been previously applied,
> THEN it is not likely that the application of I_1 will be useful.

Similarly, we can use a rule-based formalism to describe a familiar selection strategy:

> IF I_1 is an applicable instantiation matching data item D_1,
>   and I_2 is an applicable instantiation matching data item D_2,
>   and there is evidence that D_1 is inconsistent with D_2,
>   and D_1 is more recent than D_2,
> THEN I_1 should be preferred over I_2.

Several system capabilities are required to allow this. First, meta-rules must be permitted to directly access state memory. For example, this would be required to determine whether or not an instantiation has already been applied. In traditional systems, this is not permitted. However, it seems reasonable to allow this, provided that rules are *not* permitted to explicitly modify the contents of state memory.

In addition, rules must be able to directly access the rule base. Specifically, rules must have the ability to easily extract information about rules which is useful with respect to control. In TEIRESIAS, control was **content-directed;** that is, meta-level rules were permitted to describe the contents of target object-level rules. Alternatively, meta-level rules might match against some set of **control attributes,** specified for each rule by the programmer. For example, we saw that it was useful to explicitly represent the fact that a rule decomposes a problem into subproblems, or that a rule provides an immediate solution to a subproblem. In the most general scheme, rules themselves might be treated as data objects. They might be described by arbitrary data items, in the same way that object-level data is described in working memory.

Explicitly representing conflict resolution strategies using a rule-based formalism has several advantages. Most importantly, the conflict resolution scheme is accessible by the programmer, and can be modified to meet the needs of each application. Thus, the programmer can develop control schemes in a **domain-specific** fashion, taking advantage of semantic characteristics of the problem solving environment which are not available in more traditional, generalized approaches.

There is, however, one important problem to be solved before this scheme can be used: what method is used to resolve conflicts between conflict resolution rules? For example, one meta-rule might prefer instantiation I_1 over I_2, whereas another meta-rule prefers I_2 over I_1.

One possible solution is to provide for multiple levels of meta-rules. That is, first order meta-rules are used to resolve conflicts between object-level rules; second order meta-rules are used to resolve first order meta-rules, and so on.

One advantage of this approach is that the control scheme can be made to change based on characteristics of the execution context. In effect, second order rules may be used to select a first order control scheme.

Although this approach has been suggested (see [Davis, 1977]), it is not practiced in real systems. One reason is that in most systems, one level of meta-rules is more than sufficient, since the first level constrains the search space to the point where the second level can be replaced by exhaustive search.

In addition, although providing the programmer explicit access to the control mechanisms is important, it is not desirable to force the programmer to completely specify the control scheme. Requiring the programmer to specify two or even three levels of meta-rules is often too much of a burden.

For this reason, a set of system-defined conflict resolution rules must be available for resolving conflicts which cannot be resolved by user-specified rules. These **primitive** rules are necessarily domain independent, and are probably the same sort of rules which we have discussed previously. However, the burden placed on these rules with respect to enforcing control has been greatly decreased. Most important control decisions are made in a more intelligent fashion, through the use of the domain specific rules. The higher the level at which an unintelligent control decision is made, the less likely it is that a mistake will have a detrimental effect on the problem solving process.

In any case, we have seen that the use of meta-level rules to explicitly represent control knowledge provides many advantages over the more simplistic approaches to control previously discussed.

4.2 Goal Directed Systems

A **goal**, in the context of rule-based systems, is a problem to be solved, a task to be performed, or a state to be achieved. A **goal directed** system is one which uses information about goals and the relationships between goals to guide control.

In section 2.5, we saw an example of the use of goals in a forward chaining system. Here, goal directedness was **implicit**; that is, there was no real distinction between data elements serving as domain objects, and those serving as control tokens. Some data items functioned as goals by virtue of the fact that they were manipulated by the system in a particular way.

Backward chaining systems are also implicitly goal directed. Problem solving begins with the goal of deriving a particular data item. This is matched against the consequents of rules, in order to determine which rules are able to derive the desired data item (and, therefore, achieve the desired goal). The antecedents of rules which meet this criterion then become **subgoals,** which need to be achieved recursively.

Alternatively, a rule-based system can be **explicitly** goal directed. A good example of such a system is GRAPES [Sauers and Farrell, 1982]. In GRAPES, goals are recorded in an explicitly defined **goal memory**, which is distinct from working memory. Goals are organized hierarchically; each goal may have arbitrary sequences of subgoals organized into **AND/OR** branches. Rule antecedents may match against goals, and rule consequents may insert new goals, or declare existing goals successful.

An explicitly represented goal hierarchy has several advantages with respect to control. First, each rule may specify the goal context in which it is relevant. This assures that rules are applied only in situations in which they are potentially useful.

In addition, this greatly decreases the portion of the rule base which needs to be tested on any particular cycle. In effect, the rule base is **partitioned** according to the goal context in which the rules are relevant. When a given goal is pursued by the system, the relevant partition becomes **active**. System resources are not wasted processing rules which are relevant in other problem solving contexts.

In a goal directed system, attention is always focused on a single problem, known as the **current goal**. Changing the focus of attention during problem solving occurs when the goal context is changed. For example, if a goal is decomposed, we may want to pursue its subgoals. The mechanism used by the system interpreter to decide which goal in goal memory should be pursued on any given cycle is known as the **goal selection** mechanism.

An explicitly represented goal hierarchy imposes structure on the problem solving environment. This structure is taken into consideration by the goal selection mechanism. For example, one of the simplest goal selection mechanisms is one which traverses the goal hierarchy in a depth-first, left-to-right fashion. This simple scheme is the one used in most implicitly goal directed systems.

Explicit representation of goals has another important advantage. When goals are represented explicitly, they themselves may be manipulated as data objects. Thus, in addition to creating new goals, rules may describe characteristics of existing ones. For example, it may be useful for a rule to decide that two given goals must be pursued in sequence, or that they may be pursued independently. This information may be explicitly represented and inserted into working memory, or attached to the goals themselves.

One important use of this technique is to describe conditions under which a particular goal should be considered a success or a failure. We can declaratively attach a success criteria to each goal; then, a goal succeeds when the associated success criteria are met.

The explicit representation of success and failure criteria has several advantages. First, it is often the case that the pursuit of one goal has the side effect of achieving another goal. Similarly, the pursuit of one goal may inadvertently undo a previously successful goal. The system can recognize such situations by examining the success criteria of the individual goals in the system.

In addition, failure situations may have an interesting effect on the control mechanism. Suppose two rules are applicable towards the solution of a particular goal. One is selected, resulting in the decomposition of the goal into an **AND** sequence of subgoals. Now, if one of the subgoals fails, it may mean that we have made an incorrect decision somewhere in the problem solving process. In this situation, we may want to back up to the parent goal, and try applying the second of the two applicable rules. Thus, if we have an explicit measure of goal failure, we also have a natural way of providing an automatic **backtracking** mechanism.

We have seen that information describing goals is important with respect to control. Now, if this information is represented explicitly, it becomes available for use by the goal selection mechanism. For example, if two subgoals may be pursued independently, then the goal selection mechanism is free to choose either one.

We have also seen that the use of domain-specific control knowledge is often required in a control scheme. Domain-specific knowledge is also important in the goal selection process. In the most general scheme, goal selection may be accomplished through the use of a set of **goal selection strategies**, similar in style to conflict resolution strategies. Individual strategies may be domain-independent, or they may be provided by the applications programmer.

The specification of goal selection strategies is an ideal application for the use of **meta-rules** (see section 3.1). Traditionally, meta-rules are used to describe how object-level rules should be used by the system. Similarly, meta-level control rules may be used to describe how control knowledge should be used. For example, the following is an example of a meta-rule used for the purpose of goal selection:

$$
\begin{aligned}
&\text{IF}\quad G_1 \text{ is an active goal,} \\
&\quad\text{and } G_2 \text{ is an active goal,} \\
&\quad\text{and } G_3 \text{ is a failed goal,} \\
&\quad\text{and } G_3 \text{ is similar in function to } G_1, \\
&\quad\text{and there is no failed goal } G_4 \text{ such that } G_4 \text{ is similar to } G_2, \\
&\text{THEN } G_2 \text{ should be preferred over } G_1.
\end{aligned}
$$

Under this scheme, the programmer has a means for providing goal selection rules specific to each particular application. In addition, the system may provide a set of domain-independent goal selection rules to be used as a last resort. For example, the **depth-first-left-to-right** strategy might serve a similar function with respect to goal selection as did the **random** strategy in conflict resolution. Conflict resolution meta-rules may be used to select among conflicting goal selection meta-rules.

Notice that we have now distinguished between two types of control knowledge. Some control knowledge is represented **procedurally**. For example, conflict resolution mechanisms, meta-level rules, and goal selection strategies are all procedurally represented forms of control knowledge. Alternatively, control knowledge may be represented **declaratively**. An explicit goal hierarchy is an example of declarative control knowledge, as is data describing relationships between the individual goals in the hierarchy.

The use of goal selection strategies is an example of a particularly interesting control mechanism. Declarative control knowledge is used to drive a procedurally encoded control mechanism. In general, when we refer to a **higher-level control mechanism**, we refer to a control mechanism driven by other explicitly represented control knowledge. Explicit goal directedness is the first example we have seen of the use of such a higher-level control mechanism.

The provision of a higher-level control mechanism is one of the most important methods we will find for enforcing control on a rule-based system. Many expert system development efforts have found that constraints imposed through the use of a higher-level control mechanism make rule based programming easier (see, for example, [Lewy, Gohring, and Sauers, 1984]. Thus, higher-level control mechanisms will become increasingly important in our discussion.

4.3 Prototypes in CENTAUR

CENTAUR [Aikins, 1980] is a system which performs diagnosis of pulmonary diseases through interactive consultation sessions with the user. It is basically a re-design of the PUFF system [Kunz, et al, 1978], designed to solve previous problems resulting from the implicit representation of control knowledge.

In CENTAUR, control knowledge is represented explicitly and separately from object-level knowledge, in structures called **prototypes**. A prototype is a frame-like representation of typical patterns of knowledge inherent in the application domain. In CENTAUR, they are used to represent various pulmonary disorders, subclasses and degrees of disorders, and prototypical diagnostic situations.

Each prototype contains a series of **slots**, used to hold knowledge about the domain. Rules may be procedurally attached to various slots, which completely specify the function of the attached rules. Thus, each rule is applied in a specific context: it is applied during the consultation when the system needs to determine the value of a particular slot.

CENTAUR takes a hypothesize and match approach to problem solving. Each prototype may contain a **components** slot, which specifies links to other related prototypes. Thus, when a disorder is hypothesized, the system attempts to match prototypes related to this disorder.

Prototypes also contain explicit control knowledge about how to pursue the various hypotheses. This control knowledge is represented in the form of a set of

control tasks. The consultation process itself is represented as a prototype; this high-level prototype specifies how the various control tasks in lower-level prototypes should be executed.

One advantage to representing control knowledge in this fashion is that control knowledge is prototype-specific; that is, the control structure can be changed based on the hypothesis being pursued.

In addition, the frame-based approach provides contextual control knowledge which helps in the selection of rules to be applied. In this respect, the use of prototypes to guide control has much in common with the use of explicit goals in goal directed systems. Hypothesizing a pulmonary disorder to be matched is much like the creation of a goal. The prototype associated with the hypothesis explicitly specifies which subgoals should be pursued.

In CENTAUR, a best-fit matching approach was taken to solving the problem of determining which of the current set of active prototypes should be pursued at any given time. The match was based on certainty measures associated with each prototype. Thus, a particular symptom might indicate one of several possible disorders, each with some relative certainty.

The main problem with the use of certainty factors in this way is that the certainty of a symptom indicating one disorder is relative to the certainties of the other indicated disorders. Thus, this scheme has many of the same problems as does a pure rule prioritization conflict resolution strategy (see section 2.3). As the number of prototypes increases, certainty factors become increasingly difficult to maintain. CENTAUR contained approximately 50 rules. In a more complex system, a more sophisticated prototype selection strategy may have been required.

The control scheme used in CENTAUR is specific to the hypothesize and match problem solving methodology. The interpreter performed three main tasks in sequence: hypothesis formation, followed by hypothesis refinement, followed by a cleanup phase. One control slot specified by the prototypes is the **if-confirmed** slot, which describes what action should be taken if the hypothesized pulmonary disorder associated with that prototype is confirmed.

It has not yet been shown that this approach is generalizable to more complex task domains. However, the use of prototypes in CENTAUR does provide an important example of the integration of rule-based technology with a more sophisticated knowledge representation scheme than is used in traditional systems. It also shows that, in many applications, the development of a domain specific architecture is a viable alternative to the use of a generalized rule-based development system.

In fact, it is often the case that the use of a sophisticated knowledge representation scheme *requires* the development of a domain specific architecture. Increasing numbers of expert systems are being constructed in this fashion. The state of the art in expert system development tools is such that complex systems are often too awkward when expressed using a domain independent formalism.

Much of this is due to the fact that existing domain-independent control architectures are frequently proven inadequate. Furthermore, current methods for representing domain-specific control knowledge in a domain-independent framework are difficult to use. What is really needed is a scheme which facilitates the addition of domain-specific control knowledge into a existing generalized system.

4.4 Hearsay-III

Hearsay-III [Balzer, et al, 1980] is a domain-independent architecture for the development of rule based expert systems. It is based, in part, on ideas derived from the Hearsay-II Speech Recognition System [Erman, et al, 1980].

A system developed in Hearsay-III is constructed using **knowledge sources.** A knowledge source is basically a generalized production rule. Many of the constraints imposed on traditional rule formalisms were relaxed, resulting in rules with a larger conceptual grain size.

Knowledge sources communicate via a **blackboard** mechanism. The blackboard may be partitioned hierarchically into several areas, providing a flexible means for structuring knowledge to be manipulated by the various knowledge sources.

The Hearsay-III blackboard is initially divided into two main areas. The **domain** blackboard is used for communication between what in other systems would be referred to as object-level rules. The **scheduling** blackboard is used by knowledge sources which manipulate control knowledge.

The Hearsay-III system was designed for applications in which the process of selecting knowledge sources to be applied is complex. Thus, the control mechanism supports the use of domain-specific scheduling knowledge sources, developed by the applications programmer.

Domain knowledge sources are triggered by matching data which appears on the domain blackboard. However, unlike more traditional rule based architectures, the Hearsay-III architecture does not immediately execute rules which have been triggered. Instead, an **activation record** is created for each triggered rule. These are placed on the scheduling blackboard. Scheduling knowledge sources are then used to decide which activation record should be executed at any given time. Activation records may be tagged with domain-specific control knowledge at the time they are created; this knowledge may then be used by the scheduling knowledge sources to help guide the selection of activation records to be applied.

The Hearsay-III system also includes a user-accessible **context mechanism,** which allows for the construction of multiple models of the problem solving domain. This is coupled with a **choice mechanism**, which allows the system to select among the various contexts. A choice can be **deduced**: the system irreversibly selects a single domain model to be the correct problem state representation. Alternatively, a choice can be **assumed**: the system assumes a domain model to be used, while at the same time maintaining the representation of alternate models to be used later.

It is useful to compare the Hearsay-III control scheme to that of the more traditional expert system building architectures. In the traditional approach, the recognize/act cycle (see section 2.1) begins with the matching of rules in the rule base. In Hearsay-III, this corresponds to the triggering of domain knowledge sources.

In the traditional approach, matched rule instantiations enter the conflict set. In Hearsay-III, a set of activation records is maintained on the scheduling blackboard. The most important difference here is that the more traditional conflict set is internal to the system, and is accessible only by the interpreter. The scheduling blackboard is accessible by all scheduling knowledge sources. This is similar in effect to allowing rules to manipulate instantiations in the conflict set, making them accessible to the applications programmer.

Note that the use of meta-level rules (see section 3.1) serves a similar function, in that it provides access to the control mechanisms in a way which allows for the creation and manipulation of domain specific control knowledge. However, meta-level rules traditionally manipulate rules, not instantiations. In our discussion of conflict resolution, we found that rule-level control strategies were often insufficient to make intelligent control decisions. The Hearsay-III architecture allows scheduling rules to access instantiation-level control knowledge, as well as other domain-specific control knowledge describing the triggering environment.

In more traditional systems, conflict resolution is performed on the conflict set, and a single instantiation is selected for application. This is independent of whether a domain independent approach to conflict resolution is taken, or a meta-level rule based approach is taken. In Hearsay-III, scheduling knowledge sources have complete control over which activation records are executed. Activation records are explicitly added and removed from the scheduling blackboard by knowledge sources. Thus, we are able to obtain the effect of selecting any number of instantiations from the conflict set to be applied, in whatever order is desirable.

Furthermore, scheduling knowledge sources may make use of the Hearsay-III context mechanism. Thus, it is possible for the system to apply multiple, competing knowledge sources by executing each in a different problem solving context. This allows an application system to propose multiple solutions to a given problem, and compare the solutions in a domain-specific fashion.

Note that the use of scheduling knowledge sources, manipulating explicitly represented control knowledge written on the scheduling blackboard, fits our definition of a higher-level control mechanism. Also note that, through the use of this higher-level control mechanism, the programmer may develop a control scheme which suits any given application domain.

One problem with the use of the Hearsay-III control architecture, however, is that the programmer must develop the *entire* control scheme for each particular application domain. Many of the low-level control functions provided automatically in most systems must be developed from scratch using the Hearsay-III scheduling facilities.

Now, Hearsay-III was designed as a testbed for the rapid development of expert systems. The control scheme was intentionally generalized to maximize its utility across application domains. It was intended that a set of fairly general schedulers be developed in house over time, such that they might be used, with possible minor alterations, in other application efforts.

The main point here, then, is that there is a tradeoff between the amount of flexibility provided to the programmer in developing a control scheme, and the ease of development of each particular application. The more flexible the formalism, the more effort must be spent by the programmer in tailoring the control scheme to fit the needs of a particular domain. In designing a control methodology, we must be careful balance the flexibility of the system with its ease of use.

4.5 Controlled Production Systems

Each of the control schemes which has been investigated in this section calls for the explicit representation of control knowledge. The notion of a **controlled production system** [Georgeff, 1979] was introduced as a means for formalizing this representation of control knowledge.

Traditional production system architectures consist of a set of productions (the rule base), a set of data items (working memory), and an interpreter (see section 1). A controlled production system is augmented with a control mechanism known as a control language. This can be described as a formal language (see, for example, [Hopcroft and Ullman, 1979]) defined over the set of productions, which specifies the set of legal rule sequences.

For example, suppose a rule-based system contained the productions P_1, P_2, P_3, and P_4. A control language specified over this set of productions might be

$$P_1 (P_2 + P_3)^* P_4$$

This **regular expression** defines a control language described as follows: production P_1 must be applied first, followed by any number of applications of either P_2 or P_3 (including no applications), terminated by an application of P_4.

It can be shown (see [Georgeff, 1979]) that the set of control languages which can be described using regular expressions (that is, **regular** control languages) are sufficiently powerful to represent such traditional control mechanisms as external sequencing, iteration over sets of productions, and context switching in partitioned production systems.

If the control language formalism is extended to allow **context-free** control languages, this scheme can be used to describe recursive control mechanisms, such as goal directedness (see section 4.2). For example, consider again the small production set defined above. A context-free control language defined over this set of productions might described with the following grammar:

```
S    --> G1 G2   |   G3
G1   --> S   | P1
G2   --> P2 | G2 G2
G3   --> P3 | P4
```

Here, S is the **root** symbol of the grammar. We might think of it as being analogous to the top goal, or the main problem to be solved, in a goal directed system. Each G_i is a **non-terminal** symbol, which is described in the grammar in terms of other sequences of symbols. The G_i might be thought of as subgoals. For example, the top goal can be solved either by solving *G1* and *G2* in sequence, or by solving *G3*. Note that *G1* may be solved by recursively solving a problem of type *S*.

Each rule P_i in the above grammar is a **terminal** symbol. When all non-terminal symbols have been expanded into terminal symbols, we have identified a legal rule sequence.

Note the rule-like characteristic of the context-free grammar specification. Each line in the language specification is, in fact, itself referred to as a production.

In a controlled production system, the conflict resolution process is theoretically trivial. It can be described with the following strategies:

[1] Eliminate instantiations of rules whose application produces a rule sequence not defined by the control language;

[2] Select a random instantiation.

Thus, the entire burden for enforcing control is placed on the definition of the control language. Deciding whether or not the controlled production system scheme is desirable, from the point of view of the programmer, depends entirely on the ease with which the control language can be specified.

Representing the control language using a formal description of the grammar, as in the examples above, has several serious drawbacks. In a system with an extremely small number of rules, the construction of such a formal description may be trivial. However, in a real expert system, with hundreds of rules, requiring a formal description of the grammar is unreasonable.

In addition, the formal approach to describing the control language greatly restricts the modularity and flexibility of the rules in the rule base. When a new rule is added, the control language grammar must be updated to specify changes in the set of legal rule sequences. This is similar in spirit to the problems inherent in strict rule prioritization schemes (see section 2.3), except that the changes required in the control grammar are potentially much more extensive and difficult to derive. Thus, we have gained explicit representation of control information, at the expense of system modularity.

Finally, recall that, in our discussion of conflict resolution strategies (see section 2), we determined that selecting among rules to be applied often requires reasoning on the instantiation level. Similarly, determining whether a sequence of rules is legal may require examining the instantiations of those rules.

Alternatively, we might examine contextual information about the environment which will allow us to distinguish between two rule instantiations. Consider again our example of a context-free grammar description, presented above. Deciding whether we should apply rule P_1 or rule P_3 depends on whether we should be pursuing goal $G1$ or $G3$. That is, we must decide which is the best method for solving S in the given problem solving context. Thus, we might make the following changes in our grammar definition:

```
x y S     -->   G1 G2
    z S     -->   G3
        .   .   .
```

Here, x, y, and z embody contextual information about the problem solving environment required to decide between the two alternate methods of solving S. The resulting grammar is now **context sensitive**. What we are leaning towards, in effect, is a complete rule-based model of the process of controlling the object-level rule base.

This model is now very close to the explicitly goal directed model of control presented in section 4.2. Rules match against a goal context, and data in working memory. As a consequence, they may declare subgoals.

Another constraint on the formal grammar specification which we may want to relax is the requirement that the terminal symbols be productions. For example, we may want a terminal symbol to represent a description of a class of productions. This new scheme is one which is very similar to the use of **meta-level** control rules (see section 4.1), where rule invocation was **content-directed**.

What we are finding here is that all explicitly represented control mechanisms, in effect, impose a control language on the rule base. However, explicit representation of control knowledge does not require explicit definition of the control grammar. Thus, formalizing the notion of a controlled production system, in terms of a formal grammar imposed on the rule base, is a conceptualization which may be replaced by more practical explicit representations to be used in real systems.

One such representation is described in [Georgeff, 1983]. Here, the concept of a **procedural expert system** is introduced, where procedural knowledge describing sequences of tasks to be performed is explicitly represented.

A procedural expert system is constructed of **knowledge areas**. Each knowledge area contains two main components. The **invocation** part is used to trigger a knowledge area, by testing against goals and data in the problem solving environment. Thus, it is similar in function to the antecedent of rules in traditional systems. The **body** is used to establish new goals, or infer new facts. Thus, it is similar in function to the consequent of traditional rules.

The form which the body of a knowledge area takes, however, is significantly different from the traditional representation of rule consequents. The body contains large amounts of domain-specific procedural knowledge, encoded in the form of a **Recursive Transition Network**. Recursive transition networks, or

RTNs, are frequently used as a means for representing some subset of a **Natural Language** (for example, English) for syntactic parsing (see, for example, [Winograd, 1983]). They are also used for representing the syntactic structure of computer programming languages to be processed by a translator or compiler.

An RTN consists of a set of named **networks**. Each network consists of a set of **states**, connected together with directed **arcs**. Each network has a single **initial state**, from which processing of the network begins. In the Natural Language domain, arcs are labelled with lexemes (words and punctuation symbols), or lexical categories (such as noun, verb, adjective, etc). In order to process a given input sentence, we begin at the start state of some network, and attempt to traverse arcs by consuming symbols in the input stream which match the labels on the arcs. Processing continues in this fashion, until a **final state** of the network is reached. In addition, arcs may be labelled with **phrasal** level syntactic categories. Each such category corresponds to a named network in the RTN. In order to traverse these phrasal arcs, we must be able to parse the corresponding named network, beginning at the current input stream position. This capability gives the RTN its recursive nature.

In the body of a knowledge area, an RTN is used to represent the decision making process required to solve a particular subproblem in the task domain. Arcs in the network are **augmented** with tests and actions (similar in style to those in an Augmented Transition Network (**ATN**); see [Winograd, 1983]). Test augmentations on an arc are arbitrary functional predicates used to test characteristics of the problem solving environment. Some tests may be used to set up goals to determine whether or not a particular fact is true. Action augmentations may be used to infer new facts to be added to the data base.

Thus, the body of a knowledge area can potentially incorporate much more knowledge of the expert domain than the consequents of traditional rules. Control is represented explicitly in the arcs of the RTN.

The use of knowledge areas provides an interesting combination of heuristic and algorithmic programming. Knowledge areas are triggered heuristically by matching the invocation part of the knowledge area against an explicit goal stack. Triggering a knowledge area signals its applicability to the current problem. However, no order is imposed on the triggered knowledge areas. Thus, the invocation part of a knowledge area serves a role which is similar to that of a meta-level rule, since it determines utility without ordering.

Once a knowledge area is triggered, it may be executed. Execution occurs by algorithmic, exhaustive search of the RTN. Thus, executing the body of a knowledge area corresponds to problem solving in a well-structured area. When a more heuristic approach is again required, we can invoke a subgoal from within the RTN body. This subgoal is then processed recursively, by determining which knowledge areas are relevant to solving that goal.

The use of an RTN in the body of a knowledge area imposes a control language on the tests and actions to be executed within the body, in much the same way that an RTN is used to define a language for Natural Language processing. Furthermore, this control mechanism is much closer in spirit to a formal language definition than the previously presented mechanisms.

More importantly, this scheme is much more extendible than the formal definition approach. New knowledge areas may be developed, and they are automatically incorporated into the problem solving process when they become relevant to a particular problem solving goal.

It is not as easy to extend the body of a particular knowledge area. However, this is to be expected. The various sequences of tests and actions in the RTN are closely coupled, in that there is a strict order in which they must be applied in order to correctly solve problems in the applicable domain.

This is the only example of a control scheme we have seen where **coupling** between rules (or, in this case, test/action pairs) is explicitly represented. Thus, although the modification of problem solving information represented in an ATN formalism may be difficult, it is not nearly as difficult as modifying a set of rules for which the coupling is not made explicit.

One important lesson should be learned from the procedural expert system formalism. Some problem solving knowledge is best represented heuristically, and is therefore a good candidate for representation in a rule-based formalism. However, much problem solving knowledge is algorithmic. This is true even in expert system application domains. When algorithmic knowledge is represented in a rule-based fashion, problems begin to occur. Rules are coupled in odd, implicit ways. Modularity is lost, and the system becomes more difficult to extend.

Therefore, a control scheme which is desirable for expert system programming must include a well-balanced scheme for representing both heuristic and algorithmic problem solving knowledge. Only then will we find a control mechanism which provides the advantages of a rule-based programming language, while at the same time allows the expert system programmer to develop an application system rapidly and effectively. This view will play an important role in the remainder of our discussion.

5 RESULTS

This section presents a summary of the important results obtained during our discussion of control mechanisms. These results should be taken as design considerations for the development of any new control mechanism to be used for expert system applications. Thus, they will play a major role in the next section, which presents some preliminary proposals for an integrated expert system control architecture.

5.1 Domain Specific Control Knowledge

We have found that in order to guarantee logically correct problem solving in complex rule-based expert systems, it is usually necessary to represent varying levels of control knowledge specific to the domain of application. Furthermore, it is difficult to obtain domain specific behavior by relying solely on domain independent control mechanisms. When the programmer is forced to rely on such mechanisms, the resulting rule-based system implementation becomes confusing, with many implicit interactions between individual rules resulting in a loss of modularity and extensibility.

Thus, it is highly desirable for an expert system control mechanism to provide a means for the expression of domain specific control knowledge. The domain specific control mechanisms must be easily integrated into the existing control framework. In addition, the new control knowledge must itself be easily modified and extended. This, we have seen, requires that the new control knowledge be explicitly represented.

We have actually identified two types of domain specific control knowledge which must be represented explicitly. The first type is the sort of control knowledge which most of the control schemes we have studied are concerned with: control knowledge which is used by the system to decide among competing rules to be applied.

Second, we want to make explicit those interactions between individual rules which affect control, but are usually made implicit. For example, it is often the case that the logic of one rule is correct only under the assumption that some prerequisite task has already been performed. The correctness of the rule base is guaranteed through the passing of control tokens in working memory from one rule to another. It is this type of implicit control knowledge which must be made explicit in order to retain coherence in the rule base over time.

5.2 Conflict Resolution and Search

Of all of the control mechanisms we have examined, conflict resolution is the most common in real systems. It is also the most unreliable of the control mechanisms, in that it is difficult to develop a logically coherent system while, at the same time, promoting extensibility.

We have found that much of this is due to the fact that traditional conflict resolution strategies rely solely on domain independent control information. There are then several ways in which this problem can be alleviated. First, we can associate various attributes with the individual rules, at the time they are developed, which might be useful in making control decisions. Conflict resolution strategies can be designed which examine these attributes.

Second, we have seen that meta-level rules can be used as a means for developing a domain specific conflict resolution scheme, which can be integrated with domain independent strategies by the system interpreter. This allows the programmer to specify control knowledge which is specific to the application domain, and is therefore consistent with the objectives described in section 5.1. In addition, we have seen that applying domain independent conflict resolution strategies to resolve meta-level conflicts will both minimize the number of incorrect control decisions, and decrease their effect on the problem solving process.

Finally, we must remember that search is an alternate to conflict resolution. By providing a backtracking scheme, we can decrease the burden placed on conflict resolution for making initially correct control decisions. Instead of forcing the use of a last resort conflict resolution strategy, we might perform a best-first search of the rules in question, allowing the system to recover from the selection of an incorrect rule instantiation.

Such a scheme is facilitated if we provide, in our formalism for the representation of control knowledge, a means for specifying information which allows the system to decide when it is relevant to search, and when it is relevant to backtrack.

Thus, explicit representation of multiple possible solution paths may be desirable, as well as the assignment of completion criteria to various system goals and tasks.

5.3 Global vs. Local Control

In section 4.2, we introduced the notion of a higher-level control mechanism. Recall that by a higher-level control mechanism, we mean a control mechanism which makes use of other explicitly represented control knowledge in making control decisions.

For example, suppose the solution to some problem P requires that task X be performed, followed by task Y. One way to represent this control information is through the use of a meta-level control rule, as follows:

```
IF   We must solve problem P,
     and Rule R_1 performs task X,
     and Rule R_2 performs task Y,
     and task X has not been performed,
     and task Y has not been performed,
THEN prefer R_1 over R_2.
```

Alternatively, in a goal-directed system, we may make use of the following rule, which basically represents the same control information:

```
IF    The goal is to solve P,
THEN  solve subgoals X and Y sequentially.
```

Now, both of these examples access explicitly represented control information. In the first case, we make use of the knowledge that each rule is used to perform a specific task, and that certain tasks have not yet been performed. In the second case, we access and manipulate goals. Thus, both examples may be thought of as higher-level control mechanisms.

However, the second method for representing this task specific control knowledge is, at least in this case, much more natural. In the latter example, the **structure** of the problem solving process is explicitly represented. That is, the fact that P decomposes into X followed by Y is explicit. In the first example, this information is implicit in the fact that X rules should be preferred over Y rules. This is, perhaps, a subtle difference; however, as we can see by comparing the two examples, the difference is important.

We have seen that the inclusion of a higher-level control mechanism in the design of an overall control scheme is advantageous in several respects. Here, we are advocating the proposal that explicit representation of the problem solving process increases the coherence of the control scheme. We will refer to a higher-level control mechanism which makes use of an explicit description of the structure of problem solving as a **global control mechanism**.

This allows us to distinguish between global and local control mechanisms. **Global control** is the process of selecting a problem solving context; **local control** is the process of selecting a problem solving procedure to be used within that global context.

Note that here, the terms *global* and *local* are not absolute measures; they are used with respect to a problem solving context. Since it is frequently the case that a problem can be decomposed into subproblems, control knowledge which is local to one context may actually be global control knowledge in another context.

Also note that, although we require that the global control mechanism be represented explicitly, we are not imposing the constraint that it be represented declaratively. In fact, since expert knowledge is often knowledge about the problem solving *process*, it may be the case that a procedural representation is more appropriate. For example, in our discussion of procedural expert systems (see section 4.5), we saw control knowledge about the problem solving process represented procedurally in the form of a recursive transition network.

5.4 Algorithmic vs. Heuristic Problem Solving

We have seen that a major advantage of rule-based expert system programming is that it allows for the representation of **heuristic** problem solving. That is, rules are used to represent knowledge used in practice by expert problem solvers in the application domain. This knowledge is likely to lead to the solution of a problem, but it is not guaranteed to do so. As the number of rules directed towards a particular subproblem increases, the amount of heuristic knowledge brought to bear on that problem increases. Thus, the probability that some combination of these heuristics will lead to a satisfactory solution for a given problem also increases.

However, it is also the case that, even in expert system applications, some subset of the problem domain is well-structured, and therefore some subset of the problem solving knowledge which must be represented is actually **algorithmic**. More importantly, we have seen that the representation of algorithmic reasoning in a strict rule-based framework is both awkward and inadequate. When programmers are forced to represent algorithmic knowledge in this fashion, the resulting system becomes incoherent and fragile. Rules are coupled through the manipulation of implicit control information, and the resulting rule dependencies decrease the degree to which the system may be extended over time.

Thus, what we are advocating here is an approach which allows for the representation of both heuristic and algorithmic control knowledge. Furthermore, our scheme must ensure that these two schemes are thoroughly integrated. In ill-structured domains, problem solving may best be represented heuristically. However, a more traditional, algorithmic formalism may be used when appropriate.

The ability to represent algorithmic control knowledge explicitly has several further advantages. First, traditional algorithmic programming, as a science, has been studied much longer than has rule-based programming. We know more about how algorithms should and should not be structured to promote readability, modularity, efficiency, and, most importantly, correctness. Although expert system programming is traditionally rule-based, these attributes are still desirable.

In addition, algorithmic programs are, in general, described on a much higher level than their rule-based counterparts. A subroutine is itself a small program, and may contain a much larger grain size of knowledge than is traditionally possible in a rule-based formalism.

Finally, algorithmic programming does not require some of the costly overhead which is required for rule-based programming. For example, there is no need to perform conflict resolution for an algorithmic reasoning process. This also means that the resulting system may be more reliable, and will require less search than would its rule-based counterpart.

Remember that we are not suggesting that heuristic programming is eliminated: it is essential that heuristic programming be used in many problem areas. However, purely heuristic programming is never required, if only for the reason that expert system problem solving in purely heuristic domains is beyond the current state of the art.

6 PROPOSALS

This section presents some preliminary proposals concerning the design of an integrated control scheme for expert system programming. The scheme described here takes into account the design considerations described in the previous section. It features explicitly represented control knowledge, and provides a unique combination of heuristic and algorithmic problem solving capabilities.

A word of caution is required: the ideas presented here are at times incomplete. This section is meant merely to present a brief sketch of some preliminary results of research currently in progress. Furthermore, the control scheme presented here has not yet been implemented in a working system. Thus, we have little empirical evidence concerning how this scheme behaves in a real expert system environment.

6.1 Contexts

The control scheme presented here is driven by **contexts**. A context is a generalized control data object, which is used to globally direct problem solving procedures. Each context can be thought of as a problem solving environment, consisting of a targeted problem to be solved, a view of working memory, and a set of attributes describing the context itself.

A context is similar, in many respects, to an explicit goal object (see section 4.2). Goals, however, are usually thought of as being organized in a particular fashion; that is, hierarchically organized sets of goals and subgoals, with explicit AND/OR relationships between siblings. Contexts are not constrained to this type of hierarchical structure, although they may be organized this way if desired.

Two types of contexts are required by our **Context-Driven Control Scheme** (CDCS). The first type will be referred to as a **GET** context. A GET context is used, conceptually, to represent a generalized condition. Thus, a GET context allows a CDCS program to access facts from the data base. For example, consider the following fragment:

```
GET =b such that
    :(is-a`=b battery)
    :(on-line =b (=t1 =t2))
```

This fragment is a GET context **descriptor**. The problem described by this GET context descriptor is to determine the set of possible values of the variable $=b$. The pattern-like conditions in the GET context descriptor are used to describe what sort of object $=b$ must be. Here, we are looking for a battery, which must be on line (that is, in operation in a power system) during some time interval $(=t1$ $=t2)$. Each pattern is preceded by a ':' to indicate that it is not a pattern in the traditional sense; as we will see later, these patterns are processed by the system in a slightly more complicated fashion.

When the fragment above is executed by the system, an instance of the described GET context is **invoked**. When a context is invoked, a specific problem to be solved is declared to the system. For example, an instance of the GET context described above may have the goal of finding all batteries which are on line in the time interval (186 192).

We will say that an instance of a GET context is **successful** if and only if at least one example of the object (or objects) specified in the context descriptor is found. Otherwise, the instance of the context is said to **fail**. Thus, a GET context descriptor has a boolean nature, which allows us to think of it as a generalized test to performed on the problem solving environment.

A **DO** context is used to represent a generalized action to be performed in the current problem solving environment. A DO context is similar in function to what would be, in more traditional algorithmic programming languages, a procedure call. For example, the fragment

```
DO (unschedule =load-name (=t1 =t2))
```

is a DO context descriptor. The variables in the context descriptor are used in a manner similar to variable parameters in a standard procedure invocation scheme. That is, they may have values at the time an instance of the DO context is created, and the values may be modified as a result of the execution of the DO context.

Together, GET and DO contexts provide the primitives required to represent the conditions and actions of standard IF-THEN rules. The antecedent of the rule is constructed using a series of GET contexts, which test features of working memory. The consequent is constructed using a series of DO contexts, which make changes to the current problem solving environment.

However, as we will soon see, contexts provide a much more powerful means for representing conditions and actions than is standardly possible, by virtue of the fact that they are manipulated by the proposed CDCS control mechanisms in an extremely powerful fashion.

6.2 Control Constructs

The context-driven control scheme advocated here provides the full range of primitive control constructs available in a traditional, block-structured programming language. Thus, a CDCS program is not strictly rule-based, in the traditional sense. It consists of a set of modular procedures, each of which might be thought of as a generalized rule.

In our proposed scheme, a GET context descriptor may be used in any situation where a condition is expected in a traditional, block structured program. Similarly, a DO contexts may be used whenever a statement to be executed is expected.

For example, the CDCS formalism might include an **IF-THEN-ELSE** construct, which may be used as follows:

```
IF  <GET-Context>
THEN  <DO-Context-1>
ELSE  <DO-Context-2>
```

This IF-THEN-ELSE fragment is executed by the system as follows. First, *<GET-Context>* is invoked, creating an instance of a GET context. If the GET context is successful, then *<DO-Context-1>* is invoked. On the other hand, if the GET context fails, then *<DO-Context-2>* is invoked.

Iteration can be explicitly represented in several ways. First, we might use one of the iterative constructs found in traditional, block structured programming languages, such as a **WHILE-DO** or **REPEAT-UNTIL** construct. For example, consider the following fragment:

```
REPEAT
   <DO-Context>
UNTIL  <GET-Context>
```

Here, the system invokes *<DO-Context>*. This may result in changes to working memory, or the modification of variable parameters in the instantiated DO context. Then, *<GET-Context>* is invoked. If it is successful, then execution of this fragment halts. Otherwise, the DO context is invoked again, and so on, until the GET context invoked is successful.

In addition, a generalized **FOR** construct, traditionally used to iterate over an enumerated type, is desirable. However, we must extend the definition of this control construct slightly, allowing iteration over the result of a GET context invocation. The resulting **FOR-EACH** control construct is used in the CDCS system as follows:

```
FOR-EACH  <GET-Context>
          <DO-Context>
```

This fragment is executed by the system as follows. First, *<GET-Context>* is invoked. If it fails, then execution halts. Otherwise, *<DO-Context>* is invoked once in the current problem solving environment for *each* solution to the GET context discovered by the system.

For example, consider the following CDCS program fragment:

```
Let =x be 0;
FOR-EACH =b such that
           :(is-a =b battery)
         DO Let =x be (=x + 1);
```

Here, traditional block-structured program statements are mingled with CDCS context descriptors. Thus, although GET and DO contexts *may* be used in place of traditional conditions and actions, the more traditional statements are still permitted. Also, note that the GET keyword in the *GET =b such that...* context description, although technically required, is assumed.

This program fragment is executed by the system as follows. First, the variable $=x$ is initialized. Then, the GET context is invoked, with the goal of determining all possible values for $=b$ such that $=b$ is a battery. For each battery found, the DO statement is executed, incrementing the value of $=x$. Thus, when the fragment has been completely executed, $=x$ is bound to the number of batteries in the problem solving environment.

Remember that when an instance of a GET or DO context is created, a problem to be solved is declared to the system. However, problems do not necessarily need to be solved when they are declared. For example, if several CDCS routines begin execution in parallel, one might result in the creation of a GET context, and one a DO context. The system must decide which of the currently active contexts should be executed.

For this reason, it is desirable to include some control constructs in the CDCS formalism which specify explicit relationships between contexts. For example, the **begin ... end** control construct might be used to indicate explicitly that a series of DO contexts (possibly intermingled with traditional programming statements and other control constructs) should be invoked sequentially. Similarly, the **par-begin ... par-end** construct might be used to indicate that a series of DO contexts may be invoked in parallel; that is, there is no ordering which must be imposed on the invocation of the various contexts.

We also need several logical operators which impose control relationships on GET contexts. These are as follows:

and (GET1 GET2 ... GETn)
> A boolean operator which returns true if all of the enclosed GET contexts are successful. The enclosed contexts may be invoked in parallel.

or (GET1 GET2 ... GETn)
> A boolean operator which returns true as soon as one of the enclosed GET contexts is successful. The enclosed contexts may be invoked in parallel.

cand (GET1 GET2 ... GETn)
> The conditional and operator. GET1 is invoked. If it does not succeed, then the entire expression returns false. Otherwise, GET2 is invoked, and so on. If all invoked contexts are successful, then the entire expression returns true.

cor (GET1 GET2 ... GETn)
> The conditional or operator. GET1 is invoked. If it succeeds, then the entire expression returns true. Otherwise, GET2 is invoked, and so on. If no invoked context is successful, then the entire expression returns false.

Note that, in each of the control constructs described here, the relationships between context specifications is explicit. However, the relationship is represented procedurally. Later, we will see that corresponding relationships between **instances** of contexts are also created. These will be represented declaratively.

One remaining control construct must be provided: subroutine invocation. The ability to call a subroutine from within a CDCS fragment is one of the most important capabilities to be provided. However, our formalism will not include an explicit invoke-subroutine construct. Instead, a more generalized method for subroutine invocation will be provided through the use of the TO control construct, to be described in the next section.

6.3 The TO Construct

The **TO** construct is also a control construct available in the CDCS formalism. However, it is in a different class than those discussed in the previous section. It is important enough to warrant a separate discussion.

The TO construct is used to specify relationships between contexts and CDCS procedures. It is used as follows:

TO <Context> <DO-Context>

Here, *<Context>* may be either a GET context or a DO context. The interpretation of a TO construct is as follows: one way that the problem described by the *<Context>* specification may be solved is by invoking the context described by *<DO-Context>*.

For example, consider the following procedure, which might be used in an expert system to perform energy management on board an automated space station (see [Lewy, Gohring, and Sauers, 1984]):

```
TO GET =x  such  that
         :(power-available (=t1 =t2) =x)
    DO begin
         Let =x be 0;
         FOR-EACH =p  such  that
                  :(is-a =p power-source)
                  :(power-provided =p (=t1 =t2) =x1)
         DO Let =x be (=x + =x1);
    end
```

This procedure is interpreted as follows. Suppose that we are trying to determine the power, $=x$, available to the spacecraft during some time interval *(=t1 =t2)*; that is, suppose a GET context matching the one in the above TO statement has already been invoked and is currently active.

Then, one way that $=x$ can be determined is to find each power source $=p$ such that $=p$ provides some amount of power, $=x1$, during the time interval in question. GET contexts may be invoked recursively, if necessary, to find the individual power sources and the amount of power provided by each one. Finally, we can sum the power provided by all of the power sources, and our original task has been successfully completed.

Thus, the TO construct in the above procedure serves to provide the system with information which is important in a specific, well-defined problem solving context. That is, a problem solving procedure has been associated with a particular problem solving task.

Several features of this procedure are important. First, note that the CDCS formalism used here allows the construction of algorithmic modules which are much more expressive than traditional IF-THEN rules. However, these procedures definitely exhibit rule-like behavior.

Second, the use of the TO control construct enables the system to easily determine in what problem solving situations this rule is applicable. In this way, the TO construct might be thought of as a higher level control construct, providing explicit control information which relates problem solving procedures to the tasks for which they are applicable.

Most importantly, note the combination of algorithmic and heuristic problem solving exhibited here. A simple algorithm can be used to solve the problem with which this rule is associated. Thus, the problem solving procedure provided is basically algorithmic in structure. However, some of the information required by this algorithm may not be readily available, and may be difficult to derive. The system is free to recursively invoke other problem solving contexts, thereby using other problem solving procedures to derive the missing data.

For example, suppose we did not know the power provided by a particular power source $=p$ in the desired time interval $(=t1\ =t2)$. Then, an instance of the GET context

```
GET  =x1  such  that
     :(power-provided  =p  (=t1  =t2)  =x1)
```

would be invoked. This allows us to determine the power available using other rules, such as the following:

```
IF  :(is-a  =s  solar-panel)
THEN  TO  GET  =x  such  that
          :(power-provided  =s  (=t1  =t2)  =x)
     DO   IF  :(night-time  (=t1  =t2))
          THEN  Let  =x  be  0
          ELSE  . . .
```

This rule is interpreted as follows. Suppose $=s$ is a solar panel. (Note that a GET context is again assumed, which allows us to determine whether or not $=s$ is a solar panel through the use of another problem solving procedure.) Then, to get the power provided by $=s$ during the time interval $(=t1\ =t2)$, we first check to see if that time interval occurs during the night. If the time interval is at night, then no power is provided by $=s$ (since solar panels require sunlight to produce power). Otherwise, etc. ...

Also, note that similar problem solving procedures may be provided to describe how to obtain the power provided by batteries, by regenerative fuel cells, and by any other type of power source which we might need to handle in our domain of expertise.

As demonstrated above, the TO construct can be used as if it was a more traditional program statement. Thus, it can called conditionally from within another control construct. We may, however, need to place some constraints on the use of TO constructs, for purposes of semantic consistency. For example, the fragment

```
TO GET =x such that ...
   DO TO GET =y such that ...
```

does not have a well-defined meaning. Literally, it might be read as follows: one way to get $=x$ such that some condition is true is to declare a method for obtaining $=y$ such that another set of conditions is true. The problem is that by declaring a problem solving procedure for $=y$, we have not directly addressed the solution of $=x$.

However, the meaning of the following rule fragment, which also has multiple TO constructs, *is* well-defined:

```
IF  :(is-a =p battery)
THEN TO GET =x such that
            :(power-provided =p (=t1 =t2) =x) ...
ELSE IF :(is-a =p solar-cell)
THEN TO GET =x such that
            :(power-provided =p (=t1 =t2) =x) ...
    . . .
```

This fragment is basically a CASE statement, which provides a method for determining the power provided by a power source based on the type of that power source. Thus, one constraint which seems to be necessary for semantic consistency is that a TO constructs may not be nested within another TO construct.

Finally, note that the use of the TO construct provides, in effect, a generalized subroutine invocation method. The instantiation of a context description can be thought of as calling a subroutine. Instead of naming the subroutine, the context description describes the *goal* of the subroutine invocation. The TO construct is used to define which subroutines can be used to solve the problem defined by the context description.

The important difference between our scheme and a more traditional subroutine calling scheme is that ours allows for heuristic selection of the actual procedure to be invoked. That is, a CDCS procedure can test features of the problem solving environment to determine which TO constructs (and, therefore, which subroutines) are most applicable in the current context. Without this capability, our formalism would not be adequate for expert system programming.

In summary, the TO construct provides a method of integrating algorithmic and heuristic reasoning processes. Furthermore, the TO construct allows us to explicitly represent all of the control knowledge relevant to a particular problem solving procedure in a single, highly modular rule. At the same time, we can easily escape to other procedures for the solution of problems which are not specifically addressed by the original procedure.

6.4 The Relationship between Contexts and Data

With the use of the TO construct, we now have two methods for solving a problem specified by a GET context. First, every data item in working memory which matches the GET context descriptor provides a solution to the problem associated with that context. For example, the data items

```
1. (is-a Battery-23 power-source)
2. (is-a Solar-Panel-2 power-source)
```

can be used to provide two possible solutions to the problem specified by the GET context descriptor

```
GET  =p  such  that
     :(is-a  =p  power-source)
```

In addition, each GET problem may be solved by a relevant rule. A rule may be relevant to a given GET context *only if* it contains a TO control construct whose context specification matches that GET context. (This condition may not be sufficient, since the TO construct may be contained in a branch of a conditional which is not reachable in the current problem solving environment.)

The fact that a rule cannot be relevant to the solution of a GET problem unless it is explicitly declared to be relevant may be a seemingly trivial point. However, as we will see in the next section, this is actually very important. In more traditional systems, it is often very difficult to determine whether or not a rule is relevant to the solution of a particular problem.

Now, when the problem specified by a GET context has been solved by a relevant rule, one side effect which may be desirable is to create a data item representing each solution. Thus, once the problem has been solved, it can now be solved again quickly by retrieving the solution from working memory.

On the other hand, this may not be desirable. In situations where the truth of a data item is likely to change frequently, we may want to impose the requirement that it be derived explicitly each time. Thus, our formalism may need to provide a means for making this an optional feature.

The major advantage of the automatic creation of data items derived as a result of solving a GET problem is that there is now a well-defined relationship between data items and the GET contexts used to derive them. From the user's point of view, tests which merely retrieve a data item from working memory are indistinguishable from tests which derive the data item using a problem solving procedure.

Thus, the invocation of a GET context can be used to derive a data item which is not represented explicitly. GET contexts are therefore used to trigger backward chaining reasoning.

In a similar way, the invocation of a DO context can be used to create data items by triggering forward chaining reasoning. TO DO X, the system may apply a procedure which is applicable to X. In the absence of such a procedure, we assume that to DO X, we merely assert X in the current problem solving environment.

By this time, it has probably become apparent that many contexts may be active simultaneously. Whenever this occurs, there is always danger of two contexts resulting in the assertion of conflicting data items. In many cases, uncertain reasoning, rather than a programming error, may be the cause of a seemingly contradictory situation. Since we want our system to operate properly in heuristic problem solving environments, we must be able to handle such inconsistencies.

Recall that we initially claimed that a context represented a problem solving environment, including a view of the data in working memory. If we take this view seriously, then the result of the invocation of a context is not *merely* a set of derivable data items; the invocation of a context really serves to identify a new set of possible problem solving environments.

Thus, we can ensure that consistency is maintained between contexts by having each operate in its own problem solving environment. Whenever the invocation of a context results in more than one solution, we can spawn multiple problem solving environments.

For example, consider the following fragment:

```
IF     :(is-a =p power-source)
       :(power-provided =p (=t1 =t2) =x1)
THEN DO Let =x be (=x + =x1);
```

Suppose also that *=t1* and *=t2* are bound to *186* and *192* respectively. Then, the evaluation of the IF construct may require the invocation of the GET context

```
GET =p such that
    :(is-a =p power-source)
    :(power-provided =p (186 192) =x1)
```

Now, if it can be determined that

```
1.  (is-a Battery-23 power-source)
2.  (power-provided Battery-23 (186 192) 24)
3.  (is-a Solar-Panel-2 power-source)
4.  (power-provided Solar-Panel-2 (186 192) 0),
```

then two problem solving environments result: one in which the power source is *Battery-23*, and one in which the power source is *Solar-Cell-2*. The *Let* statement in the above fragment is then executed twice, once in each problem solving environment:

```
Let =x be (=x + 24), and
Let =x be (=x + 0).
```

In addition to showing the relationship between contexts and data, this example also demonstrates the importance of the FOR-EACH construct. In the fragment above, our intent was probably to assign $=x$ the total value of all power provided. Thus, assigning $=x$ two different values in two different problem solving contexts does not achieve the desired result. In this example, what we really wanted was

```
FOR-EACH =p such that
          :(is-a =p power-source)
          :(power-provided =p (=t1 =t2) =x1)
    DO Let =x be (=x + =x1);
```

Recall that the FOR-EACH statement allows the execution of the DO statement repeatedly in a single problem solving environment. Thus, this achieves the desired effect.

Even with the use of the FOR-EACH statement, we may need to spawn multiple problem solving contexts in order to maintain consistency. For example, suppose that we have two methods for estimating the power provided by a solar cell, resulting in the following two possible data items:

```
(power-provided Solar-Cell-2 (186 192) 0)
(power-provided Solar-Cell-2 (186 192) 3)
```

In this case, there are two problem solving environments resulting from the execution of the FOR-EACH statement: one in which *Solar-Cell-2* contributes *0* to the value of $=x$, and one in which it contributes *3* to the value of $=x$.

Thus, consistency between data items and contexts may be maintained through the creation of multiple contexts. Maintaining multiple contexts, however, is potentially resource expensive (see section 2.7). Each time a new context is spawned, the amount of search which must be performed by the system is increased.

There are, however, methods which we can use to decrease the number of contexts which must be considered. For example, if a GET context is invoked which eventually fails, then its parent context (that is, the one from which it was spawned) may also fail. Failure may be a result of the absence of a problem solving procedure to handle a given situation. Alternatively, we may want to allow CDCS procedures to explicitly force failure.

For a further discussion of the expected efficiency of a CDCS implementation, as it relates to the cost of the context mechanism, see section 7.

6.5 Further Examples

This section presents some additional examples of rules written in the proposed CDCS formalism. These examples show how some of the familiar problems we have encountered in our discussion of control methodologies can be avoided through the use of CDCS control constructs.

First, let us examine the problem of recognizing special case relationships between rules (see section 2.6). Recall the following example:

```
Rule1:                              Rule2:
    IF     ( a  =x  =y )                IF     ( a  =x  =y )
           ( b  =x  =y )                       ( b  =x  =y )
           ( c  =x  =y )             THEN ( e  =x  =y )
    THEN ( d  =x  =y )
```

Here, it important that, for purposes of extensibility, the system be able to recognize that *Rule1* is a special case of *Rule2*. However, if *Rule1* is changed, *Rule2* must also be changed. Therefore, the system is not completely modular in either case.

This special case relationship can be represented explicitly using our CDCS formalism, as follows:

```
IF  : ( a  =x  =y )
    : ( b  =x  =y )
THEN  begin
        IF  : ( c  =x  =y )
        THEN  : ( d  =x  =y )
        ELSE  : ( e  =x  =y )
      end
```

In addition to explicitly representing the relationship between the two rules, this fragment avoids the problem of having to duplicate modifications across rules. The most important advantage to this scheme, however, is that it does not depend on rule ordering for correctness. If the c data item does not yet exist, but can be derived through the use of another rule, then the GET context invoked to derive c will be successful, and our rule still works correctly. In purely forward chaining systems, we must be able to guarantee, somehow, that the c rule is appled first.

This is related to another important point. In a purely forward chaining system, it is often difficult to determine when a rule is relevant to the solution of a given problem. For example, a rule R_2 may be relevant to the solution of a problem P, but may not be applicable because of the fact that a critical data item d is missing. Thus, the application of rule R_1, which is seemingly irrelevant to P, may actually be relevant if it creates d, therefore enabling the application of R_2. In other words, R_2 may be applied towards P only if R_1 and R_2 are applied in the correct sequence.

In our system, this problem does not arise. If R_2 is relevant to some context P, and data item d is missing, then R_1 may be applied in the context P', which was created with the explicit goal of solving the problem of deriving d.

Thus, declaring that R_1 is relevant to P' is sufficient for our purposes, since we know that P' is related to P in a well-defined manner. The combination of forward and backward chaining reasoning which we have provided makes it easy to determine when a rule is relevant to the solution of a problem.

Also, note that the **negation vs. absence** problem (see section 2.6) disappears in our system. Consider the following rule fragment:

```
IF  (not  :(c  =x  =y))
       .   .   .
```

Here, falsehood of the c data item can never be confused with the absence of c in the case that it is true, but has not yet been derived. If we do not know that *(c =x =y)* is true, the a GET context is invoked with the goal of deriving the missing data item. If c is merely absent (as opposed to false), it is derived in a backward chaining fashion. The rule functions exactly the same as if the data item had already been derived beforehand.

In our system, semantic special case relations are just as easily represented as syntactic ones. For example, consider the following rule fragment:

```
IF     :(is-a  =x  bird)
THEN begin
        IF     :(is-a  =x  penguin)
        THEN  :(waddles  =x)
        ELSE  :(flies  =x)
     end
```

Here, again, the correctness of our rule does not depend on the ability to derive the *penguin* data item beforehand.

One slightly more complex example is in order. In section 6.4, we saw an example of a rule used to determine the power provided by a solar cell in some given time interval. We claimed that, in order to extend the system to handle a new type of power source, we merely had to add an additional rule which specifies how to get the power provided by a power source of that type.

Now, there are probably many different characteristics of the new type of power source which may need to be determined. For example, we may need to determine the current drawn from the power source, the expected lifetime of the power source, etc. Thus, the likelihood is high that, when we first extend the rule base, we forget to add a rule to perform one of the required functions.

Suppose, then, we know that

$$(i s - a \ New-Power-Source-1 \ power-source),$$

but that we forget to add a rule which allows us to calculate the power provided by a power source of type *New-Power-Source*. What happens to the operation of the following rule, which calculates total power provided?

```
Let =x be 0;
FOR-EACH =p such that
         :(is-a =p power-source)
         :(power-provided =p (=t1 =t2) =x1)
      DO Let =x be (=x + =x1);
```

Here, the GET context invoked to determine the power provided by *New-Power-Source-1* fails; thus, it does not affect the value of $=x$, and is therefore is treated as if it does not provide power.

This may be a difficult bug to find. Since we want our system to be readily extendible, we may want to write a rule which recognizes the fact that there exists a power source with no method which can be used to derive the amount of power it provides. This rule would warn the user of the error situation, and is therefore extremely useful to a programmer assigned the task of extending our power management expert system to include a new power source.

Our error handling rule might be written as follows:

```
IF  :(is-a =p power-source)
     (not :(power-provided =p (=t1 =t2) =x))
THEN TO GET =x such that
          :(power-provided =p (=t1 =t2) =x)
     DO begin
          write("Can't get power provided: " =p);
          fail();
        end;
```

This rule is interpreted as follows. If $=p$ is a power source, but the power provided by $=p$ cannot be derived using any method currently known by the system, then if we are trying to derive the power provided by $=p$, enable a new problem solving method. This new method warns the user that a problem exists, and then causes the current problem solving context to fail. Thus, we still can't derive the power provided, but the user has at least been warned.

Note that this new method for determining the power provided by a power source is not enabled if there is an existing method which is successful. Thus, it is impossible for this rule to interfere with existing problem solving methods. It is treated as a rule to be used only as a last resort. At the same time, we are guaranteed that this method is enabled whenever the error situation occurs. Finally, if we never need to know the power provided by a power source missing a power provided rule, then this rule is never applied.

Thus, in summary, it appears that many of the problems we have seen in our investigation of control mechanisms have already been avoided in our newly proposed control scheme. Although this section provides a mere handful of examples, they were not contrived. Thus, they do serve to demonstrate the utility of the CDCS formalism.

6.6 Selecting Contexts

So far, we have discussed the algorithmic control constructs provided in the CDCS formalism, and have introduced the notion of context invocation. In this section, the process by which the system selects contexts for problem solving is described.

In the course of executing a statement in a CDCS procedure, a GET or a DO context descriptor may be encountered. This usually requires that an instance of the context be created by the system interpreter. In this case, we say that the context is *invoked*.

We have briefly described the invocation of a context as the declaration to the system of a new problem to be solved (see section 6.1). The invocation of a context does not, however, require that the problem associated with the context be solved immediately. Instead, the context is manipulated by the **context selection** mechanism, which is responsible for deciding which contexts should be pursued at any given time.

A context is, itself, a data object. Contexts may be described in memory by a set of **control attributes**. These attributes may then be used by the context selection mechanism in order to guide control decisions. We want control attributes to be explicitly represented, so that they are accessible to both the system interpreter, and the expert system application programmer. Our first task, then, is to specify how contexts are described in the CDCS formalism.

When a context is invoked, a new data object is created, representing a new instance of that context descriptor. For example, when the context descriptor

```
GET =x such that
    :(power-provided =p (=t1 =t2) =x)
```

is encountered, the context data object

```
(c0132 GET (power-provided Battery-23 (186 192) =x))
```

might be created. In addition, several important characteristics of the context are described at the time it is created. For example,

```
(is-a c0132 context)
```

may be created. Note that, in the current conception of the system, these data items are inserted in working memory, just as if they were ordinary domain-level data items. This is so that they may be explicitly accessed and manipulated by rules using precisely the same mechanisms used for domain-level data.

Another important attribute of every context is its **status**. When a context is first invoked, it has status **pending**. Thus,

```
(status c0132 pending)
```

would be created. The status of a context may be changed over time. At least the following status values must be recognized by the system:

pending: A context whose status is pending has been created through the instantiation of a context descriptor. However, no decision to select the context has yet been made. If a context may not yet be activated, then its status is not yet pending. For example, if context C_2 is invoked conditionally on the success of C_1, then C_2 is not pending until C_1 succeeds.

active: A context whose status is active has been selected for problem solving. Only when a context is active may rules be selected to be applied towards that context. Several contexts may be active simultaneously, which means that problem solving is currently being performed in each context. (Note that the system does not necessarily have to activate two contexts which are *permitted* parallel execution.)

successful: A context whose status is successful corresponds to a problem which has been solved. Only an active context may become successful.

failed: A context whose status is failed corresponds to a problem which we were not able to solve. Only an active context may become failed.

suspended: A context whose status is suspended has not yet been declared a success or a failure. However, problem solving is no longer permitted in this context. Suspension is intended to be a temporary status. It is useful in situations where the invocation of a proposed context of high priority requires that currently active contexts be interrupted. Only an active context may become suspended.

cancelled: A context whose status is cancelled has not yet been declared a success or a failure. However, problem solving in that context is no longer required. For example, if we must solve either problem *A or* problem *B*, then when *A* is solved, *B* might be cancelled.

Other data items are automatically created at context invocation time to describe relationships between contexts. For example:

```
(cand c0342 c0343)
(cand c0343 c0344)
```

The system describes invoked contexts explicitly in this fashion so that control information is available for manipulation by rules in the application domain.

In addition, we have seen that domain specific control knowledge is often important in selecting problems to be solved. Thus, our formalism must allow the programmer to explicitly describe domain specific characteristics a newly invoked context, at the time it is created. This may be done through the use of the **with** qualifier, as demonstrated in the following fragment:

```
GET  =x  with  :(context-priority  =C  low)
                :(total-permitted-resources  =C  =sum)
        such  that
                :(power-provided  =p  (=t1  =t2)  =x)
```

Here, the variable $=C$ is meant to be bound automatically to the instance of the GET context being invoked. The data items described by the **with** keyword are programmer defined. They will be local to the newly created context, are meant strictly for the purpose of making domain specific control decisions. Thus, when an instance of the above context descriptor is invoked, the following data items might be created:

```
(c8450 GET (power-provided Battery-23 (186 192) =x))
(is-a c8450 context)
(status c8450 pending)
(context-priority c8450 low)
(total-permitted-resources c8450 18)
```

Now, we have a scheme for explicitly representing attributes of contexts in such a way that they may be manipulated by CDCS procedures defined by the programmer. Some control attributes are user-defined; others are inherent to the system.

In order for the system-defined control attributes to be useful to the programmer, we must assign **semantics** to the individual data items. That is, system-defined control attributes have a specific meaning, by virtue of the fact that they are used by the system in a particular way. The application programmer, who knows the semantics of the control attribute data items, can explicitly manipulate the interpreter's control mechanisms by asserting new control knowledge.

For example, suppose we impose the following semantic constraint on the use of **status** data items: problem solving can be performed on a given context C if and only if

```
(status C active)
```

is true in the current problem solving environment. Both the system interpreter and the programmer abide by this convention. Thus, if the interpreter activates a particular context for problem solving, the programmer is informed of this through the assertion of the appropriate status data item. In the same way, the programmer can inform the interpreter that a given context should be activated by asserting that the status of the context is active.

The most important question concerning context selection still remains: given the explicit representation in memory of contexts and their control attributes, how does the programmer manipulate this control knowledge in order to tailor the control scheme to the needs of a particular application?

The key here is that the system manipulates control information in exactly the same way that the programmer manipulates domain level data items. Thus, when the interpreter wants to find the set of currently active contexts, a GET context is invoked, whose goal is to determine the set of contexts whose status is active:

```
GET =C such that
  :(status =C active)
```

This is extremely important, since the programmer now has a well-defined means for communication with the internal control mechanisms. For example, consider the following subroutine:

```
IF  :(not (status =any-context active))
THEN TO GET =C such that
            :(status =C active)
      DO FOR-EACH =C such that
                  :(status =C pending)
        DO begin
            :(not (status =C pending))
            :(status =C active)
          end
```

This rule is interpreted as follows. If there does not currently exist a context whose status is active, then to get the set of active contexts, simply find and activate all pending contexts.

Several characteristics of this rule are important. First, note that it is easy for the expert system programmer to define context selection procedures to be integrated into the existing control framework. Communication between the interpreter and the programmer is well-defined. In addition, new control procedures are defined using precisely those control constructs which are ordinarily used to manipulate object-level knowledge.

Second, it is easy for the programmer to specify exactly in which problem solving situations the new control rules are applicable. In the above example, the new control procedure is used *only* when there is no currently active context, and the system interpreter is trying to find new ones.

Remember that the test to see whether or not there is currently an active context behaves exactly as do all other CDCS conditions. If we know of a context whose status is active, this rule may not be applied. Otherwise, we create a GET context to try and derive the set of active contexts in a backward chaining fashion. If there are no other rules which can activate a context, then the THEN clause of this rule is executed, enabling us to activate all pending contexts.

Thus, not only is the relationship between the new context selection rule and the interpreter well-defined; the relationship to other domain-specific control rules which activate contexts is also well-defined. And, finally, note that none of this depends on any sort of conflict resolution procedure for correctness.

As another example, consider the following rule:

```
IF  :(status =C pending)
    :(context-priority =C high)
THEN begin
     FOR-EACH =activeC such that
              :(status =activeC active)
              :(not (context-priority =activeC high))
       DO begin
              :(not (status =activeC active))
              :(status =activeC suspended)
          end
    :(not (status =C pending))
    :(status =C active)
    end
```

This rule may be interpreted as follows: if a context with high priority is pending (that is, if it has just been invoked), then suspend all currently active contexts whose priority is not high, and activate the pending context.

Here, the context-priority data items are domain specific, and were defined by the programmer. Each context may be assigned a priority at the time it is created. (This is done with the use of the **with** qualifier, described previously in this section.) Note that domain dependent control attributes are easily integrated into the existing control scheme, in the same way that system-defined control attributes were handled in the previous example.

Also, notice that this rule is not tied to a particular context with the use of a TO statement; thus, it is relevant across contexts, and will allow high priority contexts to act as if they were interrupts. (Actually, this rule is relevant to the null context; see section 6.7.)

In summary, our proposed context-driven control scheme includes a well-defined method for the representation of domain-specific control information. This information can be expressed in two forms: as control attributes, which are used to describe characteristics of contexts, and as rules representing context selection procedures. Control rules are specified in a manner which is totally consistent with the representation of object-level rules. They are therefore easily expressed by the expert system programmer, and are easily integrated into the domain independent control framework provided by the system.

6.7 The Activation/Execution Cycle

Now that we have described the method by which control information is manipulated by the programmer, we are ready to examine the internal CDCS control mechanism. The system executes a sequence of what we will refer to as **activation/execution** cycles, as follows:

[1]   Activate the **null** context.

This initializes the control mechanisms. All rules which are not explicitly attached to a context (with the TO statement) are relevant to the null context. The null context is always active (this cannot be changed by the programmer).

[2] Determine the set of rules relevant to active contexts.

Associated with each rule is a set of **execution states**. Each execution state is basically a link between a rule and a problem solving environment, plus a pointer to the current statement being executed in the rule.

Initially, every rule has exactly one execution state: execution begins at the start of the rule, and the problem solving environment is the null context.

A particular execution state of a rule is relevant to the current problem solving process if the next statement to be executed is not a context descriptor (since it is then relevant to the null context), or if the next statement is a TO statement whose context description matches a currently active context.

[3] Execute relevant rules in the contexts for which they are relevant.

Each rule execution state which is relevant is executed; no conflict resolution is performed. (This is discussed further below.) Each execution state specifies both the problem solving environment to be used, and the statement at which to begin execution. Execution continues until the next context description requiring context invocation is encountered. At this point, the execution state is updated and suspended. Thus, the pointer to the next statement to be executed in each execution state is really a link to the context invocation which caused the execution state to be suspended.

In the case where a rule can be executed to completion without encountering a new context invocation, the problem solving context associated with the execution context is declared successful. Working memory is updated to reflect this. Now, we return to the rule execution state which caused the invocation of the successful context. A new execution state is created for each solution to the successfully solved problem. Each of the new execution states is, in turn, executed, in a forward fashion, until suspended or successful.

[4]   Invoke new contexts.

Each execution state suspended in step 3 has provided us with a new context to be invoked. After all execution has been completed, the system instantiates all context descriptors which need to be invoked. In addition, the attributes of each new context are described in working memory (see section 6.6). Remember that when a new context is invoked, it is given the **pending** status. Also note that there are no longer any rules which can be executed in the currently active contexts.

[5]   Activate a new context to determine the set of active contexts.

As described in section 6.6, the system creates a new instance of the following GET context descriptor:

```
GET =C such that
    :(status =C active)
```

However, this context is immediately given an active status. Thus, it is the only active status for which rules may be applicable on the next cycle.

[6]   Repeat at step 2.

Thus, we determine the set of rules applicable to the task of activating contexts, then execute them. This results in a new set of active contexts, which enable new rules on the next cycle, and so on.

In order for this to work correctly, we must rely on the fact that the system has a set of default rules which are used to activate contexts in the absence of domain-specific rules. For example, we may want to first activate contexts whose status is suspended, followed by contexts whose status is pending, etc.

This process continues until no further contexts can be activated, and no rules may be executed in the currently active contexts.

Although this control mechanism is more complex than that found in most traditional systems, it allows for well-defined communication between the system interpreter and the rule base.

Furthermore, note that we have chosen to execute all applicable rules, completely eliminating the standard conflict resolution process. As previously discussed, the ability to sprout multiple problem solving contexts allows us to do this, while at the same time maintaining internal consistency (see section 6.4).

In addition, throughout our discussion of the CDCS control scheme, we have seen examples of the coordination of rules with each other and with the problem solving process (see especially sections 6.4 through 6.6). All of the functions standardly provided through conflict resolution are provided elsewhere in our system. Thus, we are able to guarantee that rules are applied correctly without the use of conflict resolution.

Finally, the control mechanisms we have provided in the CDCS formalism seem to work better at imposing control on the rule base than do the other methods we have seen for selecting among rules. Thus, the decision to apply all relevant rules in each problem solving situation appears to be justified.

7 CONCLUDING REMARKS

A new control architecture for the development of rule-based expert systems has been proposed. This architecture is driven by explicitly represented control objects known as **contexts**.

The proposed context-driven control architecture has several important features. First, it stresses the importance of the explicit representation of control knowledge, in both declarative and procedural forms.

In addition, the CDCS formalism provides sophisticated facilities for the representation of domain-specific control knowledge. The expert system application programmer may define control procedures which tailor the control scheme to the needs of each task. This control knowledge is represented in a manner which is completely consistent with the representation of object-level knowledge. The interface between the internal control mechanisms and the domain-specific control mechanisms is well defined, facilitating the integration of new control procedures.

Finally, the CDCS formalism provides an integrated scheme for the representation of both algorithmic and heuristic problem solving procedures. Problem solving is algorithmic in well-structured problem areas. Heuristic reasoning can be used where algorithms are not appropriate.

The CDCS architecture imposes modularity on the individual rules in the rule base. It has been shown that this modularity promotes the extensibility of the system. At the same time, the control mechanisms provided by the formalism are powerful enough to impose structure on the rule base, without sacrificing modularity. Thus, the proposed control scheme seems to satisfy the requirements we have identified for a system which allows for the rapid development of expert systems which are both correct and easily extendible.

Since the proposed CDCS control scheme has not yet been implemented, and has not been used in the development of a real expert system, many of the ideas presented here are merely speculative. Thus, one obvious direction for further research is the development of a simulated CDCS system. This will allow the utility of the representation formalism to be thoroughly tested, and will provide empirical evidence concerning the degree to which our assumptions about the use of the CDCS mechanisms were correct.

We also need evidence concerning the real-time performance of a system using the CDCS formalism. The ability to represent and manipulate many contexts simultaneously is critical to the operation of a CDCS system. In addition, we have seen that other systems which provide this type of capability are impractical due to efficiency considerations. System performance is one of the major outstanding issues concerning the CDCS system which must still be addressed.

However, we must remember that the CDCS formalism is characteristically different from most backtracking systems which require the representation of multiple problem solving environments. Rules in the CDCS formalism are expressed on a much larger grain size than is possible in traditional systems; thus, it is expected that the CDCS formalism will result in a much smaller rule base.

In addition, rules in the CDCS formalism are highly constrained, in that the problem solving context in which they are relevant is explicitly defined. This means that the number of rules which must be considered for application in any given problem solving context is relatively small.

Thus, there is evidence which leads us to believe that efficiency of the targeted CDCS system is not a problem which will prevent the practical application of the formalism in real systems.

In conclusion, research in the area of control has provided much insight into the design and development of rule-based Expert Systems. The context-driven scheme proposed here is promising, in that it appears to provide solid solutions to many of the problems which programmers must face in the development of expert application systems. If the utility of the CDCS formalism is confirmed, then we will have greatly decreased the level of effort required to develop and maintain Expert Systems which operate correctly in real problem solving situations.

Acknowledgments

Some of the ideas which led to the development of the control scheme proposed here have been derived from several other research efforts. The author would like to thank the following individuals involved in these efforts: Rob Farrell and the members of John Anderson's research team at Carnegie-Mellon University involved in the GRAPES project; Jonathan Bein and others in the Artificial Intelligence Unit at Martin Marietta Denver Aerospace who have either worked on or put up with the HAPS project.

The author would also like to thank Brigham Bell and Jonathan Bein for comments on a previous draft of this manuscript. Last, but certainly not least, go thanks to Victoria for tolerating all of this.

References

Aikins, J. S., "Prototypes and Production Rules: An Approach to Knowledge Representation for Hypothesis Formation", in *Proceedings of the Sixth International Joint Conference on Artificial Intelligence*, 1979.

Aikins, J. S., "Representation of Control Knowledge in Expert Systems", in *Proceedings of the First National Conference on Artificial Intelligence*, 1980.

Allen, B. P., and J. M. Wright, "Integrating Logic Programs and Schemata", in *Proceedings of the Eighth International Joint Conference on Artificial Intelligence*, 1983.

Balzer, R., L. Erman, P. London, and C. Williams, "Hearsay III: A Domain-Independent Framework for Expert Systems", in *Proceedings of the First National Conference on Artificial Intelligence*, 1980.

Barnett, J. A., "How Much is Control Knowledge Worth?: A Primitive Example", in *Artificial Intelligence* 22:1, pp. 77-89, 1984.

Clancey, W. J., *The Advantages of Abstract Control Knowledge in Expert System Design*, Technical Report STAN-CS-83-995, Department of Computer Science, Stanford University, 1983.

Davis, R., *Applications of Meta-Level Knowledge to the Construction, Maintenance, and Use of Large Knowledge Bases*, Technical Memo HPP-76-7, Heuristic Programming Project, Stanford University, 1976.

Davis, R., "Interactive Transfer of Expertise: Acquisition of New Inference Rules", in *Proceedings of the Fifth International Joint Conference on Artificial Intelligence*, 1977.

Davis, R., "Knowledge Acquisition in Rule-Based Systems: Knowledge about Representations as a Basis for System Construction and Maintenance", in *Pattern-Directed Inference Systems*, D. A. Waterman and F. Hayes-Roth (eds.), Academic Press, New York, 1978.

Davis, R., and B. G. Buchanan, "Meta-Level Knowledge: Overview and Applications", in *Proceedings of the Fifth International Joint Conference on Artificial Intelligence,* 1977.

de Kleer, J., J. Doyle, G. L. Steele, and G. J. Sussman, *Explicit Control of Reasoning,* Technical Memo 427, Massachusetts Institute of Technology, Artificial Intelligence Laboratory, 1977.

Doyle, J., "A Truth Maintenance System", in *Artificial Intelligence* 12, 231-272, 1979.

Doyle, J., "The Ins and Outs of Reason Maintenance", in *Proceedings of the Eighth International Joint Conference on Artificial Intelligence,* 1983.

Erman, L. D., F. Hayes-Roth, V. R. Lesser, and D. R. Reddy, "The Hearsay II Speech Understanding System: Integrating Knowledge to Resolve Uncertainty", in *Computing Surveys* 12:2, 1980.

Erman, L. D., P. E. London, and S. F. Fickas, "The Design and an Example Use of Hearsay-III", in *Proceedings of the Seventh International Joint Conference on Artificial Intelligence,* 1981.

Forgy, C. L., *On the Efficient Implementation of Production Systems,* Ph.D. Thesis, Department of Computer Science, Carnegie-Mellon University, 1979.

Forgy, C., *OPS4 User's Manual,* Technical Report CMU-CS-79-132, Department of Computer Science, Carnegie-Mellon University, 1979.

Forgy, C., *OPS5 User's Manual,* Technical Report CMU-CS-81-132, Department of Computer Science, Carnegie-Mellon University, 1981.

Forgy, C., "Rete: A Fast Algorithm for the Many Pattern/ Many Object Pattern Match Problem", in *Artificial Intelligence* 19: 17-37, 1982.

Forgy, C., and J. McDermott, "OPS, A Domain-Independent Production System Language", in *Proceedings of the Fifth International Joint Conference on Artificial Intelligence,* 1977.

Georgeff, M. P., "A Framework for Control in Production Systems", in *Proceedings of the Sixth International Joint Conference on Artificial Intelligence,* 1979.

Georgeff, M. P., "Procedural Control in Production Systems", in *Artificial Intelligence* 18, 1982.

Georgeff, M., and U. Bonollo, "Procedural Expert Systems", in *Proceedings of the Eighth International Joint Conference on Artificial Intelligence,* 1983.

Hopcroft, J. E., and J. D. Ullman, *Introduction to Automata Theory, Languages, and Computation,* Addison-Wesley, Reading, Mass., 1979.

Lenat, D. B., and J. McDermott, "Less than General Production System Architectures", in *Proceedings of the Fifth International Joint Conference on Artificial Intelligence,* 1977.

Lewy, D., J. Gohring, and R. Sauers, "EMES: An Expert System for Spacecraft Energy Management", in *Proceedings of the Second Conference on Artificial Intelligence,* Oakland University, Rochester, Michigan, 1984.

McDermott, J., "R1: A Rule-Based Configurer of Computer Systems", in *Artificial Intelligence* 19: 39-88, 1982.

McDermott, J.M., and C. Forgy, "Production System Conflict Resolution Strategies", in *Pattern Directed Inference Systems,* D. A. Waterman and F. Hayes-Roth (eds.), Academic Press, New York, 1978.

Reinstein, H. C., and J. S. Aikins, "Application Design: Issues in Expert System Architecture", in *Proceedings of the Seventh International Joint Conference on Artificial Intelligence,* 1981.

Rychener, M. D., "A Semantic Network of Production Rules in a System for Describing Computer Structures", in *Proceedings of the Sixth International Joint Conference on Artificial Intelligence,* 1979.

Rychener, M. D., "Approaches to Knowledge Acquisition: The Instructable Production System Project", in *Proceedings of the First Annual National Conference on Artificial Intelligence,* 1980.

Rychener, M. D., "Control Requirements for the Design of Production System Architectures", *SIGART Newsletter* 64, 1977.

Sauers, R., and R. Farrell, *GRAPES User's Manual,* Technical Report ONR-82-3, Department of Psychology, Carnegie-Mellon University, 1982.

Sauers, R., and R. Walsh, "On the Requirements of Future Expert Systems", in *Proceedings of the Eighth International Joint Conference on Artificial Intelligence,* 1983.

Terry, A., *The CRYSALIS Project: Hierarchical Control of Production Systems,* Technical Memo HPP-83-19, Department of Computer Science, Stanford University, 1983.

Winograd, T., *Language as a Cognitive Process, Volume One: Syntax,* Addison-Wesley, Reading, Mass., 1983.

A Quantitative Approach to Approximate Reasoning in Rule-based Expert Systems*

Henri Prade

Langages et Systèmes Informatiques
Université Paul Sabatier
31062 Toulouse Cedex, France

ABSTRACT

This paper is divided in two main parts. The first one deals with the modeling of uncertainty and imprecision, while the second one is devoted to deductive inferences and to the problem of combining items of information, in case of imprecision or uncertainty. Together with probability, different kinds of uncertainty measures (credibility and plausibility functions in the sense of Shafer, possibility measures in the sense of Zadeh and the dual measures of necessity) are introduced in a unified way. The more empirical proposal used in the MYCIN expert system for dealing with uncertainty is also closely considered. The modeling of imprecise or vague information by means of possibility distributions is presented. The relation between imprecision and uncertainty in terms of possibility and necessity is also discussed as well as the notion of a degree of truth and the truth-qualification of propositions. Then, in the framework of possibility theory the representation of imprecise or fuzzy "if ..., then ..." rules and their processing by means of a generalized modus ponens are studied in detail. The particular case of uncertain rules is addressed in the same setting, and some default reasoning issues are considered. Different problems of reasoning which are specific of the treatment of uncertain information, without being dependent on a particular approach, are pointed out. In particular, it is shown that the combination of uncertain or imprecise items of information provided by different reliable sources, is not always suitable. Lastly, the Dempster/Shafer rule of combination as well as a possibilistic rule are examined. On the whole a computational approach to approximate reasoning based on   recently developed theoretical tools, is proposed.

I - INTRODUCTION

A part of the human knowledge we have to represent and to manipulate in engineering applications, such as expert systems, is often uncertain, pervaded with fuzziness (if its expression involves vague predicates) and incomplete. Indeed, during the last few years there has been an increasing interest in developing representation techniques and inference procedures capable of accommodating uncertainty. For a long ti-

---

* This paper gathers, develops and unifies results previously presented in other papers
  by the author (Prade, 1983, 1985c, 1984b, 1985a,b).

me, the Bayesian model had been the only numerical approach to inference with uncertainty, if we except the patterns of plausible reasoning analyzed by Pólya (1954) where neither any quantification nor formal treatment appear. Many researchers in Artificial Intelligence have felt a need for alternatives of the standard Bayesian approach (see Szolovits, Pauker, 1978 ; Sage, Botta, 1983, for a discussion) and have proposed and used (generally with success) empirically-based models, particularly in expert systems such as MYCIN (Shortliffe, Buchanan, 1975), PROSPECTOR (Duda, Gaschnig, Hart, 1981), CASNET (Weiss, Kulikowski, Amarel, Safir, 1978), SPERIL (Ishizuka, Fu, Yao, 1981b; Ishizuka, Fu, Yao, 1982b) (see also Weiss, Kulikowski, 1979 ; Lesser, Reed, Pavlin, 1980 ; Michalski, Chilausky, 1980 ; Friedman, 1980 ; Friedman, 1981 ; Kayser, 1979 ; Schefe, 1979). Non-quantitative approaches have been also designated for dealing with different kinds of uncertainty or imprecision, especially default reasoning (Reiter, 1980 ; Moore, 1983), non-monotonic reasoning (Mc Carthy, 1980 ; Mc Dermott, Doyle, 1980), and qualitative reasoning (Hayes, 1979 ; De Kleer, 1984 ; see also Cohen, 1985 ; Doyle, 1983b). In the same time, several mathematical models of uncertainty, which depart from the usual probability approach, have been recently proposed, particularly Shafer's belief theory (Shafer, 1976) and Zadeh's possibility theory (Zadeh, 1978a), whose favor is becoming recently increasing in Artificial Intelligence.

In the following, we try to present a synthetic view of most of the quantitative approaches which have been proposed. The paper is organized in two main parts. The first one is devoted to an unified presentation of the different mathematical approaches of uncertainty, including Shafer's belief theory, Zadeh's possibility and fuzzy set theories, and probability theory. The MYCIN model is also discussed in this framework. The second part is devoted to approximate and plausible reasoning, where patterns of deductive inferences with uncertain or imprecise premises and the problem of combining several uncertain or imprecise evidences relative to a same matter, are studied in great detail. With these results in hand, the propagation and the combination of uncertainty and imprecision in expert systems can be dealt with even if some open questions remain. A bibliography on Artificial Intelligence-oriented treatments of uncertainty is appended.

II - REPRESENTING UNCERTAINTY AND IMPRECISION
IN A COMMON FRAMEWORK

In this paper, the following distinction is made between uncertainty and imprecision. A propostion is regarded as uncertain as long as its truth (or its falsity) cannot be established with respect to the available information ; a proposition, whose contents state the value of some variable, is imprecise if this value is not sufficiently determined with respect to a given scale. Note that a precise proposition may be uncertain and a proposition, which is completely certain, may be imprecise.

1 - MODELING UNCERTAINTY

According to vocabulary several points of view should exist for estimating the uncertainty of a proposition specifying some possible event ; for instance, it may be somewhat probable, plausible, credible, possible or necessary (i.e. certain). Different mathematical theories have been proposed, some of them recently, for modeling these different kinds of uncertainty.

a) Probability

Probability theory had been the only existing mathematical approach to uncertainty until recently. Let P be a finite set of propositions, such that

i)	if $p \in P$, then $\neg p \in P$	($\neg$: negation)
ii)	if $p \in P$, $q \in P$, then $p \wedge q \in P$	($\wedge$: conjunction)

Note that the ever-false proposition 0 belongs to P (since we have the contradiction law $p \wedge \neg p = 0$) as well as the ever-true proposition $\mathbb{1}$ (since we have the excluded-middle law $p \vee \neg p = \mathbb{1}$, where $p \vee q = \neg(\neg p \wedge \neg q)$ by definition). When $p \wedge q = 0$, p and q are said to be "mutually exclusive" since if one of the proposition is true, the other is false ; $p \wedge q = 0$ is equivalent to $p \rightarrow \neg q = \mathbb{1}$ (with $p \rightarrow q = \neg p \vee q$ by definition), which reads "p entails $\neg q$". A proposition p is said to be <u>elementary</u> with respect to P if there exists no proposition $q \in P$, other than 0 and p, such that $\neg p \wedge q = 0$. In other words, 0 and p itself are the only propositions which entail p. Any proposition in P other than 0, is elementary or can be expressed as a disjunction of elementary propositions.

A probability measure P, defined on the Boolean lattice $(P, \wedge, \vee, \neg)$, is a function from P to $[0,1]$ such that

i)	$P(0) = 0$	
ii)	$P(\mathbb{1}) = 1$	
iii)	$\forall p \in P, \forall q \in P$, if $p \wedge q = 0$, then $P(p \vee q) = P(p) + P(q)$.	

These axioms have the following noticeable consequences

$. \forall p \in P, P(p) + P(\neg p) = 1$ (1)

$.$ if p entails q (i.e. $p \rightarrow q = \mathbb{1}$), then $P(q) \geq P(p)$ (2)

b) <u>Credibility and plausibility</u>

In probability calculus, the probability that p is true, P(p) and the probability that p is false, P(¬p), are linked together by the equation (1). Thus, if P(p) = 0, we must have P(¬p) = 1 ; when we have no a priori knowledge regarding the truth or the falsity of p, it may seem natural to take $P(p) = P(¬p) = \frac{1}{2}$. However, as soon as we are considering more than two alternatives (mutually exclusive in pairs), the ignorance is difficult to represent, since whatever the probability distribution we use, there exist propositions (distinct from 𝟙) which are more probable that others (distinct from 𝟘), which may seem paradoxical since no knowledge is available.

In the seventies, several alternative models, departing from probability theory where proposed by different researchers. All of them share the following minimal properties which are intuitively reasonable. Let g be a function from P to [0,1], which estimates some kind of confidence we have in the truth of an element of P ; then g must fulfil the requirements

$$\text{i)} \qquad g(\mathbf{0}) = 0$$
$$\text{ii)} \qquad g(\mathbf{1}) = 1 \tag{3}$$
$$\text{iii)} \qquad \text{if p entails q } (p \rightarrow q = \mathbf{1}), \text{ then } g(q) \geq g(p)$$

A function g which satisfies (3) has been termed "fuzzy measure" by Sugeno (1974). Note that g is not necessarily additive. However, the axioms (3) characterize a too large family of function with which it would be difficult to perform computations. Thus, axioms (3) must be particularized by adding other requirements in order to get "fuzzy measures" of practical use.

Shafer (1976) (see also Barnett, 1981 ; Lowrance, Garvey, 1982) introduced a so-called belief function (which may be preferably termed 'credibility function') which of course satisfies (3) and which can be built from a so-called "basic probability assignment" m ; m is a function from P to [0,1] such that

$$\bullet \qquad m(\mathbf{0}) = 0$$
$$\bullet \qquad \sum_{p \in P} m(p) = 1. \tag{4}$$

Then, the credibility function Cr, based on m, is defined by

$$\forall\, q \in P,\; Cr(q) = \sum_{p \text{ entails } q} m(p) \tag{5}$$

The assignment m is supposed to represent an uncertain body of evidence. A certain body of evidence would be represented by a unique proposition p_0 such that $m(p_0) = 1$ and $\forall\, p \neq p_0$, m(p) = 0. When the evidence is uncertain, several propositions (<u>which are not necessarily mutually exclusive</u>) are possible, with different probabilities, for describing the evidence. The propositions p such that m(p) > 0, which correspond to the possible contents of the uncertain evidence under consideration, are said to be 'focal'. Note that the assignment m does not satisfy (3), except if we are in the situation of total ignorance (i.e. $m(\mathbb{I}) = 1$ and $\forall p \neq \mathbb{I}$, $m(p) = 0$). $m(p)$ is the probability that the evidence is <u>exactly and completely</u> described by p, in other words the weight of evidence in favor of p, but not a probability measure on P (indeed, $m(p \vee q) \neq m(p)+m(q)$ even if $p \wedge q = \emptyset$, in general). The credibility that q is true is obtained by adding all the probabilities of the possible exact descriptions of the evidence which entails q.

By duality, a plausibility function Pl is defined from Cr

$$\forall \, p \in P, \; Pl(p) = 1 - Cr(\neg p) \tag{6}$$

We get in terms of m

$$\forall \, q \in P, \; Pl(q) = \sum_{p \text{ does not entail } \neg q} m(p) \tag{7}$$

In other words, the plausibility of q is obtained as the sum of the weights of evidence in favor of propositions which are not inconsistent with q.

It can be easily checked that

$$\forall \, p \in P, \; Cr(p) + Cr(\neg p) \leq 1 \tag{8}$$

$$\forall \, p \in P, \; Pl(p) + Pl(\neg p) \geq 1 \tag{9}$$

Thus, it is possible to have $Cr(p) = Cr(\neg p) = 0$ and $Pl(p) = Pl(\neg p) = 1$ in case of ignorance : two opposite propositions may appear both plausible without being somewhat credible. With this approach it is possible to distinguish between lack of belief and disbelief since $Cr(p) = 0$ does not entail $Cr(\neg p) = 1$ (which is equivalent to $Pl(p) = 0$) while $Cr(\neg p) = 1$ entails $Cr(p) = 0$.

Formulae (6) and (8) yield

$$\forall \, p \in P, \; Cr(p) \leq Pl(p) \tag{10}$$

The plausibility of a proposition is always greater or equal to its credibility ; a proposition is all the more credible as the opposite proposition is less plausible. All theses properties are in agreement with the intuitive meaning generally attached to the concepts of plausibility and credibility. By the way, this model does not seem in disagreement with the basic ideas used by Colby and Smith (1969) in their empirical but quantitative approach of belief.

Two important particular cases of credibility and plausibility functions are got for special structures of the set of focal propositions :

- When all the focal propositions are among the elementary propositions of P, the credibility and plausibility functions, defined by (5) and (7), reduce to a same probability measure and then (6) is nothing but (1).

- When the focal propositions form a "nested structure" with respect to the entailment relation, the credibility and plausibility functions, defined by (5) and (7) reduce to a necessity measure and a possibility measure respectively : possibility and necessity are the topic of the following section.

c) Possibility and necessity

When the focal propositions are consonant, i.e. such that they can be ordered in the following way

$$P_n \text{ entails } P_{n-1} \text{ entails } \dots \text{ entails } P_1 \tag{11}$$

It can be shown that

$$\forall \ p \in P, \ \forall \ q \in P, \ Cr(p \wedge q) = \min(Cr(p), Cr(q)) \tag{12}$$
$$\forall \ p \in P, \ \forall \ q \in P, \ Pl(p \vee q) = \max(Pl(p), Pl(q)) \tag{13}$$

A credibility (plausibility resp.) function which satisfies (12) ((13) resp.) is called a necessity (possibility resp.) measure. Necessity measures are called consonant belief functions by Shafer (1976).

Possibility measures were introduced by Zadeh (1978a) independently ; possibility measures were extensively considered by Shackle (1961) previously in economics modeling, but this author did not develop their calculus in detail. In the following, N and Π will denote necessarily and possibility measures respectively.

From (12) and (13) we deduce

$$\forall \ p \in P, \ \min(N(p), N(\neg p)) = 0 \tag{14}$$
$$\forall \ p \in P, \ \max(\Pi(p), \Pi(\neg p)) = 1 \tag{15}$$

$$\forall \ p \in P, \ \begin{cases} \Pi(p) < 1 \ \Rightarrow N(p) = 0 \\ \\ N(p) > 0 \ \Rightarrow \Pi(p) = 1 \end{cases} \tag{16}$$

Note that (6), i.e.

$$\forall \ p \in P, \ N(p) = 1 - \Pi(\neg p) \tag{17}$$

expresses that the necessity that p is true corresponds to the impossibility that p is false, the impossibility being measured by the complement to 1 of the possibility measure (cf. Dubois, Prade, 1980). The same duality exists between the modal operators 'possibly' and 'necessarily' in modal logic ; moreover, here we take into account the fact that possibility is also a matter of degree, which is ignored in modal logic.

Here the uncertainty of proposition p is represented by a pair of numbers $(\Pi(p), N(p))$ rather than by a unique number as in probability calculus where $1-P(\neg p)$ is still $P(p)$.

The constraints (16) express that a proposition must be completely possible before being somewhat necessary. A proposition whose probability or necessity is equal to 1 can be regarded as certain, while it is not the case for a proposition whose possibility is 1 since the opposite proposition may also have a possibility equal to 1.

Beside the axioms ((12) and (13) contrast with the additivity of probability measures), the difference between probability on the one hand and possibility and necessity on the other hand stands out when we consider the respective structures of the sets of their focal propositions. Possibility and necessity correspond, in terms of m, to an uncertain evidence whose possible contents are consonant while probability correspond to an uncertain evidence whose possible contents are dissonant (i.e. mutually exclusive when they are taken in pairs) ; moreover in the case of probability, a focal proposition is elementary and any compound proposition $p = p_1 \vee p_2$ $(p_1 \neq 0, p_2 \neq 0)$ cannot be focal, this situation contrasts with the case of possibility and necessity where there is at most one focal proposition which is elementary.

<u>N.B.</u> For a discussion of the axiomatics of plausibility, credibility functions, possibility, probability and necessity measures, g_λ-fuzzy measures, in a common framework, see Dubois, Prade (1982a), (1982c).

d) <u>Degrees of belief and disbelief in MYCIN</u>

In the expert system MYCIN (Shortliffe, Buchanan, 1975), a measure of belief and a measure of disbelief in the hypothesis h knowing the evidence e, respectively denoted by MB(h,e) and MD(h,e), were introduced somewhat empirically and are used in this system, as well as in many others, rather successfully. From the definitions of MB(h,e) and of MD(h,e) in terms of the probabilities $P(h|e)$ and $P(h)$,

$$MB(h,e) = \begin{cases} 1 \text{ if } P(h) = 1 \\[2ex] \dfrac{\max(P(h|e), P(h)) - P(h)}{1 - P(h)} \text{ otherwise} \end{cases} \tag{18}$$

$$MD(h,e) = \begin{cases} 1 \text{ if } P(h) = 0 \\[2ex] \dfrac{P(h) - \min(P(h|e), P(h))}{P(h)} \text{ otherwise} \end{cases} \tag{19}$$

It can be easily checked that

$$MB(\neg h,e) = MD(h,e) \tag{20}$$

and that

$$MB(h,e) > 0 \Rightarrow MD(h,e) = 0 \; ; \; 1-MD(h,e) < 1 \Rightarrow MB(h,e) = 0 \tag{21}$$

It is worth-noticing that the constraints (20) and (21) are analogous to (17) and (16) respectively, viewing MB(h,e) as a necessity measure and MD(h,e) as the complement to 1 of a possibility measure (Prade, 1980a ; Prade, 1983). The formulae used in MY-CIN for combining degrees of belief or disbelief will be given and commented in appropriate places in the following.

2 - MODELING IMPRECISION AND RELATED ISSUES

a) The concept of a possibility distribution

α) *Basic principles*

While the truth (or the falsity) of a proposition may appear to be uncertain, its contents may be imprecise. Consider the following propositions for instance

- "John is <u>very young</u>"
- "<u>Most</u> Swedes are <u>tall</u>"
- "x and y are <u>approximately equal</u>"
- "Paul's height is between 1.70 m and 1.80 m"

They are imprecise since John's age is not precisely assessed, the proportion of Swedes under consideration is only very roughly given, 'tall' is a vague predicate, the exact relationship between x and y is not given, we may want to know Paul's height more accurately.

However, a statement such as "Paul's height is between 1.70 m and 1.80 m" may be regarded as imprecise only with respect to a given standard of precision in the context of human's height, while a proposition like "John is young" is intrinsically imprecise or if we prefer fuzzy because of the presence of a vague predicate. In given contexts, vague predicates induce fuzzy sets in the sense of Zadeh (1965) ; a fuzzy set is defined by its membership function which ranges on the interval [0,1].

The contents of a proposition p of the form 'X is A', which restricts (in a fuzzy or a non-fuzzy way) the possible values of a variable X on a universe of discourse S, is represented by means of the membership function of the subset induced by the predicate A ; this subset of S will be also denoted by A and its membership function by μ_A. $\forall\ s \in S$, $\mu_A(s)$ is interpreted as the possibility that the proposition p_s = 'X takes the value s' is true, knowing that 'X is A'. Thus the proposition 'X is A' is translated into (see Zadeh, 1978a, 1978b, 1981b)

$$\forall\ s \in S,\ \pi_X(s) = \mu_A(s) \tag{22}$$

where π_X is the possibility distribution attached to the variable X ; π_X is a function from S to [0,1]. Although a fuzzy set may play the role of a possibility distribution, there is a noticeable difference between the two concepts. From a semantic point of view, the values (fuzzily) restricted by a possibility distribution π_X are more or less eligible values for the variable X and as such must be regarded as mutually exclusive since the variable is supposed to be single-valued ; a fuzzy set represents a collection of elements with an unsharp boundary and the membership of an element does not exclude the membership of another in any way. As far as S is the exhaustive set of the possible values of the variable X, at least one value must be completely possible (its possibility is equal to 1), then the attached possibility distribution π_X is said to be <u>normalized</u> ($\exists\ s \in S,\ \pi_X(s) = 1$).

Conversely, an exhaustive collection of elementary propositions (which are thus mutually exclusive) of the form 'X takes the value s' where $s \in S$, weighted by a zero or a non-zero possibility degree $\pi_X(s)$, gives birth to a fuzzy set A defined by

$$\forall\ s \in S,\ \mu_A(s) = \pi_X(s) \tag{23}$$

and the corresponding information will be interpreted as a statement of the form 'X is A' even if there does not exist a predicate in the language corresponding to A. Note that in the general case nothing is supposed concerning the set S which may be finite or not, ordered or not.

The proposition 'X is not A', which corresponds to $\neg p$ with p = 'X is A', will be represented by the possibility distribution

$$\forall\ s \in S,\ \pi_X(s) = \mu_{\overline{A}}(s) = 1-\mu_A(s) \tag{24}$$

i.e. $\neg p$ will be interpreted as 'X is $\overline{A}$'.

When the more or less possible values which may be taken by a variable Y defined on a set T, depend on the value which is taken by another variable X, this fact can be represented by means of a so-called conditional possibility distribution $\pi_{Y|X}$. The possibility distribution $\pi_{Y|X}(.,s)$ represents the fuzzy set of the possible values of Y in T when X is equal to s. A conditional possibility distribution generalizes the idea of a multivoque function which already extends the idea of a function.

β) *Inclusion and specificity*

Fuzzy set inclusion, defined by (Zadeh, 1965),

$$A \subseteq B \Leftrightarrow \forall\ s \in S,\ \mu_A(s) \leq \mu_B(s) \tag{25}$$

is in agreement with the fact that the larger A, the less restrictive the proposition p = 'X is A' (short for "the true value of X is in A") is for the possible values of X. Yager (1982a) introduced the idea of a so-called measure of specificity for estimating how precise is the information 'X is A' rather that its fuzziness. A specificity measure Sp is such that, A and B being normalized fuzzy sets :

   i) $\forall\ A \subseteq S,\ Sp(A) \in [0,1]$

   ii) $Sp(A) = 1 \Leftrightarrow A$ is singleton of S   (26)

   iii) $A \subseteq B \Rightarrow Sp(A) \geq Sp(B)$

Note that the maximum of Sp corresponds to the case where the value of X is precisely known in S, i.e. A reduces to a singleton. A crisp set can be less specific (i.e. precise) than a fuzzy set for restricting the possible values of a variable ; the maximum of specificity corresponds to a precise assessment of the value of the variable. Thus, the measure of specificity is relative to the scale of measurement which is used. Examples of measures of specificity can be found in (Yager, 1982a ; Dubois, Prade, 1984b ; Dubois, Prade, 1985d).

γ) *Representing uncertainty with possibility distributions*

It is important to notice that possibility distributions enable us also to represent uncertain items of information. A fact 'X is A' is uncertain if one is not completely sure that the value of X is restricted by μ_A. This can be understood as the existence of some possibility, graded by α, that the value of X lies anywhere "outside A" and can be represented by a possibility distribution such as the one pictured on figure 1.

Then, the possibility distribution restricting X is defined by

$$\forall\ s \in S,\ \pi_X(s) = \max(\mu_A(s),\alpha) \tag{27}$$

The smaller α, the less uncertain the information 'X is A'.
The fuzzy set A can be viewed as a default set of possible values for X in this case ; see (Prade, 1985a). When A is a singleton of S, we have a precise but uncertain information.

The <u>support</u> of a possibility distribution π_X is defined by

$$\text{support}\ (\pi_X) = \{s \in S,\ \pi_X(s) > 0\} \tag{28}$$

When the support of π_X is limited, i.e. is a proper subset of S, 'X is A' yields the certain information that X takes its value among the elements of support (π_X) since other elements in S have received a possibility degree equal to 0. When support (π_X) = S as in (27), we are only certain of the trivial information 'X is S' and of nothing else.

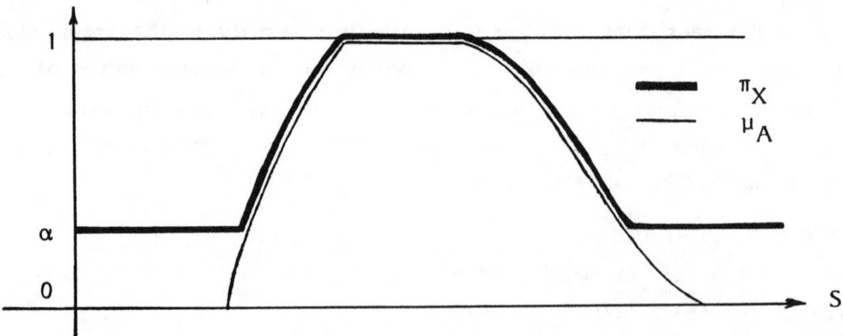

Figure 1

As it has been recalled in II.1.d, in MYCIN to a proposition p (corresponding to a non-vague or so-assumed information) is attached a degree of belief MB(p) and a degree of disbelief MD(p) which must be such that

$$\min(MB(p), MD(p)) = 0 \qquad (29)$$

due to (21). If the proposition p expresses the information 'X is A' (where A is a non-fuzzy set), then p may be represented by the possibility distribution

$$\forall\ s \in S,\ \mu_X(s) = \begin{cases} 1 - MD(p) & \text{if } s \in A \\ 1 - MB(p) & \text{if } s \notin A \end{cases} \qquad (30)$$

viewing MD as a degree of impossibility and MB as a degree of necessity (using the remark made in II.1.d and (17)) (Martin-Clouaire, Prade, 1985b). The constraint (29) guarantees that the possibility distribution defined by (30) is normalized ; this possibility distribution is a particular case of the one pictured on Figure 1 where A is an ordinary subset of S.

b) <u>Possibility and necessity measures issued from a possibility distribution</u>

α) *The case of non-vague propositions*

Knowing that 'X is A' (translated by $\pi_X = \mu_A$), we can compute the possibility $\Pi_X(F;A)$ that the proposition q = 'X is F' is true where F is a non-vague predicate represented by a crisp subset of S. Indeed, noticing that $q = \underset{s \in F}{\vee}\ p_s$ with $\forall\ s \in S,\ p_s = $ 'X is $\{s\}$'

(i.e. X = s) and viewing $\mu_A(s)$ as the possibility measure $\Pi(p_s)$ of the proposition p_s, (13) gives for S finite

$$\forall\ F \subseteq S,\ \Pi_X(F;A) = \underset{s \in F}{\max}\ \mu_A(s) \qquad (31)$$

Note that $\forall\ s \in S,\ \Pi_X(\{s\};A) = \mu_A(s) = \pi_X(s)$. We have $\Pi_X(S;A) = 1$ since $\pi_X = \mu_A$ is normalized. Then (17) defines the necessity $N_X(F;A)$ that the proposition q = 'X is F' is true

$$\forall\ F \subseteq S,\ N_X(F;A) = \underset{s \notin F}{\min}\ (1-\mu_A(s)) \qquad (32)$$

The extension of (31) and (32) to non-finite sets such that $\mathbf{R}^n$, is obvious, replacing 'max' by 'sup' and 'min' by 'inf'. When π_X is the characteristic function of an ordinary subset, expressions (31) and (32) reduce respectively to

$$\Pi_X(F;A) = \begin{cases} 1 & \text{if } F \cap A \neq \emptyset \\ 0 & \text{otherwise} \end{cases} \quad \text{and} \quad N_X(F;A) = \begin{cases} 1 & \text{if } F \supseteq A \\ 0 & \text{otherwise} \end{cases}$$

which shows the links between possibility and intersection, and between necessity and inclusion. When evaluating the possibility of an event, only the most favorable case is taken into account as it is shown by (31), which departs from probability where the evaluation is cumulative $(P_X(F) = \underset{s \in F}{\Sigma}\ P_X(\{s\}))$ in the finite case).

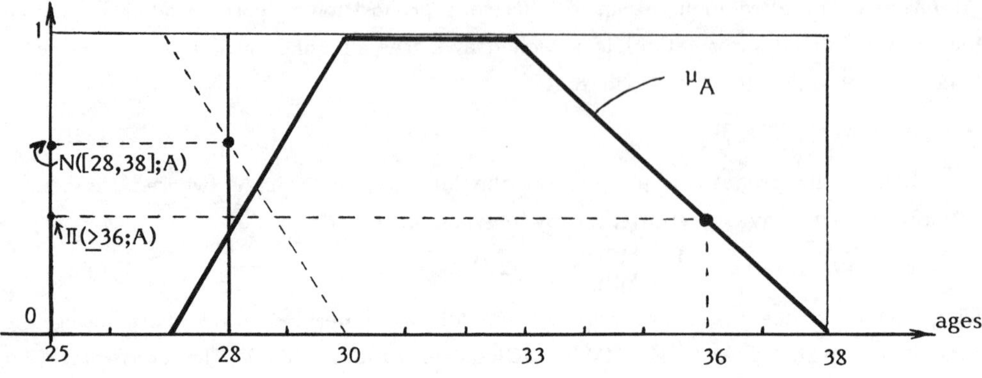

Figure 2

For example, it is known that John is about 30 to 33 years old and certainly not less than 27 and more than 38 years old. This information is represented by a possibility distribution on Figure 2. Then using (31) and (32) we can easily compute the possibility and the necessity that John is more than 36 years old (F = {age, age $\geq$ 36}), here we get $\Pi(F;A) \simeq 0.4$ and $N(F;A) = 0$. Computing the possibility and the necessity that John is between 28 and 38 years old (i.e. F = {age, 28 $\leq$ age $\leq$ 38}) will give $\Pi(F;A) = 1$ and $N(F;A) \simeq 0.65$. See Figure 2. It is important to keep in mind that these values are purely indicative, since a precise identification of the possibility distribution μ_A is generally out of reach or not meaningful. Moreover the values of $\Pi(F;A)$ or $N(F;A)$ are not very sensitive to slight variations of μ_A. What essentially matters is the identification of the regions where μ_A is equal to 1 or zero, and the assessing in the other regions, of possibility degrees which are all the larger as the associated value is considered as more possible for the variable under consideration.

The <u>core</u> of a possibility distribution π_X is defined as

$$\text{core}(\pi_X) = \{s \in S, \pi_X(s) = 1\} \tag{33}$$

It can be easily checked that $\Pi(\text{core}(\mu_A);A) = 1$ while $N(\text{core}(\mu_A);A) = 0$. Contrastedly, $\Pi(\text{support}(\mu_A);A) = 1 = N(\text{support}(\mu_A);A)$. This is in agreement with our intuition, since it is completely certain that the value of X is among the elements of $\text{support}(\pi_X)$ while it is only completely possible that X takes its value in $\text{core}(\pi_X)$. Note also that denoting by $A^{\boxed{\alpha}}$ the fuzzy set whose characteristic function is defined by $\mu_{A^{\boxed{\alpha}}}(s) = \max(\mu_A(s),\alpha)$, we have $N(\text{support}(\mu_A);A^{\boxed{\alpha}}) = 1-\alpha$; this means that in (27) our degree of certainty (necessity that X takes its value in $\text{support}(\mu_A)$ is only equal to $1-\alpha$ or that in (30) our degree of certainty that the value of X is in A is nothing but MB(p), which is satisfactory.

Since there is an isomorphism between the Boolean lattice $(P,\wedge,\vee,\neg)$ of the propositions of the form 'X is F' ($F \subseteq S$) and the set 2^S of the crisp subsets of S equipped with the usual set operations, $\Pi_X(.;A)$ and $N_X(.;A)$, which are set functions from 2^S to $[0,1]$, are a possibility measure and a necessity measure in the sense of (13) and (12) respectively ; indeed

$$\forall \ F \in 2^S, \ \forall \ G \in 2^S, \ \Pi_X(F \cup G;A) = \max(\Pi_X(F;A),\Pi_X(G;A)) \tag{34}$$

$$\forall \ F \in 2^S, \ \forall \ G \in 2^S, \ N_X(F \cap G;A) = \min(N_X(F;A),N_X(G;A)) \tag{35}$$

β) A possibility distribution as a basic probability assignment

In the isomorphism between $(P,\wedge,\vee,\neg)$ and $(2^S,\cap,\cup,^-)$, $p \rightarrow q = \mathbb{1}$ corresponds to $F \subseteq G$ where p = 'X is F' and q = 'X is G' ; $\Pi_X(.;A)$ and $N_X(.;A)$ are based (in the sense of (7) and (5)) on the basic probability assignment m, from 2^S to $[0,1]$, defined by (see Dubois, Prade, 1982c, for a proof).

$$\begin{aligned} m(\{s_1,...,s_i\}) &= \mu_A(s_i) - \mu_A(s_{i+1}), \qquad i = 1,n \\ m(F) &= 0 \text{ if } F \neq \{s_1,...,s_i\} \end{aligned} \tag{36}$$

where the n elements of S are supposed to be ordered according to the decreasing values of μ_A ; $\mu_A(s_{n+1}) = 0$ by convention. The focal elements of m correspond to the different α-cuts of A, which are defined by

$$A_\alpha = \{s \in S, \ \mu_A(s) \geq \alpha\}, \tag{37}$$

where α ranges in the set of the different values taken by μ_A.

It is also worth-noticing that $N(A_\alpha;A) = 1-\alpha$ for a continuous membership function defined on the real line. Thus a fuzzy set (and by way of consequence a possibility distribution) can be viewed as a collection of nested subsets weighted by confidence levels.

From a practical point of view, it is important that possibility and necessity measures, as well as probability measures, can be directly expressed in terms of a distribution which for S finite, requires only $|S|-1$ numerical values to be defined, while $2^{|S|}-2$ values are needed to define a function m in general.

In Dubois, Prade (1982c ; 1983), a one-to-one correspondence between a probability distribution p_X and a possibility distribution π_X is introduced on finite domains ; this transformation preserves the following inequalities

$$\forall \ F \in 2^S, \ N_X(F) \leq P_X(F) \leq \Pi_X(F) \tag{38}$$

where P_X, Π_X and N_X are the probability, possibility and necessity measures based on p_X and π_X respectively (i.e. $P_X(F) = \sum_{s \in F} p_X(s)$; $\Pi_X(F) = \max_{s \in F} \pi_X(s)$; $N_X(F) = \min_{s \notin F}(1-\pi_X(s))$. The transformation is defined by

$$\forall\ s \in S,\ \pi_X(s) = \sum_{s' \in S} \min(p_X(s'), p_X(s)) \tag{39}$$

and conversely

$$\forall\ i = 1,n,\ p_X(s_i) = \sum_{j=i}^{n} \frac{1}{j} \cdot (\pi_X(s_j) - \pi_X(s_{j+1})) \tag{40}$$

where the n elements of S are supposed to be ordered according to the decreasing values of π_X and $\pi_X(s_{n+1}) = 0$ by convention. From (36) and (40), we deduce that

$$\forall\ s \in S,\ p_X(s) = \sum_{F \supseteq \{s\}} \frac{1}{|F|} \cdot m(F) \tag{41}$$

where m is the basic probability assignment associated with π_X. Formula (41) corresponds to a natural way of approximating a basic probability assignment by a probability distribution by splitting the weights of evidence m(F) and by equally sharing them among the elementary events composing F. This is exactly what happens in traditional Bayesian inference when the lack of a priori knowledge is modeled by a uniform probability density. Moreover the inequalities (38) are very satisfactory for the intuition since they are in agreement with the motto : what is probable must be possible and what is necessary (i.e. ineluctable) must be probable. Thus, a possibilistic interpretation can be provided for frequency histograms concurrently with the usual probabilistic interpretation.

γ) *The case of vague proposition*

In section II.2.b.α, from a possibility distribution π_X, modeling an imprecise statement such that 'X is A' (A is a predicate represented by a subset of S not reduced to a singleton), we built two uncertainty measures, namely the possibility measure $\pi_X(.;A)$ and the necessity measure $N_X(.;A)$; note that when μ_A is the membership function of a singleton $\{s_0\} \subseteq S$, (i.e. when 'X is A' is a precise statement), (31) and (32) reduce to the "certainty" measure, $\Pi_X(F; \{s_0\}) = N_X(F; \{s_0\}) = \{ \begin{smallmatrix} 1 & \text{if } s_0 \in F \\ 0 & \text{if } s_0 \notin F \end{smallmatrix}$, $\forall$ F.

$\Pi_X(.;A)$ and $N_X(.;A)$ were introduced as ordinary set functions measuring the uncertainty of non-vague propositions represented by crisp (i.e. non-fuzzy) subsets of S, called "events" ; more generally, we want to evaluate the possibility, the necessity, but also the probability, of an event which is itself vaguely described ; such a fuzzy event will be modelled by a fuzzy set. In order to extent set functions to fuzzy events it is necessary to define the algebra of these events first.

Let $\tilde{P}(S)$, the set of fuzzy subsets of S. A fuzzy set F is defined by its membership function μ_F from S to [0,1]. Usual set-operations are extended to fuzzy sets in the following way (Zadeh, 1965)

. complementation $\quad\quad \forall \; s \in S, \; \mu_{\bar{F}}(s) = 1-\mu_F(s)$ (42)

. intersection $\quad\quad\quad \forall \; s \in S, \; \mu_{F \cap G}(s) = \min(\mu_F(s),\mu_G(s))$ (43)

. union $\quad\quad\quad\quad\quad \forall \; s \in S, \; \mu_{F \cup G}(s) = \max(\mu_F(s),\mu_G(s))$ (44)

The usual properties of set-operations are preserved except the noncontradiction and excluded-middle laws, weakened in $\forall \; s \in S$, $\min(\mu_F(s),\mu_{\bar{F}}(s)) \leq \frac{1}{2}$ and in $\forall \; s \in S$, $\max(\mu_F(s),\mu_{\bar{F}}(s)) \geq \frac{1}{2}$; it is not surprising that an ill-defined set somewhat overlaps its complement which is itself not-accurately defined. More generally, 'min' and 'max' may be replaced in (43) and (44) by any pair of dual triangular norm and co-norm (see the appendix for a background on triangular norms).

Then the probability $P(F)$ of a fuzzy event F is defined by the expectation of its its membership function (Zadeh, 1968)

$$\forall \; F \in \tilde{P}(S), \; P(F) = E(\mu_F)$$

$$= \sum_{s \in S} \mu_F(s).p(s) \quad\quad \text{(finite case)} \quad (45)$$

where $p(s) = P(\{s\})$. With this definition, still we have $\forall \; F \in \tilde{P}(S)$, $\forall \; G \in \tilde{P}(S)$, $P(F \cup G) = P(F) + P(G) - P(F \cap G)$ as soon as $\mu_{F \cup G}(s) + \mu_{F \cap G}(s) = \mu_F(s) + \mu_G(s)$, $\forall \; s$; it is the case with (43) and (44). Similarly, Smets (1981a ; 1981b) has defined the plausibility and the credibility of a fuzzy event in a natural way as upper and lower expectations (see Dempster , 1967, for these concepts) of its membership function.

However, the definition of the possibility of a fuzzy event proposed by Zadeh (1978a) is not a particular case of Smets' definition although a possibility measure is a particular case of plausibility function. Zadeh's proposal for extending (31) is

$$\forall \; F \in \tilde{P}(S), \; \Pi_X(F;A) = \sup_{s \in S} \min(\mu_F(s),\pi_X(s)) \quad (46)$$

with $\pi_X(s) = \Pi_X(\{s\};A) = \mu_A(s)$. (32) is extended by

$$\forall \; F \in \tilde{P}(S), \; N_X(F;A) = \inf_{s \in S} \max(\mu_F(s),1-\pi_X(s)) \quad (47)$$

$$= 1 - \Pi_X(\bar{F};A). \quad (48)$$

More generally, we may think of using any pair of dual triangular norm and co-norm instead of min and max in (46) and (47) for aggregating μ_F with π_X and μ_F with $1-\pi_X$ respectively. Since any triangular norm (resp. co-norm) is distributive with respect to max (resp. min), we still have $\forall \; F \in \tilde{P}(S)$, $\forall \; G \in \tilde{P}(S)$, $\Pi_X(F \cup G;A) = \max(\Pi_X(F;A), \Pi_X(G;A))$ and $N_X(F \cap G;A) = \min(N_X(F;A), N_X(G;A))$ using (43) and (44) for defining the intersection and the union. These characteristic properties of possibility and necessity measures would not be preserved using Smets' approach. We have

$$\forall \; F \in \tilde{P}(S), \; \Pi_X(F;A) \geq N_X(F;A) \quad (49)$$

provided that $\pi_X = \mu_A$ is normalized. However, only weaker versions of (14), (15), (16) hold, due to the lack of non-contradiction and excluded-middle laws for fuzzy sets. From a multivalued logic point of view, (46) evaluates the non-emptiness of a generalized intersection while (47) is a degree of inclusion. The fact that probability, possibility and necessity measures are increasing with respect to set inclusion as defined by (25), is compatible with the entailment principle (see Zadeh, 1979a) 'if X is F, then X is G' as soon as $F \subseteq G$ in the sense of (25). Besides, when $A \subseteq B$, viewing μ_A and μ_B as two possibility distributions, the possibility and necessity measures $\Pi_X(.,B)$ and $N_X(.;B)$ defined from μ_B are respectively greater and smaller than the possibility and the necessity measures $\Pi_X(.;A)$ and $N_X(.;A)$, defined from μ_A, which is quite natural since the proposition 'X is B' is less specific (i.e. precise) than 'X is A'. Lastly note that we have $\Pi(A;A) = 1$ and $N(A;A) \geq \frac{1}{2}$ when A is a fuzzy set ; this is due to the fact that we cannot then be completely sure that 'X is A' when $\pi_X = \mu_A$ since A and $\overline{A}$ somewhat overlap ; we have only $N(\text{support}(A);A) = 1$.

δ) Non-interactivity and compound propositions

The notion of non-interactivity in possibility theory plays a role analogous to that of independence in probability theory (see Zadeh, 1975). Two variables, X and Y, which take their values respectively on S and T are said to be non-interactive if their join possibility distribution $\pi_{X,Y}$, from $S \times T$ to [0,1], supposed to be normalized, is such that

$$\forall \ (s,t) \in S \times T, \ \pi_{X,Y}(s,t) = \min(\pi_X(s),\pi_Y(t)) \tag{50}$$

where π_X and π_Y are the marginal possibility distributions obtained from $\pi_{X,Y}$ by projection :

$$\pi_X(s) = \sup_{t \in T} \pi_{X,Y}(s,t) \ \text{and} \ \pi_Y(t) = \sup_{s \in S} \pi_{X,Y}(s,t) \tag{51}$$

Note that $\pi_X(s)$ is the possibility of the event '$\exists \ t \in T, X = s$' viewing this proposition as equivalent to the disjunction $\underset{i \in I}{\vee} p_i$ where $p_i = $ '$T = t_i \wedge X = s$' and I is an index set. The equality (50) expresses the fact that the fuzzy set of the possible values of X does not depend on the value of Y and reciprocally. We always have

$$\forall \ (s,t) \in S \times T, \ \pi_{X,Y}(s,t) \leq \min(\pi_X(s),\pi_Y(t)). \tag{52}$$

The compound propositions 'X is A and Y is B' and 'X is A or Y is B' will be represented respectively by

$$\forall \ s \in S, \ \forall \ t \in T, \ \pi_{X,Y}(s,t) = \mu_{A \times B}(s,t) = \min(\mu_A(s),\mu_B(t)) \tag{53}$$

$$\forall \ s \in S, \ \forall \ t \in T, \ \pi_{X,Y}(s,t) = \mu_{A+B}(s,t) = \max(\mu_A(s),\mu_B(t)) \tag{54}$$

provided that X and Y are non-interactive. A $\times$ B extends the Cartesian product (see Dubois, Prade, 1981) for a discussion of the extension of the Cartesian product to fuzzy sets) ; we have $A + B = \overline{\overline{A} \times \overline{B}}$.

Using the definitions (53) and (54) it can be shown that

$$\Pi_{X,Y}(F \times G \; ; \; A \times B) = \min(\Pi_X(F;A), \; \Pi_Y(G;B)) \qquad (55)$$
$$\Pi_{X,Y}(F+G \; ; \; A \times B) = \max(\Pi_X(F;A), \; \Pi_Y(G;B)) \qquad (56)$$
$$N_{X,Y}(F \times G \; ; \; A \times B) = \min(N_X(F;A), \; N_Y(G;B)) \qquad (57)$$
$$N_{X,Y}(F+G \; ; \; A \times B) = \max(N_X(F;A), \; N_Y(G;B)) \qquad (58)$$

provided that X and Y are non-interactive and where $\Pi_{X,Y}(.;A \times B)$, $N_{X,Y}(.;A \times B)$, $\Pi_X(.;A)$, $N_X(.;A)$, $\Pi_Y(.;B)$, $N_Y(.;B)$ are the possibility and necessity measures built from $\pi_{X,Y} = \mu_{A \times B}$, $\pi_X = \mu_A$ and $\pi_Y = \mu_B$ respectively. When X and Y are interactive, the sign '=' is replaced by '$\leq$' in (55) and by '$\geq$' in (58), (56) and (57) remaining unchanged. See Prade (1982a) for a proof of (55)-(56).

The following formulae used in MYCIN

$$\begin{aligned} MD(h_1 \wedge h_2,e) &= \max(MD(h_1,e),MD(h_2,e)) \; ; \\ MD(h_1 \vee h_2,e) &= \min(MD(h_1,e), \; MD(h_2,e)) \end{aligned} \qquad (59)$$

$$\begin{aligned} MB(h_1 \wedge h_2,e) &= \min(MB(h_1,e), \; MB(h_2,e)) \; ; \\ MB(h_1 \vee h_2,e) &= \max(MB(h_1,e),MB(h_2,e)) \end{aligned} \qquad (60)$$

are the exact counterparts of (55)-(58), changing MD into $1-\Pi$, MB into N, h_1 and h_2 into F and G respectively provided that the hypotheses h_1 and h_2 are logically independent, which corresponds to the non-interactivity of X and Y in (55) and (58).

ε) *Plausibility and credibility functions based on fuzzy local elements*

Yager (1982b) has introduced generalized plausibility and credibility functions defined from fuzzy focal elements (see also Ishizuka, Fu, Yao, 1982a ; Dubois, Prade, 1985a). They are respectively defined by

$$\forall \; F \in \tilde{P}(S), \; Pl(F) = \sum_{i=1}^{n} m(A_i).\Pi(F;A_i) \qquad (61)$$

$$\forall \; F \in \tilde{P}(S), \; Cr(F) = \sum_{i=1}^{n} m(A_i).N(F;A_i) \qquad (62)$$

where the A_i's, $i = 1,n$, are the focal elements (supposed to be in a finite number), m being a generalized basic probability assignment defined from $\tilde{P}(S)$ to [0,1] such that $\sum_{i=1}^{n} m(A_i) = 1$ and $m(\emptyset) = 0$; the A_i's are supposed to be normalized ; $\Pi(F;A_i)$ and

216

N(F;A$_i$) are defined by (46) and (47). Expressions (61) and (62)   clearly generalize (7) and (5), since in the isomorphism between $(P, \wedge, \vee, \neg)$ and $(2^S, \cap, \cup, \bar{\ })$, (7) and (5) are respectively transformed into PI(F) = $\sum_{A \cap F \neq \emptyset} m(A)$ and into Cr(F) = $\sum_{A \subseteq F} m(A)$ and   since

$\Pi(F;A_i)$ and $N(F;A_i)$ can be viewed as intersection and inclusion indices respectively. When the A_i's are non fuzzy, (61) and (62) correspond to Smets' proposal (Smets, 1981a, 1981b) ; see also Zadeh (1979d).

c) Fuzzy quantifiers

Zadeh (1978b, 1979a) has pointed out that a proposition of the form 'Q u's are A', where Q is a quantifier which may be crisp (e.g. '$\forall$', '$\exists$', 'at least 70 %') or fuzzy (e.g. 'most', 'some'), where the u's are elements of a set U on which an attribute X is defined which takes its values in S, and where A is a fuzzy or crisp subset of S, can be understood as 'Q restricts the possible values of the proportion of elements of U whose attribute X is A', i.e.

$$\forall \ x \in [0,1], \ \pi_{Prop(\hat{A} | U)}(x) = \mu_Q(x) \tag{63}$$

where $\hat{A}$ is the fuzzy or crisp subset of elements of U which are A, defined by

$$\forall \ u \in U, \ \mu_{\hat{A}}(u) = \mu_A(X(u)) \tag{64}$$

and where μ_Q is the characteristic function of a subset (possibly fuzzy, possibly reduced to one element) of numbers in [0,1].

<u>N.B.</u> In this framework, '$\forall$' and '$\exists$' are represented respectively by $\mu_\forall(1) = 1$, $\mu_\forall(x) = 0$, $\forall \ x \in [0,1)$ and $\mu_\exists(0) = 0$ and $\mu_\exists(x) = 1$, $\forall \ x \in (0,1]$. 'At least 70 %' is represented by $\forall \ x < 0.7$, $\mu_Q(x) = 0$ and $\forall \ x \geq 0.7$, $\mu_Q(x) = 1$. More generally Q is a genuine fuzzy set of [0,1].

When U is finite and using the scalar cardinality of a fuzzy set ($|\hat{A}| = \sum_{u \in U} \mu_{\hat{A}}(u)$), (63) induces the following possibility distribution on the possible membership functions $\mu_{\hat{A}}$ which are in agreement with the proposition 'Q u's are A'

$$\pi(\mu_{\hat{A}}) = \mu_Q(\frac{|\hat{A}|}{|U|}) \tag{65}$$

As $|U|$ increases and S becomes a continuum, (65) can be changed into

$$\pi(\rho) = \mu_Q(\int_S \rho(s) . \mu_A(s) . ds) \tag{66}$$

where ρ is a density function ($\rho(s).ds$ is the proportion of u's whose attribute X takes its value in the interval [s,s+ds]).

More generally, propositions such that 'Q u's which are B, are A' would lead to

$$\forall\, x \in [0,1], \quad \pi_{Prop(\hat{A}|\hat{B})}(x) = \mu_Q(x) \tag{67}$$

with $Prop(A|B) = \dfrac{|\hat{A} \cap \hat{B}|}{|\hat{B}|}$ and where $\mu_{\hat{A}}(u) = \mu_B(Y(u))$, Y being an attribute defined from U to T and B a fuzzy set of T.

d) Degree of truth and truth-qualification

α) Degree of truth and compatibility

After a background on the measurement of uncertainty and the representation of imprecise or fuzzy statements, we turn to a short discussion of the relation between the notion of a degree of truth and possibility and necessity measures.

A degree of truth may be viewed as a measure of the <u>conformity</u> between a representation of the contents of the proposition under consideration and a representation of what is actually known of the reality. Thus the degree of truth of a proposition is relative to our state of knowledge. See Dubois, Prade (1982b), Prade (1982b) for a detailed discussion ; see Zadeh (1981b) for a related point of view.

Let us suppose that the uncertain body of evidence is represented by a possibility distribution π_e and that the contents of the proposition $p = $ 'X is A' under consideration is also represented by a possibility distribution π_p (which is crisp if p is a non-vague statement). Then, using (46) and (47) we can compute the possibility that p is true given e :

$$\Pi(p,e) = \sup_{s \in S}\ \min(\pi_p(s), \pi_e(s)) \tag{68}$$

and the necessity that p is true given e :

$$N(p,e) = \inf_{s \in S}\ \max(\pi_p(s), 1-\pi_e(s)) \tag{69}$$

<u>N.B.</u> : Cayrol, Farreny, Prade (1980, 1982) have designed a procedure of pattern-matching where $\Pi(p,e)$ and $N(p,e)$ are used in order to evaluate the semantic similarities between patterns and data.

It has been shown that either when π_e is the characteristic function of a singleton (i.e. the evidence is precise and $\Pi(p,e) = N(p,e)$) or when the proposition p is non-vague (then either $\Pi(p,e) = 1$ or $N(p,e) = 0$),

$$v(p,e) = \frac{\Pi(p,e)\ +\ N(p,e)}{2} \tag{70}$$

can be regarded as a genuine degree of truth in the sense that the truth-functionality is preserved for the negation, the conjunction and the disjunction ; see Dubois, Prade (1982b) and also Gaines (1976). For instance, we have

$$v(\neg p,e) = 1 - v(p,e) \tag{71}$$

As pointed out in Prade (1980a), the certainty factor $CF(h,e) = MB(h,e)-MD(h,e)$ $\in [-1,+1]$, used in MYCIN, can be viewed as a degree of truth $v(h,e)$ up to a scaling effect since

$$v(h,e) = \frac{1 + CF(h,e)}{2} \in [0,1] \qquad (72)$$

coincides with (70), changing $MB(h,e)$ into $N(p,e)$ and $MD(h,e)$ into $1-\Pi(h,e)$.

<u>N.B.</u> See Prade (1984a) for the evaluation of the possibility and of the necessity that a proposition involving a quantifier (possibility fuzzy) is true.

Zadeh (1978b) has introduced a fuzzy degree of truth named 'compatibility'. The compatibility of π_p with respect to π_e is a fuzzy set $CP(p,e)$ of the real interval $[0,1]$ whose membership function is defined by

$$\forall\ x \in [0,1],\ \mu_{CP(p,e)}(x) = \sup_{x=\pi_p(s)}\ \pi_e(s)$$

$$\qquad (73)$$

$$= 0 \ \text{if}\ \pi_p^{-1}(x) = \emptyset$$

$CP(p,e)$ is nothing but the fuzzy set of the possible values of the variable $\pi_p(s)$ when the possible values of s are restricted by the possibility distribution π_e. Particularly, when π_e is a crisp possibility distribution (i.e. $\forall\ s,\ \pi_e(s) \in \{0,1\}$), $CP(p,e) = \{\pi_p(s)\ \text{such that}\ \pi_e(s) = 1\}$. Thus if π_e corresponds to the crisp set F' while p is the proposition X is F (i.e. $\forall\ s,\ \pi_p(s) = \mu_F(s)$), $CP(p,e)$ can be viewed as $\mu_F(F') = \{\mu_F(s),\ s \in F'\}$; a value s is compatible with F to the degree $\mu_F(s)$ and thus the fuzzy set of $[0,1]$, $\mu_F(F')$ represents the compatibility of the whole set F' (i.e. the evidence) with F (i.e. the proposition p). When π_p is crisp, (73) reduces to the two possibility degrees $\mu_{CP(p,e)}(1) = \Pi(p,e)$ and $\mu_{CP(p,e)}(0) = 1-N(p,e)$. Lastly, when $\pi_p = \pi_e$, (73) gives $\mu_{CP(p,e)}(x) = x$ provided that $\exists\ s,\ \pi_p(s) = x$; thus the compatibility of F with F is no longer 1 when F is fuzzy, but the special fuzzy set of $[0,1]$ defined by $\mu_\tau(x) = x,\ \forall\ x$ (μ_F being a function which takes all the values in $[0,1]$).

It can be shown (Prade, 1980b) that

$$\Pi(p,e) = \sup_{x \in [0,1]}\ \min(x, \mu_{CP(p,e)}(x)) \qquad (74)$$

$$N(p,e) = \inf_{x \in [0,1]}\ \max(x, 1-\mu_{CP(p,e)}(x)) \qquad (75)$$

Thus $CP(p,e)$ contains the information represented by $\Pi(p,e)$ and $N(p,e)$.

Using extended operations on fuzzy numbers (Dubois, Prade, 1980), $CP(\neg p,e)$ can be easily expressed in terms of $CP(p,e)$, and $CP(p \wedge q,e)$ or $CP(p \vee q,e)$ in terms of $CP(p,e)$ and of $CP(q,e)$ provided that the variables involved in p and q are non-interactive ; see (Prade, 1980b ; Dubois, Prade, 1979).

β) *Truth .qualification*

Conversely, given the possibility distribution π_p of the proposition under consideration, and its fuzzy truth-value τ viewed as a compatibility, it is possible to get the greatest solution (in the sense of fuzzy set inclusion (25)) π_e^+ of the equation $\tau = CP(p,e)$: we have

$$\forall\ s \in S,\ \pi_e^+(s) = \mu_\tau(\pi_p(s)) \tag{76}$$

π_e^+ represents what can be concluded about the reality knowing that the proposition p is τ-true. See Zadeh (1978b), (1979a). In other words, the contents of a proposition of the form 'p is τ', where p is itself a proposition and τ a linguistic truth-value, is represented by the possibility distribution defined by (76) ; note that (76) is similar to the modeling of the modification due to a linguistic hedge (see Zadeh, 1972) : for instance 'X is very A', represented by $\pi_X = [\mu_A]^2$, can be viewed as equivalent to 'X is A is τ' with $\mu_\tau(x) = x^2$, $\forall\ x \in [0,1]$. Note that $\pi_e^+ = \pi_p$ for $\mu_\tau(x) = x$, $\forall\ x$; if τ is a crisp subset of $[0,1]$ (particularly if τ is a scalar value) π_e^+ is non fuzzy.

When the proposition p is non-vague, $\pi_p(s) = 0$ or 1, $\forall\ s$; if $\mu_\tau(0) = \mu_\tau(1) = 0$, (76) yields $\forall\ s \in S,\ \pi_e^+ = 0$. Thus, the approach does not enable to take into account a proposition such that 'X is equal to 5 is almost true' and to understand it as 'X is almost equal to 5'. In order to solve this problem a modification of (76) has been proposed ; see Prade (1985c).

III - REASONING FROM IMPRECISE OR UNCERTAIN PREMISES

We successively deal with deductive inferences from imprecise or uncertain premises, and with the combination of more or less certain or more or less consonant items of information obtained or derived from different sources. The propagation of imprecision and uncertainty via deductive inferences and the combination of uncertain or imprecise items of information can be considered as the two basic patterns of reasoning which are needed in expert systems when the knowledge is not precise or certain.

1 - DEDUCTIVE INFERENCES IN RULE-BASED SYSTEMS

a) Introduction

Roughly speaking in a rule-based system, the expert knowledge is encoded under the form of a collection of "if ..., then ..." rules where the if-part of a rule states conditions, the satisfying of which allows to fire the rule and to exploit the related information stated in the then-part of the rule. The inference engine of a rule-based system determines the rules which can be fired given the data describing the current situation to manage, selects the rule(s) to fire and then modify the data base by taking into account the consequences stated in the then-part(s) of the fired rule(s).

The human knowledge expressed in the rules may be pervaded with imprecision or uncertainty. Particularly a rule will be imprecise or fuzzy if vague predicates are used in its statement. Moreover a rule may also be uncertain if its consequence(s) remain uncertain when its condition(s) are certainly satisfied. Besides the current data can be imprecise or uncertain if they are produced by using rules which are not precisely stated and/or which do not guarantee certain conclusions, or if the situation analyzed by the rule-based expert system is itself partially and imperfectly known.

In the following we present extensions of modus ponens-like patterns of reasoning when the two premises "if p, then q" and "p" are pervaded with some imprecision or uncertainty which will be propagated to the conclusion "q". A datum will be supposed to express some restriction (represented by means of a possibility distribution) on the possible values of a single-valued variable. Conjointly a rule will be seen as a piece of knowledge concerning the way how the value of a variable Y depends on the values of other variables X_i. The rules will be considered as general laws in the sense that they are supposed to always hold and not only in the case of some particular items whose attributes are denoted by the variable X_i and Y.

Thus, let us consider the following example of analogical reasoning (Winston, 1980 ; Chouraqui, 1982) taken from (Bourelly, Chouraqui,Ricard, 1983) :

The position of city T is <u>coastal</u> and its latitude is <u>medium</u> ; The climate of T is <u>temperate</u>
The position of city T' is <u>not far from the sea</u> and its latitude is <u>medium</u>

The climate of T' is <u>temperate</u>

The confidence in the result of such an analogical reasoning depends

i)   on the validity of the analogy (i.e. the similarity between the predicates and the certainty that similar or identical predicates mean the same thing in the different premises when they are vague or fuzzy ; this can be estimated using the possibility and necessity measures defined by (68) and (69) ; see (Farreny, Prade, 1982)

ii)   on the extent of the analogy taken into account in the inference and of course,

iii)   on the existence of a dependence between the attributes under consideration. In the above example the reasoning seems valid because of the similarities of the predicates and because of the dependence (<u>not stated</u> in the premises) between the climate on the one hand, and the position and the latitude on the other hand. In this example we consider two <u>singular</u> situations (the ones of cities T and T') which are paralled without any explicit statement of the possible causal link between the two propositions concerning T, i.e. we have not a possibly partial and imprecise, but general description of the relation between the nature of climate, the position and the latitude. Taking into account such a general rule will be possible with extensions of modus ponens.

In the next section we present and discuss the generalization of modus ponens to rules and facts represented by means of possibility distributions.

b) <u>Deductive inference with fuzzy or imprecise premises</u>

α) *Description of a causal link by a conditional possibility distribution*

Let X and Y be two variables whose domains are S and T respectively. A causal link from X to Y is represented here as a conditional possibility distribution (Zadeh, 1978a, 1981a) $\pi_{Y|X}$ which restricts the possible values of Y for a given value of X ; in other words $\pi_{Y|X}(.,s)$ is the membership function, from T to [0,1], of the fuzzy set of elements of T which are possibly in causal relation with $s \in S$; $\pi_{Y|X}(t,s)$ is the possibility that $Y = t$ if $X = s$. $\pi_{Y|X}$ extends the idea of a function and more generally of a multiple-valued mapping.

Let π_X be a possibility distribution which a priori restricts the possible values of the variable X. Then the possibility distribution $\pi_{X,Y}$ restricting the possible values of the pair (X,Y) is obtained by combining $\pi_{Y|X}$ and π_X, i.e.

$$\forall \ s \in S, \ \forall \ t \in T, \ \pi_{X,Y}(s,t) = \pi_X(s) * \pi_{Y|X}(t,s) \tag{77}$$

where * is a combination operation. Triangular norms (see the appendix), in particular a*b = min(a,b), a*b = a.b or a*b = max(0,a+b-1), are good candidates for this combination operation. However, due to the distinct nature of the elements to combine in (77), it does not seem absolutely necessary that the operation * satisfies symmetry and associativity requirements, which are characteristic properties of triangular norms. For other choices of * including non-symmetrical pseudo-conjunctions the reader is referred to Dubois, Prade (1984a).

By projection (see II.2.b.δ) we get the possibility distribution restricting the possible values of Y

$$\forall \ t \in T, \ \pi_Y(t) = \sup_{s \in S} \ \pi_{Y|X}(t,s) * \pi_X(s) \tag{78}$$

The formula (78) is the analogous in possibility theory of

$$\forall \ t \in T, \ p_Y(t) = \sum_{s \in S} p_{Y|X}(t,s) \cdot p_X(s) \tag{79}$$

in probability theory where p denotes a probability allocation and S is assumed to be finite.

β) Representation of the rule "if X is F, then Y is G"

As explained in II.2.a.α, "X is F" can be represented by $\pi_X = \mu_F$ where π_X is the possibility distribution restricting the possible values of X and μ_F is the characteristic function of the set F. Note that this representation applies to fuzzy sets underlain by predicates as well as to crisp sets.

In pratice, the complete description of the causal link in terms of $\pi_{Y|X}$ is not available in general. We may only have a collection of rules of the form

$$\text{"if } X \text{ is } F_i \text{, then } Y \text{ is } G_i \text{"} \qquad\qquad i = 1,n$$

which provides an incomplete description of the causal link from S to Y, each rule being viewed as

$$\text{"if } \pi_X = \mu_{F_i} \text{, then } \pi_Y = \mu_{G_i} \text{"}$$

where the μ_{F_i}'s and the μ_{G_i}'s are the membership functions of fuzzy sets in S and in T respectively, which are supposed to be normalized (i.e. $\exists\ s,\ \mu_{F_i}(s) = 1$ and $\exists\ t,\ \mu_{G_i}(t) = 1$), in the following.

We first consider the case of one rule ; then using (78) "if X is F, then Y if G" translates, as pointed out in (Prade, 1983 ; Dubois, Prade, 1984a ; Dubois, Prade, 1985b), into the inequality

$$\forall\ t \in t,\ \sup_{s \in S} \pi_{Y|X}(t,s) * \mu_F(s) \leq \mu_G(t) \qquad\qquad (80)$$

where $\pi_{Y|X}$ is unknown ; the inequality stems from the entailment principle (Zadeh, 1979a), "if Y is G, then Y is G'" as soon as G' corresponds to a larger possibility distribution (i.e. $\forall\ t,\ \mu_{G'}(t) \geq \mu_G(t)$), since the rule does not necessarily state the most restrictive possibility distribution for Y given the one restricting X.

We are interested in the greatest solution (in the sense of fuzzy set inclusion) $\pi_{Y|X}$ of (80) since it is the less restrictive one. Note that (80) always has a normalized solution since F and G are normalized. The greatest solution $\hat{\pi}_{Y|X}$ is given by

$$\hat{\pi}_{Y|X}(t,s) = \mu_F(s) *\!\!\to \mu_G(t) \qquad\qquad (81)$$

with

$$a *\!\!\to b = \sup\ \{x \in [0,1], x*a \leq b\} \qquad\qquad (82)$$

It can be noticed that $\mu_{F \times G}$ (defined by (53)) is also a solution of (80) for $* = \min$, however it is not the greatest solution generally. The expression (82) yields for

. $a*b = \min(a,b)$, Gödel implication (Rescher, 1969) : $a *\!\!\to b = \begin{cases} 1 \text{ if } a \leq b \\ b \text{ if } a > b \end{cases} \qquad (83)$

. $a*b = a.b$, Goguen implication (1969) : $a \overset{2}{*\!\to} b = \begin{cases} 1 & \text{if } a = 0 \\ \min(1, b/a) & \text{if } a \neq 0 \end{cases}$ (84)

. $a*b = \max(0, a+b-1)$, Łukasiewicz implication (Rescher, 1969) :
$$a \overset{3}{*\!\to} b = \min(1, 1-a+b) \tag{85}$$

Note that $\forall\, (a,b) \in [0,1]^2$, $a \overset{1}{*\!\to} b \leq a \overset{2}{*\!\to} b \leq a \overset{3}{*\!\to} b$. For $* = \min$, the expression (81) defines a more specific possibility distribution than with the other triangular norms. Other implication functions considered in multiple-valued logic, can be obtained in (82) with other choices for the combination operation $*$. See (Dubois, Prade, 1984a).

It is worth noticing that our representation of the rule in terms of the greatest solution of(80) does give back $\pi_Y = \mu_G$ when we apply (78) with $\pi_X = \mu_F$ and $\pi_{Y|X} = \hat{\pi}_{Y|X}$, in any case, when $*$ is a continuous triangular norm.

Note that $\hat{\pi}_{Y|X}$, defined by (81)-(82), is such that

$$\text{if } \mu_F(s) = 0, \text{ then } \hat{\pi}_{Y|X}(t,s) = 1, \; \forall\, t \in T \tag{86}$$

It means that if we consider a possible value of X outside of the support of the fuzzy set F, i.e. among the elements of $\{s \in S, \mu_F(s) = 0\}$, the possible corresponding value of Y remains completely indeterminate, when we only consider the rule "if X is F, then Y is G", which is natural. Besides, it is also worth-noticing that with the implication functions defined by (82), we have $a \overset{*\!\to}{} b = b$ as soon as $a = 1$, and thus

$$\text{if } \mu_F(s) = 1, \text{ then } \hat{\pi}_{Y|X}(t,s) = \mu_F(s) \overset{*\!\to}{} \mu_G(t) = \mu_G(t), \; \forall\, t \in T \tag{87}$$

which means that if we are certain that the value of X is among the ones compatible with "X is F", the possible values of Y are exactly restricted by the possibility distribution μ_G, which is satisfying.

γ) *Generalized modus ponens*

The so-called "generalized modus ponens" introduced by Zadeh (Zadeh, 1978b ; 1979a; 1979b) corresponds to the following pattern of reasoning.

$$\frac{\begin{array}{l} \text{If X is F, then Y is G} \\ \quad \text{X is F'} \end{array}}{\text{Y is G'}} \tag{88}$$

The possibility distribution $\pi_Y = \mu_{G'}$, which can be deduced from the two premises, is obtained by a direct application of (78) where $\pi_X = \mu_{F'}$ and $\pi_{Y|X} = \hat{\pi}_{Y|X}$ defined by (81)-(82) :

$$\forall\, t \in T, \; \mu_{G'}(t) = \sup_{s \in S} (\mu_F(s) \overset{*\!\to}{} \mu_G(t)) * \mu_{F'}(s) \tag{89}$$

In the following (89) will be symbolically denoted by

$$G' = (F \overset{*\!\to}{} G) \circ F' \tag{90}$$

The following desirable properties can be proved (Dubois, Prade, 1984a ; Dubois, Prade, 1985b) when * is a triangular norm :

. $F'' \subseteq F' \Rightarrow (F *\!\!\to G) \circ F'' \subseteq (F *\!\!\to G) \circ F'$ (91)

Thus G' obtained by (89), is all the more restrictive that F' is more restrictive itself.

. $(F *\!\!\to G) \circ F' \supseteq G$ provided that F' is normalized.   (92)

The conclusion yielded by the generalized modus ponens cannot be less restrictive than G ; it is in agreement with the situation in classical logic where, F', F, G being crisp sets, we can deduce that "Y is G" from "X is F' " and "if X is F, then Y is G" provided that $F' \subseteq F$, otherwise the value of Y remains completely indeterminate (i.e. "Y is T"). It is worth noticing that (92) holds with equality i.e. $(F *\!\!\to G) \circ F' = G$ as soon as $F' \subseteq F$, F' being normalized, since we have $(F *\!\!\to G) \circ F = G$ and the sup-* composition is monotonous.

The following compositional property holds (Dubois, Prade, 1984a ; 1985b)

. $G' \supseteq G \Rightarrow [G' *\!\!\to H] \circ [(F *\!\!\to G) \circ F'] = [(G' *\!\!\to H) \circ (F *\!\!\to G)] \circ F'$ (93)

In other words, the formal mechanism which from two rules of the form "if X is F, then Y is G" and "if Y is G', then Z is H" where $G' \supseteq G$, enables the rule "if X is F, then Z is H" to be validated in the crisp case, is preserved in the fuzzy case.

For discussing (88) in terms of truth-values, Baldwin (1979 ; 1982), has introduced the compatibilities (see II.2.d.α), CP(F;F') and CP(G;G') which are nothing but the possibility distributions attached to the values of the degrees of truth of the propositions "X is F" and "Y is G" knowing respectively that "X is F' " and that "Y is G' ". Then (89) becomes

$$\begin{cases} \cdot\ \mu_{CP(F;F')}(x) = \sup_{x=\mu_F(s)} \mu_{F'}(s) \\ \qquad\qquad\quad = 0 \text{ if } \mu_F^{-1}(x) = \emptyset \\ \cdot\ \mu_{CP(G;G')}(y) = \sup_{x \in [0,1]} f(x,y) * \mu_{CP(F;F')}(x) \\ \cdot\ \mu_{G'}(t) \qquad = \mu_{CP(G;G')}(\mu_G(t)) \end{cases}$$
       (94)

where f is the implication function which is used. (94) is equivalent to (88), provided that $f(a,b) = a *\!\!\to b$.

More generally, if a fuzzy truth-value τ is attached to the rule "if X is F, then Y is G", this must be understood as (see Prade, 1983 ; 1985c)

$$\tau = CP(F *\!\!\to G ; X \to Y)$$

with $\mu_{X \to Y} = \pi_{Y|X}$ and $\mu_{F *\!\!\to G} = \mu_F *\!\!\to \mu_G$. Then we have (from (76))

$$\hat{\pi}_{Y|X}(t,s) = \mu_\tau(\mu_F(s) *\!\!\to \mu_G(t))$$
       (95)

thus (89) is generalized by

$$\forall\, t,\ \mu_{G'}(t) = \sup_s\ \mu_\tau(\mu_F(s) \overset{*}{\to} \mu_G(t)) * \mu_{F'}(s) \tag{96}$$

For $\mu_\tau(x) = x$, $\forall\, x \in [0,1]$, (96) gives back (89) ; this fuzzy truth-value is implicitly assumed in (88).

δ) The limits of the generalized modus ponens

An important remark must be made about the generalized modus ponens and formula (89) which expresses it, concerning its scope of applicability. Since with the implication functions (83) and (84) we have $a \overset{*}{\to} 0 = 0$ if $a \neq 0$ and $0 \overset{*}{\to} 0 = 1$, the expression of $\mu_{G'}(t)$ in (89), if $\mu_G(t) = 0$ reduces to

$$\forall\, t,\ \mu_G(t) = 0 \Rightarrow \mu_{G'}(t) = \sup_{\substack{s \\ \mu_F(s)=0}}\ \mu_{F'}(s) = \mu_{CP(F;F')}(0) \tag{97}$$

and more generally

$$\forall\, t,\ \mu_{G'}(t) \geq \sup_{\substack{s \\ \mu_F(s)=0}}\ \mu_{F'}(s) \tag{98}$$

Thus we have

$$(\exists\, s \in S,\ \mu_{F'}(s) = 1 \text{ and } \mu_F(s) = 0) \Rightarrow \forall\, t,\ \mu_{G'}(t) = 1 \tag{99}$$

<u>N.B.</u> If instead of min or the product we use another operation in (78) and (89) and consequently another implication in (89), we still obtain results similar to (98), i.e. a lower bound for $\mu_{G'}$ depending only on the relative position of F and F'. For Łukasiewicz implication (85) we have

$$\forall\, t,\ \mu_{G'}(t) \geq \sup_{s \in S}\ \max(0,\ \mu_{F'}(s) - \mu_F(s)) \tag{100}$$

For other implications see (Dubois, Prade, 1984a).

When $F' \subseteq F$ (i.e. $\mu_{F'} \leq \mu_F$) (89) gives $\mu_{G'} = \mu_G$ provided that F' is normalized. What (98) or (100) points out is that a uniform level of indetermination Θ appears (in the sense that $\forall\, t,\ \mu_{G'}(t) \geq \Theta$) as soon as F' is no longer included in F. The level of indetermination is all the greater as a significant part of F' is not included in F, which is intuitively natural. As pointed out by (99), when $\mu_{F'} = 1 - \mu_F$ and $\exists\, s,\ \mu_{F'}(s) = 1$, we have $\Theta = 1$ in any case ; indeed, from "X is not F" and "if X is F, then Y is G", we cannot deduce anything concerning Y.

In some situations, it might be useful to have at our disposal a pattern of inference of the following kind.

> X is F'
>
> if X is F, then Y is G
>
> F' "differs" from F, but F' is not "far" from F $\qquad\qquad$ (101)
> ____
>
> Y is G' with G' not "far" from G

226

where "far" refers to metrics defined in S and in T and extended to fuzzy sets of S and T. Such a reasoning, which departs from the generalized modus ponens as pointed out in (Dubois, Prade, 1984a) or (Dubois, Prade, 1985b), is plausible rather than approximate. Indeed such an extrapolation can be safe only if we suppose that the relations which links the possible values of Y to the value of X and which is partially described by the rule "if X is F, then Y is G", is "continuous" in the neiborghood of the fuzzy Cartesian product F×G. The smaller the distance between F and F', the safer the result of the inference. A pattern of inference like (101) yields a conclusion which is only "plausible" in the sense that we have no information about its degree of certainty or if we prefer about the plausibility of other statements concerning Y, as long as we have no additional information on the relationship between Y and X. Contrastedly, in the generalized modus ponens, from "X is F'" and "if X is F, then Y is G", we deduce that "Y is G'" where G' is such that

$$\mu_{G'}(t) = 1 \text{ if } \mu_G(t) = 1 \tag{102}$$

$$\mu_{G'}(t) \in [\max(\Theta(F;F'), \mu_G(t)), 1] \text{ if } 0 < \mu_G(t) < 1 \tag{103}$$

$$\mu_{G'}(t) = \Theta(F;F') \text{ if } \mu_G(t) = 0 \tag{104}$$

with $\Theta(F;F') = \sup_{\substack{s \\ \mu_F(s) = 0}} \mu_{F'}(s)$ when $*$ is the min operation or the product. When F is a crisp set, F' being normalized, (103) reduces to $\mu_{G'}(t) = \max(\Theta(F;F'), \mu_G(t))$ since implication functions defined by (82) satisfy $0 \twoheadrightarrow b = 1$ and $1 \twoheadrightarrow b = b$. $\Theta(F;F')$ is the possibility that x is outside the support of F, $\{s \in S, \mu_F(s) > 0\}$, knowing that "X is F'". Thus roughly speaking (102)-(104) express that "Y is G" (or something a bit fuzzier when F is not crisp) with a certainty which can be estimated by $1-\Theta(F;F')$, viewing this certainty as the impossibility that "X is not F at all" knowing that "X is F'". The generalized modus ponens is a pattern of deductive reasoning taking into account the uncertainty due to the fuzziness of the premises.

In several papers (Fukami, Mizumoto, Tanaka, 1980 ; Mizumoto, Fukami, Tanaka, 1979b ; Mizumoto, Zimmermann, 1982) the following example of a pattern of fuzzy reasoning is given.

> "if a tomato is red, then the tomato is ripe"
> "the tomato is very red"
> ____
> then   "the tomato is very ripe"

However, the generalized modus ponens cannot enable us to obtain this conclusion from the two above premises only. Such an inference presupposes we know that the ripeness degree is an increasing function of the color intensity, which is not stated in the premises.

However it is possible to somewhat accommodate the generalized modus ponens in order to make it more flexible by enlarging F and G by means of two fuzzy tolerance relation R_S and R_T into $\tilde{F}$ and $\tilde{G}$ respectively defined by

$$\mu_{\tilde{F}}(s) = \sup_{s' \in S} \min(\mu_{\tilde{F}}(s'), \mu_{R_S}(s,s')) \geq \mu_F(s) \tag{105}$$

$$\mu_{\tilde{G}}(t) = \sup_{t' \in T} \min(\mu_{\tilde{G}}(t'), \mu_{R_T}(t,t')) \geq \mu_G(t) \tag{106}$$

where R_S and R_T model approximate equalities and are reflexive and symmetrical fuzzy relations (R is reflexive if $\forall\, x$, $\mu_R(x,x) = 1$ and symmetrical if $\forall\, x$, $\forall\, y$, $\mu_R(x,y) = \mu_R(y,x)$). When from the rule "if X is F, then Y is G" we postulate the new rule "if X is $\tilde{F}$, then Y is $\tilde{G}$"; we can then obtain non-trivial conclusions for F' not included in F, but in $\tilde{F}$ only.

ε) Case of several rules

Let us now consider a set of rules

"if X is F_i, then Y is G_i", i = 1,n

where the μ_{F_i}'s and μ_{G_i}'s are viewed as possibility distributions ; it provides an incomplete description of a causal link from X to Y.

It can be proved (Dubois, Prade, 1984a), (Dubois, Prade, 1985b) that the conditional possibility distribution defined by

$$\hat{\pi}_{Y|X}(t,s) = \min_{i=1,n} \mu_{F_i}(s) \overset{*}{\to} \mu_{G_i}(t) \tag{107}$$

is the most valid representation of a set of rules "if X is F_i, then Y is G_i", (i = 1,n) ; note that since min is idempotent, adding a new rule identical to one already there leaves $\hat{\pi}_{Y|X}$ unchanged.

With this representation, the inference mechanism works as follows. Given the statement "X is F'" and the collection of rules "if X is F_i, then Y is G_i", (i = 1,n), we deduce the statement "Y is G'" where

$$G' = F' \circ [\bigcap_i (F_i \overset{*}{\to} G_i)]$$

This way of processing a set of rules has the following properties (Dubois, Prade, 1984a), (Dubois, Prade, 1985b) : $\forall\, j$, $1 \leq j \leq n$; $\forall\, k$, $1 \leq k \leq n$,

$$(F_j \cup F_k) \circ \bigcap_i (F_i \overset{*}{\to} G_i) \subseteq G_j \cup G_k \tag{108}$$

$$(F_j \cap F_k) \circ \bigcap_i (F_i \overset{*}{\to} G_i) \subseteq G_j \cap G_k \tag{109}$$

where $\cup$ and $\cap$ translate into max and min respectively ; particularly we may take j = k in (108) or (109). These results are appealing since, if a known fact of the form "X is A" where A corresponds to a disjunction (resp. conjunction) of facts appearing as conditions in the if-parts of a set of fuzzy rules, then the disjunction (resp. conjunction) of the respective consequents is obtained.

One may think of another inference mechanism from a set of rules, where the rules are separately considered. This alternative procedure is summarized by the following expression :

$$G' = \bigcap_{i=1,n} G'_i \qquad (110)$$

with

$$G'_i = F' \circ [F_i \ast\!\!\rightarrow G_i]$$

where $\bigcap$ translates into min. It can be checked that

$$F' \circ [\bigcap_{i=1,n} (F_i \ast\!\!\rightarrow G_i)] \subseteq \bigcap_{i=1,n} [F' \circ (F_i \ast\!\!\rightarrow G_i)] \qquad (111)$$

which expresses the consistency of this second procedure with respect to the first one expressed by (107). Moreover, a counterpart of (109) holds (Dubois, Prade, 1984a ; Dubois, Prade, 1985b), when rules are kept separate :

$$\bigcap_{i=1,n} [(F_j \cap F_k) \circ (F_i \ast\!\!\rightarrow G_i)] \subseteq G_j \cap G_k \qquad (112)$$

However the counterpart of (108) is not valid generally ; for instance, if $n = 2$ and $F_1 \cap F_2 = \emptyset$, then

$$\bigcup_{i=1,2} (F_1 \cup F_2) \circ (F_i \ast\!\!\rightarrow G_i) = T$$

Hence $G' = T$ (i.e. $\forall \ t \in T, \ \mu_{G'}(t) = 1$) ; thus instead of deducing $G' = G_1 \cup G_2$ as the first procedure does, keeping the rules separate only provides a trivial conclusion.

Note that when we deal with rules of the form "if X is F_i, then Y is G_i" the collection of fuzzy sets F_i and G_i are only supposed to be normalized ; there is no requirement of mutual exclusiveness or of exhaustiveness.

ζ) Compound conditions

In section II.2.b.δ, we saw that a compound proposition "X_1 is F_1 and X_2 is F_2" where X_1 and X_2 are two variables taking their values in S_1 and S_2 respectively, can be correctly represented by the possibility distribution $\pi_{X_1,X_2} = \mu_{F_1 \times F_2}$ provided the two variables X_1 and X_2 are non-interactive. Then, a rule of the form "if X_1 is F_1 and ... and X_m is F_m, then Y is G" will be represented by the possibility distribution

$$\pi_{Y|X_1,\ldots,X_m}(t,s_1,\ldots,s_m) = (\min_{j=1,m} \mu_{F_j}(s_j)) \ast\!\!\rightarrow \mu_G(t) \qquad (113)$$

In case of interactivity the possibility distribution $\pi_{X_1,\ldots,X_m}$ cannot be expressed as the min-combination of its projections, and must be dealt with as such. In any case the generalized modus ponens can be obviously extended in order to accommodate rules with a conjunctive condition part.

c) Reasoning with uncertain premises

α) *Basic pattern*

The possibility distribution-based approach to deductive reasoning which was presented in detail in section III.1.a is now particularized in the case of uncertain premises. In a previous section (II.2.a.γ) we pointed out that a <u>non-vague</u> proposition p expressing an item of information of the form "X is F" whose uncertainty is estimated in terms of possiblity and necessity, can be represented by the possibility distribution

$$\forall \ s \in S, \ \pi_X(s) = \mu_{\hat{F}}(s) = \begin{cases} \Pi(p) & \text{if } s \in F \\ 1-N(p) & \text{if } s \notin F \end{cases} \tag{114}$$

with the normalization constraint $\max(\Pi(p), 1-N(p)) = 1$. In other words, the proposition "X is F" is possibly true at the degree $\Pi(p)$ and necessarily true at the degree N(p)" is translated in a new proposition "X is $\hat{F}$" which itself is regarded as certain, but where $\hat{F}$ is a genuine fuzzy set (while F is an ordinary subset of S).

A rule "if p, then q" is uncertain if one is not completely sure that q is true as soon as p is true. A natural way to quantify this uncertainty is to evaluate first, to what extent it is <u>sufficient</u> that p be true for having q true and second, to what extent it is <u>necessary</u> that p be true for having q true. The second evaluation can be seen as the degree to which it is sufficient to have p false in order to have q false. This way of considering a conditional relation between two propositions (Martin-Clouaire, Prade, 1985a) generalizes the notion of necessary and sufficient condition and has been used by others in some different mathematical framework ; see (Duda, Gaschnig, Hart, 1981 ; Soula, Vialettes, San-Marco, 1983). The necessity measure $N(p \to q)$ that $p \to q$ is true (where "$\to$" denotes the material implication, p and q are non-fuzzy propositions) rates to what extent one is certain to be able to deduce (by the modus ponens logical rule of inference) that q is true knowing that p is true. Thus, $N(p \to q)$ corresponds to the degree to which it is sufficient to have p true in order to infer that q is true. Likewise, the necessity measure $N(\neg p \to \neg q) = N(q \to p)$ evaluates to what extent it is necessary that p be true for having q true. The rule "if p, then q", whose uncertainty is estimated by $N(p \to q)$ and $N(q \to p)$ and where the propositions p = "X is F" and q = "Y is G" are supposed to be non-vague (F and G are ordinary subsets), can be represented by the conditional possibility distribution :

$$\forall\ s \in S,\ \forall\ t \in T,\ \pi_{Y|X}(t,s) = \begin{cases} 1 & \text{if } s \in F,\ t \in G \\ 1-N(p{\to}q) & \text{if } s \in F,\ t \notin G \\ 1-N(q{\to}p) & \text{if } s \notin F,\ t \in G \\ 1 & \text{if } s \notin F,\ t \notin G \end{cases} \tag{115}$$

which can be obtained by applying (114) to the propositions $p \to q$ and $\neg p \to \neg q$. More precisely, we get (115) by using the identities $N(p \to q) = 1-\Pi(\neg(p \to q)) = 1-\Pi(p{\wedge}\neg q)$ and similarly $N(q \to p) = 1-\Pi(\neg p{\wedge} q)$, by assuming that $N(p \to q) > 0$ and $N(q \to p) > 0$ (which implies $\Pi(p \to q) = 1 = \Pi(q \to p)$ due to (16)), and by observing that $p \to q = \neg p{\vee}q = (p{\wedge}q) \vee (\neg p{\wedge}\neg q) \vee (\neg p{\wedge}q)$ which yields $\max(\Pi(p{\wedge}q),\Pi(\neg p{\wedge}\neg q)) = 1$ using (13). $\pi_{Y|X}$ defined by (115) is the less restrictive possibility distribution compatible with the available knowledge. By applying (81), (83) and (107) it can consistently be checked that the rule "if p, then q" whose uncertainty is evaluated by $N(p \to q)$ <u>and</u> $N(q \to p)$, is equivalent to the <u>two</u> following rules :

$$\text{"if X is F, then Y is } \hat{G}\text{" with } \mu_{\hat{G}}(t) = \begin{cases} 1 \text{ if } t \in G \\ 1-N(p{\to}q) \text{ if } t \notin G \end{cases} \tag{116}$$

$$\text{"if X is not F, then Y is } \underset{\vee}{G}\text{" with } \mu_{\underset{\vee}{G}}(t) = \begin{cases} 1-N(q{\to}p) \text{ if } t \in G \\ 1 \text{ if } t \notin G \end{cases} \tag{117}$$

It can be checked that the application of (78), <u>with $* = $ min</u>, where π_X and $\pi_{Y|X}$ are defined by (114) and (115) respectively, and which corresponds to the generalized modus ponens applied to the fact "X is $\hat{F}$" and to the combination of the rules (116)-(117), yields

$$\forall\ t \in T,\ \pi_Y(t) \leq \begin{cases} \max(1-a',b') \text{ if } t \in G \\ 1-\min(a,b) \text{ if } t \notin G \end{cases} \tag{118}$$

with $N(p) \geq b$, $\Pi(p) \leq b'$, $N(p \to q) \geq a > 0$ and $N(q \to p) \geq a' > 0$. Note that it can be easily checked that π_Y is normalized (i.e. $\max(1-\min(a,b),\max(1-a',b')) = 1$) as soon as π_X is itself normalized (i.e. $\max(1-b,b') = 1$).

The result expressed by (118) can be presented under the form of the more explicit pattern

$$\begin{array}{l} N(p \to q) \geq a \\ N(\neg p \to \neg q) \geq a' \\ N(p) \geq b,\ \Pi(p) \leq b' \text{ with } \max(1-b,b') = 1 \\ \hline N(q) \geq \min(a,b),\ \Pi(q) \leq \max(1-a',b') \end{array} \tag{119}$$

where p and q are non-fuzzy propositions. This pattern of reasoning which deals with uncertain premises can be also directly established (Prade, 1985c ; Dubois, Prade, 1985d) from the axiomatic properties of possibility and necessity measures. Similarly, the following pattern, where the inequalities concerning $N(p)$ and $\Pi(p)$ are reversed in comparison with (119), can be derived (Prade, 1985c ; Dubois, Prade, 1985d)

$$N(p \to q) \geq a$$
$$N(\neg p \to \neg q) \geq a'$$
$$\underline{N(q) \leq b, \quad \Pi(p) \geq b'} \tag{120}$$
$$N(q) \leq \begin{cases} 1 \text{ if } a' \leq b \\ b \text{ if } a' > b \end{cases}, \quad \Pi(q) \geq \begin{cases} 0, \text{ if } a+b' \leq 1 \\ b' \text{ if } a+b' > 1 \end{cases}$$

The pattern (119) may be compared with its probabilistic counterparts which are easy to establish

$$\text{Prob}(p \to q) \geq a$$
$$\text{Prob}(\neg p \to \neg q) \geq a'$$
$$\underline{b \leq \text{Prob}(p) \leq b'} \tag{121}$$
$$\max(0, a+b-1) \leq \text{Prob}(q) \leq \min(1, 1-a'+b')$$

and

$$\text{Prob}(q|p) \geq a$$
$$\text{Prob}(p|q) \geq a' > 0$$
$$\underline{b \leq \text{Prob}(p) \leq b'} \tag{122}$$
$$a.b \leq \text{Prob}(q) \leq \min(1, b'/a')$$

The patterns (119), (121) and (122) are formally similar and their differences in the operations used for computing the bounds on the uncertainty of the conclusion reflects the difference of nature between the measures used for grading the uncertainty or the different modelings of the causal links between p and q in terms of material implication or in terms of conditioning. In (Dubois, Prade, 1985f) it is pointed out that the pattern (121) still holds with the same operations for computing the upper and lower bounds when the inequalities $b \leq \text{Prob}(p) \leq b'$ are replaced by $b \leq \text{Cr}(p) \leq \text{Pl}(p) \leq b'$, $\text{Prob}(q)$ by $\text{Cr}(q) \leq \text{Pl}(q)$, $\text{Prob}(p \to q)$, $\text{Prob}(\neg p \to \neg q)$ by $\text{Cr}(p \to q)$, $\text{Cr}(\neg p \to \neg q)$ respectively. This is not very surprising since a probability measure is both a credibility and a plausibility function ; besides, necessity and possibility measures are particular cases of credibility and plausibility functions respectively, which explains that we get improved bounds in (119) ($\forall a, \forall b, \min(a,b) \geq \max(0,a+b-1)$ and $\forall a', \forall b', \max(1-a',b') \leq \min(1,1-a'+b')$). Slightly different patterns of reasoning with uncertainty are presented in (Dubois, Prade, 1985a) where choices other than min are considered in (78) and in (118) and where conditional possibilities and necessities are used, and in (Prade, 1985c) where a multi-valued logic-based approach is discussed.

<u>N.B.</u> In MYCIN, the product is used, rather than the min operation as in (119), for computing the degree of belief in the conclusion of a rule from the degrees of belief in the rule itself and in the fact which triggers the rule.

β) *a matrix calculus*

The expression (78) applied with * = min to the particular case of uncertain but non-vague propositions p and q (then the universe S and T can be viewed as reduced to the set $\{p, \neg p\}$ and $\{q, \neg q\}$ respectively), can be conveniently presented in a matrix form :

$$\begin{bmatrix} \Pi_Y(q) \\ \Pi_Y(\neg q) \end{bmatrix} = \begin{bmatrix} \Pi_{Y|X}(q,p) & \Pi_{Y|X}(q,\neg p) \\ \Pi_{Y|X}(\neg q,p) & \Pi_{Y|X}(\neg q,\neg p) \end{bmatrix} \begin{bmatrix} \Pi_X(p) \\ \Pi_X(\neg p) \end{bmatrix} \tag{123}$$

where the matrix product is defined by analogy with the usual one, changing the sum into max operation and the product into min operation. It is interesting to notice that when the possibility degrees are only known to be restricted to subintervals, the matrix product can still be performed since max and min operations are extended in the following way

$$\max([a,b],[c,d]) = [\max(a,c),\max(b,d)] \tag{124}$$

$$\min([a,b],[c,d]) = [\min(a,c),\min(b,d)] \tag{125}$$

Note that a precise value is a particular case of a subinterval : a = [a,a]. Then remembering that $\forall$ p, $N(p) = 1-\Pi(\neg p)$, the pattern of reasoning expressed by (118)-(119) corresponds to the matrix product, where the inequalities translate into subintervals.

$$\begin{bmatrix} 1 & [0,1-a'] \\ [0,1-a] & 1 \end{bmatrix} \begin{bmatrix} [0,b'] \\ [0,1-b] \end{bmatrix} = \begin{bmatrix} [0,\max(1-a',b')] \\ [0,1-\min(a,b)] \end{bmatrix} \tag{126}$$

In this framework the ordinary modus ponens corresponds to the product (Prade, 1985b ; Farreny, Prade, 1985a ; Farreny, Prade, 1985a,b)

$$\begin{bmatrix} 1 \\ 0 \end{bmatrix} = \begin{bmatrix} 1 & [0,1] \\ 0 & [0,1] \end{bmatrix} \begin{bmatrix} 1 \\ 0 \end{bmatrix} \tag{127}$$

since a certain proposition p is represented in (123) by $\Pi_X(p) = 1$, $\Pi_X(\neg p) = 0$ (and thus $N(p) = 1$) and a certain rule "if p, then q" by $\Pi_{Y|X}(q,p) = 1$, $\Pi_{Y|X}(\neg q,p) = 0$ (when p is true, "$\neg q$ true" is completely impossible) while $\Pi_{Y|X}(q,\neg p)$ and $\Pi_{Y|X}(\neg q,\neg p)$ remain completely indeterminate in the absence of other information.

As pointed out in (Farreny, Prade, 1985a) and (Farreny, Prade, 1985b) and as suggested by the following small example, this matrix calculus can be used as a possible approach to some kinds of default reasoning. Suppose our knowledge base contains some information pertaining to the usual meeting behaviour of people :

(I) if Bob comes, generally Mary comes

(II) Bob comes

(III) if Mary comes, then Tom comes

The default rule (1) will be represented by

$$\Pi_I = \begin{bmatrix} \Pi_I(M,B) & \Pi_I(M,\neg B) \\ \Pi_I(\neg M,B) & \Pi_I(\neg M,\neg B) \end{bmatrix} = \begin{bmatrix} 1 & ? \\ \lambda & ? \end{bmatrix}$$

with $1 > \lambda \geq 0$, where ? stands for $[0,1]$ while the hard fact and rule (II) and (III) are respectively represented by

$$\Pi_{II} = \begin{bmatrix} \Pi_{II}(B) \\ \Pi_{II}(\neg B) \end{bmatrix} = \begin{bmatrix} 1 \\ 0 \end{bmatrix} \quad \text{and} \quad \Pi_{III} = \begin{bmatrix} \Pi_{III}(T,M) & \Pi_{III}(T,\neg M) \\ \Pi_{III}(\neg T,M) & \Pi_{III}(\neg T,\neg M) \end{bmatrix} = \begin{bmatrix} 1 & ? \\ 0 & ? \end{bmatrix}$$

By chaining, we obtain the following result concerning Mary's coming :

$$\Pi_I \circ \Pi_{II} = \begin{bmatrix} \Pi(M) \\ \Pi(\neg M) \end{bmatrix} = \begin{bmatrix} 1 & ? \\ \lambda & ? \end{bmatrix} \begin{bmatrix} 1 \\ 0 \end{bmatrix} = \begin{bmatrix} 1 \\ \lambda \end{bmatrix}$$

and finally concerning Tom's coming :

$$\Pi_{III} \circ \Pi_{II} \circ \Pi_I = \begin{bmatrix} \Pi(T) \\ \Pi(\neg T) \end{bmatrix} = \begin{bmatrix} 1 & ? \\ 0 & ? \end{bmatrix} \begin{bmatrix} 1 \\ \lambda \end{bmatrix} = \begin{bmatrix} 1 \\ [0,\lambda] \end{bmatrix}$$

Note that if Π_{III} is changed into $\begin{bmatrix} 1 & 1 \\ 0 & 0 \end{bmatrix}$ we obtain $\begin{bmatrix} \Pi(T) \\ \Pi(\neg T) \end{bmatrix} = \begin{bmatrix} 1 \\ 0 \end{bmatrix}$, which is in agreement with out intuition, since it corresponds to add the rule "if Mary does not come, then Tom comes', while changing Π_{III} into $\begin{bmatrix} 1 & 0 \\ 0 & 1 \end{bmatrix}$ (i.e. adding the rule 'if Mary does not come, then Tom does not come') would yield $\begin{bmatrix} \Pi(T) \\ \Pi(\neg T) \end{bmatrix} = \begin{bmatrix} 1 \\ \lambda \end{bmatrix}$.

This quantitative approach to default reasoning may be considered as being in the spirit of Rich (1983) and departs from the symbolic one based on formal logic developed by Reiter and Criscuolo (1980,1981,1983);see also (Moore, 1983). For more details on the approach sketched above, see (Farreny, Prade, 1985a ; 1985b).

γ) *Reasoning with fuzzy default values*

Now we consider the more general case of uncertain fuzzy facts such as "X is F with a necessity degree equal to 1-α", where F refers to a fuzzy set. As discussed in sections II.2.a.α and II.2.b.α, such an information can be represented by the possibility distribution

$$\forall \; s \in S, \; \pi_X(s) = \max(\mu_F(s),\alpha) = \mu_F^{\boxed{\alpha}}(s) \tag{128}$$

From a default reasoning point of view, F can be viewed as a fuzzy default set of possible values for X, since there remains a possibility equal to α that X takes its value outside of F. This may correspond to situations stated under the form "Generally, X is F" or "Usually, X is F".

We are now in position to apply the generalized modus ponens introduced in section III.1.b.γ, to the two premises

> Usually (α), X is F'
>
> Usually (β), if X is F, then Y is G

where α and β are respectively the degrees of possibility that X takes its value outside F' and that the default rule does not hold. Using (78) with $* = \min$, we get (Prade, 1985a)

$$\forall\ t \in T,\ \pi_Y(t) = \sup_{s \in S} \min[\max(\mu_{F'}(s),\alpha),\max(\mu_F(s)*{\to}\mu_G(t),\beta)] \tag{129}$$

Provided that F' is normalized and $\exists\ s,\ \mu_F(s) = 0$, (129) reduces to

$$\forall\ t \in T,\ \pi_Y(t) = \max(\mu_{G'}(t),\alpha,\beta) \tag{130}$$

where $\mu_{G'}$ is the result obtained by application of the standard generalized modus ponens and given by (89). It was pointed out in section III.1.b.δ that

$$\forall\ t,\ \mu_{G'}(t) \geq \sup_{s,\mu_F(s)=0} \mu_{F'}(s) \overset{\Delta}{=} \gamma$$

and thus (130) indicates that the possibility that Y takes its value outside the support of G is equal to $\max(\alpha,\beta,\gamma)$. This result is not surprising since the conclusion concerning Y may be indeterminate, if F' is not a correct fuzzy value for X, or if the default rule does not hold in the case under consideration, or if a significant part of F' is not included in F. When $F' \subseteq F$ (i.e. $\mu_{F'} \leq \mu_F$), we have G' = G (see III.1.b.γ) and then from "Usually X is F" and "Usually, if X is F, then Y is G" we conclude that "Usually Y is G" with $\pi_Y = \max(\mu_G,\alpha,\beta)$. If instead of knowing that "X is $F'^{[\alpha]}$" (using the notation introduced in (128)) we have two pieces of information "X is $F_1'^{[\alpha_1]}$" and $F_2'^{[\alpha_2]}$" for instance, with $F_1' \subseteq F$ and $F_2' \subseteq F$, we can then conclude that $\pi_Y(t) = \max(\mu_G(t), \min(\alpha_1,\alpha_2),\beta)$, which is satisfactory.

Note that (130) includes (118) as a particular case since then F and G are ordinary subsets, G' = G, and (130) corresponds to the matrix product (in the sense of section III.1.c.β)

$$\begin{bmatrix} 1 & 1 \\ \beta & 1 \end{bmatrix}\begin{bmatrix} 1 \\ \alpha \end{bmatrix} = \begin{bmatrix} 1 \\ \max(\alpha,\beta) \end{bmatrix}.$$

It must be pointed out that here our view of default values is not statistical in nature. The situation is analyzed in terms of the possibility that a default value is not correct and not in terms of the frequency with which this default value is not correct. If we assume a frequentist interpretation with a probability equal to $(1-\alpha)$ that "X is F" is true and a probability equal to $(1-\beta)$ that "if X is F, then Y is G" is true we clearly conclude, under an independence assumption, that the probability that "Y is

G" is true is $(1-\alpha).(1-\beta)$ or if we prefer that there is a probability equal to $1-(1-\alpha).(1-\beta) = \alpha+\beta - \alpha.\beta$ that Y is indeterminate. Thus with different interpretations of α and β we get $\alpha+\beta - \alpha.\beta$ in the probabilistic case and $\max(\alpha,\beta)$ in the possibilistic one. Note also that $\max(\alpha,\beta) \simeq \alpha+\beta - \alpha.\beta$ when α and β are almost zero or 1 or when one of α and β is much greater that the other. See Rauch (1984) for a related discussion dealing with the notion of independence.

δ) Probabilistic uncertainty and fuzzy premises

Finally, we consider a situation where probability and possibility are mixed together. We are supposed to have the $n+1$ rules

> if X is F_i, then Y is G_i $i = 1,n$
> if X is F_0, then Y is indeterminate

where the $F_0, F_1,...,F_n$ are non-fuzzy and form a partition of S and the G_i's are normalized fuzzy sets. A distribution of probability $p_i = P(F_i)$ ($\sum_{i=0}^{n} p_i = 1$) is known. The problem is to find what can be said of the proposition 'Y is G' in terms of probability.

As it has been recognized by Zadeh (1979d), here information consists of a probability distribution and of a conditional possibility distribution $\pi_{Y|X}(t,s) = \mu_{G_i}(t)$ if $s \in F_i$. This problem has been considered by Dempster (1967) when the G_i's are non-fuzzy. When they are, using the degree of intersection $\Pi(G;G_i)$ and the degree of inclusion $N(G;G_i)$ of G_i in G, given by (46) and (47), i.e. $\Pi(G;G_i) = \sup\limits_{t \in T} \min(\mu_G(t),\mu_{G_i}(t))$; $N(G;G_i) = \inf\limits_{t \in T} \max(\mu_G(t),1-\mu_{G_i}(t))$ we are in position to compute the plausibility

$$Pl_Y(G) = \sum_{i=1}^{n} p_i.\Pi(G;G_i) + p_0 \tag{131}$$

and the credibility

$$Cr_Y(G) = \sum_{i=1}^{n} p_i.N(G;G_i) \tag{132}$$

using (61) and (62). Lastly, when the values of the p_i's are only approximately known and represented by fuzzy numbers, expressions (131) and (132) can be generalized and remain computationally tractable using recent results in fuzzy arithmetics by Dubois and Prade (1981).

If the p_i's are replaced by possibility degrees π_i, $i = 0,n$ in the above problem, we recover the usual possibilistic scheme of approximate reasoning encompassed in the general formula (78).

236

d) <u>Some problems of reasoning under uncertainty</u>

In this section a brief account on some worth-mentioning questions related to the management of uncertain pieces of knowledge, is given

α) *Questions of transitivity*

As pointed out by Zadeh (1982 ; 1984a) (see Reiter and Criscuolo (1983) for a related discussion), from the two premises

> All the x's which satisfy property A, satisfy property B
> Most of the X's which satisfy property B, satisfy property C

we <u>cannot deduce anything</u> concerning the proportion of x's which satisfy C among the ones which satisfy A, while if we replace "Most of" by "All" in the second premise, we obviously conclude that "All the x's which satisfy A, satisfy C too". Such a brittleness is particularly striking since it happens as soon as the quantifier in the second premise is not "All", even if the proportion to which it refers is very near to 1 (but not equal to 1).

Nevertheless if we consider a particular x_0 which satisfies A, we can conclude that x_0 also satisfies B from the first premise, and then, <u>in the absence of any other information</u>, x_0 probably satisfies C with a probability which is all the greater as the referred proportion in the second premise is nearer to 1, even if nothing enables us to support the rule "Most of the x's which satisfy A, also satisfy C". See (Dubois, Farreny, Prade, 1985) for a more detailed discussion.

When we consider a rule of the form "if X is F, then Y is G", we generally implicitely assume that this rule applies to any possible item x for which the variables X and Y involved in the rule make sense as attribute values, just because the expert knowledge encoded in rules is supposed to be appropriate to analyse or diagnose any particular situation in the field of expertise. The transitivity property proved in section III.1.b.ε for the generalized modus ponens is satisfying because it is supposed to apply to a particular situation (i.e. a particular x), even if the F and G of a rule may be pervaded with imprecision of uncertainty. However in section III.2.a we shall see that the absence of any, even weak, transitivity property in the pattern of reasoning considered at the begining of this section, leads to tricky questions when combining uncertain pieces of information.

The reader is referred to Zadeh (1982 ; 1983a,b ; 1984a) for a study of different patterns of reasoning involving fuzzy quantifiers.

β) *Unequal importance of conditions*

Another intricate issue which is worth mentioning is what may be called "the unequal importance" of conditions in the if-part of a rule. Let us consider a rule of the form "if $p_1 \wedge p_2 \wedge \ldots \wedge p_n$, then generally q". By the unequal importance of the conditions "p_i true" with respect to the conclusion "q true", we mean that the uncertainty on the truth of each p_i may have unequal consequences on the uncertainty of the conclusion q. Expert system knowledge gives examples of rules where some conditions must be imperatively satisfied in order to be able to conclude, while the satisfying of others improve only the certainty of the conclusion. We may also imagine that there is some possible <u>compensation</u> between the degrees to which each condition is satisfied, when estimating the certainty of the conclusion (for instance if the rule expresses the evaluation of a complex object, see (Martin-Clouaire, Prade, 1985b) for a related discussion). In other cases, the conditions may have equal importance, but may not need to be all imperatively satisfied in order to conclude with some certainty, the satisfying of (at least) <u>most</u> of them being sufficient, see Yager (1984 ; 1985a).

For dealing with these questions we have suggested (see Prade (1984b)) for each rule to use a table giving a partial, possibly linguistic (i.e. imprecise or fuzzy) specification of the relation between the degrees of certainty (expressed in terms of possibility and necessity, or in terms of compatibility (or of probability as well) of $p_1, p_2, \ldots, p_n$ and the degree of certainty of q (similarly expressed). The information contained in this table can be viewed as a collection of metarules of the kind "if the degree of truth (or of certainty) of p_1 is restricted by the fuzzy set σ_1 and ... and if the degree of truth of p_n is restricted by σ_n, then the degree of truth of q is restricted by τ. From this collection of metarules and the actual degrees of truth $\sigma'_1, \sigma'_2, \ldots, \sigma'_n$ of $p_1, p_2, \ldots, p_n$ the (possibly fuzzy) degree of truth τ' of q can be computed using the approach of the generalized modus ponens. When p_i is of the form "X_i is F_i", the actual degree of truth of p_i can be computed as the compatibility of "X_i is F_i" with respect to the reality "X_i is F'_i" (see section II.2.d.α). More precisely, given the table which provides a rough description of the uncertainty of q in function of the uncertainty of the conditions $p_1, p_2, \ldots, p_n$, namely

p_1	p_2	$\ldots$	p_n	q
σ_{11}	σ_{12}		σ_{1n}	τ_1
σ_{21}	σ_{22}		σ_{2n}	τ_2
$\ldots$	$\ldots$		$\ldots$	$\ldots$
σ_{m1}	σ_{m2}		σ_{mn}	τ_m

the membership function of the degree of truth τ' of q could be obtained as

$$\forall \ x \in [0,1], \ \mu_{\tau'}(x) = \sup_{x_1,x_2,\ldots,x_n} \min\left(\min_{i=1,n} \mu_{\sigma'_i}(x_i), \min_{j=1,m} \left[\left(\min_{i=1,n} \mu_{\sigma_{ji}}(x_i) \right)^* \to \mu_{\tau_j}(x) \right] \right) \qquad (133)$$

With such an approach the way of combining the degrees to which the conditions of a compound condition are satisfied and of propagating the uncertainty to the conclusion-part of the rule, would be implicitly encoded in the table attached to the rule. A rough description by means of fuzzy degrees of the relation between the uncertainty of the conclusion and the uncertainty attached to the satisfying of the condition(s), might be sufficient in practice.

2 - COMBINING UNCERTAIN OF IMPRECISE ITEMS OF INFORMATION

a) <u>Is combining always suitable ?</u>

Before presenting and discussing the rules of combination which have been proposed in different framework, we start with a brief analysis of situations where it may be not suitable to combine.

When two rules having the form "if X^1 is F^1, then Y is G^*" and "if X^2 is F^2, then Y is G^{**}" respectively, are confronted with the two pieces of information "X^1 is F'^1" and "X^2 is F'^2", two conclusions about the value of Y are obtained. These two results can be combined provided the relation between X^1 and Y is independent of the relation between X^2 and Y (i.e. the rule "if X^1 is F^1, then Y is G^*" is effectively true whatever value X^2 has and vice versa, the rule "if X^2 is F^2, then Y is G^{**}" is true whatever value X^1 takes). In case of non-independence, the knowledge concerning the relation between Y and the other variables must appear in rules of the form "if X^1 is F^1 and X^2 is F^2, then Y is ..." rather than in rules considering X^1 and X^2 separately.

Several default values cannot be used simultaneously in a reasoning process if they are interacting. In other words, assuming some default value for a variable may not be consistent with assuming some default value for another variable whose value logically depends on the value of the former variable, if this interaction between the values of the two variables is not taken into account. For example, let us suppose that the value of a variable Y is at least partially determined by the values X_1 and X_2. Moreover we suppose that "X_1 is F_1 and X_2 is F_2" is almost impossible, and we have for instance the two rules "if X_1 is F_1 and X_2 is not F_2, then Y is G" and "if X_1 is not F_1 and X_2 is F_2, then Y is G". Then if from a source of information we know for sure that X_1 is F_1, we may assume the fuzzy default value $\bar{F}_2$ (where the complement is defined by $\mu_{\bar{F}} = 1-\mu_F$) for X_2, i.e. we consider that "X_2 is $\bar{F}_2^{[\beta]}$" using the notation used in III.1.c.γ. Thus we conclude using the generalized modus ponens that "Y is $G^{[\beta]}$". Now if from another source of information we know that X_2 is F_2 and then we assume that "X_1 is $\bar{F}_1^{[\alpha]}$", we conclude that "Y is $G^{[\alpha]}$". Finally combining the two partial results we shall conclude that "Y is $C^{[\alpha*\beta]}$" where * is some combining operation. This conclusion albeit uncertain, may be quite different from the actual one, since it may happen that "if X_1 is F_1 and X_2 is F_2, then Y is not G" is true in the reality.

Another kind of situation where combining is not suitable is the following one. (Dubois, Prade, 1985e). Let us consider a knowledge base where we have the certain fact

x_0 satisfies property A

and the rules

All the x's which satisfy A, satisfy B	(rule 1)
Almost all the x's which satisfy B, satisfy C	(rule 2)
Most of the x's which satisfy A, do not satisfy C	(rule 3).

Using only rule 1 and rule 2 would yield that x_0 satisfies C very probably, while the direct use of rule 3 enables us to conclude that x_0 does not satisfy C probably. However the knowledge basis is not inconsistent, since it is possible that the exceptions of rule 2 are mainly made of the x's which satisfy A (we have not any rule which would say that "Most of the x's which satisfy B, satisfy A"). In this situation we have only to consider the result given by rule 3, which is the <u>most specific</u> rule with respect to the set of items to which it applies. The result obtained from rule 1 and rule 2 has some value only if we have not the rule 3 at our disposal. See Ginsberg (1984) and Dubois, Farreny, Prade (1985) for further discussions.

b) Dempster's rule of combination

Let m_1 be two basic probability assignments (in the sense of (4)) representing two uncertain bodies of evidence relative to a same matter. Dempster's rule of combination (Dempster, 1967 ; 1968), which generalizes Bayes' rule, enables us to combine them in order to get a new basic probability assignment m defined by

$$m(\emptyset) = 0; \ \forall \ C \neq \emptyset, \ m(C) = \frac{\displaystyle\sum_{\substack{i,j \\ A_i \cap B_j = C}} m_1(A_i).m_2(B_j)}{\displaystyle\sum_{\substack{i,j \\ A_i \cap B_j \neq \emptyset}} m_1(A_i).m_2(B_j)} \tag{134}$$

Note that m does not exist when there is no common part between the focal elements of m_1 and those of m_2. Dempster's rule of combination is associative. See (Barnett, 1981 ; Garvey, Lowrance, Fischler, 1981 ; Lowrance, Garvey, 1982 ; Wesley, 1983) for application-oriented presentations of (134).

Zadeh (1979c ; 1984b) has discussed the normalization in (134) which may be unsuitable since when the denominator of (134) is not equal to 1; the quantity

$$\sum_{\substack{i,j \\ A_i \cap B_j = \emptyset}} m_1(A_i).m_2(B_j) > 0$$

evaluates the degree to which the two evidences are dissonant ; the normalization conceals the existence of this dissonance. Indeed if we consider the particular case where we only have three mutually exclusive alternatives, a, b, c and we apply (134) to the basic probability assignments

$$m_1(a) = 0, \qquad\qquad m_1(b) = 0.1, \qquad\qquad m_1(c) = 0.9$$
$$m_2(a) = 0.9, \qquad\qquad m_2(b) = 0.1, \qquad\qquad m_2(c) = 0$$

which corresponds to two extremely dissonant sources of information, we find the sharp result

$$m(a) = 0, \qquad\qquad m(b) = 1, \qquad\qquad m(c) = 0$$

as pointed out by Zadeh (1984b). However if we slightly alter m_1 and m_2 in the following way

$$m_1'(a) = 0.01, \qquad\qquad m_1'(b) = 0.1, \qquad\qquad m_1'(c) = 0.89$$
$$m_2'(a) = 0.89, \qquad\qquad m_2'(b) = 0.1, \qquad\qquad m_2'(c) = 0.01$$

then (134) yields

$$m'(a) \simeq 0.32, \qquad\qquad m'(b) \simeq 0.36, \qquad\qquad m'(c) \simeq 0.32$$

which is a very unsharp result. This "discontinuity" in the behavior of (134) may look strange and rather catastrophic at first glance. But in the first case the sources 1 and 2 assert their <u>complete</u> certainty in the total impossibility of alternatives a and c respectively and thus b remains as the only possible alternative even if both sources a priori consider b as quite improbable. Contrastedly in the second case both sources do not completely reject any alternatives a priori, even if some ones are almost impossible and if they disagree on what are so. When a source is not definitely certain of something, but only almost certain, this source basically accepts to revise its judgement in the light of new information or opinion, or at least to see that the reality gives an unexpected result in the future. Thus assessing a zero value or a very small value to a probability (or a possibility) may lead to extremely different conclusions in some cases. See (Dubois, Prade, 1985f) for further discussions.

Some particular cases of (134) are noticeable.

c) <u>Particular cases</u>

. When m_1 and m_2 reduce to two probability distributions p_1 and p_2, (134) gives back the combined probability distribution p

$$\forall \ s \in S, \ p(s) = \frac{p_1(s).p_2(s)}{\sum_{s \in S} p_1(s).p_2(s)} \tag{135}$$

If S has only <u>two</u> elements s and $\bar{s}$ (i.e. there are only two possibilities), (135) gives

$$p(s) = \frac{p_1(s).p_2(s)}{1-p_1(s) - p_2(s) + 2\,p_1(s).p_2(s)} \tag{136}$$

This aggregation operation has been extensively used by Kayser (1979) ; it is also worth noticing that (136) is the expression of an associative "symmetrical sum" * in the sense of Silvert (1979), i.e. we have $p_1*p_2 = 1-(1-p_1)*(1-p_2)$, where p_1*p_2 denotes the operation defined by (136).

. When m_1 reduces to p_1 and $m_2(A) = 1$ (which entails $m_2(B) = 0$, $\forall\,B \neq A$), (134) gives the usual conditioning $p(s) = \dfrac{p_1(s)}{P_1(A)}$ is $s \in A$ and $p(s) = 0$ if $s \notin A$ with $P_1(A) = \displaystyle\sum_{s \in A} p_1(s)$.

. If m_1 and m_2 are such that, $\exists\,A$, $m_1(A) = 1-m_1(S)$ and $m_2(A) = 1-m_2(S)$, i.e. A is the unique and common focal element (apart S) of m_1 and m_2), then (134) gives for m, whose focal elements are also A and S

$$\begin{aligned} m(A) &= m_1(A) + m_2(A) - m_1(A) \cdot m_2(A) \\ m(S) &= (1-m_1(A)) \cdot (1-m_2(A)) \end{aligned} \tag{137}$$

In MYCIN (Shortliffe, Buchanan, 1975), the belief or disbelief measures are combined in the following way

. if $MB(h,e_1) > 0$ and $MB(h,e_2) > 0$ (which entails $MD(h,e_1) = MD(h,e_2) = 0$)

$$MB(h,e_1 \wedge e_2) = MB(h,e_1) + MB(h,e_2) - MB(h,e_1) \cdot MB(h,e_2) \tag{138}$$

. if $MD(h,e_1) > 0$ and $MD(h,e_2) > 0$ (which entails $MB(h,e_1) = MB(h,e_2) = 0$)

$$MD(h,e_1 \wedge e_2) = MD(h,e_1) + MD(h,e_2) - MD(h,e_1) \cdot MD(h,e_2) \tag{139}.$$

In case of a positive measure of belief and a positive measure of disbelief, there is a conflict and another combination formula is used (Buchanan, Shortliffe, 1984). Note that (138) and (139) are similar to (137).

d) The case of possibility distributions

When m_1 and m_2 reduce to two possibility distributions π_1 and π_2, the result given by (134) is not a possibility distribution except in some noticeable particular cases (when apart of S, m_1 and m_2 have only one focal element each, but not necessarily the same). If we want to obtain a possibility distribution, several proposals can be made with some justifications (see Dubois, Prade, 1985a), among them, we have the analogous of (135) :

$$\forall\,s \in S,\; \pi(s) = \frac{\min(\pi_1(s),\pi_2(s))}{\displaystyle\sup_{s \in S}\,\min(\pi_1(s),\pi_2(s))} \tag{140}$$

242

In (140), the use of the normalization may be discussed as in the case of Dempster's rule and we may think of using another operation than 'min', although the idempotence of min seems a desirable property. The extension of (140) to k sources (k > 2) is obvious. With this extension of (140), one source which disagrees with all the others is sufficient to lead to a strongly dissonant situation. In other words, a belief is not made stronger, if it is shared by many sources. Besides, the relative importance (or reliability) of the sources might be took into account in this framework by using an approach recently proposed in multi-criteria aggregation (see Dubois, Prade, 1985d, pp. 89-90).

In the case where S has only two elements which corresponds to two opposite alternatives p and $\neg$ p, and where there are k sources of information which provide $N_i(p)$ and $\Pi_i(p)$, the rule of combination (140) reduces to

$$N(p) = 1 - \frac{1 - \max_{i=1,k} N_i(p)}{\max(\min_{i=1,k} (1-N_i(p)), \min_{i=1,k} \Pi_i(p))}$$

$$\Pi(p) = \frac{\min_{i=1,k} \Pi_i(p)}{\max(\min_{i=1,k} (1-N_i(p)), \min_{i=1,k} \Pi_i(p))}$$

$$(141)$$

with $N_i(p) = 1-\Pi_i(\neg p)$. See (Martin-Clouaire, Prade, 1985a ; 1985b).

It is worth noticing that the normalization used in (141) is very similar to the one used in the MYCIN combination formula in case of conflict (when $\exists$ i, MB_i > 0, $\exists$ j$\neq$i, MD_j > 0) (Buchanan, Shortliffe, 1984)).

IV - CONCLUDING REMARKS

In this paper, a unified treatment of imprecision and uncertainty in reasoning mecanisms has been proposed. Possibility theory is a convenient framework for dealing with vague predicates or ill-bounded categories, uncertain facts or rules, imprecisely specified quantifiers. The degrees of uncertainty might be ill-known themselves ; in this case, the available results on arithmetic operations with fuzzy numbers (Dubois, Prade, 1980 ; 1981 ; 1985d) enable us to extend the procedures used with precise degrees of uncertainty in a computational way. The knowledge representation, in terms of possibility distributions, which is used seems more suitable for representing uncertainty here than a probability-based method, since we are able to distinguish between a total lack of certainty that p is satisfied ($\Pi(\neg p) = 1$) and the certainty that p is not satisfied ($\Pi(p) = 0$), which is not possible in probability theory where $Prob(\neg p) = 1$

⇐⇒ Prob(p) = 0. Max and min are "qualitative" operations which are in agreement with the possible lack of precision of the different possibility degrees, what really matters is only that some alternatives are certainly more possible than others. Operations used in probability theory are more sensitive to changes (even limited) in probability values. The number of inference systems explicitly based on possibility theory is increasing. Among those which appeared recently, let us mention REVEAL (Small, 1984), FRIL (Baldwin, 1983 ; Baldwin, Zhou, 1984), PROTIS (Soula, Vialettes, San Marco, 1983), SPHINX (Fieschi, 1984 ; Fieschi M., Joubert, Fieschi D., Soula, Roux, 1982), PI-QL (Whiter, 1984), SPII-1 (Martin-Clouaire, Prade, 1985b), DIABETO (Buisson, Farreny, Prade, 1985) ; see also (Tong, Shapiro, Dean, Mc Cune, 1983a ; 1983b), (Whalen, Schott, 1983a ; 1983b), (Ernst, 1981), (Ishizuka, Fu, Yao, 1982a ; 1982b), (Sanchez, Gouvernet, Bartolin, Vovan, 1981). A possibility theory-based approach seems also very promising for the management of incomplete information data bases (Prade, 1984a), (Prade, Testemale, 1984).

Besides, it was pointed out that the combination of uncertain items of information pertaining to a same matter is not always suitable. This may lead to difficult control problems. Moreover it is of the highest importance, when expressing the expert knowledge under the form of "if...,then... " rules, to specify all the parameters on which the conclusion may depend, in the same way as we have to take into account all the available information concerning all its arguments for estimating the value of a function.

Several issues related to approximate reasoning have not been dealt with in this paper ; particularly the problems of the strategies to use in reasoning processes : when is it better to look for establishing a particular conclusion (backward chaining), when is it better to derive all the possible conclusions from the available information (forward chaining), for instance ? Other important issues, such as the checking and the maintenance of the consistency of a knowledge base containing uncertain or imprecise items or the learning of fuzzy production rules from particular cases (Lesmo, Saitta, Torasso, 1982 ; 1983) would deserve a particular study also.

Acknowledgements

The author wants to thank his colleagues Didier Dubois, Henri Farreny, Roger Martin-Clouaire, Claudette Testemale for fruitful discussions about many issues of this paper.

A P P E N D I X

A triangular norm * (see Schweizer, B., Sklar, A. (1963) Associative functions and abstract semigroups. Publ. Math. (Debrecen), Vol. 10, pp. 69-81) is a two-place function from $[0,1] \times [0,1]$ to $[0,1]$ such that i) $a*b = b*a$, ii) $a*(b*c) = (a*b)*c$, iii) if $a \leq b$ and $c \leq d$, then $a*c \leq b*d$, and iv) $1*a = a$, $0*0 = 0$. The greatest triangular norm is min and the least one is defined by

$$a*b = T_W(a,b) = \begin{cases} a \text{ if } b = 1 \\ b \text{ if } a = 1 \\ 0 \text{ otherwise} \end{cases} \text{ ; thus we always have}$$

$T_W(a,b) \leq a*b \leq \min(a,b)$. Other noticeable triangular norms are $a*b = a.b$ and $a*b = \max(0,a+b-1)$, moreover we have $T_w(a,b) \leq \max(0,a+b-1) \leq a.b \leq \min(a,b)$. By duality each triangular norms * is associated with a triangular co-norm defined by

$$a \perp b = 1-(1-a) * (1-b)$$

Triangular norms are conjunction operators while co-norms are disjunction operators (see (Dubois, Prade, 1985d) for instance) ; the main co-norms are, in increasing order

$$\max(a,b) \leq a+b-a.b \leq \min(1,a+b) \leq \begin{cases} a \text{ if } b = 0 \\ b \text{ if } a = 0 \\ 1 \text{ otherwise} \end{cases}$$

There exist many parametered families of triangular norms and co-norms in the literature ; among them, the one studied and identified by Frank, M.J. (On the simultaneous associativity of $F(x,y)$ and $x+y-F(x,y)$. Aequat. Mat. Vol. 19, pp. 194-226, 1979) is specially remarkable since a triangular norm * of this family is such that $a+b = a*b + a \perp b$, where $\perp$ is the associated co-norm ; the members of this family range from $\max(0,a+b-1)$ to $\min (a,b)$ and are thus the only eligible operators compatible with an expression of $Prob(p \wedge q)$ in terms of $Prob(p)$ and $Prob(q)$.

REFERENCES

Adams, E.W., Levine, H.P., "On the uncertainties transmitted from premises to conclusions in deductive inferences". Synthese, 30, 429-460, 1975.

Adams, J.B., "A probability model of medical reasoning and the MYCIN model". Mathematical Biosciences, 32, 177-186, 1976.

Adlassnig, K.P., Kolarz, G., "CADIAG-2 : Computer - assisted medical diagnosis using fuzzy subsets". In : Approximate Reasoning in Decision Analysis (M.M. Gupta, E. Sanchez, eds.), North-Holland, 219-247, 1982.

Baldwin, J.F., "A new approach to approximate reasoning using a fuzzy logic". Fuzzy Sets and Systems, 2, 309-325, 1979.

Baldwin, J.F., "An automated fuzzy reasoning algorithm". In : Fuzzy Set and Possibility Theory : Recent Developments. (R.R. Yager, ed.), Pergamon Press, 169-195, 1979.

Baldwin, J.F., "A fuzzy relational inference language for expert systems". Proc. 13th IEEE Int. Symp. on Multiple-Valued Logic, Kyoto, Japan, 416-423, 1983.

Baldwin, J.F., Pilsworth, B.W., "Axiomatic approach to implication for approximate reasoning with fuzzy logic". Fuzzy Sets & Systems, 3, 193-219, 1980.

Baldwin, J.F., Pilsworth, B.W., "Fuzzy reasoning with probability". Proc. 11th IEEE Int. Symp. Multiple-Valued Logic, Oklahoma City, 100-108, 1981.

Baldwin, J.F., Zhou, S.Q., "An introduction to F.R.I.L. - A fuzzy relational inference language". Fuzzy Sets & Systems, 14, 155-174, 1984.

Bandler, W., Kohout, L.J., "The four modes of inference in fuzzy expert systems". Cybernetic & Systems Research, 2, (R. Trappl, ed.), North-Holland, 581-586, 1984.

Barnett, J.A., "Computational methods for a mathematical theory of evidence". Proc. 7th Int. Joint Conf. Artificial Intelligence, Vancouver, 868-875, 1981.

Bonissone, P.P., "A survey of uncertainty representation in expert systems". Proc. 2nd Workshop of North-American Fuzzy Information Processing Society, GE, CR & D, Schenectady, N.Y., 1983.

Bonnet, A., Harry, J., Ganascia, J.G., "LITHO, un système expert inférent la géologie du sous-sol". Technique et Science Informatiques, 1, 393-402, 1982.

Bouchon, B., "A propos des règles de combinaison employées dans les systèmes experts utilisant le raisonnement approximatif". Actes Journées "Utilisation de l'Information, des Questionnaires et des Ensembles Flous dans les Problèmes Décisionnels", Tours, France, Sept. 14-16, 1983.

Bourelly, L., Chouraqui, E., Ricard, M., "Formalisation of an approximate reasoning : The analogical reasoning". Proc. IFAC Symp. Fuzzy Information, Knowledge Representation & Decision Analysis, Marseille (France), 135-141, July 19-21, 1983.

Buchanan, B.G., Shortliffe, E.H. (eds.), "Uncertainty and evidential support". In : Rule-Based Expert Systems - The MYCIN Experiments of the Stanford Heuristic Programming Project. Addison-Wesley, Reading, 209-232, 1984.

Buisson, J.C., Farreny, H., Prade, H., "Un système expert en diabétologie accessible par minitel. Aspects informatiques". Actes 5ème Journées Internationales sur les Systèmes Experts et leurs Applications, Avignon, France, 174-189, May 13-15, 1985 .

Cantone, R.R., Pipitone, F.J., Lander, W.B., Marrone, M.P., "Model-based probabilistic reasoning for electronics trouble-shooting". Proc. 8th Int. Joint. Conf. on Artificial Intelligence, Karlsruhe, 207-211, Aug. 1983.

Cayrol, M., Farreny, H., Prade, H., "Possibility and necessity in a pattern matching process". Proc. IXth Int. Cong. on Cybernetics, Namur, Belgium, 53-65, Sept. 8-13 1980.

Cayrol, M., Farreny, H., Prade, H., "Fuzzy pattern matching". Kybernetes, 11, 103-116, 1982.

Chouraqui, E., "Construction of a model for reasoning by analogy". Proc. European Conf. on Artificial Intelligence, Orsay, 48-53, July 1982.

246

Colby, K.M., Smith, D.C., "Dialogues between humans and an artificial belief system". Proc. Int. Joint Conf. on Artificial Intelligence. Washington, D.C., 319-324, 1969.

Collins, A., "Fragments of a theory of human plausible reasoning". Proc. of TINLAP-2 ("Theoretical Issues in Natural Languages Processing-2") (D. Waltz, ed.), 194-201, 1978.

Cohen, P.R., "Heuristic Reasoning About Uncertainty : An Artificial Intelligence Approach". Pitman, Boston (204 p.), 1985.

Cohen, P.R., Grinberg, M.R., "A framework for heuristic reasoning about uncertainty". Proc. 8th Int. Joint Conf. Artif. Intelligence, Karlsruhe, 355-357, Aug. 1983.

De Kleer, J., Brown, J.S., "A qualitative physics based on confluences". Artificial Intelligence, $\underline{24}$, 7-83, 1984.

Dempster, A.P., "Upper and lower probabilities induced by a multivalued mapping". Annals of Mathematical Statistics, $\underline{38}$, 325-339, 1967.

Dempster, A.P., "A generalization of bayesian inference". J. Royal Statistical Society, $\underline{B-30}$, 205-247, 1968.

Doyle, J., "A truth maintenance system". Artificial Intelligence, $\underline{12}$, 231-272, 1979.

Doyle, J., "Some theories of reasoned assumptions - An essay in relational psychology". Memo CMU CS-83-125, Carnegie-Mellon University, 1983a.

Doyle, J., "Methodological simplicity in expert system construction : The case of judgments and reasoned assumptions". The AI Magazine, 39-43, Summer 1983, 1983b.

Dubois, D., Prade, H., "Operations in a fuzzy-valued logic". Information and Control, $\underline{43}$, n° 2, 224-240, 1979.

Dubois, D., Prade, H., "Fuzzy Sets and Systems : Theory and Applications". Vol. 144, in Mathematics in Sciences and Engineering Series. Academic Press, New York (393 p.), 1980.

Dubois, D., Prade, H., "Additions of interactive fuzzy numbers". IEEE Trans. Automatic Control, $\underline{26}$, n° 4, 926-936, 1981.

Dubois, D., Prade, H., "A class of a fuzzy measures based on triangular norms. A general framework for the combination of uncertain information". Int. J. of General Systems, $\underline{8}$, n° 1, 43-61, 1982a.

Dubois, D., Prade, H., "Degree of truth and truth-functionality". Proc. 2nd World Conf. on Maths. at the Service of Man, Las Palmas, Spain, June 28 - July 3, 1982, 262-265, 1982b.

Dubois, D., Prade, H., "On several representations of an uncertain body of evidence". In : Fuzzy Information and Decision Processes (M.M. Gupta, E. Sanchez, eds.), North-Holland, 167-181, 1982c.

Dubois, D., Prade, H., "Unfair coins and necessity measures. A possibilistic interpretation of histograms". Fuzzy Sets and Systems, $\underline{10}$, n° 1, 15-20, 1983.

Dubois, D., Prade, H., "Fuzzy logics and the generalized modus ponens revisited". Cybernetics & Systems, $\underline{15}$, 87-125, 1984a.

Dubois, D., Prade, H., "A note on measures of specificity for fuzzy sets". Int. J. of General Systems, 10, 279-283, 1984b.

Dubois, D., Prade, H., "Evidence measures based on fuzzy information". Automatica, 21, 547-562, 1985a.

Dubois, D., Prade, H., "The generalized modus ponens under sup-min composition. A theoretical study". In : Approximate Reasoning in Expert Systems (M.M. Gupta, A. Kandel, W. Bandler, J.B. Kiszka, eds.), North-Holland, 1985b.

Dubois, D., Prade, H., "The management of uncertainty in fuzzy expert systems and some applications". In : The Analysis of Fuzzy Information (J.C. Bezdek, ed.), Vol. 2, CRC Press, to appear, 1985c.

Dubois, D., Prade, H., "Théorie des Possibilités. Applications à la Représentation des Connaissances en Informatique". Masson, Paris (250 p.), 1985d. English version publ. by Plenum.
Dubois, D., Prade, H., "Le traitement de l'imprécision et de l'incertitude dans les modèles de raisonnement des experts". In : Introduction aux Systèmes Experts de Gestion (C. Ernst, ed.), Eyrolles, Paris, 93-115, 1985c.

Dubois, D., Prade, H., "Combination and propagation of uncertainty with belief functions". A reexamination. Proc. 9th Int. Joint Conf. Artificial Intelligence, Los Angeles, 111-113, 1985d.

Dubois, D., Farreny, H., Prade, H., "Sur divers problèmes inhérents à l'automatisation des raisonnements de sens commun". Proc. 5th Cong. AFCET Reconnaissance des Formes et I.A., Grenoble, 321-328, Nov. 1985.
Duda, R., Gaschnig, J., Hart, P., "Model design in the Prospector consultant system for mineral exploration". In : "Expert Systems in the Micro-Electronic Age" (D. Michie, ed.), Edinburgh Univ. Press, 153-167, 1981.

Duda, R.D., Hart, P.E., Nilsson, N.J., "Subjective bayesian methods for rule-based inference systems". Tech. Note n° 124, SRI-International, Menlo Park, Ca., (22 p.), 1976

Ernst, C., "An approach to management expert systems using fuzzy logic". In : Applied Systems and Cybernetics (G.E. Lasker, ed.), Pergamon Press, 2898-2905, 1981.

Farreny, H., Prade, H., "About flexible matching and its use in analogical reasoning". Proc. European Conf. on Artificial Intelligence, Orsay, 11-14 july 1982, 43-47, 1982.

Farreny, H., Prade, H., "A possibility theory-based approach to default and inexact reasoning". Computers & Artificial Intelligence (Bratislava), 4, 125-134 , 1985a.

Farreny, H., Prade, H., "Mécanisation de raisonnements par défaut en termes de possibilités". Actes Cong. AFCET Informatique "Matériels et Logiciels pour la 5ème Génération", Paris, March 5-7, 353-364, 1985b.

Fieschi, M., "Intelligence Artificielle en Médecine. Des Systèmes Experts". Masson, Paris, 1984.

Fieschi, M., Joubert, M., Fieschi, D., Soula, G., Roux, M., "SPHINX : an interactive system for medical diagnosis aids". In : Approximate Reasoning in Decision Analysis (M.M. Gupta, E. Sanchez, eds.), North-Holland, 269-275, 1982.

Fox, M.S., "Reasoning with incomplete knowledge in a resource - limited environment : integrating reasoning and knowledge acquisition". Proc. Int. Joint Conf. on Artificial Intelligence, Vancouver, Aug. 1981, 313-318, 1981.

248

Friedman, L., "Trouble-shooting by plausible inference". Proc. 1st Annual National Conf. Artificial Intelligence, Stanford, Aug. 1980, 292-294, 1980.

Friedman, L., "Extended plausible inference". Proc. 7th Int. Joint Conf. Artificial Intelligence, Vancouver, Août 1981, 487-495, 1981.

Fukami, S., Mizumoto, M., Tanaka, K., "Some considerations of fuzzy conditional inference". Fuzzy Sets and Systems, $\underline{4}$, 243-273, 1980.

Gaines, B.R., "Foundations of fuzzy reasoning". Int. J. Man-Machine Studies, $\underline{8}$, 623-668, 1976. (Also in : Fuzzy Automata and Decision Processes) (M.M. Gupta, G.N. Saridis, B.R. Gaines, eds.), North-Holland, 19-75, 1977.

Garvey, T.D., Lowrance, J.D., Fischler, M.A., "An inference technique for integrating knowledge from disparate sources". Proc. 7th Int. Joint Conf. Artificial Intelligence, Vancouver, Aug. 1981, 319-335, 1981.

Giles, R., "A formal system for fuzzy reasoning". Fuzzy Sets & Systems, $\underline{2}$, 233-257, 1979.

Giles, R., "A computer program for fuzzy reasoning". Fuzzy Sets & Systems, $\underline{4}$, 221-234, 1980.

Ginsberg, M.L., "Non-monotonic reasoning using Dempster's rule". Proc. Nat. Conf. on Artificial Intelligence (AAAI-84), Austin, Tx, Aug. 6-10, 126-129, 1984.

Glymour, C., "Independence assumptions and Bayesian updating". Artificial Intelligencen, $\underline{25}$, 95-99, 1985.

Gordon, J., Shortliffe, E.H., "The Dempster-Shafer theory of evidence". In : Rule-Based Expert Systems - The MYCIN Experiments of the Stanford Heuristic Programming Project (B.G. Buchanan, E.H. Shortliffe, eds.), Addison-Wesley, Reading, 272-292, 1984.

Goguen, J.A., "The logic of inexact concepts". Synthese, $\underline{19}$, 325-373, 1969.

Halpern, J.Y., Mc Allester, D.A., "Likelihood, probability, and knowledge". Proc. Nat. Conf. Artificial Intelligence (AAAI-84), Austin, Tx, Aug. 6-10, 137-141, 1984.

Hayes, P.J., "The naive physics manifesto". In : Expert Systems in the Micro-Electronic Age (D. Michie, ed.), Edinburgh University Press, 1979.

Hempel, C.G., "Studies in the logic of confirmation". In : "Aspects of Scientific Explanation and Other Essays in the Philosophy of Sciences", The Free Press, New York, 1965.

Ishizuka, M., "Inference methods based on extended Dempster and Shafer's theory for problems with uncertainty/fuzziness". New Generation Computing, $\underline{1}$, 159-168, 1983.

Ishizuka, M., Fu, K.S., Yao, J.T.P., "A theoretical treatment of certainty factor in production systems". Memo CE-STR-81-6, Purdue University, IN., (13 p.), 1981a.

Ishizuka, M., Fu, K.S., Yao, J.T.P., "Inexact inference for rule-based damage assessment to existing structures". Proc. 7th Int. Conf. on Artificial Intelligence, Vancouver, 837-842, 1981b.

Ishizuka, M., Fu, K.S., Yao, J.T.P., "Inference prodecures with uncertainty for problem reduction method". Information Sciences, $\underline{28}$, 179-206., 1982a.

Ishizuka, M., Fu, K.S., Yao, J.T.P., "A rule-based inference with fuzzy set for structural damage assessment". In : Approximate Reasoning in Decision Analysis (M.M. Gupta, E. Sanshez, eds.), North-Holland, 261-268, 1982b.

Kayser, D., "Vers une modélisation du raisonnement 'approximatif'". Proc. of the Colloque "Représentation des connaissances et Raisonnement dans les Sciences de l'Homme" (M. Borillo, ed.), Saint-Maximin, Sept. 1979, Publ. by INRIA, 440-457, 1979.

Kayser, D., "Comment représenter la typicalité ?", Actes Cong. AFCET Informatique "Matériels et Logiciels pour la 5ème Génération", Paris, March 5-7, 177-186, 1985.

Kim, J.H., Pearl, J., "A computational model for causal and diagnostic reasoning in inference systems". Proc. 8th Int. Conf. Artif. Intelligence, Karlsruhe, Aug. 83, 190-193, 1983.

Kling, R., "Fuzzy-PLANNER : Reasoning with inexact concepts in a procedural problem-solving language". J. of Cybernetics, 4, n° 2, 105-122, 1974.

Konolige, K., "Bayesian methods for updating probabilities". In : "A computer-based consultant for mineral exploration" by R.O. Duda, P.E. Hart, K. Konolige, R. Reboh. Final Report SRI Project 6415, SRI-International, Menlo Park, 83-146, 1979.

Laurière, J.L., "Un langage déclaratif : SNARK". Int. Rep., Institut de Programmation, Paris VI, 1984.

Le Faivre, R., "The representation of fuzzy knowledge", J. of Cybernetics, 4, n° 2, 57-66, 1974a.

Le Faivre, R., "Fuzzy problem-solving". Ph.D. Thesis, University of Wisconsin, 1974b.

Lemmer, J.F., Barth, S.W., "Efficient minimum information updating for bayesian inferencing in expert systems". Proc. 3rd, Annual American Artificial Intelligence Conf., 424-427, 1982.

Lesmo, L., Saitta, L., Torasso, P., "Learning of fuzzy production rules for medical diagnosis". In : Approximate Reasoning in Decision Analysis (M.M. Gupta, E. Sanchez, eds.), North-Holland, 249-260, 1982.

Lesmo, L., Saitta, L., Torasso, P., "Fuzzy production rules : A learning methodology". In : Advances in Fuzzy Sets, Possibility Theory, and Applications, (P.P. Wang, ed.), Plenum Press, 181-198, 1983.

Lesmo, L., Saitta, L., Torasso, P., "Evidence combination in expert systems". Int. J. Man-Machine Studies, 22, 1985.

Loui, R., "A perspective on probability in A.I.", Inter. Rep., Dept. of Computer Science, Univ. of Rochester, N.Y., 1984.

Lowrance, J.D., Garvey, T.D., "Evidential reasoning : A developing concept". Proc. IEEE Int. Conf. on Cybernetics and Society, 6-9, 1984.

Lesser, V.R., Reed, S., Pavlin, J., "Quantifying and simulating the behavior of knowledge-based interpretation systems". Proc. 1st Annual Nat. Conf. on Artificial Intelligence, Stanford, Aug. 1980, 111-115, 1980.

Lu, S.Y., Stephanou, H.E., "A set-theoretic framework for the processing of uncertain knowledge". Proc. Nat. Conf. Artificial Intelligence (AAAI-84), Austin, Tx, Aug. 6-10, 216-221, 1984.

Mamdani, E.H., "Application of fuzzy logic to approximate reasoning using linguistic systems. IEEE Trans. on Computers, $\underline{C-26}$, 1182-1191, 1977.

Martin-Clouaire, R., "Infering uncertain conclusion from imprecise premises : A fuzzy set-theoretical approach applied to medical diagnosis". Proc. 6th Int. Cong. Cybernetics & Systems, Paris, Sept. 10-14, 175-180, 1984a.

Martin-Clouaire, R., "A fast generalized modus ponens". BUSEFAL n° 18, L.S.I., Univ. P. Sabatier, Toulouse, 75-82, 1984b.

Martin-Clouaire, R., Prade, H., "Managing uncertainty and imprecision in petroleum geology". In "Computers in Earth Sciences for Natural Resources Characterization" (J.J. Royer, ed.), Int. Colloq. April 9-13, Nancy, France, 85-98, 1984.

Martin-Clouaire, R., Prade, H., "On the problems of representation and propagation of uncertainty". Int. J. Man-Machine Studies, $\underline{22}$, 251-264, 1985a.

Martin-Clouaire, R., Prade, H., "SPII-1 : A simple inference engine capable of accommodating both imprecision and uncertainty". In : Computer-Assisted Decision-Making (G. Mitra, ed.), North-Holland, 117-131, 1985b.

Mc Carthy, J., "Circumscription - A form of non-monotonic reasoning". Artificial Intelligence, $\underline{13}$, 27-39, 1980.

Mc Dermott, D., Doyle, J., "Non-monotonic logic I". Artificial Intelligence, $\underline{13}$, 41-72, 1980.

Mc Dermott, D., "Non-monotonic logic II : Non-monotonic modal theories". J. of Assoc. Comp. Mach., $\underline{29}$, 33-57, 1982.

Michalski, R.S., Chilausky, R.L., "Knowledge acquisition by encoding expert rules versus computer induction from examples : a case study involving soybean pathology". Int. J. Man-Machine Studies, $\underline{12}$, n° 1, 63-88, 1980.

Mizumoto, M., "Fuzzy reasoning with a fuzzy conditional proposition "if ... then ... else ...". In : Fuzzy Set & Possibility Theory : Recent Developments (R.R. Yager, ed.), Pergamon Press, 211-223, 1982.

Mizumoto, M., Fukami, S., Tanaka, K., "Fuzzy conditional inferences and fuzzy inferences with quantifiers". Proc. 6th Int. Joint Conf. Artificial Intelligence, Tokyo, 589-591, 1979a.

Mizumoto, M., Fukami, S., Tanaka, K., "Some methods of fuzzy reasoning". In : Advances in Fuzzy Set Theory and Applications (M.M. Gupta, R.K. Ragade, R.R. Yager, eds.), North-Holland, 117-136, 1979b.

Mizumoto, M., Zimmermann, H.J., "Comparison of fuzzy reasoning methods". Fuzzy Sets & Systems, $\underline{8}$, 253-283, 1982.

Moore, R.C., "Semantical considerations on nonmonotonic logic". Proc. 8th Int. Joint Conf. Artif. Intelligence, Karlsruhe, Aug. 83, 272-279, 1983.

Negoita, C.V., "Fuzzy sets in knowledge engineering". Proc. 6th Int. Cong. Cybernetics & Systems, Paris, Sept. 10-14, 181-186, 1984a.

Negoita, C.V., "Expert Systems and Fuzzy Systems". Benjamin/Cummings, Menlo park, (224 p.), 1984b.

Ng, S.W., Walker, A., "Max-min chaining of weighted causal assertions is loop free". 1st Annual National Conference on Artificial Intelligence, Stanford, Aug. 1980, 105-107, 1980.

Pearl, J., "Reverend Bayes in inference engines : A distributed hierarchical approach". Proc. 3rd Annual American Artificial Intelligence Conference, 133-136, 1982.

Pednault, E.P.D., Zucker, S.W., Muresan, L.V., "On the independence assumption underlying subjective bayesian updating". Artificial Intelligence, 16, 213-222, 1981.

Pólya, G., "Mathematics and Plausible Reasoning". Vol. II : Patterns of Plausible Inference". Princeton University Press, 2nd edition 1968, 1954.

Prade, H., "Plausible reasoning for artificial intelligence". Proc. of Selected Papers of the 1st Int. Conf. on Artificial Intelligence and Information-Control Systems of Robots. Bratislava, June 1980, 57-64, 1980a.

Prade, H., "Compatibilité. Qualification. Modification. Niveau de précision". BUSEFAL n° 4, L.S.I., Toulouse, 71-78, 1980b.

Prade, H., "Modal semantics and fuzzy set theory". In : Fuzzy Set and Possibility Theory: Recent Developments (R.R. Yager, ed.), Pergamon Press, 232-246, 1982 a.

Prade, H., "Degree of truth : matching statement against reality". BUSEFAL n° 9, L.S.I., Univ. P. Sabatier, Toulouse, 88-92, 1982b.

Prade, H., "A synthetic view of approximate reasoning techniques". Proc. Int. Joint Conf. on Artificial Intelligence, Karlsruhe, Aug. 1983, 130-136, 1983.

Prade, H., "Lipski's approach to incomplete information data bases restated and generalized in the setting of Zadeh's possibility theory". Information Systems, 9, n° 1, 27-42, 1984a.

Prade, H., "A fuzzy set-based approach to analogical, default and other kinds of plausible reasoning". Proc. 6th Int. Cong. Cybernetics & Systems, Paris, Sept. 10-14, 187-192, 1984b.

Prade, H., "Reasoning with fuzzy default values". Proc. 15th IEEE. Int. Symp. Multiple-Valued, Logic, Kingston, May 28-30, Ontario, 191-197, 1985a.

Prade, H., "A simple inference technique for dealing with uncertain facts in terms of possibility". Kybernetes, 15, 19-24, 1985b.

Prade, H., "A computational approach to approximate and plausible reasoning, with applications to expert systems". IEEE Trans. on Pattern Analysis and Machine Intelligence, 7, (3), 260-283, 1985. Corrections in 7 (6), 747-748, 1985c.

Prade, H., Testemale, C., "Generalized database relational algebra for the treatment of incomplete/uncertain information and vague queries". Information Sciences, 34, 115-143, 1984.

Quinlan, J.R., "Consistency and plausible reasoning". Proc. 8th Int. Joint Conf. Artif. Intelligence, Karlsruhe, Aug. 83, 137-144, 1983.

Rauch, H.E., "Probability concepts for an expert system used for data fusion". The AI Magazine, Fall 1984, 55-60, 1984.

Reiter, R., "A logic for default reasoning". Artificial Intelligence, 13, 81-132, 1980.

Reiter, R., Criscuolo, G., "On interacting defaults". Proc. Int. Joint Conf. on Artificial Intelligence, Vancouver, Aug. 1981, 270-276, 1981.

Reiter, R., Criscuolo, G., "Some representational issues in default reasoning". Computers & Mathematics with Applications, 9, n° 1, 15-27, 1983.

Rescher, N., "Many-Valued Logic". Mac Graw-Hill (359 p.), 1969.

Rescher, N., "Plausible Reasoning". Van Gorcum, Amsterdam (124 p.), 1976.

Rich, E., "Default reasoning as likelihood reasoning". Proc. Nat. Conf. on Artificial Intelligence (AAAI-83), Washington, D.C., Aug. 22-26, 348-351, 1983.

Rollinger, C.R., "How to represent evidence - Aspects of uncertain reasoning". Proc. 8th Int. Joint Conf. on Artif. Intelligence, Karlsruhe, Aug. 83, 358-361, 1983.

Sage, A.P., Botta, R.F., "On human information processing and its enhancement using knowledge-based systems". Large Scale Systems, 5, 35-50, 1983.

Sanchez, E., "Resolution of composite fuzzy relation equations". Information and Control, 30, 38-48, 1976.

Sanchez, E., "Solutions in composite fuzzy relation equations : Application to medical diagnosis in Brouwerian logic". In : "Fuzzy Automata and Decision Processes" (M.M. Gupta, G.N. Saridis, B.R. Gaines, eds.), North-Holland, 221-234, 1977.

Sanchez, E., Gouvernet, J., Bartolin, R., Vovan, L., "Linguistic approach in fuzzy logic of the W.H.O. classification of dyslipoproteinemias". In : Applied Systems and Cybernetics (G.E. Lasker, ed.), Pergamon Press, Vol. VI, 2884-2889, 1981.

Schefe, P., "On foundations of reasoning with uncertain facts and vague concepts". Int. J. of Man-Machine Studies, 12, 35-62, 1980.

Schefe, P., "On representing uncertainty in A.I. systems". Mitteilung n° 69, Institut für Informatic, University of Hamburg, (30 p.), 1979.

Sembi, B.S., Mamdani, E.H., "On the nature of implication in fuzzy logic". Proc. 9th IEEE Int. Symp. on Multiple-Valued Logic, Bath, 143-151, 1979.

Shackle, G.L.S., "Decision, Order and Time in Human Affairs". Cambridge University Press, Cambridge, U.K., 1961.

Shafer, G., "A Mathematical Theory of Evidence". Princeton University Press, (297 p.), 1976.

Shafer, G., "Probability judgement in artificial intelligence and expert systems". Working Paper n° 165, The University of Kansas, Lawrence, (39 p.), 1984.

Shortliffe, E.H., Buchanan, B.G., "A model of inexact reasoning in medicine". Mathematical Biosciences, 23, 351-379, 1975.

Silvert, W., "Symmetric summation : A class of operations on fuzzy sets". IEEE Trans. on Systems, Man and Cybernetics, 9, n° 10, 657-659, 1979.

Small, M., (ed.) "Policy Evaluation Using REVEAL". ICL Knowledge Engineering, Manchester, G.B., 1984.

Smets, P., The degree of belief in a fuzzy event". Information Sciences, $\underline{25}$, 1-19, 1981a.

Smets, P., "Medical diagnosis and degrees of belief". Fuzzy Sets and Systems, $\underline{5}$, 259-266, 1981b.

Soula, G., Sanchez, E., "Soft deduction rules in medical diagnostic processes". In : "Approximate Reasoning in Decision Analysis" (M.M. Gupta, E. Sanchez, eds.), North-Holland, 77-88, 1982.

Soula, G., Vialettes, B., San Marco, J.L., "PROTIS, a fuzzy deduction-rule system : Application to the treatment of diabetes". Proc. MEDINFO 83, Amsterdam, 1983.

Sugeno, M., "Theory of fuzzy integral and its applications". Ph.D. Thesis, Tokyo Institute of Technology, Tokyo, (124 p.), 1974.

Sugeno, M., Takagi, T., "Multi-dimensional fuzzy reasoning". Fuzzy Sets & Systems, $\underline{9}$, 313-325, 1983.

Suppes, P., "Probabilistic inference and the concept of total evidence". In : "Aspects of Inductive Logic" (J. Hintikka, P. Suppes, eds.), North-Holland, 49-65, 1966.

Szolovits, P., Pauker, S.G., "Categorical and probabilistic reasoning in medical diagnosis". Artificial Intelligence, $\underline{11}$, 115-144, 1978.

Tanaka, K., "Resume on dealing with uncertainty/ambiguity in conjunction with knowledge engineering". In : Applied Systems and Cybernetics. (G.E. Lasker, ed.), Pergamon Press, Vol. VI, 2866-2876, 1981. Also in : Fuzzy Set and Possibility Theory : Recent Developments (R.R. Yager, ed.), Pergamon Press, 38-48, 1982.

Tong, R.M., Efstathiou, J., "A critical assessment of truth functional modification and its use in approximate reasoning". Fuzzy Sets and Systems, $\underline{7}$, 103-108, 1982.

Tong, R.M., Shapiro, D.G., Dean, J.S., Mc Cune, B.P., "A comparison of uncertainty calculi in an expert system for information retrieval". Proc. 8th Int. Joint Conf. Artif. Intelligence, Karlsruhe, Aug. 83, 194-197, 1983a.

Tong, R.M., Shapiro, D.G., Mc Cune, B.P., Dean, J.S., "A rule-based approach to information retrieval : some results and comments". Proc. Nat. Conf. Artificial Intelligence (AAAI-83), Washington, D.C., Aug. 22-26, 411-415, 1983b.

Tsukamoto, Y., "An approach to fuzzy reasoning method". In : Advances in Fuzzy Set Theory and Applications (M.M. Gupta, R.K. Ragade, R.R. Yager, eds.), North-Holland, 137-149, 1979.

Tversky, A., Kahneman, D., "Judgement under uncertainty : Heuristics and biases. Science, $\underline{185}$, 1124-1131, 1974.

Thöle, U., Zimmermann, H.J., Zysno, P., "On the suitability of minimum and product operators for the intersection of fuzzy sets". Fuzzy Sets & Systems, $\underline{2}$, 167-180, 1979.

Trillas, E., Valverde, L., "On some functionaly expressable implications for fuzzy set theory". Proc. 3rd Int. Seminar on Fuzzy Set Theory, (E.P. Klement, ed.), J. Kepler Univ., Linz, Sept. 7-12, 1981, 173-190, 1981.

Turksen, I.B., Yao, D.D.W., "Bounds for fuzzy inference". Proc. 6th European Meeting on Cybernetics & Systems Research (R. Trappl, ed.), North-Holland, 1982.

Umano, M., Mizumoto, M., Tanaka, K., "A system for fuzzy reasoning". Proc. 6th Int. Joint Conf. on Artificial Intelligence, Tokyo, Aug. 1979, 917-919, 1979.

Wahlster, W., "Die Repräsentation von Vagem Wissem in Natürlichsprachlichen Systemen der Kunstlichen Intelligenz". Bericht n° 38, Institut für Informatik, University of Hamburg, 1977.

Weber, S., "A general concept of fuzzy connectives, negations and implications based on t-norms and t-co-norms". Fuzzy Set & Systems, 11, 115-134, 1983.

Weiss, S.M., Kulikowski, C.A., Amarel, S., Safir, A., "A model-based method for computer-aided medical decision-making". Artificial Intelligence, 11, 145-172, 1978.

Weiss, S.M., Kulikowski, C.A., "EXPERT : A system for developing consultation models". Proc. 6th Int. Joint Conf. on Artificial Intelligence, Tokyo, Aug. 1979, 942-947, 1979.

Wesley, L.P., "Reasoning about control : the investigation of an evidential approach". Proc. 8th Int. Joint Conf. Artif. Intelligence, Karlsruhe, Aug. 83, 203-206, 1983.

Whalen, T., Schott, B., "Fuzzy production systems for decision support". Proc. Int. Conf. Cybernetics and Society, Atlanta, 649-653, 1981.

Whalen, T., Schott, B., "Decision support with fuzzy production systems". In : Advances in Fuzzy Sets, Possibility Theory, and Application, (P.P. Wang, ed.), Plenum Press, 199-216, 1983a.

Whalen, T., Schott, B., "Issues in fuzzy production system". Int. J. Man-Machine Studies, 19, 57-71, 1983b.

Whiter, A., "PI-QL : Nearer to the ideals of logic programming via fuzzy logic ? Int. Rep., Dept. of Eng. Maths., University of Bristol, England, 1984.

Wilmott, R., "On the transitivity of implication and equivalence in some many-valued logics". Proc. IEEE Int. Symp. Multiple-Valued Logic, 253-262, 1980.

Winston, P.H., "Learning and reasoning by analogy". Communications of the ACM, 23, 689-703, 1980.

Yager, R.R., "An approach to inference in approximate reasoning". Int. J. Man-Machine Studies, 13, 323-338, 1980.

Yager, R.R., "Measuring tranquility and anxiety in decision-making : an application of fuzzy sets". Int. J. Man-Machine Studies, 18, 139-146, 1982a.

Yager, R.R., Generalized probabilities of fuzzy events from fuzzy belief structures". Information Sciences, 28, 45-62, 1982.

Yager, R.R., "Quantified propositions in a linguistic logic". Int. J. Man-Machine Studies, 19, 195-227, 1983a.

Yager, R.R., "Hedging in the combination of evidence". J. of Information & Optimization Sciences, 4, n° 1, 73-81, 1983b.

Yager, R.R., "On the relationship of methods of aggregating evidence in expert systems". Tech. Rep. MII-303, Iona College, New Rochelle, N.Y., (20 p.), 1983c.

Yager, R.R., "Reasoning with fuzzy quantified statements". Tech. Rep. MII-308, Iona College New Rochelle, N.Y., (47 p.), 1983d.

Yager, R.R., "Approximate reasoning as a basis for rule-based expert systems". IEEE Trans. on Systems, Man & Cybernetics, 14, 636-643, 1984.

Yager, R.R., "Q-projections on possibility distributions". Tech. Rep. MII-501, Iona College,New Rochelle, N.Y., (11 p.), 1985a.

Yager, R.R., "Explanatory models in expert systems". Tech. Rep. MII-503, Iona College, New Rochelle, N.Y., (22 p.), 1985b.

Zadeh, L.A., "Fuzzy sets". Information and control, 8, 338-353, 1965.

Zadeh, L.A., "Probability measures of fuzzy events". J. Math. Analysis and Applications, 23, 421-427, 1968.

Zadeh, L.A., "A fuzzy set theoretic interpretation of linguistic hedges". J. of Cybernetics, 2, n° 3, 4-34, 1972.

Zadeh, L.A., "Outline of a new approach to the analysis of complex systems and decision processes". IEEE Trans. Systems, Man, Cybernetics, 3, 28-44, 1973.

Zadeh, L.A., "The concept of a linguistic variable and its application to approximate reasoning". Informations Sciences, Part 1 : 8, 199-249 ; Part 2 : 8, 301-357 ; Part 3 : 9, 43-80, 1975.

Zadeh, L.A., "Fuzzy sets as a basis for a theory of possibility". Fuzzy Sets and Systems, 1, n° 1, 3-28, 1978a.

Zadeh, L.A., "PRUF : A meaning representation language for natural languages". Int. J. Man-Machine Studies, 10, n° 4, 395-460, 1978b.

Zadeh, L.A., "A theory of approximate reasoning". Machine Intelligence, Vol. 9 (J.E. Hayes, D. Michie, L.I. Mikulich, eds.). Elsevier, 149-194, 1979a.

Zadeh, L.A., "Approximate reasoning based on fuzzy logic". Memo UCB/ERL M79/32 Univ. of Calif. Berkeley (35 p.). Abridged version in : Proc. Int. Joint Conference Artificial Intelligence, Tokyo, Aug. 1979, 1004-1010. 1979b.

Zadeh, L.A., "On the validity of Dempster's rule of combination of evidence". Memo UCB/ERL M79/24, University of California, Berkeley (12 p.), 1979c.

Zadeh, L.A., "Fuzzy sets and information granularity". In "Advances in Fuzzy Set Theory and Applications" (M.M. Gupta, R.K. Ragade, R.R. Yager, eds.), North-Holland, Amsterdam, 3-18, 1979d.

Zadeh, L.A., "Fuzzy sets versus probability". Proc. of the IEEE, 68, 421, 1980.

Zadeh, L.A., "Possibility theory and soft data analysis". In : Mathematical Frontiers of the Social and Policy Sciences (L. Cobb, R.M. Thrall, eds.), A.A.A.S Selected Symposium, Vol. 54, Westview Press, Boulder, Ca., 69-129, 1981a.

Zadeh, L.A., "Test-score semantics for natural languages and meaning representation via PRUF". Tech. Note n° 247, SRI-International, Menlo Park, Ca., (75 p.), 1981b.

Zadeh, L.A., "A computational approach to fuzzy quantifiers in natural languages". Computers & Mathematics with Applications, 9, n° 1, 149-184, 1982.

Zadeh, L.A., "Common-sense knowledge representation based on fuzzy logic". Computer (IEEE), 16, n° 10, 61-65, 1983a.

Zadeh, L.A., "A theory of common sense knowledge". In : Aspects of Vagueness (H.J. Skala, S. Termini, E. Trillas, eds.), D. Reidel, 257-295, 1984a.

Zadeh, L.A., "The role of fuzzy logic in the management of uncertainty in expert systems". Fuzzy Sets & Systems, 11, n° 3, 199-228, 1983b.

Zadeh, L.A., "Review of 'A Mathematical Theory of Evidence', by G. Shafer". The AI Magazine, Fall 1984, 81-83, 1984b.

Zadeh, L.A., "A simple view of the Dempster-Shafer theory of evidence". Berkeley Cognitive Science Rep. n° 27, (12 p.), 1984c.

Zimmermann, H.J., Zysno, P., "Latent connectives in human decision making". Fuzzy Sets and Systems, 4, n° 1, 37-61, 1980.

Structural Analysis of Electronic Circuits in a Deductive System

Takushi Tanaka

The National Language Research Institute
3-9-14 Nishigaoka Kita-ku, Tokyo 115, Japan

ABSTRACT

As a step toward automatic circuit understanding, we have developed methods for structural analysis of electronic circuits in a deductive system called Duck. We first show how circuits are represented in logic. Corresponding to each circuit elment or device, a predicate is defined. Circuits are defined using those predicates. Circuit analysis is done as an iteration of proofs which determine the basic structures in the circuit.

Next, we present a new representation method for circuits to advance our study. A circuit is viewed as a sentence and its elements as words; analysis of a circuit is thus analogous to parsing a language. A bottom-up mechanism is used to analyze impedance networks. A top-down mechanism is used to analyze electronic circuits into blocks with specific functions. Circuit structures are defined by deductive rules analogous to definite clause grammars. Using those rules, an object circuit is decomposed into a parse tree of functional blocks.

1   INTRODUCTION

When an engineer first looks at a circuit schematic, he tries to partition the circuit into familiar sub-circuits with known goals. He then tries to pursue the causality of electrical events through those sub-circuits to determine if and how it achieves the overall goal of the circuit. This is based on his assumption that every electronic circuit is designed as a goal oriented composition of basic circuits with specific functions.

Therefore, understanding a circuit means finding a hierarchical structure of functional blocks and rediscovering the designer's original intentions. Almost all designed circuits share a feature of natural language: they both carry information of the speaker/designer's intentions mapped onto their structures. In addition, a circuit schematic not only represents a physical circuit, but also functions as a written language for electronic engineers.

As a step toward automatic circuit understanding, we have developed methods for structural analysis of electronic circuits in a deductive system called Duck [McDermott 1983].

We first show how circuits are represented in logic. Predicates are defined for circuit elements and devices. Each predicate has an element name and connecting nodes as terms. Using these predicates, a circuit is defined as a conjunction of assertions representing each element or device. Specific structures in an object circuit are found by deriving a proof of an assertion representing their structure. The determination of a circuit's structure through an iteration of proofs is the key idea throughout this study.

When a specific structure is found in the object circuit, we often want to rewrite the circuit into an equivalent one. Since the object circuit is represented by a set of assertions in a Duck database, rewriting the circuit involves changing this set of assertions. The simplest method to do this is to define a meta-procedure outside the deductive system [Tanaka 1983]. However, here we have adopted a different solution to this rewriting problem.

Next, we present a new representation method for circuits to advance our study. The predicate symbols which have been used for circuit elements are now changed to function symbols. Since the same notations are used for predicates and functions, nothing changes regarding the notation. Each function forms a composite term denoting an element itself. A circuit is represented by a tuple of those terms.

In the new representation method, a circuit is viewed as a sentence and its elements as words. The circuit analysis process thus resembles language parsing process. A bottom-up mechanism is used to analyze impedance networks. The mechanism is based on equivalence transformations of circuits analogous to the reduction process from terminal symbols to non-terminal symbols in parsing strings.

A top-down mechanism is used to analyze electronic circuits with specific goals. Circuit structures with specific functions are defined by deductive rules analogous to definite clause grammars [Pereira, Warren 1980]. Using those rules, an object circuit is decomposed into a parse tree of functional blocks in terms of a logic program.

Most rules for circuit analysis correspond to context-free grammars, but we discovered several circuits which can not be generated by context-free rules. In order to parse this class of circuits, we introduce additional conditions to the rules. The conditions define the relationship between a circuit's topology and its electrical characteristics.

2 CIRCUITS REPRESENTED IN LOGIC

2.1 Syntax Used in This Study

Duck is a Lisp-based system for writing predicate calculus rules [McDermott 1983]. We use Lisp's symbolic expressions for predicates:

    (predicate -terms-)

Each term is either a constant, or an expression of the form

    (function -terms-)

or a tuple of those terms (Section 4.2).

Two kinds of expressions are available for a logical implication with antecedent p and consequent q:

    (-> p q)
    (<- q p)

We will use the term "rule" for these assertions. Assertions of the form "(-> ...)" are forward chaining rules; of the form "(<- ...)", backward chaining rules. Logically, these rules have the same meaning that p implies q, but procedurally, these rules specify forward and backward chaining respectively. In the following sections, we will show how these rules are used. The forward/backward chaining distinction is important for explicit deduction control.

2.2 Predicates for Elements and Devices

The circuit CA12 in Figure 1 is represented as follows (1) in our system. The assertion "(TERMINAL T1 #1)" states that T1 is a terminal at node #1. The assertion "(RESISTOR R1 #1 #2)" states that R1 is a resistor connecting node #1 and node #2. The node order is arbitrary because a resistor does not have polarity. On the other hand, the node order is important for elements or devices which have polarity, such as diodes and transistors. We therefore define the predicate "DIODE" such that "(DIODE D1 #2 #3)" states D1 is a diode with the anode connected to node #2 and the cathode to node #3. "CA12" is a predicate without arguments. "(CA12)" as a propositional constant states that there is a circuit called CA12. "->" is the forward chaining symbol. It means logical implication, but procedurally, it means that when "(CA12)" is added to the Duck database, then "(TERMINAL T1 #1)", "(TERMINAL T2 #2)", ... , "(DIODE D1 #2 #3)" are to be asserted (added to the database) immediately [McDermott 1980].

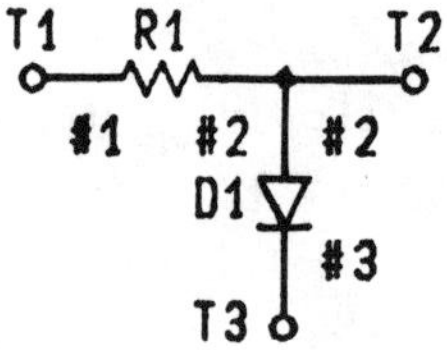

Figure 1: Circuit CA12

```
(-> (CA12) (AND (TERMINAL T1 #1)
                (TERMINAL T2 #2)
                (TERMINAL T3 #3)
                (RESISTOR R1 #1 #2)
                (DIODE D1 #2 #3)))                           (1)
```

2.3 Rules for Non-Polar Elements

If "(CA12)" is asserted, we can prove "(RESISTOR R1 #1 #2)", but we cannot prove "(RESISTOR R1 #2 #1)". Since we want to have "(RESISTOR R1 #1 #2)" implies "(RESISTOR R1 #2 #1)", we will assert the following implication:

```
(FORALL (X A B) (-> (RESISTOR X A B) (RESISTOR X B A)))
```

The implication can simply be written as follows in Duck:

```
(-> (RESISTOR ?X ?A ?B) (RESISTOR ?X ?B ?A))               (2)
```

"?"-marked variables are universally quantified. When an assertion "(RESISTOR R1 #1 #2)" is added to the database, "(RESISTOR R1 #2 #1)" is also added to the database by the above rule. Similar rules are written for the predicates CAPACITOR and INDUCTOR. If an assertion already exists in the database, the Duck system will not add it again to the database, thereby assuring that the rule is not infinitely applied. But if we use a backward chaining rule (next section) instead of the forward chaining rule, and if an objective assertion is not found in the database, the system will loop infinitely.

2.4 Predicates for Abstract Elements

We can define predicates for abstract elements. These predicates correspond to the conceptual hierarchy of circuit elements and devices. First we will define the predicate Z-ELM, so that we can refer to resistors, capacitors, and inductors as impedance elements (3).

```
(<- (Z-ELM ?X ?A ?B) (OR (RESISTOR ?X ?A ?B)
                         (CAPACITOR ?X ?A ?B)
                         (INDUCTOR ?X ?A ?B)))                (3)
```

The backward chaining symbol "<-" is used instead of the forward chaining symbol. It also means logical implication, but differs procedurally from forward chaining. The rule (3) is applied when the system tries to prove "(Z-ELM D1 #2 #3)" corresponding to the query "Does there exist an impedance element D1 connecting nodes #2 and #3?". In order to prove the assertion, the system tries to prove either "(RESISTOR D1 #2 #3)" or "(CAPACITOR D1 #2 #3)" or "(INDUCTOR D1 #2 #3)". In the same manner, we can also define predicates such as ACTIVE-ELEMENT, TWO-TERMINAL-ELEMENT, ... , ANY-ELEMENT so that we can refer to these classes of elements.

We could also write rule (3) as forward chaining rules:

```
(-> (RESISTOR ?X ?A ?B) (Z-ELM ?X ?A ?B))
(-> (CAPACITOR ?X ?A ?B) (Z-ELM ?X ?A ?B))
(-> (INDUCTOR ?X ?A ?B) (Z-ELM ?X ?A ?B))
```

When an object circuit is asserted, not only its elements, but also many abstract elements for each element are to be added into the database by these rules. The abstract elements are theorems derived from the operation of the rules on the circuit elements.

There are two ways to derive abstract elements: by the application of either forward or backward chaining rules. Forward chaining rules cause all possible abstract elements to be derived with the addition of each circuit element to the database. As a result, these abstract elements are readily available if needed at some future time; however, typically only a fraction of these abstract elements are used in analysis of the circuit. Backward chaining, on the other hand, only forms abstract elements as needed - on request, so to speak.

2.5 Predicates for Circuit Identification

In order to determine which kind of analysis can apply to the object circuit, several predicates for circuit identification are defined. They identify the global properties of an object circuit. By proving the formula

    (EXISTS (X A) (TERMINAL X A)),

we can determine whether the object circuit has terminals, or not. In the query mode of the Duck system, the formula can simply be written as follows:

    (TERMINAL ?X ?A)

A "?"-marked symbol is existentially interpreted when it appears in query mode. "OPEN-CIRCUIT", which has terminals, is defined as follows:

    (<- (OPEN-CIRCUIT) (TERMINAL ?X ?A))   (4)

"IMPEDANCE-NETWORK" is defined to prove that all the elements in the circuit are impedance elements. Predicates such as TWO-TERMINAL-NETWORK which count the number of terminals are defined using the built-in predicate TOTAL (Section 3.2).

3   FINDING STRUCTURES IN A CIRCUIT

3.1 Finding Specific Structures

Let us consider the circuit CA39 in Figure 2. In order to show the existence of resistors connected in series (Figure 3), we attempt to prove the following formula:

    (EXISTS (X Y A B C) (AND (RESISTOR X A B)
                             (RESISTOR Y B C)))

When "(CA39)" is asserted, the formula becomes true, because we can substitute constants (R1 R2 #1 #2 #3) into variables (X Y A B C), respectively, corresponding to the actual existence of a series circuit in CA39. But we can also substitute constants (R1 R1 #1 #2 #1) or (R1 R3 #2 #1 #3) for the variables, substitutions which do not correspond to series connections. In order to reject the former incorrect substitution, the predicate "(NOT (= A C))" is added to the formula.

Rejection of the latter incorrect substitution is rather difficult: a series connection demands that the central node "?B" (Figure 3) should not be connected to elements other than those in the formula. In order to represent this constraint the predicates DEGREE and CONNECTED are introduced.

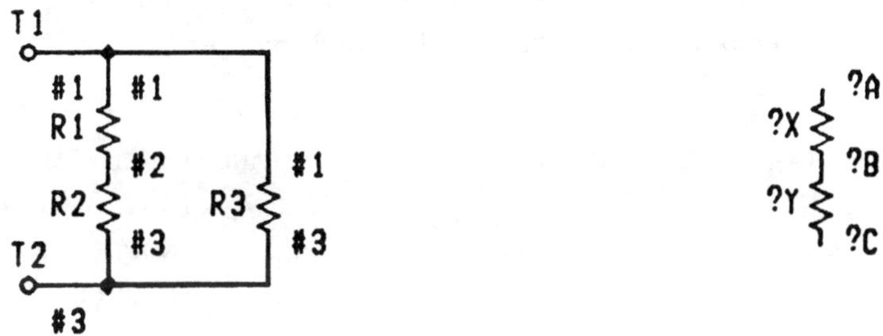

Figure 2: Circuit CA39   Figure 3: R-SERIES

3.2 Rules for Node-Degree

We will use the backward chaining rule CONNECTED to enumerate the terminals, impedance elements, and diodes ?X connected to node ?A.

```
(<- (CONNECTED ?X ?A) (OR (TERMINAL ?X ?A)
                          (Z-ELM ?X ?A ?B)
                          (DIODE ?X ?A ?B)
                          (DIODE ?X ?B ?A)))                    (5)
```

The predicate DEGREE has two arguments. It becomes true if the first is a node and the second is its degree in the object circuit. "DEGREE" is defined as follows using CONNECTED and TOTAL.

```
(<- (DEGREE ?A ?DEG) (TOTAL ?DEG 1 (CONNECTED ?X ?A)))         (6)
```

"TOTAL" is a special built-in predicate which states the first term is a sum of the second term according to all known instances of the third term. Now we can define the predicate R-SERIES for the resistors connected in series:

```
(<- (R-SERIES ?X ?Y ?A ?B ?C) (AND (RESISTOR ?X ?A ?B)
                                   (RESISTOR ?Y ?B ?C)
                                   (NOT (= ?A ?C))
                                   (DEGREE ?B 2)))           (7)
```

3.3 Circuit Structures for Impedance Networks

In the analysis of a two-terminal network, we try to discover specific sub-structures such as series, parallel, star, and delta circuits, in order to rewrite the circuit into a simpler one. In many cases we can analyze circuits without formal analysis of full circuit equations. We can define the predicates Z-SERIES, Z-PARALLEL, Z-STAR, and Z-DELTA for network analysis. The predicate Z-SERIES for a series connection of impedance elements is defined by replacing "RESISTOR" with "Z-ELM" in (7):

```
(<- (Z-SERIES ?X ?Y ?A ?B ?C) (AND (Z-ELM ?X ?A ?B)
                                   (Z-ELM ?Y ?B ?C)
                                   (NOT (= ?A ?C))
                                   (DEGREE ?B 2)))           (8)
```

"Z-PARALLEL" for a parallel connection of impedance elements is defined as follows:

```
(<- (Z-PARALLEL ?X ?Y ?A ?B) (AND (Z-ELM ?X ?A ?B)
                                  (Z-ELM ?Y ?A ?B)
                                  (NOT (= ?X ?Y))))          (9)
```

The condition "(NOT (= ?X ?Y))" is added so that an element is not found twice in proving "(Z-ELM ?X ?A ?B)" and "(Z-ELM ?Y ?A ?B)". The condition "(NOT (= ?A ?C))" in (8) also implies "(NOT (= ?X ?Y))" in the nature of circuit topology.

3.4 Procedurally Defined Circuits

There are some circuit predicates which can not be adequately defined by the methods discussed so far. Our approach faces a difficulty when we try to define a predicate SERIES-PARALLEL-CIRCUIT which refers to an infinite, recursive set of circuits. We need a finite method to define an infinite set of the circuits.

The procedure to determine whether a circuit is a series-parallel circuit of impedance elements or not is defined in the following manner.

First the circuit is identified as a two terminal network and an impedance network (Section 2.5). Then the circuit is rewritten iteratively into simpler equivalent forms each time a series or a parallel circuit is found within it. If the circuit can ultimately be rewritten into a single element, then we have shown that the original one was a series-parallel circuit. The first and last steps are realized using the predicate TWO-TERMINAL-NETWORK, IMPEDANCE-NETWORK, and TOTAL-ELEMENTS defined by the predicate TOTAL. But the middle step is not so easy to implement in a deductive system, because rewriting a circuit into an equivalent one means changing the set of assertions in the Duck database. This can be done by introducing a state term into each predicate (Section 4.1), but it is easier to consider the procedure in a total system consisting of the deductive system and its meta-procedure.

3.5 Rewriting Circuits

In order to control the deductive system procedurally, several mechanisms are provided for calling Duck from Lisp. If the formula

    (ADD '(CA39))

is evaluated in Lisp, the assertion "(CA39)" is added to the Duck database. Then by the forward chaining rule of circuit CA39 (Figure 2), "(TERMINAL T1 #1)", ... , "(RESISTOR R3 #1 #3)" are added into the database. Then by rule (2), "(RESISTOR R1 #2 #1)", ... , "(RESISTOR R3 #3 #1)" are also added.

Under this condition let us consider a procedure which finds resistors connected in series and then rewrites part of the circuit into an equivalent element. At first, corresponding to a proof of "(EXIST (X Y A B C) (R-SERIES X Y A B C))", the following formula

    (FETCH '(R-SERIES ?X ?Y ?A ?B ?C))

is evaluated in Lisp. If it finds any series circuits, it returns a stream of instances of the variables (X Y A B C).

In order to rewrite a series part, we have to remove a set of assertions corresponding to the series circuit. If the first instance is (R1 R2 #1 #2 #3), the formulas

```
(ERASE '(RESISTOR R1 #1 #2))
(ERASE '(RESISTOR R2 #2 #3))
```

are to be evaluated. When the first one is evaluated to remove the resistor R1, not only "(RESISTOR R1 #1 #2)" but also its deduced image "(RESISTOR R1 #2 #1)" is erased from the database by Duck's data dependency mechanism [McDermott, Doyle 1979]. If the first instance is (R2 R1 #3 #2 #1), the formulas

```
(ERASE '(RESISTOR R2 #3 #2))
(ERASE '(RESISTOR R1 #2 #1))
```

are to be evaluated. The deduced image "(RESISTOR R1 #2 #1)" will be erased but its original "(RESISTOR R1 #1 #2)" can not be erased. Since we want to erase the original when the image is erased, we set up an "IF-ERASED-DEMON" in Duck as a forward chaining from the erasure. The rule is written as follows:

```
(LISPRULE R-IMAGE-DELETE
    (RESISTOR ?X ?B ?A) ->
        (IF-ERASED '(RESISTOR ?X ?B ?A)
                   (ERASE '(RESISTOR ?X ?A ?B)))))
```

According to the rule, "(RESISTOR R1 #1 #2)" is erased. Then an assertion representing an equivalent resistor is to be added as follows:

```
(ADD '(RESISTOR ER1 #1 #3))
```

Now we can define the predicate SERIES-PARALLEL-CIRCUIT as a Lisp function outside the deductive system [Tanaka 1983]. The Lisp function may be called from a Duck predicate. This approach may be used for actual network analysis, but the side-effects of the predicate destroy the original circuit. Therefore we develop a new method for circuit representation in the following chapter.

4   A NEW METHOD FOR CIRCUIT REPRESENTATION

4.1 Difficulties in the Previous Approach

Assertions in the Duck database can be viewed as axioms provided by the outside world, or theorems deduced by forward chaining from those axioms. Rewriting a circuit into an equivalent one involves changing the set of those assertions. Usually a logic never erases theorems once deduced by its own rules. Thus, the set of theorems increases monotonically with the set of axioms [McDermott, Doyle 1981]. Our problem of erasing theorems originates from the method of circuit representation. As we want to rewrite a circuit in ordinary logic, we will change the method.

One solution is to never erase the original circuit, but write a new one for each equivalence transformation. We have to separate these circuits in the Duck database. This can be done by introducing a state term for each predicate such as:

    (RESISTOR R1 #1 #2 state)

The state term identifies the circuit to which the element belongs. All elements in the original circuit have the same state name such as "ORIGINAL". All elements in an equivalent circuit have another state name such as "EQUIVALENT-1". But this approach has another difficulty in determining which part of a circuit has already been rewritten and which is not.

Another solution is not to use assertions for circuit representation. We will present this new method in the following sections.

4.2 Functions for Elements and Devices

First, we change the predicate symbols which have been defined for circuit elements and devices into function symbols. Since the same notations are used for predicates and functions, the notation remains the same. Each function forms a composite term denoting an element itself. For example, the function

    (RESISTOR R1 #2 #3)

denotes a resistor itself named R1 connecting nodes #2 and #3, while the predicate states the relationship between those terms. The function "(RESISTOR R1 #2 #3)" is never evaluated in logic. It denotes a specific resistor in a circuit schematic or a physical circuit. The function

    (NPN-TR Q2 #4 #1 #3)

denotes a NPN-transistor named Q2 with the base connected to node #4, the emitter to node #1, and the collector to node #3 respectively.

268

The circuit CD83 in Figure 4 is represented as a tuple of those terms surrounded by "!<" and ">". The order of elements in the tuple is not important.

```
!<(TERMINAL T1 #1) (TERMINAL T2 #2) (TERMINAL T3 #3)
   (RESISTOR R1 #2 #3) (RESISTOR R2 #4 #1)
   (NPN-TR Q1 #4 #3 #4) (NPN-TR Q2 #4 #1 #3)>
```

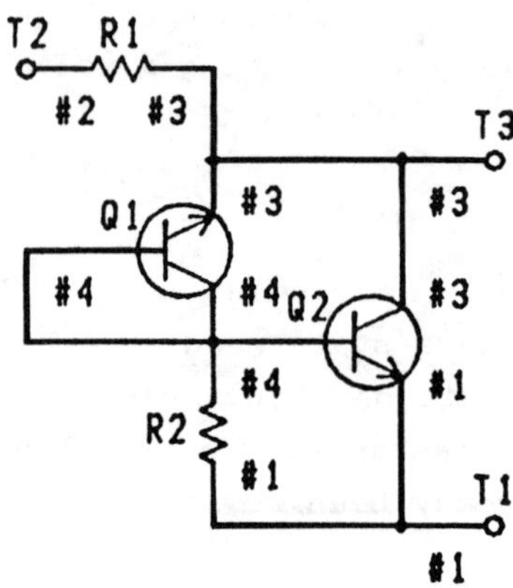

Figure 4: Circuit CD83

4.3 Predicates for Tuples

In the previous approach, an object circuit was represented as a set of assertions corresponding to its elements. So, finding a specific element in the object circuit meant proving an assertion for the element. In the present approach, an object circuit is represented as a tuple of element terms. So, finding a specific element in a circuit means identifying the element term as a member of the tuple. For this purpose, we will define two membership predicates. The predicate "MEMBER" is defined by the following assertion:

```
(MEMBER ?M !<!&?L ?M !&?R>)                                    (10)
```

"?M", "?L", and "?R" are universally quantified variables. The notation "!&?X" matches any number of elements of a tuple, binding ?X to a tuple of those elements. So "!<!&?L ?M !&?R>" matches any tuple of one or more elements, and binds ?M to a member of the tuple, ?L to the left part, and ?R to the right part of the rest [McDermott 1983]. The other membership predicate "MEM-REST" is defined as follows:

```
(MEM-REST ?M !<!&?L ?M !&?R> !<!&?L !&?R>)                     (11)
```

Unlike MEMBER, we can acquire the rest part of a tuple from the third argument of MEM-REST. Using the predicate we can separate an object circuit into an element and the rest:

    (MEM-REST element object-circuit rest)

This is an important advantage of the new approach, since we did not have an effective method to separate the object circuit into an element and the rest in the previous approach.

4.4 Sub-Circuit

In order to refer to parts of circuits, we will use the predicate SUB-CT (sub-circuit). "SUB-CT" has arguments similar to those of MEM-REST in the previous section. The difference is that the first argument is not a real element but a sub-circuit viewed as an abstract element. Here, "abstract" means that the element does not exist as a member of the tuple representing a circuit.

    (SUB-CT abstract-element object-circuit rest)

We first show a simple application of this predicate. A backward chaining rule is defined for each non-polar element:

    (<- (SUB-CT (RES ?R ?A ?B) ?CT ?REST)
        (OR (MEM-REST (RESISTOR ?R ?A ?B) ?CT ?REST)
            (MEM-REST (RESISTOR ?R ?B ?A) ?CT ?REST)))   (12)

The rule says if "(RESISTOR ?R ?A ?B)" or "(RESISTOR ?R ?B ?A)" is a member of a circuit ?CT, then an abstract element "(RES ?R ?A ?B)" exists as a sub-circuit. The function "RES" is introduced as a Skolem function which represents the existence of the abstract element. This rule enables us to refer to a resistor represented by "(RESISTOR R1 #1 #2)" or "(RESISTOR R1 #2 #1)" as "(RES R1 #1 #2)". Similar rules are written for capacitors and inductors, "CAP" and "IND", respectively. In this approach, we no longer need the "image-element method" for non-polar elements (Section 2.3). Corresponding to the predicate Z-ELM in Section 2.4, two functions Z-ELEMENT and Z-ELM are defined. "Z-ELEMENT" is used as a real element with equivalent impedance in an equivalent circuit (Section 5.2). "Z-ELM" is used as an abstract element to refer to a resistor, a capacitor, an inductor, or a Z-ELEMENT:

```
(<- (SUB-CT (Z-ELM ?X ?A ?B) ?CT ?REST)
    (OR (MEM-REST (Z-ELEMENT ?X ?A ?B) ?CT ?REST)
        (MEM-REST (Z-ELEMENT ?X ?B ?A) ?CT ?REST)
        (SUB-CT (RES ?X ?A ?B) ?CT ?REST)
        (SUB-CT (CAP ?X ?A ?B) ?CT ?REST)
        (SUB-CT (IND ?X ?A ?B) ?CT ?REST)))                    (13)
```

We can refer to an NPN-transistor or a PNP-transistor as a transistor by the following rule:

```
(<- (SUB-CT (TRANSISTOR ?Q ?B ?E ?C) ?CT ?REST)
    (OR (MEM-REST (NPN-TR ?Q ?B ?E ?C) ?CT ?REST)
        (MEM-REST (PNP-TR ?Q ?B ?E ?C) ?CT ?REST)))           (14)
```

"ANY-ELM" is defined as an abstract element to stand for any element ?X or terminal ?X connected to a node ?A:

```
(<- (SUB-CT (ANY-ELM ?X ?A) ?CT ?REST)
    (OR (SUB-CT (Z-ELM ?X ?A ?B) ?CT ?REST)
        (SUB-CT (TRANSISTOR ?X ?A ?B ?C) ?CT ?REST)
        (SUB-CT (TRANSISTOR ?X ?C ?A ?B) ?CT ?REST)
        (SUB-CT (TRANSISTOR ?X ?B ?C ?A) ?CT ?REST)
        (MEM-REST (DIODE ?X ?A ?B) ?CT ?REST)
        (MEM-REST (DIODE ?X ?B ?A) ?CT ?REST)
        (MEM-REST (TERMINAL ?X ?A) ?CT ?REST)))               (15)
```

The "sub-circuit" concept is very important and useful. Using the predicate SUB-CT, functional blocks in electronic circuits are defined as abstract elements (Section 6.3). The predicate SUB-CT has the ability to decompose an electronic circuit into a hierarchical structure of functional blocks (Section 6.4).

4.5 Predicates with Negation

We will now define predicates with negation. "NON-MEMBER" is defined as a failure of MEMBER:

```
(<- (NON-MEMBER ?X ?TUP) (THNOT (MEMBER ?X ?TUP)))            (16)
```

"(THNOT p)" succeeds if "p" can not be proven true [Sussman, Winograd, Charniak 1971].

In a similar fashion, "NON-SUBCT" is defined as a failure of SUB-CT.

(<- (NON-SUBCT ?X ?CT) (THNOT (SUB-CT ?X ?CT ?REST)))   (17)

"NON-SUBCT" succeeds if an abstract element ?X is not in the circuit ?CT as a sub-circuit, while "NON-MEMBER" succeeds if the element ?X is not a member of the tuple ?TUP. These predicates are used to express various conditions in the definitions of circuit structures.

5 BOTTOM-UP ANALYSIS FOR IMPEDANCE NETWORKS

5.1 Circuit Structures for Network Analysis

Now we can define circuit structures for network analysis using the predicate SUB-CT. A function Z-SERIES is defined for a series circuit of impedance elements:

```
(<- (SUB-CT (Z-SERIES ?X ?Y ?A ?B ?C) ?CT ?REST)
    (AND (SUB-CT (Z-ELM ?X ?A ?B) ?CT ?RST1)
         (SUB-CT (Z-ELM ?Y ?B ?C) ?RST1 ?REST)
         (NON-SUBCT (ANY-ELM ?Z ?B) ?REST)))          (18)
```

Figure 5: Z-SERIES

?X ?Y
?A ?B ?C

Unlike definition (8) in Section 3.2, the condition "(NOT (= ?A ?C))", which was added to avoid finding the same element twice, is no longer necessary. After the first impedance element ?X is found, the second element ?Y is searched for in the remainder, which does not include the first element. The condition of definition (8) which requires the central node ?B not to be connected to elements other than ?X and ?Y is replaced by the predicate NON-SUBCT (Section 4.5) and the function ANY-ELM (Section 4.4).

Functions Z-PARALLEL, Z-STAR, and Z-DELTA are defined as follows:

```
(<- (SUB-CT (Z-PARALLEL ?X ?Y ?A ?B) ?CT ?REST)
    (AND (SUB-CT (Z-ELM ?X ?A ?B) ?CT ?RST1)
         (SUB-CT (Z-ELM ?Y ?A ?B) ?RST1 ?REST)))          (19)
```

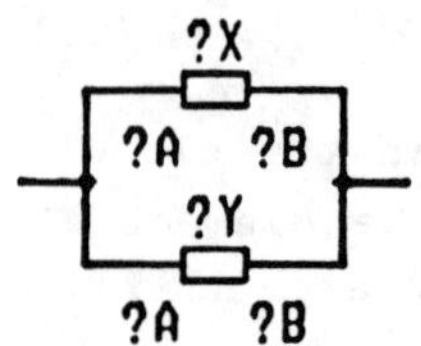

Figure 6: Z-PARALLEL

```
(<- (SUB-CT (Z-STAR ?X ?Y ?Z ?A ?B ?C ?D) ?CT ?REST)
    (AND (SUB-CT (Z-ELM ?X ?A ?D) ?CT ?RST1)
         (SUB-CT (Z-ELM ?Y ?B ?D) ?RST1 ?RST2)
         (SUB-CT (Z-ELM ?Z ?C ?D) ?RST2 ?REST)
         (NON-SUBCT (ANY-ELM ?U ?D) ?REST)))                    (20)
```

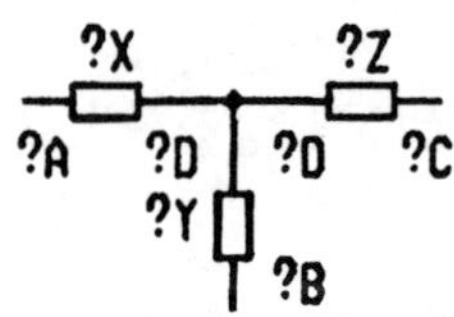

Figure 7: Z-STAR

```
(<- (SUB-CT (Z-DELTA ?X ?Y ?Z ?A ?B ?C) ?CT ?REST)
    (AND (SUB-CT (Z-ELM ?X ?B ?C) ?CT ?RST1)
         (SUB-CT (Z-ELM ?Y ?C ?A) ?RST1 ?RST2)
         (SUB-CT (Z-ELM ?Z ?A ?B) ?RST2 ?REST)))                (21)
```

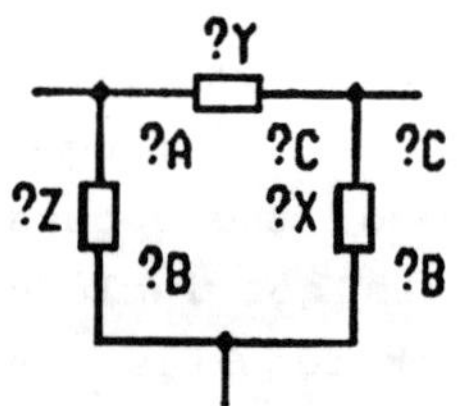

Figure 8: Z-DELTA

5.2 One-Step Equivalence Transformations

When we find impedance elements connected in series in the object circuit, we can rewrite that part into an equivalent impedance element.
We use the predicate SR-EQIVCT to implement this process:

```
(<- (SR-EQIVCT ?CT ?EQCT)
    (AND (SUB-CT (Z-SERIES ?X ?Y ?A ?B ?C) ?CT ?REST)
         (= ?EQCT !<(Z-ELEMENT (SR ?X ?Y) ?A ?C) !& ?REST)>)))
```

The rule first finds a series structure in the object circuit as a
sub-circuit, then adds a new element "(Z-ELEMENT (SR ?X ?Y) ?A ?C)"
to the rest to form an equivalent circuit ?EQCT (Figure 9). The new
name "(SR ?X ?Y)" is given to the element by the Skolem function "SR".
The rule can also be written without using the variable ?EQCT:

```
(<- (SR-EQIVCT ?CT !<(Z-ELEMENT (SR ?X ?Y) ?A ?C) !& ?REST>)
    (SUB-CT (Z-SERIES ?X ?Y ?A ?B ?C) ?CT ?REST))                 (22)
```

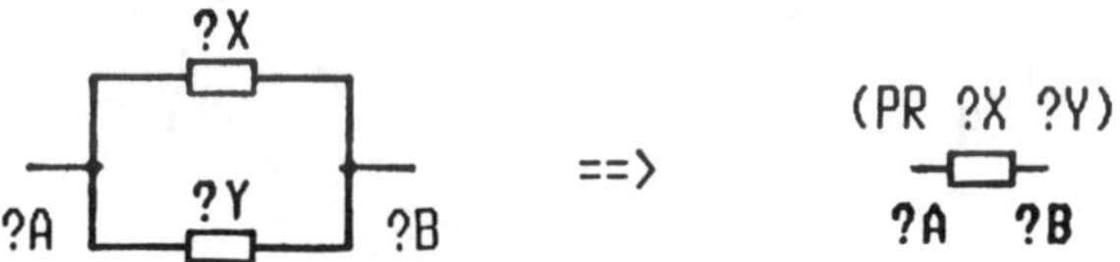

Figure 9: Series transformation

A similar rule is written for parallel connections of impedance elements. A new name "(PR ?X ?Y)" is given to the equivalent impedance
element by the Skolem function "PR".

```
(<- (PR-EQIVCT ?CT !<(Z-ELEMENT (PR ?X ?Y) ?A ?B) !& ?REST>)
    (SUB-CT (Z-PARALLEL ?X ?Y ?A ?B) ?CT ?REST))                 (23)
```

Figure 10: Parallel transformation

A predicate ST-EQIVCT is defined for the star-delta equivalence
transformation:

```
(<- (ST-EQIVCT ?CT !<(Z-ELEMENT (ST ?X ?Y ?Z) ?B ?C)
                    (Z-ELEMENT (ST ?Y ?Z ?X) ?C ?A)
                    (Z-ELEMENT (ST ?Z ?X ?Y) ?A ?B)
                    !& ?REST>)
    (SUB-CT (Z-STAR ?X ?Y ?z ?A ?B ?C ?D) ?CT ?REST))            (24)
```

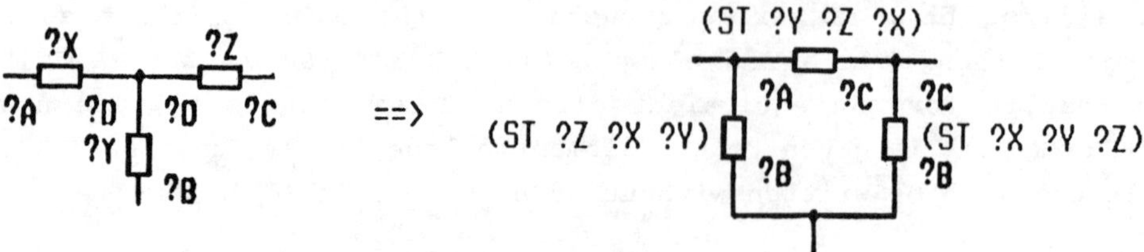

<u>Figure 11</u>: Star-delta transformation

Unlike the series and parallel transformations, the star-delta
transformation does not reduce the number of elements in the circuit.
Three elements connected in star are transformed into three different
elements connected in delta. Those elements are given new names by the
Skolem function "ST".

A similar rule is written for the delta-star transformation:

```
(<- (DT-EQIVCT ?CT !<(Z-ELEMENT (DT ?X ?Y ?Z) ?A (ND ?A ?B ?C))
                     (Z-ELEMENT (DT ?Y ?Z ?X) ?B (ND ?A ?B ?C))
                     (Z-ELEMENT (DT ?Z ?X ?Y) ?C (ND ?A ?B ?C))
                     !& ?REST>)
    (SUB-CT (Z-DELTA ?X ?Y ?Z ?A ?B ?C) ?CT ?REST))           (25)
```

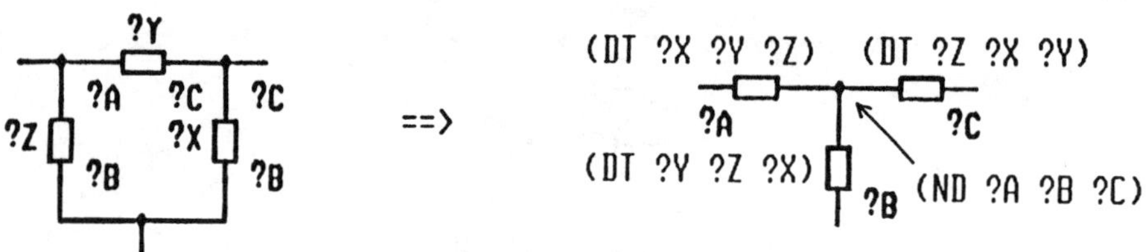

<u>Figure 12</u>: Delta-star transformation

In this transformation, we have to assume a new node for the star connection. A name "(ND ?A ?B ?C)" is given to the node by the Skolem
function "ND". New names are also given to the equivalent elements
by "DT".

5.3 Series-Parallel Circuit

We first define a predicate SP-EQIVCT for one-step transformations.
It stands for the series or the parallel equivalence transformation:

```
(<- (SP-EQIVCT ?CT ?EQCT) (OR (SR-EQIVCT ?CT ?EQCT)
                              (PR-EQIVCT ?CT ?EQCT)))          (26)
```

When a circuit ?CT is given to the predicate SP-EQIVCT, an equivalent
circuit is returned in the variable ?EQCT. Although the original circuit contains many series and parallel circuits, only one part of the
structure is rewritten into an equivalent impedance element at a time
by this predicate.

Next we define a predicate M-SP-EQIVCT which has the ability to
rewrite a circuit iteratively into simpler equivalent forms each
time a series or a parallel circuit is found in it. The predicate is
recursively defined as follows:

```
(<- (M-SP-EQIVCT ?CT ?EQCT)
    (OR (AND (SP-EQIVCT ?CT ?EQ1)
             (M-SP-EQIVCT ?EQ1 ?EQCT))
        (AND (THNOT (SP-EQIVCT ?CT ?EQ1))
             (= ?EQCT ?CT))))                              (27)
```

The first part of the disjunction says "rewrite the circuit ?CT into
an equivalent one ?EQ1 by the predicate SP-EQIVCT", then "apply the
predicate M-SP-EQIVCT to the circuit ?EQ1 recursively". The rest part
of the disjunction says "if the equivalent transform failed, return
the original circuit as an equivalent circuit".

Now we have defined the predicate SERIES-PARALLEL-CIRCUIT in a deductive manner, something we could not have done in the previous approach.

```
(<- (SERIES-PARALLEL-CIRCUIT ?CT)
    (M-SP-EQIVCT ?CT !<(Z-ELEMENT ?X ?A ?B)
                       (TERMINAL ?Y ?C) (TERMINAL ?Z ?D)>))      (28)
```

"M-SP-EQIVCT" in (28) rewrites the circuit ?CT into the simplest
equivalent circuit. If the simplest equivalent circuit consists of one
Z-ELEMENT and two terminals, then the original circuit ?CT is proven
to be a series-parallel circuit. We may replace the variables ?C and
?D with ?A and ?B or ?B and ?A respectively. Definition (28) does not
require a specific ordering of the nodes - AB or BA will do - and thus
it executes faster.

5.4 Bottom-Up Analysis for Series-Parallel Circuits

Let us consider a process of equivalence transformation by "M-SP-
EQIVCT". The circuit CA41 in Figure 13 is represented as follows:

```
!<(TERMINAL T1 #1) (TERMINAL T2 #2)
  (RESISTOR R1 #1 #3) (RESISTOR R2 #3 #2) (RESISTOR R3 #3 #4)
  (RESISTOR R4 #4 #2) (RESISTOR R5 #4 #5) (RESISTOR R6 #5 #2)>
```

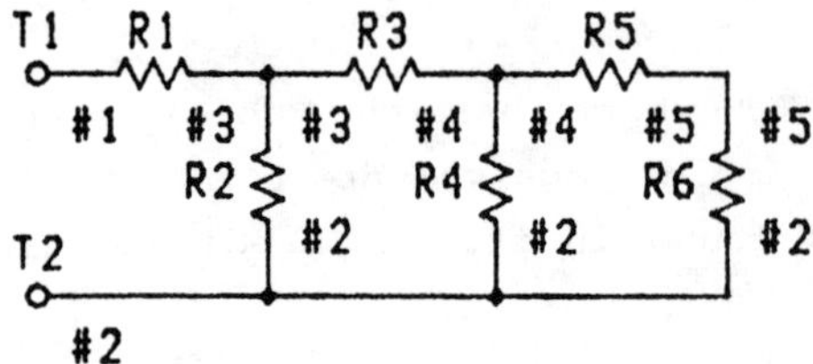

Figure 13: Ladder circuit CA41

Running the following goal form causes Duck to perform equivalence transformations. "ca41" stands for the circuit tuple of CA41.

```
(M-SP-EQIVCT ca41 ?EQCT)
```

According to the definition (27) of "M-SP-EQIVCT", the goal is decomposed into the following subgoal structure:

```
(OR (AND (SP-EQIVCT ca41 ?EQ1)
         (M-SP-EQIVCT ?EQ1 ?EQCT))
    (AND (THNOT (SP-EQIVCT ca41 ?EQ1))
         (= ?EQCT ca41)))
```

For "(SP-EQIVCT ca41 ?EQ1)", rule (26) generates the following goal:

```
(OR (SR-EQIVCT ca41 ?EQ1)
    (PR-EQIVCT ca41 ?EQ1))
```

Rule (22) transforms the first goal "(SP-EQIVCT ca41 ?EQ1)" into

```
(SUB-CT (Z-SERIES ?X ?Y ?A ?B ?C) ca41 ?REST)
```

by unifying ?EQ1 with !<(Z-ELEMENT (SR ?X ?Y) ?A ?C) !& ?REST>. The goal "SUB-CT" succeeds by substituting R5, R6, #4, #5, and #2 for the variables ?X, ?Y, ?A, ?B, and ?C respectively. Then the circuit

```
!<(TERMINAL T1 #1) (TERMINAL T2 #2) (RESISTOR R1 #1 #3)
  (RESISTOR R2 #3 #2) (RESISTOR R3 #3 #4) (RESISTOR R4 #4 #2)>
```

is derived as the remainder of the series circuit from the variable ?REST. An equivalent impedance element "(Z-ELEMENT (SR R5 R6) #4 #2)" for the series circuit is added to the remainder by unification. Then the goal "(SP-EQIVCT ca41 ?EQ1)" succeeds, binding ?EQ1 to an equivalent circuit:

```
!<(Z-ELEMENT (SR R5 R6) #4 #2) (TERMINAL T1 #1) (TERMINAL T2 #2)
   (RESISTOR R1 #1 #3) (RESISTOR R2 #3 #2) (RESISTOR R3 #3 #4)
   (RESISTOR R4 #4 #2)>
```

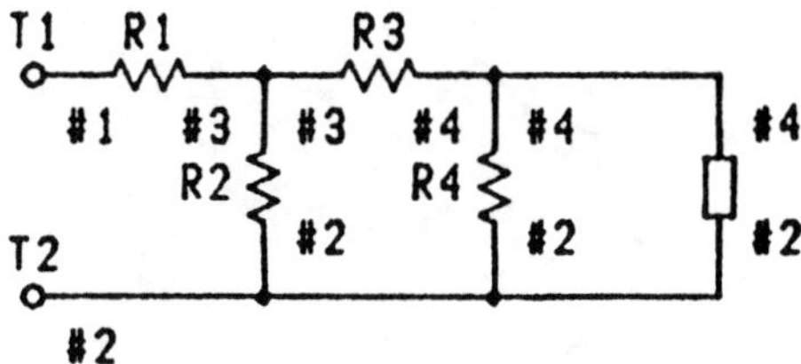

Figure 14: Transformation 1

This circuit becomes the input of "(M-SP-EQIVCT ?EQ1 ?EQCT)". The
process is repeated, and the circuit is transformed into an even
simpler equivalent form:

```
!<(Z-ELEMENT (PR (SR R5 R6) R4) #4 #2) (TERMINAL T1 #1)
   (TERMINAL T2 #2) (RESISTOR R1 #1 #3) (RESISTOR R2 #3 #2)
   (RESISTOR R3 #3 #4)>
```

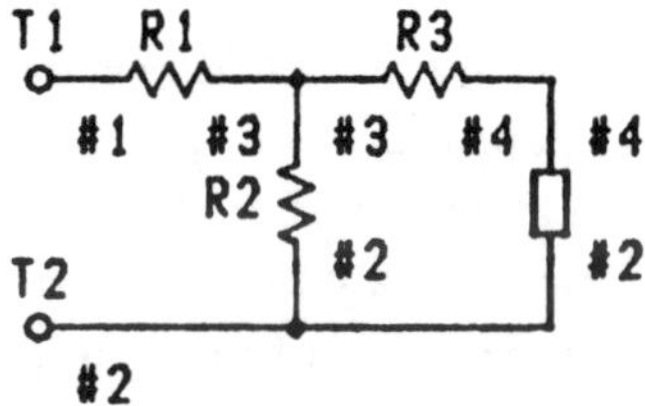

Figure 15: Transformation 2

This process continues until no series or parallel transformation can
be made.

The initial goal "(M-SP-EQIVCT ca41 ?EQCT)" succeeds, and we can eventually derive the value of the variable:

```
EQCT = !<(Z-ELEMENT (SR (PR (SR (PR (SR R5 R6) R4) R3) R2) R1) #2 #1)
          (TERMINAL T1 #1) (TERMINAL T2 #2)>
```

The name of the equivalent element keeps track of goals which succeeded. It forms a tree structure which has been constructed bottom-up as
in Figure 16.

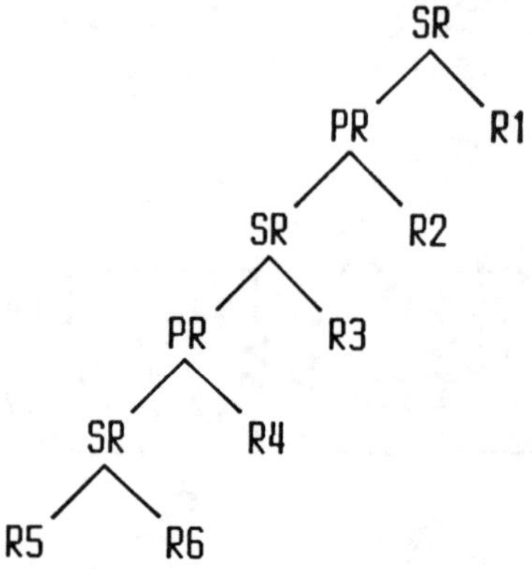

Figure 16: Parse tree for CA41

The process is similar to the bottom-up analysis of a sentence in language processing. Think of a circuit as a sentence, and its elements as words. We may call the process "parsing", and the tree structure a "parse tree". The bottom-up parsing is based on a rewriting mechanism from terminal symbols to non-terminal symbols. The mechanism is implemented as a top-down depth-first goal search.

The reverse process of equivalence transformation is viewed as a circuit generation process. The series and parallel transformations in reverse can be viewed as context-free generative grammars for circuits because, without depending on the other elements, a non-terminal symbol "Z-ELEMENT" can be rewritten into other Z-ELEMENTs or into terminal symbols such as RESISTORs connected in series or parallel. However, the star and the delta equivalent transformations have context-dependent properties; a circuit generated by these rules does not possess a simple tree structure (next section). We also present a top-down analysis method for electronic circuits in Chapter 6.

5.5 Context-Dependent Circuit Transformations

We will define a new predicate which stands for all the one-step equivalence transformations in Section 5.2:

```
(<- (SPYD-EQIVCT ?CT ?EQCT) (OR (SR-EQIVCT ?CT ?EQCT)
                                (PR-EQIVCT ?CT ?EQCT)
                                (ST-EQIVCT ?CT ?EQCT)
                                (DT-EQIVCT ?CT ?EQCT)))        (29)
```

If a circuit ?CT is given to the predicate "SPYD-EQIVCT", an equivalent circuit is bound to ?EQCT by one-step transformations. In successive applications of this predicate, the series and parallel transformations must have higher priority than the star and delta transformations because the series and parallel reduce a circuit into a simpler equivalent form, but the star and delta do not. The order of the disjunctive goals in (29) implies the priority of those goals for the first answer.

Next we define a predicate "M-SPYD-EQIVCT" which successively applies one-step transformational rules to an object circuit. The predicate can analyze most two-terminal impedance networks which electrical engineers frequently encounter.

```
(<- (M-SPYD-EQIVCT ?CT ?EQCT)
    (OR (AND (SPYD-EQIVCT ?CT ?EQ1)
             (M-SPYD-EQIVCT ?EQ1 ?EQCT))
        (AND (THNOT (SPYD-EQIVCT ?CT ?EQ1))
             (= ?EQCT ?CT))))                          (30)
```

The following goal applies the one-step transformations successively to the circuit CA45 in Figure 17, and rewrites the circuit into its simplest equivalent form.

```
(M-SPYD-EQIVCT
   !<(TERMINAL T1 #1) (TERMINAL T2 #2) (RESISTOR R1 #3 #4)
     (CAPACITOR C1 #1 #4) (CAPACITOR C2 #3 #2)
     (INDUCTOR L1 #1 #3) (INDUCTOR L2 #4 #2)>
   ?EQCT)
```

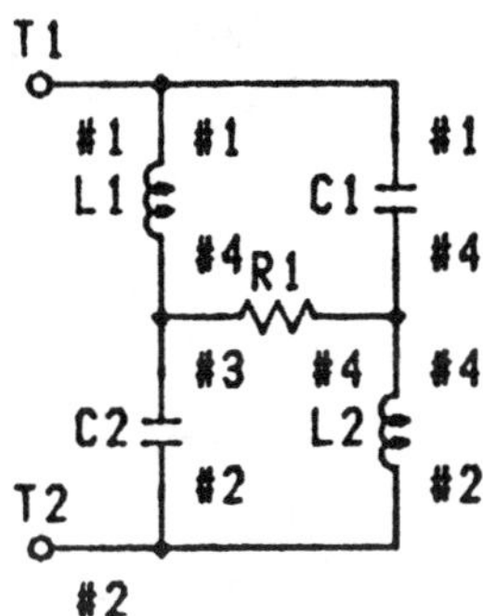

Figure 17: Circuit CA45

The first result for this goal is:

```
EQCT = !<(Z-ELEMENT (PR (ST R1 C1 L2)
                        (SR (PR (ST C1 L2 R1) C2)
                            (PR (ST L2 R1 C1) L1))) #1 #2)
           (TERMINAL T1 #1) (TERMINAL T2 #2)>
```

The equivalent circuit consists of one impedance element and two terminals. The name of the impedance element keeps track of goals which
succeeded (Figure 18). It shows that the three elements R1, C1, and
L2 connected as a star have been transformed into three elements (ST
R1 C1 L2), (ST C1 L2 R1), and (ST L2 R1 C1) connected as a delta by
the star-delta transformation at the first stage of the process. Then
those elements and the remainder in the circuit are transformed by
series and parallel transformations. Unlike the elements that appeared
in the previous section, the elements appearing in the transformation
process no longer form a simple tree structure. That is, the star-
delta and the delta-star transformations can not be viewed as context-
free circuit generation rules.

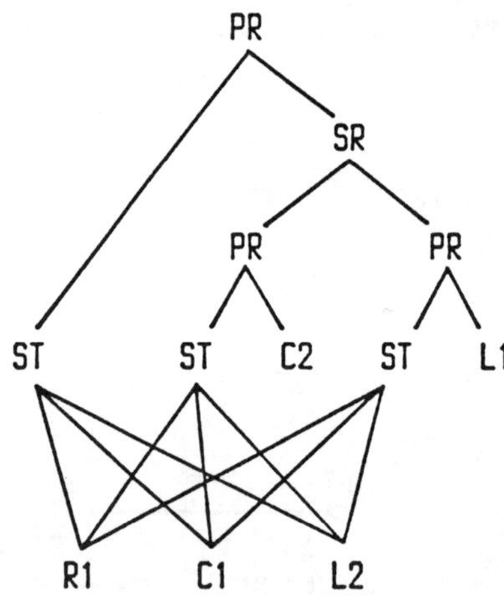

Figure 18: Parse tree for CA45

We will show another example of successive equivalence transformations. The following goal parses the circuit CA53 in Figure 19.

```
(M-SPYD-EQIVCT
   !<(TERMINAL T1 #1) (TERMINAL T2 #2) (RESISTOR R1 #1 #3)
      (RESISTOR R2 #1 #4) (RESISTOR R3 #1 #5) (RESISTOR R4 #3 #8)
      (RESISTOR R5 #3 #6) (RESISTOR R6 #4 #6) (RESISTOR R7 #4 #7)
```

```
    (RESISTOR R8 #5 #7) (RESISTOR R9 #5 #8) (RESISTOR R10 #6 #2)
    (RESISTOR R11 #7 #2) (RESISTOR R12 #8 #2)>
?EQCT)
```

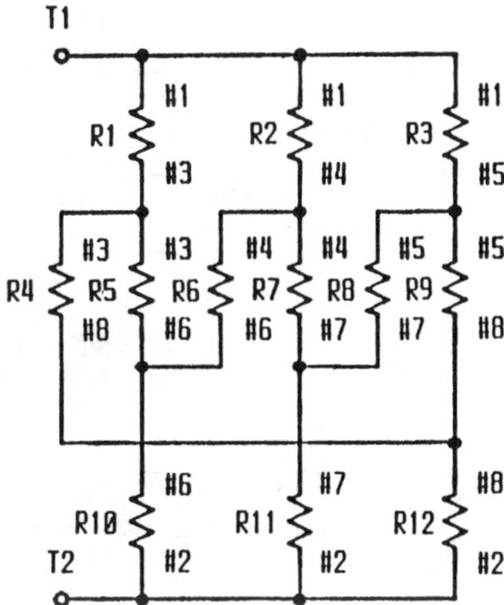

Figure 19: Circuit CA53

We can derive an equivalent circuit which consists of an impedance element and two terminals from the variable ?EQCT of the goal for the first result. The name of the element shows how equivalence transformations have been done.

```
EQCT = !<(Z-ELEMENT
    (PR
     (ST
      (PR (ST R1 (ST R10 R6 R5)
                 (DT (PR (ST R4 R12 R9) (ST R7 R11 R8))
                     (ST R12 R9 R4)
                     (PR (ST R9 R4 R12) (ST R6 R5 R10)))))
          (ST R3 (ST R11 R8 R7)
                 (DT (PR (ST R9 R4 R12) (ST R6 R5 R10))
                     (PR (ST R4 R12 R9) (ST R7 R11 R8))
                     (ST R12 R9 R4))))
      (PR (ST (ST R10 R6 R5)
              (DT (PR (ST R4 R12 R9) (ST R7 R11 R8))
                  (ST R12 R9 R4)
                  (PR (ST R9 R4 R12) (ST R6 R5 R10)))
              R1)
          (ST (ST R11 R8 R7)
              (DT (PR (ST R9 R4 R12) (ST R6 R5 R10))
                  (PR (ST R4 R12 R9) (ST R7 R11 R8))
                  (ST R12 R9 R4))
              R3))
     (DT (ST R12 R9 R4)
         (PR (ST R9 R4 R12) (ST R6 R5 R10))
         (PR (ST R4 R12 R9) (ST R7 R11 R8)))))
```

282

```
      (SR
       (PR
        (PR (PR (ST (DT (PR (ST R4 R12 R9) (ST R7 R11 R8))
                        (ST R12 R9 R4)
                        (PR (ST R9 R4 R12) (ST R6 R5 R10)))
                    R1 (ST R10 R6 R5))
                R2)
            (ST (DT (PR (ST R9 R4 R12) (ST R6 R5 R10))
                    (PR (ST R4 R12 R9) (ST R7 R11 R8))
                    (ST R12 R9 R4))
                R3 (ST R11 R8 R7)))
        (ST (DT (ST R12 R9 R4)
                (PR (ST R9 R4 R12) (ST R6 R5 R10))
                (PR (ST R4 R12 R9) (ST R7 R11 R8)))
            (PR (ST R1 (ST R10 R6 R5)
                    (DT (PR (ST R4 R12 R9) (ST R7 R11 R8))
                        (ST R12 R9 R4)
                        (PR (ST R9 R4 R12) (ST R6 R5 R10))))
                (ST R3 (ST R11 R8 R7)
                    (DT (PR (ST R9 R4 R12) (ST R6 R5 R10))
                        (PR (ST R4 R12 R9) (ST R7 R11 R8))
                        (ST R12 R9 R4))))
            (PR (ST (ST R10 R6 R5)
                    (DT (PR (ST R4 R12 R9) (ST R7 R11 R8))
                        (ST R12 R9 R4)
                        (PR (ST R9 R4 R12) (ST R6 R5 R10)))
                    R1)
                (ST (ST R11 R8 R7)
                    (DT (PR (ST R9 R4 R12) (ST R6 R5 R10))
                        (PR (ST R4 R12 R9) (ST R7 R11 R8))
                        (ST R12 R9 R4))
                    R3)))))
       (PR (PR (ST R8 R7 R11) (ST R5 R10 R6))
           (ST
            (PR (ST (ST R10 R6 R5)
                    (DT (PR (ST R4 R12 R9) (ST R7 R11 R8))
                        (ST R12 R9 R4)
                        (PR (ST R9 R4 R12) (ST R6 R5 R10)))
                    R1)
                (ST (ST R11 R8 R7)
                    (DT (PR (ST R9 R4 R12) (ST R6 R5 R10))
                        (PR (ST R4 R12 R9) (ST R7 R11 R8))
                        (ST R12 R9 R4))
                    R3))
            (DT (ST R12 R9 R4)
                (PR (ST R9 R4 R12) (ST R6 R5 R10))
                (PR (ST R4 R12 R9) (ST R7 R11 R8)))
            (PR (ST R1 (ST R10 R6 R5)
                    (DT (PR (ST R4 R12 R9) (ST R7 R11 R8))
                        (ST R12 R9 R4)
                        (PR (ST R9 R4 R12) (ST R6 R5 R10))))
                (ST R3 (ST R11 R8 R7)
                    (DT (PR (ST R9 R4 R12) (ST R6 R5 R10))
                        (PR (ST R4 R12 R9) (ST R7 R11 R8))
                        (ST R12 R9 R4)))))))))
      #1 #2)
    (TERMINAL T1 #1) (TERMINAL T2 #2)>
```

5.6 Numerical Computing

In the series transformation, a part of circuit !<(RESISTOR R1 #1 #2)
(RESISTOR R2 #2 #3)> is transformed into an equivalent impedance
element "(Z-ELEMENT (SR R1 R2) #1 #3)".

```
        R1  R2                        (SR R1 R2)
      —\/\—\/\—        ==>              —\/\—
      #1  #2  #3                     #1      #3
```

Figure 20: Series transformation of resistors

When we go into Lisp, we can easily compute the equivalent impedance.
That is, at first we include the resistance value in the name of each
resistor:

```
(SETQ R1 10)
(SETQ R2 20)
```

If we define the function "SR" as the arithmetic function "+", we can
acquire the equivalent impedance by simply evaluating the name of
equivalent element:

```
(SR R1 R2) ---> 30 ohm
```

In order to represent impedances as complex numbers, we will use the
following representation:

```
(real-part imaginary-part)
```

The Lisp-functions "C+", "C-", "C*", and "C/" are defined corresponding to the arithmetic functions "+", "-", "*", and "/" for complex
numbers.

The Lisp-functions "SR" for series impedance and "PR" for parallel
impedance in UCI-lisp syntax are defined as follows (Figure 9, 10):

```
(DE SR (X Y) (C+ X Y))                                          (31)
```

```
(DE PR (X Y) (C/ (C* X Y) (C+ X Y)))                            (32)
```

The Lisp-functions "ST" for star transformation and "DT" for delta
transformation are defined as follows (Figure 11, 12):

```
(DE ST (X Y Z)
   (C/ (C+ (C* X Y) (C* Y Z) (C* Z X)) X))              (33)

(DE DT (X Y Z)
   (C/ (C* Y Z) (C+ X Y Z)))                            (34)
```

Now we can compute the equivalent impedances of two-terminal networks such as CA41 and CA45 which have been already transformed into single equivalent elements in Section 5.4 and 5.5. To compute the equivalent impedance we evaluate the name of the equivalent element in Lisp after setting the impedances for each element in the original circuit.

6 TOP-DOWN ANALYSIS FOR ELECTRONIC CIRCUITS

6.1 Circuits Viewed as Language

Electronic circuits are designed as a goal oriented composition of basic circuits with specific functions. Consequently, an electronic circuit usually forms a hierarchical structure of functional blocks. Each element in the circuit has a given role in forming functional blocks. Each block is also given a role in forming super blocks. These blocks are hierarchically organized to achieve the overall goal of the circuit. Therefore, understanding a circuit involves finding this hierarchical structure and rediscovering the designer's original intentions.

Almost all designed circuits have the feature of language that they carry information of the speaker's intentions mapped onto their structures. A circuit schematic not only represents a physical circuit, but also functions as a written language for electronic engineers. A circuit can thus be viewed as a sentence and its elements as words. Circuit structures with specific functions are represented by deductive rules analogous to those in definite clause grammars. Using these rules, an object circuit is decomposed into a parse tree of functional blocks. Parsing circuit topology is a step toward automatic circuit understanding.

6.2 Macro Elements as Non-Terminal Symbols

In designing analog IC circuits, there are many functional blocks which can be viewed as macro elements (macro devices) [Interdesign

Inc. 1976]. The macro element "diode-connected transistor" is defined by the following rules:

```
(<- (SUB-CT (D-TRANSISTOR (FD ?Q) ?A ?C) ?CT ?REST)
    (MEM-REST (NPN-TR ?Q ?A ?C ?A) ?CT ?REST))                  (35)

(<- (SUB-CT (D-TRANSISTOR (RD ?Q) ?A ?C) ?CT ?REST)
    (MEM-REST (NPN-TR ?Q ?C ?A ?C) ?CT ?REST))                  (36)
```

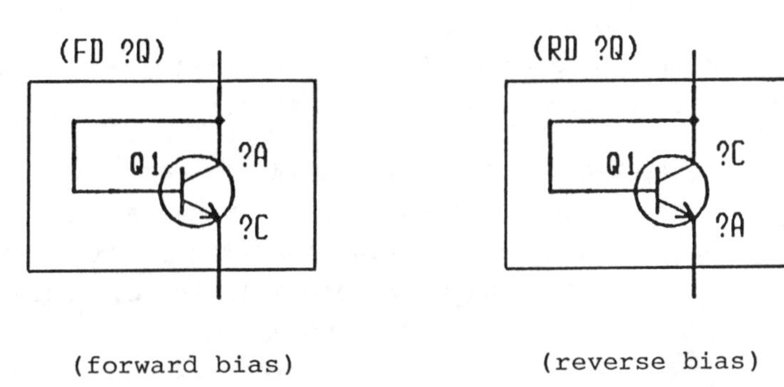

Figure 21: Diode-connected transistor

Rule (35) says that, if an NPN-transistor ?Q with the base and the collector connected to the same node ?A is a member of the tuple ?CT representing a circuit, then there exists a diode-connected transistor (FD ?Q) as an abstract element in the circuit (Section 4.4). The functions "D-TRANSISTOR" and "FD" are introduced as Skolem functions representing the existence of a diode-connected transistor and its name. That is, as a diode-connected transistor exists corresponding to the transistor ?Q, we can give a unique name (FD ?Q) to the macro element, and we can denote the macro element by "(D-TRANSISTOR (FD ?Q) ?A ?C)". The function "D-TRANSISTOR" has the same arguments as ordinary elements. The first argument (FD ?Q) is the name of the macro element. The second and the third arguments are its nodes (anode, cathode).

If we consider a circuit as a sentence in a formal language, the macro elements are non-terminal symbols, while the ordinary elements are terminal symbols. The rules can be viewed as context-free grammars which define the relationships between those symbols. Object circuits are written using terminal symbols. The non-terminal symbols appear in the process of parsing the circuit.

In analog IC design, diode-connected transistors are often used as zener diodes biased in reverse. Rule (36) is provided for this purpose.

Rule (37) recursively defines a series circuit of diodes as a macro element. The conjunctive part of the definition says "find a diode-connected transistor ?Q connected to ?A and ?B in the circuit ?CT", and "find a series connection of diodes ?D connected to ?B and ?C in the rest of the circuit ?RST1", then "give the name (S-DD ?Q ?D) to the macro element". The condition "NON-SUBCT" demands the node ?B should not be connected to any elements other than those diodes connected in series (Section 4.5, 5.1).

```
(<- (SUB-CT (S-DIODE ?NAME ?A ?C) ?CT ?REST)
    (OR (SUB-CT (D-TRANSISTOR ?NAME ?A ?C) ?CT ?REST)
        (AND (SUB-CT (D-TRANSISTOR ?Q ?A ?B) ?CT ?RST1)
             (SUB-CT (S-DIODE ?D ?B ?C) ?RST1 ?REST)
             (= ?NAME (S-DD ?Q ?D))
             (NON-SUBCT (ANY-ELM ?Z ?B) ?REST))))        (37)
```

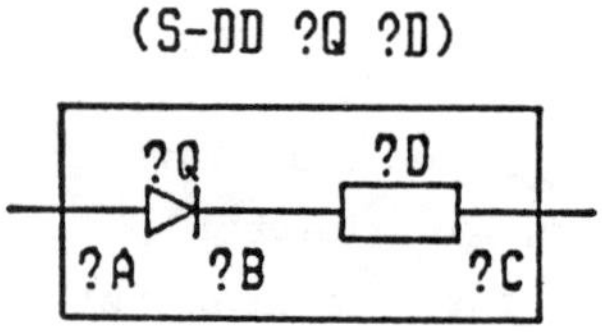

(S-DD ?Q ?D)

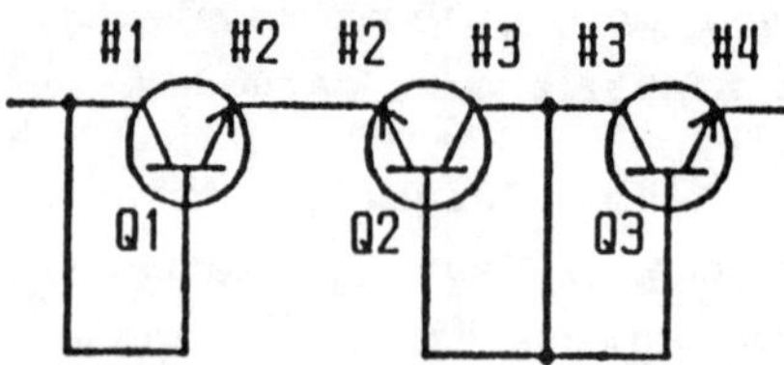

Figure 22: Diodes connected in series

According to this rule, the diodes connected in series (Figure 23) form two different parse trees (Figure 24).

Figure 23: Circuit CD7

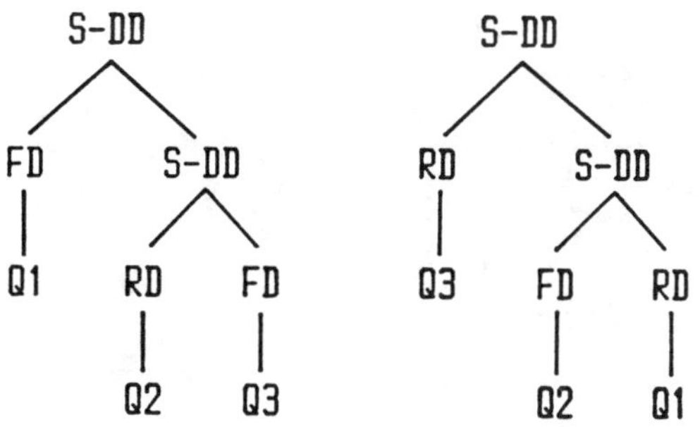

Figure 24: Parse trees for CD7

6.3 Functional Blocks in Analog IC Designs

Now we can define macro elements for the various functional blocks in analog IC designs.

Rule (38) defines the simple voltage regulator in Figure 25.

```
(<- (SUB-CT (V-REGULATOR (V-REG ?D ?R) ?IN ?OUT ?COM) ?CT ?REST)
    (AND (SUB-CT (S-DIODE ?D ?OUT ?COM) ?CT ?RST1)
         (SUB-CT (RES ?R ?IN ?OUT) ?RST1 ?REST)))            (38)
```

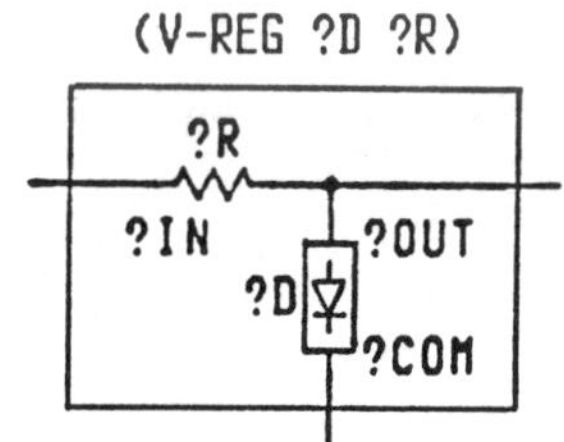

Figure 25: Voltage regulator

Rule (39) defines the voltage divider in Figure 26.

```
(<- (SUB-CT (V-DIVIDER (V-DIV ?X ?Y) ?IN ?OUT ?COM) ?CT ?REST)
    (AND (SUB-CT (RES ?X ?IN ?OUT) ?CT ?RST1)
         (SUB-CT (RES ?Y ?OUT ?COM) ?RST1 ?REST)))           (39)
```

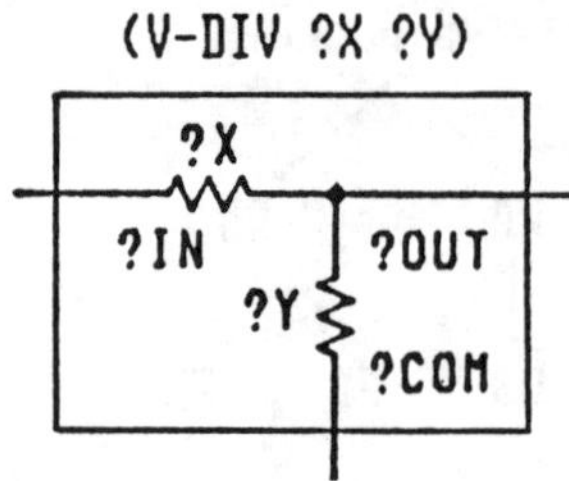

<u>Figure 26:</u> Voltage divider

A voltage source is defined by a voltage regulator or a voltage divider as shown in Figure 27:

```
(<- (SUB-CT (V-SOURCE (V-SOC ?V) ?OUT ?COM) ?CT ?REST)
    (OR (SUB-CT (V-REGULATOR ?V ?IN ?OUT ?COM) ?CT ?REST)
        (SUB-CT (V-DIVIDER ?V ?IN ?OUT ?COM) ?CT ?REST)))        (40)
```

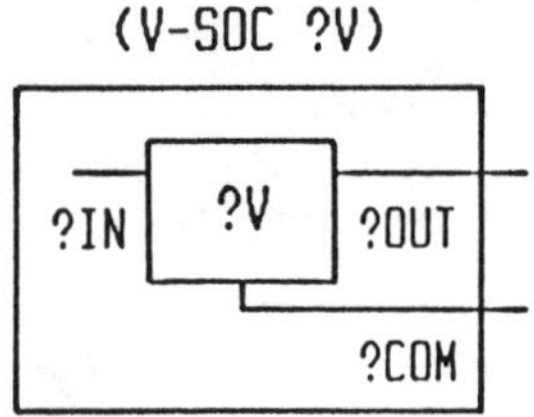

<u>Figure 27:</u> Voltage source

A current source is defined using an NPN-transistor, a resistor connected to its emitter, and a voltage source:

```
(<- (SUB-CT (C-SOURCE (C-SINK ?VS ?Q ?R) ?SINK ?COM) ?CT ?REST)
    (AND (SUB-CT (V-SOURCE ?VS ?B ?COM) ?CT ?RST1)
         (MEM-REST (NPN-TR ?Q ?B ?E ?SINK) ?RST1 ?RST2)
         (SUB-CT (RES ?R ?E ?COM) ?RST2 ?REST)))        (41)
```

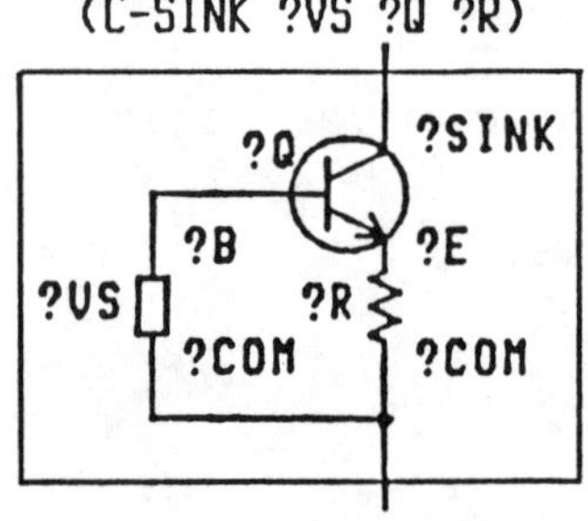

<u>Figure 28:</u> Current source

An emitter-coupled pair of NPN-transistors is defined as:

```
(<- (SUB-CT (E-COUPLE (E-CUP ?Q1 ?Q2) ?B1 ?B2 ?E ?C1 ?C2)
            ?CT ?REST)
    (AND (MEM-REST (NPN-TR ?Q1 ?B1 ?E ?C1) ?CT ?RST1)
         (MEM-REST (NPN-TR ?Q2 ?B2 ?E ?C2) ?RST1 ?REST)))        (42)
```

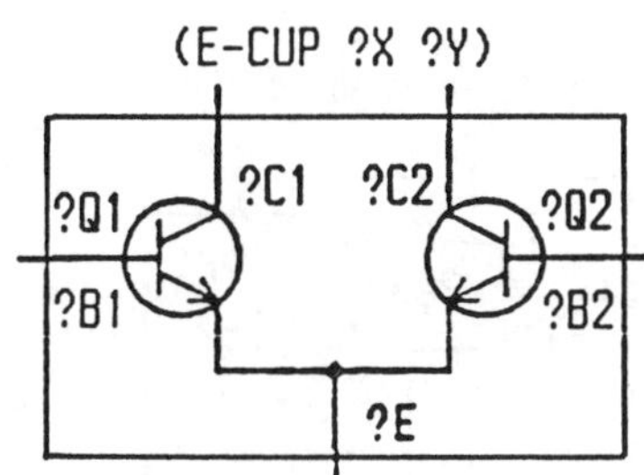

Figure 29: Emitter-coupled pair

A single-ended differential amplifier consists of an emitter-coupled
pair, a resistor for load, and a resistor or a current source connected to the emitter of the pair:

```
(<- (SUB-CT (S-DIF-AMP (SD-AMP ?EC ?R ?CS) ?B1 ?B2 ?G ?C1 ?C2)
            ?CT ?REST)
    (AND (SUB-CT (E-COUPLE ?EC ?B1 ?B2 ?E ?C1 ?C2) ?CT ?RST1)
         (SUB-CT (RES ?R ?C1 ?C2) ?RST1 ?RST2)
         (OR (SUB-CT (RES ?CS ?E ?G) ?RST2 ?REST)
             (SUB-CT (C-SOURCE ?CS ?E ?G) ?RST2 ?REST)))        (43)
```

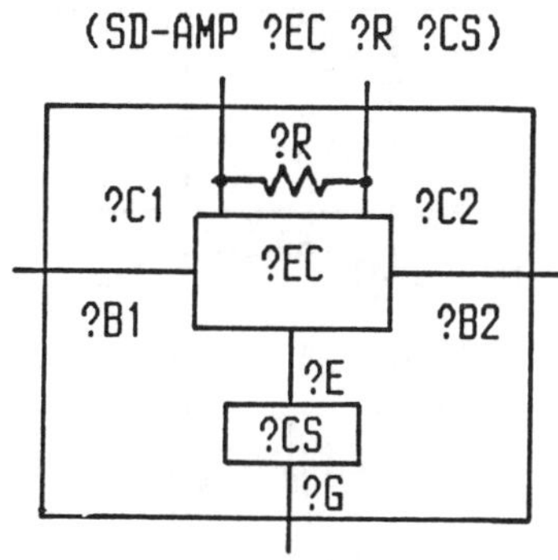

Figure 30: Single-ended differential amplifier

290

A comparator with internal reference voltage and inverted output is
defined as follows:

```
(<- (SUB-CT (I-COMPARATOR (I-COMP ?AMP ?VS) ?B1 ?C1 ?P ?G)
            ?CT ?REST)
    (AND (SUB-CT (S-DIF-AMP ?AMP ?B1 ?B2 ?G ?C1 ?P) ?CT ?RST1)
         (SUB-CT (V-SOURCE ?VS ?B2 ?G) ?RST1 ?REST)))          (44)
```

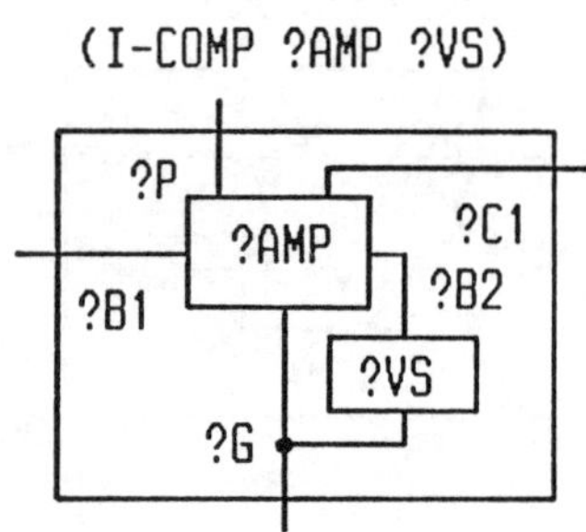

Figure 31: Comparator with
internal reference voltage

6.4 Parsing Circuit Topology

Figure 32 shows a small portion of an analog IC circuit [Interdesign
Inc. 1976]. We will call the portion of the circuit CD71. The circuit
is represented as a tuple of composite terms denoting each element or
device (Section 4.2):

```
!<(RESISTOR R1 #12 #1) (RESISTOR R2 #2 #10) (RESISTOR R3 #2 #3)
  (RESISTOR R4 #3 #1) (RESISTOR R5 #2 #4) (NPN-TR Q1 #9 #11 #10)
  (NPN-TR Q2 #3 #11 #2) (NPN-TR Q3 #4 #12 #11)
  (NPN-TR Q4 #4 #5 #4) (NPN-TR Q5 #5 #1 #5)>
```

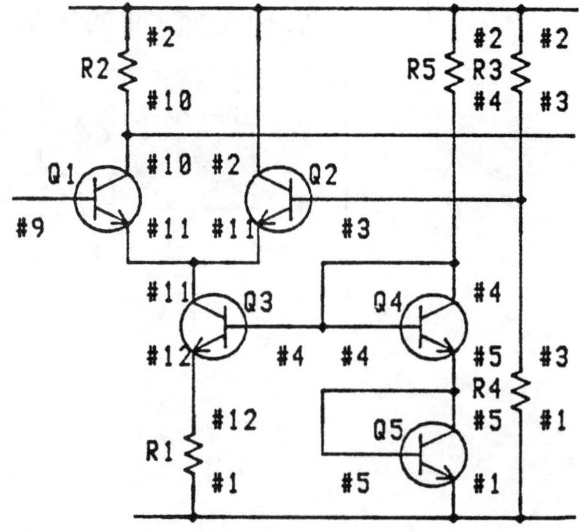

Figure 32: Circuit CD71

Now we assume that the tuple is a sentence, and its elements are words. The word order is arbitrary in our language for circuit topology.

Running the following goal form causes Duck to start parsing. "cd71" is a syntactic abbreviation standing for the circuit tuple.

    (SUB-CT (I-COMPARATOR ?NAME ?IN ?OUT ?POW ?GND) cd71 !<>)

As the variable ?REST of the predicate SUB-CT is bound to the null circuit !<>, the goal asks whether the total circuit pictured in Figure 32 is a macro element of the type "comparator with internal reference voltage". According to rule (44), the goal is decomposed into conjunctive subgoals:

    (AND (SUB-CT (S-DIF-AMP ?AMP ?IN ?B2 ?GND ?OUT ?POW) cd71 ?RST1)
         (SUB-CT (V-SOURCE ?VS ?B2 ?GND) ?RST1 !<>))

by unifying ?NAME with (I-COMP ?AMP ?VS). The goal says first "find a single-ended differential amplifier in circuit CD71", and then "find a voltage source connected to the amplifier as its voltage reference". The first subgoal "single-ended differential amplifier" is decomposed by rule (43):

    (AND (SUB-CT (E-COUPLE ?EC ?IN ?B2 ?E ?OUT ?POW)
               cd71 ?RST2)
         (SUB-CT (RES ?R ?OUT ?POW) ?RST2 ?RST3)
         (OR (SUB-CT (RES ?CS ?E ?GND) ?RST3 ?RST1)
             (SUB-CT (C-SOURCE ?CS ?E ?GND) ?RST3 ?RST1)))

by unifying ?AMP with (SD-AMP ?EC ?R ?CS). The goal says sequentially "find an emitter-coupled pair", "find a resistor connected to the collectors of the pair", and finally "find a resistor or a current source connected to the emitter of the pair". By rule (42), finding an emitter-coupled pair means proving the following goal:

    (AND (MEM-REST (NPN-TR ?Q1 ?IN ?E ?OUT) cd71 ?RST4)
         (MEM-REST (NPN-TR ?Q2 ?B2 ?E ?POW) ?RST4 ?RST2))

by unifying ?EC with (E-CUP ?Q1 ?Q2). The first subgoal succeeds by unifying "(NPN-TR ?Q1 ?IN ?E ?OUT)" with "(NPN-TR Q1 #9 #11 #10)" in tuple cd71. The second subgoal succeeds by unifying "(NPN-TR ?Q2 ?B2 ?E ?POW)" with "(NPN-TR Q2 #3 #11 #2)" in the rest circuit of the

first goal. Now the existence of a macro element "emitter-coupled
pair" is proved to be a sub-circuit of CD71 with the variables bound
as follows:

    (E-COUPLE (E-CUP Q1 Q2) #9 #3 #11 #10 #2)

This macro element works as a non-terminal symbol in parsing the circuit. The new name "(E-CUP Q1 Q2)" is given to the macro element by
the Skolem function "E-CUP". The next subgoal is to find a resistor
connected to the collectors of the emitter coupled pair. The element
"(RESISTOR R2 #2 #10)" fits this condition, and its macro element
satisfies the subgoal by rule (12):

    (RES R2 #2 #10)

The last subgoal of rule (43) is to find a resistor or a current
source connected to the emitter. This subgoal is:

    (OR (SUB-CT (RES ?CS #11 ?GND) rst4 ?RST1)
        (SUB-CT (C-SOURCE ?CS #11 ?GND) rst4 ?RST1))

where "rst4" stands for the tuple of elements associated with the circuit pictured in Figure 32, with elements Q1, Q2, and R2 removed.

    !<(RESISTOR R1 #12 #1) (RESISTOR R3 #2 #3) (RESISTOR R4 #3 #1)
      (RESISTOR R5 #2 #4) (NPN-TR Q3 #4 #12 #11) (NPN-TR Q4 #4 #5 #4)
      (NPN-TR Q5 #5 #1 #5)>

Since no resistor is connected to #11, the first goal of the disjunction fails. The second goal is decomposed into subgoals by rule (41).

The goal-subgoal decomposition process goes on iteratively until each
SUB-CT goal reaches MEM-REST goals which identify the terminal symbols.

When initial goal finally succeeds, and the values of the variables
will be follows:

```
 NAME = (I-COMP (SD-AMP (E-CUP Q1 Q2)
                        R2
                        (C-SINK (V-SOC (V-REG (S-DD (FD Q4) (FD Q5))
                                              R5))
                                Q3
                                R1))
               (V-SOC (V-DIV R3 R4)))
```

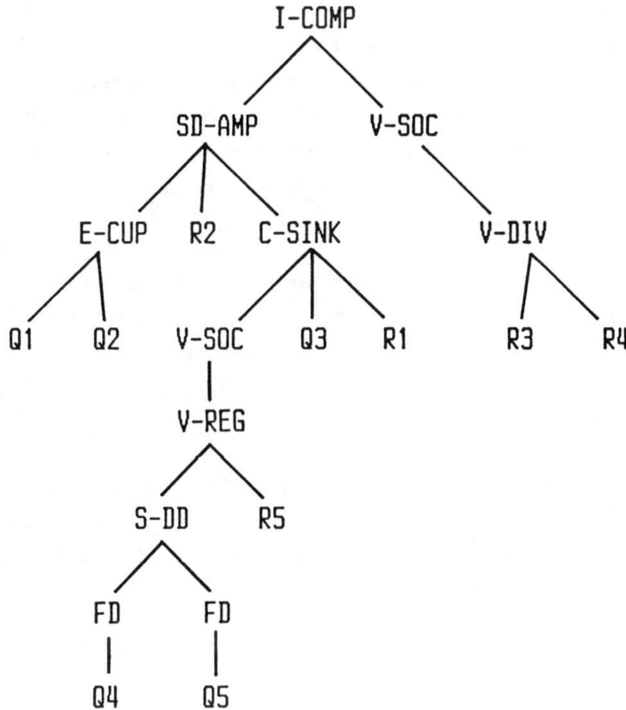

Figure 33: Parse
tree for CD71

IN = #9
OUT = #10
POW = #2
GND = #1

The name in each macro element keeps track of the goals which have
succeeded. They form a hierarchical structure of macro elements, which
can be viewed as a parse tree of the circuit, in a manner analogous
to the syntactic structure of a sentence.

6.5 Behavior of the Predicate SUB-CT

Functional blocks in analog IC designs are coded into deductive rules
analogous to those of definite clause grammars (Section 6.6) by the
predicates SUB-CT and MEM-REST. The rules define a set of circuits in
the same way that generative grammars define a language. If the object
circuit is given, and if the circuit is a member of the set, the following goal parses the circuit.

```
(SUB-CT ?WHAT-CIRCUIT object-circuit !<>)
```

In this case, the top-down method does not work efficiently, because the first argument is a variable which does not contain information about how to parse the circuit. Therefore, Duck tries to match all the SUB-CT defined abstract elements againist the circuit. As a result, if the object circuit is a member of the set defined by the rules, the goal eventually parses the circuit.

Top-down parsing works effectively when the circuit goal is already specified as in the example of Section 6.4. Usually, when an engineer encounters a circuit, it is in the context of a specified device. Therefore, the circuit goal can be inferred from the context. Thus, top-down parsing can be used effectively in actual analyses of electronic circuits.

Even if an object circuit is not a member of the set, if the null circuit !<> is replaced by a variable ?REST, the following goal can be used to identify all functional blocks which have been defined as macro elements:

    (SUB-CT ?WHAT-CIRCUIT object-circuit ?REST)

As a consequence of its realization in logic programming, data flows to the predicate SUB-CT are bilateral. If a macro element is given instead of the object circuit, the following goal works as a circuit generator.

    (SUB-CT macro-element ?CT !<>)

Then we can acquire the generated circuit from the variable ?CT. For example, the following goal generates a set of circuits.

    (SUB-CT (S-DIODE ?NAME #1 #2) ?CT !<>)

    NAME= (RD ?_3)
    CT= !<(NPN-TR ?_3 #2 #1 #2)>

    NAME= (FD ?_5)
    CT= !<(NPN-TR ?_5 #1 #2 #1)>

    NAME= (S-DD (RD ?_24) (RD ?_22))
    CT= !<(NPN-TR ?_22 #2 ?_23 #2) (NPN-TR ?_24 ?_23 #1 ?_23)>
      . . .

Variables such as "_3" are generated by the Duck system. The rules for circuit structures were defined for use in parsing circuits, not generating them. Therefor, generated circuits contain these existentially quantified variables. They are not desirable in actual circuits. The solution to this problem is not to use parsing rules for generation, but to rewrite the rules for circuit synthesis.

6.6 Differences Between This Approach and Definite Clause Grammars

In definite clause grammars [Pereira, Warren 1980], the following grammar rule

    sentence --> noun_phrase, verb_phrase.

is translated into a clause in Prolog as follows:

    sentence(S0, S) :- noun_phrase(S0, S1), verb_phrase(S1, S).

The variables S0, S1 and S are pointers which represent the beginning or ending points of phrases in a sentence. We can read the clause as "a sentence extends from S0 to S if there is a noun phrase from S0 to S1 and a verb phrase from S1 to S". Each pointer is composed of a list of words occurring after that point in the sentence (Figure 34).

This rule can be written as a backward rule in Duck:

    (<- (SENTENCE ?S0 ?S) (AND (NOUN-PHRASE ?S0 ?S1)
                               (VERB-PHRASE ?S1 ?S)))

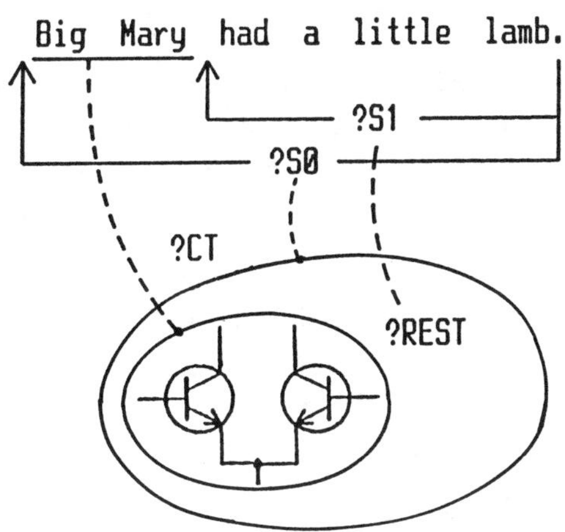

Figure 34: Sentence vs. Circuit

If we use a predicate "SUB-STRING" to refer to a part of a sentence corresponding to "SUB-CT" in Section 4.4, the rule can also be written as follows:

```
(<- (SUB-STRING SENTENCE ?S0 ?S)
    (AND (SUB-STRING NOUN-PHRASE ?S0 ?S1)
         (SUB-STRING VERB-PHRASE ?S1 ?S))))
```

If we want to acquire a parse tree for the sentence, the rule can be modified as follows:

```
(<- (SUB-STRING (SENTENCE (S ?NP ?VP)) ?S0 ?S)
    (AND (SUB-STRING (NOUN-PHRASE ?NP) ?S0 ?S1)
         (SUB-STRING (VERB-PHRASE ?VP) ?S1 ?S)))
```

This rule has the same structure as the rules in Section 6.3. The non-terminal symbols "(SENTENCE (S ?NP ?VP))", "(NOUN-PHRASE ?NP)", and "(VERB-PHRASE ?VP)" correspond to the macro elements in the previous sections. Variables such as ?S0 and ?S1 correspond to ?CT and ?REST in the predicate SUB-CT (Figure 34).

The grammar rules which generate terminal symbols are written as:

```
noun --> [mary].
```

In definite clause grammars, this would be written as:

```
noun(S0, S) :- connects(S0, mary, S).
```

In Duck, it would be written as:

```
(<- (SUB-STRING NOUN ?S0 ?S) (CONNECTS Mary ?S0 ?S))
```

The order of the first and the second arguments is changed in the definition of CONNECTS. This rule is similar to rule (35) which defines the relation between the macro element "diode-connected transistor" and the ordinary element "NPN-transistor":

```
(<- (SUB-CT (D-TRANSISTOR (FD ?Q) ?A ?C) ?CT ?REST)
    (MEM-REST (NPN-TR ?Q ?A ?C ?A) ?CT ?REST))
```

The predicate CONNECTS is defined by the following assertion:

```
(CONNECTS ?W !<?W !&?S> ?S)
```

while "connects" in Prolog is defined as:

```
connects([W |S], W, S).
```

Now we compare the predicate CONNECTS with the predicate MEM-REST
defined as:

    (MEM-REST ?M !<!&?L ?M !&?R> !<!&?L !&?R>)

The first argument of CONNECTS is the first element of the tuple which
is the second argument of CONNECTS. On the other hand, the first argument of MEM-REST is a member of the tuple which is the second argument
of MEM-REST. In both CONNECTS and MEM-REST, the last arguments are the
rest of the tuples. The difference is that the object circuit is not
a string of words, but a set of elements; furthermore, every element
has a structure which is its particular circuit topology.

7   ELECTRICAL CONDITIONS

7.1 Rejecting Undesired Interpretations

A voltage divider is defined by a pair of resistors "(V-DIV ?X ?Y)"
as shown in Figure 35-a. Duck finds ten voltage dividers in circuit
CD71 (Figure 32) by the following goal:

    (SUB-CT (V-DIVIDER ?NAME ?IN ?OUT ?COM) cd71 ?REST)

But eight of them such as "(V-DIV R1 R4)" were not thought of as voltage dividers by the circuit designer (Figure 35-b). These undesired
interpretations do not form macro elements which contribute to the
final goal of the circuit, so they should be rejected in the parsing
process.

In the case of parsing circuit CD71, most of these undesired interpretations actually do not occur, because the macro element I-COMPARATOR
(44) is defined so that it looks for a differential amplifier before
looking for a voltage source (voltage divider). When it finds the
differential amplifier first, then the remainder of the circuit will
consist of exactly the only actual voltage source. If the order of
the definition is reversed, then the undesired interpretations will
be found first, and the system will have to backtrack until it finds
the correct interpretation.

If we are informed that nodes #1 and #2 of circuit CD71 are power
nodes connected to its power supply, we can reject these undesired
interpretations more efficiently. Namely, we can use an electrical

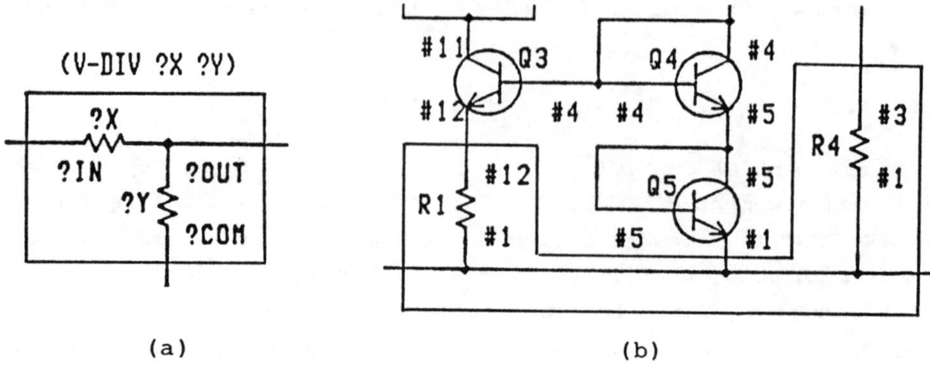

(a)   (b)

Figure 35: Undesired interpretation

condition that does not permit the node ?OUT of a voltage divider
to be connected to power nodes. We can simply add this electrical
condition "(THNOT (POWER-NODE ?OUT))" into the voltage divider
definition (39):

```
(<- (SUB-CT (V-DIVIDER (V-DIV ?X ?Y) ?IN ?OUT ?COM) ?CT ?REST)
    (AND (SUB-CT (RES ?X ?IN ?OUT) ?CT ?RST1)
         (SUB-CT (RES ?Y ?OUT ?COM) ?RST1 ?REST)
         (THNOT (POWER-NODE ?OUT)))))
```

If it is known that #1 and #2 are power nodes, the following assertions will be added into Duck database before the parsing process:

```
(POWER-NODE #1)
(POWER-NODE #2)
```

and the system will no longer generate undesired interpretations such
as "(V-DIV R1 R4)". These electrical conditions resemble selectional
restrictions in language processing. We can use the information
provided by electrical conditions to reduce syntactic ambiguities in
parsing circuits. The implementation of electrical conditions presented below is more sophisticated than the simplistic example presented
here.

7.2 Transferring Conditions Between Goals

As inputs, electrical conditions supply information that expedites the
identification of macro elements; however the system also generates
electrical conditions as outputs. If a voltage regulator (Figure 25)

is identified in a circuit, the input node ?IN and the common node ?COM of the voltage regulator must be power nodes of the circuit. This information is used afterward for identifying other macro elements such as voltage dividers (previous section) more efficiently. In other words, electrical conditions can be generated from a circuit topology as well as supplied by the outside world. The conditions can also be applied to parsing circuit topology.

In order to transfer the electrical conditions between goals, we will introduce new variables ?IN-COND and ?OUT-COND to form a new predicate "SUB-CTC" (sub-circuit with conditions) such as:

```
(SUB-CTC macro-element object-circuit rest ?IN-COND ?OUT-COND)
```

The variables ?IN-COND and ?OUT-COND are substituted by a tuple of terms denoting the electrical conditions such as:

```
!<(POWER-NODE #1) (POWER-NODE #2)>
```

The variable ?IN-COND holds conditions set by the preceding goals. The variable ?OUT-COND contains additional ones discovered in the current goal. We will give a new version of the definition "voltage regulator" using this predicate:

```
(<- (SUB-CTC (V-REGULATOR (V-REG ?D ?R) ?IN ?OUT ?COM)
            ?CT ?REST ?IN-COND ?OUT-COND)
    (AND (SUB-CT (S-DIODE ?D ?OUT ?COM) ?CT ?RST1)
         (SUB-CT (RES ?R ?IN ?OUT) ?RST1 ?REST)
         (NON-MEMBER (POWER-NODE ?OUT) ?IN-COND)
         (= ?OUT-COND
            !<(POWER-NODE ?IN) (POWER-NODE ?COM) !&?IN-COND>)))
```

The last two lines are added to the rule (38). The first line demands the output node must not be the power node, which is the same condition as in the previous section. The second line generates the output conditions which require the nodes ?IN and ?COM to be the power nodes.

The predicate SUB-CTC can be used to improve parsing efficiency as explained in the previous section. A truly important application of this predicate is the writing of parsing rules for context dependent circuits.

7.3 Context-Dependent Circuit Generation

Suppose that a goal generates two conjunctive sub-goals and each goal
generates a voltage source in designing circuits. When one of the vol-
tages is derived from the other, an engineer may combine two voltage
sources into one voltage source for simplicity. That is, he has the
ability to use context dependent circuit generation rules, while we
have developed rules corresponding to context-free grammars.

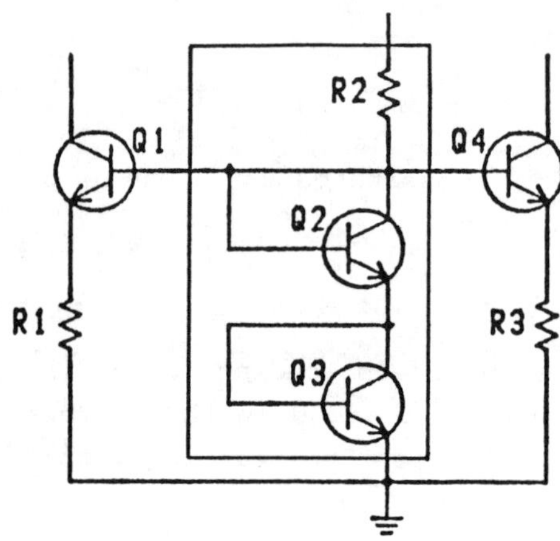

Figure 36: Current sources with
a shared voltage regulator

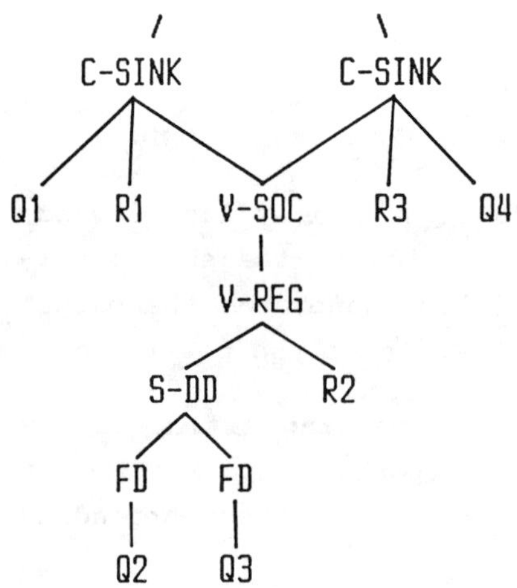

Figure 37: Parse tree for a
shared voltage regulator pair

A macro element "voltage regulator" contributes to form two current sources as a shared voltage source in the circuit shown in Figure 36. The parse tree of the circuit no longer forms a simple tree structure as shown in Fifure 37.

The predicate SUB-CT does not have the ability to represent parsing rules for context dependent circuits. Using the predicate SUB-CTC in the previous section, we can overcome the problem of combining circuits. When a subgoal finds a voltage source, the subgoal generates information pertaining to the voltage source as an electrical condition and transfers the information to another subgoal which needs a voltage source. Then the subgoal succeeds using the transferred conditions instead of finding another voltage source.

7.4 Rules for Combined Circuits

We will redefine the voltage source (40) using the predicate SUB-CTC, so that it generates a term "(CTRLD-VOLTAGE (V-SOC ?V) ?OUT ?COM)" as an electrical condition for the output:

```
(<- (SUB-CTC (V-SOURCE (V-SOC ?V) ?OUT ?COM) ?CT ?RT ?IC
            !<(CTRLD-VOLTAGE (V-SOC ?V) ?OUT ?COM) !&?OC>)
    (OR (SUB-CTC (V-REGULATOR ?V ?IN ?OUT ?COM) ?CT ?RT ?IC ?OC)
        (SUB-CTC (V-DIVIDER ?V ?IN ?OUT ?COM) ?CT ?RT ?IC ?OC)))
```

The condition says the voltage across ?OUT and ?COM is controlled by the voltage source "(V-SOC ?V)". If the goal succeeds, the rest of the circuit ?RT no longer has the voltage source, but the output condition ?OC contains the term "(CTRLD-VOLTAGE (V-SOC ?V) ?OUT ?COM)" as an electrical condition for another goal which needs a voltage source.

Using this condition, we can define a current source which shares its voltage source with another circuit:

```
(<- (SUB-CTC (C-SOURCE (C-SINK ?VS ?Q ?R) ?SINK ?COM)
            ?CT ?RT ?IC ?OC)
    (AND (MEM-REST (NPN-TR ?Q ?B ?E ?SINK) ?CT ?RST1)
         (SUB-CT (RES ?R ?E ?COM) ?RST1 ?RST2)
         (OR (SUB-CTC (V-SOURCE ?VS ?B ?COM) ?RST2 ?RT ?IC ?OC)
             (AND (MEMBER (CTRLD-VOLTAGE ?VS ?B ?COM) ?IC)
                  (= ?RT ?RST2)
                  (= ?OC ?IC)))))
```

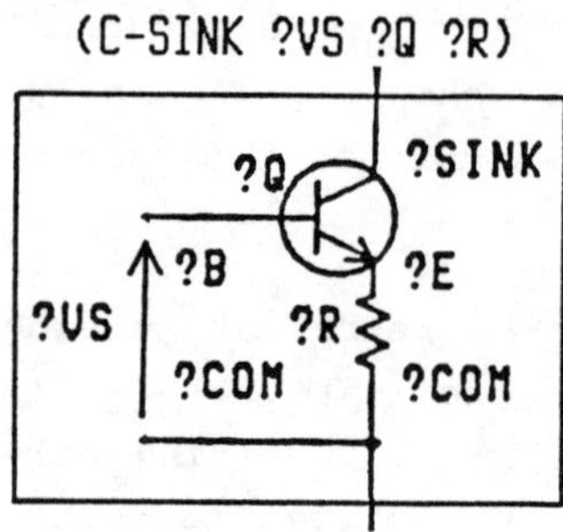

Figure 38: Current source defined by electrical conditions

The first subgoal of the disjunction forms the same topological condition as rule (41). The second subgoal is provided to take into account the context of the rest of the circuit. It succeeds when an electrical condition "(CTRLD-VOLTAGE ?VS ?B ?COM)" is a member of input conditions ?IC.

7.5 Negative Information and State Antagonism

We have tacitly employed a closed world assumption [Reiter 1978] regarding circuit topology. That is, no element or device exists without being explicitly asserted (Chapter 2) or included in the circuit tuple (Chapter 4). However, the closed world assumption is no longer appropriate for a tuple of electrical conditions. The tuple represents only a small portion of the electrical properties of an object circuit. Even if a specific term is not found in the tuple, we can not conclude that the circuit does not have the electrical property denoted by that term. Negative information on electrical conditions must be explicitly mentioned in an open world assumption.

When we found a voltage regulator, we concluded that the input node and the common node must be power nodes in Section 7.2. In the open world assumption, we can also generate a term denoting that the output node of a voltage regulator must not be a power node:

    !< ... (NOT (POWER-NODE output)) ... >

The negative information can be used to prevent other goals from mistaking the output node for a power node. As we do not want contradicting affirmative and negative terms referring to one electrical condition to exist in a tuple, we will define a predicate CONTRADICT:

```
(<- (CONTRADICT (NOT ?C) ?TUP) (MEMBER ?C ?TUP))
(<- (CONTRADICT ?C ?TUP) (MEMBER (NOT ?C) ?TUP))
```

CONTRADICT succeeds when an electrical condition in the first argument contradicts the conditions in a tuple ?TUP. Before assuming an output condition in a goal, we can use the predicate to test whether it contradicts the input conditions or not.

In order to take our study from parsing circuits to understanding them, we have to introduce more terms for electrical events and states. When we introduce terms for electrical states, we meet another kind of contradiction. If a transistor Q1 is in the active-state, Q1 is neither in the cutoff-state nor in the saturate-state. Namely, if the input conditions include "(STATE Q1 ACTIVE)", the existence of conditions attributing to Q1 any state other than the active state constitutes a contradiction. We will use a predicate ANTAGONIZE to remedy this state antagonism:

```
(<- (ANTAGONIZE (STATE ?Q ?X) ?TUP)
    (AND (MEMBER (STATE ?Q ?Y) ?TUP) (NOT (= ?X ?Y))))
```

The predicate is also used to test the conditions before assuming states in a goal.

8   CONCLUSION

We have presented three methods for the structural analysis of circuits using the Duck system. The most straightforward method was developed in Chapter 2 and 3. The other two methods utilize logic programming, and are more sophisticated.

The first method was originally developed in Lisp [Tanaka 1981, 1982]. In that system, a circuit was represented as a list of elements. In defining these elements to be assertions, Duck provided all the mechanisms necessary for circuit pattern matching. In that system, however, control mechanisms remained in Lisp.

The development of the newer methods was a consequence of a new interpretation of circuits: namely, viewing circuits as language. The problem of understanding circuits is transformed to the problem of understanding a language.

In language processing, a bottom-up parser works on the input strings. It replaces the terminal symbols by non-terminal symbols until the string is reduced to a starting symbol "S". The second method, developed in Chapter 4 and 5, corresponds to this bottom-up parsing. The bottom-up mechanism directly implements the process which engineers often employ for computing impedance networks.

A top-down parser proceeds from the starting symbol "S", finds rules that apply to it and expands it. The process is repeated until the parser generates the input string from left to right. The third method, developed in Chapter 6, corresponds to this kind of top-down parsing. Unlike a string, the order of elements in a circuit tuple is not important. On the other hand, priorities of rules have a strong impact on the efficiency with which circuits are parsed. Each rule defines what sub-circuit or element should be looked for next.

Usually every electronic circuit is designed as a goal oriented compositions of functional blocks. Therefore if a circuit goal is given, the goal contains the information needed to identify the circuit according the rules. The top-down parser effectively analyzes an electronic circuit when the circuit goal is given.

The structural analysis of electronic circuit is a step toward automatic circuit understanding similar to syntactic analysis of language. But, circuit understanding implies more than language understanding; unlike language, a circuit not only represents designer's intentions, but also represents the physical circuit itself.

For electronic engineers, understanding intentions is usually only part of understanding circuit behavior. In fact, the engineer may design a circuit with the goal "amplify" in mind, and discover additional behavior such as "oscillation" which he did not purposely include. Usually, such inadvertent behaviors arise because potential flaws such as stray capacitances are overlooked, or because all of the implications of a given topology are not clearly understood. Catching potential flaws or oversights such as these was the motivation for this study.

The electrical conditions developed in Chapter 7 define the relationship between a circuit topology and its electrical characteristics. We can introduces more terms relating electrical behavior to the definitions of functional circuits. We may introduce terms of the form "(<- q p)" or "(-> p q)" in which "p" and "q" specify electrical behavior. When a circuit goal succeeds, the argument ?OUT-COND of the predicate SUB-CTC contains rules of electrical behavior for the circuit. The set of the acquired rules will enable deductions concerning circuit behavior. Then, our study will enter a new stage of understanding circuit behaviors.

ACKNOWLEDGEMENTS

This work was started when I was studying at the Yale AI-project in 1982, and developed after I returned to Japan. I would like to thank: Prof. Roger Schank for the opportunity to study, Prof. Drew McDermott for Duck, David Littleboy for his helpful advice and criticism, and AI circle AIUEO for many fruitful discussion.

APPENDIX

If you are familiar with Prolog, you can translate backward chaining rules from Duck into Prolog. I will show several examples in C-Prolog syntax. The following clauses, though simplified, can parse the circuit CD71 in Prolog.

predicate MEM-REST:

```
memrest(X,[X|Y],Y).
memrest(X,[A|Z],[A|U]) :- memrest(X,Z,U).
```

functions:

```
subCT(res(X,A,B),CT,REST) :- memrest(resistor(X,A,B),CT,REST);
                             memrest(resistor(X,B,A),CT,REST).

subCT(vDivider(vdiv(X,Y),IN,OUT,COM),CT,REST) :-
    subCT(res(X,IN,OUT),CT,RST1),
    subCT(res(Y,OUT,COM),RST1,REST).

subCT(dTransistor(fd(Q),A,C),CT,REST) :-
    memrest(npntr(Q,A,C,A),CT,REST).
subCT(dTransistor(rd(Q),A,C),CT,REST) :-
    memrest(npntr(Q,C,A,C),CT,REST).
```

```
subCT(sDiode(Q,A,C),CT,REST) :- subCT(dTransistor(Q,A,C),CT,REST).
subCT(sDiode(sdd(Q,D),A,C),CT,REST) :-
    subCT(dTransistor(Q,A,B),CT,RST1),
    subCT(sDiode(D,B,C),RST1,REST).

subCT(vRegulator(vreg(D,R),IN,OUT,COM),CT,REST) :-
    subCT(sDiode(D,OUT,COM),CT,RST1),
    subCT(res(R,IN,OUT),RST1,REST).

subCT(vSource(vsoc(V),OUT,COM),CT,REST) :-
    subCT(vRegulator(V,IN,OUT,COM),CT,REST);
    subCT(vDivider(V,IN,OUT,COM),CT,REST).

subCT(cSource(csink(VS,Q,R),SINK,COM),CT,REST) :-
    subCT(vSource(VS,B,COM),CT,RST1),
    memrest(npntr(Q,B,E,SINK),RST1,RST2),
    subCT(res(R,E,COM),RST2,REST).
    subCT(eCouple(ecup(Q1,Q2),B1,B2,E,C1,C2),CT,REST) :-
        memrest(npntr(Q1,B1,E,C1),CT,RST1),
        memrest(npntr(Q2,B2,E,C2),RST1,REST).

    subCT(sDiffAmp(sdamp(EC,R,CS),B1,B2,G,C1,C2),CT,REST) :-
        subCT(eCouple(EC,B1,B2,E,C1,C2),CT,RST1),
        subCT(res(R,C1,C2),RST1,RST2),
        subCT(cSource(CS,E,G),RST2,REST).

    subCT(iComparator(icomp(AMP,VS),B1,C1,P,G),CT,REST) :-
        subCT(sDiffAmp(AMP,B1,B2,G,C1,P),CT,RST1),
        subCT(vSource(VS,B2,G),RST1,REST).

goal:

    ?- subCT(iComparator(NAME,B1,C1,P,G),
            [resistor(r1,$12,$1),resistor(r2,$2,$10),
             resistor(r3,$2,$3),resistor(r4,$3,$1),
             resistor(r5,$2,$4),npntr(q1,$9,$11,$10),
             npntr(q2,$3,$11,$2),npntr(q3,$4,$12,$11),
             npntr(q4,$4,$5,$4),npntr(q5,$5,$1,$5)], REST).
```

REFERENCES

Barrow, H.G., "VERIFY: A Program for Proving Correctness of Digital Hardware Design, Artificial Intelligence, Vol.24, pp.437-491, 1984.

Charniak, E., Riesbeck, C., McDermott, D., "Artificial Intelligence Programming", Lawrence Erlbaum, NJ, 1980.

Charniak, E., McDermott, D., "Introduction to Artificial Intelligence", Addison-Wesley, 1984.

Davis, R., "Diagnostic Reasoning Based on Structure and Behavior", Artificial Intelligence, Vol.24, pp.347-409, 1984.

DeKleer, J., "Causal and Teleological Reasoning in Circuit Recognition", MIT AI-TR-529, 1979.

DeKleer, J., "How Circuits Work", Artificial Intelligence, Vol.24, pp.205-280, 1984.

Doyle, J., "A Truth Maintenance System", Artificial Intelligence, Vol.12, pp. 231-272, 1979.

Fu, K.S., "Syntactic Methods in Pattern Recognition", Academic Press, NY, 1974.

Genesereth M.R., "The Use of Descriptions in Automated Diagnosis", Artificial Intelligence, Vol.24, pp.411-436, 1984.

Kowalski R., "Logic for Problem Solving", North-Holland, NY, 1979.

McDermott, D., "Circuit Design as Problem Solving", in Latombe (ed.), Artificial Intelligence and Pattern Recognition in Computer Aided Design, IFIP, North-Holland, Amsterdam, 1978.

McDermott, D., Doyle, J., "Non-Monotonic Logic I" Artificial Intelligence, Vol.13, 1980.

McDermott, D., "Duck: A Lisp-based Deductive System", Yale Univ., Dept. of Computer Science, 1983.

Nagasawa, I., "A Design System with Logic Programming", Japan Annual Reviews in Electronics, Computers & Telecomunications,OHM,Tokyo,1985.

Nilsson, N.J., "Principles of Artificial Intelligence", Tioga Pub., Palo Alto, CA, 1980.

Pereira, F., Warren, D., "Definite Clause Grammars for Language Analysis", Artificial Intelligence, Vol.13, pp. 231-278, 1980.

Reiter, R., "On Closed World Data Bases" in Gallaire, Minker (eds.), Logic and Data Bases, Plenam Press, 1978.

Schank, R., Riesbeck, C., "Inside Computer Understanding", Lawrence Erlbaum, NJ, 1981.

Stallman, R.M., Sussman, G.J., "Forward Reasoning and Dependency-Directed Back-tracking in a System for Computer Aided Circuit Analysis" Artificial Intelligence, Vol.9, pp.135-196, 1977.

Sussman, G.J., Winograd, T., Charniak, E., "Micro-Planner Reference Manual", MIT AI-memo No. 203A, 1971.

Sussman, G.J., Steele, G.Jr., "Constraints: A Language for Expressing Almost-Hierarchical Descriptions", Artificial Intelligence, Vol.14, pp.1-39, 1980.

Tanaka, T., "Pattern Directed Circuit Recognition I, II", 23rd, 24th Convention of Information Processing Society, 1981,1982 (in Japanese).

Tanaka, T., "Representation and Analysis of Electrical Circuits in a Deductive System", Proc. of IJCAI-83, Karlsruhe, W.G., 1983.

Tanaka, T., "Parsing Circuit Topology in a Deductive System", Proc. of IJCAI-85, Los Angeles, CA, 1985.

Tanaka, T., "Representation and Analysis of Circuit Structres by Logic Programming", Trans. of Institute of Electronics and Communication Engineers of Japan, Vol.J68-A, No.12, pp.1350-1356, 1985 (in Japanese)

Tanaka, T., "Structural Analysis of Electronic Circuits using Definite Clause Grammars", Trans. of Institute of Electronics and Communication Engineers of Japan, Vol.J69-D, No.3, pp.443-450, 1986 (in Japanese).

Williams, B.C., "Qualitative Analysis of MOS Circuits", Artificial Intelligence, Vol.24, pp.281-346, 1984.

"101 Analog IC Designs - Functional Blocks for Monochip Custom Integrated Circuits", Interdesign, Inc., Sunnyvale, CA, 1976.

Building Expert Systems Based on Simulation Models: An Essay in Methodology

José Cuena

Facultad de Informática, Universidad Politécnica
Madrid, Spain

ABSTRACT

This paper presents a methodological essay on building expert systems based on simulation models. This type of expert system can be very useful because there is an important existing body of work on modelling applied to engineering problems, and the expert system structure may allow a synthesis of the knowledge of different models and expert criteria to be used on line and to be applied to daily operation in engineering problems.

The first part of the paper deals with a methodology of knowledge base construction:

. The first step of knowledge structuring based on a conceptual grid and an operation reasoning scheme

. The second step of automatic operation rule generation for two types of rule formulation (propositional and functional formulation)

. The final step of analysis by the experts of the rules proposed through the automatic process and choice of the most significant ones. The final knowledge base is made up of the definition rules from the conceptual grid and basic and generalized operation rules from the automatic learning process, complemented by rules introduced by the experts.

The second part of the paper deals with the application of these methods to the being developed specification of two expert systems now:

Example 1: an expert system providing advice during river floods

Example 2: an expert system for control and advice in urban freeway traffic

1 INTRODUCTION

Through extensive work in the sixties Computer Science has made possible the implementation of sophisticated models of complex processes applied to design and management. The use of these models allows the establishment of the degree to which every decision factor affects the final behavior, and by stepwise refinement allows the best values for these factors to be found, to meet the goals.

The problem is that the efficiency of the couple user-system greatly depends on the capacity of the user to understand the computer's behavior and to decide on the right way to modify the decisions at every step. If the user is not expert enough, even with very sophisticated models the process of finding the right decisions may be very costly.

One of the major computer science application areas, besides management, is engineering where the problems to be solved are:

- The design (form and dimension) of facilities (building structures, etc)
- The operation of these facilities at two levels:
  . previous planning of the operation
  . real time problem solving during incidents in the operation, in order to meet the given goals

Given the complexity of the physical behavior of the elements to be designed or operated, it is not an easy task to determine the best design or operation decisions based only on projective formulation. The conventional way of defining these decisions is:

- Definition of a first set of decisions (preliminary dimensions in design problems)
- Application of one or more mathematical models of the behavior of the facility to be designed or to be operated
- Evaluation of the resulting behavior versus the objectives. Analysis of the differences and decision to accept or reject; in the latter case, definition of a new set of decisions and return to second step

When the problem is to take "almost" real time decisions in the daily operation of the facilities (for instance: the modification of previously optimized operation plans caused by incidents) it is not possible to repeat the iterative process of decision-simulation-evaluation for the new decisions:

- Because model manipulation needs specialized people not directly available to the decision maker at the time the problem occurs
- Because the iterative process, even with specialized operating people, is time consuming and the decision makers cannot wait

The result is that, for these cases, the decisions are taken by the persons responsible, based on personal criteria, and the important investments made in automatic data collection and modelling are not compensated by the value they add in daily operation.

Artificial Intelligence techniques can be very useful in compensating for such deficiencies by means of:

- Expert systems to guide the design process, by proposing the best guesses about the decision factor changes to meet the objectives
- Expert systems to help the decision makers in real time by means of recommendations for operation and diagnostics of problematic situations

These expert systems are not an alternative to using models that can be utilized in finding the best operations in the planning phase, off line, with greater accuracy for the a posteriori evaluation and improvement of the decisions proposed by the expert systems. The models can, furthermore, be used to create an artificial experience to be abstracted in rule form for the expert system.

In summary, the knowledge base of this kind of system embodies knowledge about the definition of concepts, about model operation and, more importantly, about the previous use of models in finding the right decisions to meet different goals. It can be argued that in synthesizing the models and the decision-goals relationship, there are losses of information that can affect the quality of the answers from the expert system. This solution is interesting because it makes all the synthesized on line knowledge for daily operation.

One of the critical aspects of the application of Artificial Intelligence is the existing gap between the tools for knowledge representation and application and the real knowledge of existing theories and expertise: there is no sequence of steps allowing progression from primary knowledge formulation to the operative formulation of a system. When there is previous modelling work this is easier.

This paper deals with a general methodology for building this type of synthesized expert system and its application to the design of two systems (one for real time flood prediction and advice and another for real time advice and control of urban access freeways). These systems are now in the course of execution, their final versions being the final step of a long process of information and conventional modelling.

2 GENERAL OVERVIEW OF THE METHOD

The main tasks for building a rule based system are:

- To establish a set of basic concepts (objects or contexts) and attributes for reasoning purposes
- To identify the deductive relationships between attributes more significant for building the different reasoning processes
- To evaluate the degree to which every conceptually significant relationship is supported

The main conceptual lines may be arranged in a network built between frames (or contexts) of discernment integrating attributes and their values. The following may be distinguished:

- The basic context defined by couples of values of the controlled variables, resulting from information systems or from model simulation runs
- The problem context defined by the set of possible problems of a predefined type (for instance the frame of transport problems, the frame of urban problems, agricultural problems, etc.)
- The operation context defined by:
  . The set of possible operation recommendations
  . The set of operations under way
- Other intermediate concept contexts

The knowledge is defined by the set of links between attribute-value couples:

- In the same context
- In different contexts (as has been defined, the attribute in a context may depend on attributes of another context)

The links between attributes may be of three types:

- Representing definition relationships (for instance establishing the criteria to decide whether there is an accident on a freeway, or a town is isolated, or a road closed by the waters)
- Representing relationships derived from the operation of the system
- Representing strategical definitions: the preconditions to deciding social operation (town evacuation, gate manipulation, signal change)

The conceptual grid of the system incorporates the first and third type of relationship, which have to be based on the criteria of the experts and decision makers. For establishing the conditions of the second type, a method of rule inference based on the experience resulting from model runs has to be applied. This is a special feature of complex systems where the criteria of experts is not an accurate enough source of knowledge.

For the learning of these rules an Operation Reasoning Scheme has to be previously defined from the model simulation runs as a framework for the learning process.

The learning process produces the deductive relationships between attribute values of the different frames or contexts.

Finally the knowledge of the system is built by the definition rules from the conceptual grid and by the operation rules from the model synthesis learning process.

The general procedure with possible feedback is:
- Definition by discussion between experts and knowledge engineers of a conceptual grid relating the concept structures in different contexts or frames of discernment
- Definition based on the understanding of physical behavior of an operation reasoning scheme
- Production, by means of a set of model runs, of a sample of cases described by concepts belonging to the conceptual grid. This artificial sample has to be produced oriented to the process of knowledge acquisition
- Application to the subsets of the artificial experience of an automatic rule induction system useful for quantifying the basic rules of the operation reasoning scheme
- Supervision by the experts of the proposed rules, and choice of the significant ones
- Addition of new rules, modelling the experts' understanding in two aspects:
  . including new knowledge to complement the knowledge synthesized from the model runs
  . including knowledge about the way of interpreting the model results (there are models that overestimate or underestimate some of the behavior features. The expert should include rules to take account of these modification criteria)

It is possible that the quality of the proposed rules may not be good enough. For these cases a new conceptual grid and operation reasoning scheme, taking account of new and previously discarded concepts and attributes, should be defined.

The overall process is represented by the flow chart of figure 1.

In the next paragraphs the significant features of this general method are described.

GENERAL METHODOLOGY APPLICATION FLOWCHART

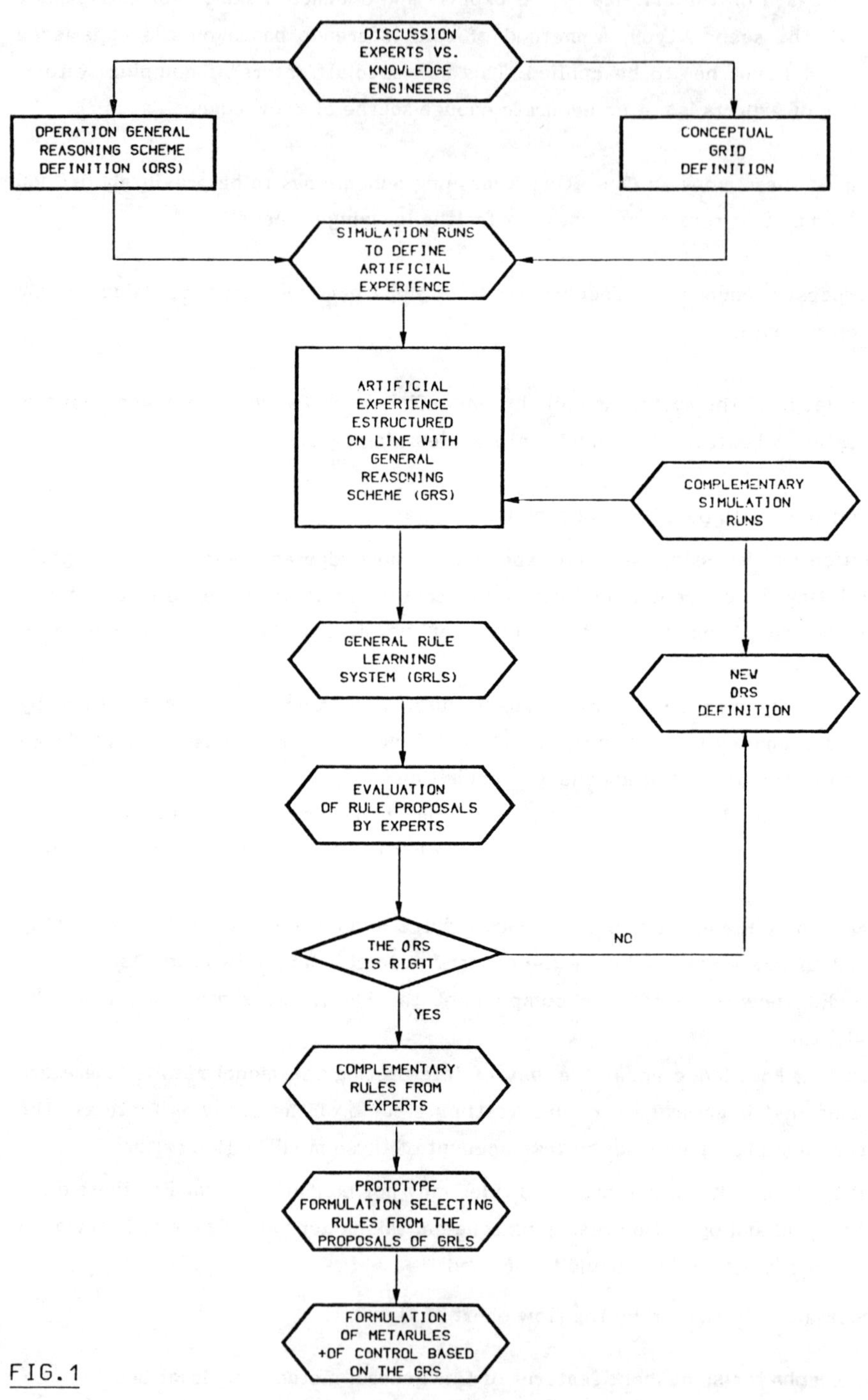

FIG.1

3 THE CONCEPTUAL GRID

As has been stated, the conceptual grid includes the concept definition of the different frames or contexts. Usually it is not possible to give precise definitions of the concepts; a traditional approach for imprecise definition is that of the certainty factors. These factors are in many cases difficult for the experts to establish. Given that the proposed method evaluates the certainty factors from model runs, for definition at the conceptual grid level the proposed method substitutes these factors by logic intervals based on:

- An "if" definition to give the sufficient condition for the concepts established
- An "only if" definition to give the necessary conditions for the concepts

For instance the following can be defined:

Q if A, B, C
Q only if A, B

That means anything like a logic interval for Q

$$A \wedge B \wedge C \to Q \to A \quad B$$

That corresponds to the Venn diagram:

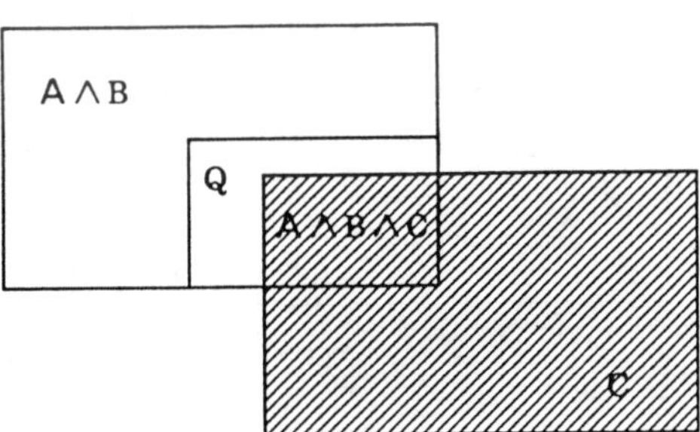

It may be possible that for some concepts only one of the two formulations is available and, also, the case of symmetrical formulation of both definitions: $Q \leftrightarrow A \vee B$ is possible.

The structure of the conceptual grid will be based on the attribute-value nodes, organized by frames of the kind described in figure 2, where intermediate nodes L, P allow the connective representations.

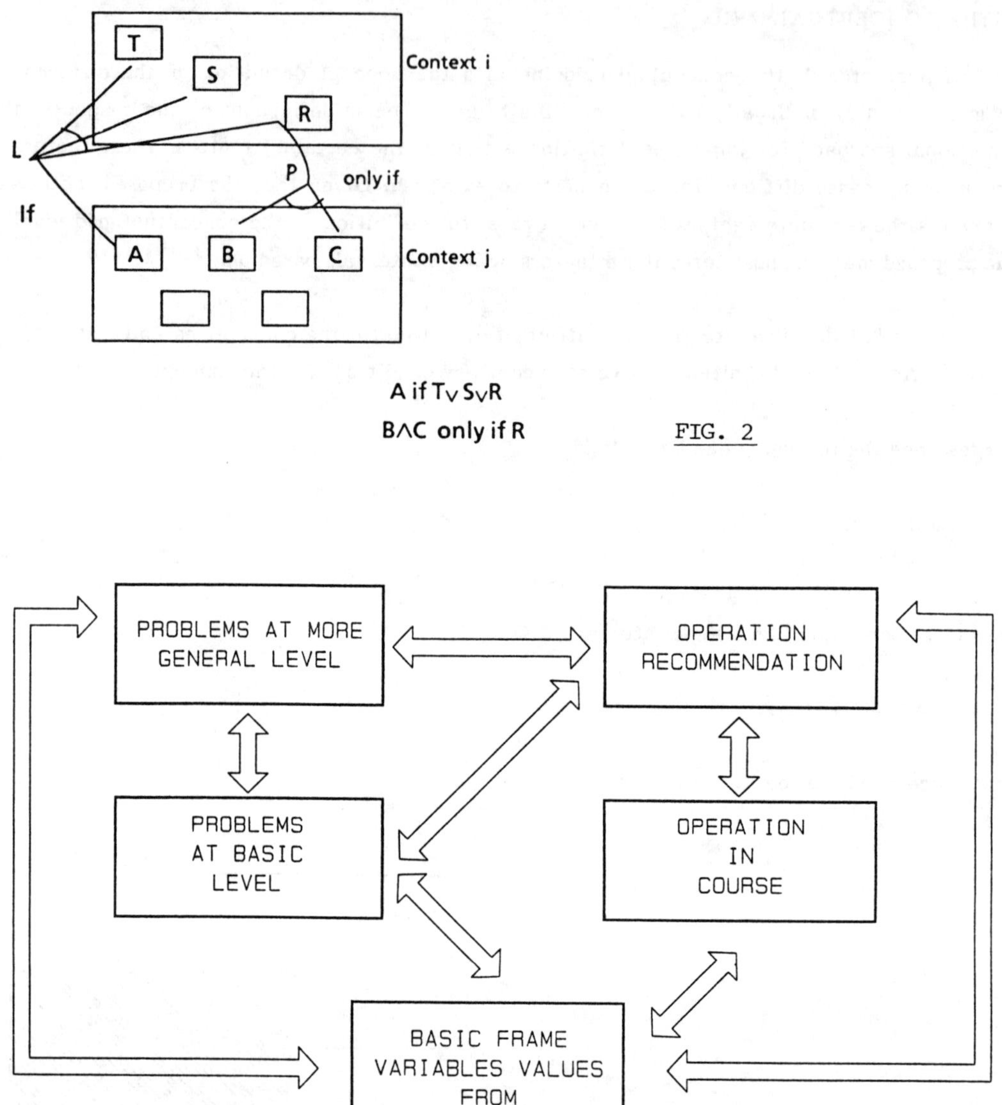

FIG. 3 CONCEPTUAL GRID GENERAL STRUCTURE

Figure 3 shows an example of a general frame structure for the conceptual grid: the more general frames include concepts for reasoning at decision level, in contrast with the basic frame where the more technical aspects are included. As will be shown, the behavior relationships may induce rule formulation between concepts at general frame level.

4 OPERATION REASONING SCHEME

The definition of the structure of reasoning about the behavior of the systems is based on:

- The theory used in the different models which are to be synthesized by the system
- The complementary knowledge of the experts about:
  . the limitations of the theories
  . the limitations of the computing method

As a result of these basic knowledge sources, the operation reasoning scheme is defined by:

- A set of classes of concepts; the elements of every class are concepts which play roles similar to causes or effects
- A set of rule formats, in each of which the concept elements of one class are potential effects produced by cause elements of the other classes of the group. A rule format will be defined in the general form:
$$C_1, C_2, \dots\dots\dots C_K \Rightarrow E_S$$
where the C_i are the potential cause classes and E is the class of potential effects
- A partial order between groups describing every line of reasoning (forward and backward)

The concepts to be used for this reasoning scheme must be elements of the basic frame so that the reasoning scheme is an abstract and logical description of the different simulation models.

The structure of the reasoning scheme plays the role of a pattern director of the learning process: the rules to quantify are the rules possible in every rule format. Once the rules are formulated by means of the learning procedure described in the next paragraph, it may be possible that the low significance of some rules indicates that the reasoning scheme was wrong. In this case, analysis of the results, and further thinking, may recommend a new scheme configuration and a new application of the learning procedure.

The definitive operation reasoning scheme is a basis for the control strategy definition in the inference engine of the system. The possible metarules may be defined based on the ordering of rule formats resulting from the scheme definition.

For instance, reasoning forward in the explanation of the flood plain water levels the ordering is:

1) rules "rain - at watersheds ⟶ flows from watersheds"
2) rules "flows from watersheds ⟶ flows at surface drainage network"
3) etc.

while for backward reasoning:

1) to explain flood plain levels, rules with river levels as antecedents may be used
2) to explain river levels, rules with flows and other river levels as antecedents may be used
3) etc.

In summary, the conceptual grid and the operation reasoning scheme represent a first level of knowledge structuring to the learning process application. Also, they can be used for control strategy definition.

5 ARTIFICIAL EXPERIENCE

By means of simulation models it is possible to obtain a sample of values of the basic frame variables that may be:

- simultaneous (values for the same instant t)
- corresponding to different time intervals

For the sake of a more precise formulation it is interesting to reason from absolute values and value increases, the value increases to be obtained as consequents. For instance, rule formulation for time intervals is:

IF the effect variable values at t are:
$$Ve_1, Ve_2 \ldots\ldots Ve_n$$
and the cause variable values at t are:
$$VC_1, VC_2 \ldots\ldots VC_r$$
and the cause variable increment values between t and $t + \Delta t$ are:
$$\Delta C_1, \Delta C_2 \ldots\ldots \Delta C_r$$

THEN the increment values of effect variables between t and $t + \Delta t$ are:
$$\Delta e_1, \Delta e_2 \ldots\ldots \Delta e_r$$
An analogous format may be defined for simultaneous rules

IF the cause variable values are:
$$VC_1, VC_2, VC_3 \ldots\ldots VC_r$$

THEN the effect variable values are defined by incrementing the present effect variables:
$$Ve_5 = Ve_5 + \Delta e_5$$

The artificial experience is defined by the set of instances of these rule structures for the sets of cause and effect variables in every rule format and for different Δt values.

In summary, the artificial experience will contain:

For every rule format of the operation reasoning scheme, a set of:

- Simultaneous observations

    $VC_1.....VC_r \ Va_1 \ Va_2.....Va_p \ Ve_1 \ Ve_2 \ .....V_h$

    VC_i : cause variables

    Ve_1 : effect variables

    Va_i : variables that can be used as cause and effect
- Interval observations for every t value considered

    $VC_1 \ VC_2 \ .... \ VC_r$

    $\Delta C_i \quad C_2 \ .... \ \Delta C_r$

    $Ve_1 \ Ve_2 \ .... \ Ve_n$

    $\Delta V_1 \quad V_2 \ .....\Delta V_n$

VC_i, Va_i, Ve_i are variables of the rule format considered

Obviously, the sample selected as artificial experience must be representative of the modelled behavior (the histograms and statistical parameters of the sample must fit those produced by the models)

The variables may have real and discrete values (states of valves, etc). For propositional rule formulation a set of intervals for the real value variables may be defined; every interval will be an attribute-value couple as in EMYCIN. [Van Melle, 80]

6 RULE INDUCTION

There are two classic approaches to rule generation from examples [Cohen, Feigenbaum, 82]:

- Data driven methods, where the artificial experience is processed instance by instance and the learning process modifies the rule structure to be adapted at every instance. The version space method [Mitchell, 79] and the AM System [Lenat,76] are significant examples of this approach
- Model driven methods, where the artificial experience is used to test the plausibility of different rule structure hypotheses. The works of [Buchanan, Mitchell, 78] , [Quinlan, 79], [Dietterich, Michalski, 81] are examples of this approach

When the possible relationships represent complex processes, as happens in engineering problems, it is difficult to apply data driven methods. The operation reasoning scheme is a source of models to be tested by the model driven method; this is the reason why the proposed method is model driven, using the ideas of Michalski, Dietterich and Quinlan.

The process of rule induction has two main steps:

- Choice of the instances of a rule format of the ORS from the artificial experience at two levels
  - simultaneous
  - with different Δt time lags
- Formulation of the rule and evaluation of the rule parameter (measure of the strength of the rule or degree of deductivity)

There are two types of rules to be induced:

- propositional rules, based on the paradigm concept-attribute-value
- functional rules of the type

$$P(V_1, V_2 . V_r), O_m . A_1 . V_i, O_s . A_2 . V_k, ... O_f . A_h . V_r \Rightarrow O_n . F(V_i, V_k ... V_r) \qquad (2)$$

  where:

  $P(V_i, V_k, ... V_r)$ is a precondition to be verified by the values of the considered attributes $A_1, A_2, ... A_h$ and where

  $f(V_i, V_k, ... V_r)$ is a function for the computation of the resulting value of the attribute A_s of the object O_n

The formulation (2) constitutes an element of flexibilization and simplification of the paradigm concept-attribute-value since, although when the values are of a continuous type, an individualization of the interval of variation can be considered, when significant precision is required, an excessive number of rules would be necessary, otherwise some intervals of greater length would be accepted in the individualization with consequent loss of precision. Formulation (2) contributes a criterion that may be of interest, since it establishes , for each attribute, a set of rules whose number is equal to the number of different functions to be utilized in calculating the corresponding value of the attribute.

This type of formula demands an inference engine distinct from the case of concept-attribute-value. These themes are dealt with in the following paragraphs.

6.1 FORMULATION OF PROPOSITIONAL RULES

Given a rule format defined by:

$C_1, C_2, ...C_m$ Cause attributes concept

$E_1, E_2, ... E_r$ Effect attributes concept

$D_1, D_2, ... D_s$ Ambiguous type attributes concept (they can be both cause and effect)

the problem of rule formulation can be considered on two levels:

- Identification of rules governing the definition of the values of each attribute considered with a sufficient degree of implication g_i (above a significance threshold), for example:

$$C_i.X, \ C_j.Y, ...C_l.Z \underset{g_1}{\Rightarrow} E_m.\ W$$

$$C_i.X, C_j.Y, ...D_f.Z \underset{g_2}{\Rightarrow} E_p.W$$

$$C_i.X, C_j.Y, ...C_1.Z \underset{g_k}{\Rightarrow} D_k.W$$

$$D_m.X, D_r.Y, ... \underset{g_r}{\Rightarrow} E_f.W$$

where X,Y,Z,W, are value variables, which can be determined in specific values within the discrete sets of possible values, giving rise to the different rules of definition of each one of them

- Identification of rules of definition of mixed concepts, for example, of the type:
$$C_iX, \ C_j.Y, ...D_s.\ t \underset{g}{\Rightarrow} L(E_p.Z, ...D_k.W....)$$

where L is a logical formula that relates different effect attributes by means of connectives of conjunction and disjunction, and g is the level of implication

This latter type of formulation has the disadvantage of not being, in general, usable by simple inference processes due to linking not being possible, for which however the structure of the consequent of the rule, based on one attribute only, is ideal. However, it is of interest that the learning system be capable of inferring this type of rule. This is because it is possible that, if important implication levels were reached, these rules could, on being presented to the experts, induce either the introduction of a new concept whose values will be defined by the consequent logical function obtained, or the formulation of rules that approximate the structure obtained with a sole attribute consequent.

Therefore, it is also interesting for the process of generation of this type of rule, relating attribute values with logical functions of other attribute values, to be mechanized to a certain degree.

6.1.1 RULES FOR DEFINITION OF ATTRIBUTE VALUES

The ID3 system focus [Quinlan 79] consists in the selection, and subsequent classification within the different branches of the training sample corresponding to the format under study; the classification is made according to the different values, first of the cause attributes and then of the ambiguous attributes, until branches are found in which subsamples may be obtained, sufficiently classified according to any effects or ambiguous aspects.

The process will become defined if criteria for the ordering of attributes and the criterion for the termination of the branches in the generation of the classification tree are established.

As criterion for selecting which attribute is to extend a determined vertex of the classification tree, a generalized formulation of the entropy, in line with method ID3, can be used, taking into account that in ID3 the elements were classifiable into classes with a sole attribute, while in the case under analysis, it is possible to classify according to the specifics D_i and E_j.

Given a sample for each one of the classification criteria, the improvement in information for each one of them, contributed by each attribute, can be evaluated in such a way that a matrix may be obtained:

ΔI_{ij} = improvement in generated information, classifying according to j, with respect to effect i

i = 1,....n = number of attributes being examined (that is, the unused D and the E)

j = 1,....n = number of cause attributes under study (that is, the unused C and the D)

The following are defined:

$$I_M = \text{average of } \Delta I_{ij}$$
$$Mx = \text{max. } (\Delta I_{ij})$$

where i_x, j_x are the indices corresponding to an element with $\Delta I_{ij} = Mx$.

The criterion for the construction of the possible rule tree for a prefixed depth limit will be the following:

- The nodes are extended in the order from greater to lesser ΔI_M.
- The attribute which produces Mx, that is jx, is elected to be classified, but a list of candidates, formed by the K attributes which can be considered for classification, whose ΔI_{mk} is different from the Mx by less than a prefixed percentage, is also selected.
- A node is successfully terminal if the level of significance in the node-associated sample of the value of an attribute is greater than a threshold. (The level of significance is evaluated by the frequency.)
- However, a successful terminal node can be a backtracking one if, in preceding nodes, there exist elements awaiting development on the list of candidates.
- A node can be a backtracking one due to lack of success if a prefixed level of the classification tree is passed without finding a sufficient frequency of attribute values.
- For the purposes of order in the expansion development process, when backtracking to a vertex is made, the average value is taken of the ΔI_{ij} of the nodes waiting in the vertex when backtracking is carried out.

If it has not been possible to explain, with the level depth limitation, all the artificial experience of the rule format under study, it will be necessary to expand the limit until more complex rules with sufficient explanatory capacity are obtained.

The calculation of ΔI_{ij} is made in the form

$$\Delta I_{ij} = H_{ij} - H_i$$

where:

$$H_i = \sum_m p_m \log p_m$$

p_m = probability of the value m in the attribute i

$$H_{ij} = \sum_k (\text{probability of the value of attribute } A_j = k) \times H_{ijk}$$

where H_{ijk} is the entropy of the attribute effect i in the subsample in which the attribute j takes its value number k.

The probabilities are estimated by the frequencies in the experience subsamples, exactly as was done in ID3 [Quinlan 79].

6.1.2 CREATION OF NEW ATTRIBUTES

To get the formulation of the suggested attributes, it is possible to use the next method of rule formulation and probability estimation using artificial experience:

- The artificial experience, for a given order of the concepts, can be described by a tree, where the links at a given level from a node are the possible values of the concept at this level in the given order of concepts

- Every path of the tree represents a subset of the total experience

- To every node i of the tree may be assigned a weight w_i equal to the number of observations, with values equal to these included in the path from the root node. Then

$$w_i = \sum_{d(i)} w_j$$

$d(i)$: set of node concept descendants from i

- To every link i-k may be assigned
  . an antecedent statement:
  $$SA = CV_{01} \wedge CV_{12} \wedge \ldots \wedge CV_{mi} \qquad (1)$$
  defined by the conjunction of concept value associate to every link in the path from the root node to i

  . a consequent statement defined by
  $$SC_k = SC_j \vee SC_r \vee SC_m \vee \ldots SC_p \qquad (2)$$

  i e. the consequent statements of the nodes next to k : j, r, m, ... p, with weights $W_j > 0$, $W_r > 0$, $W_m > 0$, ...$W_p > 0$

If the sample is complete at every node there will be weight 0 for every concept value and the consequent statements will be estimated as being reduced to tautologies.

If the sample is not complete there may be complete subtrees where the tautology reduction may be done. Then by application of recursive definition (2) taking account of the tautology reduction, it is possible to get the consequent statement for the link i-k (if some SC_1 is a tautology, obviously (2) is a tautology).

If the link i-k statement is CV_{ik} the link ik may induce the rule :

$$SA \rightarrow CV_{ik} \wedge SC_k$$

Based on the experience that verifies SA_i CV_{ik} SC_k and the experience that verifies SA_i the degree of implication g may be estimated by

$$g = \frac{n(SA_i \wedge CV_{ik} \wedge SC_k)}{n(SA_i)} \qquad (3)$$

n (F) means the number of observations that satisfy F

In (3)

$$n (SA_i \wedge CV_{ik} \wedge SC_k) = W_k$$
$$n (SA_i) = W_i$$
$$\text{then } g_{ik} = \frac{W_k}{W_i}$$

- For proposing rules for every rule format:

    . the order of the possible causes considered in the format has to be fixed
    . the order of the effects can be changed
    . for every order of effects the g_{ik} of the links corresponding to concepts that can be cause and effect is evaluated
    . the rules with g_{ik} fixed threshold are discarded
    . the rules with a consequent degree of complexity (number of connectives) bigger than a threshold are discarded
    . the selected rules are ordered by g_{ik} and degree of complexity of the conclusion

The rule for the QT link will be proposed as:
    . Antecedent formula SA_T: $C_{11} \wedge C_{21}$
    (C_{ij} : value j of the i concept)

    . Consequent formula SC_Q
    $(C_{41} \wedge F_M) \vee (C_{42} \wedge F_N) \vee (C_{43} \wedge F_P)$
    F_M : Tautology
    F_N : $(C_{63} \wedge C_{51}) \vee C_{52}$
    F_P : Tautology

Example of rule formulation

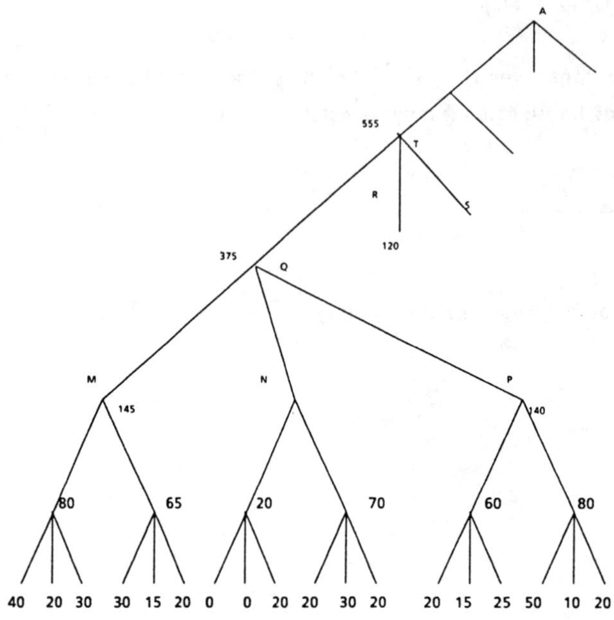

$$SC_Q : C_{41} \vee \left[C_{42} \wedge (C_{52} \vee (C_{51} \wedge C_{63})) \right] \vee C_{43}$$

Rule formulation:

$$C_{11} \wedge C_{21} \Rightarrow C_{31} \wedge \left[C_{41} \vee (C_{42} \wedge (C_{52} \vee (C_{51} \wedge C_{63}))) \vee C_{43} \right]$$

degree

$$g = \frac{375}{555} = 0,68$$

The order of the concepts in the rule definition tree depends on the rule format to be computed. For instance, for prediction rules the order may be:

$$\text{present state, decisions} \Longrightarrow \text{predicted state}$$

For decision rules, the same sample values may be ordered:

$$\text{present state, desired future state} \Longrightarrow \text{decisions}$$

Also the samples may be different based on the rule format. Obviously the sample for this second rule format may be chosen to be a subset of the possible changes in state: the set of state transition cases needed from the control point of view of the responsible persons (i.e. there is no interest in knowing the decisions to increase the flood level or the traffic congestion). The suitable transitions in state are the ones that define problems (there are problems when the present state is different from the desired state; every element of difference between present and desired state is a problem).

The rules proposed by this method at the basic frame level may be generalized by introducing concepts from other frames that simplify the formulation, and they may be more powerful because they use more general concepts. For generalization purposes, the "if" and "only if" relationships of the conceptual grid may be used:

- by rewriting, using equivalence definitions:

    If a rule formulation includes at the antecedent or consequent a subformula A and the following is defined:

    $$B \text{ "if" and "only if" } A$$

    the replacement of every A occurrence by a B occurrence is possible

- by antecedent chaining:

    If it is defined that A "if" B and A is a premise of the rule, by syllogism A can be substituted by B in the rule formulation

- by consequent chaining:

    If it is defined that A "only if" B and A is a part of the conclusion of the rule, such that the conclusion may be written as $A \wedge F$ (F:formula), the conclusion may be written $B \wedge F$

The rules obtained after this generalization process can be of the concept-attribute-value type unique in the consequent or with a more complex formula in the consequent.

In the first case, an alternative would be obtained to the rules generated by the methods in Sect. 6.1.1. which possibly might be more complex, since in the construction of the tree, optimizing criteria based on the entropy have not been taken into account.

In the second case, analysis by experts when the levels of implication obtained are important can detect whether the consequent formula can induce the creation of a new concept by the experts.

For all cases the degree g of the resulting rule is estimated in a similar way starting from the basic experience.

6.2 FUNCTIONAL RULES

The structure of these rules will be of the type:

$$P(y, r, ...w) \underset{p}{\Rightarrow} V_{x,t} = f(u_1, 2,.....u_n) + \Delta 1$$
$$-\Delta 2$$

where:

Δ_1 is the interval of variation on the right and Δ_2 on the left, associated at the level of significance p, prefix of the rule. Supposing that the distribution of errors may be symmetrical, then $\Delta_1 = \Delta_2$.

The transmission of evidence, through functional formulation, requires not only the formulation of the f functions but also of the transmission form of the extension of the associated intervals.

In effect, although the starting values of the inference mechanism are defined with precision, on applying successive functions, intervals of variation keep appearing whose incidence in the final values it is necessary to transmit throughout the tree.

Therefore, three functions associated with each real variable f_f, f_l, f_r will be defined for application in the inference engine. For example, in the case of a function f of three variables r, s, t, with respective intervals $\Delta 11$, $\Delta 12$, $\Delta 21$, $\Delta 22$, $\Delta 31$, $\Delta 32$, the evaluation would be for a given probability p (Δ_{i1} interval to the right, Δ_{i2} interval to the left):

$$V = f_f(r,s,t)$$
$$\Delta 1 = f_1 (\Delta 11, \Delta 12, \Delta 21, \Delta 22, \Delta 31, \Delta 32, p)$$
$$\Delta r = f_r (\Delta 11, \Delta 12, \Delta 21, \Delta 22, \Delta 31, \Delta 32, p)$$

The process of inference of a determined value consists in applying these functions. If the variables of some are primary values, their value is known and their intervals are null, so that the process is finished. Otherwise, for each variable, depending on the conditions in each situation, a new application of definitory functions can be brought up. The interpretation process terminates when variables with primary values are reached, with which the intended reply values will become defined, by recurrent application of the different functions with the intervals resulting from the application of f_r and f_1.

The connection between both inference mechanisms (functional and based on discrete intervals) must be made through concepts that have a double expression: functional and starting from discrete values. In these cases, once the continuous value and the intervals of variation have been obtained, a standard distribution can be assumed and the probabilities obtained of the different values, that is, if $A.v = a(\Delta_1, \Delta_2)$ is obtained, with probability p, $A.v_1$, $A.v_2$....$A.v_m$ can be generated; here v_j, v_s...,v_m are the discrete values of the attribute V in the interval $(a - \Delta_2, a + \Delta_1)$ to which are associated degrees of certainty consistent with a prefixed form of distribution in the interval $(a - \Delta_2, a + \Delta_1)$ whose total density must be p.

In accordance with the definition given of this type of rule, the process has two steps:
- formulation of the functions f_f that establish a value as a function of the others
- formulation of the functions f_l, f_r, that transmit the errors to the left and right of the value calculated by the previous function

6.2.1 FORMULATION OF FUNCTIONS

The rules to be formulated are structured on the basis of a precondition defined from the attributes with discrete values and a consequent formula in which a numerical function of a set of real numerical values appears.

In a general way, as a precondition, limitations of intervals of continuous value variation, used in the formulation of the consequent function, could appear; in this case, a discrete image attribute of the attribute evaluated as continuous should be created. The hypothesis that, in the antecedent to the rule attributes may appear with discrete values does not constitute a restriction, although it is necessary to introduce into the knowledge base a specific type of rule on value definition of a discrete image attribute or of a continuous one. For example:

$$x < 50,\ x > 15,\ y > 20,\ y < 30 \Rightarrow A.V_4$$

For the purpose of learning, the values of the created attributes can be directly incorporated into the initial experience in such a way that for each rule format, a sample is defined whose generic units are:

$$A_j.\ V_j,\ A_k.\ V_r,\ A_t.\ V_d,.......D_k.D_t.V_e,.....R_k.X,\ R_s.y,\ ....$$

where:

$A_j.\ V_j....$ = pre-existing discrete attribute-value pairs
$D_k.\ V_s....$ = discrete attribute-value pairs created to define value intervals
$R_k.\ x.......$ = continuous attribute-value pair (explanatory variables and to be explained)

On the basis of this type of experience, a process of learning can be defined, a generalization of the method of Quinlan, whose structure is the following:

- Procedure formula-rule (E, F_j, h, p, n. Var)

    n: level of tree in course

    E: is the set of initial experiences

    F_j: is the list of formulated functions

    h: criterion figure for selection of attributes

    p: depth limit level in the introduction of antecedent attributes

    I: identification of the most informative h attributes unused in the E experience

    Var: is the continuous variable to be explained

- First loop: j = 1 to h

    · evaluation of the improvement in information contributed by the A_j attribute

    · if the improvement in contributed information is not acceptable, go to end of loop 1

- Second loop from m = 1 to k (k = number of values A_j)

    · select in E the subset E' in which $A_j.V_m$ is verified

    · correlation analysis formulating $V = f(x_1.....X_n)$

    · if the correlation coefficient is good enough go to end of loop 2 and include the formulation in the list F_j

    · if it is not good enough, two options are possible:

    .. if the number of antecedent attributes is equal to p, go to end of loop

    .. if it is inferior to p, recursive call: formula-rule (E, F_j, h, p, n+1)

In order to complete the definition of the process, it is necessary to establish the form in which it is decided which one is the most informative attribute, that is, with greater discernment value. An estimate of the increase in variance explained in the classified sample with respect to the initial of the following type, is utilized as a heuristic criterion for planning:

- E is classified according to the different values of the attribute in study $A_j....$; for each value k a frequency Pk is obtained

- In each subsample, corresponding to each V_k, the r_k value is obtained, the coefficient of multiple correlation of the variable to be explained with respect to the explanatory variables in the subsample

- A measure of the informative quality of A_j is defined:

    $$I_j = \leq P_k.r_k^2 - r^2$$

    where r is the coefficient of multiple correlation of the variable to be explained previous to the classification

Once ΔI_j is obtained, the attributes are ordered according to this value and the results of the correlation analysis are put by to be used in formula-rule.

6.2.2 FORMULATION OF ERROR INTERVALS

For the inference of error intervals it is obtained, from the subsample defined by the precondition of each rule, the distribution of residues in the form of a table or histogram, with the frequencies of the distinct levels of difference prefixed in percentage with respect to the function value.

Inference of error intervals can be made by means of direct composition of these histograms or by a more global procedure in the cases in which the composition of histograms is excessively inefficient.

In order to compose histograms, the following process can be brought up:

- If the function with respect to which the errors are defined is $y = f(x_1, x_2, ...x_n)$ the form of the distribution of the errors of y from the distribution of the errors of the x_i must be established. Therefore, an approximation can be made, through the linear function:

$$\Delta y = \Sigma \frac{\delta f}{\delta xi} \Delta x_i + \delta \qquad (1)$$

(δ = random variable of error in f)

in such a way that for a given point the coefficients of Δx_i are those derived from f in the point. The problem consists in obtaining the distribution of a random variable, formulated linearly from the distributions of others. If it is assumed that the histograms are classified in m intervals, the probability of Δy formulated according to (1) is:

$$P_0^k . P_1^r . P_2^1 ,.....P_n^P$$

$$k, r, 1, ... \quad \varepsilon \left\{ 1,2,........m \right\}$$

where:

P_0^k = probability in the histogram that the value of δ is in class k

P_i^1 = probability in the histogram of the variable x_i that the value belongs to class 1

332

The value resulting from y would be that corresponding to applying (1) to the representative values of the intervals, which would give a value to be classified, in whose class the calculated joint probability would be accumulated.

The number of possible combinations of classes to combine is m^{n+1} and, therefore, whenever a definition is considered of the histograms in more than five classes, and with more than five variables, the volume of calculation can be important if it is made in real time. When this occurs, which is a frequent case, rules can be synthesized which relate the width of intervals corresponding to a given level of probability, on both sides, that is, the value exceeding the calculated one that has a probability p of not being passed, and the lower value that has a probability p of being passed.
Once the resulting histogram is known, it can serve as a basis for evaluating the intervals on different levels of probability by excess or by defect.

To do this, the previously described method of histogram composition can be applied to create a sample consisting of:

- value of x_i
- values of $\Delta_l x_i$, $\Delta_r x_i$ in the explanatory variables with probability p   (2)
- values of Δ_l and Δ_r resultants with probability p

For this it is necessary to simulate a range of cases with the inferential version in histograms of the set of rules of this type, since histograms which have input frequencies to the previously mentioned application of the function f result from the accumulation of previous reasoning steps and subsequent generation of a new frequency table.

Sample (2) can be extracted from the histograms resulting from the simulation of a range of cases.

If the values of x_i are classified according to a discrete range, a process of formulation of preconditions and adjustment of functions, of the same type as that described in Sect. 6.2.1. for calculation of $\Delta_l y$ and $\Delta_r y$, can be applied to the above-mentioned sample. There is room for the alternative, if the possible values $\Delta_l y$, $\Delta_r y$, $\Delta_l x$, $\Delta_r x_i y$ are made discrete, of applying the Quinlan method. In all cases, sufficient approximations can be reached so as to make an inference be carried out in real time in a more efficient way.

The concept of this system is summarized in the figure.

STRUCTURE OF A CONTINUOUS FORMULATIONS LEARNING PROCESS

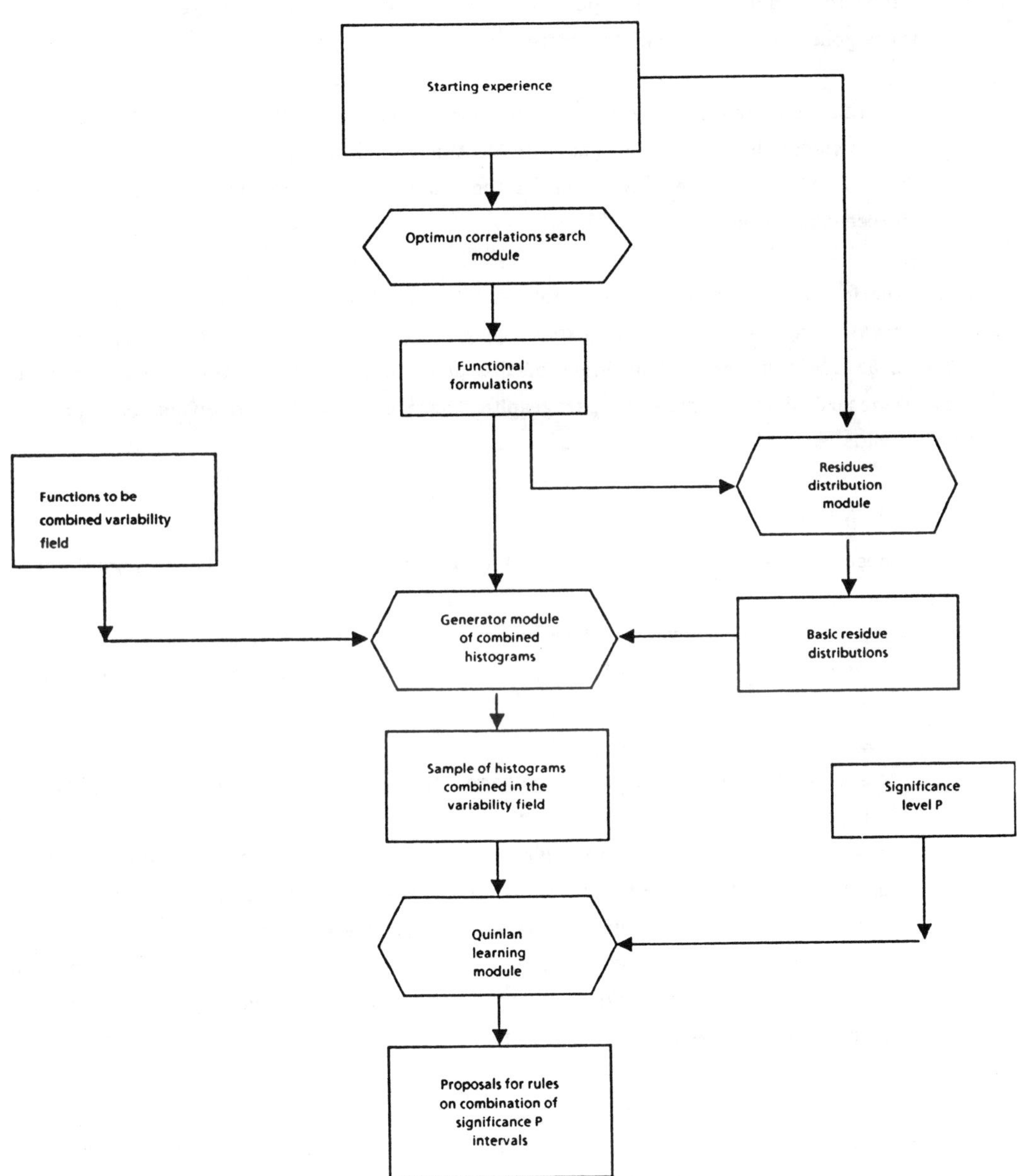

7 CASE EXAMPLE 1: EXPERT SYSTEM FOR FLOOD PREDICTION AND ADVICE

In the autumn of 1982 there were very extensive floods on the Spanish Mediterranean coast. The Spanish Ministry of Public Works decided on the design of an automatic hydrologic information system (SAIH). This investment program, based on an automatic data collection network, aims to produce real time operation recommendations and damage prediction. To achieve these goals the elements of the system are:

- a data base of the meteorological and hydraulic variable values
- a knowledge base able to "understand" the values of the variables in time and space, and to produce answers about the problematical aspects of the present and foreseeable situation

The construction of the automatic data collection network is now under way at the Jucar basin (near Valencia). An outline of an expert system for this kind of problem was presented in [Cuena, 83]. A summary of the ideas of this paper is presented within the conceptual framework described in the previous paragraphs. These are also the specifications for the system which is now being built.

7.1 THE DATA BASE

For the purposes of information about the flood area, two subsystems may be distinguished:

- The hydrographic subsystem where the causes of the problems are made up of:
  - a catchment watershed with long slopes that receives the rain, and is described as:
    - a set of catchment areas
    - a treelike network of rapid drainage formed by the streams from important slopes
  - a low zone, whose axis is the river producing the floods. This can be considered as the axis of the river together with a series of floodable storages connected to the river through the temporary water courses created during flooding
  - a flood plain near the sea that can be represented as a set of interconnected cylindrical cells. The links between cells represent the main flow lines in the flood plain produced by the influence of the substructures (railways, highways)

- The social-territorial subsystem made up of the system of towns, agricultural exploitations and road/rail networks connecting them. This is the system where the problems are located (flooding of agricultural exploitations and of towns, blocking of roads and railways, etc)

The data base incorporates an image of both subsystems with:

- . real time information about rain intensity, water levels and state of the operation elements
- . a simplified geographical information system with the locations of problematic areas and hydrographic subsystem

7.2 THE CONCEPTUAL GRID

The final elements of the reasoning process are:

- The foreseeable problems:

  - . flooding of agricultural zones
  - . flooding in the different districts of the different towns (districts in the big cities)
  - . cuts in road, railway and phone network
  - . isolation of towns because of the cuts in transport and communication network

- Recommendations for operation:
  - . concerning technical control:
    - . actions on reservoir gates, by-pass channel gates to guide the process of flooding, blasting of barriers (sediments or roads producing backwaters)
  - . concerning civil defense:
    - . alternative routes to the interrupted communications
    - . evacuation of towns or districts
      - . recommendation to start operations
      - . monitoring the development of operations

The basic concepts of the reasoning process are:

- . the rain intensities at the pluviometers
- . the water levels at the river control points
- . the state of the elements of operation

The intermediate concepts of the reasoning process are:

- the total rainfall in every area
- the flows in the rapid drainage network
- the state of levels at important transport network links, threshold for the decision of the isolation of towns

The conceptual grid represents the definition relationships between initial, final and intermediate concepts that can be defined directly by the experts; the contexts for concept definition are:

- the basic context including the resulting data from automatic control:
  - rain intensities
  - water levels
  - state of the elements of operation

- the derived contexts
  - rain context with the total rain at every reception area
  - flow context with the flows in the different elements of the rapid drainage network
  - level context with the levels at points not controlled by the automatic systems
  - problem context with every problem considered (cuts in networks, isolation of cities, levels of damage in cities and agricultural exploitations)
  - recommendation context with the different possible actions on technical or social elements (evacuation, alternative routes, etc).

As has been explained, not all the concepts included in these contexts can be defined at the level of conceptual grid; for instance the relationship between flows in the rapid drainage network and the rains at reception areas has to be defined by synthesis of the catchment response modelling results. This also happens for the relationship between the levels. In this case, the relationship between them has to be established by synthesis of the surface modelling.
It is possible to define at the conceptual grid level:

- the total rain in reception areas from individual rainfalls, measured at pluviometers
- the problems based on the current and past states of levels and rainfalls
- the recommendation based on the state of the elements of operation, past, present and predicted water levels and the problems detected

The conceptual grid will be defined by the set of definition relations on the general graph:

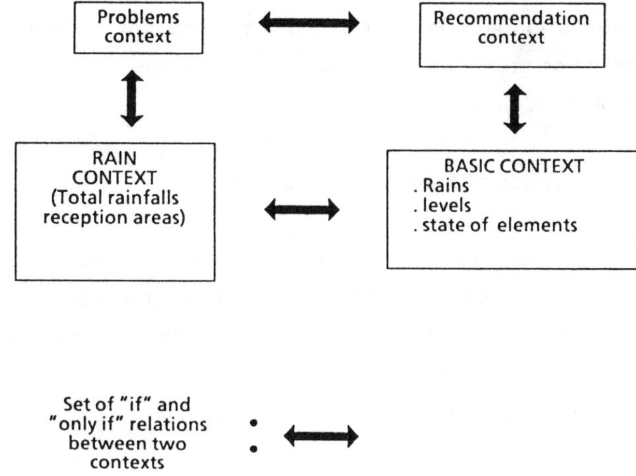

7.3 THE OPERATION REASONING SCHEME

There are three patterns of reasoning:

- reasoning about the situation at an instant t
- reasoning about the situation at t+Δt based on the situation at instant t
- reasoning about the actions to recommend, based on the known and predicted situations

The first line of reasoning deals mainly with the condition for establishing spatial relationships or the definition of concepts based on other concepts at the same instant. The rules are:

A. Rain intensity at pluviometers $\Rightarrow$ rain intensity at reception areas

B. Water levels at control points $\Rightarrow$ water levels at significant uncontrolled points

C. Water levels at control points and significant points $\Rightarrow$ problem identification

Type A and C rules can be obtained from the definitions of the conceptual grid; type B rules need to be inferred from the free surface water model, in such a way that, given the levels at some points, the levels at other points may be established by using rules that synthesize the model estimated.

The second line of reasoning deals with the physical sequence of phenomena in time, by describing the behavior of the hydrologic basin and the meteorological environment. To build the rules with numerical conclusions and premises in a more accurate way, an incremental formulation is recommended, namely, the kind of reasoning that uses the present state and known or predicted variations of some concepts in order to deduce the expected variations of other variables.

The elements of knowledge are:

- representation of the evolution of the meteorological environment; it uses the current rain intensity state at the reception areas and the different average variation in past time intervals to deduce the rain intensity variations

D. $I_i, I_j, \ldots I_e, \quad I_i/\Delta t, \Delta I_j/\Delta t \ldots \Rightarrow \Delta I_n$

$$I_i \qquad \text{rain at t at reception area i}$$
$$\Delta I_i/\Delta t \qquad \text{average variation of intensity at i in the last } \Delta t \text{ minutes}$$
$$\Delta I_n \qquad \text{predicted variation at area n in the next } \Delta t \text{ minutes}$$

- representation of the evolution of the flows in the rapid drainage network. The flows in this network are null at the beginning of the storm. At every application of the rules an increment of flow can be obtained, based on the present rain intensity and past accumulated total rain at different time intervals and the flow increments at backwater links. The scheme of the rules is:

E. $\quad I_i, \Delta I_j, \Delta I_j, \Delta Q_k, \Delta Q_1 \Rightarrow Q_n = f(I_i, I_j, \quad I_j \ldots \Delta Q_k, \Delta Q_r) + \Delta f$

where:

$I_i, \Delta I_i$ = present rain intensity and past increment at reception areas draining on reach i

ΔQ_k = flow increment at reach k of the drainage network

Δf = error interval

These rules are an inferential formulation of the classic recursive models of flow routing of the Muskingum type

- Representation of the level behavior at unsteady flow links of the river, based on present   levels and differential input flows

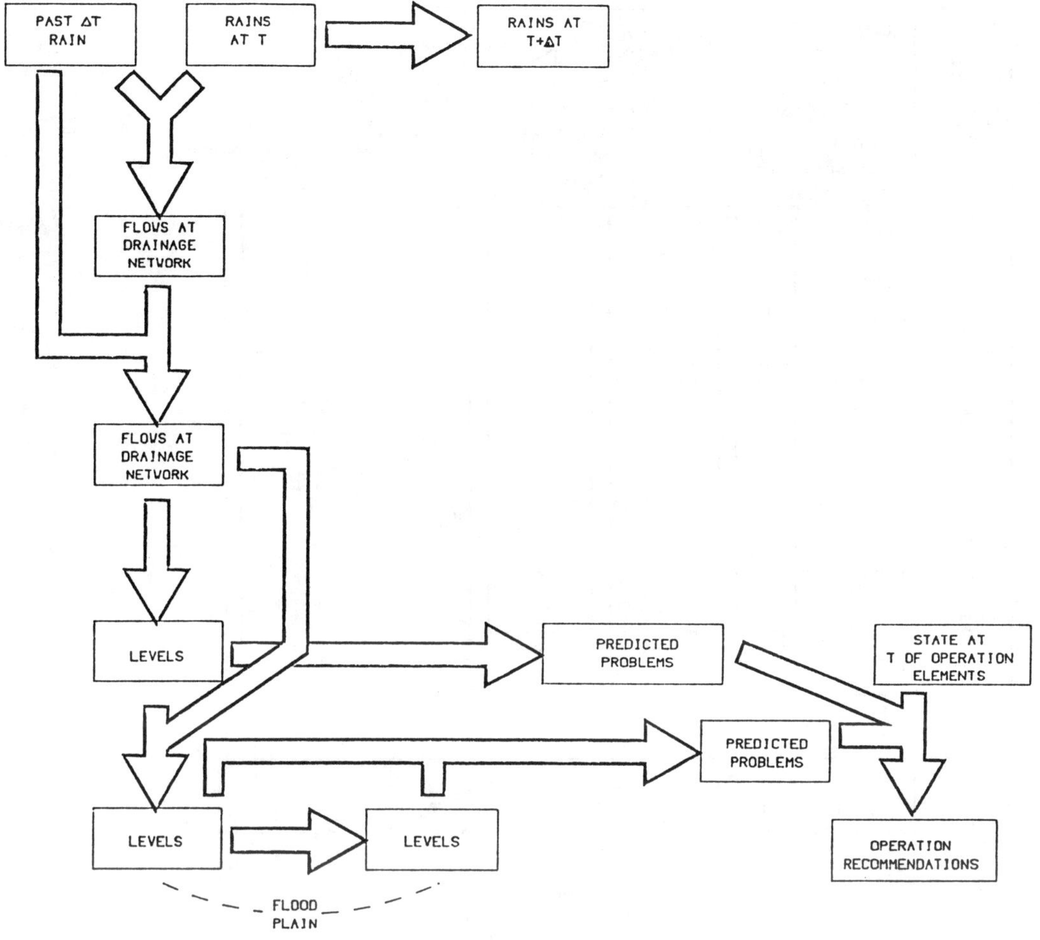

FIG.4 FLOW DIAGRAM OF REASONING ALONG TIME

F. $Y_i, \Delta Q_i, \Delta Q_j \Rightarrow Y_n = f(\Delta Q_i, \Delta Q_j, \ldots) \pm \Delta f$

. Representation of the level behavior at the flood plain based on present levels

G. $Y_i, Y_j, Y_k, \Delta Y_k, \Delta Y_j \Rightarrow \Delta Y_i = f(\Delta Y_k, \Delta Y_j) \pm \Delta f$

The third line of reasoning is based on the features of the present and predicted situation in order to recommend the different operations and civil defense decisions. The general form is:

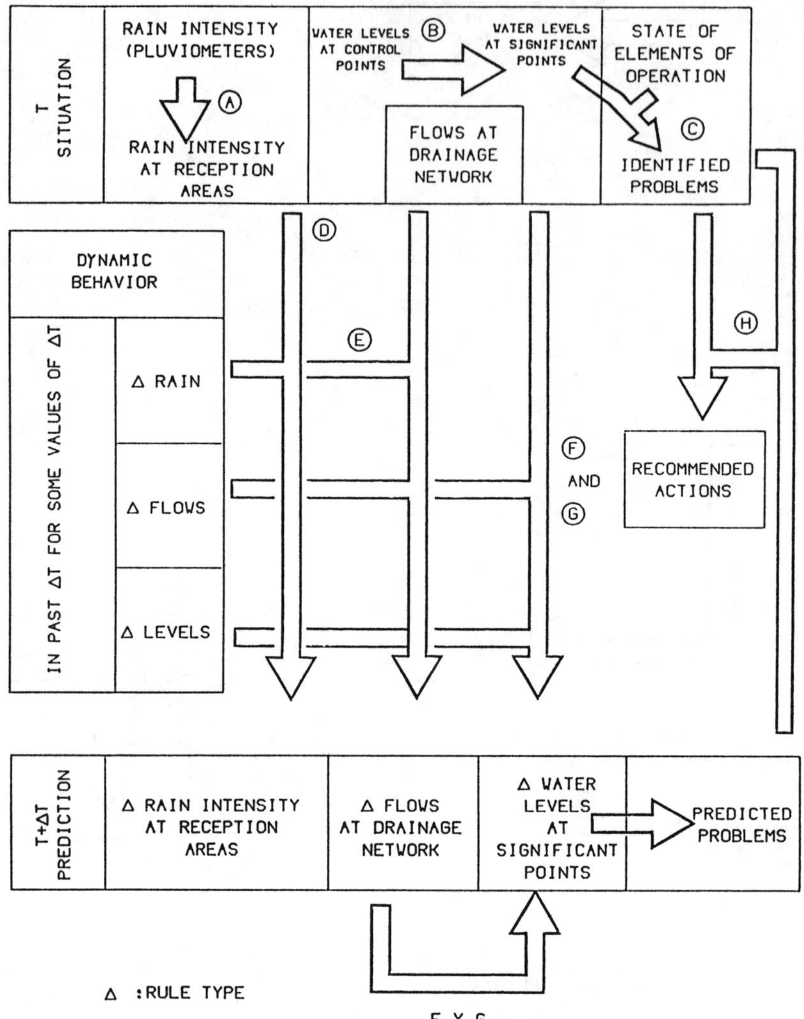

FIG. 5 RULE RELATIONSHIP BETWEEN PRESENT AND PREDICTED
SITUATION AND RECOMMENDED ACTIONS

H. State of operation elements, present and predicted problems, operation decision, civil
defense decisions

In figs. 4 and 5 the general reasoning scheme is synthesized

7.4 BUILDING THE KNOWLEDGE BASE

Once the classes of rules have been integrated into the general reasoning scheme, it is necessary to develop a method for building the rules of every class. As has been discussed before, there are two kinds of rules:

- Propositional rules relating context-concept-value triple conditions for the definition of some values. These rules are to be established mainly by the experts and responsible people. Rules of this kind are:

  - rules for estimation of total rain intensity in the reception areas, based on the rain intensities at the pluviometers

  - rules for problem identification
    - in agricultural exploitation (height of water levels → economic damage)
    - in transport and communication network (water levels → degree of closure risk)
    - in urban areas (water levels → degree of population damage risk)

  - rules for operation and civil defense
    - at technical elements like gates and pipes at reservoirs and channels
    - at social units (towns and transport network)

The technical operation rules are established, not only based on the experts and responsible persons' criteria, but also formulated with the help of the results of the different operation strategy simulations with models.

- Propositional rules about physical behavior. These rules relate discrete spaces of causes and effects, described by context-concept-value triples; this structure is used for:

- Type D rain rules, given that the meteorological phenomena are referable to discrete patterns of behavior, describe the different patterns of situation in the paest and then define the kind of temporal variation in the future

- Type H rules for recommending operation and actions, because the situation patterns for operation recommendations are well suited for discrete description in a decision table format

- Functional rules about physical behavior; these rules relate cause values and effect values through functional evaluation, corrected by confidence intervals of the kind described in Sect. 6.2. This structure is used for:

. Type D rain rule alternative formulation, when the propositional formulation is not well suited (for instance when the patterns of causes and effects take values over too large intervals)

. Type E rules for flow routing along the rapid drainage network; given the large field of variation of the flow values along the drainage network, it is not well suited to discrete modelling

. Type F and G rules for level inference based on flows and related levels. This kind of numerical modelling is adequate because the interval division would be at the cost of precision. It is given that problem identification is based mainly on the rule structures

The general method to get these formulations is presented in Sects. 6.1 and 6.2. The rules are the final result of a systematic process of knowledge generation and synthesis. The tasks to be carried out are:

. building a set of models of the catchment behavior:
  . formulation of the simulation process
  . calibration of model parameters to get an evaluated behavior (levels, flows, rains) close enough to observed behavior
. synthesis of the calibrated model behavior in a set of rules operating in real time, by using the procedure presented above.

This process takes a long time, significantly longer than the delays in the classical-knowledge engineering approach (building and calibrating the models for a basin takes one year at least), but it is important to point out that the knowledge encoded in the final system is of a higher quality than that based simply on the expert judgements about more simple questions than the overall physical behavior of a hydrologic basin.

The models used to explain the physical behavior are:
- the Sacramento model to explain the flow from reception areas to drainage network
- the Muskingum model for the routing of flows through the rapid drainage network
- the numerical implicit scheme integration model for Saint Venant's equations of the unsteady flow in open channels for the explanation of levels in the flooded areas near the river axis
- the grid of rectangular basis cylindrical cells for the levels in the flood plain

The Sacramento model [Burnash, Ferral, 1973] is a representation of the complex phenomena inside a hydrologic basin by means of an analogy with a system of five reservoirs:

- the upper reservoir representing the initial storage behavior of the soil surface: from this reservoir a part of the water infiltrates and a part runs off directly to the surface drainage network
- two intermediate reservoirs representing the behavior of the soil "humidity" water by tension and free water subsurface flow
- two deep reservoirs to represent the gravity storage

The model formulates the relationships between these reservoirs and the surface runoff by means of functions describing the flows between reservoirs and the output flow to the drainage surface network.

For the sake of modelling the response to sudden storms it is not necessary to take account of the deep reservoirs. It is then possible to calibrate the parameters of a restricted set of functions so that the computer behavior can be close enough to the observed behavior. Once a model has been calibrated it is possible to generate an artificial sample of computed behavior for different scenarios of rain, to be used as a basis for the knowledge acquisition procedure. As has been previously explained with respect to the most accurate formulation of rules, this artificial sample must include relationships between increments of cause and effect variables.

The Muskingum model for rapid drainage network formulation is perhaps the best known and the most widely used of the simplified routing methods. It was first developed by the U.S. Army Corps of Engineers for the Muskingum river. [Cunge, 1969] improved the criteria for the definition of parameters, establishing their theoretical background [Mahmood, Yevjevitch, 75].

The final rule of the Muskingum method is the equational relation between the states of a reach of the rapid drainage network at successive instants.

The state of a reach is described by:

I_i^n, O_i^n - Input and Output at the reach at instant n

The recurrent relationship between states on a reach is described by:

$$O_i^{n+1} = C_1 \cdot I_i^{n+1} + C_2 I_i^n + C_3 O_i^n \qquad (1)$$

344

C_1, C_2, C_3 are coefficients depending on the time step t and K, parameters that describe the reach.

Given a law of input at the first reach the iterative application of the equation (1) allows the computation of the flows along the network if

$$I_i = \sum_{K \epsilon S} O_k$$

S being the set of reaches that drain to the reach i.

The equation (1) is really an inference rule of the functinal type.

The Saint Venant equations are:

i) the continuity equations:

$$\frac{\partial Q}{\partial X} + T \frac{\partial Y}{\partial t} = q$$

ii) the dynamic equation

$$V \frac{\partial Q}{\partial X} + \frac{\partial Q}{\partial t} + (GA - V^2 T) \frac{\partial Y}{\partial X} = V \frac{\partial A}{\partial X}_y + g\ A (S_0 - S_f)$$

Where:

y(x,t)   depth of flow in the cross section of the river
(x, abscissa along the river axis)
(t, time)

Q(x, t)   flow

V(x, t)   average velocity

A(x, t)   cross sectional area,   Q = V.A

$\dfrac{\partial A}{\partial X}_y$ partial derivative, y value remaining constant

T   upper width of the cross section

S_0 geometric slope

S_f roughness slope which can be defined by the Manning formula:

$$S_f = \frac{n^2 V^2}{R^{4/3}}$$

g gravitational acceleration

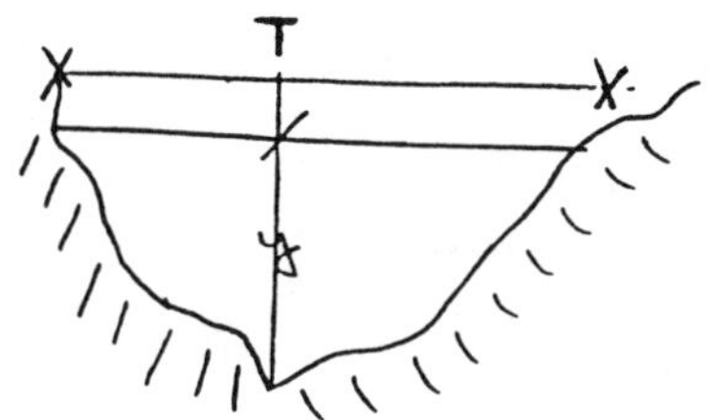

There has been a great number and variety of numerical techniques for integration of these hyperbolic equations divided in two main lines:

. characteristic curve methods (integration in a characteristic curve grid)

. finite difference methods (integration on a grid in the x, t plane)

$\bigl[$Preissman, Cunge 61, Vasiliev et al., 63$\bigr]$ present different schemas. The incremental formulation of implicit finite difference methods is the most accurate and effective class of techniques. It requires the solution of a linear system of equations at every interval of time integration.

Linked with the definite difference formulation of Saint Venant equations, it is possible to include equations for the simulation of bed load transport and for the operation of side storages to the main river axis, in such a way that the effect of the flood wave can be reproduced with this kind of model, when the main sense of flow is along the river axis, with lateral local flooding episodes.

For the flood plain simulation when there is not a main line of flow propagation, the kind of model to use is based on a generalization of Saint Venant equations.

Continuity equations:

$$\frac{\partial h}{\partial t} + \frac{\partial (V_x h)}{\partial x} + \frac{\partial (V_y h)}{\partial y} = 0$$

dynamic equation in the y axis direction:

$$\frac{1}{g}\left(\frac{\partial V_y}{\partial t} + V_x \frac{\partial V_y}{\partial x} + V_y \frac{\partial V_y}{\partial y}\right) + \frac{\partial z}{\partial y} + K_y V_y \sqrt{V_x^2 + V_y^2} = 0$$

dynamic equation in the x axis direction

$$\frac{1}{g}\left(\frac{\partial V_x}{\partial t} + V_x \frac{\partial V_y}{\partial x} + V_y \frac{\partial V_x}{\partial y}\right) + \frac{\partial z}{\partial x} + K_x V_x \sqrt{V_x^2 + V_y^2} = 0$$

where V_x, V_y are the water velocities in the x and y directions,

h: water depth

z: water level

$\bar{k}$: the overall resistance coefficient

As water velocities are not very important at the flood plain the inertia terms

$$\frac{1}{g}\left(\frac{\partial V_x}{\partial t} + V_x \frac{\partial V_x}{\partial x} + V_y \frac{\partial V_x}{\partial y}\right)$$

$$\frac{1}{g}\left(\frac{\partial V_x}{\partial t} + V_x \frac{\partial V_y}{\partial x} + V_y \frac{\partial V_y}{\partial x}\right)$$

may be dropped.

Even with this simplification the numerical solution of these equations involves great difficulty. The alternative method is to use a finite set of cylindrical cells to describe the flood plain and to define a system of the physical relationships among them to represent the hydraulic behavior (continuity and dynamic equilibrium). This method was proposed by [Preissman, Cunge, 1961] for the Mekong delta.

Based on one of these schemes it is possible to formulate a computational procedure to simulate the evolution of the flood plain: from the state of levels and velocities at t to the state of levels and velocities at t + Δt.

These flood routing models (flows, one dimensional unsteady flow and flood plain) are too complex to be worked on line, but, as has been stated, it is possible to define a set of runs to establish, in rule form, the significant relationships between the levels and the flows at different time lags (the significant relationships are investigated by having as a base the general reasoning schema predefined).

Although previous work on model implementation, calibration, etc., is necessary, this kind of synthesis knowledge base is possible, as is shown by the number of implemented models of the kind described in previous paragraphs, and the important added value of the final system makes them economically and socially interesting.

The methods described are part of the preliminary system project. The building of the model system and expert system are now under way at the Direccion General de Obras Hidraulicas of the Ministry of Public Works of Spain.

8 CASE EXAMPLE 2: EXPERT SYSTEM FOR FREEWAY TRAFFIC CONTROL

The Direccion General de Tráfico of Spain is now beginning the AURA project (AURA: Accesos Urbanos Regulados Automaticamente) (automatically regulated urban accesses) whose goal is the automatic collecting of information on and control of the traffic on the main access freeways to important Spanish urban areas. The project begins with the installation on two freeways for access to Madrid and another two freeways for access to Barcelona.

This project is now beginning and the general structure of the system for implementation is:

- a set of sensors along two-way lanes
- a network of data collection which includes local capacity for control at degraded situations
- a data processing center with two computers interconnected receiving the information from the network
- a set of signal screens placed on frames over the freeway for speed recommendation

The system receives the information from the network and carries out the tasks:

- data collection and synthesis
- data presentation through data base facilities (tables and graphics)
- freeway incident detection
- real time situation forecasting
- operation recommendations
- automatic control (sending to the signal screens speed recommendations for the drivers, opening and closing of new lanes for two-way traffic, turning on and off of stop lights for access to the freeway, etc.)

The latter four tasks are to be done by a knowledge-based system operating in real time; at the beginning the control tasks will be developed under human control but the greater the experience of working with the system the greater will be the number of control tasks carried out directly by the system.

The expert system to be built, as in example 1, will integrate a synthesis of the behavior models, the resulting conclusions of the model being used to define strategies, and the experts' knowledge.

The general methodology to be used is the same as in example 1; given that the work on this system has not advanced so far, a briefer presentation is made of the main issues of the development process.

8.1 THE DATA BASE

For the purposse of information two subsystems may be distinguished:

- . the physical environment subsystem describing the structure of the road network, the pavement state, meteorological conditions, and the date
- . the operation system describing the traffic and signal states

The data for the physical environment system are:

* Structure of the road network

- A list of cross sections at the freeway being controlled
- A set of entry and exit control points
- A set of control points of alternative paths

* State of pavement (at every 500 m)

- Dry
- Wet
- Frozen

* Meteorological conditions (at one or two meteorological stations for every freeway)

- Visibility (meters)
- Temperature
- % humidity

* The date (day, day of the week, hour)

- The operation environment data are variables

* Traffic taken at every cross section (500 m):

- Intensity (veh/hour) at every sensor
- Occupancy (% of time vehicles passing over the sensor)
- Speed (km/h)
- Structure (% three vehicle categories)

* Signalization

- Speeds at every frame (with or without red ring)
- State of access stop lights (semaphores)

8.2 THE CONCEPTUAL GRID

The final elements of the reasoning process are:

- The foreseeable problems:
  . levels of traffic
  . incident detection
  at the freeway trunk and accesses and alternative paths

- Control recommendations:
  . speed recommendations at panels
  . state of access semaphores
  . monitoring direction switching at lanes

- Complementary operations (proposals of patrols for safety at incidents or diversions via alternative itineraries)

The basic concepts for the reasoning process are:

- The state of pavements
- The meteorological conditions
- The observed traffic at different lanes at the control cross sections
- The date (hour, day of the week)
- The state of the signal systems

350

The intermediate concepts for the reasoning process are:

- Traffic patterns (holiday, labor day, Saturday night, etc., at different seasons, times and meteorological conditions)

- Attitude patterns (in different situations drivers react differently to speed recommendations):

For the system to recommend the speed level (with or without red ring) assumptions are needed about drivers' responses: as a parameter for this response the attitude context can be defined that reflects the degree of concern of the driver about the traffic. This is an aspect to develop during the period of system formulation; as a previous definition it can be considered to be based on two concepts:

. fatigue
. patience

The attitude context may be defined by the different combinations of the values of these concepts. Based on these values, rules can be formulated to define the desired speed of the drivers corresponding to the different speed recommendations as will be shown in the following paragraphs.

- The incident definitions

- The operation recommendations (the criteria for deciding the changes at speed panels)

The conceptual grid embodies some of these definitions: those based on the criteria of the experts and responsible people. Two main contexts can be distinguished:

- The basic context including the elementary concepts for the reasoning process described above

- The derived contexts:
  . traffic patterns
  . attitude patterns
  . meteorology patterns

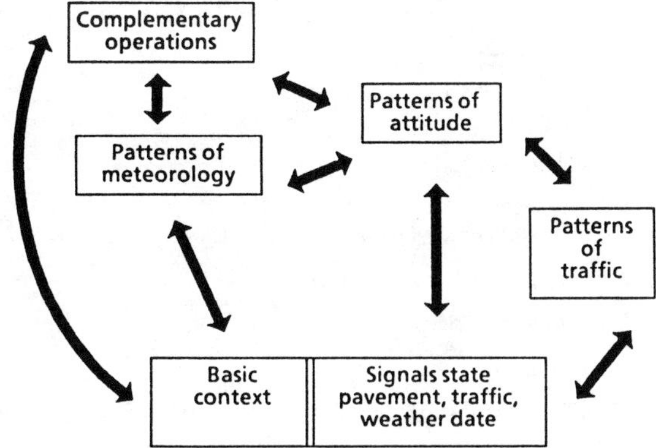

Fig. 6

- complementary operations context (definition of the patrol operations based on patterns of situation)
- congestion level definition at the significant points

The incident detection and operation contexts depend on the system behavior, and the definition of their concepts have to be established based on the model synthesis.

The context diagram at the conceptual grid level is summarized in Fig.6, with the possible links of if and only if definitions. The concepts included in every context refer to the present and past values at predefined time intervals (for instance there is a very short time lag for incident detection and one not so short for the complementary operations definition)

8.3 THE OPERATION REASONING SCHEME

As in the flood system three main lines of reasoning could be defined:

- Reasoning about the time t situation
- Reasoning about the situations at $t + \Delta t$ based on the situation at t
- Reasoning about the control of panels and lights

Given that the information system sensors are close enough, there is no need in this case of rules to interpolate elements of the present situation based on the control data. The rules about the t situation are mainly those for incident detection, which are really rules between situations very close in time ($\sim$ 20 sec.) to detect the sudden changes of traffic flow in a lane. Their general format for every cross section i will be

A. PT, PM, $PS_i H$, T_i, T'_i, T''_i, T_{i-1}, T'_{i-1}, T''_{i-1}, T_{i+1}, T'_{i+1}

$T''_{i+} \Rightarrow$ incident $_{ik}$

g

where:

PT : pattern of traffic

PM : pattern of meteorology

PS_i : state of pavement at i

H : hour

T_i, T'_i, T''_i: state of traffic variables at t, $t-\Delta t$ and $t-2\Delta t$

(Δt time step for incident detection)

(the traffic variables are those of the basic frame for every lane)

incident$_{ik}$:concept with values of the different levels of incidence: accelerating, applying brakes, stopping, stop, accident, etc., (at lane k of cross section i)

The second line of reasoning deals with the physical sequence of events describing the behavior of traffic in time. The main elements of knowledge are described as rule formats:

. Predicted traffic arrivals. Representing the evolution of the traffic environment arriving at the controlled freeway. The general rule format is

B. SL, PT, PM, H, I'_E, $\Delta I'_E / \Delta t' \Rightarrow \Delta I_E$

where:

SL : state of light ($\Delta I_E = =$ is SL = Red)

I'_E : intensity at the entry at t

$\Delta I'_E$: intensity variation at the last Δt

ΔI_E : predicted intensity variation

. Predicted traffic at exits. Representing the evolution of the traffic out of the freeway, based on the known pattern and the possible incidence of freeway traffic situations: The general rule format is:

C. PT, PM, H, I_A, $(\Delta I_A / \Delta t)$, I_w, $\Delta I' / \Delta t \Rightarrow \Delta I_n$

where:

I_A : intensity at t at the freeway trunk in the cross section near the exit

$\Delta I_A / \Delta t$: variation in the past Δt of freeway intensity

I_w : intensity at the way out at t

$\Delta I'_w / \Delta T$: variation in the past Δt of the way out intensity

. Desired speed at every cross section. This knowledge allows the estimation based on the attitude of the drivers, the traffic situation and the recommended signals. The general format is:

D. $PM, PT, AT, H, RV, I_A, V_A \Rightarrow DV_A$

where:

AT   : attitude

RV   : recommended speed at signal panel

. Predicted traffic at cross sections based on the present state behavior, at the current and adjacent cross sections, the predicted increments at the previous cross sections, the desired speed at the cross section and entries to the freeway. The general rule format is:

E. $PT, PM, H, I_E, I_A, V_A, DV_A, I_{A-1}, V_{A-1}, I_{A+1}, IV_{A+1}, \Delta I_{A-1}, \Delta V_{A-1}$
       $I_e \Rightarrow \Delta I_A, \Delta V_A$

where:

$I_{A\pm K}$: intensity at cross section +K of the cross section A

$V_{A\pm K}$: speed

  I, V : resulting increments of intensity and speed

$I_E, \Delta I_E$: intensity and increment predicted at back entries

DV_A : desired speed at A

. Future level of incidents. The detection of future incidents is based on statistics applied to predicted situations. This rule should be a translation to rule format of the statistical tables of incidents for different patterns of simulations:

F. $PI_A, PV_A, PI_{A+1}, PV_{A+1}, PW, PT, AT, H \Rightarrow PINC_A$

where:

PI_A, PI_{A+1}: predicted intensity at cross section A and next

PV_A, PV_{A+1}: predicted speed at cross section A and next

$PINC_A$: probability of incidents at A

. Speed recommendations to decide the set of speeds to recommend at panels. Reasoning must be based on the present and predicted states, taking into account the drivers' attitude. The general rule format will be

STATE AT T
CROSS SECTIONS
TRAFFIC VARIABLES
SIGNALS STATES
ARRIVALS
INTENSITY
EXITS
INTENSITY
DATE
HOUR DAY MONTH
WEATHER
CLIMATIC VARIABLES
PAVEMENT
LEVEL OF WATER
TRAFFIC VARIATION IN LAST ΔT
CROSS SECTION
ARRIVALS
EXITS
DEF.
DEF.
PATTERN OF TRAFFIC
PATTERN OF WEATHER
PATTERN OF ATTITUDES
PREDICTED ARRIVALS EXITS
INCIDENT DETECTION LEVEL
DESIRED SPEED
PREDICTED TRAFFIC VARIATIONS AT CROSS SECTIONS
PROPOSED NEW SIGNALS
PREDICTED PROBABILITY OF INCIDENTS
A
B
C
D
E
F
G
H

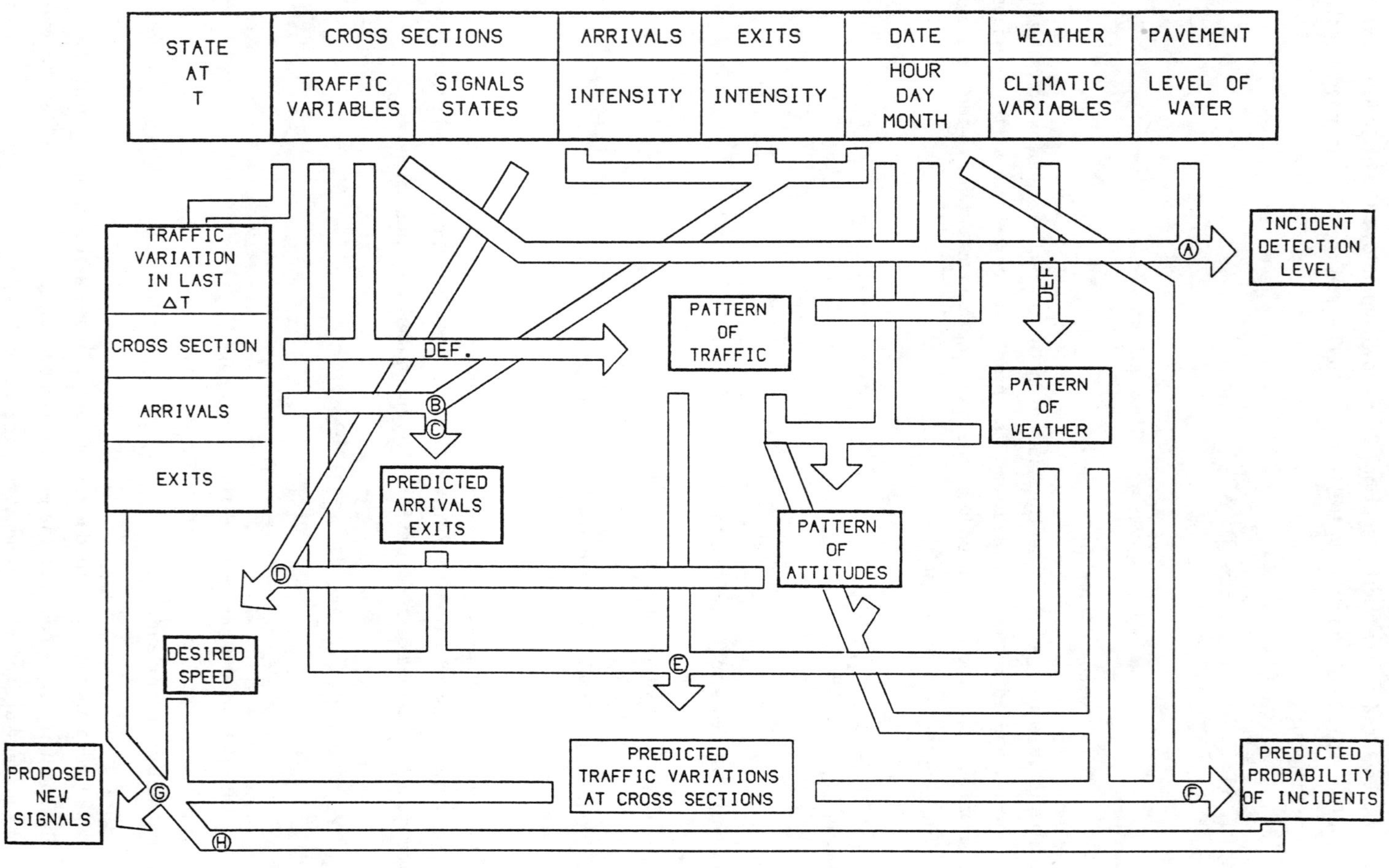

FIG. 7

G. PM, PT, H, RV_A, RV_{A+1},ΔT_A, $PINC_A$, AT, $\Rightarrow$ ΔRV_A

where:

RV_A : recommended speed at present in signal panel A.

T_A,ΔT_A : present and predicted traffic variables

. Semaphore recommendation. To decide the new state of semaphores at freeway access, based on the queue at the access and the present and predicted traffic at the first cross section after the access

H. PW, PT, H, SL, Q, T, $\Delta T \Rightarrow$ SL

where:

SL : state of the light

Q : queue of vehicles at the access

T, Δt : present and predicted traffic variable values

As in the flood system, these rule formats must be considered as groups of concepts for investigating rules by some knowledge acquisition method. From every rule format a set of alternative or conjunctive rules can be produced for getting evidence in favor of or against the conclusions of the rule format.

The general reasoning scheme for designing the knowledge base, taking account of the behavior and control rules explained, and the conceptual grid is summarized in fig. 7.

There are other aspects of reasoning to take into account (such as the complementary operation definitions and late direction sense switching monitoring); these are still to be defined.

8.4 BUILDING THE KNOWLEDGE BASE

As in example 1, this base will be based on expert definitions and rule synthesis of model runs. The models to be used are of two types:

- Microsimulation models, where the behavior is obtained as a result of the composition of individual vehicle strategies

- Macrosimulation models, based on transition functions between the flow variables in space and time obtained by numerical integration of flow equations

Given the length of the freeways to be simulated (≈ 50 km) the use of microsimulation is forbidden by efficiency criteria. The solution retained combines the two types of models with local models for the functions (entries and exits), and a macromodel for the general simulation. The results of the local micromodels are introduced as boundary conditions in the macromodel.

The microsimulation models are based on a file describing the set of vehicles in the system, with variables position, speed, acceleration, etc. The models represent the behavior of every vehicle, based on a standard strategy for every vehicle type. General traffic performance is evaluated by statistical analysis of the simulated sample.

The macrosimulation models are based on the numerical integration of two functions:

q(x,t) : traffic flow at section x at instant t (veh/hour)
p(x,t) : traffic density (veh/length) at section x at instant t
The speed function v(x,t) can be obtained by:

$$V(x,t) = q(x,t)/p(x,t)$$

also written as:

$$q(x,t) = p(x,t) \cdot V(x,t)$$

The equations governing the flow are as in hydrodynamic models:

$$\frac{\partial p}{\partial t} + \frac{\partial (pv)}{\partial x} = B(x) \qquad \text{(1) continuity equation}$$

$$V = V(p) \qquad \text{(2) dynamic equation}$$

(B(x) veh/hour/m input or output in the freeway axis)

The dynamic equation is the result of the vehicle strategy based on the traffic density. There are different representation techniques based on car following [Chandler et al., 65] [Isaksen, Payne, 73] [Goldstein, Kumar 82]. Once a dynamic formulation is selected, the model is based on the numerical integration of the system of equations (1) and (2).

The models are calibrated with the behavior data obtained in traffic surveys and specific flow measure campaigns at the significant dates.

Once the models are calibrated to represent the behavior without the control system, an assumption of the effect in the dynamic equation of driver behavior, taking account of the speed recommendations, will be made and these versions of the model will be run to generate the artificial experience in a set of predefined traffic situations and for different signal control strategies.

The resulting sample will be used for the generation of the traffic prediction rules (rule B, C, D, E, formats).

The signal recommendation rules (rule F, G formats) will be defined after analysis by the experts of the results for every simulated strategy, and the rules proposed by the learning process.

The incident detection rules (A format) will be a synthesis of the existing procedures for incident detection (California model, Texas Institute method, Sakasita, etc.) [Sakasita, May 75]. The synthesis formulation may be done by calibration of every model selecting the best mix of models. The rules define the preconditions of the situation for applying the different models.

CONCLUSIONS

An outline has been presented of a method for building expert systems for synthesis of the knowledge of existing simulation models, the knowledge about the results of using the models to simulate situations, and the experts' knowledge about the concepts, methods and results of utilizing the models.

The use of the models allows the application of model driven learning techniques for building the knowledge base:

- By producing the training sample through previous simulation runs

- By providing the base for the conceptual definition of an operation reasoning scheme, sources of the different rule formats to be tested by the learning method

An alternative rule formulation has also been proposed which allows the application of regression analysis to defining the rules.

Finally, the general application of the method for building two systems has been specified. The final version of these systems will be produced once the information and model calibration tasks are finished. The production of this type of expert system is time-consuming because of the necessary previous work but the important level of knowledge contained therein makes them very interesting.

Acknowledgements

The author is grateful to Miss Margarita Pardo for her efforts in typewriting the English manuscript.

REFERENCES

Buchanan B.G., Mitchell T.M. "Model directed learning of production rules". "Pattern directed inference systems". Waterman D.A., Hayes-Roth F. (Eds.). Academic Press 1978

Burnash R.J.C., Ferral L. "A generalized stream flow simulation system conceptual modelling for digital computers". National Weather Service & State of California Department of Water Resources. 1973

Chandler R.E., Herman R., Montroll E.W. "Traffic dynamics: studies in car following" Operation Research 6. 1965

Cohen P.R., Feigenbaum E.A. "The Handbook of Artificial Intelligence" Vol. 3. W. Kaufman Inc. 1982

Cuena J. "The use of simulation models and human advice to build an expert system for the defense and control of river floods". IJCAI 83. Karlsruhe. 1983

Cunge J.A., 1969. "On the subject of a flood propagation computation method (Muskingum method)". Journal of hydraulic research, 7. 1969

Dietterich T.G., Michalski R.S. "Inductive learning of structural description" Artificial Intelligence Vol 16. 1981

Goldstein N.B., Kumar K.S.P. "A decentralized control strategy for freeway regulation" Transportation Research. 1982

Isaksen L., Payne H.J. "Suboptimal control of linear systems by augmentation with applications for freeway traffic regulation" IEEE Trans. Automatic Control AC-18. 1983

Lenat D.B. "AM: Artificial Intelligence approach to discovery in Mathematics" PhD Dissertation Stanford University. 1976

Mahmood K., Yevjevich V. "Unsteady flow in open channels" Vols. I, II. Water Resource Publications. Fort Collins. Colorado. 1975

Mitchell T.M. "Version Spaces: An approach to concept learning" Stanford C5 Report Stan-78-711, HPP-79-2. 1979

Preissman A., Cunge J.A. "Calcul des intumescences sur machines electroniques" IX meeting of the IAHR. Dubrovnik 1961

Quinlan J.R. "Discovering rules from large collections of examples: A case study" "Expert systems in the micrelectronic age" Michie D. (Ed.). Edin burgh University Press. Edin burgh 1979.

Sakasita M., May A.D. "Development and evaluation of incident-detection algorithms for electronic-detector systems on freeways" Transportation Research 1975

Van Melle W. "EMYCIN: A domain independent system that aids in constructing knowledge based consultation programs". T. Report HPP 80-22. Heuristic programming proyect. Department of Computer Science. Stanford University. 1980

Vasiliev O.F., Godunov S.K. et al "Numerical method of computation of wave propagation in open channels: application to the problem of floods" Dokl. Akad, Nauk SSSR 151. No. 3. 1963

An Approach to Designing an Expert System Through Knowledge Organization

Jue Wang

Institute of Automation, Academia Sinica
Beijing, China

Abstract

KORG (Knowledge ORGanization) is an approach to establishing an expert system. Its tasks are concerned with the following: (1) An expert system consists of both the domain expert's knowledge and the AI expert's knowledge. (2) These two sorts of knowledge have to be mapped to a set of symbols in a computer. (These symbols are called CONCEPTS in this paper.) They are combined in terms of rules (called the connections of the semantic network). (3) Any of these concepts may be described either by other concepts or by constants which are also concepts. Based on these points, a kind of semantic network, with semantic attributes and relational attributes is presented to represent the expert's knowledge. An algorithm called DESCRIBE is also proposed. It changes this knowledge into the semantic network. An automatic programmer, in which the connections of the semantic network serve as knowledge, transforms the semantic network into an expert system program.

In order to support the approach, some tools are presented: ETL (Expert Tool Language), ETN (Expert Tool Network), and ETAP (Expert Tool Automatic Programmer).

1 Introduction

One of the difficulties in the creation of an expert system lies in the difference in knowledge background between the AI expert and the domain expert. It is problematic that domain experts do not know how to encode their knowledge for a computer, although they are able to write textbooks on their knowledge and apply it to solving difficult problems in their domain. The difficulties for AI experts are that they cannot estimate the special characteristics of some domain efficiently in advance and they are often unable to react appropriately to these characteristics immediately. These difficulties result in a bottleneck in transforming the expert's knowledge into computer code. In view of the complexity and magnitude of a practical expert system, this bottleneck becomes a serious problem. Unfortunately it will be hard to solve the problem completely before new progress is achieved in natural language processing and learning.

362

    This paper will present an approach to establishing an expert system – Knowledge Organization, abbreviated to KORG – for reducing these difficulties. The idea of the approach is that we make an environment in which the expert is prompted with some information and even with examples, while the expert's knowledge is encoded by the environment.

    The principle of KORG is concerned with the following:

(1) An expert system consists of both the domain expert's knowledge and the AI expert's knowledge.
(2) These two sorts of knowledge have to be mapped to a set of symbols in a computer. (These symbols are referred to as CONCEPTS in this paper.) They are combined in terms of rules (called the connections of the semantic network).
(3) Any of these concepts may be described either by other concepts or by constants which are also concepts.

A kind of semantic network with semantic attributes and relational attributes is the kernel of this work. Experts might apply an algorithm provided by KORG to transform their knowledge into the network and then an automatic programmer alters the semantic network to an expert system program by means of the connections of the network.

    KORG divides this knowledge into banks, denoted by KBN1, KBN2, ..., KBNi (Knowledge Bank Network), according to its roles within the expert system. If i>1, KBNi is a knowledge bank which defines the relational attribute concepts of KBNi–1; otherwise it is called the domain KBN. An expert system program will be created if the nodes in this network are transformed into a LISP model and combine these knowledge banks. So the expert's knowledge will be represented as LISP functions. The process of knowledge compilation is thus possible.

    In order to support the approach, we adopt some tools: ETL (Expert Tool Language), ETN (Expert Tool Network), and ETAP (Expert Tool Automatic Programmer).

    KORG embodies the following ideas.

(1) The root concept is provided by the domain expert; a set of concepts is used to describe the root concept, and some relational attribute concepts are generated at the same time. The concepts (Domain Concepts) are described continuously by other concepts until they are either constant concepts or procedures. A network with semantic attribute concepts and relational attribute concepts (all of them are symbols, denoted by SAC and RAC, respectively) will be created. This is a layer of the integrated network of the expert system, called the domain layer or original layer.
(2) A special language is derived from the above process. Its primitives are SACs which are selected carefully in the domain layer, so that other experts in the domain are able to employ this language to construct an expert system. Similarly, a new layer is created once again when the expert describes the SACs. A new set of SACs is used in the process to describe old SACs until all the SACs are described by either procedures or primitives. A KBN is generated. It is composed of the domain layer and semantic attribute layers as mentioned above.
(3) The RACs generated in the above process are considered as the new root concepts. By repeating this process, a new KBN is created until all these RACs are described by primitives and procedures.
(4) By combining these KBNs rationally by means of a group of program models, called FORMWORK, which describe the connective types of the network, many LISP functions can be produced. This is the automatic programmer, called ETAP in this paper.

(5) The 0-ETN must be constructed so that AI experts are able to design a variety of control structures and the solution space. The 0-ETN has the same characteristics as the above network, so it is also transformed into LISP functions by ETAP.

The advantages of KORG are:

(1) An expert system is represented as a kind of semantic network with semantic attributes and relational attributes. The creation process is just based on the description of concepts. Therefore, an algorithm used to establish the network should easily be obtained. Experts can apply the algorithm to transform their knowledge into an ETN.
(2) AI experts can design control and knowledge structures by means of the above process.
(3) Owing to the adoption of the concept for showing attribute roles, i.e., there are RACs between SACs in every arc in this network, these roles can be obtained via describing SACs. It might avoid unnecessary confusion arising from the different knowledge backgrounds of the AI experts and the domain experts.
(4) The expert system program built with the automatic programmer neither loses its flexibility in reasoning nor reduces the capability for modification of knowledge. However, the program can be compiled.

1.1 Major Points

So far we have briefly discussed the motivation of KORG, its ideas for establishing an expert system, and its advantages.

The main techniques used in KORG are as follows:

(1) A framelike structure is used to represent knowledge. The rule model and the procedure model are considered as two particular categories of frame.
(2) The assumption that any concept in an expert system is described by a set of other concepts including constant concepts, is used in KORG. (In fact, this assumption is a basic method by which a human specifies a concept. In addition, a human uses other methods to describe the concept such as figures, graphs, and examples. However, figures, graphs, or examples must be transformed into a group of concepts, if they are to be encoded in a computer. This assumption is uniform with the idea of programming.) It is natural to transform knowledge into a kind of semantic network, with semantic attributes and relational attributes for the relationships between these concepts. The transformation is supported by an algorithm, called DESCRIBE in this paper.
(3) The various concepts in the network play different roles in an expert system. In order to clarify clearly the structure of the network, the ideas of "LAYER" and "KBN" are sketched out in the paper.
(4) The connective types of the network become the kernel of the ETAP in theory. This ensures that we design a transformation model to generate LISP programs from the network directly.

In order to realize our approach, three basic problems must be solved: (1) the method of knowledge specification; (2) the structure of the semantic network; (3) the method which transforms the network into a LISP program based on the connective types in the network. Three programs – ETL, ETN and ETAP – are the solutions of these basic problems.

ETL is a framelike structure in form. However, its basic sentences are rooted in MYCIN [25], that is,

$$(A \text{ of } O \text{ is } V) \tag{1.1}$$

It will be changed into a framelike structure. A is a SAC in ETN. O and V are object and value. ETL is composed of several categories of frame; PROCEDURE and RULE are two particular categories of these. Their advantages are: (1) the knowledge represented as RULE and PROCEDURE is constructed uniformly in the semantic network with other categories of framelike structures; (2) the reasoning mechanisms are obtained via the same algorithm (DESCRIBE). The source of the structure of ETN has two aspects: (1) the semantic-syntax pattern description in pattern recognition [32], and (2) the semantic network with multilayer, multiblock and bidirectional pointer proposed by us [36]. The main contribution of ETN is that the relational attribute is drawn into the traditional semantic network [33] together with the semantic attribute.

The relational attribute is represented as

$$r = R \ (a1 \ a2 \ ... \ ai) \tag{1.2}$$

where aj is the definition of a SAC "Aj". The relational attribute is drawn in the traditional semantic network. We obtain some useful features for the design of an expert system:

(1) When an expert describes a concept, RACs are automatically generated. These concepts may provide inspiration in the discussion between AI expert and domain expert. The concepts, in general, are metaknowledge which specifies the control structure and the control strategies within the system. So the knowledge in an expert system will come from the description of concepts.

(2) The relational attribute is described by experts, it is modified easily and avoids unnecessary confusion. So an expert might design a system which possesses quite flexible reasoning.

(3) A complete model of knowledge representation is obtained. And the expert system program might be automatically designed through the definitions of the connective types of the network.

We should point out that this network is an expansion of an AND/OR graph. An AND/OR graph is only a special form of this network. If the description of all RACs in the system is only "AND" and "OR", the network degenerates into AND/OR graph. The structural definition of this network will be discussed in Sect. 3.

ETAP is an automatic programmer based on the connective types in the ETN. It consists of two parts: (1) the connective types of the semantic network; (2) the selective rules for the program generator (see Sect. 6). According to the connective types, ETAP transforms the ETN into LISP functions.

We do not attempt to discuss how to acquire the experts' knowledge here, even though the approach implies such a function. This is a very difficult problem. For example, the problem of how to select SACs often depends on the tradition in which domain experts describe knowledge; it even relates to the history of the development of a certain domain. Sometimes this is only due to a designer's partiality for a special form. So, work such as the selection of SACs in a system has to be done by the expert personally in KORG.

MDM – a Medical Decision-Making model – is regarded as an example specifying the approach, including the selection of the set of SACs, the representation of RACs, as well as the descriptions in the RACs.

1.2 Outline

The next section will discuss the ETL. The network representing the experts' knowledge is described in Sect. 3. Sections 4 and 5 consider the medical decision-making model MDM as an example for the specification of KORG. Section 6 will deal with ETAP. A summary and discussion are given in Sect. 7.

2 A Language for Describing Knowledge

There are two ways of describing knowledge in AI, i.e., formal language and natural language. Using entirely natural language to describe knowledge still leads to many difficulties in application. Currently, most systems often adopt a trade-off restriction which is called natural-language-like. This enables users to employ a language which is like natural language in syntax and sentence pattern to describe knowledge; this might be a good method to employ before a real breakthrough in natural language processing is made. ETL is just such a language. It takes the form of "filling in blanks" to lead users to describe their knowledge.

ETL is a language based on a framelike structure. It has been provided with five categories of frame for the description of knowledge with the difference characteristic. We consider that RULE and PROCEDURE do not differ from the traditional framelike quantities in data type at all. Although it is more profound to separate knowledge representation in AI into that based on rules and that based on frames, in the application, the main reason for the separation is that two different program models are needed for the interpretation of RULE and FRAME. However, in KORG these are not different, because the interpretation of the structures of these knowledge representations depends completely on the selection and the definition of SACs as well as the definition of RACs in the network. Moreover, the network will be created by an algorithm which is used for dealing with ETL (see the next section). For example, a traditional frame can select SACs X1, X2, ..., and RULE might be IF, THEN, and ELSE. The advantages of the technique have been mentioned in Sect. 1.

In this section we will briefly discuss the principle and structure of ETL. A complete understanding of ETL, especially the syntax definition of the language, is unnecessary for an understanding of the approach given in this paper. Here, we only intend to give the simplest case to specify the principle of ETL. For stricter and more complete definitions, see [35].

2.1 The Basic Structure of ETL

In the medical consulting system MYCIN, a sentence pattern has been given as follows.

$$(A \text{ of } O \text{ is } V) \tag{2.1}$$

ETL accepts this sentence pattern as its basic sentence for describing knowledge. In (2.1), "O" is a specified concept given by the expert; "A" is a SAC; "V" is an ETL sentence for describing the concept "O" (see Sect. 2.2). Experts may employ a group of basic sentence patterns to describe their knowledge, for example, to specify the concept "C" as follows:

$$\begin{aligned}
&A1 \text{ of } C \text{ is } V1\\
&A1 \text{ of } C \text{ is } V2\\
&A2 \text{ of } C \text{ is } (K \text{ is } Q)
\end{aligned} \tag{2.2}$$

The formula is changed into a framelike model such as that of the language model of ETL. (2.2) is demonstrated in Fig.2.1.

```
C
  A1
       V1,  V2
  A2
       (K is Q)
```

Figure 2.1

The formal definition of the language model so far can be given as in (2.3):

```
<ETL-frame>::=<frame-category concept> <slot-block>
<slot-block>::=<SAC><ETL-sentence>
```
$$(2.3)$$

where frame-category is the class of frame of the described concept, which will be discussed in Sect. 2.3. ETL-sentence may be conceived of as a set of sentences which is permitted in ETL; they will be introduced in Sect. 2.2.

Although ETL is a language which takes a frame as an independent unit, there are structures embedded in it, for example,

(1) Several slot-blocks compose a frame
(2) Several frames make up a course
(3) There may be many courses in an expert system (see Sect. 2.3).

The advantage of this language model is that once the domain expert has provided a concept (the root concept), the construction of knowledge can be continuous, like the processes of describing and generating concepts.

2.2 The Sentence Pattern in ETL

If the permitted sentence "V" in Fig. 2.1 is restricted to only one concept, the capability of ETL to specify knowledge will be reduced greatly. Actually, "V" is an ETL sentence, which is a set of sentences with various concepts. For example, an ETL sentence can be used to express the following sentences.

(1) The sign of shock is SBP < 90 mmHg.
(2) The symptom of infection is fever.
(3) The non-trigger of fault depends on there not being diffraction at the right of ep.
(4) The data in the list "L" is employed to count the P-wave value of ECG.

To transform these sentences into ETL form, their ETL sentences are listed in Table 2.1

Table 2.1

sentence number	ETL sentence
(1)	SBP < 90mmHg
(2)	fever
(3)	there is no diffraction at right side of ep
(4)	a procedure with "L" as input and P-wave as output

ETL sentences have recently been considered as being made up of three types of sentence:

(1) Data sentences
(2) Algorithm sentences
(3) Declarative sentences

The formal definition of an ETL sentence is given in the formula (2.4).

```
<ETL-sentence> ::= <data-sentence>/
                   <algorithm-sentence>/
                   <declarative-sentence>              (2.4)
```

The data sentence is mainly used in the procedure frame as an ETL sentence of both INPUT and OUTPUT which are two semantic attributes. The types of data are logic, real, integer and list. For instance, "L" is a list and P is real in the fourth sentence of Table 2.1. Its formal definition in ETL is:

```
<data-sentence> ::= ((NAME var.)(TYPE var.))          (2.5)
```

The algorithm sentence is only applied to the SAC "ALG" in the procedure frame. This ETL sentence has to be written in the form of a LISP function. Its formal definition is:

```
<algorithm-sentence> ::= (LISP function)              (2.6)
```

The declarative sentence is the most complex type of sentence in the definition of ETL-sentence. Its formal definition is:

Table 2.2

(1)	K
(2)	K is B
(3)	there is K prep B
(4)	K > (< , =) D
(5)	K is (declarative sentence)

where "K" and "B" are concepts, "D" is a number (real or integer), and "prep" is a preposition. The third sentence in Table 2.2 has a stronger capability for knowledge representation. According to "prep", it can represent:

(1) finding all the elements where K is true in B;
(2) evaluating $\forall(x \in B)K(x)$;
(3) evaluating $\exists(x \in B)K(x)$.

These features will be realized by means of the definition of the RAC that shows the relationship between K and B. The fifth sentence represents an embedded structure in ETL, i.e., a declarative sentence can be represented as a framelike structure. The formal definition of the declarative sentence is written as:

```
<declarative-sentence> ::= (K)/
                           (K B)/
                           (K prep B)/
                           (K > [< , =] D)/
                           (FACET <declarative-sentence>)    (2.7)
```

where FACET is a key word in ETL. The sentences in (2.7) correspond to the sentences given in Table 2.2.

2.3 The Frame Categories in ETL

Five frame categories are provided by ETL as follows.

(1) COURSE frame
(2) CONCEPT frame
(3) RULE frame
(4) PROCEDURE frame
(5) SET frame

These frames are referred to as knowledge frames.

The COURSE frame is a partitioning mark in the semantic network. Its name is a root concept in ETN (see Sect. 3). In the process of establishing a BLOCK (see Sect. 3.2.1), COURSE frame collects all concepts that users present and that the system generates automatically. These concepts fill in the distinctive blanks of the COURSE frame so that the system can employ this information to construct the connection between concepts, to guide the user to describe SACs and RACs. It can also employ COMPATIBLE MECHANISM to set up a layer (see Sect. 3.3.2).

The CONCEPT frame is similar to a prototype in the structure. The process of building a CONCEPT frame is determined by the description (definition) of a concept, which may be the domain concept or another concept in an expert system. It is the most difficult task in KORG to decide which aspects should be defined for a concept. These aspects are abstracted as SACs. Once they are determined, the process of defining knowledge for other experts in the same domain will be simplified. It looks like the students in a school are doing exercises on filling in blanks. Therefore, if these SACs are selected and the generally recognized definitions of them can be given, a special purpose language will be generated for this domain. This is an important side-product of ETL.

The RULE and PROCEDURE frames used in an expert system can be considered as framelike structures. Their SACs are IF and THEN for the RULE frame, and INPUT, ALG and OUTPUT for the PROCEDURE frame. This means that an expert system based on RULE is conceived of as the system which brings only two SACs – IF and THEN. It is a special case of ETL.

Summing up, two special frames form a uniform structure describing the expert's knowledge with the aid of the other categories of frame. It is clear that there are some fixed logical relationships between them. In a traditional system, the interpretation of these relationships is an important part of the performance program. In KORG, the relationships between these semantic attributes are generally described by relational attributes (see Sects. 3 and 5).

In general, the RULE frame is applied to describe the control knowledge as well as the simple relation of cause and effect. The PROCEDURE frame can be considered as being the expansion of primitives. These two categories of frame are the most important structures in ETL.

The purpose of designing the SET frame is to solve the problem of the communication between particular BLOCKs in the network, such as between ECG in medicine and the medical consulting system. SET can be used when these particular BLOCKs have one of the following properties:

(1) In the process of integrated reasoning, there are several requisitions for a certain BLOCK, and each requisition needs only to employ a subset of the collected data in executing this BLOCK; or

(2) It is possible to pay some costs (even large or dangerous) for executing this BLOCK; such a BLOCK should execute only once in an integrated reasoning process. It will collect all data no matter what this requisition needs. (Of course, if this BLOCK is related to time [3], SET frame can also be used, but the user has to give a semantic attribute which indicates time in this frame.)

This particular BLOCK is similar to the TEST experts mentioned in [6]. Sometimes, these TEST experts can be considered as being a knowledge source (KS). A KS could use the SET frame to describe how KSs interact. In addition, the SET frame can use some semantic attributes defined by the user to describe special aspects, for example, the conditions used in this particular BLOCK. If the users want to employ the SET frame in cases without one of these properties, the reasoning efficiency will be reduced greatly, even though this use is rational in principle.

3 ETN: A Kind of Semantic Network

Like the model of knowledge representation, the semantic network has already been widely adopted in the expert system. The common characteristic of these networks is that semantic attributes are attached to an arc of the network. The relationship between arcs is defined by AND/OR or is implicitly described in a reasoning program. The strategies using knowledge often employ metaknowledge which depends on domain knowledge. This metaknowledge should come from the interplay between the AI expert and the domain expert. They have to carefully look for these relations in the domain knowledge, then describe them. This work has a higher price and also leads easily to confusion. It is important that we should find a method which generates and names these concepts automatically, to help the expert to describe them. This might lead to lower costs. This section will present a method which attaches the relational attributes in the traditional network to overcome the difficulty.

3.1 The Basic Principle of ETN

ETN is a network with semantic attributes and relational attributes. The nodes and arcs of ETN are labelled with concepts. Such a network is illustrated in Fig.3.1, where C, Vj, Aj and R are concepts $(0<j<i+1)$; C and Vj are called the domain concepts, the Aj are SACs and R is a RAC.

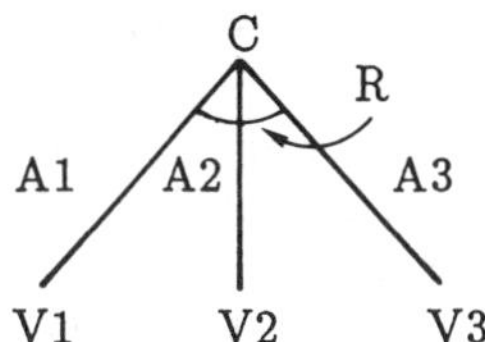

Figure 3.1

First, we employ the attribute-grammar to clarify the form of the network in theory; then a definition is given the structure of the ETN. The definition, in fact, implies an algorithm we describe below. This paper does not attempt to give a theoretical description, but rather a structural one, even though it is not difficult to give a theoretical definition for ETN. The structure should be the solution of how to create the production rules of the grammar.

Let "C" be a concept in an expert system. Its description, denoted "C", consists of a group of concepts. These concepts are distinguished into three categories, Domain Concept (DC), Semantic Attribute Concept (SAC), and Relational Attribute Concept (RAC), denoted Vj, Aj, and R, respectively. According to some rules, they are expressed as a structure (see Fig.3.1) and play different roles in the expert system.

A semantic attribute aj is a result defining a SAC which shows the relationship between two domain concepts:

$$aj = Aj(C\ Vj) \tag{3.1}$$

Similarly, a relational attribute r is a result defining a RAC which shows the relationship between semantic attributes:

$$r = R(a1\ a2\ ...\ ai) \tag{3.2}$$

ETN is a set of networks which are defined by (3.3):

$$B = (S\ Vn\ Vt\ P\ (aj\ r)) \tag{3.3}$$

where S is a root concept given by the expert or generated by the system, Vn is a set of nonterminal node concepts in B, Vt is a set of terminal node concepts, i.e., procedures or constant concepts, and P is a group of expanded production rules which should be observed in defining a concept. B is called BLOCK (see Sect.3.2.1). The expanded production rule is represented in (3.4),

$$C \xrightarrow{\ r = R(a1, ..., ai)\ } V1, V2, ..., Vi \tag{3.4}$$

where aj is Vj's semantic attribute $(0 < j < i+1)$.

An interesting fact is that the network will degenerate into the traditional "AND/OR" graph if every r in the network is defined by AND or OR only.

The nodes in the network are concepts. Their relations are described by SACs and RACs which are also concepts. This implies that attribute concepts can be defined by (3.3), as long as Aj in (3.1) and R in (3.2) become root concepts in (3.3), which is an interesting and useful idea.

When an expert wants to use ETL to define knowledge, s/he has to explicitly specify how the concept "C" is defined by "Vj" and "Aj"; but "R" is a implicit concept, and the expert only realizes that such a concept exists in the growing network.

We can design an algorithm to establish the network. It is important that the algorithm should automatically collect and name these RACs. While an expert defines these RACs, the system will provide some information as guidance cue, so that the expert defines them. This is one of the important characteristics of ETN.

According to the above discussion, there are three categories of concept – DC, SAC, and RAC – in ETN. They play different roles in an expert system. Although the attribute concepts are the labels and the relations in the network, they are considered as being concepts. If they become the root concepts, some independent BLOCKs are then able to be created via the algorithm. This is another important characteristic of ETN. However, there are relationships between these independent networks called the connective types of the network.

In order to specify the structure of the semantic network clearly, we define "LAYER" and "KBN" (Knowledge Bank Network), and attempt to employ them to get the definition of ETN on the structure.

Definition 3.1 Node Concept (NC). The label of a node in the network is called Node Concept.

Definition 3.2 LAYER. A layer is a semantic network with SACs and RACs. It is created in the following process. The process starts from the root concepts (a set of NCs). Only NCs are described by other NCs and SACs according to the assumption in Sect. 1. The process is teminated when all NCs become the constant concepts the expert considers. If the root concepts are given by either the domain expert or RACs the created layer is called the original layer. And if the root concepts are given by the domain expert only, it is then called the domain layer.

Definition 3.3 KBN. A KBN consists of a set of layers. It is created in the following process. The process starts from the original layer, denoted L0. Let Lj be the jth layer in KBN. Sj is a set of SACs which is collected in describing Lj. All elements of Sj serve as the root concepts. The process in Definition 3.2 is applied to construct a new layer Lj+1 and to generate a new set of SACs, Sj+1. The process is terminated when all elements in Si ($0<j<i$) become primitives or procedures. If the original layer in the KBN is the domain layer, the KBN is called the original KBN.

Definition 3.4 ETN. An ETN is a semantic network. The process which constructs ETN is the following. The process starts from the original KBN, denoted K0. Let Kj be the jth KBN in ETN and Rj a set of RACs generated automatically in defining Kj. All elements of Rj serve as the root concepts. The process in Definition 3.3 is applied to construct a new KBNj+1 and to generate a new set of RACs Rj+1. The process is terminated when all elements of Ri ($j<i$) become primitives or procedures.

According to the definitions, an ETN can be drawn as in Fig.3.2.

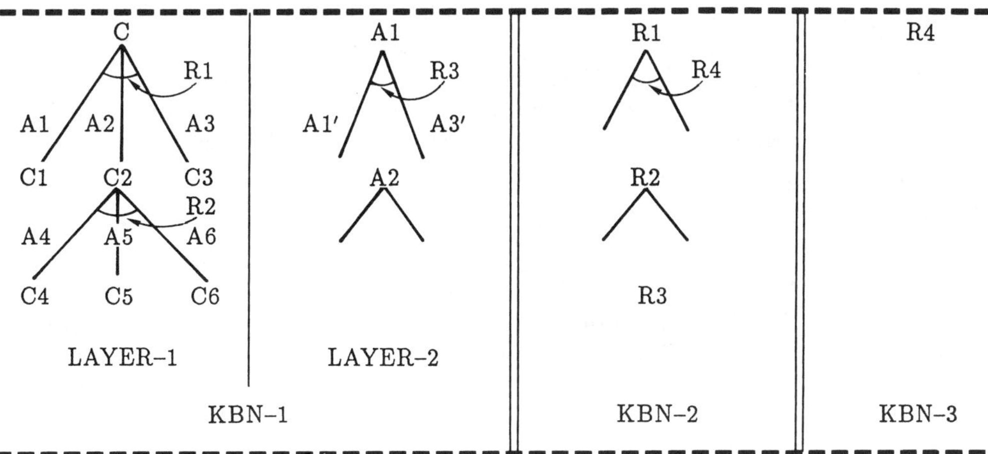

Figure 3.2

There are three connective types in ETN:

(1) ARC connection, C and C1 (see Fig.3.2);
(2) MAPPING connection, A1 in LAYER-1 and A1 as the root concept in LAYER-2;
(3) COMBINATION connection, R1 in KBN-1 and R1 as the root concept in KBN-2.

Besides the above three connective types in KORG (N.B., not in ETN), there is a fourth type we must consider – the 0-ETN connective type. The 0-ETN connective type says: sometimes, an expert hopes to construct several ETN for describing certain parts of knowledge independently, such as the solution space and control structure, etc. so that these structures might become independent models that other users can employ. The 0-ETN connection provides this convenience.

All of these connective types in KORG will be the basic knowledge of the automatic programmer (ETAP). ETAP utilizes them to transform the above semantic network into a executable program. (Recently, we have designed a generator in which the target language is LISP.)

3.2 The Structure of ETN in Practice

A good expert system is often the collection of knowledge of several experts. This knowledge, theoretically, can be constructed in a layer, but this is not a good way of doing things. It is like demanding that we edit a textbook without any chapters; nobody would think that this was an acceptable task. In addition, it is well known that "A single knowledge source is too weak" [29].

It is necessary to provide a function establishing a multiknowledge source for a tool system. KORG has provided such a function – BLOCK – to ensure that experts can independently describe their knowledge. Then COMPATIBLE MECHANISM may put together these BLOCKs to form an ETN. BLOCK is one of the features of the ETN structure. The bidirectional pointer is another technical feature of ETN. The purpose of such a pointer is based on "It does not pay to employ a single reasoning model in an expert system". Many expert systems , such as SU/P, create two reasoning models – model (event) driven and data driven – denoted by CALL and DRIVEN in KORG.

3.2.1 BLOCK

BLOCK is the most basic unit in ETN. Its structure is defined by (3.3) (see Sect.3.1). On the other hand, BLOCK has only a root concept at the beginning. It is different from LAYER. The relations between BLOCK and LAYER should observe the following rules:

(1) There is at least one BLOCK in a LAYER;
(2) A BLOCK cannot cross two LAYERs;
(3) A BLOCK can be shared by two LAYERs.

So, each SAC and RAC will be the root concept in a BLOCK.

In ETN, each BLOCK has to bring with it a COURSE frame. These BLOCKs can be described independently by different experts, and connected by the connective types of ETN.

3.2.2 The Bidirectional Pointer [16]

In order to support a variety of reasoning processes, KORG has provided a bidirectional pointer in ETN. If these pointers are used directly in the domain layer, KORG will automatically construct two kinds of reasoning chaining – backchaining and forwardchaining. If they are used in another layer, the expert system will obtain a very complex reasoning structure. Of course, it must be connected with some global structure for reasoning.

According to the assumption that "A concept is described by another concept", it is natural to set up the Back-Chaining-Pointer (BCP). However, the process of creating a BLOCK will set up a Forward-Chaining-Pointer (FCP). FCP is distinguished into two types:

(1) UP: If a DC is true, UP will point out the fired hypotheses;
(2) F-UP: If a hypothesis is considered, F-UP will first evaluate the value of the fact in the light of the hypothesis corresponding to it.

Therefore, UP is executed after a concept is proved, and F-UP is executed before it is proved.

3.2.3 The Middle Nodes

Sometimes, an attribute may have several different values associated with different relationships. For this reason, KORG has provided the middle nodes to describe multivalues and the relationships between elements in them. These middle nodes will automatically be generated by the DESCRIBE algorithm, as long as the expert defines the multivalue by an ETL sentence. The middle nodes include ?–#OR and ?–#AND. One should note:

(1) The middle node has the same meaning as the original semantic attribute.
(2) The relational attribute represents not only AND/OR, but also other knowledge, such as the selected strategy.
(3) There are no FCPs in the middle nodes.

Some advantages of the middle nodes are that the expert can describe more complex and more complete relationships by defining these RACs.

3.3 DESCRIBE – An Algorithm

An algorithm can be designed easily, according to the assumption that "A concept is described by other concepts". However, we have to consider the data types of nodes in ETN for matching. So far, the node type has been drawn up as follows:

(1) Knowledge type: all concepts which have already been described
(2) Instance type: all "Temporal Constant Concepts"*
(3) Middle-node type : all middle node frames

DESCRIBE is an algorithm for creating a LAYER. If there is only a root concept at the beginning, DESCRIBE becomes the algorithm which creates a BLOCK. By the definition of ETN on the structure of the ETN network, the layer is the most basic unit. So, we will only present this algorithm.

---

* Whether a concept needs to be defined depends on the requirements of the expert system. For example, if "fever" does not need to be defined in a system, then "fever" is a "Temporal Constant Concept". But if "fever" is defined as "the temperature is greater than 38°C" by another expert, "fever" is not a constant.

3.3.1 Temporal Constant Concept (TCC)

We have been using the word "constant" in the definition of ETN. In fact, it is only a symbol which is not defined temporally while the network is growing. An expert can describe it if the system requires. The "constant" is called Temporal Constant Concept (TCC).

TCC is constructed as the form which is uniform with knowledge type in KORG. But like the constant, we have to distinguish TCCs into data types so that some of them can be defined via DESCRIBE and be matched while they are used. TCCs is called Instance in ETN. ETN has provided four types of instances:

(1) L-INSTANCE gives a logical value (YES, NO, NONE)
(2) S-INSTANCE consists of two variables, one a logical value, the other a list
(3) D-INSTANCE gives a real or integer
(4) LIST-INSTANCE gives a list

S-INSTANCE and LIST-INSTANCE specify the fact that the expert can employ a list to describe a concept, such as a multivalue.

3.3.2 Compatible Mechanism

"Compatible" is an important mechanism in DESCRIBE. Its tasks are concerned with two roles: (1) to ensure that the network can be grown in the process of describing TCC; (2) to ensure there exists one and only one concept with the same name in the network. Compatible mechanism consists of a group of rules which are divided into two types, according to the above roles; they are called Unique Rule and Substitution Rule, respectively. Some of the rules are shown in Table 3.1.

Table 3.1

RULE NO.	NEW NODE TYPE	OLD NODE TYPE	TYPE OF RULE
1.	CONCEPT	L-INSTANCE	SUBSTITUTION
2.	CONCEPT	S-INSTANCE	SUBSTITUTION
10.	L-INSTANCE	L-INSTANCE	UNIQUE
11.	L-INSTANCE	CONCEPT	SUBSTITUTION
12.	D-INSTANCE	D-INSTANCE	UNIQUE

The first rule in the table can be read as: If there is a CONCEPT, whose name is "C" (CONCEPT is a type of node) in ETN, then the use of a new TCC named "C" will not create a new instance node. Only the FCP in the old node will be modified. This is a substitution rule. The tenth rule can be read as: If there is a node "C", whose type is L-INSTANCE, then a new TCC named "C" will not create a new instance, and only FCP in the old node is modified.

The Compatible Mechanism ensures that unnecessary redundance in the network is decreased and checks some of the contradictions in time.

3.3.3 DESCRIBE

"DESCRIBE" is the most basic algorithm for establishing ETN. This algorithm will accomplish the following tasks:

(1) Maintaining the growth of the network by the compatible mechanism;
(2) Collecting all SACs and RACs.

Table 3.2

```
 1.  (defun DESCRIBE (CONCEPT-LIST)
 2.     (cond ( (null CONCEPT-LIST)
 3.              (PUT-KNOWLEDGE-IN-COURSE)
 4.              (PUT-TCC-IN-COURSE)
 5.              (PUT-SAC-IN-COURSE)
 6.              (PUT-RAC-IN-COURSE)  )
 7.            (t  (COMPATIBLE  (car CONCEPT-LIST))
 8.                (cond ( (IS-CC  (car CONCEPT-LIST))
 9.                         (DESCRIBE  (cdr  CONCEPT-LIST))  )
10.                       (t  (DEFINE-TCC  (car CONCEPT-LIST))
11.                           (ADD-PRODUCED-TCC-TO  CONCEPT-LIST)
12.                           (COLLECT-SAC)
13.                           (NAME-RAC)
14.                           (DESCRIBE  (cdr  CONCEPT-LIST))
15.                     ) )
16.        ) )
17.  )
```

The algorithm is constructed as a recursive model in Table 3.2, where

(1) COMPATIBLE (step 7) uses the rules (see Table 3.1) to maintain the network.
(2) IS-CC (step 8) is a predication which decides whether the first element in CONCEPT-LIST needs to be defined. It is a query-answer program.
(3) DEFINE-TCC (step 10) is a function which guides the user in defining a concept with other concepts.
(4) COLLECT-SAC (step 12) is a function which collects all SACs employed in defining a TCC.
(5) NAME-RAC (step 13) is a function. It will automatically name all RACs which are generated in growing the network.

The algorithm is a recursive program. It will terminate when CONCEPT-LIST is null.

The algorithm has provided a way of growing a layer, but SACs and RACs are only collected. They will become root concepts which apply this algorithm to generate other layers. Clearly, it is easy to design a program to offer information which helps the user to define RACs and SACs.

If there is only a concept in the CONCEPT-LIST at the beginning, the algorithm will construct a BLOCK. This is a very important fact, because a layer consists of a group of BLOCKs.

4 The Specification on KORG. Part 1

In the introduction, we pointed out that the description of domain concepts depends on the selection for SACs. How to automatically select SACs is an important and complex problem which is not solved thoroughly in theory.

In this section, a medical application is chosen as an example to show how the problem described above is solved. KORG can transform the describing knowledge into a selection of SACs. For domain experts, looking for a set of SACs to define domain concepts is simpler than defining directly their knowledge according to an AI model, because SACs are only concerned with several aspects that need to be specified in defining domain concepts, which is not too difficult for a first-rate expert. However, automatic selection by learning is not easy. Once SACs have been determined, a special purpose language can be derived from ETL, which will bring us some benefits for establishing subsystems in this domain. So far, the experts in this domain can construct their knowledge in the same way as children do exercises on filling in blanks, by means of this special purpose language. The other tasks of this section are concerned with some skills that apply KORG to building an expert system; they have appeared in the medical consulting system SHOCK [37].

4.1 Medical Consulting System

Medical consultation is a very complex, and typical, problem in AI. In comparison with other domains, the medical domain possesses the advantage that a new principle of AI can be easily examined. This might be the reason why the medical consulting domain has been taken notice of by researchers in the field of AI. When we worked on KORG, we also first selected the medical consulting domain as an example, and then expanded to other domains, such as pattern recognition for Chinese characters, etc.

In general, the set of knowledge of a medical consulting system is so large that we have to look for an efficient approach to dealing with such a vast amount of knowledge. For example, PIP is a consulting system for nephrotic syndrome, including about 60 frames [24], and MYCIN is for diseases due to infection by bacilli; it consists of 200 rules [25]. We made the system SHOCK, which is for shock syndrome and a subset of its causes of disease has about 100 frames. So we need a system which should include as much knowledge as possible and whose hardware costs are as low as possible. This is a very important problem in China.

There is no physician who can be called a first-rate expert for the integrated problems in the medical world. What we often do in diagnosing a complex case is to invite several experts with different skills for consultation. Therefore, we have to consider the problem of how to collect knowledge from different physicians, who are first-rate experts in their fields, i.e., we need a tool to take to these experts to define their respective systems, and then these systems can be rationally assembled to form a large system, so that the consulting system is large enough to include the knowledge of several medical experts.

The process of consultation in one complex case, needs, in general, only part of the integrated medical knowledge, if the system is large enough. The intersection of knowledge that is used in the consulting process for several complex cases is small. So we have to have some efficient methods for getting knowledge and methods for interacting between these subsystems.

These problems stem from the fact that the amount of knowledge is too much for a practical expert system. This means that we have to solve the problem of the bottleneck in transforming knowledge into computer code and in search efficiency. The BLOCK in ETN supports experts in defining their subsystem independently. The bidirectional pointer can be applied to raise the efficiency of the search.

The description of concepts is simple in the medical consulting domain. The descriptions of disease and manifestations, in general, adopt concepts or numbers. Of course, some of the special tests need to employ graphics or figures (which is not considered in this paper). The difficulty in making a medical system is not the description of domain knowledge, but the principle of reasoning.

4.2 The Selection of SACs and Their Definition

Selecting SACs in a certain domain is the first task in making an expert system in KORG. The selection depends on the tradition of describing this domain. Generally, we could not find a simple method to select SACs for all domains automatically. Although learning appeals strongly to us, it is a very complex method for the work. Fortunately, experts are able to find out these concepts. If they meet the difficulties, they can adopt a method such as the UNIT system [28], which is also supported by ETL, to define their knowledge.

One of the purposes of selecting these concepts is to create a special purpose language so that other experts can apply it to define subsystems. These concepts are not bound by the particular concept or by the special subsystem. There is no difficulty in the selection of SACs in the medical domain. When we open any medical textbook, it is found that the descriptions of diseases are almost the same for diagnosis, i.e., any disease is described by several fixed aspects, such as sign, symptom, cause, complication, etc. These are just concepts generally recognized by the medical world in the description of disease. These concepts should be selected as SACs in the medical consulting domain.

Our Medical Decision-Making Model, MDM, has selected, in addition to these SACs, some concepts that represent the control strategies, such as the condition of considering a hypothesis called trigger and the condition of refusing a hypothesis called non-trigger. We list here the semantic attributes in MDM:

(1) SIGN and SYMPTOM: The manifestations of the disease "D" that should be observed in diagnosis. For example, the sign of shock is (SBP < 90mmHg).
(2) TEST: The evidence necessary that should be obtained from the test in the diagnosis, such as ECG, X-ray.
(3) CAUSE and INDUCED: The cause of disease "D" and disease induced by "D", respectively. For example, the disease induced by infection is sepsis.
(4) COMPLICATION and COMPLICATED: The complications of disease "D" and diseases complicated by "D", respectively.
(5) RECOMMEND-TREAT: The recommended treatment for "D".
(6) DIFFERENCE-DIAGNOSIS: To apply rule-out to diagnose "D".
(7) TRIGGER and NON-TRIGGER: The conditions considering "D" and the conditions refusing "D". For example, the male sex is non-trigger of post-labor hemorrhage.
(8) SUBKIND: To classify for "D". For example, shock can be classified as cardiogenic shock, hypovolemic shock, etc. Some books call it AKO.

The semantic attribute should be defined in two aspects: (1) the reasoning model (MDL): there are two possible models in MDM, CALL and DRIVEN. (2) The operation (OP), for example, the counting operation. This results in a form for defining semantic attribute concepts shown in Table 4.1, where MDL has two possible aspects; CALL is used to count semantic attributes, and then return a result as Ai's value. DRIVEN does not need to return a result as its value, because this class of semantic attribute is not related to proving "D" at all. On the contrary, if "D" is proved to be true, then new tasks will be generated. Two such concepts are considered as primitives in MDM. Obviously, it is necessary to design two such reasoning models in an efficient expert system. DRIVEN is adopted in "from fact to hypothesis", and CALL is applied to prove a hypothesis. OP expresses the counting forms of these semantic attributes possible. MDM abstracts five classes of forms (Table 4.2).

Table 4.1

```
(CONCEPT Ai)
(        MDL)
   ------
(        OP)
   ------
(FIN)
```

Table 4.2

(1)	MUST-NOT-HAVE	MUST-NOT-HAVE → A
(2)	MUST-HAVE	MUST-HAVE → A
(3)	COUNT	UNCERTAINTY COUNT
(4)	LOGIC	LOGICAL OPERATION
(5)	EVENT	GENERATING NEW TASK

According to the definition of the middle node in ETN, some new SACs can be automatically derived from SACs. For example, TRIGGER can generate TRIGGER-#ORi and TRIGGER-#ANDj (i,j>0). Figure 4.1 is a graph of ETN transformed by shock-frame. N0, N1, and N2 are the middle nodes.

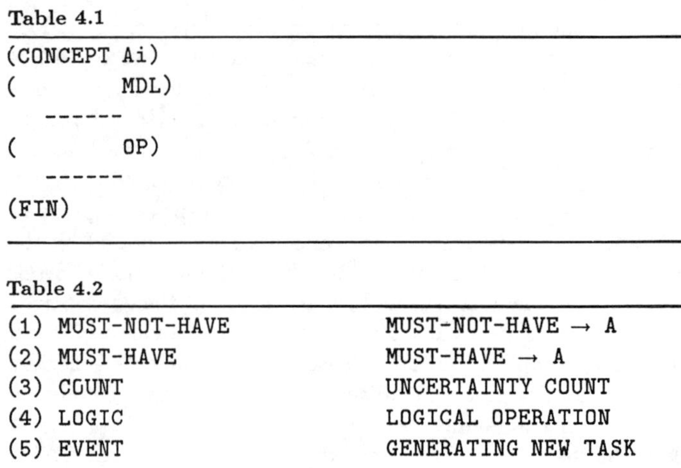

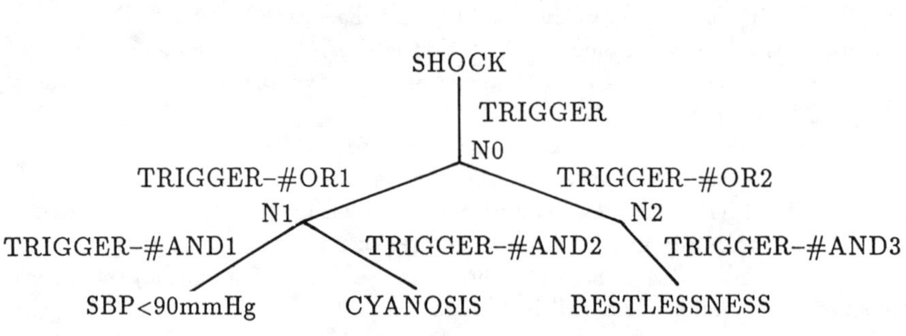

Figure 4.1

In addition to the features mentioned in Sect. 3, these middle nodes give a good method for solving universal quantifiers and existential quantifiers, i.e., they can be described in relational attributes (see Sect. 5). G.G.Hendrix has worked on this problem, by use of a partitioning network [15]. Our contribution is to regard the relational attributes as a factor which represents network structure, and can be added to a set of nodes in the network. Certainly it has the ability to represent more complex knowledge. The advantage is that the knowledge can be generated in the process of defining RACs (note, defining concept!). The problem of how to define RACs is left to the next section.

Table 4.3

(CONCEPT TRIGGER)	(CONCEPT TRIGGER-#OR)	(CONCEPT-TRIGGER-#AND)
(CALL)	(CALL)	(CALL)
(NO)	(Ni)	(-Kj)
(END)	(END)	(END)
(MUST-HAVE)	(MUST-HAVE)	(MUST-HAVE)
(NO)	(Ni)	(-Kj)
(END)	(END)	(END)
(FIN)	(FIN)	(FIN)

Table 4.3 shows the definitions of TRIGGER and some concepts derived from TRIGGER according to Fig. 4.1. In the table $0<i<3$, $0<j<4$, k1 is (SBP<90mmHg), K2 is cyanosis, and K3 is restlessness in Fig. 4.1.

Note: (1) The definitions of any SAC and the concepts derived from SAC have the same MDL and the same OP. (2) These definitions come from MDM. Of course, we can give other definition models, but we will not discuss them here in detail (see [34] and [37]). The same method can be applied to define other SACs. If the reasoning model is DRIVEN, it is designed as a structure in MDM which interacts with 0-ETN. This will be discussed in the next section.

4.3 MDML: A Special Purpose Language for a Medical Consulting System [34]

Although the relational attributes have not been introduced in detail until now, this will not hinder us in describing "a special purpose language for establishing a medical consulting system". This work has involved the medical consulting domain only, but the idea, i.e., deriving a special purpose language from a mother language, may be applied to other domains, as long as the domain experts can select a set of SACs. This is an important side-product of KORG.

The idea of deriving a special purpose language was first shown in RLL [13] for AI. Our contribution is that the method of deriving such a special purpose language is based on the selection of SACs. Its advantage is that the selecting SACs are concerned with describing domain concepts, and the description of these SACs may produce a new special purpose language such as MDL and OP presented in Sect. 4.2.

Since the selection of SACs and their definition in MDM have been discussed in Sect. 4.2 in detail and the mother language ETL has also been described in Sect. 2, it is unnecessary to explain the structure and the meaning of this language. Here, we give only the formal syntax for the language MDML. The definition of MDML syntax is illustrated in Table 4.4.

Table 4.4

```
   <COURSE>  ::= <name>{<set1><ETL-sentence>}n
  <CONCEPT>  ::= <name>{<set1><ETL-sentence>}k
     <RULE>  ::= (see Sect. 2)
<PROCEDURE>  ::= (see Sect. 2)
      <SET>  ::= <name>{<set2><ETL-sentence>}m
     <set1>  ::= (See Sect. 4.2)
     <set2>  ::= RISK/SUBEXPERT/
```

In MDM, some of the tests can be defined by SET frame. These SET frames have two SACs – RISK and SUBEXPERT. The former is the condition that the SUBEXPERT refuses to take the test, e.g., if a disease case satisfies the conditions of RISK, the test will be refused for the patient's safety; otherwise the system will execute this SUBEXPERT (note: we have described a rule on the relationship between semantic attributes in the SET frame). The latter is the name of a certain test. All data collected by this test will be put together in a special semantic attribute – DOWN.

4.4 SHOCK: A Medical Consulting System*

SHOCK is a medical consulting system defined by means of MDML. Its purpose is to be consulted for shock syndrome and its causes. It is easy to diagnose shock syndrome, but sometimes it is not significant for the treatment of the complex case. So physicians must diagnose its causes. If the set of causes is large and complex, it is not easy to draw the correct conclusions. The SHOCK system includes only a part of this large set of causes. Here, we do not discuss this system in detail, because our purpose is to introduce the method of how to apply the conclusions drawn in Sects. 4.2 and 4.3 to make a practical expert system.

According to the pathophysiologic process, shock can be separated into cardiogenic, hypovolemic, anaphylactic and traumatic shock. This can be represented by the semantic attribute SUBKIND as follows:

```
(SUBKIND)
(cardiogenic-shock)
(hypovolemic-shock)
(anaphylactic-shock)
(traumatic-shock)
(END)
```

Clearly, they are connected with different causes. For example, causes of hypovolemic shock may be infection, hemorrhage, etc. A series of BLOCKs can be created by defining these causes (concepts). Of course, shock is also a BLOCK.

But the causes of infection could be urinary infection, respiratory infection, etc., and they may be just conceived of as some new BLOCK. Table 4.5 is the definition of infection. It can be found from this table that experts describe their knowledge by MDML as if they were doing exercises on filling in blanks.

---

* This system was designed by J.C. Cheng, Physician-in-Chief of Internal Medicine, Beijing 2nd Municipal Hospital, China.

Table 4.5

```
(COURSE infection)
(SIGN)
(temperature > 38°C)
(infection-present)
(WBC > 10000/cumm)
(END)
(SUBKIND)
(biliary-infection)
(urinary-infection)
(respiratory-infection)
    ------
(END)
(INCLUDE)
(peritonitis)
(sepsis)
(END)
    ------
(FIN)
```

In the KORG application, how to divide the domain knowledge into BLOCKs is a skilled problem. There is a variety of complex relationships in the medical consulting domain; how to create BLOCKs will directly relate to the efficiency in reasoning and to the cost which should be paid for the hardware. For example, the cause of hemorrhage may be "gynecologic hemorrhage", but this may only be a part of "gynecologic condition". If "hemorrhage" and "gynecologic condition" become two BLOCKs, their intersection is non-empty. This implies that there are the following methods of solving this problem: either the non-empty set constructs an independent BLOCK, or the system allows the user to employ a part of any BLOCK. The former will simplify the method of maintaining BLOCK, except for increasing the number. The latter is just the opposite of the former. SHOCK adopts the former. The reasons are: (1) for ETN, increasing the number of BLOCKs does not bring with it any difficulties in representing knowledge and dealing with knowledge; (2) ETN allows the network to be constructed as an embedded structure; (3) according to the principle of ETN, it does not raise the cost of hardware and does not reduce the efficiency in reasoning, but it omits the program of maintaining BLOCK. We feel that the former is more rational. Although domain experts have to construct these BLOCKs by hand, we can design a program to accomplish this task.

5 The Specification on KORG.   Part 2

We have specified the process that applies KORG to a concrete domain, and that produces the domain KBN of MDM in Sect. 4. It has already been pointed out that the basic principle is suitable to describe RACs which are produced in defining the domain KBN. We attempt to specify how to define RACs in this section. In order to discuss the roles of relational attributes in an expert system, we might conceive two cases which do not contain the relational attributes in an expert system.

First, an expert system could consist of all the knowledge which is provided in Sect. 4. After an automatic programmer has transformed this knowledge into LISP functions, the system will be established. Because the reasoning is a fixed sequence, it neither cuts an impossible path nor does it select the best path of reasoning. The efficiency of reasoning will be low.

Second, if the relational attributes are not introduced in the network, the knowledge of the efficiency of the reasoning has to be implicitly contained in a performance program; the user cannot define any control structure or any control knowledge.

According to the definition of ETN, the relational attributes come from the process of defining concepts which can be automatically produced in establishing the domain KBN. Experts can be guided to define their knowledge. The KBNs which are produced in defining these RACs will be combined by an automatic programmer with the domain KBN to form an integrated system.

Another subject covered in this section is the problem of the 0-ETN structures. For an expert system, the solution space is an indispensable feature for the explanation, but the solution space should be located in the top level of an expert system. So the semantic attribute and relational attribute cannot generate the concepts related to it. The solution space has the property of a global variable for the integrated system. Based on it, a system needs to independently define a structure called 0-ETN in the top level of an expert system. The other structures which relate to the global variable, such as BLACKBOARD [17] and AGENDA [8,18], can define in terms of 0-ETN. It is interesting that 0-ETN satisfies the definition of ETN in the structure of the network.

5.1 The Description of Relational Attribute Concepts

We will use MDM to specify the definition of RACs that are produced in defining the domain KBN of MDM.

The knowledge which is described by relational attributes plays the role of control reasoning in an expert system. This knowledge will decide the selection of the reasoning path. The control knowledge, in general, is very complex. It can be separated into two cases: (1) the reasoning has a fixed sequence that is determined by experts in advance; (2) the selection of the path that is decided by the particular reasoning situation. This leads to two models of the description. The former adopts the rule frame, the latter adopts the concept frame. If the concept frame is adopted, it is certain to produce SACs and RACs. According to the definition of ETN, these concepts will generate a new layer and a new KBN, respectively.

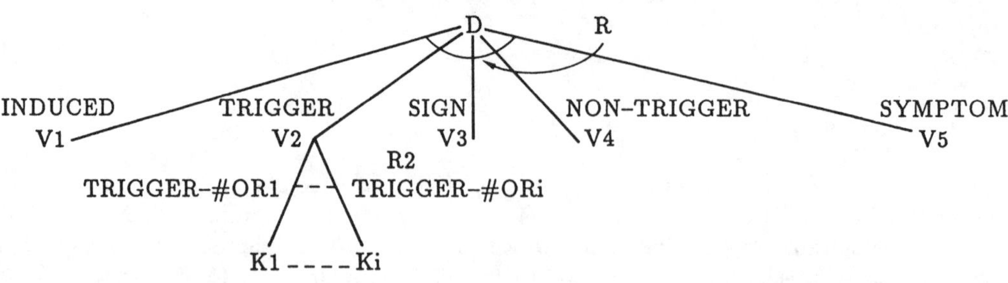

Figure 5.1

Because the DRIVEN model in reasoning is involved in 0-ETN, it will be illustrated in Sect. 5.2. In this part, we attempt to specify the description of the RACs in the "CALL" model of reasoning. Figure 5.1 is part of an ETN in MDM. Five arcs starting from node concept "D" are labelled, including TRIGGER, NON-TRIGGER, SIGN, SYMPTOM and INDUCED. The relational attribute concept, R1, is defined by experts as follows.

```
(1) IF:   NON-TRIGGER
    THEN:   TRIGGER
(2) IF:   TRIGGER
    THEN:   SIGN
(3) IF:   SIGN
    THEN:   INDUCED
```
$$(5.1)$$

While D is being executed, the group of rules indicates the conditions that execute semantic attributes in D. For example, if NON-TRIGGER is true, the TRIGGER will be executed, otherwise the value of NIL is returned to D.

Formula (5.1) shows the control knowledge with fixed sequence control knowledge. There is another case in an expert system. For example, we cannot determine the sequence of sign and symptom beforehand. This sequence depends on the reasoning situation.

In order to represent these relationships, we modify (2) and (3) in (5.1) to the following:

```
(2') IF:   TRIGGER
     THEN:   MANIFESTATION
(3') MANIFESTATION

        | eval1
        |     SYMPTOM
        | eval2
        |     SIGN
(4') IF:   MANIFESTATION
     THEN:   INCLUDE
```
$$(5.2)$$

Therefore, the relationship between SYMPTOM and SIGN is described by the definitions of SACs eval1 and eval2, and their relational attributes, denoted R'. Defining eval1 and eval2 leads to a new layer; defining R' produces a new KBN.

The middle nodes in ETN will derive some new SACs from old SACs, such as TRIGGER–#ORj in Fig.5.1. A new RAC R2 will describe the control knowledge more precisely.

We pointed out in Sect. 2 that ETL-sentence is a set of sentences. The result of evaluating semantic attributes should satisfy some formula, for example, TRIGGER.

$$\text{trigger} = \forall\, x(\text{MUST-HAVE}\,(x)) \tag{5.3}$$

This specifies that TRIGGER is equal to the value of evaluating MUST-HAVE(x) for all of x, where x is a sentence of ETL-sentence in TRIGGER.

According to the definition of the middle node, (5.3) can be separated into two parts:

$$\text{trigger-\#orj} = \text{MUST-HAVE}\,(Kj) \tag{5.4}$$
$$\text{trigger} = \text{MUST-HAVE}\,(M1) \tag{5.5}$$
$$\text{r2} = R2\,(\text{trigger-\#or1} - \text{trigger-\#ori}) \tag{5.6}$$

The formulas (5.4) and (5.5) are applied to define the SACs TRIGGER and TRIGGER-#ORj (1<j<=i) and formula (5.6) is applied to describe the RAC R2.

The RACs can be described by RULE frame, CONCEPT frame and PROCEDURE frame so that experts can represent two cases as mentioned above. R3 is a RAC which is defined by PROCEDURE; the procedure is described in formula (5.7).

```
                P1
   ┌─────────────────────────────
   │  INPUT
   │       SIGN-#ORj   (1<=j<=i)
   │  ALG
   │       COUNT
   │  OUTPUT
   │       M2
```
$$\tag{5.7}$$

This formula defines the method to evaluate M2 from SIGN–ORj, which is a terminal node in this KBN. If we hope that R3 has the capability of selecting SIGN–#ORj, which will first be executed by means of the reasoning situation, R3 has to contain the knowledge which describes the capability, such as that given in (5.8).

```
   IF:  SIGN-#ORj > 60
   THEN:  P1 (j)
```
$$\tag{5.8}$$

The rule can be considered as framelike in Sect.2. The relationship between IF and THEN (SACs) in RULE frame is just that of a relational attribute. It can be directly represented as (cond ((IF A)(THEN b))), i.e., it is regarded as a primitive. KORG will describe it in ETAP by means of FORMWORK.

Through introducing the relational attributes we obtain two advantages: (1) Knowledge can be separated into units, which experts can independently define. The relationships between this knowledge can be transformed into the description of combinative connections in ETN. (2) Experts are enabled to describe complex problems by the formal method with only simple syntax.

5.2 The Description of Control Structure and 0-ETN

The control structure is an indispensable part in any expert system (although some expert systems take the structure in the performance program implicitly). The typical structure of these is OPEN list [23], which can be considered as a queue list or a stack list. If this is maintained by the different methods, it will derive distinctive search models. Now the more complex structures, such as BLACKBOARD and AGENDA, have already been developed, and their principles are based on OPEN list. These lists and their maintaining programs are independent of the knowledge hierarchy; they are the global variables. The purpose of the control structure is to build a task schedule structure for reasoning. The principle of the schedule is the knowledge of the control structure for the search.

How can we describe the control structures in KORG? Before answering the question, we first specify the SAC "UP", which expresses the forward-chaining-pointer (FCP) from which we give the DRIVEN model.

For efficiency, the strategies of the DRIVEN model are different from those of the CALL model. The CALL model hopes to prove that a node is false, i.e., to cut a reasoning path as soon as possible, but DRIVEN hopes that it can find the shortest path, which reaches the goal quickly. Obviously, the latter is more difficult than the former.

UP and F-UP are related to the DRIVEN reasoning model. Although they indicate the FCPs that reduce the search for a knowledge base, a loop is produced in the ETN. This is a weak method. In order to make sure that either the strategies in the DRIVEN model are described or a network that has no loop is produced, we have to give an independent structure. For example, Fig.5.2 is a network to be established by the algorithm DESCRIBE.

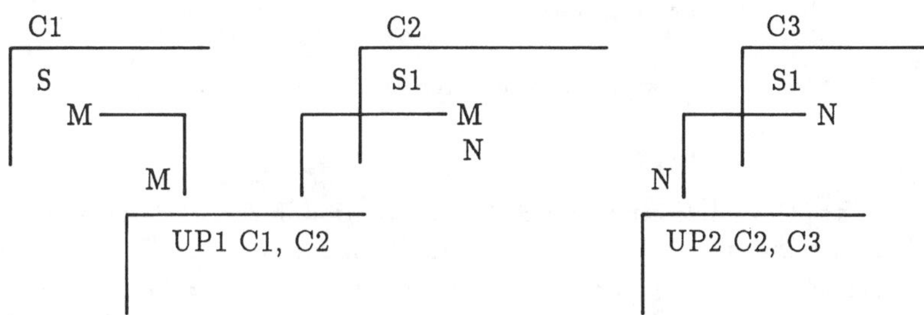

Figure 5.2

The ETN-sentence of UP has two sentences C1 and C2 in the node M. If M is true, C1 and C2, as hypotheses, are proposed. Which hypothesis should be executed first? The answer involves the problem of how to represent the control knowledge in forward deduction; see Fig.5.3.

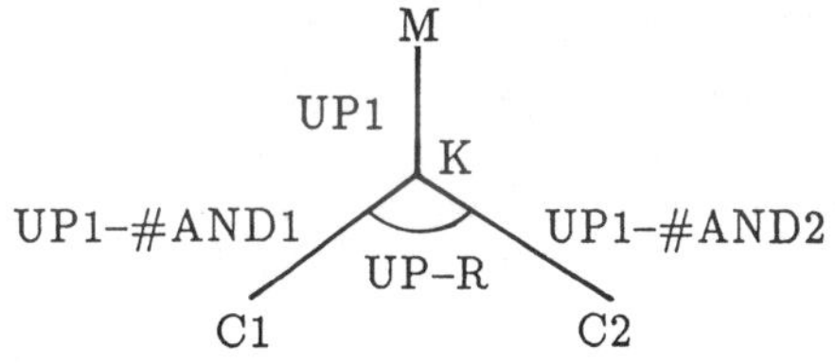

Figure 5.3

We cannot add the network to a certain layer of the ETN, because it would make a loop in the layer, as mentioned above. It would construct a new independent structure which is related to the definition of UP1. So, while a system executes UP1 of M, it seems to execute the CALL reasoning model, not the DRIVEN model. If the definition of UP1 did not connect with the global variable structure, the structure could accomplish the task of forward deduction. However, we have to consider two cases: (1) If M and N are true simultaneously (see Fig.5.2), the model in Fig.5.3 cannot solve the problem of the sequence of C1 and C3. In fact, C1, C2, and C3 have to compete with each other in reasoning. (2) We have to produce a series of different UPs, denoted UP1, UP2, etc. This is quite terrible for a practical expert system. So, the rational method, which solves these problems, is to adopt the global variable structure, such as BLACKBOARD. In addition, the solution space should be of this structure. These solution spaces are called 0-ETN in KORG.

These are constructed as another ETN; its root concepts should be BLACKBOARD and SOLUTION-SPACE. To define these concepts, 0-ETN will be formed. They can be written in the form of frames, but these frames differ from the frames that were applied previously to defining knowledge. They require a refinement mechanism to maintain them in reasoning, i.e., some of them have to be built dynamically. Obviously, we can use SACs and RACs to define them, because they are concepts. A general model is given for SOLUTION-SPACE as follows.

```
(CONCEPT solution-space)
    (refinement)
       ------
    (language generator)
       ------
    (FIN)
```

After the solution is carried to the solution space, the refinement mechanism connects them together in 0-ETN (various methods might be used). The words and the sentences are carried to the language generator to construct the complete sentences for the explanation. Of course, the SACs "refinement" and "language generator" as well as their relational attribute should be defined, but we do not discuss them in detail here. However, it must be pointed out that (1) constructing a 0-ETN is just like establishing a new ETN; (2) the commands carried to the solution space come from the nodes in the old ETN. By means of the 0-ETN connection, these commands will be added to every node in the old ETN.

Finally, we will briefly describe the design of BLACKBOARD which is rooted in SU/P. According to the definition of ETN, there are five semantic attribute concepts, CBH, EVENT-LISTS, EVENT, PROBLEM-LIST and EVENT-HISTORY-LIST, in the BLACKBOARD frame. We will not repeat the definitions of these SACs which have been given in the paper [22]. Their relational attributes should contain (1) the conditions executing these semantic attributes; (2) the conditions moving the element in one semantic attribute to another. KORG can easily describe such a control structure. As for AGENDA, we can also adopt the same method to describe it.

6 ETAP: An Automatic Programmer

We have discussed the principle of knowledge representation including the domain experts' knowledge and the AI experts' knowledge. Up to now, we have not yet solved the problem of how to apply the knowledge to reasoning. If we design an interpreter for ETN, an expert system will be accomplished. However, we do not attempt to apply the method as mentioned before to establishing an expert system, but do this by means of an automatic programmer based on the connective types in ETN instead of the traditional method. We do this in order to obtain a set of LISP functions. This process is the last step of KORG.

The subject of automatic programming is essentially the same as "compiler" in computer science. N.J.Nilsson has called it supercompiler. This subject is so important that A.Barr and E.Feigenbaum have even written "All of AI is a search for appropriate methods of automatic programming" [2].

This section will introduce the method of transforming the description of the experts' knowledge (here it is ETN) into LISP code. We adopt an automatic programmer, called

ETAP, to accomplish this task. ETAP is not involved in the design of data and optimization, because these problems, in general, do not relate directly to the described program itself, but depend on the supporting environment of the computer and the programmer's preference for a certain program model.

In view of the similarity of both the framelike and the LISP models, ETAP regards a frame as a unit in LISP functions. And three categories of the connective types as well as the 0-ETN connective type correspond to a group of models of functions called FORMWORK in this paper. They will be applied to produce the target program.

6.1 Principle

We have established the ETN structure. The task of ETAP is concerned with transforming the structure into an executable program. From ETN, first, the automatic programmer needs mainly to solve the problem of how to represent the three connective types of ETN and the 0-ETN connective type in the form of a LISP model, because once these four connective types are expressed as LISP models, we will obtain the condition transforming ETN into a LISP model. Second, it must solve the problem of how to use the connective types of ETN.

These connections in ETN specify the relationships of the concepts the expert system requires. ETAP expresses the connections as a group of LISP models called FORMWORK, then some rules in ETAP apply FORMWORK to transform ETN into an expert system program.

The arc connection is the simplest type in ETN. Assume that there is only arc connection in an expert system. If any node is represented as a LISP function and the relationship between Vj ($0<j<i+1$) and C is assumed to be "CALL" for programming, the evaluation of a node in ETN can be written as

```
(defun C ()
  (V1)
  (V2)
  ------
  (Vj)         )                                        (6.1)
```

This specifies the fact that the relationship between Vj and C is: the value of C depends on the evaluation for Vj according to such a sequence, and the result of Vi is regarded as the value of C. Clearly, this program is not useful. It can only represent the "CALL" relationship, but not others. And it cannot describe the relationship between V1, V2, ..., Vi. However, it is a basic program model, and all of the other program models evolve from it.

In order to represent the other relationships, we have to improve the assumption that C and Vj are CALL relationships only. According to the definition of ETN, it needs to add a semantic attribute SAj to these arcs in the network so that the user represents those relationships. Since each SAj comes from the process defining SACj, SAj is a new layer whose SACj is a root concept. If we consider SACj as a function name whose object is the SAj, we may obtain (6.2) from (6.1).

```
(defun C ()
  (SAC1   V1)
  (SAC2   V2)
  ------
  (SACi   Vi) )                                         (6.2)
```

Therefore, this function can represent not only the "CALL" relationship, but also the others such as "DRIVEN" through defining SACj. The formula (6.2) has given the description of ETAP for mapping connections in ETN.

However, this function is not enough to represent ETN, because we do not yet describe the relationship between SACj ($0<j<i+1$). The current state of the relationship is implicitly represented as a sequence like (6.2). This implies that it is a search using no heuristic information in the reasoning.

The relational attribute shows the way for adding heuristic information to a search process as pointed out in Sect. 3. The relational attribute will be constructed as a new KBN, as was the domain KBN. So, we can at least transform the relational attribute KBN in (6.2) into LISP functions. If we add this relational attribute to (6.2), (6.3) will be obtained. (This relational attribute is from the process of defining a RAC.)

```
(defun C ()
            (R
            (SAC1  V1)
            ------
            (SACi  Vi) )    )
```

$$(6.3)$$

The formula (6.3) is a LISP model which expresses the combinative connection of ETN. It is a theoretical result of ETAP. Either SACj or R, even Vj, still need more careful transformations.

A 0-ETN connection is more complex than an ETN connection. First, because it is an ETN, it will be transformed into a LISP model by means of an ETN connection. Second, it involves the problem of how to deal with global variables that show in 0-ETN. Third, part of an ETN connection in 0-ETN is dynamic, i.e., the connections have to be made in the process of reasoning. So, the connection cannot act independently as in the process above.

The first problem has been discussed previously, while the second can be solved by global variable connections. The last relates to the definition of the control structure. If the control structure is designed as BLACKBOARD or AGENDA, the DRIVEN model has to use global variables to interact with them in reasoning. This implies that we need to set up a mechanism in the 0-ETN connection to solve the problem. Obviously, this can be designed.

6.2 FORMWORK

Formula (6.3) provides the theoretical model that transforms ETN into a LISP model. In order to design a practical automatic programmer, we cannot use (6.3) directly. We have to consider its evolved models, called FORMWORK in ETAP. The set of these FORMWORK models is really a LISP program generator.

6.2.1 The Basic FORMWORK

We will briefly list the basic FORMWORK models here, then use them to describe the various connections in ETN.

```
FORMWORK 0.1        (defun  C    ()   )
FORMWORK 0.2        (defun  C    (L)  )
FORMWORK 0.3        (cond ( (  )  (  ) (  ) )   )
FORMWORK 0.4        (dolist I  () () () --- ()  )
```

```
FORMWORK 0.5      (V)
FORMWORK 0.6      (S  V)
FORMWORK 0.7      (prog  (Qj)   (steq  Qj  (Ij))  )
FORMWORK 0.8      (csetq  CAj   (K)    )
FORMWORK 0.9      (eval   'A)
```

ETAP will use these nine basic FORMWORKs to represent the connections of ETN, and the various categories of nodes in ETN are mapped to this form.

This paper will only consider these basic FORMWORKs which relate to the ETN connections; others will be left to another paper.

6.2.2 The Knowledge on Using FORMWORKs

Although we have given a set of FORMWORKs and have described the principle of the automatic programmer based on connections of the network, we do not discuss the problem of the utilization of FORMWORK, i.e., the conditions for using FORMWORK.

First, we have to consider the basic knowledge of ETAP including:

(1) A frame is transformed into a LISP function by means of FORMWORK 0.1 or FORM-WORK 0.2.
(2) By FORMWORK 0.3, RULE frame can be written to (cond (() () ---)).
(3) By FORMWORK 0.8 and 0.7, PROCEDURE frame is translated to

```
(prog (Aj)
      (setq  Aj  (Ij))
      (algorithm)
      (csetq  Qk  (OUTk))  ).
```

The latter two rules are the definitions of RACs – between IF and THEN for RULE frame, between INPUT, ALG, and OUTPUT for PROCEDURE frame.

Then we have to consider the conditions on using FORMWORKs.

The arc connection is the simplest of the connections of ETN. It can use FORMWORK 0.1 and 0.5 to transform these connections. In this technique, it is not rational that a pure arc connection be regarded as an independent step; it should combine with the mapping connection to become a step. So, a rule is given for the transformation step.

RULE
  IF   A SAC (SACj) is unique in the integrated system,
  THEN   FORMWORK 0.1 and 0.5 are used.   (6.4) is formed.

```
              (defun  C  ()
                    (SACj)   )                                    (6.4)
```

and FORMWORK 0.1 and 0.5 are used to construct SACj function
  ELSE   FORMWORK 0.1 and 0.6 are used.   (6.5) is formed.

```
              (defun  C  ()
                    (SACj  Vj)  )                                 (6.5)
```

and SACj function is constructed by FORMWORK 0.2 and 0.9.

```
              (defun  SACj  (L)
                    (eval  'L)  )                                 (6.6)
```

We conclude that there are two subsets of FORMWORK. One is composed of FORM-WORK 0.1 and 0.5, another is FORMWORK 0.1 and 0.6 for the domain frame and FORM-WORK 0.2 and 0.9 for the semantic attribute frame. The condition for using them is that SAC is unique in the integrated system.

The conditions for using FORMWORK are more complex for combinative connections, because they are concerned with the model of knowledge representation used in RACs. RULE frame, PROCEDURE frame, and CONCEPT frame can be used to define these RACs.

Since CONCEPT frame and PROCEDURE frame can be transformed into LISP functions (theoretically, RULE frame could be also transformed into a LISP function, but this is not reasonable, see below), they have the same form in the program model. This subset includes FORMWORK 0.6 for RAC in KBN, and FORMWORK 0.2 and 0.9 for the object of relational attribute.

If the RAC is described by RULE frame, FORMWORK 0.3 is used as follows

```
(cond ( SAC1  V1)
       (SAC2  V2)
       ------
       SACi  Vi) )   )
```
$$(6.7)$$

Clearly, if RULE frame is transformed into LISP functions, as is CONCEPT frame, it will bring us unnecessary trouble.

It is possible for these two forms to be combined to define RACs. This problem can be solved easily, as long as FORMWORK 0.3 and the subset of FORMWORK 0.2 and 0.6 are alternatively used to form the program according to the definition of the RAC by the expert. For example, the RA0 which is a RAC is defined as follows.

```
FRAME 1.
         IF      SAC1
         THEN    SAC2

FRAME 2.
         IF      SAC2
         THEN    SACM

FRAME 3.
         SACM
        |________________
        |select-max
        |       SAC3, SAC4, SAC5

FRAME 4.
         IF      SACM > 80
         THEN    SAC6
```

These four frames are transformed into the formula (6.8),

```
(cond ( SAC1  V1)
       (SAC2  V2)
       (>  (SACM)   80)
       (SAC6)
         )      )
```
$$(6.8)$$

where frame SACM will be transformed into a LISP function by means of FORMWORK 0.1 and 0.5.

Similarly, we can conclude that there are two subsets of FORMWORK. One is FORM-WORK 0.3, another contains FORMWORK 0.1, 0.5 and FORMWORK 0.2, 0.6. The condition for using these two subsets is that a RAC be defined by RULE frame.

Since 0-ETN is an ETN, it can be translated into a LISP model by means of the above process. In general, the object of this function is empty when execution of this system begins; the 0-ETN connection will be shown in the reasoning, i.e., it will fill the object in the value list of the function. We must find a method for solving the problem. MDM adopts FORMWORK 0.2 and 0.9 to establish "AGENDA". The newly produced tasks are filled in the variable "L", then (eval 'L) executes these tasks in L. As the solution space, we use the refinement mechanism to construct a LISP function directly. The above actions must be put to an expert system together, as a part of it.

Another problem of the 0-ETN connection is the global variables that will be solved in ETAP. These global variables must be collected in transforming 0-ETN into a LISP model. All the places using them in ETN apply FORMWORK 0.8 to produce a LISP model. (It includes the object of ALG in the PROCEDURE frame.)

6.3 Some of the Primitives Defined by ETAP

In Sects. 4 and 5 we have used several SACs, such as IF and THEN in RULE frame, and INPUT, ALG, and OUTPUT in PROCEDURE frame.

CALL and DRIVEN are applied to define SACs of the domain layer. They are primitives in KORG. They possess common characteristics: first, they have the same definition in any expert system; second, all of them are the procedure knowledge. These concepts are described by LISP functions.

KORG has provided two reasoning models – CALL and DRIVEN. They are shown as: (1) a function invokes other functions; (2) a function generates an event or a group of events which is the function name. These events are invoked by the schedule program in the top level of the system (the schedule program is described in 0-ETN). These two models are just in accordance with two subsets of FORMWORK in ETAP. CALL contains FORMWORK 0.5 and 0.6; DRIVEN is FORMWORK 0.7 and 0.8. The problem of using these FORMWORKs depends on the knowledge defined by ETAP. For example, if ETL-sentence in DRIVEN is a global variable (BLACKBOARD), FORMWORK 0.8 will be used to define this DRIVEN.

The FORMWORKs that are used in defining RULE frame and PROCEDURE frame have been specified in Sect. 6.1, and we do not repeat them here.

7 Summary

An approach to establishing an expert system (KORG) has been presented in this paper. It includes three models – ETL, ETN, and ETAP. Establishing the expert system is based on a series of transformations from experts' knowledge to LISP codes. Its kernel is ETN – a kind of semantic network with semantic attributes and relational attributes. The relational attribute in particular plays an important role in these transformations.

The acquisition of knowledge is based on the assumption "A concept is described by other concepts". So, we can design an algorithm, DESCRIBE, to collect experts' knowledge.

A large tool system based on this principle is being designed including natural-language processing, knowledge acquisition and explanation, etc.

Acknowledgements

This paper has resulted from the work of many people. J.W. Tai and X. Chen have been involved in the ETN model. Z.Y. Chen , L.C. Yin, and F. Fang have helped me to develop the principle and the program of ETAP. C. Ho proposed the bidirectional pointer. X.L. Ji has helped me to design the ETL model. Thanks to J.W. Tai for early reading of this paper and for providing many helpful suggestions. Thanks also to Q.H. Hu and C.M. Lou for encouraging this work.

References

[1] Akins, J.: Prototypes and production rules: an approach to knowledge representation for hypothesis formation, IJCAI-6, 1-3, 1979

[2] Barr, A. and Feigenbaum, E.A.: The handbook of artificial intelligence, Vol.2, William Kaufmann, Los Altos, 1982

[3] Blum, R.L.: Discovery confirmation and incorporation of causal relationship from time-oriented clinical data-base: the RX project. Computer and Biomedical Research 15(2), 164-187, 1982

[4] Barstow, D.R.: A knowledge-base system for automatic programming consultation. IJCAI-5, 382-388, 1977

[5] Barstow, D.R.: A perspective on automatic programming. Schlumberger-Doll Research, Palo Alto, CA, sys-004, 1983

[6] Chandrasekaran, B., Gomez, F., Mittal, S. and Smith, J.: An approach to medical diagnosis based on conceptual structure. IJCAI-6, 134-142, 1979

[7] Dahl, O.J., Dijkstra, E.W. and Hoare, C.A.R.: Structure programming. Academic Press, New York, 1972

[8] Davis, R. and Lenat, D.B.: Knowledge-base system in artificial intelligence. McGraw-Hill International, New York, 1982

[9] Davis, R., Buchanan, B.G. and Shortliffe, E.H.: Production rule as representation for knowledge-based consultation program. Artificial Intelligence, 8(1), 15-45, 1977

[10] Davis, R.: Panel on dealing with uncertainty. IJCAI-6, 1101-1102, 1979

[11] Dilger, W. and Womann, W.: Semantic network as abstract data types. IJCAI-8, 321-324, 1983

[12] Georgeff, M. and Bonollo, U.: Procedure expert system. IJCAI-8, 151-157, 1983

[13] Greiner, R. and Lenat, D.B.: A representation language language. AAAI-1, 165-169, 1980

[14] Guiho, G.: Automatic programming using abstract data types. IJCAI-8, 1-9, 1983

[15] Hendrix, G.G.: Expanding the utility of semantic network through partitioning. IJCAI-4, 115-121, 1975

[16] Ho, C. and Bai, Y.C.: Oil-well prospecting data interpeter system – principle and performance. Tech. Rep. Institute of Automation, Academia Sinica, Beijing, China, 1983 (In Chinese)

[17] Lesser, V.R. and Erman, L.D.: A retrospective view of the HEARSAY-2 architecture. IJCAI-5, 790-800, 1977

[18] Lou, C.M. and Wang, J.: Structure based on control strategy, IJCAI-8, 222-224, 1983

[19] Melle, W.V.: A domain-independent production-rule system for consultation program. IJCAI-6, 923-925, 1979

[20] Minsky, M.: A framework for representation knowledge. In: Winston, P.H. (ed.): The psychology of computer vision. McGraw-Hill, New York, 1975

[21] Nii, H.P. and Aielle, N.: AGE (Attempt to Generalize): A knowledge-base program for building knowledge-base programs. IJCAI-6, 645-655, 1979

[22] Nii, H.P. and Feigenbaum, E.A.: Rule-based understanding of signal. In: Waterman, D.A. et al.(eds): Pattern-directed inference system. Academic Press, New York, 1978

[23] Nilsson, N.J.: Principles of artificial intelligence. Springer-Verlag, Berlin, Heidelberg, 1982

[24] Pauker, S.G., Gorry, G.A., Kassirer, J.P. and Schwartz, W.B.: Toward the simulation of clinical cognition: taking present illness by computer: Am. J. Medicine 60, 981-995, 1976

[25] Shortliffe, E.H.: Computer based medical consultation: MYCIN. North-Holland, Amsterdam, 1976

[26] Smith, B.G.: A model for learning system. IJCAI-5, 338-343, 1977

[27] Smith, D.E. and Clayton, J.E.: A frame-based production system architecture. AAAI-1, 154-156, 1980

[28] Stefik, M.: An examination of a frame-like structure representation system. IJCAI-6, 845-852, 1979

[29] Stefik, M., Akins, J., Balzer, R., Benoit, J., Birnbaum, L., Hayes-Roth, F. and Sacerdoti, E.: The organization of expert systems, a tutorial. Artificial Intelligence, 18(2), 135-173, 1982

[30] Swartout, W.R.: XPLAIN: A system for creating and explaining expert consulting programs. Artificial Intelligence, 21(3), 285-325, 1983

[31] Szolovits, P. and Pauker, S.G.: Categorical probabilistic reasoning in medical diagnosis. Artificial Intelligence, 11(1,2), 115-144, 1978

[32] Tai, J.W. and Fu, K.S.: Semantic syntax directed translation for pictorial pattern recognition. School of Electrical Engineering, Purdue University, Tech.Rep. TR-EE81-38

[33] Wang, J. and Tai, J.W.: A semantic network for pattern description and knowledge representation. (To be published in Acta Automatica Sinica)

[34] Wang, J.: MDM: A medical decision-making model. Tech.Rep. Institute of Automation, Academia Sinica, Beijing, China, 1981 (In Chinese)

[35] Wang, J. and Ji, X.L.: ETL: A tool language for establishing knowledge-base. Tech.Rep. Institute of Automation, Academia Sinica, Beijing, China, 1984 (In Chinese)

[36] Wang, J. and Ji, X.L.: A semantic network and the method for forming it. CAAI-4, in Guayong, 1984

[37] Wang, J. and Cheng, J.G.: MDM model and medical consultation system defined by MDM – SHOCK. Tech.Rep Institute of Automation, Academia Sinica, Beijing, China, 1983 (In Chinese)

[38] Weiss, S.M. and Kulikowski, C.A.: EXPERT: A system for developing consultation model. IJCAI-6, 942-947, 1979

Garden Path Errors in Diagnostic Reasoning

Paul E. Johnson[1], James B. Moen[2] and William B. Thompson[2]

[1]Department of Management Sciences and
[2]Computer Science Science Department
University of Minnesota, Minneapolis, MN 55455, USA

ABSTRACT

An efficient strategy for fault diagnosis relies upon specific symptoms to activate only a small portion of the available diagnostic knowledge. However, expert systems and humans using this strategy often commit characteristic errors. These errors occur because significantly different faults may manifest similar symptoms. If these symptoms are confused, the wrong portion of diagnostic knowledge can be activated. This paper discusses such errors and describes a strategy for reducing their incidence based upon an investigation of expertise in the Galen expert system.

1 Introduction

Highly expert problem solvers are prone to characteristic mistakes on certain classes of problems. In one such class, early information in the problem statement typically suggests a solution that is incorrect. Our experience indicates that these *Garden Path Problems* are distinct from other classes of problems that are difficult to solve due to lack of experience in a domain, or where the knowledge needed to solve them has not yet been developed. Individuals faced with Garden Path problems often make what we shall term Garden Path errors, which consist of proposing a solution based upon initial cues and then disregarding, ignoring, or "explaining away" later conflicting information which would tend to disconfirm the initial solution. Research at the University of Minnesota is being directed at understanding the basis for Garden Path errors and discovering heuristics which will enable them to be avoided. This paper discusses Garden Path errors both in the context of expert problem solvers and expert systems. The discussion concentrates on two generations of expert diagnostic systems, the second of which contains specific mechanisms intended to avoid such errors.

The research reported here was accomplished with the cooperation of the SUMEX-AIM computing facility at Stanford University and the Department of Pediatrics in the University of Minnesota Medical School. Preparation of this report was supported in part by funds provided by the University of Minnesota Microelectronics and Information Sciences Center.

One area in which Garden Path errors have been studied is physics problem solving (Johnson & Thompson, 1981; Cohen, 1975). Here the initial solution has often been linked to prior misconceptions about physical phenomena, as well as incomplete knowledge of the subject matter (Clement, 1982). A second area that has been examined for the occurrence of Garden Path mistakes is medical diagnosis. Studies have shown that a physician's knowledge of diseases may be grouped in memory into sets of competing alternatives (Johnson, et al., 1981). When one member of such a group is suggested by specific data (cues), the others are often overlooked. Because the initially considered member of the set is incorrect, confusion among the other members due to the signs and symptoms they have in common is often sufficient to prevent the identification of a subsequent, correct alternative.

Research at the University of Minnesota over the past several years has been conducted in both these areas. We shall concentrate here on the work in medical diagnosis because it has been developed most extensively, and because it has resulted in a cognitive simulation model, as well as an expert system that avoids Garden Path mistakes. The hypothesis that has guided much of the work we shall present is that Garden Path errors occur because a problem solving process that works most of the time is applied to a class of problems for which it is not well suited. So powerful is the mechanism underlying this process that even individuals with specific training in a field are unable to overcome it in tasks where they have not been trained beforehand on the appropriate response.

We begin with a brief description of a particular domain of Garden Path problems within the medical subspeciality of Pediatric Cardiology, a branch of medical practice concerned with the diagnosis and treatment of congenital heart diseases. We then describe our attempt to develop a cognitive simulation model of expertise in diagnostic reasoning (called Diagnoser) and a subsequent expert system for avoiding Garden Path errors (called Galen).

We close with an argument on the need for linking research on the study of expertise in human problem solving with the developing interest in building computer programs that embody human expertise on specific complex tasks.

2 Background of Work

One interpretation of medical diagnosis is as a problem solving process in which individuals attempt to classify data by matching it against known patterns of patient signs and symptoms. These patterns comprise a vocabulary of disease types built up in response to specific teaching and learning experiences. The process of performing a diagnosis with such patterns can be divided into two parts. Initially, patient data suggest candidate disease hypotheses. Although the process of hypothesis generation can continue throughout the examination of data, it tends to be most pronounced in the early stages of the task. As data are examined and hypotheses are considered, a second stage called hypothesis evaluation occurs. Here expectations associated with disease patterns are compared with specific patient data in order to determine whether some specific hypothesis might be true in the present situation.

The process of diagnosis as it has been described in empirical studies at Minnesota (Johnson, 1982) and elsewhere (e.g. Elstein et al., 1978) indicates that physicians tend initially to hypothesize disease possibilities and then seek either confirming or disconfirming evidence as they continue examining the data of a case. One strategy for doing this is to generate all or most of the disease possibilities early and then get rid of all but one of the competing alternatives. A somewhat different strategy is to hypothesize a much smaller number of alternatives (sometimes only one) and consider only these alternatives until they are either proven or disproven correct.

In the work at Minnesota, experts (board certified medical faculty), trainees (individuals who have completed a residency and are training to become specialists), and novices (medical students) are asked to solve cases of congenital heart disease drawn from the files of the University of Minnesota Heart Hospital. Subjects from each of the three groups are given the cases and asked to perform diagnoses while giving verbal thinking aloud protocols. These "concurrent" protocols are then tape recorded and transcribed for analysis, and comprise the basic data of the research.

Based upon a series of such studies, a model of expertise was formulated (Swanson et al., 1977). This model was written as a computer simulation model consisting of two programs (Swanson, 1978). The first program, called Deducer, was designed to generate disease templates from input data describing various pathophysiological states of the circulatory system (e.g. misconnections, obstructions, etc.). Templates produced by Deducer consisted of patterns of internal hemodynamic states (e.g. blood flows, pressures) and patient signs and symptoms resulting from these states (e.g. murmurs) and represented predictions of what should appear in a given disease. These templates were validated against patterns of comparable patient data provided by a consulting cardiologist.

The second program, Diagnoser, used the disease templates generated by Deducer plus a number of disease specific heuristics to initiate and evaluate each template in response to data of a case. A set of training cases was developed in order to tune the behavior of Diagnoser to the performance of an expert consultant. Following this phase, a new set of cases was selected. These cases were given to Diagnoser and also to a new sample of experts.

In subsequent studies (Johnson et al., 1981) performance of Diagnoser was compared with the performance of human physicians. As part of the research, a difficult case was selected and a set of plausible diagnoses for the case was determined in collaboration with an expert physician. This set contained the correct diagnosis for the case, as well as other diagnoses with which it might plausibly be confused. The data of the original case was then systematically varied to produce a group of related experimental cases. When physicians were given these new cases, they frequently gave the wrong diagnosis, but always chose from the set of plausible diagnoses. In a subsequent study (Feltovich, 1981), naturally occuring cases with these characteristics were found in hospital files. When these cases were given to expert physicians, they made errors like those made in the experimental cases. When Diagnoser was run on these cases, it made errors like those of the expert physicians.

At this point, a systematic study of the case files was undertaken and it was discovered that while the base rate of errors in diagnosis (defined as the difference between a pre and post-heart catheterization diagnosis) was quite low for most diseases (1-2%), it was as high as 40% for certain diseases. In cases where there was a discrepancy between the physician's initial diagnosis and that reported from the heart catheterization, the actual diagnosis was typically a member of the set of plausible diagnoses for the initially diagnosed disease.

Two lines of research followed. An empirical study of expert diagnosis was undertaken by Hassebrock (1985) in an effort to document more thoroughly the structure of disease sets in the field of pediatric cardiology. At the same time, a new model of diagnostic problem solving was created. This new model, implemented in a computer program called Galen, imposed a more explicit structure on the organization of diagnostic knowledge. By making knowledge organization explicit, Galen allowed us to investigate the relationships between knowledge organization and performance. The model of diagnosis implemented in Galen thus provided a mechanism for solving difficult problems using limited computational resources, and permitted the investigation of both the cause of errors in diagnosis and a possible approach to minimizing their occurrence.

To understand the nature of Garden Path errors better, why they occur, and how they might be avoided, we shall first examine the expertise embodied in the Diagnoser program and where it failed. We shall then consider in more detail the Galen program and how its expertise addresses the weaknesses in the earlier program.

3   The Diagnoser Model

The Diagnoser program was our first effort and an extensive system for diagnostic reasoning in Pediatric Cardiology. Diagnoser represents its knowledge in terms of frames (Minsky 1975; Swanson, 1978). Each frame has a unique *name*, a list of *slots,* and a *type.* A slot is an attribute-value pair. The slot's attribute is a name that uniquely identifies it within the frame. The slot's value is usually a piece of Lisp code or some simple object like a name, a number, or a pointer to another frame. The frame's type is a pointer to a type frame that specifies permissible slots for that frame, and also that contains general information about all frames of that type.

Diagnoser works by selecting a known *disease template frame* as its diagnosis. As their name suggests, disease template frames represent the disease templates that were discussed earlier. A disease template frame contains a large number of *expectation frames*, which each describe a symptom or a condition of the circulatory system that should be observed if the patient has the disease represented by the template. Diganoser selects the disease template frame whose expectation frames best match the available patient data. Selecting templates is fairly complex and involves three additional kinds of intermediate frames: *data frames, test frames*, and *hypothesis frames.*

Diagnoser builds a new *data frame* to internally represent each new piece of patient data that it collects. The data in a data frame differs from raw data in that it is expressed using a canonical set of terms and units. The data frame is also associated with many small *test frames* which act something like rules. Each test frame contains a pattern. The patterns of each test frame are matched against the newly created data frame. Most of this matching is done by a general match procedure, but some test frames contain Lisp code that acts as a special purpose matcher instead. Lisp code must be used if the test frame must examine the original input data before it was transcribed to a frame, if it must examine more than one data frame, or if it must examine program variables inaccessible to the pattern matcher. If the match is successful, more Lisp code in the test frame is executed to perform operations on *hypothesis frames.*

Hypothesis frames represent intermediate conjectures about the patient's condition. A hypothesis frame contains pointers to one or more template frames which contain detailed expectations about what should be observed if the conjecture is true. Hypothesis frames also contain Lisp code that is executed in response to specific operations being performed on the hypothesis.

There are four possible operations on hypothesis frames: **trigger, reject, accept,** and **further-specify.** *Triggering* a hypothesis frame retrieves it from the knowledge base and brings it into initial consideration. *Rejecting* a hypothesis frame asserts that it is incorrect, removing it and its associated template frames from further consideration. *Accepting* a hypothesis frame asserts that it is correct and optionally rejects some of its competing hypothesis frames. *Further specifying* a hypothesis frame selects another template frame pointed to by the hypothesis frame for further consideration. The name comes from the fact that the template frames pointed to by a hypothesis frame usually represent more specific forms of the hypothesis.

Diagnoser uses three distinct types of hypothesis frames. A *Disease hypothesis frame,* like **ASD** (Atrial Septal Defect), represents a disease. It points to template frames that represent how the circulatory system should appear in possible variants of the disease, (e.g. **ASD-mild, ASD-moderate,** and **ASD-severe**). These represent possible diagnoses. The Lisp code in a hypothesis frame selects one of these template frames to be considered in response to specific sets of circumstances.

A *Pathophysiological hypothesis frame,* like **PBF-increased** (Pulmonary Blood Flow increased), represents an important condition of the circulatory system. It points to a template frame that describes what the circulatory system is like in such a state. It contains Lisp code that triggers hypothesis frames involving the state. For example, Lisp code in **PBF-increased** selects diseases in which the pulmonary blood flow is expected to be increased.

A *Category hypothesis frame,* like **cyanotic-diseases,** represent a significant group of pathophysiological or disease hypotheses. It points to a template frame that describes features of the circulatory system that are common to members of the group. Its Lisp code triggers hypothesis frames that are members of the group in much the same way that disease hypothesis frames select template frames. It is also typically used to rule out diseases. For example, Lisp code in **cyanotic-diseases** is capable of rejecting all disease hypotheses not involving cyanosis.

Diagnoser begins a diagnosis by accepting a piece of patient data and transcribing it to a data frame. The data frame then is matched against an appropriate set of test frames. This selects one or more hypothesis frames for consideration. Lisp code in each hypothesis frame next selects a template frame which represents the current best approximation about how the hypothesis should present itself. For example, the hypothesis frame **ASD** would select the template frame **ASD-moderate** if the case mentions a murmur that would be heard if the patient has a moderate atrial septal defect.

The data frame is matched against all comparable expectation frames in each hypothesis' template frames. If it does match, the template frame is said to have *violated expectations*. Lisp code in the hypothesis frame that points to the template frame identifies the violation and takes action to correct it. The action usually involves applying **further-specify** to the hypothesis frame, selecting another template frame that does not exhibit the violation.

When all template frames have been matched in this way, Diagnoser obtains another piece of data and repeats the process already described. After the last piece of data has been processed, Diagnoser assigns a numeric weight to each template frame belonging to a nonrejected hypothesis. The weight increases with the number of its correctly matched data frames and decreases with the number of its violations. The template frames are then sorted by weight, and the disease template frame with the highest weight is taken to be the correct diagnosis.

4 Limitations of the Diagnoser Model

Although somewhat lengthy, the above discussion of Diagnoser is necessary to understand the reasons for Diagnoser's success as well as its susceptibility to error. One reason for the model's success is that its architecture effectively embodies the task of diagnosis in simulated cases in pediatric cardiology. In this respect Diagnoser works by repeatedly alternating between two phases. In the first phase new data cues suggest new hypotheses, while in the second phase old hypotheses are evaluated in terms of the newly obtained data. These two phases complement each other and compensate for each other's limitations.

The first phase quickly chooses a plausible hypothesis frame without much search by simply matching patterns in data type frames and following associated pointers to hypothesis frames. Some data cues suggest individual circulatory malformations without suggesting a single accompanying disease. These cues are modeled in Diagnoser by a data frame that triggers a pathophysiological hypothesis frame. Some data cues are extremely general, suggesting some member of a class of diseases is present. These cues are modeled by a data frame triggering a category hypothesis frame. Finally, some data cues suggest possible diagnoses, and are modeled by a data frame triggering a disease hypothesis frame. Hypotheses can be accepted, rejected, or further specified in the same way.

Although the first phase of diagnosis is fast and often yields correct results, it is not always guaranteed to choose a correct final diagnosis. Not only are some data cues misleading, but early case data sometimes suggest hypotheses refuted by later data. The second phase compensates for this by considering several levels of intermediate hypothesis frames before reaching a template frame suitable as a diagnosis. For example, information about handling violated expectations available in the intermediate hypothesis frames allows Diagnoser to detect bad choices and rapidly redirect attention to better hypothesis frames, provided that the knowledge base designer has foreseen the potential problems.

In effect, the network of frames in Diagnoser's knowledge base is carefully constructed so that the right knowledge is available in the right place at the right time. The topological structure of this network, and the locations in the network where knowledge about violated expectations is placed, represents an important kind of implicit strategic knowledge that is worth studying in its own right.

We originally believed that most of Diagnoser's expertise resulted from the detailed expectations found within template frames. As mentioned above, template frames are synthesized in isolation from Diagnoser by Deducer (Swanson, 1978). Deducer uses a causal model of the human circulatory system to predict expected blood flows, pressures, and observable symptoms that result from a given set of physiological defects.

When comparing the performance of a consulting cardiologist with that of Diagnoser, however, we were often surprised to see the cardiologist obtain correct diagnoses even though he ignored many of the expectations produced by Deducer. The expectations were correct, but many were simply irrelevant to a successful diagnosis of the case ("the murmur is all you need here to tell you the diagnosis"). At other times, the cardiologist seemed to use a priority ranking of expectations that changed from case to case. For example, he ignored certain unmatched expectations ("we hardly ever hear a split second heart sound") or treated some unexplained data as being more important than others ("if you hear this murmur, you can't reach that diagnosis").

Examining output from the program in more detail, we found that Diagnoser generally got the right answer, but sometimes for reasons different from those used by the consultant. In such cases the correct hypothesis frame was triggered by examination of case data, and the correct template frame received the highest numeric weight at the end of the run. But the actual confirmed expectations contributing to its high weight were not always the ones the consultant felt to be important. Apparently, once the rule-like pieces of Lisp code directed the program's attention to the right hypotheses, the hardest part of the diagnosis was done.

We eventually concluded that these problems resulted from inadequacies in the way expectations were represented in template frames. Most of these inadequacies were traceable to the fact that expectations are automatically derived from circulatory defects by the causal model in Deducer. Although the expectations are finely detailed and almost always correct, they are sometimes inappropriate for use in diagnosis because they represent how diseases should canonically present themselves to the physician, not how diseases actually do present themselves.

Diagnoser represents expectation frames as if they were all of equal importance. In contrast, an expert physician knows not only that expectations vary in importance, but that the presence or absence of certain expectations have specific consequences for a given diagnosis. Some of this knowledge about importance is represented in Diagnoser using Lisp code to handle important violated expectations. Specific actions are associated with specific violations: for example, violating a mildly significant expectation causes a hypothesis frame to be further specified, whereas violating a highly significant one causes it to be rejected. But only significant violations, not confirmations, are associated with actions in this way. The majority of expectations in template frames are not treated this way either, suggesting that their effect on the final diagnosis is minimal.

Diagnoser represents expectation frames not as patterns that can match data frames in multiple ways, but as objects that resemble data frames, matching in only one way. An expectation frame may fail to match for trivial reasons which a human physician could easily explain away as being the result of noisy data or variations in the way that a referred case is reported. Because expectations resemble data frames, they also cannot represent things that are not expected to be observed. Such knowledge is only representable in Diagnoser by resorting to Lisp code.

5 Diagnoser Reasoning Errors

In the experiment referred to earlier (Johnson et al., 1981), a diagnosed Garden Path case of Total Anomalous Pulmonary Venous Connection (TAPVC) was selected from hospital files and modified to create sixteen separate versions. These versions were based upon the manipulation of four specific cues judged to be the most significant in achieving a correct diagnosis. The sixteen versions were given to expert diagnosticians and the Diagnoser program; the experts and the program made similar responses.

One type of incorrect response resulted from simply not ever thinking of the correct alternative; if it was not considered, it could not be concluded. This kind of error was observed for both the experts and for Diagnoser. Errors of this type in Diagnoser were due either to inadequate triggering rules, or in some cases to a lack of appropriate information about violated expectations so when one alternative is incorrect, another better one can be selected. A variation on this kind of error was to think of a compelling but incorrect alternative initially and then not be able to generate the correct alternative when later cues appeared. In some cases this error in Diagnoser was due to a lack of connections from an initial disease to a plausible variant, and in other cases a triggering rule was omitted. In still other cases the error was due to the template for a disease candidate having too many expectations so that when many of them were not present the number of unmatched data frames kept the match for the correct alternative from being strong enough to override the match obtained for the initial, incorrect alternative.

A second type of error found in the behavior of human diagnosticians as well as the Diagnoser model was to think of the correct alternative as well as others but not be able to evaluate the evidence of the case correctly. Two forms of such errors were observed. In one instance the expectations for a given disease were too general so that when the critical cues appeared they were missed as confirmatory. In the second instance the expectations employed by both the model and a human problem solver were too specific, so that evidence that would be sufficient to conclude the correct alternative was ignored because it was not realized that too much exactness was not warranted in these circumstances.

The Diagnoser model made errors because its triggering rules were incomplete, or in some instances incorrect, and because its expectation frames were too specific in some places and too general in others. But in addition, the model made errors because it was not able to differentiate between different hypotheses which were both confirmable given the data of the case. In a sense the model behaved much like human diagnosticians (including experts) who allocated too many resources to the wrong alternatives. Garden Path problems are interesting and potentially important precisely because their solution requires a strategic allocation of resources based upon an awareness that things are not always as they seem.

6 The Galen Model

Based on our experiences constructing and experimenting with Diagnoser, a new diagnostic system called Galen was designed. The original reason for building Galen was to re-implement Diagnoser in a form that would be a better vehicle for studying the strategic organization of diagnostic knowledge. As a result, the first version of Galen (Thompson et al., 1983) resembled Diagnoser in that it selected *models* of the circulatory system and matched their expectations against patient data. Galen's models were constructed by hand translating Diagnoser's template frames, classifying each expectation frame as a *major* or *minor* finding to express the relative importance of individual expectations. Experiments suggested that this scheme had the same problems as Diagnoser in representing expectations. In many cases it did not even work as well, since it lacked the extensive tuning and adjustment of its predecessor. Although we could have tuned Galen in the same way we did Diagnoser, we chose instead to re-examine our assumptions about how diagnosis should be preformed by computer.

Part of the reason Diagnoser was successful was that it quickly identified relevant frames and used the knowledge those frames contained without having to search extensively. As mentioned earlier, the right knowledge is available in the right place at the right time. Each frame in Diagnoser contains small pieces of Lisp code, all immediately available when the frame is examined for relevance to a case. Some of those pieces of code act like rules, making decisions by examining known data and by examining expectations found in the template frames. Other pieces introduce new hypotheses for later processing. Using Lisp code in this way is a source of power, since it is easy to perform complex tests on the execution state of the program and perform complex actions as a result. For example, it is possible to make decisions based on both accumulated data and current hypotheses by writing code that examines Diagnoser's internal data structures.

Although the use of Lisp code is a source of power, it results in a knowledge base that is not easy to change and understand without detailed knowledge of the inference procedure's internals (Richie et al., 1984). To avoid these problems, we decided to express Galen's knowledge base entirely in a rule oriented language embedded in Lisp which does not allow including Lisp code. The resulting system would be easier to understand and modify.

If Galen's rules are to represent the same knowledge that Diagnoser represents in Lisp, the expressive power of its rule language must be comparable to that of the Lisp fragments used by Diagnoser. It is therefore not sufficient that rules only detect patterns of input data and conditionally operate on hypotheses. They must be able to detect whether a hypothesis is still in contention, whether it has been accepted or rejected, and why. They must also be able to gather evidence for and against hypotheses and to take appropriate action when sufficient evidence has accumulated.

This is accomplished using three techniques. First, a data structure called an *object* is used to represent all computationally relevant facts about data and hypotheses. Objects also satisfy several additional requirements, based on experience with Diagnoser frames: (1) it must be possible to examine objects at varying levels of detail, (2) it must be easy to determine what rules are applicable to a given object (just as in Diagnoser it was easy to tell what rules were associated with a given frame), and (3) it must be easy to implement objects in Lisp.

Conceptually, objects are n-ary trees, where the root of each subtree names the kind of information to be found in its branches. Objects have a natural representation in Lisp as nested lists, of the form $(C\ E_1\ ...\ E_n)$, where $n \geq 0$. C is a symbol called the object's context, and represents the name at the root of the subtree. E_1 through E_n are called the object's elements, and represent the branches of the tree. These elements are usually objects, but can also be symbols or numbers.

For example, we represent the loudness of a murmur as an object whose context is *loudness* and whose elements describe loudness in more detail:

(loudness moderate)

This object could appear as an element of a more complex object that describes the murmur completely:

```
(systolic_murmur
  (loudness moderate)
  (time ejection)
  (location
    (aortic_area)))
```

Each successive level of nested parentheses describes the murmur in greater detail. The outermost level simply states that a systolic murmur exists. The next level states the murmur's loudness, time (where it occurs in the cardiac cycle) and location (where the murmur is heard on the chest). The deepest level gives actual values for what is known about the murmur: the murmur is moderately loud, occurs during the ejection phase of the cardiac cycle, and is heard in the aortic area. The extra set of parentheses around *aortic_area* indicate that more detailed information could be given (the place in the aortic area where the murmur is heard best, for example), but is not given in this object.

The second technique involves introducing a structure called the scratchpad, as a globally available repository for all computationally relevant facts about the current problem, somewhat like the *blackboard* used in Hearsay (Erman et al., 1980). The scratchpad is an object, of the form:

```
(scratchpad
  (data D_1 ... D_m)
  (hypotheses H_1 ... H_n))
```

It represents all accumulated problem data as the objects D_1 through D_m, and all hypotheses ever considered during the current problem as the objects H_1 through H_n. Initially the scratchpad is empty, without any D's or H's, but new data objects and hypothesis objects are added as the case is diagnosed.

The third technique involves design of Galen's rule interpreter. Each rule contains a pattern part that describes an object and an executable action part. Since the scratchpad is itself an object, rules can be written which detect any set of computationally relevant facts about the problem. When a rule is applied, its pattern part is matched against a portion of the scratchpad, and if the match succeeds, its action part is executed.

The resulting complexity of some rule patterns can cause problems if the usual view of a production system as being a flat, unstructured collection of rules is taken. In such systems, all antecedents are checked for potential matches each time a significant event occurs in the computation. This potentially expensive procedure is usually implemented by restricting the complexity of antecedents (e.g. by forcing all data to be represented as n-tuples or property lists) and by using clever indexing or hashing techniques (Allen, 1983; Forgy, 1982) to minimize the amount of matching done at run time.

Restricting the complexity of antecedents is not feasible in Galen, since they must be able to detect fairly complex situations as represented on the scratchpad. Using hashing or indexing to minimize the number of rules that must be examined is possible, but unnecessary given our model of diagnosis, which suggests that rules are strongly bound to the classes of data and the individual hypotheses they affect. We can therefore partition all rules into small rule teams and assign a team to each class of data and each hypothesis before any diagnosis is done (Aikins, 1980). In this way only the rules associated with the object currently receiving attention from Galen need to be considered at any one time. This also allows the rule interpreter to avoid using complex conflict resolution mechanisms, since potential conflicts have been resolved as a by-product of rule team creation.

Pattern matching in rules is done by a recursive procedure that takes advantage of the fact that objects can represent facts at several levels of detail. The context of an object can be regarded as a summary of the information that its elements describe. When the pattern matcher searches a large nested object (like the scratchpad), it can can ignore irrelevant objects if it examines an object's context before examining its elements (and it can hardly help doing so, because of the way Lisp lists are implemented). An object whose context names an irrelevant fact can be ignored and attention can be diverted to a different object. An object whose context names a relevant fact can have its elements searched in greater depth, but only as deeply as necessary to match the pattern or to determine that the pattern does not match.

For example, if a moderately loud systolic murmur at the aortic area that is loudest under the right clavicle is detected during a physical examination, the scratchpad would appear as:

```
(scratchpad
  (data
    (auscultation
      (systolic_murmur
        (loudness moderate)
        (time ejection)
        (location
          (aortic_area
            (heard_best under_right_clavicle))))))
  (hypotheses))
```

A rule that should act in the presence of an unspecified systolic murmur could then use the pattern:

```
(auscultation
  (systolic_murmur))
```

for this purpose. The surrounding contexts *scratchpad* and *data* are assumed to be present in a pattern if they are not explicitly mentioned.

Similarly, a pattern that detects a systolic ejection murmur whose location is somewhere in the aortic area, but is not concerned with loudness, is:

```
(auscultation
  (systolic_murmur
```

```
        (time ejection)
        (location
          (aortic_area))))
```

The pattern:

```
        (auscultation
          (any
            (systolic_murmur
              (time ejection)
              (loudness (any moderate loud))
              (location
                (aortic_area)))
            (thrill SS_notch)))
```

matches either a moderate to loud systolic ejection murmur in the aortic area, or a thrill at
the suprasternal notch. The name *any* introduces a series of alternative matches. In addition to alternatives, portions of the pattern that must not match, or that may optionally
match are possible, as are patterns that test for numbers that fall within specific ranges.

When a rule's pattern part matches the scratchpad, its action part is executed, typically
performing one or more operations on hypotheses. Some operations modify the hypothesis
objects on the scratchpad, representing the hypotheses that Galen is currently considering.
These operations are analogous to those in Diagnoser. They include **propose**, which introduces a new hypothesis into consideration, **accept** and **reject**, which respectively assert the
truth or falsity of hypotheses, and **confirm** and **oppose**, which respectively associate
confirmatory and disconfirmatory evidence with a hypothesis. The matching portion of the
scratchpad is regarded as evidence supporting the execution of an operation. In general,
when a hypothesis is operated upon, a record of the operation is written on the scratchpad as
an element of the affected hypothesis object, and the rules associated with the object are
applied to determine the effects of the operation. Each such record specifies the name of the
operation, the name of the hypothesis it affected, and the matching portion of the scratchpad
that led to its being performed. Some operations ignore hypotheses that are not yet being
considered or that are known to be false. For example, **confirm** will not work on a
hypothesis that has been rejected or one that has not yet been proposed. Similarly, it is possible to reject an accepted hypothesis but not possible to accept a rejected one.

Other operations do not modify hypotheses, but act to stop the program. One such
operation is **succeed**, which asserts that the current problem has been solved. The other is
fail, which asserts that the current problem cannot be solved.

Galen works by using data directed rules to suggest a small set of plausible hypotheses,
then using hypothesis directed rules to refine these hypotheses until one of them can be
shown correct (Miller et al., 1984). This is done by executing a series of three step cycles.
Initially the scratchpad is empty. The first step of each cycle obtains a piece of problem
data from the outside world, translates it to an object, and writes the object on the data
page of the scratchpad (Fig. 1).

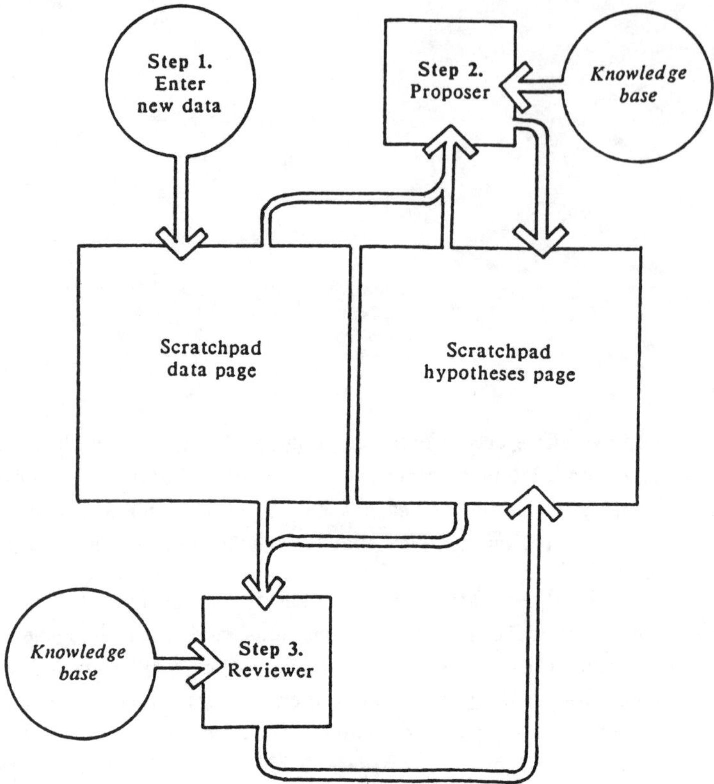

Fig. 1. Major Components of Galen

The second step involves running a procedure called the *proposer*. The proposer applies all rule teams associated with newly arrived data objects on the scratchpad. Typically, these rules act to propose new hypotheses (hence the name) but it is possible for them to execute the other operations as well.

When the proposer has finished, the *reviewer* is called. The reviewer is a procedure that applies the rule teams associated with all nonrejected hypothesis objects appearing on the scratchpad. Hypothesis objects are visited in arbitrary order and their rule teams are applied until no more rules are successful.

When the reviewer has finished, Galen checks to see whether a succeed or fail operation has been performed, or whether there is no more data available. If either of these is true, the program stops, otherwise a new cycle is started.

It is convenient to imagine that the hypotheses in Galen's knowledge base form a directed graph, where vertices are hypotheses and edges are rules. One hypothesis "points to" another if the first hypothesis contains a rule whose action part operates on the second. This provides a useful pictorial notation for knowledge bases. It also emphasizes potential relationships between competing hypotheses, an understanding of which has proven critical in realizing expert performance.

In terms of this analogy, Galen works by using the proposer and the reviewer to investigate hypotheses (search the graph) by applying rules (following edges from one vertex to another). The proposer selects one or more hypotheses (vertices) that are worthy starting points for further search. The reviewer applies rules associated with these hypotheses (propagates search along outward pointing edges) until a solution hypothesis (vertex) has been found or until no more plausible hypotheses (vertices) remain to be searched.

Although this procedure could conceivably search very large portions of the graph, it does not do so in practice, and explicit mechanisms to limit search have not been necessary. An examination of the pediatric cardiology knowledge base suggests three reasons. First, only the most promising vertices in the knowledge base are ever used to initiate search. This is equivalent to saying that the rules used by the proposer seldom make serious mistakes. Second, only a small number of edges are ever followed. This is equivalent to saying that most rules associated with hypotheses describe very specific states of affairs. Third, many edges point back to their originating vertex. This is equivalent to saying that many rules associated with a hypothesis act on the hypothesis itself, typically to gather evidence. Since the number of effectively outward pointing edges is small, it is hard to search very far.

7 Galen's Reasoning

Although all rules in Galen are untyped and represented in the same formalism, different rules perform different functions. There are four main classes of rules: *triggering* rules, *evaluation* rules, *refinement* rules, and *monitor* rules (Fig 2.).

Triggering rules examine features of problem data and introduce new hypotheses as a result. Most triggering rules are associated with specific classes of data and are therefore handled by the proposer. Their pattern parts typically match features of problem data and their action parts execute propose or accept operations.

In the graph analogy suggested above, triggering rules are edges originating outside the hypothesis graph and terminating at specific hypotheses. They suggest plausible initial starting points for further initial search within the graph.

Evaluation rules are typically associated with individual hypotheses and are handled by the reviewer. Their pattern parts examine the scratchpad for specific confirmatory or disconfirmatory evidence, and their action parts execute **confirm** and **oppose** operations on their containing hypotheses, respectively. In this way they accumulate evidence for later use by refinement rules.

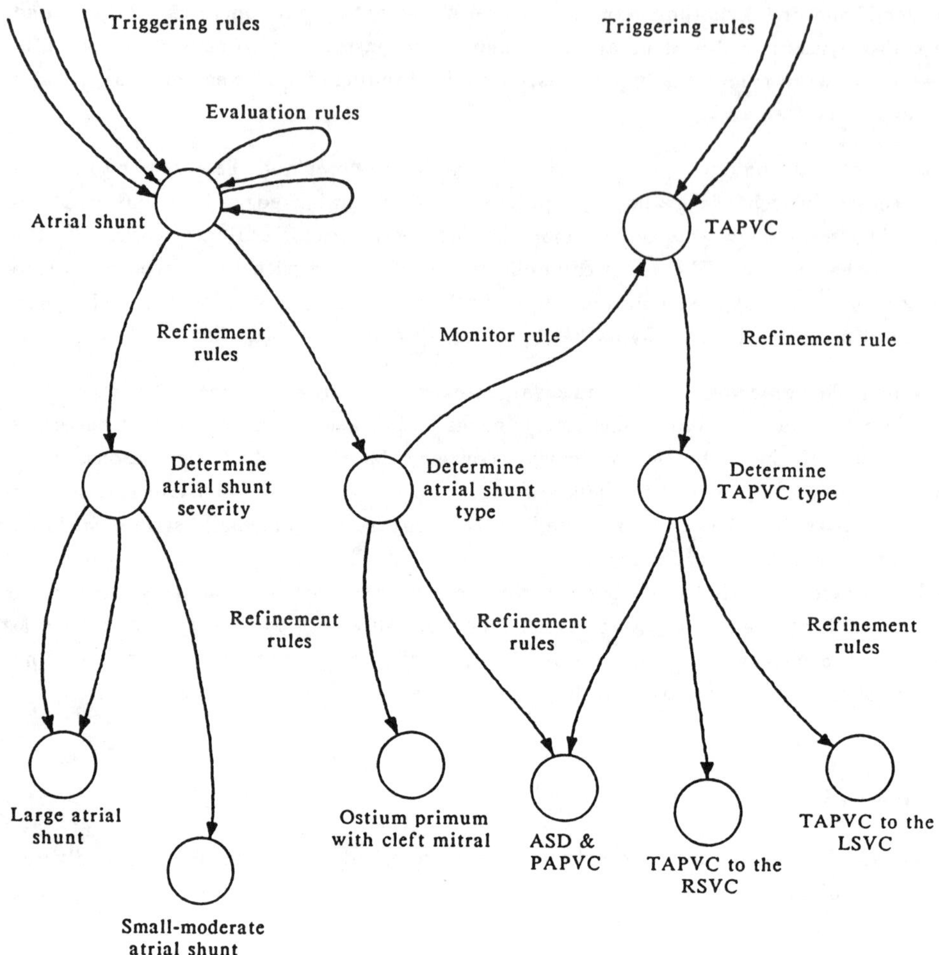

Fig. 2. A Portion of Galen's Knowledge Base Graph

Evaluation rules appear as edges in the graph that both originate and terminate at the same vertex. In this way they prevent the graph from being searched beyond the vertex until enough evidence has accumulated.

Refinement rules are associated with individual hypotheses and are handled by the reviewer. Their pattern parts typically match significant configurations of evidence about a hypothesis that was accumulated by evaluation rules, or features of problem data and other hypotheses. Their action parts execute **accept** or **reject** operations on their containing hypotheses, or **propose** or **accept** operations on other hypotheses that are more specific variants of them.

Refinement rules that accept or reject their containing hypotheses appear much like evaluation rules in the graph. Refinement rules that propose or accept variant hypotheses are edges connecting short linear chains of vertices. Each vertex in the chain represents a hypothesis that is a more specific form of the one that precedes it. Partitioning the graph into stages of vertices helps keep the search from going too far unless the evidence suggests that it should.

Monitor rules are also associated with individual hypotheses and are handled by the reviewer. Unlike refinement rules, they do not operate on more specific forms of the hypotheses that contain them. Their action parts introduce previously unrelated hypotheses that should be considered un addition to, or instead of, their containing hypothesis.

In the graph, the edge corresponding to a monitor rule originates at a vertex in the chain of vertices established by refinement rules. The edge terminates at a vertex that is not in the same chain. Alternatively, a monitor rule may appear in an unrelated hypothesis, but may "watch" the scratchpad for the presence of certain hypotheses, rejecting or otherwise modifying them if they appear. Monitor rules thus act to lead search away toward new parts of the graph if the evidence suggests that it should and are particularly useful when confronted with a Garden Path problem. It is important that the number of monitor rules be small, or their pattern parts be very specific, to avoid an exploding uncontrolled search of the entire graph.

8 Garden Path Reasoning

If a class of rules in the knowledge base is inadequate in some respect then an error can occur. As described earlier, one kind of error is due to inadequate triggering rules that result in a diagnostician missing the correct diagnosis because he or she simply did not think of it: "I never considered disease **X**." Inadequate evaluation rules can also allow the diagnostician to consider the correct diagnosis but not know what to do about investigating it: "It looks like disease **X** but I don't know why symptom **A** is there." Inadequate refinement rules can allow the diagnostician to consider the correct diagnosis, but be unable to choose the final diagnosis from its competitors: "Diseases **X**, **Y**, and **Z** explain the symptoms, but I don't know which one it is."

Garden path errors can occur as a result of inadequate monitor rules. A hypothesis can be triggered and enough evidence gathered for it so that it can be accepted as the final diagnosis, even though it is wrong. The problem is that an easily overlooked piece of patient data should have been detected and acted upon by a missing monitor rule. (As described above, monitor rules are so called because they "monitor" the usual diagnostic process, interrupting it if necessary.) A human diagnostician who made such an error might have said: "Disease **X** is the answer, and symptom **A** is irrelevant," although it is as likely that **A** would not have been noticed at all.

In order to examine Galen's reasoning on Garden Path cases of congenital heart disease it was first given the versions of the TAPVC case described earlier. In each version the model reached a diagnosis of TAPVC. Galen concluded a diagnosis of TAPVC in some cases because its triggering rules were more powerful than those of Diagnoser so that even in the face of relatively weak evidence it proposed TAPVC. In other cases Galen's monitor rules forced the TAPVC hypothesis to be considered despite early strong evidence for one of the alternatives in its competitor set.

As a means of further testing the power of Galen's knowledge base, a number of "natural error" cases were selected from hospital files. These cases were ones in which the pre and post catheterization diagnoses differed. Galen was given these cases to diagnose. Its response on such a case of TAPVC is shown in Examples 1 and 2. In TAPVC, a hole is present between the left and right atria of the heart and the vessels normally feeding blood to both atria are misconnected so that only the left atrium receives blood from the body.

The case in Examples 1 and 2 was initially misdiagnosed by a human physician as ASD (Atrial Septal Defect), a disease in which only the hole between the atria is present. One key to distinguishing the two diseases is to note the presence of cyanosis, which is characteristic of TAPVC but not of ASD. This can be difficult not only because cyanosis is sometimes hard to identify in a patient, but also because if its significance is not appreciated the symptoms seem to point toward ASD, effectively leading the physician down a garden path.

Since Galen does not have any perceptual mechanisms, and must rely on a human to interpret sensory data, it cannot deal with Garden Path errors resulting from a failure to detect weak or marginal cyanosis. The addition of monitor rules to Galen can, however, deal with errors resulting from overcommitment to ASD in the presence of possible cyanosis. In Example 1, which follows, a version of Galen without these rules repeats the physician's error by following a line of reasoning apparently similar to that in the original misdiagnosed case.

Commentary appears in this type face.

Output produced while the program is running appears in this type face.

{ This is Galen 3.1, running at U of MN CSci Vax on Wed Apr 17 18:42:13 1985. Galen is using the Garden Path Pediatric Cardiology 0.85 knowledge base. }

In this example, we have removed all monitor rules relating ASD to cyanosis from Galen's knowledge base. When given this case of TAPVC that was originally misdiagnosed as ASD by a human physician, Galen repeats the original misdiagnosis.

Galen works in a series of three-step cycles. In the first step of each cycle, Galen obtains a new piece of case data (the patient is seven months old) and writes it on the scratchpad, as shown below.

1. Obtaining the following data:

(age 7)

In the second step, the Proposer applies rules associated with the new piece of data. These rules determine if the new data immediately suggests any new hypotheses of if it requires any changes to old ones.

1.1. Determining immediate effects of the new data.

In the third step, the Reviewer applies rules associated with each nonrejected hypothesis currently on the scratchpad. These rules determine if the new data suggests any changes to their containing hypothesis.

1.2. There are no hypotheses yet.

2. Obtaining the following data:

(sex female)

2.1. Determining immediate effects of the new data.

2.2. There are no hypotheses yet.

3. Obtaining the following data:

```
(when_recognized
  (age_when_recognized 0.01)
  (reason_for_recognition symptoms))
```

3.1. Determining immediate effects of the new data.

3.2. There are no hypotheses yet.

4. Obtaining the following data:

```
(initial_symptoms
  (rhythm rapid)
  (CHF_symptoms tachypnea))
```

4.1. Determining immediate effects of the new data.

Every time a rule is successfully applied, a message is printed. The message contains a unique number for the application (e.g. 4.1.1.), the class of data or hypothesis that the rule is associated with (e.g. initial_symptoms), the portion of the scratchpad the rule's pattern matched (the parenthesized structure), and a statement describing the action that the rule is executing (e.g. suggesting congestive heart failure).

The symbol "$unspecified" means that some objects deeply nested in the data were not examined by the rule's pattern.

414

4.1.1. In initial_symptoms, the presence of

    (initial_symptoms
      (CHF_symptoms $unspecified))

suggests congestive_heart_failure.

4.2. Determining how the new data affects current hypotheses.

5. Obtaining the following data:

    (present_symptoms)

    No information about present symptoms was reported in this case.

5.1. Determining immediate effects of the new data.

5.2. Determining how the new data affects current hypotheses.

6. Obtaining the following data:

    (physical_examination
      (cyanosis
        (central_cyanosis
          (varies_in_some_circumstances)))))

6.1. Determining immediate effects of the new data.

    A triggering rule notes that the patient is cyanotic, ignoring the fact that the cyanosis is variable.

6.1.1. In physical_examination, the presence of

    (physical_examination
      (cyanosis
        (central_cyanosis $unspecified)))

causes the acceptance of cyanosis.

6.2. Determining how the new data affects current hypotheses.

7. Obtaining the following data:

    (heart
      (location_of_cardiac_apex
        (position_relative_to_MCL LAT-MCL)
        (intracostal_space 5LICS))
      (systolic_murmur
        (location
          (pulmonary_area))
        (loudness moderate)

```
      (time ejection))
    (diastolic_murmur
      (location
        (LSB))
      (loudness soft)
      (time mid))
  (s2
    (splitting
      (fixed))
    (p2 loud)))
```

7.1. Determining immediate effects of the new data.

A triggering rule notes that this systolic murmur suggests a shunt at level of the atria. This defect is present in both ASD and TAPVC. The hypothesis about atrial shunt contains evaluation rules that will begin gathering evidence in its favor, and refinement rules that will accept it if enough evidence can be found.

7.1.1. In heart, the presence of

```
(heart
  (systolic_murmur
    (location
      (pulmonary_area $unspecified))
    (time ejection)
    (loudness moderate)))
```

suggests atrial_shunt.

Another triggering rule notes that this diastolic murmur also suggests an atrial shunt.

7.1.2. In heart, the presence of

```
(heart
  (diastolic_murmur
    (location
      (LSB $unspecified))
    (time mid)))
```

suggests atrial_shunt, which is already being considered.

Galen detects that the patient's pulmonary arterial pressure (PAP) is increased.

7.1.3. In s2, the presence of

```
(heart
  (s2
    (p2 loud)))
```

causes the acceptance of increased_PAP.

416

7.2. Determining how the new data affects current hypotheses.

Two evaluation rules determine that the systolic and diastolic murmurs are consistent with an atrial shunt.

7.2.1. In atrial_shunt, the presence of

```
(heart
  (systolic_murmur
    (location
      (pulmonary_area $unspecified))
    (time ejection)
    (loudness moderate)))
```

is consistent with atrial_shunt.

7.2.2. In atrial_shunt, the presence of

```
(heart
  (diastolic_murmur
    (location
      (LSB $unspecified))
    (time mid)))
```

is consistent with atrial_shunt.

Enough evidence for an atrial shunt has been detected so that the hypothesis can be accepted.

7.2.2.1. In atrial_shunt, the presence of

```
(hypotheses
  (atrial_shunt
    (confirmed
      (data
        (heart
          (diastolic_murmur
            (location
              (LSB $unspecified))
            (time mid))
          (systolic_murmur
            (location
              (pulmonary_area $unspecified))
            (time ejection)
            (loudness moderate)))))))
```

causes the acceptance of atrial_shunt.

Since the patient is now assumed to have an atrial shunt, a refinement rule proposes a hypothesis that enough data has been seen to determine its type (the disease associated with the shunt) and its severity. Note that Galen has not yet committed itself to a diagnosis of ASD.

7.2.2.1.1. In atrial_shunt, the presence of

    (hypotheses
      (atrial_shunt
        (accepted $unspecified)
        ($non
          (rejected))))

suggests determine_atrial_shunt_type and determine_atrial_shunt_severity.

A refinement rule detects the diastolic murmur and determines that the shunt must be large. Note that the rule's pattern did not examine any specific information about the murmur.

7.2.3. In determine_atrial_shunt_severity, the presence of

    (heart
      (diastolic_murmur $unspecified))

causes the acceptance of large_atrial_shunt.

At this point, a monitor rule in determine_atrial_shunt_type would normally have detected cyanosis and shifted Galen's attention to TAPVC.

8. Obtaining the following data:

    (abdomen
      (palpable_liver
        (cm_below_RCM 2)))

8.1. Determining immediate effects of the new data.

8.2. Determining how the new data affects current hypotheses.

9. Obtaining the following data:

    (EKG
      (axis
        (deviation right))
      (atrial_enlargement right)
      (ventricular_hypertrophy right))

9.1. Determining immediate effects of the new data.

9.1.1. In EKG, the presence of

    (EKG
      (ventricular_hypertrophy right))

causes the acceptance of right_ventricular_hypertrophy.

418

9.1.2. In EKG, the presence of

```
(EKG
  (axis
    (deviation right)))
```

causes the acceptance of right_axis_deviation.

9.1.4.1. In right_axis_deviation, the presence of

```
(hypotheses
  (right_axis_deviation
    (accepted $unspecified)))
```

suggests right_ventricular_hypertrophy, which is already accepted.

·9.2. Determining how the new data affects current hypotheses.

10. Obtaining the following data:

```
(X-ray
  (pulmonary_vasculature
    (abnormal
      (pulmonary_arterial_markings increased)))
  (cardiac_size moderately_enlarged))
```

10.1. Determining immediate effects of the new data.

10.1.1. In X-ray, the presence of

```
(data
  (EKG
    ($non
      (atrial_enlargement left)))
  (X-ray
    ($non
      (left_atrial_enlargement
        (non none)))))
```

causes the acceptance of no_left_atrial_enlargement.

10.1.2. In X-ray, the presence of

```
(X-ray
  (cardiac_size moderately_enlarged))
```

causes the acceptance of cardiomegaly.

A triggering rule concludes that the patient's pulmonary blood flow is increased. If there were more information, Galen would be able to estimate the degree of increase.

10.1.3. In X-ray, the presence of

```
(X-ray
  (pulmonary_vasculature
    (abnormal
      (pulmonary_arterial_markings increased)))))
```

causes the acceptance of increased_PBF.

10.2. Determining how the new data affects current hypotheses.

10.2.1. In congestive_heart_failure, the presence of

```
(hypotheses
  (cardiomegaly
    (accepted $unspecified)))
```

is consistent with congestive_heart_failure.

10.2.2. In increased_PBF, the presence of

```
(hypotheses
  (cyanosis
    (accepted $unspecified))
  (increased_PBF
    (accepted $unspecified)))
```

causes the acceptance of admixture_lesion.

The hypothesis admixture_lesion *refers to the general class of diseases being diagnosed. ASD is not an admixture lesion, but TAPVC is.*

One of the missing monitor rules would have accepted TAPVC at this point because the patient is cyanotic, has increased PBF, and has no left atrial enlargement.

11. Obtaining the following data:

```
(end_of_data)
```

11.1. Determining immediate effects of the new data.

Triggering rules associated with end of data will now make a final diagnosis.

The patient has increased PAP and PBF but Galen is unable to estimate the degree of increase.

11.1.1. In end_of_data, the presence of

```
(hypotheses
  (increased_PBF
```

```
(accepted $unspecified)
($non
  (rejected))))
```

is sufficient to conclude increased_PBF.

The patient has increased pulmonary arterial pressure.

11.1.2. In end_of_data, the presence of

```
(hypotheses
  (increased_PAP
    (accepted $unspecified)
    ($non
      (rejected))))
```

is sufficient to conclude increased_PAP.

If the patient has an atrial shunt with no relevant complications (i.e. no "complex atrial shunts") then diagnose ASD. A monitor rule that detects cyanosis would ordinarily prevent this from happening.

11.1.3. In end_of_data, the presence of

```
(hypotheses
  (atrial_shunt
    (accepted $unspecified)
    ($non
      (rejected)))
  ($non
    (con
      (type complex_atrial_shunt)
      (accepted)
      (non
        (rejected)))))
```

causes the acceptance of atrial_septal_defect.

The rule that does the actual diagnosis also provides an estimate of the severity of the disease.

11.1.5. In end_of_data, the presence of

```
(hypotheses
  (atrial_shunt
    (accepted $unspecified)
    ($non
      (rejected)))
  ($non
    (con
      (type complex_atrial_shunt)
```

```
(accepted)
(non
   (rejected)))))
```

is sufficient to conclude large_atrial_shunt and atrial_septal_defect.

11.2. Determining how the new data affects current hypotheses.

{ Galen 3.1 has finished running on Wed Apr 17 18:51:03 1985. }

In Example 2, three monitor rules are added to the Galen knowledge base used above. One such rule appears in the cyanosis hypothesis itself and acts to reject all hypotheses that may not be accompanied by cyanosis. Another appears in the hypothesis corresponding to an atrial level shunt, which checks if cyanosis is being considered and introduces TAPVC if the check succeeds. A third is associated with a group of hypotheses that recognize an atrial shunt in the presence of cyanosis in a different way, as a precaution against error. Galen uses the last two rules to avoid making an erroneous diagnosis of ASD.

{ This is Galen 3.1, running at U of MN CSci Vax on Wed Apr 17 18:11:18 1985.
Galen is using the Pediatric Cardiology 0.85 knowledge base. }

In this example, the three monitor rules that were removed from Galen's knowledge base are replaced, and Galen is given the case from Example 1 again. Galen now correctly diagnoses TAPVC.

There are no differences between this example and Example 1 until the point where the atrial shunt hypothesis is accepted. We omit output until that point.

7.2.2.1. In atrial_shunt, the presence of

```
(hypotheses
  (atrial_shunt
    (confirmed
      (data
        (heart
          (diastolic_murmur
            (location
              (LSB $unspecified))
            (time mid))
          (systolic_murmur
            (location
              (pulmonary_area $unspecified))
            (time ejection)
            (loudness moderate))))))))
```

causes the acceptance of atrial_shunt.

7.2.2.1.1. In atrial_shunt, the presence of

```
(hypotheses
  (atrial_shunt
    (accepted $unspecified)
    ($non
      (rejected))))
```

suggests determine_atrial_shunt_type and determine_atrial_shunt_severity.

7.2.3. In determine_atrial_shunt_severity, the presence of

```
(heart
  (diastolic_murmur $unspecified))
```

causes the acceptance of large_atrial_shunt.

TAPVC presents itself with symptoms of an atrial level shunt accompanied by cyanosis. A monitor rule associated with one of the atrial shunt hypotheses detects cyanosis and diverts Galen's attention to TAPVC.

7.2.4. In determine_atrial_shunt_type, the presence of

```
(hypotheses
  (cyanosis
    ($non
      (rejected))))
```

causes the acceptance of TAPVC.

A refinement rule associated with the TAPVC hypothesis suggests that there is enough information present to determine the type of TAPVC that the patient has. As in this case, there often isn't enough evidence to make such a determination.

7.2.4.1. In TAPVC, the presence of

```
(hypotheses
  (TAPVC
    (accepted $unspecified)))
```

suggests determine_TAPVC_type.

There are no more differences between Example 1 and this example until the hypothesis about admixture lesion is accepted. We omit output until that point.

TAPVC is a member of the class of admixture lesions, but ASD is not.

10.2.3. In increased_PBF, the presence of

```
(hypotheses
  (cyanosis
```

```
    (accepted $unspecified))
  (increased_PBF
    (accepted $unspecified)))
```

causes the acceptance of admixture_lesion.

Another monitor rule causes acceptance of TAPVC. Using rules that accept the hypothesis in different ways is a protection against error.

10.2.4. In no_left_atrial_enlargement, the presence of

```
(hypotheses
  (cyanosis
    ($non
      (rejected)))
  (increased_PBF
    (accepted $unspecified)))
```

causes the acceptance of TAPVC, which is already accepted for other reasons.

11. Obtaining the following data:

```
(end_of_data)
```

11.1. Determining immediate effects of the new data.

Rules associated with end of data will now offer a final diagnosis. As in Example 2, the patient has increased PBF and increased PAP.

11.1.1. In end_of_data, the presence of

```
(hypotheses
  (increased_PBF
    (accepted $unspecified)
    ($non
      (rejected))))
```

is sufficient to conclude increased_PBF.

11.1.2. In end_of_data, the presence of

```
(hypotheses
  (increased_PAP
    (accepted $unspecified)
    ($non
      (rejected))))
```

is sufficient to conclude increased_PAP.

Galen now comes to a correct diagnosis of TAPVC. The rules applicable to the severity of a simple atrial shunt are not relevant to TAPVC so no information about severity is provided.

11.1.3. In end_of_data, the presence of

```
(hypotheses
  (TAPVC
    (accepted $unspecified)
    ($non
      (rejected))))
```

is sufficient to conclude TAPVC.

11.2. Determining how the new data affects current hypotheses.

{ Galen 3.1 has finished running on Wed Apr 17 18:25:01 1985. }

Additional cases have been used to demonstrate the value of monitor rules in avoiding the situations that lead to garden path errors. The monitor rules are able to recognize the special situations in which it is necessary to reevaluate the relevance of initially triggered hypotheses. It is still unknown whether a small set of specific rules is adequate to recognize all these situations. If this is not the case, many monitor rules will have to be added and Galen will need to perform a much broader search of its knowledge base.

9 Conclusion

Because human experts are the ones we turn to when we need solutions to hard problems, we sometimes forget that upon occasion they make mistakes. While errors in an expert's thinking may occur due to the lack of some specific piece of knowledge, they more often occur due to what can be viewed as a strategic misallocation of problem solving resources. This situation occurs in problems that contain what we have called Garden Paths in which early cues strongly suggest incorrect answers, and later, usually weaker cues suggest answers that are correct. Study of such problems can give us valuable insight into the deeper nature of the problem solving process as well as provide practical knowledge for overcoming reasoning errors in specific fields of interest.

In the work presented here we have outlined an approach to the study of Garden Path errors in an area of medicine concerned with the diagnosis of congenital heart diseases. We have employed a methodology for building expert systems based upon the intensive study of human experts and the development and testing of a theory of expertise in the form of a cognitive simulation model. The virtue of our approach is that it provides a clear means of identifying and testing hypotheses about the content of expert knowledge, as well as a means for developing knowledge which can lead to performance at an expert level and beyond. As an added benefit the approach can provide insight into the kind of knowledge needed to provide explanations of solution paths to system users. The weakness in our approach is that it is time consuming and may not result in the most efficient system. Clearly its value is greater when the expertise of interest is found among professional problem solvers (physicians, lawyers, managers, etc.) for whom the answers to problems have considerable societal and personal significance. When the result of errors made in using a system are sick patients, convicted clients or reduced profits, the quality of the problem solution as well as the means of reaching it weigh heavily on the user's mind.

A critical aspect of our approach is the process of interacting with human experts. Although we have not dealt with this in any detail in the present paper, it is our ultimate source of success. In building the Galen system, for instance, we worked intensively with a single expert over a period of several months in order to identify the knowledge (in this case the monitor rules) that would enable Galen to avoid Garden Path errors. Because experts are not fully or in some circumstances even dimly aware of what they know, the process of acquiring knowledge, especially that which can add to performance in the field, is difficult indeed (Johnson, 1983; 1984).

In contrast with a number of other systems, particularly in the medical area (e.g. MYCIN, Buchanan & Shortliffe, 1984; INTERNIST, Miller et al., 1984), the Galen system was developed from a study of tasks in which human expertise "almost" works. When we give experts tasks to which their knowledge applies, we run the risk of learning principally about the task and its demands, rather than about the expertise that accomplishes it. Instead of using tasks in which experts perform well, we have investigated expertise through tasks in which the expert makes mistakes. We believe that the knowledge gained from this approach offers considerable promise for the development of systems which are less susceptible to error and more robust in their domain of application. But more than this, we believe that the study of Garden Path reasoning offers the opportunity for understanding and improving the knowledge which is brought to bear on tasks in the first place.

In some respects the approach we describe is reminiscent of work done over a decade ago by Churchman, Lederberg and Feigenbaum (Churchman, 1971; Lederberg & Feigenbaum, 1968) in which the attempt was to develop a program that would embody expertise in chemical analysis (Dendral) as well as provide insight into the nature of the inquiry process itself. Though less ambitious than the Dendral project, our work has also focused on the dual problem of achieving a high level of program performance while at the same time attempting to gain an understanding of an important human intellectual activity.

REFERENCES

Aikins, J., "Prototypes and production rules: A knowledge representation for computer consultations," Ph.D. dissertation, Rep. #STAN CSD 80-814, Stanford University, 1980.

Allen, E., "YAPS: A Production System Meets Objects," *AAAI-83*, March 1983.

Churchman, C.W., "The Design of Inquiring Systems: Basic Concepts of Systems and Organizations," Basic Books Inc., 1971.

Clancey, W.J., "Classification Problem Solving," *Proceedings of the National Conference on Artificial Intelligence,* pp. 49-55, 1984.

Clement, J., "Student's Misconceptions in Introductory Mechanics," *American Journal of Physics,* 1982, 50 (1), 66-71.

Cohen, H.A. "The Art of Snaring Dragons," MIT A.I. Memo 338, May 1975.

Elstein, A., Shulman, L. and Sprafka, S., *Medical Problem Solving,* Harvard University Press, 1978.

Erman, L.D., Hayes-Roth, F., Lesser, B.R. and Reddy, D.R., "The HEARSAY-II speech understanding system: Integrating knowledge to resolve uncertainty," *Computing Surveys,* 1980, 12(2):213-253.

Feltovich, P., "Knowledge Based Components of Expertise in Medical Diagnosis," Unpublished doctoral dissertation, University of Minnesota, 1981.

Forgy, C.L., "Rete: A Fast Algorithm for the Many Pattern/Many Object Pattern Match Problem," *Artificial Intelligence,* 1982, 19, 17-37.

Johnson, P.E., "What Kind of Expert Should A System Be?" *The Journal of Medicine and Philosophy,* 1983, 8, 77-97.

Johnson, P.E., "The Expert Mind: A New Challenge for the Information Scientist," In Th. M.A. Belemans (Ed.), *Beyond Productivity: Information Systems Development for Organizational Effectiveness.* Elsevier Science Publishers, B.V. (North Holland), 1984, 367-386.

Johnson, P.E., Duran, A.S., Hassebrock, F., Moller, J., Prietula, M., Feltovich, P.J., & Swanson, D.B., "Expertise and Error in Diagnostic Reasoning," *Cognitive Science,* 1981, 5, 235-285.

Johnson, P.E., Thompson, W.B., "Strolling down the garden path: Detection and recovery from error in expert problem solving," *Proceedings of the Seventh International Joint Conference on Artificial Intelligence,* Vancouver, British Columbia, August 1981.

Lederberg, J., Feigenbaum, E.A., "Mechanization of Inductive Inference in Organic Chemistry," in B. Kleinmuntz (Ed.), *Formal Representation of Human Judgment,* New York: John Wiley & Sons, Inc., 1968.

Miller, R.A., Pople, H.E. Jr., and Meyers, J.D., "INTERNIST-1: An experimental computer-based consultant for general internal medicine," in *Readings in Medical Artificial Intelligence: The First Decade,* Clancey, W.J. and Shortliffe, E.H. (eds.), Addison Wesley, 1984.

Minsky, M., "A Framework for the Representation of Knowledge," in P.H. Winson (Ed.), *The Psychology of Computer Vision,* New York: Cambridge University Press, 1975.

Richie, G.D., & Hanna, F.K., "AM: A Case Study in A1 Methodology," *Artificial Intelligence,* 1984, 23, 249-268.

Swanson, D.B. "Computer Simulation of Expert Problem Solving in Medical Diagnosis," Unpublished doctoral dissertation, University of Minnesota, 1978.

Swanson, D.B., Feltovich, P.J. and Johnson, P.E., "Analysis of Physician Expertise: Implications for the Design of Decision Support Systems," in D.B. Shires and H. Wolf (Eds.), *Medinfo 77*, Amsterdam: North-Holland Publishing Co., 1977.

Thompson, W.B., Johnson, P.E., and Moen, J.B., "Recognition-based Reasoning," *Proceedings of the Eighth International Joint Conference on Artificial Intelligence,* Karlesruhe, West Germany, August 1983.

Knowledge Organization and Its Role
in Temporal and Causal Signal Understanding:
The ALVEN and CAA Projects

John K. Tsotsos and Tetsutaro Shibahara

Department of Computer Science
10 King's College Road, University of Toronto
Toronto, Ontario, Canada M5S 1A4

ABSTRACT

This paper describes the ALVEN and CAA projects. These projects share many basic concepts particularly with respect to the representation of knowledge and to the hypothesize and test nature of the control strategy. They both deal with temporally rich data interpretation tasks. However, they focus on very different aspects of interpretation. ALVEN processes images of a time-varying sequence in a real-time fashion (although not in real time), while CAA considers an entire signal, as if time were a second spatial dimension. ALVEN deals with the assessment of the performance of the human left ventricle from an X-ray image sequence, while CAA considers the causal relationships of the electrophysiology of the human heart and the resulting electrocardiogram signal, and tries to detect and classify anomalies of rhythm. The contributions of these works lie in the elucidation of a representation and control structure for the knowledge-based interpretation of time-varying signals.

1 INTRODUCTION

The development of the ALVEN and CAA systems represents a long-term research effort over the past 12 years. The basic approach involves exploiting frame-based representations for interpretation. Frames are organized into a semantic network and a control strategy was developed that is driven by the knowledge organization. ALVEN uses the generalization/specialization, aggregation/decomposition, similarity and temporal precedence organizational relations, while CAA adds a causal relation to this set. This paper will discuss aspects of the two systems, with the bulk of the discussion devoted to the CAA system. Details on ALVEN have appeared in several previous publications [Tsotsos et al. 80], [Tsotsos 81], [Tsotsos 85], [Tsotsos 87]. All of the examples presented in section 2.0 are from the ALVEN system, and examples from the CAA system all appear in section 5.0. The discussions in sections 2.0 and 3.0 summarize features that the two systems have in common.

2 THE REPRESENTATION SCHEME

2.1 Knowledge Packages: Classes

Packaging up knowledge leads to a modular representation, with all the advantages of modularity, particularly the enhancement of clarity and flexibility. Most knowledge package representation schemes borrow strongly from the frame concept of [Minsky 75]. Our frames are called classes and borrow much from the Procedural Semantic Networks formalism (PSN) of [Levesque & Mylopoulos 79]. A class provides a generalized definition of the components, attributes and relationships that must be confirmed of a particular concept under consideration in order to be able to make the deduction that the particular concept is an instance of the prototypical concept. Classes also have embedded, declarative control information, namely exceptions and similarity links. These features will be described shortly. Note that there is a distinction between the "prerequisites" of the class, those components that must be observed in order to instantiate the class, and the "dependents" of a class, those components that must be derived on instantiation. Dependent slots carry their own computation information. Classes exhibit large grain size, and translating their contents to rules would require many rules. An obvious advantage over a rule-based scheme is that elements that conceptually belong together are packaged together into a class. Other frame-based schemes for medical consultation systems include the MDX system [Chandrasekaran et al. 79] and CADUCEUS [Pople 82].

2.2 Knowledge Organization

When confronted with a large, complex task, "divide and conquer" is an obvious tactic. Task partitioning is crucial, however, arbitrary task subdivision will yield structures that are unwieldy, unnecessarily complex or inappropriately simple. Furthermore they have poorly defined semantics, lead to inefficient processing, and lack clarity and perspicuity. Within the existing representational repertoire, there exist two common tools for domain sub-division and organization, namely the IS-A relationship (or generalization/specialization relation), and the PART-OF relationship (or the part/whole relation or aggregation/decomposition). [Brachman 79], [Levesque & Mylopoulos 79], [Brachman 82] provide discussions on their properties, semantics and use. The IS-A was included in order to control the level of specificity of concepts represented. IS-A provides for economy of representation by representing constraints only once, enforcing strict inheritance of constraints and structural components. It is a natural concept organizational scheme, and provides a partial ordering of knowledge concepts that is convenient for top-down search strategies. In conjunction with another representational construct, SIMILARITY, IS-A siblings may be implicitly partitioned into discriminatory sets. The PART-OF or aggregation relationship allows control of the level of resolution represented in knowledge packages and thus the knowledge granularity of the knowledge base. It provides for the implementation of a divide-and-conquer representational strategy. It too forms a partial ordering of knowledge concepts that is useful for both top-down and bottom-up search strategies. Concept structure can be represented using slots in a class definition. The slots form an implicit PART-OF relationship with the concept. Representational prototypes (classes) are distinguished from and related to tokens by the INSTANCE-OF relationship. Instances must reflect the structure of the class they are related to; however, partial instances are permitted in association with a set of exception instances (the 'exception record') for that class. In addition, another type of incomplete instance is permitted, namely the potential instance or hypothesis. It is basically a structure that conforms to the "skeleton" of the generic class, but may have only a subset of slots filled, and has not achieved a certainty high enough to cause it to be an instance or partial instance.

2.3 Multi-Dimensional Levels of Detail

The term "level of detail" seems to denote different things to different people. In most schemes, it is used to express problem decomposition only [Nilsson 71]. We present two separate views of abstraction "level". These views are related to the fact that all concepts have both IS-A and PART-OF relationships with other concepts. Thus the level of specificity of detail can be controlled by, or examined by traversing, the IS-A hierarchy, while the level of resolution of detail (decomposition in other schemes) is reflected in the PART-OF hierarchy. In [Patil et al. 82], only the decomposition view of level is present, while in CADUCEUS, [Pople 82], (it seems that) the level of specificity is employed and level of resolution is restricted to causal connections. In [Wallis & Shortliffe 82] rule complexity is used which may be likened to our view of level of resolution; however, its use is restricted to explanation.

2.4 Time

Several interacting mechanisms are available for the representation of temporal information. This multi-pronged approach differs from other schemes that embody a single type of construct for handling temporal information. The complexity of time necessitates several special mechanisms. Our approach differs from others [Allen 81], [Mittal & Chandrasekaran 80], in that we were motivated by problems in signal analysis rather than in representing natural language temporal descriptions and their inherent ambiguity and vagueness. It is not clear, for example, what kind of control strategy can be employed along with Allen's scheme of temporal representation. Fagan [Fagan 80] is concerned with a temporal interpretation situation. However, there are a number of issues, primarily in control, that are not considered by his system, VM:

- using the rule-based approach, only a data-driven recognition scheme is incorporated, and thus, VM cannot instigate a search for temporally expected events;

- the handling of noise is not formalized, but is rather ad hoc;

- the complexity of temporal relationships among rules seems limited, and arbitrary groupings of temporal events and their recognition are not addressed;

- expectations in time are table-driven, and no distinction is made between them and default values or expected ranges. Expectations in AL-VEN are computed from such information but current context is taken into account as well so that expectations are tailored for the task at hand;

- partial satisfiability of temporal event groupings cannot be handled.

In addition, Long and Russ also address the problem of time-dependent reasoning [Long and Russ 83]. Their scheme is closer to Fagan's than to ours. The control is data-driven exclusively. Their representation of time, however, shares some similarities with ours in that both points and intervals are used, and special meaning is assigned to the variable "now".

A brief description of the representation of time used by ALVEN follows. A TIME_INTERVAL class is defined that contains three slots, namely, start time, end time and duration. This class can then be included in the structure of any other class and would define its temporal boundaries and uncertainty in those values. Using those slots, the relations before, after, during, etc., (similar to [Allen 81]) are provided. In constraint or default definition, sequences of values (or ranges of values) may be specified using an 'at' (@) operator, so that in effect a piecewise linear approximation to a time-varying function can be included. In this case of course, constraint evaluation must occur at the proper point in time. Tokens of values such as volume or velocity for which use of this operator is appropriate, have two slots, one for the actual value and the other for the time instant at which that value is true. The time instant slot is a dependent slot whose value is set to the value of the special variable "now" (current time slice). Note that this kind of mechanism could easily be expanded if required to multi-dimensional functions.

Finally, arbitrary groupings of events can be represented. The set construct (which may be used for any type of class grouping, not only for events), specifies elements of a group, names the group as a slot, and has element selection criteria represented as constraints on the slot. [Patil et al. 82] describe a version of temporal aggregation similar to ours, but do not seem to have a time-line along which selection of values can occur, nor do they distinguish between aggregations of events and sequences of measurements.

Since knowledge classes are organized using the IS-A and PART-OF relations, their temporality is as well. By constructing a PART-OF hierarchy of events, one implicitly changes the temporal resolution of knowledge classes (as long as not only simultaneous events are considered). For example, suppose that the most primitive events occur with durations on the order of seconds. Then groupings of those may define events that occur with durations in the minute range, and then groupings of those again on the order of hours, and so on. Yet, many kinds of events cannot be so decomposed, and there is no requirement that all events have such a complete decomposition. Those events however, are not left hanging, since they will also be related to others in the knowledge base via the IS-A relationship. The control scheme makes use of the temporal resolution with respect to sampling rates and convergence of certainties.

In the following examples, first the TIME_INTERVAL class is shown, followed by the class for the concept of SEQUENCE, followed by a constraint on volume of the left ventricle from the normal left ventricle class, showing the use of the @ mechanism for both default and constraint definition.

example 1

```
class TIME_INTERVAL with
prerequisites
   st : TIME_V such that [st >= 0];
   et : TIME_V such that [et >= st];
dependents
   dur : TIME_V with dur ← et - st;
end
```

This provides the basic definition of a time interval for the system, and each concept in the knowledge base has a time interval as part of its definition. The TIME_INTERVAL class has three slots, a start time (st), an end time (et) and a duration (dur); thus, each entity of the knowledge base has these three slots as well.

example 2

```
class SEQUENCE is-a MOTION with
prerequisites
   motion_set : set of MOTION such that [
      for all m : (MOTION such that
         [m element-of motion_set])
       verify [
         m.subj = self.subj,
          ~ find m1 : MOTION where [
         m1 element-of motion_set,
         (m1.time_int.st during m.time_int or
         m.time_int.st during m1.time_int) ],
         find m2 : MOTION where [
            m2 element-of motion_set,
            (m.time_int.st = m2.time_int.et or
            m2.time_int.st = m.time_int.et ) ] ] ,
         card(motion_set) > 1,
         strict_order_set(motion_set,time_int.st) ] ;

dependents
   first_mot : MOTION with
      first_mot ← earliest_st(motion_set) ;
   last_mot : MOTION with
      last_mot ← latest_st(motion_set ;
   time_int : with time_int ←
      ( st of TIME_INTERVAL with st ← first_mot.time_int.st ,
      et of TIME_INTERVAL with et ← last_mot.time_et );
end
```

The SEQUENCE example demonstrates how a set of motion concepts from the knowledge base can be grouped into a sequence of motions. Basically, a set of motion instances is proposed, and for all of the elements of that set, a set of constraints are defined that must be observed if that particular set is a temporal sequence of motions. The constraints are that all the motions of the set refer to the same motion subject, there is no motion in the candidate set whose start or end times are during another motion instance's time interval, that the cardinality of the set is greater than one, and that there is a strict temporal order among the elements of the set. If a given set does not satisfy these constraints, another one is tried. Once a satisfying set of motions is found, the dependent slots of first motion, last motion, and the time interval for the sequence are computed. Specialized sequences of events, specific to heart motions, are then defined in terms of the generic SEQUENCE class. The specific classes would provide types of motions and other constraints so that the number of candidate motion sets is greatly reduced.

example 3

```
volume : VOLUME_V with
    volume ← (vol of VOLUME_V with
      vol ← (minaxis.length @ now ) ** 3
        default(117 @ m.systole.time_int.st,
               22 @ m.systole.time_int.et,
               83 @ m.diastole.rapid_fill.time_int.et,
              100 @ m.diastole.diastasis.time_int.et,
              117 @ m.diastole.atrial_fill.time_int.et)
      such that [
    volume @ m.diastole.time_int.et >= 97
      exception [TOO_LOW_EDV with volume ← volume ],
    volume @ m.diastole.time_int.et <= 140
      exception [TOO_HIGH_EDV with volume ← volume ],
    volume @ m.systole.time_int.et >= 20
      exception [TOO_LOW_ESV with volume ← volume],
    volume @ m.systole.time_int.et <= 27
      exception [TOO_HIGH_ESV with volume ← volume] ] ,
    time_inst of VOLUME_V with time_inst ← now ) ;
```


The VOLUME example is included to demonstrate how a piecewise linear approximation to a function, in this case, the volume versus time function, can be encoded. There are 5 points specified for the function, that is, five volume values with corresponding time instants. Further, a number of constraints with associated exceptions are given, and these basically provide the envelope of acceptable values around the function, whereas the function itself gives average or default values.

2.5 Exceptions and Similarity Relations

The recording of exceptions to slot filling and constraint matching has proven to be valuable. Exceptions are classes in their own right, with slots to be filled on instantiation, i.e., when raised. Each slot constraint (or group of constraints) of a class may have an associated exception clause. This clause names the type of exception that would be raised on matching failure, and provides a definition for filling the exception's slots, since these slot fillers identify the context within which the exception occurred and play an important role in the determination of the action to take on the exception. Each slot has an implicit exception associated with it for cases where a slot filler can not be found. Exceptions are used in two ways: 1) to record the matching failures of current hypotheses, recording the failures of the reasoning process; and 2) to assist in directing system attention to other, perhaps more viable hypotheses. The prototypical exception class is shown below along with one of its specializations, followed by an example from a stroke volume slot. Other examples have already appeared.

example 1

```
class EXCEPTION with
dependents
   subj : PHYS_OBJ ;
   time_int : TIME_INTERVAL ;
   source_type : CLASS ;
   source_id : INTEGER ;
end
```

This is the basic EXCEPTION class, and each other exception type in the system is a sub-type of this one. Thus, each exception class requires slots defining the subject of the motion for which the exception has been raised, the time-interval during which the exception was raised, and the class name and internal identifier for the class that raised the exception during matching.

example 2

```
class TOO_MUCH_MOTION is-a EXCEPTION with
dependents
   seg : STRING ;
   disp : LENGTH_VAL with disp ←
```

```
            (len of LENGTH_VAL with
        len ← dist(subj.centroid @ source_id.time_int.st,
              subj.centroid @ source_id.time_int.et ) ,
        time_inst of LENGTH_VAL with time_inst ← now) ;
end
```

TOO_MUCH_MOTION is a specific type of exception, adding two slots, 'seg' and 'disp', to the set of slots inherited from the EXCEPTION class. Thus, when the exception is raised, the exception will record in addition to the inherited information described above, the name of the heart segment that caused the exception, and the actual displacement that represented too much motion.

example 3

```
stroke_vol : VOLUME_V with
        stroke_vol ← (vol of VOLUME_V with
            vol ← self.volume @ m.diastole.time_int.et -
                    self.volume @ m.systole.time_int.et
                default(95) such that [
                vol >= 70
                    exception [LOW_STROKE_VOLUME with
                        volume ← vol ],
                vol <= 120
                    exception [HIGH_STROKE_VOLUME with
                        volume ← vol ] ] ,
        time_inst of VOLUME_V with time_inst ← now) ;
```

The volume exceptions show how one may encode constraints and their corresponding exception types. So for the first one of this example, if the volume is not greater than or equal to 70, the exception LOW_STROKE_VOLUME is raised, and an additional slot, 'vol', is filled with the actual volume, in addition to the slots predefined by the exception class.

Similarity measures that can be used to assist in the selection of other relevant hypotheses on hypothesis matching failure are useful in the control of growth of the hypothesis space. These measures usually relate classes that together comprise a discriminatory set, i.e., only one of them can be instantiated at any one time. As such, they relate classes that are at the same level of specificity of the IS-A hierarchy, and that have the same IS-A parent classes. Similarity links are components of the frame scheme of [Minsky 75], and a realization of SIMILARITY links as an exception-handling mechanism is presented in [Tsotsos et al. 80] based on a representation of the common and differing portions between two classes. This view is contrasted with the sets of competitors described for the ABEL system [Patil et al. 82]. In that formulation, the level of specificity of the competing set is not represented. Similarity links enable explicit discussion of class comparisons, not only between the connected classes, but also by traversals of several links [Gershon 82]. Thus they are an element of embedded declarative control, and add a different view of class representation, thereby enhancing redundancy of the representation. The three major components of a SIMILARITY link are the list of target classes (given first), the "similarities" expression (the important common portions between the source and target classes), and the "differences" expression (the time-course of exceptions that would be raised through slot constraints in the source class or in parts of the source class). During interpretation, the target classes are not active when the SIMILARITY link is being evaluated. Thus, in time-dependent reasoning situations, the components of the target class that are the same as in the source class before activation of the SIMILARITY link, or that the source class may not care about that may have already 'passed in time', are included in the similarities expression. There is an implicit conjunction of the differences in the exception record, while the similarities form a disjunction. Many SIMILARITY links will be shown in subsequent examples.

2.6 Partial Results and Levels of Description

Partial instances are permitted with an accompanying exception record. More importantly, since instance tokens are produced for each verified hypothesis, and since hypotheses maintain the organization exhibited by the classes from which they are formed, interpretation results also exhibit the same structure. That is, there are levels of description that may examined as appropriate by a user.

It is important to realize that the instantiation of a hypothesis is achieved only when its certainty has reached a threshold value. (The thresholds are not set in an ad hoc fashion, but rather depend on a number of factors relating to the context of interpretation and knowledge structure - see [Tsotsos 87] for details). Thus, even though not all components of a hypothesis have been verified, instantiation may still take place if that hypothesis has significantly more successes than its competitors over the same time period.

This would then create a partial instance, including the verified components, the final certainty, and a set of exception records specifying what was not observed.

3 THE INTERPRETATION CONTROL STRUCTURE

ALVEN and CAA employ hypothesize and test as the basic recognition paradigm. The activation of a hypothesis sets up an internal goal, that is, the class from which the hypothesis was formed, that tries to verify itself. However, activation of hypotheses proceeds along each of several dimensions concurrently, and hypotheses are considered in parallel rather than sequentially. These dimensions are the same class organization axes that are described above. Specifically, we define: *goal-directed* search to be movement from general to specialized classes along the IS-A dimension, the goal being to find the appropriate sub-class definition for the data in question; *model-directed* search to be movement from aggregate to component classes along the PART-OF dimension; *temporal* search to be a specific form of model-directed search in that a temporal ordering among components controls the time of activation; *failure-directed* search to be movement along the SIMILARITY dimension; and *data-directed* search to be movement from components to aggregates of components upwards along the PART-OF dimension. For a given set of input data, in a single time slice, activation is terminated when none of the activation mechanisms can identify an unactivated viable hypothesis. Termination is guaranteed by virtue of the finite size of the knowledge and the explicit prevention of re-activation of already active hypotheses. The activation of one hypothesis has implications for other hypotheses as well, as will be described below. Because of the multi-dimensional nature of hypothesis activation, the "focus" of the system also exhibits levels of attention. That is, in its examination, the focus can be stated according to desired level of specificity or resolution (the two are related), discrimination set, or temporal slice. The control structure is illustrated in Figure 1.

Each newly activated hypothesis is recorded in a structure that is similar to the class whose instance it has hypothesized. This structure includes the class slots awaiting fillers, the relationships that the hypothesis has with other hypotheses, and an initial certainty value determined by sharing the certainty with the hypothesis that activates the new hypothesis.

In other aspects the systems differ and these differences are highlighted in upcoming sections of this paper.

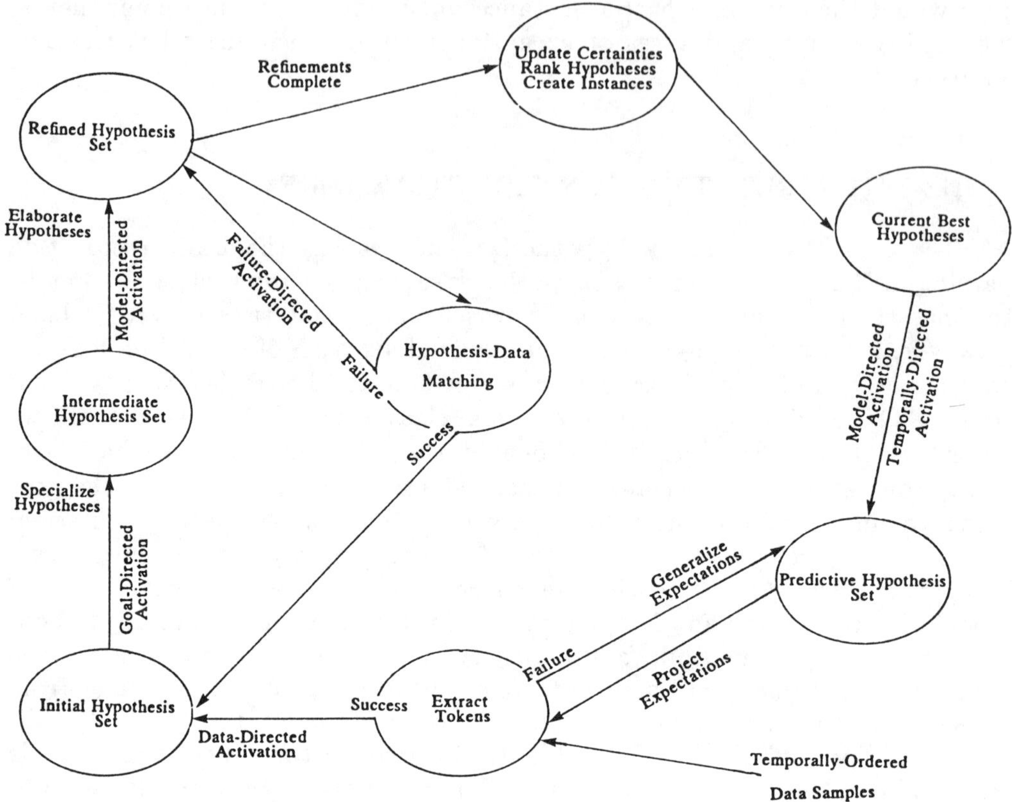

Figure 1. The Control Structure

4 THE ALVEN PROJECT

4.1 Overview

The ALVEN project was an experiment in the design of a framework for the integration of time into high level (attentive) vision. The key elements are an organization of knowledge along several dimensions, including time, several search modes facilitated by the knowledge organization, a hypothesize and test reasoning framework and a temporal cooperative process, driven by the knowledge organization, for hypothesis ranking. The major aspects of the cooperative process, namely, the definition of consistency, process neighbourhoods, initial certainties, compatibility factors, are all defined in terms of the knowledge organization. Iterations are tied to temporal measurements, and this allows temporal sampling to be discussed quantitatively. A qualitative analysis that includes hypothesis response rise and fall times is presented in addition to guidelines for setting compatibilities such that performance is appropriate. The scheme subsumes previous relaxation methods in that iterations are performed in time for either dynamic or static situations, and because the structure over which the cooperative process operates is allowed to change with time. It is further shown that the dimensions of knowledge organization, IS-A, PART-OF, SIMILARITY and Temporal Precedence, have uses far beyond their desirable structuring and access properties, and that they play important other roles in a knowledge based interpretation scheme. These are all discussed in detail in [Tsotsos 87].

The evaluation of left ventricular (LV) performance by computer from cine representations of LV dynamics is a difficult and long-studied problem. A large number of heuristics have been proposed for measuring shape changes [Brower & Meester 81], following anatomical landmarks [Slager et al. 79], computing segmental volume contributions (for a comparison, see [Gerbrands et al. 79]), etc., all performing with varying degrees of success, but being applied independently of each other. Although such heuristics are indeed valuable quantitative measures, we propose that their limited performance is due to two key considerations: 1) it is unlikely, given the complexity of the domain of LV dynamics and the amount of training that a clinical specialist in this area receives, that any single heuristic can capture all the important facets of the evaluation and be successful in all applications; 2) the heuristics are purely quantitative in nature, contrasting with the fact that clinicians, and for that matter humans in general, deal in qualitative or descriptive terms combined with numerical quantities. That is, relational quantities are necessary components of the interpretation process, while numerical ones are secondary. The key here is that a computer system that is to solve the difficult problems present in the domain of LV dynamics interpretation must integrate the above mentioned numerical heuristics as well as consider the symbolic processing aspects of the interpretation. We distinguish our approach from those whose goal is to provide some intermediate visual representation that must still be subjectively interpreted by a clinician, (the work described in [Hoehne et al. 80] is a particularly good example of such a representation). Our goal is to perform this interpretation, in much the same way as the clinician does, and to do it in an objective and consistent manner.

In [Aiello 83], three incarnations of the PUFF system were compared each with the same knowledge, but different control schemes. The result of the comparison was that for PUFF's specific problem domain, expectation-driven (what is called model-driven below) was the best strategy, yet it too had drawbacks. Its analysis was strongly influenced by the initial hypothesis, and was not able to recover from bad initial states, and moreover could not respond to all input data, only that which was required by the model. The control scheme of ALVEN does not rely on a single mechanism. We recognize that a single scheme may not be adequate for all situations, and thus several interacting dimensions are included. Specifically, our control scheme does not suffer from the above-mentioned drawback because of its incorporation of model-driven, data-driven and lateral failure-driven search, reflecting traversals of the knowledge base along the IS-A, PART-OF or SIMILARITY dimensions.

Matching is defined as successful if all slots that should be considered for filling are filled and no matching exceptions are raised. Otherwise, the match is unsuccessful. Using this binary categorization of matching, and the relationships amongst hypotheses, a certainty updating scheme based on relaxation processes [Zucker 78] is used. Details of this scheme appear in [Tsotsos 87], and the definition of temporal relaxation is considered as one of the major contributions of the ALVEN project. Basically, hypotheses that are connected by knowledge organizational relationships that imply consistency support one another, and those linked by relationships that imply inconsistency compete with one another by removing support. The IS-A relationship is in the former group, while the SIMILARITY is in the latter group. The focus of the system is defined as the set of best hypotheses, at each level of specificity, for each set of structural components being considered in the given time slice. The focus, due to the slow change of certainties inherent in relaxation schemes exhibits inertia, or procrastination, i.e., it does not alter dramatically between certainty updates. Both global and local consistency is enforced through the contributions of hypotheses to one another via their organizational relationships.

4.2 LV Dynamics Knowledge and its Representation

Although there is still much work to be done in the determination of the knowledge of LV dynamics, much can be found in current literature which can be incorporated into our formalism. Two examples will be given. This knowledge is used as a starting point for knowledge base construction only. Moreover, although the exact numerical quantities may differ between imaging techniques, the *qualitative* descriptions do not.

The left ventricular beat is comprised of 2 major phase, systole (contraction) and diastole (expansion). In turn, systole is divided into 3 phases: isovolumic contraction; rapid ejection; and, slow ejection. Diastole is made up of 4 phases: isovolumic relaxation; rapid filling; diastasis; and, atrial filling. The physical structure of the left ventricle is divided into three segments: the anterior segment; the apical segment; and, the posterior segment. Each LV motion phase is defined by specific characteristics for each segment as well as for the LV as a whole. It is clear that there is thus a PART_OF structure both in terms of the physical entity as well as in terms of the events it exhibits.

In the series of papers by Gibson and his colleagues, (for example [Doran et al. 78], [Gibson et al. 76]), several investigations were carried out that determined quantitative aspects of specific LV motions. In the second paper quoted, the segmental motions of the LV during isovolumic relaxation were examined in normal and ischemic LVs using echocardiography in order to determine dynamic differences between these two cases. Without describing technical details of their method, we will briefly summarize their findings. They discovered that in normal LVs an outward wall motion of 1.5 - 3.0 mm. could be present in any region during isovolumic relaxation. In abnormal cases, i.e., patients with coronary artery disease, affected areas show inward motion, 2mm. or more for posterior or apical segments, and any at all for anterior regions, and non-affected areas, due to a compensatory mechanism, may exhibit an increased outward motion of up to 6mm. over normal. The key feature to note here is that the description given does not have a mathematical form at all - it is a combination of quantitative and qualitative measures. The term "outwards" does not specify any precise direction as long as the motion of the segment is away from the inside of the LV. It is not impossible to set up a mathematical model of this knowledge; the model will be both cumbersome and will bury the pertinent facts in its equations. The knowledge class for this information (and more) follows and its description follows the example:

```
class N_ISORELAX is-a NO_VOLUME_CHANGE with
prerequisites
  subj : N_LV  such that [

      (find ant_mot : NO_TRANSLATION where [
         ant_mot.subj = self.subj.anterior ,
         ant_mot.time_int = self.time_int
         ]
      or
      find ant_mot : OUTWARD where [
         ant_mot.subj = self.subj ,
         ant_mot.time_int = self.time_int ,
         dist(ant_mot.subj.centroid @ ant_mot.time_int.st,
             ant_mot.subj.centroid @ ant_mot.time_int.et) < 3
```

444

```
                exception [TOO_MUCH_MOTION with seg ← "anterior" ,
                                        direction ← "outward",
            disp ← dist(ant_mot.subj.centroid @ ant_mot.time_int.st,
                    ant_mot.subj.centroid @ ant_mot.time_int.et) ]
        ]
    ) exception [TOO_MUCH_MOTION with seg ← "anterior",
                            direction ← "inward"] ,

    (find post_mot : NO_TRANSLATION where [
        post_mot.subj = self.subj.posterior ,
        post_mot.time_int = self.time_int
        ]
    or
    find post_mot : INWARD where [
        post_mot.subj = self.subj ,
        post_mot.time_int = self.time_int ,
        dist(post_mot.subj.centroid @ post_mot.time_int.st,
            post_mot.subj.centroid @ post_mot.time_int.et) < 2
            exception [TOO_MUCH_MOTION with seg ← "posterior",
                            direction ← "inward",
            disp ← dist(post_mot.subj.centroid @ post_mot.time_int.st,
                    post_mot.subj.centroid @ post_mot.time_int.et) ]
        ]
    or
    find post_mot : OUTWARD where [
        post_mot.subj = self.subj ,
        post_mot.time_int = self.time_int ,
        dist(post_mot.subj.centroid @ post_mot.time_int.st,
            post_mot.subj.centroid @ post_mot.time_int.et) < 3
            exception [TOO_MUCH_MOTION with seg ← "posterior",
                            direction ← "outward",
            dist(post_mot.subj.centroid @ post_mot.time_int.et,
                post_mot.subj.centroid @ post_mot.time_int.et) ] ]
    ) ,

    (find ap_mot : NO_TRANSLATION where [
        ap_mot.subj = self.subj.apical ,
        ap_mot.time_int = self.time_int
        ]
    or
    find ap_mot : INWARD where [
        ap_mot.subj = self.subj ,
        ap_mot.time_int = self.time_int ,
```

```
                dist(ap_mot.subj.centroid @ ap_mot.time_int.st,
                    ap_mot.subj.centroid @ ap_mot.time_int.et) < 2
                  exception [TOO_MUCH_MOTION with seg ← "apical",
                                        direction ← "inward",
                  disp ← dist(ap_mot.subj.centroid @ ap_mot.time_int.st,
                          ap_mot.subj.centroid @ ap_mot.time_int.et) ]
              ]
          or
        find ap_mot : OUTWARD where [
          ap_mot.subj = self.subj ,
          ap_mot.time_int = self.time_int ,
          dist(ap_mot.subj.centroid @ ap_mot.time_int.st,
              ap_mot.subj.centroid @ ap_mot.time_int.et) < 3
            exception [TOO_MUCH_MOTION with seg ← "apical"
                              direction ← "outward",
              disp ← dist(ap_mot.subj.centroid @ ap_mot.time_int.st,
                      ap_mot.subj.centroid @ ap_mot.time_int.et) ] ]
        )
      ] ;


dependents
  time_int :  with time_int ← (dur of TIME_INTERVAL with
                          dur ← default(0.093*(30/(0.8*HR))) )
          such that [
            time_int.st ≥ 0.24*(30/(0.8*HR)) ,
            tim_int.et ≤ 0.43*(30/(0.8*HR)) ,
            time_int.dur ≥ 0.08*(30/(0.8*HR)) ,
            time_int.dur ≤ 0.12*(30/(0.8*HR))
              exception [TOO_LONG_ISORELAX]
          ] ;


similarity links

  sim_link1 : ISCH_AP_ISOVOL_RELAX
    for differences :
      d1 : TOO_MUCH_MOTION where [
          seg = "apical" ,
          direction = "inwards" ,
          time_int = ap_mot.time_int ];

      d2 : TOO_MUCH_MOTION where [
          seg = "anterior" ,
          direction = "outwards" ,
```

```
            disp < 9 ,
            time_int = ant_mot.time_int ];
        d3 : TOO_MUCH_MOTION  where [
            seg = "posterior" ,
            direction = "outwards" ,
            disp < 9 ,
            time_int = post_mot.time_int ]; ;


sim_link2 : ISCH_ANT_ISOVOL_RELAX
    for differences :
        d1 : TOO_MUCH_MOTION where [
            seg = "anterior" ,
            direction = "inwards" ,
            time_int = ant_mot.time_int ];

        d2 : TOO_MUCH_MOTION where [
            seg = "apical" ,
            direction = "outwards" ,
            disp < 9 ,
            time_int = ap_mot.time_int ];
        d3 : TOO_MUCH_MOTION where [
            seg = "posterior" ,
            direction = "outwards" ,
            disp < 9 ,
            time_int = post_mot.time_int ]; ;


sim_link3 : ISCH_POST_ISOVOL_RELAX
    for differences :
        d1 : TOO_MUCH_MOTION where [
            seg = "posterior" ,
            direction = "inwards" ,
            time_int = post_mot.time_int ];
        d2 : TOO_MUCH_MOTION where [
            seg = "anterior" ,
            direction = "outwards" ,
            disp < 9 ,
            time_int = ant_mot.time_int ];
        d3 : TOO_MUCH_MOTION where [
            seg = "apical" ,
            direction = "outwards" ,
            disp < 9 ,
            time_int = ap_mot.time_int ]; ;
end
```

The definition states that for a normal isovolumic relaxation phase to be recognized, normal motions for each segment must be present. There are three main clauses in the definition. The first defines the expected normal motion of the anterior segment, the second for the posterior segment and third for the remaining segment, the apical one. So for example, in the first clause, the definition reflects Gibson's characterization: the anterior segment during this phase, must either not display any translational movement, or could display an outward motion of displacement less than 3 mm. A larger displacement than this in the outwards direction would be recorded as the exception TOO_MUCH_MOTION, with specific additional contextual information recorded as well. If the anterior segment were displaying motion and it were not outwards, then it must be inwards and this fact too would be recorded as an exception. The dependent portion specifies relevant timing information for the temporal placement of the phase within the left ventricular cycle. *HR* is in units of beats/sec. so that the right hand side of the timing expressions is in units of number of images. Also, using the information derived from [Gibson et al. 76], the similarity links provide definitions of the exceptions to normal that must be instantiated if a hypothesis representing an ischemic segment is to be activated. Note that only the connections to possible ischemic states detectable by considering only the characteristics of the isovolumic relaxation phase, are included above; a set of similarly formed constraints would have to be present for other disease states as well, for those cases where the isovolumic relaxation phase plays a role in their definition. The three similarity links relate the normal phase to the ischemic motions of abnormal phases in each of the three LV segments. For example, an ischemic apical segment, according to Gibson's definition, is shown by either the apical region itself having too much inward motion during this phase, and/or one of the other regions (posterior or anterior) exhibiting too much outward motion during the phase. Note that the set of differences does not define a necessary set; any one of the conditions is sufficient.

It should be clear that the above is not complete; it requires the remainder of the definitions for the other phases and motions since the entire definition of each class of LV motion is defined as a hierarchy of abstraction, each level adding more detail to the previous one. Some of the types of information that are represented are: volume changes where known for normal phases; ejection fractions; and, measures of degrees of abnormalities, derived heuristically; and others.

A second body of knowledge of the form necessary for interpretation can be found in [Fujii et al. 79]. These researchers investigated, eight different clinical cardiac disease states with the intent of discovering posterior wall motion differences and similarities among the diseases, as well as global LV characteristics. The diseases were: pericarditis, congestive cardiomyopathy, hypertrophic cardiomyopathy, valvular aortic stenosis, aortic insufficiency, mitral stenosis, mitral insufficiency, and systemic hypertension. Normal LV's were also studied. The measurements made for each of the above LV states were: stroke volume, rapid filling volume, slow filling volume, atrial filling volume, the percent filling for each of the previous three phases with respect to the stroke volume, posterior wall excursion in total, and for each of the three phases of diastole, as well as the percentage excursion in each phase, diastolic posterior wall velocity, rapid filling rate, LV end diastolic dimension, and ejection fraction. It is, of course, difficult to verify their results. However, they are important - they provide at least a starting point for the further elaboration and verification of such detailed dynamic information. In addition to the large amount of numerical information, that they derived, they attached to the significant findings qualitative descriptors - such as whether or not this quantity should be higher or lower than in the normal case. This was rather fortunate from our point of view: the representational formalism that we had designed can handle description via common components and differences very well, and uses such information to advantage during the decision phases of the interpretation. It should be clear from the previous example how such information would be included into the representation, and this fact alone raises another important advantage of this scheme. The addition of information into a mathematical model may require a complete redefinition of the model. In our case, information is easily inserted, as long as one understands the semantics of the representation.

4.3 The ALVEN System

Examples of the ALVEN system have appeared previously and thus will not be repeated here [Tsotsos 85]. The results were very satisfactory. Each analysis produced by ALVEN was completely consistent with the reports that radiologists produce for those films. The major difference is in detail. ALVEN produces very detailed descriptions at a number of levels of abstraction. The information that is produced is beyond the capability of analysis by human observation. Moreover, it seems that most of quantities computed are beyond the capability of the science of cardiology to incorporate into routine patient care. It is encouraging that we can make predictions for quantities and analyses that may also advance the state-or-the-art of heart patient care.

5. THE CAA PROJECT

5.1 Overview

The CAA system uses a causal model of the electrophysiology of the heart in order to explain observed abnormalities in rhythm in terms of the corresponding abnormalities of causal events and electrical relationships in the heart. In the domain of electrocardiology, this causal reasoning process is especially important because the domain involves causal and temporal knowledge about the cardiac conduction system. It is clear that cardiologists analyze ECGs using this type of knowledge and thereby provide diagnostic interpretations of abnormal events in the underlying physiological mechanism of the heart. The recognition problem of ECG rhythm disorders, above all, is interesting because the overall performance of existing ECG programs is at most 80% reliable for abnormal ECGs [Hagan et al. 79] and we believe a basic reason for this unreliability is that current systems lack underlying physiological knowledge to handle the complexity inherent in cardiac rhythms. The ECG wave identification is much complicated by its "antenna" nature, that is, leads on the patient's chest receive only the aggregated electrical activity of the heart, and there is no simple correspondence between signal features and individual electrical discharges in the heart.

Our approach to the problem of building such a system is to construct a knowledge base stratified by several distinct knowledge bases (KBs) each representing different perspectives of the domain. Its control structure, therefore, supports a guiding mechanism between corresponding concepts in different KBs as well as another guiding mechanism between causally related concepts in each KB. In representational terms, the former mechanism uses "projection links" and the latter uses "causal links". These links together contribute to the generation of hypotheses and the decision of overall interpretations in the recognition of ECG signals. This approach also integrates several established AI techniques. The system inherited the basic control framework from the ALVEN system, including the attention mechanism for specialization and aggregation, which is supported by the implementation of similarity links, and the exception handling mechanism. The hypothesize-and-test paradigm is used as in ALVEN and other systems like PIP [Szolovits & Pauker 78] and HEARSAY-II [Mostow et al. 78]. The knowledge organizational method is based on the IS-A, PART-OF, and INSTANCE-OF hierarchies as used in the PSN formalism.

To prove the efficacy of our methods, a prototype system called CAA (Causal Arrhythmia Analysis system) has been designed and implemented using a frame-input PSN system on Franz LISP (and UCI LISP) [Shibahara 83], [Shibahara 86]. The prototype with a limited size of knowledge base was tested and yielded satisfactory results.

5.2 Representation of Causal Connections

Rieger and Grinberg distinguished "one-shot causality" where the cause event(s) is required only at the start of the effect event(s) from the "continuous causality" where the continuous presence of the cause is required to sustain the effect [Rieger & Grinberg 76]. CAA causal links are based on these features: first, they specify the existential dependency of an affected event on its causative event(s); second, they impose temporal constraints between causative and affected events. Thus, the affected events cannot occur without the occurrence of the corresponding causative events, with effects temporally following their causes. Interested in representing the dependencies of causal connections among events more precisely, we look at causality from the viewpoint of whether a causal influence is internal to a subject or it influences other distinct subject(s). One-shot causal links, therefore, are specialized into the following:

(1) **Transfer:** the subject of the event normally completes the current event and proceeds to the following event.
(2) **Transition:** the subject is forced to terminate its current event and proceed to a new event.
(3) **Initiation:** the causative event, due to a given subject, triggers a new event of another subject.
(4) **Interrupt:** the causative event, due to a given subject, interrupts and forces the termination of an event by another subject.
(5) **Causal-block:** the causative event of a subject, fails to influence an event of another subject due to a blockage of the causal flow.

The above CAA causal links include implicit temporal constraints; thus, causal structures are described more qualitatively without specifying time coordinate values. Causal events are aggregated at several levels and may involve an arbitrary number of causal links. However, causal links themselves remain atomic lest the semantics of causal connections should become ambiguous.

5.3 Use of Causal Links

To interpret real ECG signals, the knowledge base must contain the causal knowledge about normal and abnormal connections among cellular events, which produce particular ECG tracings in the observable signal domain. We represent such causal activities using CAA causal links. Fig. 2 illustrates a typical ECG tracing for a normal cardiac cycle in (a), its electrical conduction path in an anatomical diagram in (b), and the corresponding causal conduction model with causal links in (c).

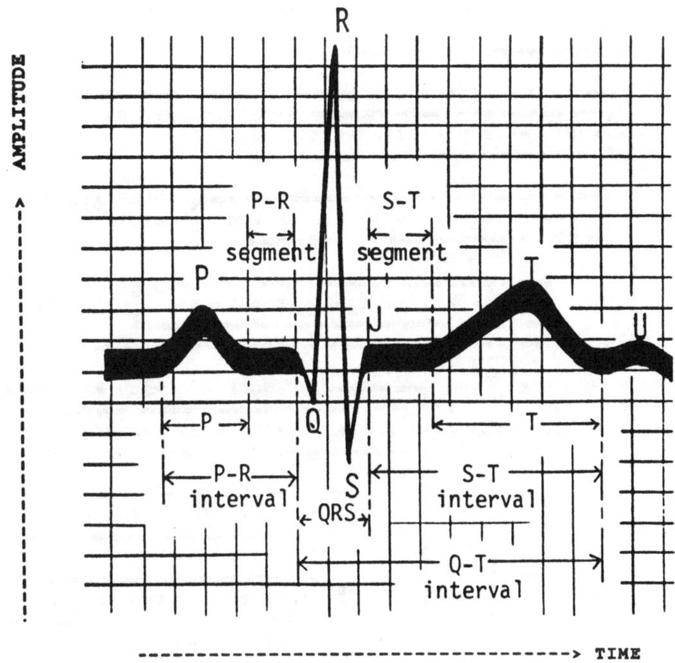

Figure 2. (a) A Typical Single Beat ECG Tracing

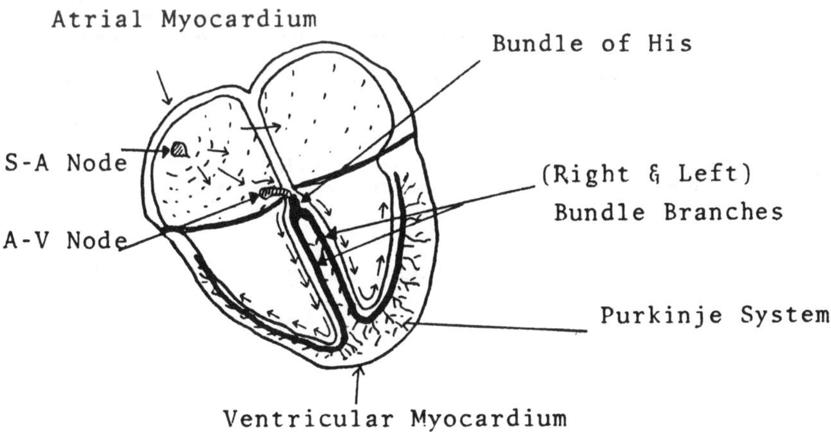

Figure 2. (b) The Cardiac Conduction System

452

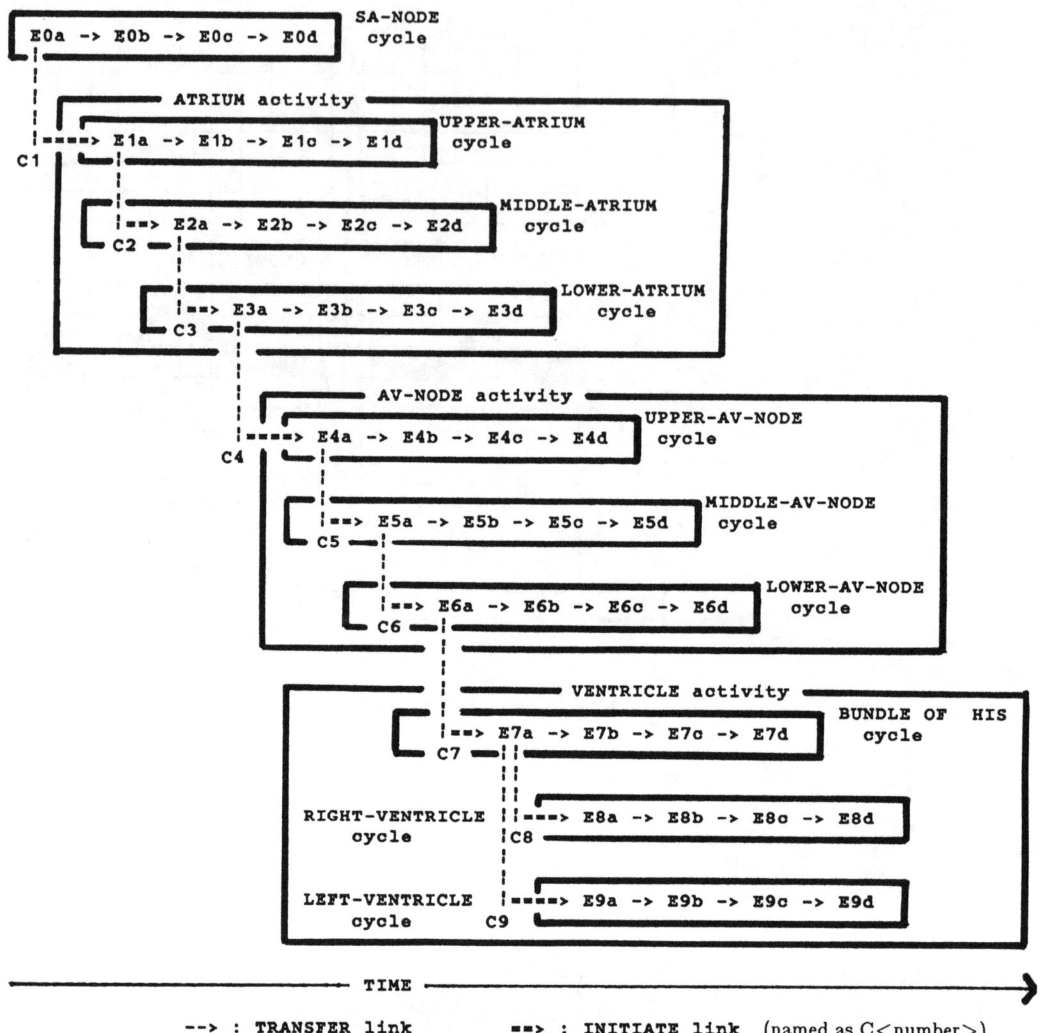

Symbols E<number>a, E<number>b, E<number>c, and E<number>d denote a depolarization phase event, an under-repolarization phase event, a partial-repolarization phase event, and a full-repolarization phase event, respectively.

Figure 2. (c) Internal Causal Structure of a Normal Cardiac Cycle

In this causal model, short symbols like E0a are used to denote one of four basic events (phases) in a small portion of the cardiac conduction system; these phases are "depolarization" [with symbol a], "under-repolarization" [with symbol b], "partial-repolarization" [with symbol c], and "full-repolarization" [with symbol d]. Such basic phase events are successively aggregated into "cycle", "activity", "beat", and "beat-pattern" events in the physiological event KB to describe more global and complex causal structures.

Note that causal links across beat events (not shown) are TRANSITIONs and INTERRUPTs except pace-making parts (normally, the SA-Node) because the overall oscillation of the conduction system is controlled (or triggered) by such self-oscillating cells. Also, since the current model is rather devoted to supraventricular arrhythmias, the bundle branches are included in the ventricles.

ABEL and CADUCEUS are recent medical expert systems that use causal notions. The ABEL system provides multiple levels of descriptions of medical hypotheses and hierarchically organizes disease structure [Patil 81]. In the CADUCEUS system, analyzing differential diagnoses and causal graphs of diseases, Pople proposed sophisticated control links for efficient decision making [Pople 82]. In spite of the sophistication in expressing causal mechanisms in ABEL and CADUCEUS, these systems do not seem to provide a means to construct a recognition system of time-varying signals due to the weakness in the representation of precise timing contexts among events.

Causality has been recently approached from the standpoint of "qualitative reasoning" [Forbus 82], [Kuipers 82], [deKleer & Brown 83], [Long 83]. In particular, Long's work addresses the same domain of electrocardiogram interpretation, but was not specifically interested in the arrhythmia problem. He introduced qualitative times to describe the causal relations that might or must have taken place. He interestingly proposed four causal templates that give an extension of "continuous causality", while our causal links are specialized in "one-shot causality". We have taken a different approach because original signals are input to the system as real-valued data and the use of some quantitative analysis is inevitable at the measurement level so that unnecessary ambiguity is avoided (as Kunz noticed in his AI/MM system [Kunz 83]).

Based on the methods of multivariate analysis Blum approached causality statistically [Blum 82]. However, our problem domain includes mostly exact causal relationships. Therefore, we limit the use of statistical standards to the estimation of inherently spontaneous variables such as event durations.

5.4 Representation of Domain Knowledge

The normal activity of the ventricles is decomposed into three cycle events, *i.e.*, bundle-of-his-cycle-event, right-ventricle-cycle-event, and left-ventricle-cycle-event. Figure 3 exemplifies the use of a class frame and causal links. (The dot "." notation is used to specify the component of the referred slot.) Two INITIATE links represent the conductions from the bundle of His to the left and the right ventricles, respectively. Note that the information related to the class itself, in this case, the subject part name and the activation type, is given as the instantiation of a metaclass ACTIVITY-CONCEPT.

```
class VENT-ALL-MATURE-FORWARD-ACTIVITY
  is-a VENT-ACTIVITY
  instance-of ACTIVITY-CONCEPT instantiated-with
              subject: VENTRICLE;
              activation: FORWARD;;
with   components
  bundle-of-his-cycle-event: BHIS-MATURE-CELL-CYCLE;
  right-ventricle-cycle-event: RV-MATURE-CELL-CYCLE;
  left-ventricle-cycle-event: LV-MATURE-CELL-CYCLE;
  bhis-rv-delay: NUMBER-WITH-TOLERANCES
      calculate := /* delay set-up expression */;
  bhis-lv-delay: NUMBER-WITH-TOLERANCES
      calculate := /* delay set-up expression */;
causal-links
  bhis-rv-propagation: INITIATE
  causative-starting-event:       bundle-of-his-cycle-event.depolarization-phase-
event;
   initiated-event: right-ventricle-cycle-event.depolarization-phase-event;
   delay: bhis-rv-delay;;
  bhis-lv-propagation: INITIATE
  causative-starting-event:       bundle-of-his-cycle-event.depolarization-phase-
event;
   initiated-event: left-ventricle-cycle-event.depolarization-phase-event;
   delay: bhis-lv-delay;;
end
```

Fig. 3 Class Frame for Normal Activity of the Ventricles

Statistical information, so commonly used in medical reasoning systems, has particular importance when insufficient information is available about the disease status of a patient [Szolovits & Pauker 78]. In our case, the recognition system uses statistical standards to create expectations for unknown attributes of events and to estimate the goodness-of-fit of hypotheses. Since statistical standards about a class are not the attributes of any particular instance of the class but the attributes of the class itself, such standards could be defined in appropriate metaclasses and instantiated as properties of the class itself. In other words, event statistics are good examples of meta-knowledge or "knowledge about knowledge" and such knowledge is organized along the INSTANCE-OF axis. In fact, to provide "mean" and "standard-deviation" values to all the physiological phase events, CAA has the following metaclass CELL-PHASE-CONCEPT (Fig. 4-(a)).

In Fig. 4-(a), default functions, MEANFUNC and DEVFUNC, are generic functions that are supposed to generate mean and standard deviation about durations of phase events. Such statistical standards about phases are functions of "subject", "maturity", "phase", and a state variable HR$ (heart rate). Therefore, such a standard, for example, a mean value, is given by the expression "(mean subject maturity phase HR$)" in a particular phase event class (Fig. 4-(b)). In the evaluation of this expression, the slot-names such as "mean" and "subject" are replaced by real properties of the class, such as "MEANFUNC" and "SA-NODE". This is considered as the tailoring process of the general "mean" expression to the definitional context of this event; *i.e.*, such statistics may change to fit into each event hypothesis. On the other hand, HR$ is a global variable that reflects the current state of the model, where hypotheses are being instantiated; in other words, such global variables are used to make statistical standards sensitive to the current recognition context. Heart rate, blood pressure and breathing rate are examples of dynamic or time varying global variables while age-group, sex, race, and types of medications are static global variables. Obviously, default functions, MEANFUNC and DEVFUNC, may be replaced by any appropriate function if necessary.

The role of the function DURATION-ESTIMATE is similar to that of causal links in that the equation "end-time = start-time + duration" is used to estimate any unknown values among them. In this case, however, the standard mean and deviation values of the duration must be explicitly supplied for the calculation of the consistency (or reasonableness) of the estimated duration value, based on the physiological knowledge.

---

metaclass CELL-PHASE-CONCEPT
with components
    subject: HEART-PORTION;
    maturity: DEGREE-OF-MATURITY;
    phase: PHASE-NAME;
    mean: EXPRESSION *default* MEANFUNC;
    deviation: EXPRESSION *default* DEVFUNC;
end

Fig. 4.(a) A Metaclass to Describe Phase-concepts' Own Properties

---

class SAN-COMP-DEP-PHASE
 instance-of CELL-PHASE-CONCEPT
  instantiated-with
  subject: SA-NODE;
  maturity: COMPLETE;
  phase: DEPOLARIZATION;
  mean: ;/* default is MEANFUNC */
  deviation: ; /* default is DEVFUNC */
is-a PROTO-EVENT
with
 components
 consistency: NUMBER;
 start-time: NUMBER-WITH-TOLERANCES; /* inherited */
 end-time: NUMBER-WITH-TOLERANCES; /* inherited */
 duration: NUMBER-WITH-TOLERANCES
    such-that NON-NEG-CONSTR:
    [NOT [GT 0 VALUE$.central-value]]; /* inherited */
 constraints
 duration-estimation:
  (DURATION-ESTIMATE start-time end-time duration
   (mean subject maturity phase HR$)
   (deviation subject maturity phase HR$));
end

Fig. 4.(b) A Phase Class as an Instance of CELL-PHASE-CONCEPT

5.5 Knowledge-base Stratification and Projection Links

Due to our causal model approach, we at least distinguish two subdomains, i.e., the ECG morphological (shape) domain and the electrophysiological domain. Therefore, the system's knowledge base is stratified by the ECG waveform KB and the physiological event KB. The idea of stratifying a

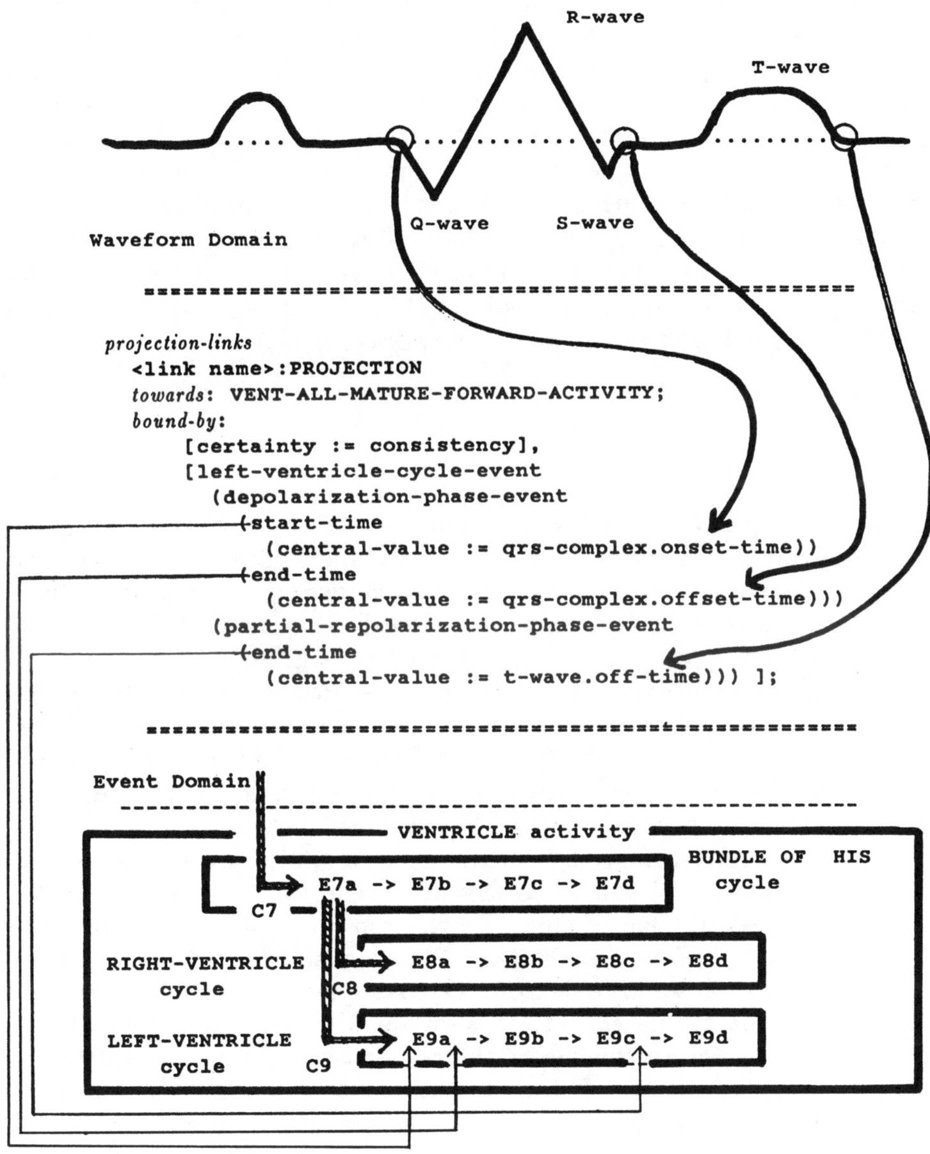

Figure 5. Bindings Using Projection Links

458

knowledge base resembles Rich's "overlays" since it provides different perspectives to the problem [Rich 81]. In our method, however, the linking mechanism between different KBs is biased to recognition purposes.

Projection links have been introduced into the CAA system to relate corresponding concepts in distinct domain KBs. In our model based approach such links are essential since they relate temporal and/or morphological abnormalities in waveforms to corresponding abnormalities in physiological causal structures. The diagram in Fig. 5 illustrates a projection link that defines the correspondence between the corner point information of a normal QRST waveform and the timings of a normal activity event of the ventricles. This projection link must be defined in the class frame of the normal QRST waveform. For recognition, the most important aspect of projection links is that they provide guiding paths to map concepts across differently organized KBs and support the synchronization of recognition activities in different domains. In our system, projections from established waveform hypotheses result in the basic data set (hypotheses) in the underlying event domain, on which the recognition of causal events works.

5.6 Recognition Strategies and Control

Signals are processed by three functional modules in the following order:

(1) The **peak-detection module** extracts wave segments and slopes from sampled ECG input signals and emits peak tokens with the measured parameters. This module uses the syntactic method given by Horowitz [Horowitz 75] based on piecewise linearization and parsing techniques using a context-free grammar.

(2) The **waveform analysis module**, for each cardiac cycle, forms waveform hypotheses on the peak tokens and refines the hypotheses to describe the given set of tokens best. Once established, such hypotheses are projected into the physiological event domain to form their corresponding event hypotheses.

(3) The **event analysis module** accepts projected events as a starting data set and generates rhythm event hypotheses in a more global context of time to elucidate rhythm abnormalities in the underlying cardiac conduction system. Since most of physiological events do not have observable counterparts (waveforms), the event analysis module makes expectations on the attributes of unseen events using the causal knowledge of the conduction system and statistical standards of events. If the system encounters a lack of information because of missing waves, it may request the peak-detection module to search for such missing tokens based on the expectation of such waves.

Our recognition strategy is based on the hypothesize-and-test paradigm, in particular, the attention mechanisms of ALVEN. The focus-of-attention mechanism proceeds from the generic to the specific along IS-A hierarchy. When a class hypothesis succeeds matching, a focusing action is taken by choosing and hypothesizing an appropriate specialized class of the successful class. When the current hypothesis fails, the change-of-attention mechanism chooses alternative hypotheses through similarity links, examining the similarities and the differences between classes.

Let us examine how the above specialization and aggregation process works for QRST waveforms. After all peaks are detected and measured, the waveform analysis module chooses groups of consecutive prominent peaks with high amplitude and steep slope as *anchoring shapes.* These anchoring shapes are candidates for QRST-COMPOSITE-SHAPE. The wave analysis for an anchoring shape starts with hypothesizing the class QRST-COMPOSITE-SHAPE on the prepared set of basic peak tokens, as the first step. This class is most generic for all the shapes composed of Q, R, S, and T waves and only requires the existence of any QRS complex wave as the sole component; thus, this component class is hypothesized and its instantiation follows using the prepared Q, R, and/or S wave tokens. If there is one of Q, R, or S wave tokens is missing, the hypothesis of QRST-COMPOSITE-SHAPE fails. As the second step, one of specialized QRST composite wave classes under QRST-COMPOSITE-SHAPE is hypothesized and all its attributes are tested. Since all the specialized classes are connected by similarity links, using exceptions raised by test results the system may choose the next appropriate hypothesis and finally reach the valid hypothesis for the given anchoring shape. The test procedure for each attribute slot, however, triggers an independent process to recognize the token of the slot. For example, class STANDARD-QRST-COMPOSITE-SHAPE has a slot named qrs-complex and this slot is of type NORMAL-QRS-COMPLEX. In turn, this is an IS-A parent to the classes STANDARD-QRS-COMPLEX-SHAPE, STANDARD-QR-COMPLEX-SHAPE, STANDARD-RS-COMPLEX-SHAPE and STANDARD-R-ONLY-COMPLEX-SHAPE. Thus, the previous qrs-complex token must be specialized along the IS-A relationship. With such a specialized QRS wave token and a separately specialized T wave token, the second step decides the most appropriate hypothesis among QRST composite shapes for the given set of wave tokens.

Similarly but independently, in the physiological event domain, the specialization and aggregation process starts with the most generic beat pattern and eventually provides several specialized patterns as probable overall interpretations.

A beat pattern (rhythm) is a complex time-varying event aggregated from more local events such as beats, activities, cycles, and phases. Causal links in such an aggregated event imply connections among its component events. Thus, once projections are made to some of these components, the system can produce **expectations** of unknown components from the known components. Therefore, when the system hypothesizes such an aggregated event, it looks ahead or looks back for its component events which are causally linked to "already-established" component events. Most frequently, causal links are used to locate the temporal positions of "to-be-expected" events by their inherent temporal constraints. This expectation is made by the following basic equality implicitly imposed over starting or ending times of participating events.

$$\langle \text{effect-time} \rangle \ = \ \langle \text{cause-time} \rangle \ + \ \langle \text{delay-period} \rangle .$$

Let us look at the above mechanisms in a clear small case where a QRST composite wave is seen but the P wave has not been recognized for the current wave group. Fig. 6 illustrates the case and the interval "Area #1" is the probable area where a P wave would appear if the beat is a normal sinus-pacing beat. To estimate such an area under a particular beat hypothesis is important since the peak-detection module may search for a P wave intensively in this area, again. The area is estimated using the projection and the expectation mechanisms in the following fashion:

(0) A hypothesis of NORMAL-QRST-COMPOSITE-SHAPE is established.

(1) A projection to a normal ventricle activity event (Fig. 5):

(a) The onset and offset times of the QRS complex are bound to the starting and ending times of the depolarization phase of the left ventricle. The off-time of the T wave is bound to the ending time of the partial-repolarization phase. These phase events are generated immediately and two other phase events are expected by three TRANSFER causal links and event statistics. Thus, the left ventricle (LV) cycle event is generated.

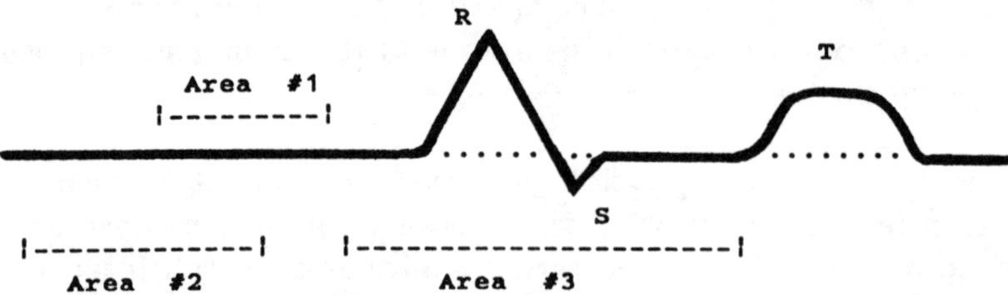

Figure 6. Expected Regions for the P Wave

(b) By the INITIATE causal link to the Bundle of His (BHIS) and subsequent TRANSFER links, the BHIS cycle event is generated. Also, by the INITIATE link from the BHIS to the right ventricle (RV), the RV cycle event is generated.

(c) With the above three cycle events, the projection to the normal ventricle activity event is completed.

(2) Expectation of the AV-Node activity, the Atrium activity, and the SA-Node activity under a hypothesis of the normal sinus-pacing beat (Fig 2-(c)) :

(a) The INITIATE link C7 is invoked to expect the phase E6a, then E6b, E6c, and E6d phases are expected by three TRANSFER links, and finally, the lower AV-Node cycle event is generated. Similarly, using C6 and C5 INITIATE links, the middle and the upper AV-Node activity events are generated. Thus, the AV-Node activity event is formed with these component cycle events.

(b) Starting with the INITIATE link C4, the atrium activity event is expected in the same as above, and, next, the SA-Node cycle event is expected.

(c) A hypothesis of the normal sinus-pacing beat is completed.

Under this hypothesis, the on-time and the off-time of the P wave correspond to the starting time of the upper-atrium cycle and the ending time of the lower-atrium cycle, respectively. Therefore, the search area for a probable P wave is given as the interval between theses times [e.g., from 110 +/- 16ms to 40 +/- 15ms before the QRS complex]. The request of the search for the P wave is fed back to the peak-detection module to repeat the detection with different sensitivity parameters.

The above CAA expectation mechanism is characterized by the following features:

(1) The expectation is made from the known to the unknown, forward or backward in time, and upward or downward in a PART-OF class structure.

(2) The expectations propagate to make a closure of temporal and/or structural dependencies and complete the PART-OF structure of the hypothesis.

Projections are made in the following fashion:

(1) Projections may be made between differently structured classes as seen in Fig. 5.

(2) To eliminate unnecessary instantiations of projections, any projected class is instantiated only when a current global hypothesis requests the class as a component.

To recognize a periodic or successive arrhythmia, its repetitive behavior is defined by the recursive definition of beat-pattern frames. By such a frame, recognition may proceed one beat to the next along the time axis instantiating successive beats to form the beat-pattern.

In the process of forming beat-patterns, causal links between adjacent beats allow the system to verify the causal relationship that govern the pace-making mechanism on a beat-to-beat basis. The overall consistency of a beat-pattern is calculated based on the consistencies of these causal links and beat components. As well as the causal consistency among beats, overall characteristics and tendencies are observed and used to recognize individual arrhythmias. For this purpose, most beat-pattern classes include a component that monitors the changes of variables from one beat to another. A typical example is to monitor the change of the R-R interval or the P-R interval.

In arrhythmia beat-patterns, similarity links must also be defined to relate beat-patterns that have some features in common and handle situations where one or more matching exceptions have been raised. Fig. 7 shows ECG wave configurations that correspond to three different AV-Block arrhythmia patterns and the matching exceptions used by similarity links. Such similarity links between repetitive beat-patterns enable the system to switch beat-pattern hypotheses from one pattern to its alternatives according matching exceptions.

The recognition of particular arrhythmia patterns such as the AV-Block beat-patterns must be initiated by more general classes in the IS-A hierarchy.

The most generic class for repetitive arrhythmias is REPETITIVE-RHYTHM-PATTERN, and this class is immediately specialized according to heart rate into one of three rate-specific classes: FAST-RHYTHM-PATTERN, MODERATE-RHYTHM-PATTERN, and SLOW-RHYTHM-PATTERN. If we assume a normal heart rate between 60 and 100 beats per minute, MODERATE-RHYTHM-PATTERN is selected and one of its more specialized classes must again be chosen; most normally, the first choice is NORMAL-SINUS-RHYTHM-PATTERN because it represents the most generic rhythm that has only NORMAL-SINUS-PACING-BEATs. If any abnormality is found in the recognition of such normal beats, other rhythm pattern(s) are triggered through a similarity link. For the cases of AV-Blocks, an exception must be raised on the recognition of a prolonged atrium-ventricle-interval in one of the component beats. Then the similarity link which contains this exception triggers the rhythm pattern AV-PROLONGED-RHYTHM-PATTERN, which is the immediate IS-A class of the three AV-Block beat pattern classes.

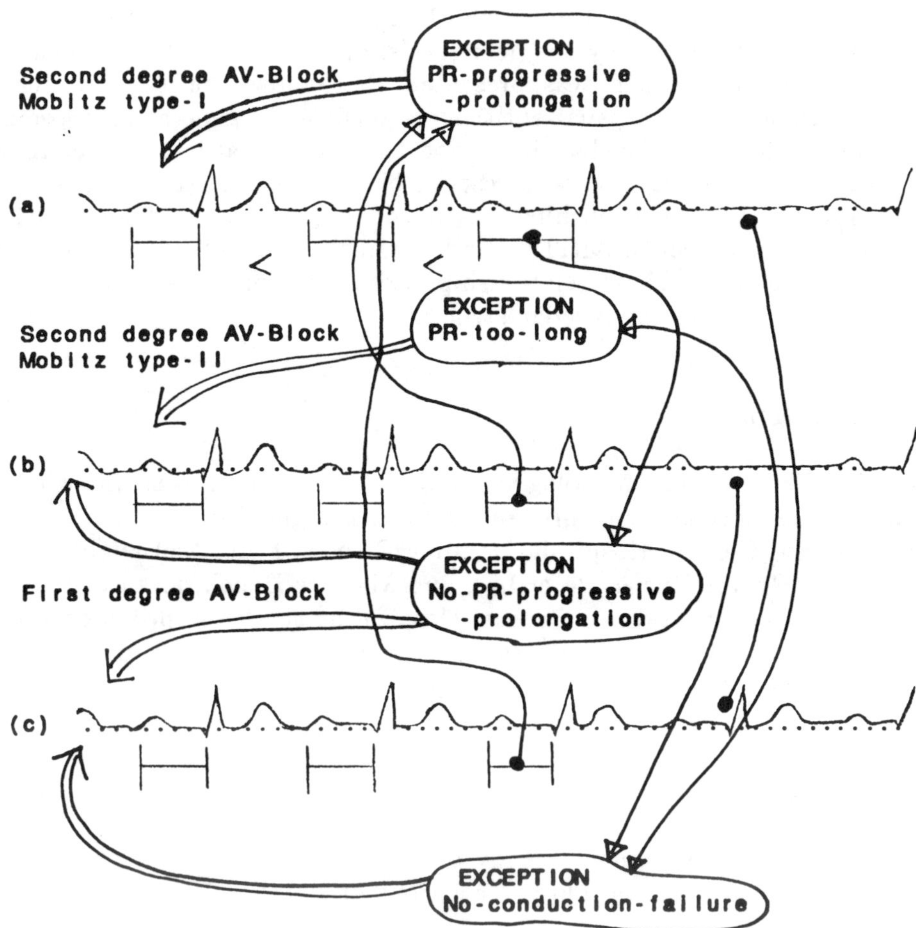

Figure 7. Exceptions Among AV-Block Beat Patterns

The final interpretation is given by the set of all surviving beat-patterns with high overall consistency factors. The consistency is calculated using event statistics and a test-score function, which is similar to fuzzy constraints in [Zadeh 83].

6 CONCLUSIONS

We conclude that frame-based representations are appropriate for complex time-varying signal interpretation tasks. We have presented aspects of representation, knowledge organization and control, that has led to success-ful implementations of two systems, ALVEN and CAA, that deal with temporally rich medical signal domains. In the case of CAA, a further contribution was described namely the deep model of the heart's electrophysiolgy and a projection mechanism was presented that allows for the relating signal characteristics to conceptual entities responsible for generating those signals. A final basic claim is that it is not the frame nature of the knowledge representation per se that was responsible for the success of these systems, but rather, the relationships of frame organization, IS-A, PART-OF, INSTANCE-OF, SIMILARITY, and Temporal Precedence, that drive the control structure. These relationships drive the control structure as well as provide for desirable knowledge structure.

Acknowledgements

The applications to cardiology would not have been possible without the constant support and encouragement of E. Douglas Wigle, Chief of Cardiology, Toronto General Hospital. Dominic Covvey, Peter McLaughlin, Menashe Waxman, Robert Burns, Peter Liu, and Maurice Druck, all of of the Division of Cardiology, at Toronto General Hospital at the time, provided much useful guidance and data. The first author is a Fellow of the Canadian Institute for Advanced Research.

References

Aiello, N., "A Comparative Study of Control Strategies for Expert Systems: AGE Implementation of Three Variations of PUFF", Proc. AAAI-83, Washington, 1983.

Allen, J., "Maintaining Knowledge about Temporal Intervals", TR-86, Dept. of Computer Science, University of Rochester, 1981.

Blum, R., "Discovery and Representation of Causal Relationships from a Large Time-Oriented Clinical Database: The RX Project", Springer-Verlag, Lecture Notes in Medical Informatics 19, 1982.

Brachman, R., "On the Epistemological Status of Semantic Networks", in *Associative Networks,* ed by Findler, Academic Press, 1979.

Brachman, R., "What IS-A is and Isn't", Proc. CSCSI-82, Saskatoon, 1982.

Brower, R., Meester, G., "The Shape of the Human Left Ventricle: Quantification of Symmetry", Proc. Computers in Cardiology, Florence, 1981.

Chandrasekaran, B., Gomez, F., Mittal, S., Smith, J., "An Approach to Medical Diagnosis Based on Conceptual Structures", Proc. IJCAI, Tokyo, 1979.

Doran, J., Traill, T., Brown, D., Gibson, D., "Detection of Abnormal Left Ventricular Wall Movement During Isovolumic Contraction and Early Relaxation", *British Heart Journal,* Vol. 40, 1978.

Fagan, L, "VM: Representing Time-Dependent Relations in a Medical Setting", PhD Thesis, Computer Science Department, Stanford University, 1980.

Fujii, J., Watanabe, H., Koyama, S., Kato, K., "Echocardiographic Study on Diastolic Posterior Wall Movement and Left Ventricular Filling by Disease Category", *American Heart Journal,* Vol.98, 1979.

Forbus, K., "Modeling Motion with Qualitative Process Theory", Proceedings of the Second National Conference on Artificial Intelligence, American Association for Artificial Intelligence, Pittsburgh, August 1982.

Gerbrands, J., Booman, F., Reiber, J., "Computer Analysis of Moving Radiopaque Markers from X-Ray Films", in *Computer Graphics and Image Processing,* Vol.11, 1979.

Gershon, R., "Explanation Methods for Visual Motion Understanding Systems", M.Sc. Thesis, Dept. of Computer Science, University of Toronto, 1982.

Gibson, D., Prewitt, T., Brown, D., "Analysis of Left Ventricular Wall Movement During Isovolumic Relaxation and its Relation to Coronary Artery Disease", *British Heart Journal,* Vol. 38, 1976.

Hagan, A., et al. "Evaluation of Computer Programs for Clinical Electrocardiography Computer Techniques in Cardiology", ed. by D. Cady, Jr., Marcel Dekker, Inc., New York 1979.

Hoehne, K., Boehm, M., Nicolae, G., "The Processing of X-Ray Image Sequences", in *Advances in Digital Image Processing,* ed. by Stucki, Plenum Press, 1980.

Horowitz, S., "A Syntactic Algorithm for Peak Detection in Waveforms with Applications to Cardiography" *Communications of the ACM 18-5,* Association for Computing Machinery, May 1975.

de Kleer, J., Brown, J.S., "The Origin, Form and Logic of Qualitative Physical Laws", Proceedings of the 8th International Joint Conference on Artificial Intelligence, Karlsruhe, August 1983.

Kuipers, B., "Getting the Envisionment Right", Proceedings of the Second National Conference on Artificial Intelligence, American Association for Artificial Intelligence, Pittsburgh, August 1982.

Kunz,J.C., "Analysis of Physiological Behavior using a Causal Model based on First Principles", Proceedings of the Third National Conference on Artificial Intelligence, American Association for Artificial Intelligence, August 1983.

Levesque, H., Mylopoulos, J., "Procedural Semantic Networks", in *Associative Networks,* ed. by Findler, Academic Press, 1979.

Long., W., "Reasoning about State from Causation and Time in a Medical Domain", Proceedings of the Third National Conference on Artificial Intelligence, American Association for Artificial Intelligence, August 1983.

Long, W., Russ, T., "A Control Structure for Time-Dependent Reasoning", Proc. IJCAI-83, Karlsruhe, Germany, 1983.

Minsky, M., "A Framework for Representing Knowledge", in *Psychology of Computer Vision,* ed. by Winston, McGraw-Hill, 1975.

Mittal, S., Chandrasekaran, B., "Organizing Data Bases involving Temporal Information", Proc. IEEE SMC Society, 1980.

Mostow, D.J., Hayes-Roth, F., "A Production System for Speech Understanding System", *Pattern Directed Inference Systems,* ed. by Waterman and Hayes-Roth, Academic Press, 1978.

Nilsson, H., *Problem-Solving Methods in Artificial Intelligence,* McGraw-Hill, 1971.

Patil, R.S., "Causal Representation of Patient Illness for Electrolyte and Acid-Base Diagnosis", Laboratory for Computer Science, Massachusetts Institute of Technology, Technical Report MIT/LCS/TR-267, PhD Thesis, 1981.

Patil, R., Szolovits, P., Schwartz, W., "Modeling Knowledge of the Patient in Acid-Base and Electrolyte Disorders", in *Artificial Intelligence in Medicine,* ed. by P. Szolovits, Westview Press, 1982.

Pople, H., "Heuristic Methods for Imposing Structure on Ill-Structured Problems: The Structuring of Medical Diagnostics", in *Artificial Intelligence in Medicine,* ed. by P. Szolovits, Westview Press, 1982.

Rich, C., "A Formal Representation for Plans in the Programmer's Apprentice", Proceedings of the 7th International Joint Conference on Artificial Intelligence, Vancouver, British Columbia, 1981.

Rieger, C., Grinberg, M., "The Causal Representation and Simulation of Physical Mechanics", TR-495, Univ. of Maryland, Nov. 1976.

Shibahara, T., Tsotsos, J., Mylopoulos, J., Covvey, H., "CAA: A Knowledge-Based System Using Causal Knowledge to Diagnose Cardiac Rhythm Disorders", Proceedings of the 8th International Joint Conference on Artificial Intelligence, Karlsruhe, W. Germany, August 1983.

Shibahara, T., "On Using Causal Knowledge to Recognize Vital Signals: A Study of Knowledge-Based Interpretation of Arrhythmias", PhD Thesis, Dept. of Computer Science, University of Toronto, 1986, also LCM-TR-86-1.

Slager, C., et al., "Left Ventricular Contour Segmentation from Anatomical Landmark Trajectories and its Application to Wall Motion Analysis", Proc. Computers in Cardiology, Geneva, 1979.

Szolovits, P., Pauker, S., "Categorical and Probabilistic Reasoning in Medical Diagnosis", *Artificial Intelligence 11,* 1978.

Tsotsos, J.K., Mylopoulos, J., Covvey, H.D., Zucker, S.W., "A Framework For Visual Motion Understanding" *IEEE Trans. on Pattern Analysis and Machine Intelligence,* Nov. 1980.

Tsotsos, J., "Temporal Event Recognition: An Application to Left Ventricular Performance Assessment", Proc. International Joint Conference on Artificial Intelligence, Vancouver, 1981.

Tsotsos, J., "Representational Axes and Temporal Cooperative Processes", in *Vision, Brain and Cooperative Computation,* ed. by Arbib and Hansen, MIT Press/Bradford Books, 1987.

Tsotsos, J.K., "Knowledge Organization and its role in representation and Interpretation for Time-Varying Data: The ALVEN System", *Computational Intelligence 1,* 1985.

Wallis, J., Shortliffe, E., "Explanatory Power for Medical Expert Systems: Studies in the Representation of Causal Relationships for Clinical Consultations", STAN-CS-82-923, Stanford University, 1982.

Zadeh, L., "Commonsense Knowledge Representation Based on Fuzzy Logic", *IEEE Computer 16-10,* October 1983.

Zucker, S., "Production Systems with Feedback", in *Pattern-Directed Inference Systems,* ed. by Waterman and Hayes-Roth, Academic Press, 1978.

Subject Index